MEDITERRANEAN SEA

SEA

S E A

CRETAN SEA

MEDITERRANEAN SEA

100 kil.

100 m.

SAMOS

ICARIA

CHIOS

MYKONOS

TENOS

NAXOS

C Y C L A D E S

PAROS

ANDROS

SIPHNOS

MELOS

KEA

CRETE

Hierapetra

Herakleion

Mylopotamos

Rethymnon

Canea

Kastelli

Thebes

Levadia

ATTICA

Megara

Athens

Hexamilion

Corinth

Tarsos

CORINTHIA

MEGARIS

ARGOLIS

Argos

Nauplia

Monemvasia

C.Malea

KYTHERA

Patras

Aigion

ACHAIA

Kalavryta

Mt.Erymanthos

Glarentza

Chlomoutsi

ELIS

Olympia

Santameri

P E L O P O N N E S E

ARCADIA

Tripolis

Leondari

Pylos

Modon

MESSENIA

Kalamata

Coron

Sparta

Mistra

KYNOURIA

TSACONIA

LACONIA

C.Tainaron

CEPHALONIA

ZACYNTHUS

RUTGERS BYZANTINE SERIES

PETER CHARANIS, *General Editor*

ORIGINS OF THE GREEK NATION

The Byzantine Period, 1204–1461

By APOSTOLOS E. VACALOPOULOS

Translation by Ian Moles, revised by the author

RUTGERS UNIVERSITY PRESS
New Brunswick, New Jersey

*To the memory of my parents and of
my uncle Eustathios Vacalopoulos*

CONTENTS

Illustrations, including Maps   xi

Abbreviations   xiii

Note on Sources   xv

Foreword by Peter Charanis   xxi

Introduction   xxv

CHAPTER 1   *Byzantine Ethnic Infusions*   1
    Fallmerayer's Theory   1
    The Slavs   2
    The Albanians   6
    The Vlachs   12
    The Franks and Turks   15

CHAPTER 2   *The Survival of Greek Civilization*   17
    From the Roman Conquest to the Tenth Century   17
    From the Tenth Century through the Thirteenth   21

CHAPTER 3   *Origins of National Consciousness*   27
    Various Theories   27
    Political Decentralization after Fourth Crusade   28
    Rivalry between Epirus and Nicaea   31
    Political and Intellectual Developments in Nicaea   36
    Cultural Activity during the Latin Period   43

CHAPTER 4   *The Palaeologian Period*   46
    Classical Revival in Literature and Art   46
    The Cultural Prominence of Thessalonica   49
    The Effect of *Pronoia* on the Peasantry   54
    The Hesychast Controversy   57

CHAPTER 5   *Turkish Conquest of Asia Minor*   61
    Effect on Greek Population   61
    Nature of Invasion   64
    Crypto-Christianity and Greek Apostasy   66

CHAPTER 6   *Turkish Invasion of the Balkan Peninsula*   69
    Piracy in the Aegean and Ionian Seas   69
    The Ottoman Landings in Thrace   71
    The Extension of Turkish Control   73
    Conditions in the Greek World, 1354–1402   78

CHAPTER 7   *The Church at Bay*   86
    The Crisis of Faith   86
    Eschatological Teaching after 1204   90
    The "New" Martyrs   93
    The Church in the Latin Dominions   95
    The Question of Union of the Churches   99

CHAPTER 8   *The Catalyst of Conquest*   104
    Hellenism in the Frankish Dominions   104
    Hellenism in Epirus and Thessaly   111
    Hellenism in Macedonia   116

CHAPTER 9   *George Gemistos*   126
    Prospectus for Reform   126
    Gemistos' Influence   132

CHAPTER 10   *The Byzantine and Ottoman Empires after Ankara*   136
    Some General Observations   136
    Murad II   144

CHAPTER 11   *Impressment of Christians*   151
    Reorganization of the Janissaries   151
    Christian Spahis   152
    The Greek Armatoles   157

CHAPTER 12   *Turkish Colonization and Economic Reconstruction*   161

CHAPTER 13   *The Last Protagonists of Neo-Hellenism*   169
    The Morea under Constantine Palaeologus   169
    Bessarion   172
    Constantine and the Turkish Peril   178
    Constantine as Emperor   180

CHAPTER 14 *The Turks at the Gates of Constantinople*   187
   Preparations for War and the Union Controversy   187
   Siege of the City   193
   Capture of the City   198
   Echoes of the Fall in Legend and Tradition   202

CHAPTER 15 *Completion of the Turkish Conquest*   206
   Structure of Ottoman Empire after 1453   206
   Fall of the Despotate of Morea   207
   Seizure of the Gattilusi Possessions   216
   Overthrow of the Empire of Trebizond (1461)   221
   A Greek Historian Looks to the Restoration of His Nation   231

CHAPTER 16 *Greek Scholars in the West*   234
   Italy as a Greek Refuge   234
   Manuel Chrysoloras   237
   Gemistos and Bessarion   241
   Argyropoulos and Chalcocondyles   245
   Greek Scholars outside Italy   250

CHAPTER 17 *The Question of National Liberation*   256

Notes   265

Index   369

Maps, by Dorothy deFontaine   403
   (See also endpapers)

ILLUSTRATIONS

FIGURES

1. Castle of Trikkala, 14th-century Byzantine, with later Turkish repairs. Photo: A. Koulouridas.   9
2. Ascension of Alexander the Great, 12th-century relief, St. Mark's, Venice. Photo: Fratelli Alinari, No. 20697.   25
3. Church of St. Elias, mid-14th century, Thessalonica, after restoration. Photo: Lykides Studio.   51
4. St. George the Swift, 14th-century fresco, Church of St. Nicholas of the Orphans, Thessalonica. Photo: Lykides Studio.   52
5. The Monastery of the Metamorphosis, 14th century, at Meteora. Photo: Nick Stournaras.   70
6. Janissary, 15th century, drawing by Gentile Bellini, reprinted by courtesy of the Trustees of the British Museum. Photo: British Museum.   75
7. Peribleptos Monastery, 14th century, Mistra. Photo: Erika Cruikshank.   83
8. (a) and (b), Palace of Mistra, 13th or 14th century. Photos: Author.   84
9. John Ouroš Palaeologus as the Monk Ioasaph, detail of fresco in the Monastery of the Metamorphosis at Meteora, executed in 1483. Photo: M. Lascaris, in *Byzantion*, XXV–XXVI–XXVII (1955–1957), fasc. 1, planche 2.   115
10. Manuel II Palaeologus (1391–1425), between his father and eldest son. Pen drawing, *Cod. gr. 1783*, f. 2, Bibliothèque Nationale, Paris. Photo: Spyridon Lambros, in Λεύκωμα βυζαντινῶν αὐτοκρατόρων (Athens, 1930), fig. 86.   117
11. The Walls of the Citadel of Thessalonica, 4th century, with later repairs. Photo: Lykides Studio.   119
12. Cenotaph of G. Vibius Quartus, n.d., near Philippi. Photo: Author.   122
13. John VIII Palaeologus (1425–1448), 15th-century bronze bust, Vatican Museum. Photo: Spyridon Lambros, in Λεύκωμα βυζαντινῶν αὐτοκρατόρων (Athens, 1930), fig. 87.   140
14. Constantine XI Palaeologus (1448–1453), detail of a pen and wash drawing on parchment of the Palaeologian emperors,

FIGURES

15th century, *Cod. S. f. 5.5* (*Gr. 123*), f. 294^v, Biblioteca Estense, Modena. Photo: Author. 182

15. Mohammed II the Conqueror, from a portrait by Gentile Bellini, National Gallery, London. Photo: Author. 189

16. View of Walls of Constantinople, 5th century. Photo: Cyril Mango. 195

17. Acrocorinth, with Byzantine and Frankish architecture and many later additions. Photo: Elisabeth Brownstein. 210

18. Castle of Modon (Methone), Venetian, with minor Turkish repairs. Photo: Author. 214

19. Manuel Chrysoloras, pen drawing No. 9849, the Louvre, Paris. Photo: Giuseppe Cammelli, in *I Dotti byzantini e le origine dell' umanesimo* (Florence, 1941–1954), vol. 1, frontispiece. 238

20. Cardinal Bessarion kneeling before a reliquary of the Holy Cross, detail from a painting by Gentile Bellini in the Kunsthistorisches Museum, Vienna. Photo: Kunsthistorisches Museum. 242

21. John Argyropoulos, pen drawing, from the Greek *Cod. Baroccianus 87*, f. 35, Photo: Émile Legrand, *Bibliographie hellénique* (Paris, 1885), reprinted by Culture et Civilisation (Brussels, 1963), vol. 1, frontispiece. 246

22. Demetrius Chalcocondyles, from Paolo Giovio's *Elogia virorum literis illustrium* (Basel, 1577). Photo: Giuseppe Cammelli, in *I Dotti byzantini e le origine dell' umanesimo* (Florence, 1941–1954), III, 133. 248

MAPS FOLLOWING INDEX:

Asia Minor in the 14th Century

The Extension of the Ottoman Turks to the Greek Mainland (14th and 15th centuries)

Main Points of Albanian Penetration

Settlements of Turcoman Tribes (Yuruks) in Western Thrace, Macedonia, and Thessaly (end of 14th, beginning of 15th century)

The Greek Peninsula from 1402 to 1425

The Greek Peninsula and the Islands from 1453 to 1460

Constantinople during the Siege

Expeditions of the Turks against the Empire of Trebizond

ENDPAPERS

The Greek Peninsula and the Islands

ABBREVIATIONS

AAEEG	*Annuaire de l'Association pour l'encouragement des études grecques en France*
AE	'Αρχαιολογική ἐφημερίς
ΑΕΑΣ	'Αρχεῖον ἑταιρείας αἰτωλοακαρνανικῶν σπουδῶν
ΑΠ	'Αρχεῖον Πόντου
ΑΘΓΛΘ	'Αρχεῖον θρακικοῦ γλωσσικοῦ λαογραφικοῦ θησαυροῦ
ΑΧ	'Ανδριακά χρονικά
BNJ	*Byzantinische Neugriechische Jahrbücher*
BSA	*Annual of the British School of Athens*
BSOAS	*Bulletin of the School of Oriental and African Studies*
Byz.-Sl.	Byzantinoslavica
BZ	Byzantinische Zeitschrift
ΔΙΕΕ	Δελτίον ἱστορικῆς καί ἐθνολογικῆς ἑταιρείας
DOP	*Dumbarton Oaks Papers*
ΔΧΑΕ	Δελτίον χριστιανικῆς ἀρχαιολογικῆς ἑταιρείας
ΕΕΒΣ	'Επετηρίς ἑταιρείας βυζαντινῶν σπουδῶν
ΕΕΦΣΠΑ	'Επιστημονική ἐπετηρίς Φιλοσοφικῆς Σχολῆς Πανεπιστημίου 'Αθηνῶν
ΕΕΦΣΠΘ	'Επιστημονική ἐπετηρίς Φιλοσοφικῆς Σχολῆς Πανεπιστημίου Θεσσαλονίκης
EMA	'Επετηρίς Μεσαιωνικοῦ 'Αρχείου
Hell. Contemp.	*L'Hellénisme contemporain*
HME	'Ημερολόγιον Μεγάλης 'Ελλάδος
HX	'Ηπειρωτικά χρονικά
JHS	*The Journal of Hellenic Studies*
JÖBG	*Jahrbuch der Österreichischen Byzantinischen Gesellschaft*
KX	Κρητικά χρονικά
ΛΑ	Λαογραφικόν ἀρχεῖον

MEE   Μεγάλη ἑλληνική ἐγκυκλοπαιδεία
MOG   *Mitteilungen zur Osmanischen Geschichte*

NE   Νέος Ἑλληνομνήμων
NJKA   *Neue Jahrbücher für das klassische Altertum, Geschichte
               und deutsche Literatur*

OCP   *Orientalia christiana periodica*

ΠΑΑ   Πρακτικά 'Ακαδημίας 'Αθηνῶν
PG   *Patrologia graeca*, ed. Jacques Migne

RE   *Real Encyklopädie Pauly-Wissowa*
REB   *Revue des études byzantines*
REG   *Revue des études grecques*

SBN   *Studi bizantini e neoellenici*

Viz. Vrem.   *Vizantiiskii Vremennik*

ZDMG   *Zeitschrift der Deutschen Morgenländischen Gesellschaft*

NOTE ON SOURCES

The difficulties which confront any student of the history of the modern Greek nation are many and various. They begin with the lack of any systematic introduction to the sources of modern Greek history [1] as well as the lack of a study of modern Greek historiography [2] of the sort that would acquaint the student with the state of historical studies in Greece. There is no comprehensive bibliography capable of guiding the student through the forest of hundreds, nay thousands, of published sources and studies, long or short, significant or insignificant. And that is to say nothing of the vast range of material, known and unknown, which resides in official archives, or the enormous volume of articles (most of them, fortunately, small and unimportant) which have been, and are being, continually published in inaccessible local newspapers and magazines. The whole comprises an incredible bulk of material, which is especially discouraging for the inexperienced researcher.

The sheer variety of studies and references precludes their classifica-

1. See the brief surveys by M. B. Sakellariou, "Πηγές τῆς νέας ἑλληνικῆς ἱστορίας [Sources of Modern Greek History]," Νέα Ἑστία, xxxix (1946), 26–28, 106–109, 156–161, 234–236, 307–309; and Nikolaos B. Tomadakis, "Περί ἀρχείων ἐν Ἑλλάδι καί τῆς ἀρχειακῆς ὑπηρεσίας [On the Archives in Greece and the Archives Service]," ΔΙΕΕ, xi (1956), 1–32 (with the relevant bibliography). Cf. Peter Topping, "The Public Archives of Greece," *The American Archivist*, xv (1952), 249–257.

2. Spyridon Lambros wrote an interesting work entitled Αἱ ἱστορικαί μελέται ἐν Ἑλλάδι κατά τόν πρῶτον αἰῶνα τῆς παλιγγενεσίας μετά προεισαγωγῆς περί τῶν ἑλληνικῶν ἱστορημάτων ἐπί τουρκοκρατίας [Historical Studies in Greece during the First Century of "Regeneration," with an Introduction concerning Greek Narratives during the Turkish Rule]. However, the work has bibliographical deficiencies and remains unpublished. See George Charitakis, "Σπυρίδωνος Π. Λάμπρου τά μετά θάνατον εὑρεθέντα [Spyridon Lambros' Posthumous Works]," ΝΕ, xiv (1917), 208–209, 267–269; Spyridon Lambros, "Ἡ ἱστορική σχολή τῆς Ἑπτανήσου [The Historical School of the Seven Ionian Islands]," ΝΕ, xii (1915), 319–347 (a good outline); and M. B. Sakellariou, "Νεοελληνικές ἱστορικές σπουδές [Modern Greek Historical Studies]," Νέα Ἑστία, xxxii (1943), 26–31, 102–106, 158–162, 233–236, 290–295, 359–364, 435–440, 495–498, 548–552, 615–618, 804–813.

tion within a few categories and, consequently, the easy formulation of judgments on their worth. Not to be overlooked also is the investigator's quandary when confronted by the work of amateur historians who disregard the canons of historical research, carelessly perpetuate false conclusions, embellish their texts with statements which the evidence does not warrant, and conceal genuine findings in a maze of obliquity.

Nevertheless it is possible, by way of essaying at least a tentative classification of sources, to offer a few simple and fairly general comments. The most important and reliable material consists, of course, of the primary sources: all those written muniments (public or private documents, inscriptions, and the like) which were compiled contemporaneously with the historical event, or hard upon it. Since they are the creations of the historical moment, they have an intimate relationship with the society in which they appear. Of course a great many of these, both Greek and foreign, have been lost, or destroyed by war and natural calamities, or by the neglect or ignorance of their owners. But a great many are still extant in Greek and foreign archives (state, monastic, in Turkish courts, titles' offices, and so on). The Turkish archives in particular contain much valuable information, a good deal of it unexplored, on the history of the Greek nation during the period of Turkish domination.[3]

Where the primary sources are incomplete or entirely lacking, we must have recourse to secondary sources. Of these, undoubtedly the most trustworthy for their attention to detail are the reports of ambassadors and consuls from West European countries. A great deal of sound and worthwhile information about the political, and especially the economic, situation in the Greek lands under Turkish occupation can be garnered from these. The Vatican archives, the Spanish archives,[4] and

3. For a Turkish historical bibliography, see *Türkiye Tarih Yayınları Bibliografyası, 1729–1950* (Ankara, 1952)—the second edition covers 1729–1955 (Istanbul, 1959)—compiled by Enver Koray. An interesting review of historical studies in Turkey since 1923 appears in *Anadolu (Revue des études d'archéologie et d'histoire en Turquie)*, in the series *Turquie médiévale et moderne*, ɪ (Paris, 1952). There is an important and comprehensive bibliographical survey of Turkish history and civilization in Jean Sauvaget's *Introduction to the History of the Muslim East*, based on the second edition as recast by Claude Cahen (Berkeley–Los Angeles, 1965), pp. 193–215. The relevant Greek bibliography, however, is most deficient.

4. Spyridon Lambros, " Ἑλληνικά ἱστορήματα ἐν τοῖς ἀρχείοις τῆς Ἱσπανίας [Greek Narratives in the Spanish Archives]," NE, vɪ (1909), 263–272. This is an anthology of notes dealing with Greek national history taken from Isidoro Carini, *Gli archivi e le biblioteche di Spagna in rapporto alla storia d'Italia in generale, e di Sicilia in particolare. Relazione* (Palermo, 1884),

the Venetian archives in particular also contain much material that will be of inestimable value in throwing light on the many dim areas of Greek history. Greek and foreign historical investigators have long emphasized the singular significance for Greek history of the Venetian archives,[5] and have accordingly concentrated on publishing the reports of Venetian provincial governors (*provveditori*) and other official personages. The reports of Venetian plenipotentiaries to the Porte are equally valuable for the accuracy with which they survey the internal situation throughout the Ottoman Empire. They are also fine examples of the accomplished art of Venetian diplomacy. For both these reasons, foreign historians, long before their Greek counterparts, recognized them as funds of historical information. Whole series of the reports are published in the voluminous collections of Albèri, Fiedler, Barozzi, and others.

Among other secondary sources are the annals, especially those of the late Byzantine period, which were written at the same time or shortly after the events they describe actually occurred; the various narratives and chronicles by Greeks and by Turks and other foreigners, notably the

2 vols. The first Greek report on that subject is by Ioannis K. Hassiotis, "Fuentes de la historia griega moderna en archivos y bibliotecas españoles [Sources on Modern Greek History in Spanish Archives and Libraries]," *Hispania*, xxix (1969), 133–164.

5. See Constantine Sathas, Μεσαιωνική βιβλιοθήκη [*Library of the Middle Ages*] (Venice, 1872–1874), iii, vi, fn. 1; Constantine Mertzios, Θωμᾶς Φλαγγίνης καὶ ὁ μικρὸς Ἑλληνομνήμων [Thomas Flangines and the Minor "Hellenomnemon" (Greek Remembrances)] (Athens, 1939), pp. 186–187; Spyridon Lambros, "Κώδικες ἑλληνικῶν ἱστορημάτων ἐν τῇ κατά τήν Βενετίαν Fondazione Quirini Stampalia [Codices of Greek Narratives of the Fondazione Quirini Stampalia in Venice]," NE, viii (1911), 482–488; William Miller, "Le Rubriche dei Misti del Senato, libri XV–XLIV [Summaries of the Senate Decrees, Vols. XV–XLIV]," ΔIEE, vii (1910–1918), 69–119; Spyridon Theotokis, Εἰσαγωγὴ εἰς τὴν ἔρευναν τῶν μνημείων τῆς ἱστορίας τοῦ Ἑλληνισμοῦ καὶ ἰδίᾳ τῆς Κρήτης ἐν τῷ Κρατικῷ Ἀρχείῳ τοῦ βενετικοῦ κράτους [*An Introduction to Research into Documents of the History of Hellenism, Especially that of Crete, in Venice's State Archives*] (Corfu, 1926), and his "Κατάλογος χειρογράφων τῆς βιβλιοθήκης τοῦ Ἀγ. Μάρκου ἐν Βενετίᾳ κατ' ἐπιλογήν ἐκ τῆς VI καί VII ἰταλικῆς σειρᾶς [Catalogue of Manuscripts in the Library of St. Mark's in Venice Chosen from the Sixth and Seventh Italian Series]," Ἑλληνικά, iii (1930), 89–114, 347–380; iv (1932), 173–190, 394–424; v (1933), 17–38. See also Freddy Thiriet, *Les Archives vénitiennes et leur utilisation pour l'étude de l'Orient greco-latin jusqu'à la conquête turque*, in the series *Mémoire de l'École pratique des Hautes-Études* (1949–1950). I have not myself seen this. I think it is unpublished.

Italians, as well as memoirs, speeches, poems, and so on. A list of European books dealing with the Turks, which were in circulation during the sixteenth century, may be found in Carl Göllner, *Turcica, Die europäischen Türkendrucke der XVI. Jahrhunderts* (*Turcica, The European-Published Works of the XVIth Century on the Turks*), I (1501–1550), Bucharest-Berlin, 1961. The large number of Greek chronicles and chronological accounts, both published and unpublished,[6] need to be examined for their consistency with one another and with the various chronologies (*Chronikai ektheseis*), as well as with the history of the *Pseudo-Dorotheos*[7] and the various West European works on Ottoman and Byzantine history.[8] Finally, our knowledge of intellectual developments during the late Byzantine and Ottoman periods will remain sketchy until the bibliographers and codifiers of those periods have been thoroughly investigated. A most useful index to catalogues and collections of Greek manuscripts is that of Marcel Richard, *Répertoire des bibliothèques et des catalogues de manuscrits grecs* (*Index of Libraries and of Catalogues of Greek Manuscripts*), Paris, 1958.

Separate mention must be made of the "Brief Chronicles" (*Enthymeseis*) which are usually to be found on the flyleaves at the beginning or end of the texts of ecclesiastical works—in breviaries or missals, for

6. See Constantine Amantos, "Τρεῖς ἄγνωστοι κώδικες τοῦ χρονογράφου [Three Unknown Codices of the Chronicler]," Ἑλληνικά, ι (1928), 45–70; Gyula Moravcsik, "Ἄγνωστος κῶδιξ τῆς ἐκθέσεως χρονικῆς [One Unknown Codex of the Ekthesis Chronicle]," Ἑλληνικά, ιι (1929), 119–123; George Zoras, Χρονικόν περί τῶν Τούρκων σουλτάνων (κατά τόν Βαρβερινόν ἑλληνικόν κώδικα 111) [*The Chronicle of the Turkish Sultans* (*according to the Greek Barberinus Codex CXI*) (Athens, 1958), which has the relevant early bibliography.

7. After the initial publication of my book in Greek, a study was published by Elizabeth Zachariadou, "Μία ἰταλική πηγή τοῦ Ψευδο-Δωροθέου γιά τήν ἱστορία τῶν Ὀθωμανῶν [One Italian Source of Pseudo-Dorotheos for the History of the Ottomans]," Πελοποννησιακά, ν (1961), 46–59.

8. See the doctoral thesis by Elizabeth Zachariadou, Τό χρονικό τῶν Τούρκων σουλτάνων (τοῦ Βαρβερινοῦ ἑλληνικοῦ κώδικα 111) καί τό ἰταλικό του πρότυπο [The Chronicle of the Turkish Sultans (the Greek Barberinus Codex CXI) and Its Italian Model] (Thessalonica, 1960); Chr. G. Pantelidis, "Χειρόγραφος μετάφρασις τοῦ Χρονικοῦ τοῦ Δουσινιανοῦ [Handwritten Translation of the Chronicle of Lusignan]," NE, ΧΙΙΙ (1916), 472–475; chapter V of Nectario's Ἐπιτομῆς τῆς Ἱεροκοσμικῆς ἱστορίας [Epitome of Sacred-Secular History] (1677); and Manoussos Manoussacas, "'Ἐπιτομή τῆς Ἱεροκοσμικῆς ἱστορίας' τοῦ Νεκταρίου καί αἱ πηγαί αὐτῆς ['Epitome of the Sacred-Secular History' by Nectarios and Its Sources]," ΚΧ, ι (1947), 319–325.

example—and which also appear, though more rarely, in the pages of ledgers or registers, and sometimes as inscriptions or engravings on Byzantine and post-Byzantine monuments. These "Brief Chronicles" are directly connected with the daily lives of the people, commonly recording misfortunes such as invasion, epidemic, earthquake, violent weather, war, banditry, assassination, drought, and fire. The events described were generally of such magnitude as to make a profound impression on the masses, and the "Brief Chronicles" were written while the recollection of the event was fresh. Thus, they are more precise and reliable than the annals—indeed, often more so than any other secondary source— since they were the spontaneous revelations of the popular memory. Many have been published in various journals, historical and otherwise, though some are virtually inaccessible to the researcher.[9] Unfortunately, they were not collected until comparatively recent times; then only in a most unsystematic fashion and not in all the Greek lands.

Another fruitful source of information is the travel descriptions written by foreigners who visited Greece or passed through it on the way to other countries: [10] pilgrims to the Holy Land, collectors of antiquities or Byzantine manuscripts, merchants, diplomats, artists, scientists, and others. Sometimes the impressions of their distant and dangerous travels were set down immediately; most often, they were written up at home from brief notes taken on the spot. There was usually a good market for such curiosities in their homelands. Invariably, the narrators spoke of exciting adventures in strange lands plagued by disease, banditry, and piracy, where the conquerors attached little importance to the lives of the conquered. Some of the most interesting pages in these books contain descriptions of the ruins of ancient Greek cities. Of course, the information is of very uneven quality, depending on the personality, education, and occupation of the traveller, as well as the length of time he actually spent in Greek lands.[11] Most of the information in any case

9. The most important collections are in NE, vols. 7, 8, and 16. Cf. Spyridon Lambros, Βραχέα χρονικά [Brief Chronicles], ed. Constantine Amantos, in Μνημεῖα τῆς ἑλληνικῆς ἱστορίας (Athens, 1932), vol. I, part I.

10. For information on the routes taken by travellers in the late Byzantine period, see Bertrandon de la Brocquière, *Voyage d'outremer et retour de Jérusalem en France par la voie de terre, pendant le cours des années 1432 et 1433*, ed. Pierre Legrand D'Aussy, in *Mémoires de l'Institut national des sciences et arts; sciences morales et politiques* (Paris, fructidor an XII), v, 460 ff.

11. For an analysis of the works of certain travellers, see Helen Vourazeli, Ὁ βίος τοῦ ἑλληνικοῦ λαοῦ κατά τήν τουρκοκρατίαν [*The Life of the Greek People under Turkish Rule* (Athens, 1939), part I, Introduction. See also Eugène Lovinesco, *Les Voyageurs français en Grèce au XIXe siècle (1800–*

refers to Turkish matters and thus provides only incidental enlighten-
ment, if any, on the Greek situation.

Various historical and geographical works designed mainly for teaching purposes offer useful information, particularly on the periods during
which they were written.

The most unique collection of travel books on Greece belongs to the
Gennadius Library in Athens.[12] This same library possesses many other
sources, published and unpublished, which are vital to our knowledge
of the history of modern Hellenism. It is also a veritable storehouse of
photos, maps, sketches, tableaus, aquarelles, and the like. The importance
of the Gennadius collection, particularly for nineteenth-century history
and the period of Turkish occupation, is readily perceived from even
the most casual perusal of the pages of the first two catalogues. These
were published by the Library's former curator, Shirley Howard Weber,
as (1) *Voyages and Travels in the Near East Made during the XIXth
Century* (Princeton, New Jersey, 1952); and (2) *Voyages and Travels in
Greece, the Near East and Adjacent Regions Made Previous to the Year
1801* (Princeton, New Jersey, 1953). The second volume contains an
annotated bibliography of travel books (pp. 1–5) and similar works that
appear in anthologies of travel literature (pp. 5–14).

When the written evidence is fragmentary or nonexistent, it is permissible of course to resort, though guardedly, to historical traditions,
legends, popular songs, and folklore generally, both those which have
been published and those which are preserved unwritten in the memories of the people. "The history of the past will never be found wholly
in books," as the French archaeologist, G. Perrot, correctly observed.[13]
At the same time, it is very frequently the case that the origins of ancient
Greek history and of modern Greek history are clouded by tradition and
legend. The truth is difficult, if not impossible, to find when tradition
not only disguises the real event so as to make it almost unrecognizable
but is itself susceptible of exasperating modification. For this reason,
tradition should be accepted only when backed up by written evidence,
or when it appears to complement and corroborate the written source.
Otherwise, tradition properly belongs to folklore rather than history.

1900) (Paris, 1909). On visitors to Athens, see James Morton Paton, *Chapters
on Medieval and Renaissance Visitors to Greek Lands* (Princeton–New York,
1951), which contains the early bibliography.

12. See Peter Topping, "La Bibliothèque Gennadeion. Son histoire et ses
collections," Hell. Contemp., ix (1955), 121–148.

13. See George Perrot, "Quelques Croyances et superstitions populaires des
grecs modernes. Notes recuillies en Grèce," AAEEG, viii (1874), 373.

FOREWORD

A work of synthesis, the result of many years of research and reflection, this book by Apostolos Vacalopoulos has as its general thesis the cultural continuity of the Greek people. Its more immediate objective, however, is to analyze the conditions and events which led to the disintegration and final obliteration of the Byzantine Empire. At the same time it delineates the forces which emerged from the catastrophe to constitute the basis for the formation of the modern Greek nation. The period covered has as its chronological limits 1204, when Constantinople fell to the Western Crusaders, and 1461, when the last Greek independent political unit was absorbed by the Ottoman Turks. The author, however, does not confine himself strictly within these limits; he goes beyond them when some particular subject requires.

The fundamental fact about the Byzantine Empire, whatever the ethnic origins [1] of its population may have been, is that its civilization, with allowance for Roman political antecedents, was Greek. On this point there can be no argument at all. Greek was so much the general language of communication that whoever within the Empire did not speak it was considered strange.[2] It was the language of commerce, of education, of culture in general, and also of the state.

As the language of education and culture, it oriented its speakers towards the original forms of Greek literature and thought. This is what gave Byzantine secular literature and the intellectual life of the Empire in general their dominant cultural role. And if, as is generally believed, the reading of the ancients did not for a long time strike a vital chord among the Byzantines, that was not because they did not appreciate or understand them: "Surely there is no blame," remarked an observer of Sclerena, the mistress of the Emperor Constantine IX; when asked to explain, he completed [3] the Homeric verse: "Surely there is no blame on

1. Cf. Peter Charanis, "Ethnic Changes in the Byzantine Empire in the Seventh Century," *Dumbarton Oaks Papers,* 13 (1959), pp. 25–44.

2. Charanis, *The Armenians in the Byzantine Empire* (Lisbon, 1963).

3. Michael Psellos, *Chronographie,* ed. and trans. E. Renauld, I (Paris, 1926), p. 146; English trans. by E. R. A. Sewter, *The Chronographia of Michael Psellos* (London, 1953), p. 136.

Trojans and strong-greaved Achaeans/ if for long time they suffer hardship for a woman like this one." [4] If indeed the reading of the ancients struck no vital chord it was because the ethos of the Byzantines, an ethos developed over a long period of time with the hellenistic cultural amalgam as its basis, had become quite different from that of the classical period. The cultural Greekness of the Byzantine Empire was undeniably different from that of the classical period, but it was a Greekness which, with some elements drawn from the Orient, particularly Judaism, had evolved from it.

The Oriental elements, especially Judaism, refer, of course, to religion. Since Byzantine society was profoundly Christian, there is much in the culture of Byzantium which derives from the Bible. But the Bible was read in Greek, and the theology which developed in the effort to interpret it was based on ideas and concepts drawn in the main from Greek philosophy, and was given expression in Greek. Even hagiography, the most popular form of literature developed by the medieval Greeks, had its ancient Greek antecedents.[5] Christianity, as it finally crystallized into Byzantine Orthodoxy, was—allowance being made for its biblical traditions—essentially Greek in inspiration. In time the Church, despite the spread of Orthodoxy into non-Greek lands, came to be looked upon as a national institution.

Precisely when the Church began to be regarded as such may not be easy to establish, but by the first quarter of the thirteenth century this concept had taken hold. It was by then also that the Greekness of the Empire began to be given articulate expression. Hellenism as a term was used in late classical antiquity to refer to things characteristically Greek. But with the triumph of Christianity the term assumed a religious connotation and was used to refer to any religion essentially pagan in character. For this reason, the Byzantines, who called themselves Romans, as, politically, they were, did not for centuries use it to refer to any of the features of their civilization. But all this began to change unmistakably in the course of the first quarter of the thirteenth century. Pressed by both Western Christianity, which appeared and was indeed hostile, and an invigorated Islam, which threatened them with extinction, the Byzantines turned to the ancient Greek past. That past now struck a vital chord, and terms such as Hellenism, Hellen, Hellas, were consciously applied by the Byzantines to their country, to

4. Homer, *Iliad*, III, 156–157; English trans. by Richard Lattimore, *The Iliad of Homer* (Chicago, 1951), p. 104.

5. H. A. Musurillo, S.J., ed., *The Acts of the Pagan Martyrs* (Oxford, 1954). See pages 236 ff. and 260 ff. for a discussion by the editor of possible connection of these acts with Christianity.

themselves, to their civilization. This is not to say that they sought to break completely with their antecedents. "What happened was simply this, that the consciousness of being 'Roman' gradually faded and was supplanted by a sense of 'Greekness,' though without any obvious break with historical tradition or the immediate past." Nevertheless a new hellenism was born.

The components of this new Hellenism were two: a national church, basically Greek in character, free from foreign ecclesiastical political control; and a pride in Greek antiquity, whose literary and philosophical treasures were eagerly searched for inspiration. In the development of these components there was opposition, even mutual antagonism, but in time they joined to produce the modern Greek nation. How they were formed and the conditions and disasters out of which they evolved is the tale that Vacalopoulos tells. The tale is fascinating and well told. Given the fragmentary state of the sources, details in the narrative may be questioned by some, but on the soundness of its essentials there can be no argument at all.

There is another tale, however, which Vacalopoulos tells—the tale of the refugee. "For a good man . . . to leave his city and his rich fields and go a-begging is of all things the most miserable, wandering with mother dear and aged father, with little children and wedded wife. For hateful shall such an one be among all those to whom he shall come in bondage to want and loathsome penury and doth shame to his lineage and belie his noble beauty, followed by all evil and dishonor." [6] So wrote the ancient poet Tyrtaeus in his efforts to encourage the Spartans to stave off defeat. The role of the Byzantine refugee scholars in Western Europe is well known. They did not create the Italian Renaissance, but they enriched it—enriched it considerably by opening up the inexhaustible treasures of Greek literature. A few of these scholars won honor and respect and position, but even so exile remained bitter. How much more bitter it must have been for the vast and less fortunate majority. "It would be a mistake," writes Vacalopoulos, "to assume from the prominence of some of the more notable Greek scholars and the praise heaped upon them by both contemporary and later admirers that all Greek scholars in the West were equally fortunate. Most of them, even those who found it expedient to acknowledge papal primacy and to profess the Roman Catholic faith, toiled long and hard as teachers, copyists, and translators . . . often wandering the streets of cities destitute and poor, each day having to sell more of [their] books." Having come "a-begging . . . in bondage to want and loathsome penury," they

6. J. M. Edmonds, ed. and trans., *Elegy and Iambus*, 1 (London, 1946) (Loeb Classical Library), pp. 68 ff.

were loathed by those among whom they came and "followed by all evil and dishonor." Vacalopoulos does not tell their story as fully as he does that of the more fortunate. The reason for this is very simple: the information on the latter is much more plentiful than that on the former.

Vacalopoulos, born in Greece in 1909 and now for many years Professor of Greek History at the University of Thessalonica, is one of the most distinguished of Greek scholars. His numerous works have won world-wide scholarly recognition. His work on refugees and refugee problems during the Greek Revolution of 1821 won an award of distinction from the Academy of Athens, and more recently he was honored by the same Academy for his contribution to historical knowledge.

The book is presented as a translation of the Greek original published in 1961 in Thessalonica under the title Ἱστορία τοῦ νέου Ἑλληνισμοῦ. In actual fact, however, it is a new book. It is new not only because of the numerous revisions effected by the author, but also because it has been appreciably reorganized. We are happy that we have been able to publish it as a volume in the Rutgers Byzantine Series.

Peter Charanis
General Editor, Rutgers Byzantine Series

INTRODUCTION

It is a fact that there is a paucity of knowledge about the history of Neo-Hellenism, especially the beginnings and the period of Turkish domination, because the investigators have been so few. Although the material available is vast and various, very little systematic groundwork has been done. A lot of time, patience, and effort are required to study the Greek sources so far published, Byzantine or post-Byzantine, as well as the rich mine of material in other languages, and to evaluate the information in them. There is also a vast store of unpublished material which must be collected and published before the requisite monographs and specialized studies on particular subjects and periods can be written. Only then will our historical knowledge become reasonably accurate and complete.

Whatever the difficulties, they must not be allowed to forestall the writing of a history of Neo-Hellenism, any more than they have forestalled previous attempts (when the available material, of course, was much less extensive). In our own troubled times, the Greek people have felt a need, greater perhaps than ever before, to assimilate the solid findings of the social sciences, particularly those of the historical sciences, so as to dispel the feeling of being suspended in the void of centuries. They have demanded to know the historical origins of their nation and its place in contemporary civilization. To some extent this is because the Greek is conscious of the weight of the past. Anyone who studies modern Greek history cannot help but be astonished to discover how close the past is to the present: the influence of the past is constant and all-pervasive. To the Greek, the events of the past seem as recent as *perysi,* "last year," or *properysi,* "the year before last."

There are enough histories, Greek and foreign, to satisfy a normal intellectual curiosity. Most of them, however, and certainly the best—K. Paparregopoulos, K. Hopf, George Finlay, and G. F. Hertzberg, for instance—were written more than a hundred years ago, and the more recent exhibit a variety of defects ranging from an unbalanced presentation of material to a dearth of critical interpretation to bibliographical ignorance. Lack of the spirit of research has too often led to slipshod history.

Consequently, the reader, whether Greek or foreign, is not aware of the results of new researches and merely goes over the same old material. Accordingly, the need to collect, carefully examine and classify new material has become urgent. Sources and references must be searched, historical facts must be gathered and checked, old points of view must be revised, and new problems formulated before the study of Greek history can achieve a proper momentum. It is a formidable task but one which must be carried out expeditiously if the essential characteristics of Neo-Hellenism are to yield the important lessons at present hidden in them.

There is an equal need for the preparation of historical maps to accompany the texts. The lack of such maps and atlases constitutes a sizeable gap in Greek historical knowledge.

The Greek nation has been harmed by this absence of an explicit, scientific knowledge of history and the ignorance of crucial historical problems. The unawareness of even the most prominent outlines of modern Greek history has led to national myopia in the face of some of the most serious contemporary problems and has severely hampered the nation's intellectuals, politicians, and military leaders. Secondary school teachers do not even have reliable history texts to quote from. The children, the hope of the nation, continue to receive their education from a series of carelessly written manuals. Their historical and social education in school, so essential to modern life, is either inadequate or worthless.

Thus, there is a manifest need for a history of Neo-Hellenism methodically constructed, scrupulously expounded, and illustrated with sufficient maps. Even if such a work should have various imperfections and sooner or later be made obsolete by the appearance of new knowledge, the need is surely no less great, since obsolescence inheres in human work. What is needed in particular is a history that stresses man's continuous preoccupation with the necessities of life, with the vicissitudes of war, with religion, with the problems of daily life, and the problem of choice. History's proper aim, the study of mankind, has been too much neglected. There simply does not exist any history of modern Greece that seeks to probe deeply into human psychology and to explain to the modern Hellene his nation, his ancestors, and himself. Only this kind of history can provide a proper background for the education of every human being and a true understanding of one's fellow man. History, in this sense, then, is not merely a social science: it is the very foundation of the social sciences, the source both of social understanding and of a broad social view.

Within this theoretical framework, I began in 1943 (from the very outset, that is, of my academic career, and parallel with other research) to devote a large part of my energies to the preparation of an historical synthesis of Neo-Hellenism and the compilation of suitable maps. In writing this history, I have relied on my long experience with historical problems and materials, materials which have become comprehensive in recent years. With a view to tracing the historical process as accurately as possible, I tried to return to the roots of the modern Greek nation, where I was confronted with the fascinating and difficult problem of determining at which precise point the modern Greek nation began to emerge. A search for those essential characteristics which determined the evolution of the modern Hellenic nation finally led me to the late Byzantine period (from 1204). The development of the characteristics of Neo-Hellenism at that time has not been noted in even the most authoritative of Byzantine histories. Medieval Hellenism, in other words, proved to be a transitional stage in the formation of Neo-Hellenism.

It soon appeared that an analysis of the last centuries of the Byzantine Empire from this particular vantage point, while raising a number of new and complicated problems, opened up many new horizons and led to the very heart of the historical process. I simply eschewed the usual narrative approach to the late Byzantine period and tried to view it in terms of the emergence of Neo-Hellenism. According to the conventional view, this took place when the old world was on its way out. In reality, however, what happened was that the old world, under pressure from powerful internal and external forces, was transformed into a new world. Thus was Neo-Hellenism born. It suffered and struggled in the difficult conditions which surrounded it; it tried to find itself, to survive, and to chart a better future. The historian follows this story with mounting interest and involvement.

The Palaeologian period has had a deep effect on the modern Hellenic nation and is therefore central to an understanding of it. We must frequently go back to this period if we are to understand fully, for instance, the ethnic composition of the Greek nation, the historical precedents for those types of social organization which evolved under the Turkish occupation, the aspirations and pursuits of the Greek people, their customary religious observances, their artistic and intellectual orientations, their legends and traditions. Similarly, it is in the Palaeologian period that we find the causes of the devastation of the Greek lands, the flight of populations, and the founding of new settlements, and that we learn

of some of the more ancient communal institutions and the first appearance of the armatoles, or guerrillas. These institutions were all vital in
determining the evolutionary course of Neo-Hellenism, and they therefore constitute a powerful reason for fixing the starting-point of modern
Greek history at the beginning of the thirteenth century (1204).

However, we have chosen to narrate at length only those dramatic
events associated with the reign of Constantine XI Palaeologus. Our
justification here is that Constantine's reign has always been closely
identified in the popular mind with the spirit of Neo-Hellenism and is
therefore in that sense the real vinculum between medieval and modern
Hellenism. The popular assessment is a valid one: Constantine, like the
Neo-Platonist philosopher Gemistos and his disciple Bessarion, consciously aimed at the rebirth of the state. To the extent that men like
these have come to incarnate the idea of Neo-Hellenism, I have accordingly stressed their importance as the progenitors of the nation.

The period that marks the beginning of the modern Greek nation was
turbulent indeed. The collapse of the Byzantine Empire was accompanied by cries of despair and distraught pleas for political and social
deliverance. But the murmurings of hope, the new artistic and intellectual voices which heralded the dawn of a new era, could not be entirely
drowned out. Such is the canvas of our history.

ORIGINS OF
THE GREEK NATION

BYZANTINE ETHNIC INFUSIONS

Fallmerayer's Theory

The fundamental problem of modern Greek history may be fairly epitomized in the form of two related questions. What are the ethnic origins of the Greek nation? What are the sources and components of Greek culture? Both have provoked widespread discussion and contention. Both have raised a number of additional questions concerning which scholars have sometimes disagreed completely. Indeed agreement may not be possible on many details. Yet surely it is now possible, particularly in view of the moderation of nationalistic sentiment, for reason and research to guide us to some definite conclusions, and even perhaps to a solution of the basic problem.

The question of ethnic origins was first formulated by the German historian, Fallmerayer,* in 1830, just a year after the successful consummation of the Greek struggle for independence. This was a time when philhellenists and the civilized world in general still had great hopes for the political regeneration of Greece. Fallmerayer's theory,[1] initially advanced in his *Geschichte der Halbinsel Morea wahrend des Mittelalters* (*A History of the Peninsula of Morea during the Middle Ages*) and later developed in other works, immediately attracted widespread attention. According to him, the ancient Greeks had disappeared completely and the modern Greeks were merely descendants of Slavs and Albanians.[2] Naturally, there were repercussions throughout the academic world.

* All superior numbers in the text refer to footnotes which have been collated in the section *Notes* towards the end of the book.

Scholars everywhere tried to analyze such an important ethnological postulate. The outcome of these exhaustive investigations, in spite of certain
disagreement on particular points, has generally been that Fallmerayer
grossly exaggerated in his interpretation of the sources, sources which
consist of a few brief and tantalizing texts drawn from Evagrius, Menander, John of Ephesus, a letter from Patriarch Nicholas III (1084–1111)
to Alexius I (1081–1118), and the "Brief Chronicle" usually referred to as
the *Chronicle of Monemvasia.*[3] Fortunately, historians of today know
only too well how the impressionable and unsophisticated chroniclers of
the past, for all their sensitivity and perception, were prone to embroider
the facts of history for special effect. Nor have the recent investigations
of the *Miracula Sancti Demitrii,* because of its imprecise nature, especially
with respect to chronology, led to any conclusive results.[4] Finally, the
archaeological findings in Corinth that have been regarded by some as
traces of Avaro-Slav settlement[5] are in fact Byzantine; on the other hand
the recently discovered remains of funeral pyres at Olympia do indeed
point to the appearance of the Slavs in the Peloponnese by the second
half of the seventh century.

The Slavs

Certain positive results of historical research, however, can be confidently
set down. The incursions of the Avaro-Slav peoples started in the sixth
century. By the end of that century,[6] but more especially in the early
years of the seventh century, following the overthrow of the Byzantine
Emperor Maurice (582–602), the northern regions of the Balkan peninsula had been permanently settled. The period of anarchy and internal
chaos that followed the death of Maurice provided the Slavs with further
opportunities to invade the south,[7] and it is these subsequent waves of
invasion that are difficult to follow with any reasonable degree of accuracy. The Slavs finally reached the Peloponnese by the middle of the
seventh century.[8] The Slav migrations were effected not only by invasions
of force but also by peaceful means, although it is true that the migrations
may have been due in part to certain extraneous factors such as the
plague of 746, which decimated the indigenous population of these regions.[9] In any case, their peaceful progress south can only have been a
slow one. They moved as isolated groups of peasant farmers and shepherds, and the various place-names they left behind indicate that the
line of their march was through the mountainous highlands of the west.
Indeed, the very gradual, almost imperceptible, nature of their progress
is probably the most important reason why contemporary sources did
not record it more fully. The Slav tribes which settled down in Epirus,
Macedonia, Thessaly, and the Peloponnese originally spoke a Slav dialect

related to Bulgarian.[10] Although definite proof is lacking, the Slav migrations which took place at the time of Maurice probably displaced many Greeks from the Peloponnese and northwestern Greece, who then sought refuge in Sicily and Italy.[11]

From the very outset, the assimilation and hellenization of the Slavs proceeded apace. In the first place, they suffered military reverses in 688 and 783 during the reigns of Justinian II (685–695; 705–711) and Constantine VI (780–797) and again during the reign of Irene (797–802). At the same time, the Church continued to proselytize. In the words of Dvornik,

the Christianization and hellenization of the Slavs in Macedonia, Thrace, and Epirus—at least in those parts of these provinces which remained under Byzantine rule—were pressed on with vigor during the first half of the ninth century, and it is interesting to follow the different stages of the ecclesiastical reorganization of those regions after Christianity had been utterly destroyed there. This meritorious activity of the Byzantine Church reaped its best harvest under the Patriarch Photius.[12]

The defeat which the Slavs suffered before Patras in 805,[13] when they had risen up in arms, finally sealed their fate. A deliberate program of hellenization then began in the Peloponnese. Under the aegis of the Byzantine Emperor Nicephorus (802–811), settlers drawn from other parts of the Empire were moved in, Greek émigrés were persuaded to return, and whole towns were rebuilt.[14] But the process of hellenization was slow. Not even by the reigns of Leo VI (886–912) and Alexander (912–913) had the Christianization of the Slavs been fully accomplished.[15]

The process of hellenization was not brought about merely by religious conversion and military defeat. On the contrary, the Slavs were simultaneously exposed to a variety of intellectual, political, and economic influences. The big cities of Constantinople, Thessalonica, Corinth, and Patras were obvious centers of continuous cultural diffusion, as Vasmer correctly points out.[16] Yet Hellenic culture did not emanate solely from these places; it emanated too from a few small towns which preserved their Greek names, such as Caesarea, southwest of Kozane.[17] Greeks were also to be found in small, isolated, and frequently inaccessible places, in remote island and peninsula strongholds, or secure mountain fastnesses. One may surmise that a few of Justinian's celebrated fortresses may have served some useful purpose in providing refuge for the custodians of Greek civilization.[18] These last places of refuge are mentioned by the anonymous writer of the life of St. Luke the Younger (tenth century), who gives a reliable narration [19] of the invasion of central Hellas by

Symeon, the Bulgarian Czar, and refers to the flight of the inhabitants of Phocis to the towns: "whereupon those in the towns became shut in like prisoners, while those who went to Euboea and the Peloponnese found safety." [20] Chalcidice is a notable example of a place which lay outside the path of the invader and which was not subsequently settled by him because of its mountainous situation. The plateau of Arnaea (as it is known today) was celebrated in oral tradition until the end of the eighteenth century as having been densely populated by Greeks throughout the period of the Bulgarian invasions. Other places which avoided inundation by the Slavs and therefore continued to harbor Greeks were probably the mountainous districts of southern Macedonia, Pieria and Vermion, as well as parts of eastern Macedonia.[21] Indeed the Greek population was not entirely uprooted even from the plains; various toponyms suggest that the Greek inhabitants returned to their lands as soon as the invasion ended.[22]

The *Chronicle of Monemvasia* speaks of the people of Corinth who found sanctuary on Aegina, the people of Argos on the island of Orobe (?), the people of Laconia in the surrounding mountains and in Monemvasia. Such references are typical, though in fact they occurred in different places at different times. The persistence of archaic Greek peculiarities in such districts as Tsakonia [23] indicates that the Taygetus and Parnon mountains, especially the latter, served as places of refuge. The *Chronicle of Galaxidi,* although it was not written until about 1703, similarly offers us a good deal of insight into the manner of Greek resistance to the onslaughts of the Bulgarians and other invaders. It is based on personal reminiscences as well as official Byzantine sources. Here we have a saga of heroism and bloody conflict, of retreat to fortresses, islands, and mountain peaks, of harassed pursuit, of days of hardship lengthening into years. Here we watch the Greeks, finally driven by necessity, desperation, and the desire for freedom, and fortified at last by the Byzantine armies, rushing forth to reoccupy their lands.[24]

The spiritual vitality of the Church was centered in the monasteries and the seats of numerous bishops and metropolitans. Her intellectual energy was attested in the works of leading clerical scholars. Monasteries and bishoprics were both effective in the work of proselytism.

A variety of ordinary needs brought the Slav into daily intercourse with the Greek. There were commercial transactions to be made and the financial inducements which work offered. Undoubtedly, too, the search for winter quarters brought many Slav shepherds down into the plains. Whatever the reason, they came into increasing contact with Greeks—peasants, big landowners, ecclesiastical administrators, and civil officials. The urban centers where they came principally to sell their goods were all predominantly Greek. Naturally, it is difficult to ascertain the precise nature of the relationships which were formed; but, at the same time, it is unlikely that this seminomadic people retained a completely self-sufficient mode of existence. Not that their institutions and tribal allegiances were suddenly abandoned: it is probable that they held to these while paying homage through their chiefs to the functionaries of the Byzantine Empire.[25]

References can only rarely be found to Slav settlements surviving into the tenth century, and these are only to settlements in Achaia and Elis and on the slopes of the Taygetus Mountains, where the people came to be known as Melingoi and Ezeritai.[26] The small district of Zygos, where the Melingoi lived, has been subjected to a good deal of interesting comment. As early as the fifteenth century the Greek traveller, Lascaris Kananos, remarked that the people of this district spoke a dialect similar to that of Lübeck in northern Germany, which was called "Slavia," "Sclavinia," and "Sclavonia."[27] The Slavs of the Taygetus were last mentioned by Chalcocondyles in the fifteenth century.[28] Professor Socrates Kougeas has this interesting comment to make on the assimilation of the Melingoi people:

The way of life of the people of Zygos, called Melingoi, was in many respects similar to that of the inhabitants of the neighboring fortress of Maina—those who were later called Maniatai. According to Porphyrogenitus "the Maniatai were descended not from Slavs but from ancient Romans (Byzantines), who were always called Hellenes by the local populace." The Maniatai, like the Melingi, had acknowledged fealty to the imperial authority from very early times. During the period of the Despotate [of Morea] the Maniatai and the people of Zygos, though of different racial lineage, had clearly begun to amalgamate as a consequence of racial intermixing during the Palaeologian period. Eventually, the fusion of these two peoples resulted from the assimilation of the remaining Slav elements by the preponderant Greek population. There emerged a way of life that reflected certain reciprocal influences but that was at the same time thoroughly Hellenic. This way of life, influenced by the traditions of ancient Sparta, exhibited many of the characteristics today so typical of the Maniatai—a fierce and vengeful nature, a predilection for army life, a passion for political independence . . .[29]

By the beginning of the Turkish occupation, it would appear that the total assimilation of the Slavs had been effected. This was certainly the case in southern Greece,[30] although there may have been a few remnants in western Thessaly and Epirus. All this is not, however, to suggest that the influence of the Slavs ceased forever. On the contrary, the peaceful penetration of parts of northern Greece, especially Thrace and Macedonia, continued until the Balkan wars of 1912–1913. These later immigrants were mostly Bulgarians, who came as itinerant rural workers, building craftsmen, or laborers.[31]

The comparative facility with which the Bulgarian language could be learned meant that occasionally the process of assimilation was reversed.[32] The Patzinaks in Ardea were one people so affected. But this process has to be carefully examined. The study of linguistics has shown that Slav languages were unable to influence the morphology and syntax of the Greek language in any significant way.[33] Insofar as vocabulary is concerned, Meyer maintains that this influence is restricted to the loan of no more than 273 words, of which only a few are in everyday speech. Most of these borrowed words are concrete nouns dealing with some aspect of a bucolic existence.[34] On the other hand, the Greek inheritance in certain Slav languages, especially Bulgarian, is considerable.[35]

Since most Slav toponyms allude to some aspect of nature, they obviously derive from a peasant and shepherd culture. It is not always clear whether they were brought into Greece by Slavs who settled down permanently, by tenants situated on monastic and lay estates, or by the Vlachs, Arvanito-Vlachs, and Albanians, who became thoroughly intermixed with the Slavs, particularly in the western districts. The matter is further complicated by the fact that the toponyms represent the residual deposits of successive layers of history,[36] which, in the case of Greek Macedonia at least, have been proved to belong to virtually every chronological period down to the twentieth century.

Nevertheless, at least the broader ramifications of the problem of Slav influence on Greece can now be seen against a background of scientific knowledge that permits the virtual abandonment of Fallmerayer's theory. Only in Soviet Russia has there been any recent enthusiasm shown for it [37]—an enthusiasm which must surely now be muted, however, in view of the findings in 1960 of the Greek anthropologist, Ares Poulianos, who did his investigations while in Soviet Russia. Using the methodological standards of the Soviet Anthropological Institute, Poulianos showed by means of a series of exhaustive measurements and analyses that an unbroken racial affinity existed between the ancient and modern Greeks.[38]

It must be admitted, however, that the precise extent of Slav influence on each successive stratum of the Greek ethos is, by its very nature, extraordinarily difficult to determine.

The Albanians

When the controversy surrounding Fallmerayer's theory was at its height, Thomas Gordon, the Scottish philhellenist and participant in the Greek revolution of 1821 to 1829, observed that certain scholars had looked for traces of Slav settlement and influence in the Peloponnese. But he found that these really belonged to the hellenized descendants of Albanians, who were not only still living there but also still spoke their own language.[39] Gordon, who at least knew the Peloponnese at first hand, maintained that these people were definitely not descendants of Slavs but rather of Albanians, who had come into Greece during the fourteenth and fifteenth centuries. It is now known that these new immigrants settled down in the Peloponnese and Epirus, particularly in the region of the Pindus Mountains. It is also known that many of these Illyrian Albanians spoke a Latin dialect. They were, in other words, Arvanito-Vlachs, who, besides their own Vlach language, also spoke Albanian fluently.[40] Their subsequent impact on Greece, especially in the south, was much more lasting than that of any of the preceding Slav migrations.

Many opinions have been advanced as to when the Albanians first appeared. At the more dubious extreme the migrations have been placed as early as the eighth century.[41] At the more plausible extreme they have been placed closer to the fourteenth century.[42] However, the weight of evidence would seem to point to an intermediate period. At any rate, at the end of the thirteenth century, official acknowledgement was made of the peaceful settlement of Albanians in mountainous western Thessaly near Karditsa—specifically, in the district of Phanarion. In view of this fact, it seems likely that they may have begun to move in as early as the twelfth century, sporadically and peacefully at first, occasionally with official sanction, though not always with the approval of the indigenes. In 1295, for example, Michael Gabrielopoulos, lord of Thessaly, received the entreaty of his people "not to bring in, thou nor thine heirs, any more immigrants, or to have Latin soldiers in thine employ."[43] The document exemplifies the usual national distrust of all foreign intruders.

After 1318, the peaceful Albanian infiltration came to an abrupt halt. A leaderless horde of twelve thousand people, comprising the three tribes of the Malakasioi, Bouïoi, and Mesaritai, descended upon Thessaly and ravaged the countryside. Greek and Catalan authorities in this area were forced to withdraw to the immediate vicinity of castle strongholds.[44] Some of these raiders spoke Albanian, others Arvanito-Vlach, which would seem to suggest that they came from southern Albania.[45] Indeed, the survival of certain oral traditions concerning the origin of the Albanians reinforces such a conclusion. In particular, the Arvanito-Vlachs of Acarnania, or Karagounides (which is the name applied today even to the Greek-speaking inhabitants of the plain of Thessaly), believed that their ancestors left the area of Avlona (Valona) some four or five hundred years before. Thence they had dispersed throughout the district of Metsovon, in Epirus along the Aspropotamos River (Achelous), and in Kalarites.[46] Whether or not this is so, it is definitely known that the Albanians who plundered Thessaly were eventually pacified by the Byzantine emperor Andronicus III, to whom they swore allegiance in 1333.[47]

The year 1348 marked the end of Byzantine sovereignty in Thessaly and the beginning of Serbian domination.[48] Under their leader, Stephen Dušan (1331–1355), the Serbs conquered a large area of northern Greece including parts of Macedonia, Epirus, and Thessaly.[49] The principal side-effect of the Serbian conquest was that the penetration of Albanians further towards the south was facilitated, the more so since many of them served in the Serbian armies as mercenaries.[50] As the Serbian conquest advanced, Stephen Dušan settled many Albanians on the domains of Greek military and lay magnates. Later on Greek and Latin rulers used these Albanians as mercenaries.

On the whole, it would seem that the inroads of the Albanians, accompanied as they were by yet another wave of Slavs—on this occasion Serbs and Bulgarians—contributed significantly to the diminution of the former Greek element in southern Albania and Epirus.[51] Simultaneously, there was a marked dispersal of the Greek population of Thessaly, Aetolia, and Acarnania (the two latter comprising southern Epirus),[52] which took the form of disorganized flight towards the coast.[53] On one occasion, shortly after the death of Stephen Dušan in 1355, an abortive attempt was made to stem the Albanian advance and to rehabilitate the Greek refugees of Epirus. Nicephorus II, Despot of Epirus (1356–1359), son of John II Ducas Orsini, led an army against the invaders, but was defeated and killed at the battle of the Achelous (spring 1359).[54] Thereafter, Serbs and Albanians held undisputed sway throughout the whole of north-western Greece, virtually as far as the Gulf of Corinth. Only the castles of Naupactus and Vonitsa were still in the hands of the Angevins and the Toccos. Albanian colonization in Greece was thus further extended.[55] Yet the displacement of Greek families was by no means universal. The Greek element remained in the ascendant in Vagenetia,[56] where the coastal littoral of Epirus opposite Corfu is broad and isolated and where numerous wealthy monasteries are to be found. Some noble families certainly sought refuge in Ioannina,[57] but the supposition that most of the Greek population remained on their land would seem to be borne out by the fact that this same district today coincides almost exactly with an area where the language retains a number of Greek archaisms.[58]

Many of the events of this period can be only hazily reconstructed. After the death of Stephen Dušan, the situation in Epirus and Thessaly became more and more confused.[59] Symeon Uroš, Dušan's half-brother, who conferred upon himself the title of "King and Emperor of the Romans, Serbs, and all the Albanians," [60] ruled in Thessaly and Epirus from 1356 to 1371(?).[61] He established his court in Trikkala and then pro-

Figure 1. Castle of Trikkala.

ceeded to divide his territorial inheritance. In 1367, Ioannina was assigned to his kinsman, Thomas Preliumbović, and Aetolia and Acarnania (that is, southern Epirus) went to the Albanian tribes of Boua and Liosa respectively.[62] Serb influence extended throughout the western plain of Thessaly as far as Pharsala and Domokos,[63] while Albanians and Arvanito-Vlachs were the dominant element in western Thessaly and southern Epirus. This situation remained largely unchanged until the appearance of the Turks towards the end of the fourteenth century, although there was constant friction between the two groups. Indeed, it was because Preliumbović wished to prevent Albanian dominance that he finally called upon the Turkish army for direct military support. In this way, he facilitated the expansion of Turkish hegemony in Epirus.[64]

The descent of the Albanians into Attica and the Peloponnese took place after 1382 during the last years of Catalan control (1311–1388). Attica had been recently devastated by a company of Navarrese soldiers of fortune, and as a step towards the repopulation of this region King Peter IV of Aragon gave official consent to Albanian colonization, which subsequently extended to the highlands of Boeotia, thence to Euboea, and, finally, during the Turkish occupation, to the islands of Salamis, Aegina, Angistri, and Andros.[65] Albanians may have made their first appearance in the Peloponnese during the despotate of Manuel Cantacuzenus (1348–1380), but colonization on a large scale did not take place until the time of Theodore I Palaeologus (1383–1407). In 1394, he retook Corinth after its occupation by the Franks, and mention is made of the sudden appearance at the Isthmus of 10,000 Albanian men, women, and children, with their animals. It is reasonable to suppose that such a large number could only have been in flight from the Turk. Thereafter, the colonization of the Peloponnese followed a predictable pattern. Settlements were made with official concurrence in Achaia, Elis, and Arcadia, whence they later spread into Messenia and Argolis. Much later, after the collapse of the Despotate of Morea (1461), Albanians appeared on Hydra, Spetsai, and Poros,[66] where their hellenized descendants form substantial segments of the present-day populations. It is likely that Arvanito-Vlachs and Vlachs were also caught up in the migratory stream of Albanians to the Peloponnese. In this regard Cousinéry calls our attention to the fact that there were certain peoples in the mountainous parts of Argolis who, besides speaking Greek, spoke a language which was practically identical with that of the Macedonian Vlachs.[67]

At the end of the fourteenth century, thousands of Greeks sought refuge from the Turks in the Peloponnese. These, together with the Albanian immigrants, greatly increased the military capability of the Peloponnese, which was a crucial factor in the subsequent history of the region. It is also worthy of comment that this diverse and swollen population yet managed to preserve and to perpetuate its essential Greek character.

Turkish pressure was not the only cause of Albanian migration towards the Peloponnese. At the beginning of the fifteenth century, Carlo I Tocco (1381–1429), ruler of Cephalonia and Zacynthus, had an ambition to re-establish the Greek Despotate of Epirus. With the support of the local Greek element, he proceeded to march through Epirus and western central Hellas. According to the anonymous author of the *Panegyric to Manuel and John Palaeologus,* he pushed back the "barbarians" by a combination of intrigue, persuasion, and force.[68] Who were these "barbarians"? What districts were subjugated along the route of Carlo's march? The answers to these questions are supplied by Venetian sources, which refer to the expedition of the ruler of Cephalonia against the Albanian leader, Boua Sgouros, and his house in 1405. The small town of Anatolikon, with its rich fishing grounds, was taken by a mixture of intrigue and guile. Dragomesto (now Astakos) and Angelokastron were conquered by force. In this way, the permanent occupation of southern Epirus, Acarnania, and Aetolia by the Albanians was hampered, and many of them were propelled towards Attica and the Peloponnese.[69]

However, some Albanians remained. At the very time the *Panegyric* was being written mention is made of the survival of some Albanian settlements in southern Epirus: "These people are never content to settle down in cities, towns, or castles. They retain their nomadic habits and are scattered throughout mountain and plain." However, the coastal plain itself, together with the more important urban centers such as Arta and Ioannina, was inhabited by Greeks.[70] A good deal of this kind of information, which can be culled from the *Panegyric,* is therefore valuable for the light it throws on the essential differences between Greeks and Albanians. The Greeks were mainly townspeople and farmers; the others were nomads who moved from mountain to plain with the fluctuation of the seasons. Even so, the hinterland was not inhabited solely by Albanians. Strong evidence points to the survival of ancient tribes of Epirus,[71] who spoke a quaint and colorful form of Greek, retained popular traditions about ancient Greece, and possessed discernible Greek characteristics—not the least of which was a fervent passion for freedom and independence.[72]

If the evidence of the *Panegyric* is seen in conjunction with the Venetian accounts of the military undertakings of Carlo I Tocco, it is quite apparent that this invasion contributed materially to the movement of Albanians and Arvanito-Vlachs towards eastern central Hellas and the Peloponnese.[73] Final proof, if necessary, would seem to be provided by the fact that the twenty-year-old Paul Spata, brother of the ruler of

Aetolia, Gin Boua Spata, was dislodged from his fortress of Naupactus by the Venetians in 1407 and accepted the asylum offered by his father-in-law, Theodore II Palaeologus, Despot of Morea.[74]

Amicable relations generally subsisted between those Greeks and Albanians who lived in close proximity with one another. Indeed, as a result of this, it may be presumed that whole Greek villages were assimilated by the Albanians, particularly in those areas which were predominantly settled by Orthodox Christian Albanians. Certain manifestations of the reaction to Turkish rule may be relevant to an understanding of this process of reverse assimilation. For instance, Sourmelis suggests that one of the reasons why certain Greek villages in Attica were assimilated more readily in the seventeenth and eighteenth centuries was that their inhabitants observed that the Moslem Albanian mercenaries of the Turks refrained from molesting Christian Albanians.[75]

In much the same manner as the Slavs, Albanians continued to infiltrate Greece throughout the entire period of Turkish occupation. Most of these were Moslems who came sometimes as peaceful immigrants, sometimes as brigands, and sometimes as mercenary soldiers in the Turkish army. However, much research has still to be done before the precise degree of Albanian influence in Greece is known. To what extent did the Albanians merely serve as bearers of Slav toponyms?[76] Of the various toponyms, later subject to linguistic corruption by the Greeks, which were genuinely Albanian, which Turkish?[77]

The Vlachs

The question of the extent to which the Albanians merely acted as bearers of Slav toponyms raises an analogous question about the nature of Vlach influence in Greece. These people had certainly intermixed with the Slavs, and it is likely that many Slav names which have survived in Greece are a legacy of Vlach settlement.[78]

There is a copious literature dealing with the origins of the Vlachs, and a number of conflicting theories have been put forward. Some contend that the Vlachs were descended from colonists of the Roman Empire or from an admixture of Romans and Thracians. This particular viewpoint was initially advanced by the amateur Vlach historian, Rozias, in 1808.[79] In other words, he considered the Vlachs merely as brothers of the Rumanians.[80] Another theory holds that they were latinized Dacians or Thracians, or even a single branch of this larger family—that is to say, the tribe known as Bessoi. Some postulate an Illyrian origin. Still others maintain that, in the case of those dwelling in Greece, they were no more than latinized native Greeks. This last point of view has been upheld in a very simple, yet convincing, manner by the Greek historian, Constantine

Koumas (1777–1836), himself probably of Vlach extraction. However, his theory has gone virtually unnoticed to this day, in spite of the fact that it was advanced at the beginning of the last century, probably in reply to Rozias:

If the extraordinary hero of Macedonia succeeded in spreading the Greek language throughout the whole of the East, even as far as India, in a period of only ten years, it scarcely puts a strain on our credulity to imagine that the Romans might have accomplished the same thing! Indeed, it seems but perfectly natural that over eight centuries the Latin language should also have taken root in precisely those places where Latin colonies were planted—from England to the Euphrates and from the Elbe to the deserts of Africa. For almost six centuries before the fall of Rome, the whole of what is now European Turkey was filled with Roman armies, Roman prefects, Roman lords and magnates. The result of such continuous contact between the Romans and their subject peoples was that whole peoples like the Macedonians, Thessalians, and Greeks not only learned the language of their masters but in many cases completely forgot their own mother tongue. Only in the big cities did the Greek language live on. Only the mountains of Illyricum impeded to some extent the irresistible progress of the Latin language. Even here, in mountain and valley, the village inhabitants mixed their language with Latin and so formed the bizarre, hybrid dialect which is still extant in certain districts of Epirus, Thessaly, and Greece.[81]

There is much to support Koumas' opinion. Latin, after all, was the official language of administration for more than seven hundred years, and this, as Koumas suggests, necessarily affected the local population. An important source dating from the reign of Justinian asserts that many of the European parts of the Empire spoke Latin, even in those areas where Greek predominated. This was especially true in the case of civil servants. Evidence provided by numerous Latin and Greek inscriptions attests to the establishment of Roman settlements in Greece. These settlements no doubt were conscious of their Roman citizenship and no doubt also sought to impress their civilization on the autochthonous inhabitants. It is not unreasonable to suppose, therefore, that many of the latter adopted the Latin speech. The speech of their descendants today is clearly derived from this early form. Adoption of the Latin speech must have been especially prevalent in the isolated and undeveloped western districts, which were oriented towards Italy.

The problem, however, is more complicated. If there were Vlachs, particularly in the Greek regions, whose original background may have been, as we believe, Greek, there were others whose origin was quite different. An undated source of the seventh century, describing the Avaro-Slav migrations, refers to a Latin-speaking people from the regions of the Danube, which sought refuge in the northern parts of Greece.[82] In this people we have the origin of another branch of the Vlachs, among whom we may include the Vlachorynchini of later documents as well as the Vlachs north of Lake Langadha (Koroneia) near Thessalonica, mentioned by the seventeenth-century traveller Evliya Tschelebi, and possibly also those of Moglena, who still exist and who differ somewhat from the Vlachs of the Pindus in language, customs, and traditions, a difference which may be explained by their Danubian origin.[83]

The arrival of this latinized people, to which we have referred above, took place at a time when the Latin language was still being spoken by the inhabitants of the districts involved. Regular intercourse between the newcomers and the local inhabitants was thereby facilitated, and in this way a new element, which came to be known as Vlach, gradually evolved. This new element spoke a Neo-Latin dialect, resembling that spoken in the Danubian regions. This resemblance served during the Turkish occupation as an inducement to migrate to these rich northern regions.

The intricacies of the problem of Vlach origins become even more apparent when it is realized that successive waves of Slavs and, later, Albanians settled down in those areas which were already occupied by Vlachs.[84] Later still, during the Turkish occupation, Greek-speaking immigrants from the plains and highlands of central and western Greece also found shelter in the inaccessible complex of the Pindus Mountains. All of these people came into daily contact with one another. However, the exact nature of this intercourse and the manner in which they all finally succumbed to Hellenic culture still lie hidden in unexplored history. Vague oral traditions refer to Vlach migrations from northern Epirus to the Aspropotamos River district. Besides these, there is only the tentative evidence of G. Weigand, who has attempted to construct a picture of settlement in the Pindus Mountains by reference to the traces which its peoples have left. From a total of 65 toponyms that he described, 29 were attributed to the Slavs, 22 to the Vlachs, and 15 to the Greeks. The last predominated in the region from Kerassovo to Karpenision; the first were confined mainly to the western slopes of the Pindus and to the south of Lake Ioannina.[85]

The patriot of 1821, Kasomoulis, has referred to the Vlachs of Pindus as Greco-Vlachs in order to distinguish them from the Arvanito-Vlachs (neighbors of the Colonia Albanians), who lived in the villages around Moscopolis (now Voskopojë) such as Grammousta and Nicolitsa. The influence of these Greco-Vlachs upon the development of the Greek nation is somewhat more palpable. Towards the end of the Byzantine Empire they united with the Greeks in order to confront the Turks more effectively. Throughout the period of the Turkish occupation they continued to make common cause against the invaders.[86] Subsequently, they took the lead in the establishment of Greek schools and in the propagation of Greek education, and their talents as craftsmen, merchants, and warriors enriched the life of Greece. From this racial crucible in the mountain fastnesses of western Greece, among the Latin-speaking Greco-Vlachs, the Greek-speaking nomads called Sarakatsans,[87] and the intractable guerrillas and brigands of Acarnania, came one of the sparks which rekindled the flame of Greek nationalism.

The Franks and Turks

The Latin occupation from 1204, when Constantinople fell during the Fourth Crusade, to 1566 left almost no permanent ethnic imprint on the Greek nation. This was especially so in the north, where Latin influence prevailed during the very brief period from 1204 to 1224. Even in the south, where the Latin presence made itself felt for a much greater length of time, assimilation tended to be rapid because of the small numbers of the invaders. The Latins established themselves in hastily constructed fortresses whose aspect of impermanence contrasted starkly with the august solidity of their counterparts in western Europe. The petty states set up under Latin rule were finally swept away by Byzantine and Turkish armies. Thereafter, such influence as the Latin rule may have had on Greek society faded rapidly and the Latin element was completely ingested. In time even the immediate products of racial intermixture, the Gasmuli or Vasmuli, similarly disappeared.

It is possible to find the hellenized descendants of a Latin ethnic infusion on the Aegean islands of Tenos, Naxos, Syros, and Santorini. However, the only indications of their origin are the survival of foreign names and some vestiges of Roman Catholicism. The persistence of Roman Catholicism, however, is hardly a reliable criterion of ethnic descent, since conversion of Orthodox islanders to the Latin rite occurred during the late Byzantine and Turkish periods. During the last two centuries of the Byzantine era and throughout the Turkish occupation there were no less frequent cases of Catholic apostasy to Orthodox dogma. Proof of the Greek ethnic origin of most Aegean Roman Catholics exists in the structure of their language, which followed the normal morphological development of the southern, and in particular the Cycladic, dialect: the names of trees, shrubs, wildflowers, fruits, and the like, are the same, and most importantly the customs and traditions remain entirely similar.[88]

The Turkish component in the ethnic structure of the Greek nation was limited [89] by the fundamental differences in religion which always separated these two peoples. Indeed, the influence was rather of an inverted kind, since thousands of Greeks who were converted to Islam wrought a subtle transformation in the character of the Turkish nation and permanently affected its development.

The persistence of Hellenism must be ascribed to the fact that the newcomers remained in the minority at all times. This minority suffered a gradual and imperceptible transmutation by the dominant Hellenic tradition. Neo-Hellenism, as such, began to emerge after the appearance of the last intruders, the Albanians and Arvanito-Vlachs. Its center of gravity was to be found in the Peloponnese, where most of the Slavs and Albanians had settled down. Here, in spite of the heterogeneous character of the population, the process of hellenization and cultural diffusion continued, even during four centuries of Turkish occupation.

There were many potent forces at work. Greek civilization itself was an irresistible inducement. The Greek language survived as the vital living organism through which the essence of this civilization was preserved and transmitted. In the Balkan Peninsula and Asia Minor Orthodox Christianity provided a common framework of religious belief, which was constantly propagated by the Greek clergy, especially those in the monasteries and principal ecclesiastical centers. Finally, there was the whole complex of social and economic relationships, which tended to promote the interdependence of all peoples under the Turkish yoke, and the bond of common resistance to the Moslem invader, which everywhere brought raias, or non-Moslem subjects, ever closer together. On the other hand, the religious polarity between Greek and Moslem always remained fundamental: it not only prevented the conjunction of the two groups but indeed virtually precluded any close and viable relationship.

The resemblance between certain aspects of ancient and modern Greek society has been sufficiently striking to attract the attention of numerous foreign observers since 1821.[90] There is a remarkable consensus among foreign observers as to what the more notable traits of the modern Hellenes are—nimbleness of perception, easy adaptability, depth of feeling, fervent patriotism, hatred of occupation by foreigners, and passion for politics.[91] It is also widely accepted in academic circles today that a knowledge of the customs and traditions of the modern Greeks provides an understanding both of the ancient past and of the essence of the Greek ethos. Thus the evidence found in folklore and language is the most reliable guide to a study of the overall impact of foreign elements on Greece. While our knowledge of these varied influences is incomplete, it can certainly be extended by intensive comparative studies of the folklore of particular districts in combination with detailed historical and geographical research.[92]

2

THE SURVIVAL OF GREEK
CIVILIZATION

From the Roman Conquest to the Tenth Century

From the time of the Roman conquest of Greece in 146 B.C., the Greeks,
like so many other conquered peoples, lived for centuries on the periphery
of political life in a sprawling empire whose center was Rome. The Greek
peninsula, especially southern Greece, was no longer a political center of
importance. This situation was not substantially altered by the establishment of Constantinople in 330 A.D., since Constantine's purpose in founding the city was, in part, the strengthening of Roman influence throughout
the provinces of the East. When the division of the Empire between East
and West was formalized by Theodosius in 395 the focus of the eastern
segment of the Empire was fixed even more clearly upon the Bosphorus
and Asia Minor. Southern Greece constituted, geographically, a large
province of the new empire, but it remained remote in a political sense.[1]
Nevertheless the act of Constantine as well as that of Theodosius contributed to the survival and consolidation of Hellenism in the area. "For
long centuries," writes Gregorovius,

the peculiar significance of Constantine's creation was understood by neither
the Greeks of that time nor their descendants. The building of Constantinople
in itself not only ensured the perpetuation of the Greek nation but the preservation for posterity of the incomparable treasures of Greek civilization. Without
Constantinople, indeed, Greece and the Peloponnese would have been conquered and colonized by barbarous peoples. Without this mighty fortified city
and the protection which it offered it is impossible to conceive of the conserva-
tion of Greek culture, or of the emergence of the Greek Church, or even of the

existence of the Byzantine Empire. In Constantinople, however, was born not only a rival of Athens but an enemy of pagan Hellenism.[2]

During the reign of Constantine the Great and his successor there was a spirit of toleration towards the diverse religions of the Empire. The new capital was in constant intellectual intercourse with Athens and probably with Corinth and Thebes.[3] Yet the very name Hellene, because of its connotation with the ideas and religious beliefs of the ancient Greeks, was already becoming synonymous with pagan. As adherents of the Christian religion gradually multiplied in Greece they tended to eschew the appellation Hellene in favor of *Romaios,* Roman, the more so because of an overriding sense of imperial citizenship. The pejorative overtones of the word Hellene only inhibited its use, thus destroying its function as the primary symbol of national identity. A few writers continued to use the national label; [4] others, particularly during the sixth, seventh, and eighth centuries, adopted the variant *Helladikoi.*[5]

In time, the national appellation acquired additional connotations. With the ruins of imposing buildings and monuments everywhere to be seen, the ancient Greeks, according to the testimony of generations, could only have been a people of towering physique and transcendent intellectual qualities bordering on the supernatural. "Hellene" therefore took on a further meaning, "giant," [6] which persisted in the popular mind down to the twentieth century.

The heterogeneous races and peoples of the Roman Empire lived for centuries within a social and political framework variously composed of elements of the ancient cultures of the East, the Hellenistic empire of Alexander the Great, Christianity, and the Roman polity. But since Greek civilization was deeply rooted in the East it was the Greek-speaking element which exerted the most profound and lasting influence upon the civilization of the Eastern Roman Empire. The artistic and intellectual life of the Empire was predominantly Greek, and some of its manifestations could be readily detected in the early Byzantine state. Elements of Greek drama, for instance, were absorbed into the tragic and comic styles of the popular Byzantine theater.[7] An overwhelming majority of the inhabitants of the Byzantine Empire spoke the Greek language, and intellectual, and indeed political, activity was largely governed according to the standards embodied in Greek education.

This far-reaching influence of Hellenism, whose very spirit and apotheosis were incarnate in the city of Athens, was shorn of its overtly pagan forms after the establishment of the Roman imperium in Constantinople. A definite reaction against Hellenism coincided with the extension of Christianity throughout the Eastern Empire. It was characterized by a vigorous attempt to extirpate all forms of idolatry. During the reign of

Theodosius (379–395) particularly, the official campaign to stamp out pagan worship was sedulously pursued. Many statues and works of art, formerly sacred to the ancient Greeks, were deliberately destroyed, among them the Sarapeum of Alexandria. In emulation of Constantine the Great, others—Praxiteles' "Lindia Athena" and "Knidia Athena," and Phidias' "Zeus"—were removed to Constantinople. For the time being Athens was spared, probably because of the city's cultural renown. Yet it was here that the fires of pagan worship burned most brightly; it was here, too, that various philosophical schools constituted the principal intellectual bulwark against the new religion.[8] The invasion of the Goths under Alaric dealt another destructive blow to paganism. It is quite possible that Christians collaborated in the destruction. One of the victims was Eleusis, which ceased thereafter to be a center of pagan rites.

It is by no means clear exactly how Christianity spread through Greece and especially to Athens. In the absence of more conclusive evidence it seems that it must have spread by a process of gradual infiltration over the years. Certainly by 529 it had advanced so far as to convince Justinian that, the splendor of Athens notwithstanding, the ultimate prosecution of paganism might be pursued with impunity. In that year the teaching of all pre-Christian philosophy in Athens was placed under interdict and the lands of Plato's Academy were confiscated. "Thus," writes Gregorovius, "the ancient religion was finally effaced from the cities, although its practice was surreptitiously preserved by the Neo-Platonists. For centuries afterwards Greek idolatry found adherents in the inaccessible regions of Greece, especially the Taygetus Mountains. Something of the pagan spirit, moreover, continued to be communicated to each successive Christian generation. Even the modern Greek's mind is steeped in the forms and observances of ancient mythology."[9]

In spite of the near disappearance of pagan worship the cities of Athens, Corinth, and Patras lived on as centers of a vital Hellenic culture. The Slav invasions had a negligible impact upon the culture of Attica, as the virtual absence of Slav toponyms of any kind, to which allusion has already been made, sufficiently attests. The racial strain of Attica was slightly adulterated by the Slav infusion of the sixth century and after, but its civilization remained almost intact.[10] According to legend, St. Gislenos, who came from a prominent family in Attica, studied in Athens [11] before founding the famous monastery at Hennegau, Germany, in 640. Hopf, who was the first to bring this information to the attention of scholars, believes that during the reign of Heraclius (610–641) Athens was a center for the study of Greek culture.[12] In a letter of Pope Zachary's, reference is also made to Theodore of Tarsus, Archbishop of Canterbury (668–693), as "a Greek philosopher who studied in Athens and then be-

came Latin." In Canterbury Theodore established a school for the teaching of Greek.[13] One source mentions that St. Stephen of Surozh visited
Athens in the eighth century and there met a number of local philosophers and orators.[14]

Between the seventh and tenth centuries, the assimilation of foreign
peoples was aided not only by the progressive consolidation of Byzantine authority but, most importantly, by the spread of Greek learning
which emanated from the monasteries. Monastic libraries were reposi-
tories of the ancient knowledge to which many had access. Cedrenus,
for example, mentions that the famous mathematician Leon, having been
instructed in rhetoric, philosophy, and mathematics by a distinguished
ninth-century mentor from Andros and having been enormously stimulated by this induction into intellectual pursuits, then journeyed to several
monasteries in search of more knowledge: "When he found the right
books he immersed himself in them, and eventually attained great heights
of erudition." [15]

This assimilation extended throughout the entire geographical extent
of the Byzantine Empire, in Asia Minor, continental Greece, and the
islands of the Aegean. During the middle Byzantine period (the seventh
through the eleventh centuries) the whole of Asia Minor became, cul-
turally as well as politically, an integral part of the Byzantine state.[16]
The absorption of diverse national groups, not only in Asia Minor but
throughout the whole Empire, occurred along with the dissemination of
the Greek language and Greek learning. Ultimately, it was this fusion
of many peoples, all possessing a common culture, the most important
ingredients of which were Greek, that gave form and coherence to that
distinctive civilization we now call "Byzantine." [17]

The Greek language continuously preserved the priceless treasures of
Greek literature, both ancient and medieval, at the same time that the
demotic tongue kept alive many of the most ancient cultural traditions.
Customs, habits, crafts, songs, even architectural forms,[18] all survived
the ravages of time in the folklore and common memory of the people.
The modern Greek language is replete with words and expressions that
deal with archaic social situations or that are fossilized remnants of
ancient modes of expression.[19] In Theocritus' Idylls [20] and in the works
of Byzantine scholars such as Eustathius and Joseph Bryennios, it is by
no means uncommon to find references to proverbs, popular sayings,
oaths, curses, superstitions, and so on,[21] which have been faithfully
handed down through the centuries to the present.[22] Their persistence
stresses the continuous and uninterrupted tradition of the Greek way
of life.

From the Tenth Century through the Thirteenth

An important sign of a national culture is the existence of forms of literary and artistic expression that are overtly national in character and origin. Such forms of expression, which were specifically and self-consciously Greek, arose within the civilization of the Byzantine world. They were at once cause and effect of a growing consciousness of Greek national identity.

However, it was in Asia Minor, not Greece proper, that these new manifestations first appeared. To be sure, the ancient centers of Greek civilization, notably Athens, continued not only to preserve but to propagate certain elements of the intellectual heritage of the past.[23] The study of ancient Greek writers never ceased. Michael Choniates, for instance, the twelfth-century Archbishop of Athens, declaimed eloquently upon the intellectual decadence of the Athenians, though his critical faculties could still be fed by the books which he procured in Athens, indicating the existence of some scholarly activity in that distinguished city.[24] Yet it is not possible to accept unreservedly the testimony of Master John of Basingstoke (thirteenth century) that Athens remained a fertile oasis of learning during the period of Latin domination.[25] Quite definitely, the intellectual activity of Athens decreased and, although it did not entirely disappear, its influence was then of a subsidiary, or at most a complementary, nature.

The survival of traditional folk songs, especially the ballads (*paralogai*), similarly implied that the memory of ancient times was never completely erased from the popular mind. The ballads provide a definite link with the ancient world, for their thematic material is often identical with legends which were used constantly in the classical theater. The very word "song," *tragoudi*, was derived from "tragedy," *tragodia*.[26]

By the eleventh century the Greek people had already developed some sense of a national commonalty. Towards the end of the eleventh century an anonymous commentator on Aristotle's *Rhetoric* spoke of the pillage of Asia Minor by Danişmend, the Emir of Kastamonu, and of the duty of Athenians to support their courageous compatriots in their unhappy predicament: "It is necessary, therefore, that we Athenians look to the glory of other Greeks in their desperate struggle." [27] Although Michael Choniates himself was more concerned with disparaging the intellectual achievements of his fellow Athenians, it is obvious that he considered them to be the direct descendants of the ancient Greeks.

The people of Asia Minor who attracted the attention of the Athenians in the eleventh century lived in the highlands and valleys of the Taurus and Anti-Taurus mountains. For centuries they had been engaged in conflicts with the Arabs [28] and later the Turks. These struggles had fired the imagination not only of the common people but of poets, and thus was born a series of stirring epic cycles which extolled the valor and fortitude of the several protagonists. The Arabs had their *Seyyid Battal,* the Turks their *Danişmendnāme,* which drew extensively on the former,[29] and the Greeks their *Digenis Akritas.*

The *Digenis Akritas* occupies a position of almost unique importance in the popular affections of the Greeks. A good deal of the folklore upon which it draws, together with the epic itself, is still current in the Greek world. For centuries, the bravery of the *Akritai* had been praised in tales which were kept vividly alive in the vernacular. Gradually, the vernacular established itself as a vehicle of literary expression, until by the tenth century, or perhaps as early as the ninth century, Akritic poetry had evolved definite forms not unlike those of today.[30] It would seem from the language used in its construction that the *Digenis Akritas* was written during the tenth or eleventh century by an unknown poet, who may have been a priest or monk from Cappadocia.[31] Whatever its authorship, it may be said without exaggeration that modern Greek literature stems from popularly inspired epic poetry of the kind epitomized by the *Digenis Akritas.* Since the struggles of the people of Asia Minor not only inspired the poetry but also aroused the impassioned sympathy of the Greeks of continental Greece and the Aegean,[32] the very awakening of Greek nationalism may be said to coincide with the rebirth of epic poetry. The deeds of the principal Akritic heroes such as Digenis, Constantin, Armouris,[33] Porphyris, Andronicus and his sons, and others,[34] transcended the narrow limits of the particular districts in which their exploits took place. They appeared as symbols of bravery in a national struggle.

It would seem that other forms of popular expression, songs, novels, prose narratives of various kinds, developed simultaneously with Akritic poetry. However, we have little knowledge of these.[35] In 1180, the French poet Aimé de Varennes, author of *Florimont,* maintained that he listened to Greek songs in Philippopolis (now Plovdiv) which recounted the adventures of Florimont and of Philip, "great-grandfather" of the great Alexander. He also said that he returned to France with a version of the original novel, or historical romance, of *Florimont.*[36] However, this statement must be treated with caution; it is probably an example of the kind of prevarication to which poets of this time were especially prone.[37] It is more credible that de Varennes refers to a copy of the Byzantine version of the *Alexander Romance,* which derives from an original publication of the third or fourth century, the Pseudo-Callisthenes.[38] This novel about Alexander the Great was translated into at least twenty-four languages during the Middle Ages and became generally known throughout the East as well as in Western Europe. Indeed, no other mere literary work was copied and translated so extensively at that time. Its influence upon the literature of various European and Eastern countries is a subject which falls outside the scope of this study, although we may remark its very considerable impact upon the Greek-speaking world down to the end of the period of Turkish sovereignty.[39] The widespread oral currency of various narratives associated with the *Alexander Romance*—that is to say, the Byzantine version—gave rise to numerous popular beliefs and traditions which are held to this day by the inhabitants of the peninsula and islands of Greece.[40]

The Byzantines commonly depicted Alexander as a Byzantine king, or "as a saint, or at any rate as a holy person who establishes monasteries and churches in the manner of the actual Byzantine Emperors." [41] They also represent Philip of Macedonia as the first Christian king, in accordance with a tradition which persisted in Philippopolis at least until the time when it was recorded by the English chronicler, Walter Vinsauf.[42] In Byzantine times, scholars often evoked the examples of Alexander and Philip when it was their intention to exhort or flatter the influential and the mighty. Indeed, the legends which surrounded the person of Alexander were so pervasive as to affect even the Turks. By the twelfth century a tradition had grown among them that "the Turks were finally to be crushed by those with whose assistance Alexander had once crushed the Persians." [43]

Today it is apparent that the reputation of Alexander the Great and even of his father Philip was much greater among the Greeks of the Middle Ages than many scholars have hitherto assumed. Literary and archaeological research constantly furnishes new proof that the deeds of these remarkable Macedonians reverberated down through the ages and that vivid impressions were left in the minds of each successive generation. According to the novel, Alexander was the dominant military genius of the Greek and Oriental worlds, and his example served as a model of bravery, wisdom, and, to a lesser degree, shrewdness. A common memory of Alexander in these terms and of Philip and Macedonia in general was always present, as we shall again have occasion to notice.

Finally, recent research has revealed the close connection between Byzantine painting and its classical and Hellenistic counterparts. The classical and Hellenistic methods of representation served as perennial models for Byzantine artists. The *Alexander Romance* is only one of the many novels illustrated with miniatures that circulated widely during the late Hellenistic and Roman periods. However, it was the most beloved, and accordingly survived the longest. Nothing is known of the other novels of the middle Byzantine era, but the miniatures of the *Alexander Romance* are alone sufficient to provide a concrete connection between the classical age and the Byzantine. They closely follow the style of the classical originals, using the same special artistic technique. They belong to one of the most interesting genres of antiquity. Illustrated manuscripts of the tenth and eleventh centuries also show that iconographic skills were transmitted from generation to generation. Many of the manuscripts of this period—for example, the Pseudo-Nonnus and the Pseudo-Oppian—recount episodes clearly derived from the traditional legends of antiquity. The miniatures of the *Alexander Romance* in the Pseudo-Oppian have a definite expository value in that "they still reflect classical style, thus providing evidence for the existence of an illustrated Pseudo-Callisthenes in the late classical period." [44]

The popularity of the *Alexander Romance* is evinced in numerous portrayals of its hero's life in Byzantine pottery, marble and ivory bas-reliefs, and various manuscripts which are still extant. Especially striking examples of pottery are the vases produced by lay artisans from the eleventh to the fourteenth centuries, fragments of which have been unearthed in Athens, Thessalonica, and Constantinople, the three principal centers of Greek civilization.[45] Of the several examples of marble bas-reliefs, probably the most celebrated, that of the Ascension of Alexander the Great, is to be found in the Cathedral of St. Mark's in Venice. However, others come from Thebes (late tenth or early eleventh century), Constantinople (twelfth or thirteenth century) and Mistra (fourteenth century). Yet another exists in the narthex of the main chapel of the monastery of Docheiariou on Mt. Athos. Each work of art is characterized by a scene representing the craftsman's interpretation of an episode from the illustrated text of the various Byzantine versions of the *Alexander Romance*. These illustrations are themselves derived from another version, which originated in the Roman-Hellenistic period.[46]

An increasing regard for the civilization of ancient Greece was especially discernible throughout the period of the Macedonian dynasty (867–1057). It was actively encouraged by the Emperor Constantine VII Porphyrogenitus. Classical inspiration was conspicuous in the writing of men like Michael Psellus, historian and philosopher, who contemplated the Acropolis with the utmost reverence and whose admiration for Plato knew no bounds; Arethas (ninth and tenth centuries); the twelfth-century Homeric scholar, Eustathius, Archbishop of Thessalonica; and his disciple Michael Choniates, Archbishop of Athens, who was so disillusioned with his fellow Athenians as to develop an extravagant, almost fanciful, veneration for the ancient Greeks.[47]

Such veneration was not without its disadvantages. Almost without

Figure 2. Ascension of Alexander the Great.

exception these scholars wrote in classical Attic and disdained the vernacular then being developed as a literary medium through Akritic and other poetic genres. The results of such antiquarianism, in terms of the evolution of the Greek nation and its culture, were far from salutary, for a crucial moment had arrived in the transition from medieval literature to that written in modern Greek. The historian Spyridon Lambros recognized this when he commented upon Michael Choniates' adherence to the traditional Attic language: "Byzantine literature would have assumed a better national literary mode if writers at that time had chosen to express their ideas and feelings in the more natural, living language of the people. Byzantine letters generally would have appeared more vivid and dynamic if, instead of imitating Attic Greek to the detriment of many of their literary endeavors, writers had courageously set about the literary formulation of the language of the streets and of the home. They would have been wise to eschew the eclectic and highly symbolic official language of the Church and the state." [48]

When scholars and artists turned towards antiquity, the people generally followed. They did so readily because the revival of ancient Greek influence in no way provoked the opposition of the Christian Church; on the contrary, the Church gradually assimilated it into the Christian tradition.

Each memory and practice of ancient Greek civilization handed down through the centuries contributed to a process of cultural fermentation by which the Byzantine world was imperceptibly transformed into the Greek nation. The Byzantine Empire created new conditions and needs which necessarily determined the character of modern Hellenism. Innumerable complex forces were at work. The task of delineating the principal landmarks and stages of growth in what was, after all, a slow and intricate process of evolution, is a formidable one. Nevertheless, a convention exists, as we have already pointed out, that the year 1204 marks the point from which the new Hellenism was projected. It is now our immediate concern—difficult, or even impossible, as the undertaking may well turn out to be—to examine further into the reasons for this choice.

ORIGINS OF NATIONAL CONSCIOUSNESS

Various Theories

The question of determining the origins of Greek national consciousness arose as a corollary of the nineteenth-century controversy surrounding the racial derivation of the modern Greeks. Obviously, Greek historians have been principally concerned with the matter, and it is with their views that we may conveniently begin an analysis of the problem.

The first tentative hypotheses were advanced by Zambelios, who considered that the origins of this Greek feeling of a national consciousness could clearly be traced back to the Byzantine period. This particular scholar's approach is distinguished more by an a priori belief in that which he sets out to prove than by concrete evidence. Nevertheless, he points to the continued existence of language and folk songs as sufficient indication of the early awareness of a Greek cultural identity.[1] Paparrhegopoulos later expressed the same view, though with greater clarity and precision. Recognizing the essential continuity of the Greek language and the existence of a popular literary heritage, he believed that the origins of modern Hellenism would have to be sought amid the anarchy and confusion which accompanied the Fourth Crusade (1204). He saw too that there was a marked revival of communal institutions during the later Byzantine period (brought about chiefly by the progressive deterioration of central authority) and that a spirit of popular resistance to the Latin conquerors was in the air. All these factors indicate that modern nationalism derives from the medieval Greeks.[2]

Although yet another historian, Sathas, attempted to embellish Paparrhegopoulos' theory, the latter's version is generally accepted by most

modern Greek historians.³ Two of these in particular, Amantos and Voyat-
zides, have supplemented a primary interest in the history of the Byzantine Empire with studies on modern Greek history and are therefore
well qualified to trace the relationship between the two eras. Amantos,
in his *History of the Byzantine Empire,* thinks of the year 1204 as the
terminal point of the Byzantine Empire,⁴ while Voyatzidis suggests that
the Palaeologian period (1261–1453) does not constitute the end of Byzantine Hellenism but the beginnings of Neo-Hellenism. New political
forces, he says, arose in the Eastern Roman Empire and presaged the
establishment of a new Hellenic state.⁵ Which of these interpretations
comes closest to the truth is, however, a question that need not concern
us here, since both authorities are in full agreement that many of the
forms of the political and cultural expression of modern Greece are essentially derivative of Byzantine Hellenism. In this sense, the year 1204
marks a watershed in the history of modern Greece and the civilized
world.

Political Decentralization after Fourth Crusade

The Byzantine Empire was laid low by the Crusaders from the West, but
its structure had already been undermined by a combination of ruinous
taxation, rapacious taxgathering, and the consequent decrease in the
amount of land owned by peasants.⁶ The dislocation of agricultural life
brought misery and confusion, and the rapidity with which the Empire
collapsed brought on an acute moral crisis for the Greek population: the
choice between submission and loss of freedom, or resistance and loss of
property.

Certain cities, such as Thessalonica, submitted meekly in order to preserve a nominal independence: a promise from the conquerors that local
institutions would be respected.⁷ Many nobles offered no resistance in
the expectation that their privileges and property would remain intact; ⁸
others chose to flee the enemy with the aim of finding secure hiding
places from which resistance could be organized. Nevertheless the comparative ease with which the conquerors were able to impose their will,
particularly upon the nobility, aroused the patriotic ire of at least one
contemporary observer, Nicetas Choniates: "They felt neither degrada-
tion nor dishonor in bowing their heads to the invader. They felt not a
single pang of shame in disdaining to fight—if only for their children's
sake. Not then, nor later, were they aroused by thoughts of freedom."
Indeed, his resentment was so impassioned that he accused some—in particular, the descendants of old military families—of intriguing actively
for the destruction of their country: "worthless men, corrupt and licen-

tious, who were consumed by an ambition to destroy their country" solely
in order to advance their own interests. (Even at that time, Choniates
seems to have had the vision of a unified nation.) In the general turmoil,
nobles ensconced themselves in castles and surrounded themselves with
all the pomp and panoply of sovereign princes. This practice was most
pronounced throughout the Peloponnese, where petty nobles vied constantly with one another for the perquisites and appendages of princely
power.[9] Their factious spirit was not finally curbed until the Turkish
conquest of the Peloponnese.

The situation of constant antagonism and actual armed conflict between
Greek and Latin states naturally made it all the easier for these petty
principalities to assert their sovereignty, and this political fragmentation
of the Empire in turn facilitated Turkish domination. The Fourth Crusade
brought about political chaos and physical ruin at precisely the time
when the Empire was in most need of political unity. Whole communities were uprooted. Some were displaced, only to re-establish themselves
somewhere else. Others completely disappeared. Some centers of population were swollen by the addition of refugees. Others were depopulated.[10]

Some indication of the extent of the dislocation of the population may
be gleaned from events in Nicaea, where large numbers from Constantinople took refuge, and in Ioannina. The city of Ioannina was fortified by
Michael I Comnenus Ducas (1206–1215), founder of the Despotate of
Epirus. Many Greeks sought the security of its walls and, until they found
new homes, there received the solicitous attentions of its ruler, this new
"Noah." [11] Probably no fewer than half of the refugees from Constantinople found their way to Epirus; others came from the Peloponnese through
Aetolia.[12] This mountainous and isolated region of western Greece served
not only as an impregnable fortress against the Latin invaders but also
as a focal point of active resistance, as much in the thirteenth century as
in the Second World War. This new infusion of Greek refugees, sharing
with all the inhabitants of the region the experience of resistance to a
common enemy, constituted yet another factor in the assimilation of im-
migrant Slavs.

The importance of the Crusades and of the Fourth Crusade in particular is therefore not that they provided a connecting link between the two
principal segments of European civilization. Rather, they set up an inter-
action between East and West, which thereafter characterized all relations
between the two and resulted ultimately in the emergence of a new
Greek nation. After 1204—even after the recapture of Constantinople by
Michael VIII Palaeologus in 1261—the Byzantine Empire was never more

than a simulacrum of its former self, because of the persistence of cen-
tripetal influences. In its place appeared a series of separate Greek states,
Nicaea, Trebizond, Epirus, Macedonia, and later, the Peloponnese.

Individual rulers derived such authority as they possessed from alliances with the local nobility. Yet, for precisely the reason that the traditions of Hellenism were most sturdy among the peasants, the process of
political decentralization tended to revivify the sense of Hellenism in the
everyday lives of the people. The shifting of the loci of power, that is,
tended to magnify and clarify what might otherwise have remained dif-
fuse. Roman traditions withered in the courts of the new sovereign states;
Greek traditions throve in proportion. At the same time, in the islands
and mainland areas which lay under Latin domination, the vitality of
Greek intellectual life continued to encourage a spirit of resistance.

As we shall presently see, resistance to a succession of conquerors, Bulgarian, Serbian, and Turkish, as well as Latin, greatly heightened the
Greek national consciousness. Indeed, the unrelenting struggle for survival, sustained by the knowledge of an illustrious past, constituted the
principal ingredient of Greek nationalism. The writings of all of the important historians of this period—Nicetas Choniates and Nicephorus Gregoras, for example—bristle with allusions to antiquity, proclaim the nobility of struggle, and always exalt the name Hellene. Choniates implored
God "to keep our people intact." He strove to inculcate in Greeks an
awareness of the glorious nature of their struggle, even to the extent of
referring to their defeat only with the most obvious reluctance: "How
is it possible for history to recount the great deeds of barbarians when
history itself is the greatest achievement of the Greeks?" [13]

Greek nationalism therefore began to assume a more definite form during the period of Latin conquest. It was manifest in the deeds and aspirations of the people. It was even evident to some extent in the life of the
Orthodox Church, especially in the period of Turkish domination. To be
sure, the nationalist awakening was counteracted to some extent, after
the twelfth century, by the persistence of a sense of Roman citizenship
within the decrepit framework of the restored Byzantine Empire. But this
became more and more tenuous and artificial because it no longer corresponded to reality. For example, the Byzantine armies which had offered
such ineffectual resistance to the Crusaders [14] had been composed mainly
of foreign mercenaries; but now, in the struggle with the Latin invaders,
at least in the beginning, their character was completely transformed.
Greek soldiers increasingly filled out the ranks, and it was the example
and inspiration of their ancient forebears which sustained their martial
ardor.

National resistance to the Latin conquerors was especially fierce in the

Despotate of Epirus (comprising Epirus, Acarnania, Aetolia, and parts of Thessaly), the Empire of Nicaea, the Peloponnese, and Crete. In each, we see a microcosm of the larger struggle. From each, we may therefore offer graphic illustrations of the importance of this period in the historical evolution of the new Hellenism.

Rivalry between Epirus and Nicaea

Apart from the several conflicts between Greek and Latin states, the rivalry between two important Greek states, Epirus and Nicaea, was a crucial factor in the development of Hellenism. Unfortunately, little is known about the political pursuits of the "Grand Comneni" of Trebizond and their contribution to the growth of Hellenism. Although Trebizond became the center of an intellectual movement renowned for its scientific achievements,[15] the political influence of the "Grand Comneni" in the Greek world was dissipated in a series of futile struggles with the emperors of Nicaea.[16]

The historiography of Epirus is regrettably deficient. Most of our knowledge of this state is derived from Nicaean historians, who naturally tended to interpret events from their own point of view.[17] Apart from these, virtually the only known records are the writings of a single monk, Isaac Mesopotamites. Nevertheless, a careful sifting of both sources enables us to reconstruct a fairly accurate picture of the political situation in Epirus. The aims and ambitions of the rulers of that state seem especially clear-cut.

Beginning with Theodore Comnenus Ducas (1215–1230), who had lived for a long time in the royal court of Nicaea, a contest developed between Epirus and Nicaea for hegemony over the former territories of the Byzantine Empire. Rulers competed for the right to be regarded as the legitimate successors of the Emperor in Constantinople and for the titles and honors which stemmed therefrom.[18] At first, the controversy crystallized around the status of the Church in Epirus. Political circumstances had already conferred a kind of *de facto* independence upon the Epirotic Church, and Theodore saw that his own political authority could be enhanced by maintaining this separation from the Church in Nicaea.[19] He therefore appointed or encouraged the election of local prelates without reference to the hierarchy of the Church, thereby promoting further estrangement between the two states. Since the Oecumenical Patriarchate supported the principle of ecclesiastical unity and thus, indirectly, the primacy of the Empire of Nicaea, Theodore also found himself in open conflict with the central organization of the Church.[20]

The head of the Epirotic Church was the Metropolitan of Naupactus, John Apocaucus (1155–1233), one of the most prominent figures of his

time. Apocaucus had received a sound classical education in Constantinople and was particularly influenced by the philosopher-historian Michael
Psellus. He was also, like his contemporary, Archbishop Michael Choniates
of Athens, an ardent admirer of the ancient Greek world generally.
Indeed, his role in Naupactus was entirely analogous to that of his friend
and colleague in Athens. After 1219, Apocaucus became an eager sup-
porter of and apologist for the ruler of Epirus. His letters to his patron
are paeans of praise for Theodore's audacious military exploits. They
record Theodore's conquests of Neopatras, Prosakon, Platamon, and,
finally, Thessalonica (1224). There, Theodore brought to an end the rule
of the Montferrat family; and there, in the spring of 1224, he was anointed
emperor by Archbishop Demetrius Chomatianus of Achris (Ochrida).
This event dramatized Theodore's emergence as a redoubtable rival of
the emperors of Nicaea,[21] and Apocaucus thought that nothing could be
more fitting than that Theodore assume the imperial mantle in the Great
City.[22] In a letter to Patriarch Germanus of Nicaea he extolled the
virtues of his emperor: "Here, in the West this man has looked un-
tiringly to the interests of his people. We already know him to be a
gift from God, a savior of the Christians of Epirus. He has reconquered
many towns, bringing back those citizens who had fled and reuniting
those who had been separated from one another. The religious in churches
and monasteries can again perform their proper duties as shepherds of
the people and custodians of the Church. All rejoice as before in shep-
herding the people, and the sheep listen to them and gather together in
an ever increasing flock—thanks only to our emperor." [23]

John Apocaucus and two other Church hierarchs who owed their positions mainly to his influence, Demetrius Chomatianus, Archbishop of
Achris, and George Vardanis, Metropolitan of Corfu, formed a brilliant
intellectual coterie in the Despotate of Epirus. All were acutely conscious
of being Greek.[24] Apocaucus, particularly, made constant use of the term
Hellas when referring to the southern regions of Greece.[25] Vardanis [26] was
an Athenian and had studied under Michael Choniates. As a young man
he found Latin rule insufferable and subsequently left for Epirus with a
letter of recommendation from his mentor. "No longer," it said, "could he
bear living among us here. We have been humiliated, and our country
has become a barbarous land of impious people." [27] Later, while a deacon
in the bishopric of Grevena, Vardanis declined to accept the episcopal
see of Vonitsa [28] despite the fact—at least according to Apocaucus—
that Vonitsa lay in the midst of a Greek-speaking population and was
exclusively Greek.[29] He preferred the more challenging apostolate in Grevena among a people who were predominantly uncivilized and spoke a
foreign language.

Learned men such as these served as the standard-bearers of Greek civilization in the remote areas inhabited by foreign settlers.[30] In the cities, such as Arta, their role was not only a clerical one. Bishops and nobles frequently sat in conclave [31] to discuss and direct the affairs of the city.

As the conquests of Theodore Comnenus Ducas extended to Macedonia and Thrace, it appeared that he would be the first to enter Constantinople and thus triumph over the emperors of Nicaea in their struggle for supremacy. However, his political ambitions were suddenly cut short by his defeat at Klokotnitsa in April 1230 at the hands of the Bulgarians. Still, Epirus retained its intellectual life and cultural orientation towards ancient Greece.[32] Some time later the poet Ermoniakus was commissioned by his patron, John Ducas Orsini (1323–1355), to paraphrase the *Iliad* in modern Greek verse. His trochees were not the work of a competent craftsman,[33] but at least they reflected the interest in the Homeric epics that was current at this time. This literary movement was probably stimulated by Eustathius' commentaries on Homer in his *Parekvolai* and seems to have gathered momentum at the end of the twelfth century.

By the end of the thirteenth century, mounting Greek resistance to alien intruders was also evident in those parts of Thessaly which had become detached from the Despotate of Epirus. The secular and ecclesiastical lords of Phanarion combined to extract from their overlord, Michael Gabrielopoulos, a promise that Albanians would be prevented from settling in their district. Greek nobles feared the consequences of clandestine infiltration by foreigners. Their petition also contained the specific entreaty, quoted previously, that Latin soldiers be excluded from the castle garrison of the "Lord of Thessaly." The Greek petitioners demanded that they should themselves garrison the castle, that they should be entitled to certain tax exemptions, and that they should have the right to trial by all their peers in the event of being charged with breach of discipline— demands of a sort that could be made only because of the power and influence which they already wielded. In addition, it was further vouchsafed to them that they might take possession of the monastery of Lefkousias and the "Megale Porta, together with all lands appertaining to it." [34] According to the Gabrielopoulos document, their influence also extended to the exercise of civil jurisdiction in particular localities. All rights were jealously guarded. It was therefore an accretion of many vested interests which accounted for the common front which many Greek nobles, of high and low rank alike, presented to foreign intruders.

The defeat of Theodore Comnenus Ducas at Klokotnitsa removed the only formidable rival to the emperors of Nicaea in their struggle to regain the capital of the Empire. Although themselves refugees from the Latin

usurpers, the policy of reconquest remained uppermost in the minds of
the rulers of Nicaea. The founders of the Nicaean empire, Constantine
Lascaris (1204–1205) [35] and his brother Theodore were capable, indeed
intrepid, leaders of the Greeks of northwestern Asia Minor. Theodore
(1204–1222)—"a generous man, and one who moved with the celerity of
an eagle in flight" [36]—was especially unrelenting in his efforts to imbue
his people with a spirit of militant resistance. Although the inhabitants
of this region were generally peaceable in outlook and neophytes in the
art of war,[37] they gradually became a fearless and efficient fighting force.[38]
It was there "in the Bithynian camp," as Sathas so accurately observed,
that the Byzantines were truly transformed into Greeks.[39] After 1204,
Hellenism's center of gravity shifted to the Empire of Nicaea.

Theodore I Lascaris was forced by the circumstances of his time to
appeal for assistance directly to the people and to individual nobles.
Towns and villages had completely severed all ties with Latin-dominated
Constantinople, were separate and self-contained communities, and had
revived their own local institutions, which had fallen into decay during
periods of imperial control. This situation required the rulers of Nicaea
to descend into the market place to plead their higher cause. The people
could only be aroused against the conquerors by a process of cajoling,
haranguing, and shaming; by being engaged in a hundred different bar-
gains with the nobles of a hundred different places; by being convinced
of the suffering and humiliation which would attend passive submission.
Evidence, unnoticed until now, that Theodore I frequently convoked
assemblies of the people and representatives of crafts' guilds (*ta laode
systemata*) [40] from various districts, conferred and ate with nobles in
private, and generally apprised all of the need for concerted military
action,[41] would seem to suggest that the efforts of the Nicaean emperors
were not all unavailing. Many nobles, including those who were refugees
from Constantinople, were won over by receiving grants of land for life.
This policy of making grants in *pronoia* over both public and ecclesiastical lands was continued by Theodore's heir, John III Ducas Vatatzes.
The condition of free farmers on these estates, however, grew steadily
worse with the passing of the years, until it became indistinguishable
from serfdom.[42]

The nature of Theodore's appeal, and especially his manner of approach, had the effect of blurring social distinctions and awakening in
all, peasant and noble alike, a sense of personal concern about the dis-
memberment of the Empire. His purpose, like that of his counterpart in
Epirus, Theodore Comnenus Ducas, was to inflame and direct the spirit
of national resistance to foreign oppression. His efforts met with the un-
stinted approbation of Nicetas Choniates, who was never slow in finding

classical analogies and who compared Theodore I with Alexander the Great. If zeal alone were the principal touchstone of fame the comparison was apt, for Theodore's ambition was the total expulsion of the Latin invaders and the liberation of Constantinople. Expulsion of foreign invaders was the goal of the Greek raias throughout the period of Turkish occupation until, by the beginning of the nineteenth century, it had become known, quite simply, as the "Great Idea." "These ancient, natal lands, where our homes have always been, seem as Paradise to us; and our Great City, which is the pride of all the earth and so much coveted by all the nations, seems verily the city of Almighty God." [43]

Theodore I also fought valiantly against the Seljuk Turks, who exerted continual pressure upon the Greeks of western Asia Minor. It was a struggle which, to the people of Nicaea, bore every resemblance to that of Digenis and the *Akritai* against the invaders. In the popular mind, Theodore seemed to embody the spirit of Digenis Akritas. It is therefore entirely conceivable that contemporary events brought about the revival of the written tradition of the *Digenis Akritas* and that it came to be cherished at least as much by the people of Nicaea as by people in later Palaeologian times.[44] It is even probable that the form of the epic may have undergone conscious literary renewal at this time and that the extant versions of it were in fact derived from those which appeared in the Empire of Nicaea.[45] If such is the case, we may presume that the oral traditions and songs of the Akritic Cycle were also popular and widespread.

In sum, the light of Hellenism apparently gave off a bright glow in the Empire of Nicaea. Its increasing brilliance attracted an ever increasing stream of refugees from Constantinople—scholars, monks, and ordinary people. Among them were the historians George Akropolites and Nicetas Choniates; Demetrios Karykes, the "Supreme Philosopher"; Monasteriotes who later became Archbishop of Ephesus; Theodoros Hexapterygos, tutor of Nicephorus Blemmydes; Blemmydes who, in his role as teacher of the children of noble families, exerted a profound influence upon the intellectual life of Nicaea, and, in addition to his poems, autobiography, and correspondence, left behind manuals on logic and physics and also wrote prolifically in the fields of theology, geography, medicine, and rhetoric.[46]

John III Ducas Vatatzes (1222–1254), the son-in-law and successor of Theodore I, was no less assiduous than his predecessor in seeking to expel the invaders. He fought vigorously against Turk and Bulgarian, as well as against Latin, and successfully freed large segments of the Empire.[47] His sphere of operations also reached into the far-flung Greek islands. In 1230 the two noble Cretan families of Melissinoi and Skordylai rebelled against their Venetian overlords. Emissaries from the rebellious Greeks

appeared at the court of John III and promised to merge their island with
the Empire of Nicaea in return for assistance. John III immediately dispatched thirty-three galleys to Crete, which disembarked a military detachment under the leadership of the Grand Duke Auxentius. However,
the combined Greek forces met with only limited success. After two years
of fighting, Rethymnon, Mylopotamos, and Kainourgion (Castel Nuovo)
were occupied, but Greek fortunes were eventually confounded by the
shipwreck of thirty of their galleys, the resistance of the Venetian castle
of Boniface, and the diplomatic astuteness of the dukes Bartolomeo and
Angelo Gradenigo. The rebellion finally sputtered out in 1236.[48]

Venice, to be sure, was never as easily defeated as the other Latin
powers. She possessed virtually unquestioned superiority at sea, important outposts throughout the Aegean and the entire eastern Mediterranean, and almost unlimited financial resources. Nevertheless, the Venetians, like the Turks and Germans after them, were never able to break
the stubborn and implacable will to resist for which the Cretans became
renowned. Unfortunately, since our knowledge of Crete in this period is
necessarily derived from Venetian sources, the details of Cretan resistance
and the precise nature of the Cretan connection with the Empire of
Nicaea are largely hidden from us.

Within the context of the formation of the new Hellenism, mention
should be made of the oracles and prophecies in circulation concerning
the Lascarids and John III Ducas Vatatzes in particular.[49] Although these
prophecies were substantially the same as those which had widespread
popular currency around 1200,[50] after that date they were related more
and more to the splendid deeds of the Lascarids. Greeks who lived under
the Latin occupation looked to them as sources of courage and inspiration, thereby contributing to a cult of the Lascarids which bordered on
hero worship. After his death, John III was rapidly canonized, at least in
the popular imagination.[51] Later, if for no other reason than that Vatatzes
had donated considerable tracts of land to the Church, that canonization
was officially confirmed.[52]

Political and Intellectual Developments in Nicaea

If Greek nationalism was born under foreign occupation, it was nourished
by the increasing consciousness of past greatness which appeared simultaneously in the Empire of Nicaea. The political and intellectual leaders
of the Greek people looked upon classical civilization as an ideal expression of their national individuality and therefore identified themselves
ever more closely with it. The past seemed all the more brilliant and distinguished in view of the chaos and disunity which surrounded them; a
past which afforded a paradigm of achievement and courage; a past which

thus could inspire the Greeks to overthrow their oppressors. However, the crucial role that reverence for the past played in the formation of Neo-Hellenism does not seem to have been fully grasped, even by Nicaea's principal historians, Anthony Meliarakis and Alice Gardner.

The revival, after 1204, of the name Hellene together with its various derivatives,[53] its widespread adoption in place of *Romaioi,* was naturally stimulated by a heightened awareness of cultural differences in the presence of alien conquerors. A marked fascination for the word can be traced in the writings and utterances of emperors and scholars, although its general use in everyday life was still inhibited because of religious distaste for its pagan overtones. In a letter to Pope Gregory IX between 1231 and 1237, John III Ducas Vatatzes was clearly conscious of being Greek in spite of the apparent obligations of his imperial title, "John Ducas, by the Grace of Jesus Christ, Faithful King and Emperor of the Romans." He proudly acknowledged the Pope's admission that "wisdom reigns supreme among the Greeks . . . Wisdom, and the good which flows from it, first flowered among the Greeks, whence it spread to all others who cared anything for its acquisition and its practice." Vatatzes bristled at the Pope's oversight in failing to mention that the Roman *imperium* had been bequeathed to the Greeks from the time of Constantine the Great: "for who in all the world gainsays the fact that the Greeks are the only heirs and successors of Constantine? . . . The progenitors of Our House, the Comneni and the Ducases—to say nothing of the many other rulers—were all of Hellenic stock, and it is they who have reigned in Constantinople for hundreds of years." Vatatzes believed that the Roman Empire had truly become a Greek empire from the time of Constantine the Great. To him, the official designation of the Byzantine Emperors, "King and Emperor of the Romans," had been retained solely out of the respect due to tradition and to the name of Constantine.

Thus, Vatatzes' claims to the territories held by the Frankish usurpers were based upon the rights of legal succession and historical continuity. "Although We have been driven forcibly from Our lands, We preserve Our rightful authority in them, which, under God, is inalienable and irrevocable." His refusal to accept the sovereign pretensions of John de Brienne (1231–1237), the Frankish Emperor of Constantinople, was unequivocal. "Moreover," he remarked with more than a trace of sarcasm, "we are at a loss to comprehend where on sea or earth the dominion and jurisdiction of the said Emperor could possibly lie." He then announced his intention to resist the conquerors: "We shall never stop fighting or resisting the usurpers in Constantinople, for if We did not fight them with all Our might We should be sinning against Nature, Our Fatherland, the graves and sacred temples of Our Forefathers." His letter to Pope Gregory

concluded with the threat that Greek arms were not to be despised: "We
have cavalry and a whole host of soldiery whose valor and fine martial
qualities have already been tested against the Crusaders and have not
been found wanting." [54]

A consciousness of Greek nationality is similarly proclaimed by Vatatzes' successor, Theodore II Lascaris (1254–1258) and the latter's tutor,
Nicholas Blemmydes. Blemmydes referred to the Empire of Nicaea as an
"Hellenic Dominion." [55] Theodore II called it simply "an Hellenic country" or Hellas.[56] It included within its borders parts of present-day Yugoslavia, the whole of southern Albania, Greek Macedonia, and Thrace, and
a great part of southern Bulgaria.[57] Theodore II was familiar with the
ethnic composition of the Balkans and knew each national group by name.
As in the case of the various invasions, the antagonism between the Greeks
and the nationalities of the region sharpened the national consciousness
of each. The feeling was naturally most intense in the ranks of the opposing armies. The relations between the Greek and Bulgarian soldiers were
particularly acrimonious. When Theodore II wrote to inform his tutor of
his victories over Michael of Bulgaria, whose armies were pillaging eastern
Rumelia (now part of southern Bulgaria) and Macedonia, he spoke excit-
edly of the "remarkable feats of Greek arms and exemplary Greek bravery
which could only elicit your deepest admiration." Since Theodore II was
constantly in the midst of his soldiers, he can hardly have failed to infuse
in them at least a modicum of his passion for Hellas. It is possible to form
some idea of the depth of his Greekness from certain literary and philosophical fragments which are still extant. These are significant, not merely
for the fervor they express, but for the way in which they reflect the essential character of Greek nationalism. In one place, he speaks of his delight
in using the language of ancient Greece and says he prefers it to the
ecclesiastical language of the period, which, because of its innumerable
biblical expressions he has not been able to master. He looks upon the
classical language as "more dear to him than life itself." [58] He also admires
the ancient monuments of Pergamon, which he considers to be "replete
with the genius of the Greeks—very images of Wisdom itself." The city
of Pergamon, "which so reflects the glory of our ancestors, is for that reason a constant reproach to us as their descendants." [59] To Theodore II it
seemed that the people of his empire should feel forever humble in the
presence of such artistic greatness.

The Nicaean interest in the physical heritage of the past extended to a
preoccupation with archaeology not equalled until the Renaissance. It was
also paralleled by a dedication to "all the arts and sciences." In spite of
the external menace which the emperors of Nicaea faced at all times,
they found time to collect manuscripts, establish libraries,[60] and generally

encourage intellectual and artistic pursuits.[61] Theodore II himself received an extensive education in literature, theology, and philosophy, and dreamed of making his capital the center of Greek learning. He praised its accomplishments lavishly and believed, in fact, that it had surpassed ancient Athens because classical learning and Christian theology had been brought into harmony with each other. "This glorious city of the Nicaeans prides itself precisely on this point. It has doubly enriched philosophy by reconciling objective wisdom, which is the fundamental achievement of ancient Greece, with the knowledge of God, which transcends it. Although there are many schools of philosophy here, they are all concerned with one or the other of these two sources of truth. Thus, they philosophize in the manner of Aristotle and Plato and Socrates, combining ancient philosophy with theology in a novel fashion, though, having been nurtured on the divine words of Scripture, the Apostles, and the Church Fathers, the premises with which they begin are the divine doctrines of Christ." [62] Nor was the influence of Nicaea confined to urban centers alone: "Its learning was diffused far and wide, and even peasants were educated in its ideals."

Thus, from an intellectual as well as from a political and military point of view, Nicaea not only shone as a symbol of cultural unity but served as a rallying point of active resistance to the Frankish conquerors. "Many cities have acquired power, many have gained renown, many have magnified the glory of their people; but you, Nicaea, surpass them all. You alone remain to shore up the mighty Roman Empire, which has been shattered by the armies of so many different nations." [63] In yet another encomium, Theodore II Lascaris extolled the brilliance of philosophical thought which was to Nicaea "what music is to Corinth, weaving to Thessaly, and tanning to Philadelphia." [64] If this analogy seems to descend to a proletarian level in sharp contrast to his customary grandiloquence, this was perhaps because Theodore II had reason to suspect the dedication to philosophy of many of his countrymen. In a letter to his teacher Blemmydes, he bewailed the indifference many young people seemed to show towards philosophy, despising it as a foreign science, although no form of knowledge was more essentially Greek. Theodore II certainly had this in mind when he predicted that philosophy would depart from Greece and find refuge among the "barbarians" of the West, where it would eventually make them famous. Those who denigrate philosophy, he said, or who would alienate it from its proper home will only bring disaster and barbarity to the inhabitants of Greece. "Those who were once proud of their philosophical inheritance would then become the laughing stock of the entire world." [65]

Theodore II Lascaris regarded these symptoms with uneasiness. He knew from discussions with a number of the Western "barbarians" that they were becoming adept in every aspect of philosophy.[66] It was inconceivable for reasons of national prestige that they should be allowed to challenge, let alone excel, the Greeks. Thus, on one occasion when he worsted Berthold von Hohenburg, emissary of the German Emperor Konrad IV Hohenstaufen, in a philosophical debate, he considered this no less than a national triumph, "a victory of the Greeks over the Italians."[67] Instances such as this demonstrate the projection of national feeling among the Lascarids and the scholars of Nicaea.

Theodore II Lascaris, by the quality of his administrative and military reorganization,[68] had almost created a viable Greek empire. In the task of administration he had relied exclusively upon men of ability, many of whom were not of noble birth. Indeed, he deliberately tried to limit the power and influence of the nobility and thus to lessen class divisions. This undivided attention to the welfare of all his people eventually provoked the opposition of the nobility, as Pachymeres[69] has most convincingly pointed out. Yet, though many of his efforts were rendered vain by his early death, Theodore II Lascaris remains a figure of fundamental importance for Greek history through his love of Greek civilization, his strength of character, and his impressive intellectual powers. More important historically, given his faith in the destiny of the Greek nation, which was symbolized by a steadfast ambition both to reconquer Constantinople and to reunite all Greeks under the imperial scepter, he may be regarded as the true originator of the "Great Idea." He was the first Greek emperor to be pictured with the double-headed eagle of the Byzantine Empire, which, in the opinion of Voyatzidis, represented a projection of imperial claims towards the Greek lands of both Europe and Asia. The double-headed eagle thereafter became the emblem of the Byzantine state. Later, during the Turkish occupation, the eagle became the cherished motif of the Greek raias, signifying the national aspiration of all Greeks to be free from foreign domination—or for the "Great Idea."[70]

If many of the actual reforms of the Lascarids soon disappeared, the "Great Idea" certainly inspired the Palaeologian usurper, Michael VIII (1259–1282). This, in itself, was an indication of its power and pervasiveness, even at so early a time. However, the work of internal reorganization that had so distinguished the reign of Theodore received a setback. The nobility enjoyed a resurgence of power, and this was accompanied by progressive deterioration and demoralization of the army and the civil service. When, in 1261, Michael VIII captured Constantinople, which then became the capital of the new Byzantine Empire, his ephemeral triumph, far from arresting the deterioration, even contributed to it. His subsequent successes in Mistra, Monemvasia, and Maina (1262)[71] certainly established important bridgeheads from which the Latin invader was finally driven out of the Peloponnese; but, on the other hand, through his lack of concern with the Turkish menace in Asia Minor, the Greek foothold in this vitally important region was gradually pried loose. Michael VIII threatened not only to complete the reconquest of the Peloponnese but also to occupy Crete. Here, the Greek inhabitants still offered resistance to the Venetians. Venetian apprehension in the face of what seemed to be an impending invasion led the Doge Ranieri Zeno to implore Pope Urban IV in a letter dated 8 September 1264 to organize a new crusade against the Greeks. The Venetians were naturally concerned over the fate of their colonies, especially Crete, with its vital strategic position, and wanted desperately to secure their ramified economic interests throughout the eastern Mediterranean. For this reason, they also addressed similar appeals to the rulers of other countries.[72]

For the time being, however, the recapture of Constantinople led to a revival of hope among all Greeks under foreign domination. In Crete, for example, the Venetians experienced considerable difficulty in renewing alliances with those local elements which, for reasons of profit or security, had seen fit to acknowledge fealty to Venice. The prospect of restoring the Byzantine Empire prompted the Orthodox clergy to reemphasize its attachment to Emperor and Patriarch. Many of the clergy preached sermons which were distinctly nationalistic in tone. They stressed the legality of Michael VIII's succession to the throne and exhorted all those still under foreign rule to redouble their efforts against the conquerors and thereby hasten the fulfillment of imperial reunification. From 1264 to 1299, Crete was convulsed by revolutions led by George Chortatzes and Alexius Kallerges.[73] This protracted struggle must have greatly stimulated feelings of fraternal compassion among all Greeks.

However, Venetian determination to thwart the ambitions of Michael VIII, together with the reappearance of the Turkish menace on his flank, was sufficient to induce him to open negotiations with Venice. In two agreements of 1268 and 1277 he seems not only to have abandoned his plans for Crete, but also for the Messenian strongholds of Modon (Methone) and Coron (Korone). This utterly discouraged even the most resolute of the Greek fighters, and Cretan resistance effectively collapsed. Chortatzes and many of his followers sought refuge in the imperial court at Constantinople.[74] It is not known how large this stream of refugees was or how long it lasted. Most of them, including Chortatzes himself, settled in the eastern marches of the Empire towards the end of the thirteenth century. Andronicus II Palaeologus (1282–1328) rewarded them with "salaries to be fixed annually." [75] There they joined the fight against the Turks.

Venetian power therefore remained firmly entrenched in Crete and throughout the eastern Mediterranean. Yet a subtle change in relations between the new Byzantine Empire and Venice occurred at this time. A number of Venetians who were especially well acquainted with the political situation in the Empire saw that the two states could mutually benefit from a united front against the Turks. They believed that any diplomatic overtures made with the aim of effecting such an alliance with the Byzantine Empire would be warmly received. Marino Sanudo Torsello (1270?–1343?), in his work relating to the Venetian possessions and the projected crusade, also recognized that any co-operation between the two states would most likely prove doubly useful to Venice: it would not only lead to successful confrontation with the Turks, but would also assist in the pacification of her Greek possessions.[76]

Michael VIII Palaeologus and his heirs proved in the end to be powerless to resist the Turkish flood. Quite apart from the egregious error of allowing the administrative reorganization effected by Theodore Lascaris to fall into decay, the removal of the throne from Nicaea to Constantinople meant that the center of government was isolated from the nerve-center of Greek civilization. Here, in the ancient capital of the Eastern Roman Empire, the old Roman traditions quickly reasserted themselves and the Orthodox Church resumed its traditionally close association with the imperial polity. In these circumstances the growth of an Hellenic outlook, exemplified in, for instance, the use of the national name, Hellene, was temporarily suspended.

However, the national spirit was rekindled in direct proportion to the extent to which the Empire was forced to contract to the predominantly Greek regions of the Empire in Europe and Asia Minor, to Hellas as Theodore II Lascaris had called them. Actual use of the words Hellas and Hellene tended to become more widespread [77] towards the end of the fourteenth century despite the imperial restoration. For example, although Demetrius Kydones generally used the words Greek and Roman [78] interchangeably, he once tried to explain the gap between East and West on the assumption that educated people could not really be interested in what was happening in the West, because "anyone who is not a Greek is a barbarian." [79] Thus, whatever meaning he attached to the word Roman, it was clear from this context that he at least regarded the Greeks as the indisputable heirs of ancient Greek civilization.

The Westerners had no doubt in their minds who the Greeks were. In various official documents, Popes and Western kings invariably used the words *Graecia* and *Graeci,* or the latter's then-current French equivalent, *Grieu.*[80] Nor do they appear to have doubted where these *Graeci* lived. In the fifteenth century, Thrace was explicitly identified as being part of Greece; [81] and it is precisely in Thrace, of course (or Eastern Rumelia, as it came to be called), that overland travellers in later centuries first became aware of their arrival in Greece.[82] Even in the thirteenth century Theodore II Lascaris wrote: "You will have arrived in Greece from Europe when first you arrive in Thrace." [83] Thus, in spite of a certain imprecision which surrounded the use of the word Hellene after the Palaeologian restoration, it is apparent that the inhabitants of the Byzantine Empire were Roman in only the most formal sense. If the majority did not fully appreciate this fact, the Western Europeans certainly did; so, too, did the writer of the *Chronicle of Morea*, a Gasmulus, when he said: "Long ago, these 'Romans' were called 'Greeks.' They were always distinguishable by their extreme arrogance; indeed, they still are. It was only from Rome that they took the name 'Roman.' " [84]

This period then, from the thirteenth through the fifteenth centuries, was a seminal one in the formation of Hellenic nationalism. It was at this time that the words Hellene and Hellas came into use in conjunction with the word nation. John III Ducas Vatatzes appears to have been the first to effect this conjunction (see above, page 37) and the word *genos* also recurs constantly in various texts during the last two centuries of the Byzantine Empire.[85] It was used with increasing frequency during the period of Turkish occupation (1453–1821) and was especially prominent in the writings of scholars towards the end of the eighteenth century and at the beginning of the nineteenth. What this signified, of course, was that the cultural and racial equation, the essential strength of the nationalist mystique, was established by the time of John III.

Cultural Activity during the Latin Period

Although the Greeks were reduced to a condition of political subservience during the period of Latin domination, their national cohesion was never really broken. There were, for example, a variety of cultural manifestations. Marino Sanudo Torsello had this to say of the underlying importance of religion in Greek life: that the inhabitants of the Despotate of Morea, of Cyprus, Crete, Euboea, Rhodes, and many other islands, being Greek, remained faithful to the Orthodox Church even though they were dominated by the Franks and fell technically within the ecclesiastical jurisdiction of the Pope; but their hearts and minds were immutably Greek, and whenever they were free to do so they never hesitated to show it.[86] Torsello specifically mentioned a number of places throughout the Aegean where nationalism was in constant ferment. His information is reliable and corroborates the conclusions of modern literary researchers, who, by methods of linguistic analogy, have identified the local origins of some of the Greek literature of the period. Both sources underline the point that specific forms of nationalist expression were never stifled, even in those places where the Latin conquest appeared to be most complete.

The theme of Greek bravery permeates these diverse works. There was, for example, the chivalric novel, *The Trojan War*, which was written by an unknown Greek poet, probably about the middle of the thirteenth century. Based upon Benoît de Sainte-Maur's romance of the same name (1180), its purpose in the Greek version was to extol the well-known Homeric heroes who triumphed over their adversaries.[87] It was a source of direct inspiration for the writer of the *Narrative of Achilles* and it helped to catalyze national feeling.

The *Narrative* bears no relation to the *Iliad*. Its author is concerned solely with lifting the morale of his compatriots by using Achilles as a universal symbol of Greek bravery. Thus, the hero, "in whom all Greeks take pride," is transplanted to the period of Latin conquest, where he confronts the knights of the West with all the courage of his ancient counterpart. Indeed, it is probable that the *Narrative* was written as a Greek response to the *Chronicle of Morea*, whose author, as we have seen, was given to lavish praise of the Latin conquerors. If such is the case, the *Narrative* was probably written towards the end of the thirteenth century or at the beginning of the fourteenth century. This, to be sure, is not the conclusion of Hesseling, one of the editors of the *Narrative*. Although he detects *un orgueuil national assez fort,* a strong national pride, he considers rather that it was written at the beginning of the fifteenth century [88] as a narration of "past grandeur" and only incidentally as an anodyne to the feelings of a resentful, conquered people. In other words, he overlooks the fact that a conscious evocation of the past was one of the essential springs of Greek national feeling and that both were invariably aroused in circumstances of foreign occupation. It would seem that Sathas came closer to the truth when he said that Achilles personified the Greek desire for revenge against the Crusaders.[89] The Achilles of the *Narrative* is demonstrably a medieval hero, a second Digenis Akritas. The very similarities in their lives suggest a common inspirational background. Both possessed heroic qualities which determined their subsequent achievements; both received a classical Greek education; both wore the armor of Byzantine soldiers; both abducted their wives and were pursued by their brothers-in-law, whom they defeated. The influence of popular legend and poetry in each work is plain. Although the *Narrative* has never had the same vogue [90] as the *Digenis*, it may be considered as the connecting link between the *Digenis Akritas* and the popular seventeenth-century romance, *Erotocritus*. Some of the images and episodes of the *Erotocritus* are obviously derived from it, for example the duel of Achilles with the Frankish knight.[91]

The appearance of five romantic poems between the thirteenth and fifteenth centuries may also be regarded as possible expressions of the cultural nationalism of this period. Written in a demotic language and fifteen-syllable iambic verse, they are all landmarks in the development of modern Greek literature: *Callimachus and Chrysorrhoe* (thirteenth century), *Velthandrus and Chrysantza* (thirteenth century), *Lyvistros and Rhodamne* (fourteenth century), *Florius and Platziaflora* (end of fourteenth, or beginning of fifteenth century) and *Imberius and Margarona* (fifteenth century). The oldest of the five, *Callimachus*, was written by Andronicus Comnenus Ducas Palaeologus. The authorship of *Velthandrus* and *Lyvistros* is unknown. Many incidents in these poems can be traced to the ballads and love songs of troubadours who sang in the courts of the Latin rulers in Greece and the eastern Mediterranean. These songs were learned by the indigenous Greeks and were gradually adapted to the Greek mode. They contain, of course, many episodes and allusions which reflect the social and cultural environment of Western Europe; nevertheless, they have become an authentic part of the modern Greek literary tradition.[92]

Thus, the period of Latin conquest witnessed not only the reinforcement of the oral traditions of the Greek people, but also the establishment of the demotic language as a formal literary vehicle. Vivid and alive, the language of the people insinuated itself into the courts of the Latin rulers against all their efforts to preserve and to impose their own. The conquerors found it necessary to use Greek, in both its written and spoken forms, in order to regularize their relations with the conquered. Thereafter, most of the official documents, seals, and proclamations were in modern Greek, as were the inscriptions on all Venetian coins destined for colonies. In these ways the invaders gradually "succumbed to the ever growing demands of Greek national feeling." [93]

4

THE PALAEOLOGIAN PERIOD

Classical Revival in Literature and Art

The tenth century, despite its splendid artistic and literary achievement, was surpassed by a series of advances in literature, philosophy, and art under the Palaeologian dynasty during the thirteenth and fourteenth centuries. This Palaeologian Renaissance occurred throughout the entire Hellenic world, but particularly in the three cities of Constantinople, Thessalonica, and Mistra. As was the case in Nicaea, the principal hallmark of the Renaissance was a renewed interest in classical civilization, resulting in a marked emphasis upon the traditions, forms, and practices of classical education.

In the realm of literature, a group of literateurs dedicated themselves to the elucidation and exposition of the masterpieces of antiquity. Their work is considered philologically sound by modern specialists. Four names, especially, stand out during the reigns of Michael VIII Palaeologus (1259–1282), Andronicus II (1282–1328), and Andronicus III (1328–1341): the monk Maximus Planoudes (born in Nicomedia about 1255) and his pupil Manuel Moschopoulos, both of whom taught in Constantinople; Thomas Magistros and his pupil Demetrius Triclinios, both of whom taught in Thessalonica.[1] Each pair formed a distinct literary school in the two chief centers of Greek civilization, and each attracted a multitude of students and disciples. Together, they laid the foundations of modern textual criticism. Demetrius Triclinios, for example, who is perhaps the best known of the four, developed the technique of collating and comparing a variety of manuscripts before publishing his final text. Modern philologists express approbation of his methods, his powers of perception, and the entire critical acuity of his approach.[2]

Other distinguished scholars, notably Nicephorus Gregoras and Nicholas Kavasilas, advocated the use of ancient rhetorical methods in the education of youth and constantly drew upon historical examples and precedents in their own writing, even in the case of religious subjects. In his eulogy of St. Demetrius, for instance, Nicephorus Gregoras compared the saint with Alexander the Great.[3] An encomium to St. Demetrius by Nicholas Kavasilas was entitled *Paean to the Handsome Demetrius*.[4] Secular themes, such as a paean to the city of Thessalonica, were treated in the declamatory style of the ancients. The lives of other saints were written in a manner even more clearly derivative. These were, in fact, closely modelled on Plutarch's biographies, although, to be sure, this was a technique which had been used by earlier writers when recounting the lives of Byzantine Emperors.[5] Nevertheless, Gregoras and Kavasilas enriched the tradition of hagiographical writing with new conceptions and novel devices of expression which in many respects foreshadowed a new literary epoch.

Consciousness of the enormous debt owed to the past also provided the basis for a number of parallel developments in the sciences. Theodore Metochites initiated them by recognizing the importance of mathematics for the systematic study of astronomy. At the age of forty-three, he received his first lessons from the mathematician Manuel Bryennios and was instructed in the works of Theon, Ptolemy, Euclid, Theodosius, Apollonius of Perga, and Serenus, on which all of his subsequent publications in astronomy depended. The importance of Metochites is such that all further work in astronomy during the fourteenth century by George Chrysococces, Isaac Argyros, Theodore Meliteniotes, and Nicholas Kavasilas is either directly or indirectly dependent on Metochites. In medical science, the names of John Actuarius and Nicholas Myrepsos are prominent, the latter for his contributions to pharmacology in particular. In the field of philosophy, Manuel Olovolos (born *ante* 1250) and Joseph of Ithaca (*c.* 1280–1330) were both admired and emulated by their contemporaries.[6]

Theodore Metochites is certainly the outstanding figure of the period, not only for his contributions to so many fields of knowledge, but also because he both personified and expressed the skeptical spirit of his age. His genius was a universal one—mathematician, astronomer, politician, philosopher, restorer of the monastery of Chora, renowned for its magnificent mosaics, and profound Christian thinker. Sensitive and concerned, he perceived many signs of decadence in the Byzantine world, all of which deeply troubled him. His first twenty years had been spent in Nicaea (he was born in 1260 or 1261),[7] and much of his early literary output was concerned with reconciling, in the manner of the Nicaeans,

the apparently contradictory natures of the ancient Greek literary heritage and Christianity. However, he was later shaken by an inner crisis
of religious faith, which among other things raised doubts about the
intrinsic worth of ancient Greek civilization and the value to mankind
of intellectual pursuits deriving from it. This was the kind of spiritual
disturbance that affected many of his contemporaries in an era of uncertainty and even men like Demetrius Kydones a full century later.
Characteristically, those who were tormented by it, Metochites among
them, took refuge in the ancient Greek belief in omnipresent Fate.[8] This
belief had never ceased to be a part of the Greek consciousness, and its
overtones have persisted down to the present day. Since the essential
element in this belief is an awareness of the reality of change and the
transitoriness of mankind, its reappearance among those who watched
and lamented the decay of a once mighty empire was perhaps only to
be expected.

If there is a distinctive style of the Palaeologian Renaissance, it is
possible that painting brings us closest to its essence. Artists looked to
antiquity not only for a solution to their technical problems but also as
a fount of experience and inspiration through which their own feelings
could be expressed. The extent of this preoccupation was as evident in
Bulgarian and Serbian art as in Byzantine art. Radojčić has correctly
remarked that "the touching expressionism which reached its climax in
the fourteenth century and which was not only the last representation
of the final style of Byzantine art but also the last art form in Eastern
Europe directly descended from ancient times is now disintegrating in
remote caves in Bulgaria." [9]

Much has still to be learned about the respective contributions of
various painters to this *soi-disant* Palaeologian style and the different
roles of the major centers of art. For all that, there appears to be general
agreement that a "revolution in art" [10] did in fact take place. Although
it bore the unmistakable imprint of Christian and monastic influences
and many of its manifestations were purely imitative of ancient art, its
originality consisted in the development of new forms of expression, for
which antiquity merely provided the inspiration. As Demus says: "never
before in the history of Byzantine art, not even in the tenth century, was
the past viewed so intently. If the term 'renaissance' be used with the
meaning that it has acquired in the West—that is to say, in the sense of
creative adjustment towards antiquity—it is true that it may be similarly
applied to the evolution of Byzantine painting from 1260 to 1300. . . .
Their painting was based upon absolute mastery of Hellenistic methods,
but they eschewed imitation; rather, they explored the inner substance
of their medium and thereby created entirely novel art forms." [11]

The intellectual and artistic life of the Palaeologian period therefore contributed to the birth of modern Hellenism and, in part, to the birth of the modern era throughout Europe generally. Many historians—art historians, in particular—nonetheless tend to view these phenomena in isolation or to regard them at most as the first signs of emergent nationalism. Demus, for instance, is prepared to acknowledge the signal importance of Nicaea in preparing the ground for the Palaeologian Renaissance and admits that national resistance to the Franks was a significant factor in its growth.[12] Yet, for him, these are secondary considerations. The Greek spirit was active elsewhere at the same time. The Despotate of Epirus, for example, long a thriving center of Hellenism, was the scene of vital architectural activity. Various ecclesiastical monuments of this period are constantly being discovered today in places remote from the mainstream of modern life. It is likely that future archaeological finds, particularly in Macedonia, will increase our knowledge of the cultural achievements of the period.

However, sufficient evidence has already been adduced to indicate the Greek awakening and its characteristic orientation towards antiquity. Yet, it was the Empire of Nicaea, not the Palaeologian Empire, which provided pre-eminent leadership in this moment of national retrospection and rededication. As Theodore Metochites writes, Nicaea was the real seed-bed of national revival (*diesosen hysteras anabioseos spermata*)— "the repository" [13] of a great civilized inheritance, whose seeds, as we have seen, required only a favorable environment in which to germinate and fructify.

The term renaissance as applied to the cultural quickening of the Palaeologian period must therefore be used with considerable prudence, since the cultural influence of ancient Greece never at any time ceased. It merely contracted or expanded with the political and social circumstances of the Empire, which were themselves constantly changing.

The Cultural Prominence of Thessalonica

The chief city of Macedonia, Thessalonica, was especially noted for its intellectual mettle during the Palaeologian period. The city had stood secure on the periphery of the storms of foreign invasion throughout the centuries. A certain degree of self-government (*to koinon*) had always been maintained, and the traditions of ancient Greek civilization had been preserved better than in other cities of the Eastern Empire. There are relatively few periods after ancient times in which the history of Thessalonica is hidden from us. It may be said, however, that except for the very brief occupation of the city by the Saracens in 904 and by the Normans in 1185, Thessalonica, until 1204, escaped occupation by foreigners, except, of course, the Romans, and her institutions were therefore permitted to evolve in a regular and organic way. When, in 1204, Thessalonica submitted to her Latin conqueror, Boniface Montferrat, it was only on condition that the corporate rights of the city guaranteed by the Byzantine Emperors would be respected and maintained. The traditions of ancient Hellenism and of Hellenistic civilization as well as the laws and customs of the city also survived the Latin invasion.[14]

Thessalonica's intellectual and artistic vitality throughout the fourteenth century, especially in architecture, painting (miniatures and frescoes), and calligraphy,[15] derived from the influence of older artistic techniques, notably those of the eleventh and twelfth centuries. This is most evident in the field of fresco painting, where the dramatic intensity of scenes in Church frescoes (for example, the Holy Virgin of the Church of Chalkeon), far from being Palaeologian, is a direct inheritance of the twelfth century monastic art of Asia Minor, especially that of Cappadocia.[16] The same quality of vigorous realism in Macedonian Church frescoes is now regarded as the main distinguishing feature of Macedonian painting.

The excellence of painting was by no means confined to Thessalonica. Veroia, Achris, Kastoria, as well as the ancient center of Orthodoxy, Mt. Athos, were equally celebrated for the skill of their artists. Even in distant Serbia, at the time of Milutin (1282–1321), painters whose signatures proclaim their Greek ancestry [17] practiced their art. A number of Greek painters and goldsmiths also settled in Ragusa (Dubrovnik) between 1365 and 1386, where they exerted some influence.[18]

Throughout the fourteenth century, Thessalonica was an important center of Greek scholarship and learning, ambitious to emulate in her own time the glory of ancient Athens.[19] Demetrius Kydones spoke of his city as the home of poets and orators and suggested that God had endowed the city with a certain "intellectual, almost spiritual, pre-eminence." [20] The scholars of Thessalonica were keenly aware of their Greek descent and contributed in a variety of ways to the diffusion throughout the Palaeologian Empire of a heightened consciousness of ethnic identity. "I think that there does not exist in the whole of Greece," wrote Nicholas Kavasilas, "a single Greek who does not honor this city and who does not feel within his heart that it has assumed the mantle of cultural leadership. There are even those who believe their stature is increased merely by saying that they come from Thessalonica. This is the city which produces worthy orators and students of Plato and Aristotle . . . her character is no less than that. No city has preserved so faithfully the laws of the ancient Greeks. Nor must we forget those who have practiced philosophy; nowhere else in the whole of Greece

Figure 3. Church of Saint Elias.

Figure 4. Saint George the Swift.

have there been so many." [21] There was a host of writers: Nicephorus Choumnos; Thomas Magistros; the brothers Demetrius and Prochoros Kydones, and Theodore and Nicephorus Kallistos Xanthopoulos; the jurist, Constantine Armenopoulos; [22] the archbishops Gregory Palamas and Neilos Kavasilas; [23] the latter's nephew, Nicholas Kavasilas; [24] and many others. [25] The monk, Matthew Blastares completed a legal treatise (*Syntagma kata Stoicheion*) which was quite as important as the more famous *Hexabiblos* by Armenopoulos: it exerted a profound influence throughout Eastern Europe, particularly in Serbia, Bulgaria, and Russia. [26] Of all these considerable writers, none, however, was more steeped in the traditions of classical antiquity than Demetrius Kydones. "As long as he was alive," wrote his pupil, Manuel Calecas [27] in 1398, shortly after Kydones' death, "one had the impression that the language and wisdom of ancient Greece still lived and flourished." About four hundred and fifty of the letters of Kydones are extant. Each was written with classical elegance, and together they constitute a not insignificant historical archive from which to approach a study of the second half of the fourteenth century. Kydones' classical erudition notwithstanding, he was a profound believer in Christianity. In common with many other Byzantine scholars, he apparently saw no intrinsic incompatibility between classical and Christian learning.

Most of the scholars of this period were interested in problems of social inequality and injustice. They were particularly concerned with finding some means of ameliorating the lot of the peasants and never hesitated to denounce the evils of usury and the cupidity of the nobility. [28] All of their writings on such subjects are characterized by extensive study, careful argumentation, and a broad outlook. They tended to regard these problems as symptoms of a deeper infirmity which afflicted Byzantine society as a whole. Their ideas spread to Constantinople, [29] and the influence they had on Byzantine society was another landmark in the development of modern Hellenism. In the autumn of 1371 (some years after he had opposed the democratic movement of the Zealots in Thessalonica against the nobles and rich landowners) Kydones addressed himself to John V Palaeologus as follows: "Those who live in bondage cannot properly be called human beings, for it is not possible for one who belongs to another to belong also to himself. Yet man is created for the sake of himself, which is clearly demonstrated by his possession of free will. If he loses it, it were better that he no longer claim to be a human being." [30] These words embody the idea that became in the fourteenth century the animating force of Greek nationalism. The ideas about the reformation of society and the state which originated in Thessalonica in the fourteenth century were an important inspirational source for the eventual projection of the Greek national character.

The Effect of "Pronoia" on the Peasantry

Unhappily, the artistic and intellectual achievements of this period were short-lived, for the Byzantine state underwent a social crisis from which it never recovered. This was brought about by the insatiable land hunger of the big landowners, lay and ecclesiastic. At the same time, there was increasing external pressure on the Empire from the Ottoman Turks.

Emperors had long conferred grants of public land for life to the care (*pronoia*) of landowners, statesmen, and particularly soldiers in recognition of distinguished public service. Originally, the *pronoiarioi*, the recipients of such grants, were obliged to continue their service to the state in the same capacity in consideration of which the right had been bestowed. However, from the time of the Comneni (1081–1185)—a period which was characterized by an increasing assertion of power by a military oligarchy—grants in *pronoia* came to be associated exclusively with a definite obligation of military service.[31] There is an important distinction to be made, however, between land held in *pronoia* and an older system of direct land grants, which had been made primarily as a means of reward to loyal and deserving soldiers: these latter constituted a class of soldier-farmers who worked their own lands,[32] whereas the land held in *pronoia* usually consisted of vast estates cultivated by farmers who were bound to the soil and therefore utterly dependent upon the *pronoiarios*. Nevertheless, a new class of powerful landed magnates came into being on the basis of their steady acquisition of public lands under the system of *pronoia*. The development of the system of *pronoia* along these lines became the dominant characteristic of social organization during the late Byzantine period.[33] The *pronoiarioi*, or soldiers (*stratiotai*) as they were officially called, occupied a position of overriding importance and influence in Byzantine society, which, of course, was still overwhelmingly based on an agricultural economy. On the other hand, small free farmers and soldier-farmers were being reduced to a condition of poverty and subservience. As Nicetas Choniates remarked, the provincial inhabitants were deprived of "their money, their clothes, even their loved ones by the avarice of the military class." Choniates implored divine intervention to deliver the people from their miserable circumstances.[34]

After the Fourth Crusade (1204) and the introduction of Western European feudalism into the Byzantine world, the system of *pronoia* penetrated the Empire much more thoroughly. As we have already noticed, the collapse of central authority was generally conducive to the growth of a military oligarchy.[35] This oligarchy soon exerted a vigorous and decisive influence upon the political, social, and economic life of the Empire. The military class constituted a definite ruling oligarchy in the sense that its members monopolized the control of such public affairs as were still being conducted and offered the only protection to local communities and indigenous institutions. To be sure, it was not an exact equivalent of its feudal counterpart in Western Europe. On the contrary, it was intimately involved in the life of the cities of the Empire, with which important economic contacts were maintained. The military oligarchs spent something less than half their time on their rural estates, except in rare instances.[36] The Byzantine world, however, though obviously influenced to a degree, never accepted the ideas of its Latin overlords as to the proper organization of society.[37]

The national struggle against foreign invaders also had the effect of reinforcing the strength of the local nobility mainly because the exigencies of defense led to increasing use of grants in *pronoia*. Emperors made substantial grants to local magnates as a means of enhancing their own authority, increasing the effectiveness of military resistance, and providing suitable rewards to co-operative nobles.[38] During the Palaeologian period (1261–1453), the *pronoiarioi* continued not only to consolidate but to advance their positions vis-à-vis the imperial administration. In order to gain support for his policies, Michael VIII Palaeologus established the heritable and inalienable character of the *pronoia*,[39] and in addition to the normal revenues of the estate the *pronoia* now carried with it generous exemptions from taxation.[40] It was no more than the formal acknowledgement of a social fact when the *pronoiarioi* were dignified with such titles as despot, caesar, and *sebastokrator*. Never, before the Palaeologian period, writes Charanis, "was the Byzantine Empire dominated and ruled by a number of great families—families which were related to each other and to the ruling dynasty." [41] Before official recognition of the inheritable character of the *pronoia* was accorded, it had naturally tended, in confused and unsettled times, to become inheritable in practice. However, by granting official patents of heritability, the imperial administration merely encouraged the *pronoiarioi* to seek further means of personal aggrandizement. The small free peasant and soldier-farmer were forced to sell their lands [42] and more and more were driven to abject subservience as tenants on large estates. Under the Palaeologi, the great estate held in *pronoia* became the *ne plus ultra* of social development in an agricultural society; it was not only the basic form of agricultural tenure but provided the principal means of military security for the state. Yet, even so, the small landholder did not entirely disappear. Side by side with the great landowning oligarchy, middle-class farmers apparently continued to exist who, to the extent that they were also granted land in *pronoia*, fulfilled a definite civil function within the state. Many of the representatives of this class suffered extinction as free-holders along with the small peasant landholders. Many of them sought refuge in a monastic life. But a number survived as farmers.[43] Some of the latter settled in Thrace, and it was chiefly they who were resettled in Karasi (Asia Minor) by the Turks in 1354.[44] It would seem that the *pronoiarioi* had a definite obligation to furnish the state with a specified number of light soldiery in proportion to the amount of land held.[45]

The position of peasant smallholders and the middle-class *pronoiarioi* gradually deteriorated. Unfortunately, though, the relationship of one class with the other is difficult to determine precisely because of a con-fusion of terms used for the various categories of smallholders—free farmers; *paroikoi* (free peasants, though to a degree dependent); *douloparoikoi* (free peasants, though in a very low social and material position, which put them just above slaves); *proskathemenoi* (tenants only recently established on the land); and so on.[46] Though the villages of free peasants decreased in number and size, a free communal life was preserved in many places in Thessaly, Macedonia, and Asia Minor.[47]

During the period of the thirteenth and fourteenth centuries, the ex-tent of land owned by monasteries was enormously increased by royal grants, occasional bequests, and outright purchases. Monastic properties were notorious for the economic inefficiency with which they were run, yet their steady physical growth merely absorbed more and more people who might otherwise have turned their hands to increasing the yield of the soil or assisting in the defense of the Empire. This constant accretion of monastic land was yet another factor which contributed to the demise of the free peasantry as a class; also, since it was usually accompanied by a decline in agricultural productivity,[48] the misery of the peasant's plight was invariably aggravated.

The management of most monastic estates was frequently character-ized by scandals involving simony and nepotism in the disposal of Church lands. It was not unknown even for *paroikoi* and *anakamptikos echontes* (these were in effect sharecroppers)[49] to engage in these practices during times of disturbance. Sometimes the lands would be safely restored to the Church when bishops or metropolitans placed the offender under threat of excommunication or invoked the assistance of the secular au-thority.[50] On other occasions, however, a powerful noble, taking advan-tage of the confusion of the moment, would free tenants bound to Church lands who chose to become his own soldier-farmers and grant them the land to which they were formerly bound. Thus, at one time, the tenants of the monastery of St. George of Zavlantia, in Thessaly, with the help of the local governor, the *sebastokrator* John, were enrolled as his soldiers.

In this instance, however, the monastery was successful in thwarting their intentions and recovered both the estate and its tenants (1348).[51]

The growth of the military oligarchy and the enlargement of monastic estates led to economic paralysis of the Byzantine Empire and therefore contributed immensely to its eventual demise. Thus the Empire may be said to have succumbed finally to a kind of hypertrophy of two of its most important limbs, the Church and the military oligarchy. Above all, the vast cleavages which had opened between the classes prevented the development of a united front against the Turks, and the realization of Greek nationalism was thereby indefinitely postponed.

The Hesychast Controversy

The social imbalance which appeared to be destroying the Byzantine state was promoted by violent religious turmoil and a series of civil wars that convulsed Eastern Christendom from 1339 until virtually the end of the fourteenth century. Although many of the details surrounding the Hesychast controversy have still to be learned, it stemmed essentially from the introduction into the body of Greek monasticism of an extreme form of asceticism known as Hesychasm. This movement had far-reaching repercussions on Orthodox Christianity; it reappeared at various times with greater or lesser impact on successive generations throughout the Byzantine era. In the fourteenth century, it arose as a particular manifestation of the uncertainty and despair which were the inevitable accompaniment of social dissolution and foreign invasion.

According to Meyendorff:

Hesychasm profoundly affected monastic life on Mt. Athos and in Thessalonica, especially after it found an ardent protagonist in the person of the monk, Gregory Palamas, who later became Archbishop of Thessalonica. Palamas was descended from an aristocratic family of Asia Minor which migrated to Constantinople towards the end of the thirteenth century. The family atmosphere in which he grew up was characterized by a deep respect for the monastic ideal and, in particular, the life of pure prayer and contemplation. He completed a brilliant academic career in the court of his patron, Andronicus II, and later followed his monastic vocation. Subsequently, he came to be regarded as the perfect exemplar of the life to which he had dedicated himself. He was particularly admired for the breadth of his erudition, the sharpness of his intellect, and the severity of his asceticism. Palamas completely discarded the Platonist world of ideas. He considered it utterly incompatible with the Christian conception of a God who was the only source of creation and who alone had absolute freedom to exist and to will. To him, Aristotle's proof of creation was unconvincing. To him, all life was in Christ, through whom alone came revelation—by ceaseless prayer and contemplation.

The chief adversary of the mysticism of Palamas was the Calabrian monk,

Barlaam, who represented the final glow of Byzantine civilization in Italy. Although faithful throughout his life to Orthodox Christianity, he was at the same time steeped in the spirit of the Italian Renaissance. An eminent scholar both of Western theology and ancient Greek philosophy, Barlaam visited Greece, where his arrogance and ambition succeeded only in alienating Byzantine scholars.

For a time, he taught in Thessalonica and there became interested in the Hesychast movement. However, the prevailing ignorance of Hesychast monks, who were unable to satisfy his sharp and inquisitive mind, led to rapid disaffection. . . . Barlaam regarded the study of Plato and Aristotle as the essential prerequisite for communication with God: philosophical knowledge was mankind's finest achievement and most useful tool. This attitude towards philosophy constitutes the basic difference between the outlooks of Palamas and Barlaam.[52]

Barlaam's lectures in Thessalonica and Constantinople at least made scholars aware of the importance of Western philosophy. "Those who listened to the Calabrian monk," writes Schirò, "could not help but realize that the West had also progressed, that it had reached an advanced stage of philosophical development, even that traditional Byzantine scholarship ought to be re-examined in the light of contemporary philosophical thought in the West. The teachings of Barlaam helped to bring about this revision."[53] Anyone who studies the intellectual history of Thessalonica cannot fail to be impressed with the central importance of theological and philosophical discussion. Indeed, from this time forward, each of the two civilizations, Western and Byzantine, began slowly to rediscover the arts, science, and literature of the other; and, on the Byzantine side, it was largely through a new respect for the West, which exposure to its religio-philosophical ideas initially brought about, that the impetus towards rediscovery occurred. The leaders of the opposing parties, Palamas and Barlaam, engaged in endless polemics, and oecumenical synods met one after the other in an attempt to adjudicate the disputes and placate the troubled souls of the Orthodox masses.

In spite of Barlaam's opposition, the mysticism of Gregory Palamas prevailed. The influence of Hesychasm was so pervasive that philosophical studies and classical education fell into abeyance. Its eremitic and introspective outlook affected many who would otherwise have devoted themselves to the philosophy of ancient Greece. Hesychasm was therefore inimical to the development of a liberal spirit, which might have regenerated the Byzantine world. Even the enthusiasm of so fervent an apostle of Hellenism as Nicholas Kavasilas (see above, page 50) grew mute under Hesychastic influence. Doubtless Demetrius Kydones was referring to this debasement of philosophical studies in Thessalonica and

Constantinople when, in 1376, he wrote to his former pupil Radenos that "the Macedonian (that is, the Thessalonian) and the Byzantine (that is, the Constantinopolitan) despise philosophy." [54]

On the other hand, Hesychastic mysticism represented the last attempt to revivify Byzantine monasticism and monastic art. Its influence in both respects was particularly marked in Russia and the Balkans.[55] Hesychasm does not appear to have stifled artistic inspiration or inhibited the veneration of antiquity, both of which persisted at Mt. Athos even after the fall of the Empire.[56]

Although for a long time the Hesychast controversy remained confined to the realm of theological disputation, it suddenly acquired political importance when, in 1341–1342, John Cantacuzenus, leader of the military oligarchy and pretender to the throne, was invited by the monks of Mt. Athos to support Hesychasm against the teachings of Barlaam. In return, the monks supported his claims to the throne. His principal rival in the struggle for political ascendancy was Alexius Apocaucus, who relied upon the masses and had the backing of Empress Anna of Savoy (mother of the minor, John V Palaeologus). This personal contest between John Cantacuzenus and Alexius Apocaucus gradually assumed the aspect of a class struggle in which one side fought for the preservation of its privileges and the other for freedom from oppression. The plight of the peasants exacerbated the struggle.

The civil war was fierce and indiscriminate. The countryside was ravaged and, in some areas of Thrace, Macedonia, and Thessaly, utterly devastated. Peasants crowded into castles and towns—Thessalonica and Adrianople, for example—in an attempt to escape the general turbulence. The presence of these hungry masses in the already overcrowded cities merely hastened the process of social disintegration, which was already well advanced. In these cities, a middle class had grown strong on the profits of a lucrative trade with Italy, principally the cities of Venice and Genoa. Many families had enriched themselves, and, incidentally, their wealth contributed to the development of education and the arts. They saw civil war and turmoil as providing an appropriate opportunity for the assertion of their independence from the nobility and the exercise of a definite role in the direction of public affairs.

The struggle between John Cantacuzenus and Apocaucus assumed a particularly cruel and vicious form in Thessalonica from 1342 to 1347.[57] The social ferment left its mark on the people of Thessalonica. Kydones knew this when he advised the dignitary Phacrases in 1372 that the notables should not greedily extract profits from the people or provoke the exhausted citizenry in any way, but should handle public affairs in a spirit of amiability and good will and attempt to come as close as possible to the people.[58] Although rebellion had been crushed, the need felt for social change had not. There were many in Byzantine society who believed that, if its enemies were to be stayed, the financial wherewithal for its armies had to be found at all costs, even if this meant the wholesale alienation of monastic and ecclesiastical lands and the confiscation of the Church's plate. Consciousness of the need for drastic and continuing social change was suffused throughout the Empire. Its scholars were aware of it, and its leaders, such as Manuel II, were aware of it, as we shall presently have occasion to see.

It was not only political and social disturbances that were leading the Empire inexorably to disaster. The Ottoman Turks, who were recent converts to Islam, had proclaimed their Holy War against all infidels at the very time when the seeds of Neo-Hellenism had begun to sprout. Their primitive society adjusted itself swiftly and simply to the socio-religious changes consequent upon adoption of the new religion. They burst over the frontiers of the Byzantine Empire with frenetic zeal. Certainly, the influence of Arab-Persian civilization had softened many of their barbaric customs;[59] but in the intoxication of a Holy War, the Turks reverted to their wild atavistic instincts and to a display of barbarism of the kind so vividly described in the epic of Danişmende.

TURKISH CONQUEST OF
ASIA MINOR

Effect on Greek Population

At the beginning of the eleventh century, the Seljuk Turks forced their way into Armenia and there crushed the armies of several petty Armenian states. No fewer than forty thousand souls—the largest mass exodus in Armenian history [1]—fled before the organized pillage of the Seljuk host to the western part of Asia Minor. From the middle of the eleventh century,[2] and especially after the battle of Malazgirt (1071), the Seljuks spread throughout the whole Asia Minor peninsula, leaving terror, panic, and destruction in their wake.[3] Byzantine, Turkish, and other contemporary sources are unanimous in their agreement on the extent of havoc wrought and the protracted anguish of the local population.

The dearth of adequate documentary evidence makes it difficult to measure precisely the contraction of Hellenism in Asia Minor or to analyze the process of its total obliteration in some places. Yet such evidence as we have proves that the Hellenic population of Asia Minor, whose very vigor had so long sustained the Empire and might indeed be said to have constituted its greatest strength, succumbed so rapidly to Turkish pressure that, by the fourteenth century, it was confined to a few limited areas. By that time, Asia Minor was already being called Turkey.[4]

The most reliable sources from which a reconstruction of the Turkish conquest of Asia Minor may be attempted are the synodic *Acta* of the Oecumenical Patriarchate,[5] the various reports of bishops and metropolitans, and the hierarchical lists of patriarchal and metropolitan sees.[6] In these we read of the agony of the Church as she contemplated the effects of Turkish conquest: the ruin of her people in so many ecclesiastical provinces, poverty and deprivation, and the consequent inability of the faithful to support their metropolitans and bishops. Many of these ecclesiastics were given, in addition to their own sees, other sees which had become vacant. These too, however, were overtaken by the same fate. In the end these ecclesiastics retained nothing but their titles. If we essay a comparative study of the records of various dioceses, we discover that, one after another, bishoprics and metropolitan sees which once throbbed with Christian vitality became vacant and ecclesiastical buildings fell into ruins. The metropolitan see of Chalcedon, for example, disappeared in the fourteenth century, and the sees of Laodicea, Kotyaeon (now Kutahya), and Synada in the fifteenth.[7]

With the extermination of local populations or their precipitate flight, entire villages, cities, and sometimes whole provinces fell into decay. There were some fertile districts like the valley of the Maeander River, once stocked with thousands of sheep and cattle, which were laid waste and thereafter ceased to be in any way productive.[8] Other districts were literally transformed into wildernesses. Impenetrable thickets sprang up in places where once there had been luxuriant fields and pastures. This is what happened to the district of Sangarius, for example, which Michael VIII Palaeologus had known formerly as a prosperous, cultivated land, but whose utter desolation he afterwards surveyed in utmost despair.[9]

The mountainous region between Nicaea and Nicomedia, opposite Constantinople, once clustered with castles, cities, and villages, was depopulated.[10] A few towns escaped total destruction—Laodicea, Iconium, Bursa (then Prusa), and Sinope, for example—but the extent of devastation elsewhere was such as to make a profound impression on visitors for many years to come.[11] The fate of Antioch provides a graphic illustration of the kind of havoc wrought by the Turkish invaders: in 1432, only three hundred dwellings could be counted inside its walls, and its predominantly Turkish or Arabian inhabitants subsisted by raising camels, goats, cattle, and sheep. Other cities in the southeastern part of Asia Minor fell into similar decay.[12]

Whether the Hellenic element survived or disappeared depended to a very large degree on its geographical situation. The eastern provinces of the Empire, for instance, such as Melitene and Keltzene, were generally devastated because they lay in the path of the Seljuk advance. This area was also to become a battleground between Seljuk and Mongol.[13] But in Cappadocia the Hellenic element was fortuitously preserved because in moments of peril the local inhabitants were able to find refuge in the caves which abounded in that region.[14] Other areas in which the Greek populace managed to survive were the eastern marches of the Empire towards Upper Mesopotamia,[15] the rough and barren districts of

Pisidia and Cilicia,[16] and the impassable mountain regions of the Pontic Alps. In all these places, Greek populations lived on, secure and intact.[17] As a general rule, too, the inhabitants of coastal towns and districts, especially those which remained in contact with Constantinople and the maritime states of Genoa and Venice, suffered much less than those who lived in the hinterland. Hellenism was therefore not totally extinguished in Asia Minor. But the few Greeks who survived lived under the most trying conditions, in great deprivation. So at any rate we conclude from a study of contemporary ecclesiastical documents.[18] The presence of Greeks in certain regions during modern times is by no means an indication of their survival from Byzantine times. The eventual reappearance of Greek communities and the re-establishment of ecclesiastical sees in Asia Minor usually resulted from the subsequent migration of settlers from other parts of Asia Minor [19] and the Aegean islands, or from continental Greece itself.

However, the survival of compact Greek communities, especially in Pontus, Cappadocia, and southeastern Asia Minor, is definitely proven by the evidence of anthropogeography and the combined results of linguistic, anthropological, and folk research. The dialects of Pontus, for example, particularly those of Amisus, Oenoe (Turkish Unye), and Ophis (Turkish Of), together with those of almost twenty Greek-speaking villages in Cappadocia, form a distinct linguistic entity characterized by archaic constructions incomprehensible to the speaker of modern Greek. The Cappadocian language is very close to medieval Greek and stems from Hellenistic times. There is no evidence to suggest, as Karl Dieterich does, that it derives from a period of monastic colonization in the district of Caesarea during the fourth century.

These people also exhibit interesting anthropological characteristics. Those in the coastal region of the Pontic Alps are distinguishable as a rule by their fine Greek features and dignified bearing, while those in the interior, towards Armenia, reveal a strong Armenian strain, not only in their looks but in language, manners, and customs. This Armenian influence is most pronounced in Cappadocia, where the features and body structure are strikingly Armenian—large and excessively high foreheads, big fleshy noses, and short strong bodies. The prevalence of such features in the Greek provinces of eastern Asia Minor must be due to the extensive intercourse between Byzantines and Armenians during the ninth and tenth centuries, when a dynasty of Armenian origin reigned in Constantinople. As for the Greeks of southeastern Asia Minor, the marked Semitic influence apparent in their features can most likely be explained in terms of the large Syrian migrations into Asia Minor during the Isaurian period (717–867).[20]

NATURE OF INVASION

The success of the Ottoman Turks in Asia Minor was principally due to the daring and ardor of their attacks and the inability of Byzantine generals and field commanders to cope with their disorderly method of fighting. The quality of resistance by the military and *Akritai* of the eastern provinces tended also to be less effective by reason of the heavy taxes imposed by Michael VIII Palaeologus at the instigation of his provincial governor, one Chadenos.[21]

The first wave of Ottoman Turks, the nomad Yuruks,[22] settled in the district of Sogut, southeast of Bursa, under their ruler, Ertoghrul, in the middle of the thirteenth century. The descendants of the Greek refugees of 1922 from that district still talk of that invasion.[23] The Sultan of Iconium, Alā ed-Din I Kaikobad, had granted Ertoghrul (or Etourel Ghazi, as the refugees called him) the Ermeni Mountains and the group of villages known as Domanits, near Byzantine Angelokoma, for part of his summer domain.[24] This established the Ottomans in a frontier region, as it were, of the Seljuk state, close by the most advanced of their fortified positions at Eskisehir. Beyond this point lay the Byzantine Empire and the first of her defenses at the fortress of Belokoma (Bilecik).[25] This district, then thinly populated, formed the tiny but dynamic nucleus of the later great Ottoman Empire, which absorbed and assimilated so many Moslem and Christian peoples. Ottoman activity assumed a threatening aspect under Osman, son of Ertoghrul. In particular, there were those known as ghazis,[26] indefatigable in war, zealous in religion, and with an insatiable lust for plunder and booty, who, as the principal standard-bearers in a Moslem holy war against Christians, confronted the *Akritai*. Initially, under Osman Bey, the ghazi leaders appeared to act with a certain unity and accord, though they soon gave way to the marked freedom of action which was always thereafter their most notable and fearsome characteristic. Not only did they claim the right to expropriate Byzantine lands, but Osman himself and his successor, Orchan (1324–1362),[27] were forced to acknowledge these claims by distributing the land among those ghazis who had most distinguished themselves. Although these fiefs were revocable, they bore in every other respect an aspect of feudal organization. Fief-holders, for example, or *timar-erleri* as they were called in the old Ottoman chronicles (still later to be known as *timar-sipahiler*), exacted tribute from vassals, who were obliged to render military service also.[28] These fiefs produced incomes ranging from 2,000 or 3,000 to 19,999 *ake*. Larger fiefs producing incomes up to 99,999 *ake* were called *ziamet*, and their proprietors *zaim*. This procedure of granting fiefs to fighters was not in itself Osmanic, but appears to have derived from an older Seljuk institution.[29]

The continuous attacks and pillaging by Turkish warriors naturally spread devastation and dread throughout the countryside. For some, especially peasants, the choice between capitulation or flight was not quite as bitter as it was for others: they were already suffering under the oppressive rule of their own local nobility and to accept the conqueror often seemed merely the exchange of one master for another.[30] When the spread of the Ottoman dominion appeared not only inevitable but sometimes welcome, resistance was frequently no more than token. Thus, after the fall of Nicaea (2 March 1331), some towns which were still free hastily acknowledged vassalage and paid heavy tribute (haraç). Even so, Turkish assaults by land and sea and the capture of prisoners continued and were often the necessary preludes to surrender by the inhabitants of other towns.[31] Tradition has it, for example, that, in the time of Orchan, Rysion and its neighboring villages capitulated, but only after the forcible seizure of Libyssa (Dakybiza) made their position untenable. The nobility, unable to cultivate their lands, could either abandon their estates or accept the fait accompli of conquest. Those who optimistically seized the estates of departed landowners were eventually faced with the same option. They, too, were caught up in the torrent of flight; they, too, became "the poor, the naked, and the homeless." [32]

Men, women, and children followed in the wake of retreating armies in an effort to reach the safety of European shores or the coastal cities of the Sea of Marmara, which offered the last places of refuge. They walked until they collapsed. Pachymeres gives us a vivid description of the pitiful caravans of refugees in northwestern Asia Minor that were continuously arriving in Nicomedia: old people, women, and babies lay in the streets of the city or outside its walls on the seashore, weeping and wailing for a lost husband, son, daughter, brother, or sister.[33] Under such conditions, some of the greatest families of Anatolia became extinct. Some fortunate ones joined the flight to Constantinople. Among these were the Phocas, Scleros, Bryennios, Comnenus, Angelos, Vatatzes, Tarchaniotes, and Philanthropenos families.[34]

However, there were some landed magnates, military leaders, and governors,[35] who, by signifying their willingness to submit and co-operate and subsequently by entering into special agreements with the Turks, were allowed to remain in their towns and castles. In this way many retained their lands and received other privileges. Among the Christian populace, too, there were adventurers who took an active part in the Turkish invasion in Asia Minor in the hope of being rewarded with a share of the plunder. It is difficult to evaluate the precise nature of the role these Christians played (the Kâfır-sipahiler as they are known in the old Ottoman chronicles) in the Ottoman state; it is even more difficult to define the nature of their obligations. Probably the most that can be said is that the Ottomans were prepared to tolerate Christian fief-holders in their midst in the hope that they, or their descendants, would one day be converted to Islam.[36]

Crypto-Christianity and Greek Apostasy

All the Turkish peoples were tolerant and conciliatory towards the "people of the Bible" (*Ahl al Kitab*), both Christians and Jews, when they submitted quietly and peacefully. This was a most important factor in the rapid spread of Turkish domination. However, this attitude did not prevent the Turks from frequently confiscating Christian churches or from behaving in other respects with singular barbarity.[37] Hence Christians were never able to move about with complete freedom or to express themselves with impunity. Their descriptions of their sufferings reveal a repressed fear that was never far below the surface.[38] "Orchan extended compassion towards the faithful; but towards the unfaithful, oppression." So wrote the Turkish historian, Şükrüllāh, adviser to Murad II (1421–1451) and Mohammed II (1451–1481).[39] The raias, for instance, were afraid to approach other Christians, even their own priests, who had been taken captive by the Turks, or to broach religious subjects. In such circumstances, most Christians, especially those who lived in remote areas in constant proximity to the Turks, eventually lost their own language and adopted the Turkish language.[40] Indeed, if Christians were to live as free men and to enjoy wealth, honors, dignity, and office, they had to become assimilated with their rulers by professing Islam or else attempt to escape to mountainous and inaccessible regions or to Christian states. The combination of physical suffering and concern for personal and material well-being thus led many families, or even whole peoples, to accept conversion to Islam. However, there were other pressures at work: fanatical dervishes and other devout Moslem leaders like the ghazis constantly toiled for the dissemination of Islam.[41] They had done so from the very beginning of the Ottoman state and had played an important part in the consolidation and extension of Islam. These dervishes were particularly active in the uninhabited frontier regions of the east. Here they settled down with their families, attracted other settlers, and thus became the virtual founders of whole new villages, whose inhabitants invariably exhibited the same qualities of deep religious fervor. From places such as these, the dervishes or their agents would emerge to take part in new military enterprises for the extension of the Islamic state. In return, the state granted them land and privileges under a generous prescription which required only that the land be cultivated and communications secured. The monasteries (*zaviye* or *ribât*) that were customarily built over dervish graves served as small caravansaries where travellers were able to find food and shelter.[42]

Ottoman religious tolerance, however, all but ceased to exist during times of actual fighting. From the time when the Ottoman Turks first settled in the district of Sogut and then spread out towards Bithynia, cases of forcible conversion and, coincident with this, of clandestine Christianity have been recorded. Oral traditions also are replete with instances of both.[43] In general, the tendency towards individual and mass conversion seems to have been directly related to the resumption of military activity: Greeks and other Balkan people often sought to evade anticipated destruction at the hands of rampaging Turks by announcing their religious capitulation. The Turkish avalanche always left behind the detritus of Greek apostasy, but it never buried the Greeks. Quite the contrary, in fact: these renegades from Greek religion often became the bearers of Byzantine institutions to the Ottomans. Their influence thereafter on Turkish thought and manners (in spite of Köprülü's claims to the contrary [44]) was manifest in many aspects of private and public activity.

There were also many "converts" to Islam who merely maintained a pretense of Moslem belief while secretly practicing the rites of Christianity, sometimes throughout their whole lives. Of these we shall presently have more to say. Their descendants, however, in time found themselves unable to withstand the effects of constant association with Moslems, and the eroding influences of daily social and economic contact slowly and subtly affected the doctrines and practices of Islam. "Crypto-Christianity" thus frequently constituted an intermediate stage in the process of ultimate conversion to Islam. It was certainly one of Hellenism's greatest tragedies.

In commenting upon the disappearance of the Greek population of Asia Minor, it is well to point out again that very little relevant historical evidence has been preserved. Suffice it here to mention the interesting comments of a distinguished voice on Anatolian and Turkish affairs, that of the German, A. D. Mordtmann. On a journey to Cappadocia in the interior of Asia Minor, he observes in his diary:

We know precisely the size of the Seljuk and Ottoman migrations. We also know with reasonable certainty that, far from being prolific peoples, their reproductive energies were dissipated for a variety of reasons. From this we may correctly assume that the major part of the Moslem population in Asia Minor did not stem from the Turkish migrations, but rather from the Gallo-Greek population which had become converted to Islam. The same may be presumed to have occurred, *mutatis mutandis,* in the other provinces of Asia Minor. Also, a number of other factors have led me to believe that, while in many places the people may have ostensibly professed Islam, they are in fact still secretly Christian. I have had many interesting conversations and have visited many places, which shall nevertheless go unreported because the people trusted in my discretion not to reveal things which could only expose them to danger. Frequently, I would be engaged in a serious dispute with certain persons and, not knowing the Koran well, sought ways to explain myself. At that, my rivals would suddenly burst into laughter, open their shirts, and show me a cross. Or again, when sometimes my stock of words in Turkish was exhausted during the course of our mutual altercation, to my great astonishment they would suddenly begin to express themselves very correctly in the Greek language— ancient Greek, but with modern Greek pronunciation. Who could betray such a people? [45]

Yet Turkish domination over so long a period must have considerably reduced the Greek Orthodox population, not only by uprooting it but also by the process of individual and mass conversion to Islam, as we have noted. This seems to have been true in Bithynia and in those parts along the west coast of Asia Minor, the fertile valleys of the Maeander, Cayster, and Hermus rivers.[46] The fact that very few oral traditions and very little folklore mention the conversion of the inhabitants of Anatolia to Islam [47] can be explained in part by the extreme rapidity with which the Turks asserted their predominance. Even at the end of the fourteenth century, for example, Demetrius Kydones lamented the substitution of Turkish place-names for Greek; by 1454 as many as four-fifths of the place-names may have been changed.[48]

Kydones described the fate of the Christian peoples of Asia Minor thus: "The entire region which sustained us, from the Hellespont east-wards to the mountains of Armenia, has been snatched away. They [the Turks] have razed cities, pillaged churches, opened graves, and filled everything with blood and corpses. And they have ravaged the very souls of the inhabitants by forcing them to ignore the true God and to practice their own infamous rites. Alas, too, they have even abused Christian bodies. And having taken away their entire wealth they have now taken away their freedom, reducing them to the merest shadows of slaves. And with such dregs of energy as remain in these unfortunate people, they are forced to be the servitors of the Turks' personal comforts." [49]

TURKISH INVASION OF THE BALKAN PENINSULA

Piracy in the Aegean and Ionian Seas

During the thirteenth and fourteenth centuries Turkish operations expanded rapidly into the Aegean and Ionian seas. In this area, indeed, piracy had been a very common phenomenon from the time of the Arab conquest and the beginnings of the Crusades.[1] In the fourteenth century, from places such as the Emirate of Menteşe [2] on the coast of Asia Minor, hordes of Turkish pirates descended upon the Dodecanese, plundering livestock and crops and carrying off the inhabitants.[3] Even the northern coasts of continental Greece did not escape the depredations of Moslem pirates. The monasteries of Mt. Athos were especially singled out as targets, and many monks fled westward to other monastic centers and to places like Veroia and Meteora.[4] Nor were the Turks alone. Taking advantage of the general confusion, Spanish, Catalan, Venetian, Genoese, Slavic, and Greek pirates also roamed the Aegean with impunity, attacking and capturing ships and generally behaving with gross savagery and cruelty towards crews and passengers. These corsairs also penetrated into the Sea of Marmara [5] and looted the islands and coastal areas of continental Greece from Thrace to the Peloponnese.[6] Many coastal villages were devastated, and their inhabitants sought refuge in more secure places. According to oral tradition, a number of new settlements in the interior were founded by these refugees. By the time of the Fourth Crusade, many islands were depopulated,[7] though the depopulation was temporary in most cases.

However, in 1383 Tenedos was left utterly devoid of human life as a result of Genoese and Venetian rivalry; [8] Astypalaia was laid waste in

Figure 5. Monastery of the Metamorphosis, Meteora.

the time of Murad I (1362–1389), and it was not until 1415, at the time of the Council of Constance, that it was rehabilitated by the Venetian nobleman, John Quirini.[9] The traveller Clavijo (1403–1406) mentions the existence of many uninhabited islands in the Dodecanese, though Psara and Antipsara apparently still retained their populations. According to him, there were Turks living on Samos.[10] Caumont passed through the Cyclades in 1418 and noted that a number of those islands were completely depopulated.[11] But it is to Buondelmonti that we must go in order to appreciate the full extent of devastation in the Aegean and to understand fully the fear and afflictions of its peoples. Buondelmonti alludes constantly to the Turkish pirates who sailed as far as the Ionian Sea, even to Corfu, with the local inhabitants retreating before them into the security of isolated and fortified castles, where some of the most ancient family lineages were preserved and popular traditions more readily survived. At sunrise, occasionally at a given signal, these people would open the gates and go down to their fields, always to return at night. This tedious pattern of life continued, in some cases, for whole centuries. The islands around Paros seem to have suffered particularly at the hands of the Turks. Here again, the inhabitants would leave their homes for varying lengths of time, to return only when the danger was past. In other cases—Siphnos and Naxos are two in point—the balance of the population was seriously disturbed when a large proportion of the men either emigrated or were shipwrecked. Many marriageable women died unmarried.[12]

Such conditions obviously favored a recrudescence of the slave trade, and Greek, Turkish, Albanian, Tartar, and other peoples were sold in the slave markets of the East. The Catalans developed a particularly lucrative trade in Greek slaves after their conquest of part of Hellas in 1311. From their principal market in Majorca, a vital line of communication stretched across the Mediterranean all the way to the East. Of these Greeks we know little, except that they demonstrated great skill in various fields ranging from commerce and the fine arts to farming and handicrafts.[13]

The Ottoman Landings in Thrace

Piracy at sea was but one of the ways the Turks extended their dominion. Civil war between John V and John Cantacuzenus, as well as Serbian, Bulgarian, and Turkish participation in that war, also contributed to the dislocation of the northern provinces of continental Greece and to widespread ruin throughout the countryside.[14] Turkish mercenaries in the Greek armies of this period proved to be forerunners of the Turkish host which overflowed the European provinces of the Empire. Refugees from

Asia Minor looked to Europe for their safety with less and less hope.[15] The Greeks in Europe did not fare much better under their own rulers. As Kydones despairingly wrote in the autumn of 1352: "Those who govern in our land have the power of earthquake and of plague—and are of no more use. Everyone seems to wish his neighbor dead. Where there is peace, it is more often than not with the enemy; and where there is war, it is between brother and brother. Everyone shamelessly takes up weapons against his own kind." But he realized that his complaint was futile and gloomily predicted in the spring of 1352 that the attitude of his countrymen would "surely bring to our cities today the same fate that befell Perinthos, an immortal monument to our thoughtlessness; tomorrow we will listen to the strange language of the Turks in high places." [16] There was little exaggeration in this prophecy. Already, villages in Thrace and Macedonia were being transformed into rubbish heaps (*palaiochoria*), farmers were crowding into castles and cities [17] and leaving the fields untended.

From the time the Ottoman Turks first set foot in Thrace under Suleiman, son of Orchan, the Empire rapidly disintegrated. The first cities to fall were Tzympe in 1353 and Callipolis in 1354, the latter after an earthquake had toppled the walls of the city. "The earthquake consumed not only buildings and property," wrote a contemporary observer, Archbishop Gregory Palamas of Thessalonica, "but the lives of the people: their mangled remains were tossed quite impartially, as the poet says, to the dogs and vultures." The Archbishop was passing by chance through the Hellespont in 1354 and was an appalled witness of an event which was to have such great consequences for all the Balkan peoples: large numbers of Turkish ships, almost as if bridging the two continents, were milling about and disgorging their cargoes of rapacious troops on the European shore.[18] There were many Greek scholars thereafter who reflected upon the debacle and left for posterity a fascinating record of their feelings and thoughts.[19]

Outright civil war and the internecine struggles of semi-independent regional governors in Thrace who failed to co-ordinate their efforts either with one another or with the capital contributed to the ease with which the Turks extended their sway. Suleiman first conquered the peninsula of Thrace and then used it as a bridgehead for his advance on Rhaedestos and inland.[20] Oral traditions, preserved to this day among Thracian refugees who settled in Greece, indicate the immediate flight of the populace to the safety of the mountains. Most of the inhabitants of Plagiarion (Turkish Bulayır) in Thrace escaped into the rough country of Kuru Dag on the northern shore of the Gulf of Saros. The descendants of these people of Plagiarion still talk of "Ghazi Suleiman" and many of his works (for example, the *imaret* or asylum for the poor which he founded, his mausoleum, the great mosque, formerly Hagia Sophia, all of them places of pilgrimage for later sultans). Another place of refuge for the Greeks at this time was Mt. Hieron,[21] and there were no doubt other mountains and isolated refuges as well.

From the very beginning of the Turkish onslaught under Suleiman, the Turks tried to consolidate their position by the forcible imposition of Islam. If Şükrüllāh is to be believed, those who refused to accept the Moslem faith were slaughtered and their families enslaved. "Where there were bells," writes the same author, "Suleiman broke them up and cast them onto fires. Where there were churches he destroyed them or converted them into mosques. Thus, in place of bells there were now muezzins. Wherever Christian infidels were still found, vassalage was imposed upon their rulers. At least in public they could no longer say *'kyrie eleison'* but rather 'There is no God but Allah'; and where once their prayers had been addressed to Christ, they were now to 'Mohammed, the prophet of Allah.'" [22]

The conquests of Suleiman were continued by some of his most distinguished generals, whose services were usually rewarded by the granting of a fief.

The Extension of Turkish Control

The Turkish conquests from Ankara to the Hellespont and the rapid consolidation of the landings in Thrace were soon followed by further extensions of the boundaries of their influence. The extent of their far-flung territories immediately raised manifold problems of organization and control. The ghazis, of course, had been the principal instrument of Turkish conquest, but with their loose organization they were of little help in the stage of consolidation. Recognizing this, Orchan had attempted to forge another military force both more disciplined than the ghazis and more dependent upon himself, the infantry (*yaya*), and later, the cavalry (*müsellem*). However, these had not developed in accordance with his expectations and had certainly not displaced the ghazis. The ghazis were still the main force of the Turkish army, and their fanatical spirit still determined its character, though Orchan's reorganization had the effect of making them a more orderly and tractable corps. Indeed, it was to one of the leaders of the ghazis that Orchan entrusted the task of carrying out the invasion (*akın*), and so it was still a relatively undisciplined army that spread terror among the inhabitants of the Balkan peninsula, Hungary, Transylvania, and Slavonia.[23]

The problem therefore still remained of building up a strong and, above all, loyal permanent army to guard the vast Ottoman nation. This was finally achieved by Murad I (1362–1389), whose qualities as man and ruler still provoke violent differences of opinion. Şükrüllāh extols him for his faith, his justice, his mercy, and a variety of other virtues; [24] the Bulgarian author of the life of the Despot, Stephen Lazarević, while acknowledging Murad's power, characterizes him as savage and brutal.[25] Be that as it may, Murad I was responsible for taking the crucial step which ultimately transformed the Turkish army. Early in his reign, probably in 1363,[26] Kara Roustem, a theologian from Karaman, offered a solution to the problem of what to do with the burdensome excess of prisoners of war.[27] He suggested that one-fifth be assigned to the personal use of the Sultan. In this way the janissaries came into being, youths between the ages of fifteen and twenty who were trained as an elite corps of the Sultan's and in time became not only a legend but a terrible scourge to the Christian nations.[28]

Murad deployed his power and asserted it more efficaciously among his subjects. It was from this time that the Turkish state began to lose its primitive tribal character and to take on the trappings and characteristics of an Asiatic despotism. The janissaries were the slaves of the Porte (*Kapı Kulları*) [29] and became the principal support of the state. From the time of Bayezid I (1389–1402), these personal slaves of the Sultan were occasionally granted fiefs or installed as governors in certain provinces with the specific purpose of staving off any attempts by the older Turkish families to reassert their positions of influence in the state.[30]

As rapidly as the Ottoman Empire grew in strength, so the Byzantine dissolved. The Byzantine throne was occupied by a series of incapable and profligate emperors whom the patriot monk of Magnesia characterized thus: "They are 'slaves'—of their bellies, their lusts, their bile. They are nefarious, lazy, cowardly, garrulous, braggart, shameless, arrogant, and utterly disdainful of everything. Because they are devoid of brains and sanity they have submitted to vile slavery and pay tribute to the barbarians, whom they meekly obey. Those who before were merely rude, haughty, and hateful to their own people now compound their ignominy by appearing ridiculous to their enemies . . ."

The same writer also records the shame of the Byzantine armies. "These were no longer the organized and well-disciplined armies of yore, but rather a rabble led by arrogant men who oppressed the people; they had forgotten their function as protectors. These leaders commanded nothing but disrespect. They were weak and effeminate in their behavior, cowardly, stupid, licentious, insolent, dissolute, predatory, traitorous, reckless —men who pillaged the property of others and left fields, gardens, vineyards, and forests desolate; men who knew only how to destroy those who were 'weaker.' Words did not exist to describe the wickedness of

Figure 6. Fifteenth-Century Janissary.

these insensate, obdurate, callous, ungrateful men—if, indeed, they could be called men and not beasts. . . . That was why God had forsaken them and the enemy rejoiced . . ." [31]

The Turkish peril took many grotesque forms. Turkish sympathizers, whether out of weakness or opportunism, began to exert an ever increasing influence on the life of the free cities of Thrace and even of Constantinople. These were the collaborators and black-marketeers of the period, whose numbers normally swelled as the Turkish menace loomed larger. Such men had no compunctions about giving direct assistance to the Turks in exchange for material rewards such as money, sheep, and cattle. They also had commercial dealings with the enemy, came and went openly in his camp, even caroused with him before returning to the capital to spread alarm among their fellow citizens. They intimidated the populace with threats that they would report anti-Turkish attitudes or activities to their "masters." They spoke and behaved with such audacity that many Greeks, the more timorous, perhaps, believed it better to obtain immediate conditions for the surrender of the city than await conquest by the Turks and their flunkies. Not only treason but defeatism was therefore prevalent in Constantinople and in all those cities which came under siege. The inhabitants of the once gay capital felt as if incarcerated in prison. Almost from the towers of its walls, they could watch the enemy lay waste the earth, slaughter, pillage, burn houses, churches, and public buildings, insult the faith, and mock the religious. Grief, poverty, and hunger crowded in upon the capital. People had no heart even to try to cultivate the land. Citizens and soldiers seemed to have been divested of all morale, and slaves abandoned their masters, who themselves were already "enslaved." Many sought to escape by fleeing to the more secure islands of the Aegean. The city was losing its very life. [32]

From the time of the conquest of Adrianople by Murad I in 1361 [33]— an event that left a permanent mark in demotic legend and poetry— Turkish conquest spread throughout Thrace, Bulgaria, and the entire Balkan peninsula. [34] If not required for their own military use (as in Didymoteikhon, for example), the Turks razed almost all castles lest they serve as bases for local rebellion. [35] If by chance some were left standing, they were ungarrisoned and unattended and fell into ruin with the passing of the years. [36] Vainly, Byzantine scholars attempted to warn prominent men in the West of the dangers they would face were Constantinople to fall. [37] Vainly, they tried to apprise the grandees of the court of John V Palaeologus of the consequences if those in authority continued to disregard the plight of the masses.

But the exploitation of the masses continued, greatly aided by the venality of the judges, [38] whom Demetrius Kydones called "thieves." [39]

Yet the masses remained loyal to the state. There may have been restive-ness and incipient rebelliousness, but the people still turned to Constan-tinople for their ultimate deliverance. It did not come, of course. The Empire was rotten at its core, and the Turks gnawed easily through its soft and putrescent pulp.

The failure of the Balkan peoples, Greek, Bulgarian, Albanian, and Serbian, to unite against the Turk and the weakening of their military forces by constant internecine warfare and by sporadic political and social upheaval were their final undoing. After the defeat of the Serbs at Çirmen or Cernomen near the Hebrus River in 1371, Serbia, Bulgaria, and the Byzantine Empire became tributaries of the Ottoman Empire and were obliged to render assistance in Ottoman campaigns. Panic gripped Frank-ish and Greek rulers everywhere in Greece, and for the first time, on the initiative of Pope Gregory XI, plans were mooted for some kind of con-certed resistance against the Turks. One plan was to call an assembly of Christian rulers in Catalan-controlled Thebes on 1 October 1373, to devise ways and means of combatting the Turkish threat. The plan failed.[40] Then Manuel (later Manuel II Palaeologus), who was at that time the ruler of Thessalonica and who of all the sons of John V was especially noted for his combative spirit as well as his strength of char-acter, wisdom, and literary bent, himself seized the initiative. Taking advantage of the defeat of the Serbs, he freed parts of Macedonia from the heirs of Stephen Dušan, who still maintained tenuous control in that region, and entered Serrai in November 1371.[41] He inflicted a number of defeats on the Turks, both at sea and on land, occupied several fortified positions, and liberated many prisoners, all exploits which delighted his teacher, Demetrius Kydones.[42] Although Manuel's successes proved to be only ephemeral, they were sufficient to rekindle the flame of Greek resistance, as we shall presently observe.

In spite of these temporary setbacks, the Turkish armies continued their advance westwards through Thrace. General Evrenos Bey con-quered the town of Komotine (Turkish Gumuljina) in 1364 or 1365 and from there moved into Macedonia [43] with Tsantarli Kara Halil, the hon-ored and celebrated "Torch of the Faith" (Haïreddin). The Turks won Serrai in 1383. It was here, two years later, outside the southwest wall of the city, that the Sultan, Murad I, built the famed mosque called Atık, or Eski Mosque. Until the very end of Turkish domination in Serrai, some of the twenty-four Turkish quarters of the city preserved the names of several of the most illustrious individuals and families in Turkish history—such names as Ghazi Evrenos, Basdar Haïreddin, Bedreddin Bey, and Simavnaoglou.[44]

Using Serrai as their major operational base, the Turks captured Veroia in 1385–1386, Bitola (Turkish Monastir) in 1382–1383, Christoupolis in 1387, exacted tribute from Thessalonica after four years of siege in 1387, and conquered Kitros in 1386. They then struck south and subjugated Thessaly in 1393. They invaded Epirus for the first time in 1385, then Aetolia and Acarnania (Karleli), where Albanians and Arvanito-Vlachs put up some resistance. The Peloponnese was overrun by successive waves in 1380(?), 1387, 1388, and 1395.[45] During the reign of Bayezid I, the monks of Mt. Athos declared their submission,[46] and in 1397 Athens capitulated and was subjected to temporary occupation.[47]

Some slight, yet tantalizing, evidence regarding the situation in northern Epirus appears in the *Chronicle of Dryopis,* which, though almost certainly based on earlier sources, cannot be fully relied upon since the sources themselves have been lost. However, it would seem that after the conquest of that area the Turks tolerated the existence of Christian feudatories, both secular and ecclesiastic, which were even recorded in the official Turkish land registry.[48] These registrations in northern Epirus and southern Albania were probably effected during the time of Bayezid I, after his campaigns of 1394 and 1397. They were begun in the districts of Prëmeti and Koritsa.[49]

Conditions in the Greek World, 1354–1402

The last fifty years of the fourteenth century are probably the most obscure in Balkan history. It is a period characterized by an indiscriminate terror inflicted by hordes of undisciplined ghazis. Savage forays against the Greeks by these warriors were designed to spread demoralization and panic as a prelude to actual invasion. Of course, it had never been easy, even in more settled times, to travel any great distance across the lands of peoples who, after all, spoke many different languages.[50] How much more difficult with the constant likelihood of encountering the ubiquitous Turk! This peril was compounded by an almost unparalleled outbreak of lawlessness and banditry.[51] For there were many who refused to bow under the yoke of Turk, Frank, or Albanian and who had no other recourse but to enter into a life of brigandage and rapine.

Adrianople in 1389 provides a typical example of the disorder of the times. When the city was free, according to a contemporary patriarchal document, the metropolitan had sufficient means from the income of the ecclesiastical lands of his province to support large numbers of the poor; in 1389, about twenty-eight years after its capture, he was deprived not only of land and income but even of a cell in which to live. The cathedral and all the "prominent churches" of the city had been seized. Many of the inhabitants of the city had been taken into captivity, with a resultant decline in the Christian population. Eventually, it was decided to move the metropolitan seat to nearby Agathopolis "until Adrianople should once again be restored to the Greeks." [52] The word "restoration" (*apokatastasis*) was on the tongues of Greeks everywhere.

As in Asia Minor, many property owners espoused Islam with the intention of obtaining certain social and material advantages. Religious conversions in continental Greece and in other Balkan lands seem to have been on as large a scale as in Asia Minor. The sources, though, are generally silent on this point, and very little contemporary evidence exists. At any rate Kydones referred in distress to the small remnant of the Greek race and to the fact that increasingly large numbers of Greeks were being caught up in the stream of Islam.[53] Again, too, as popular tradition and the evidence of nomenclature in places like Thrace amply attest, Moslem priests were notably successful in proselytizing and in catechizing their faith among the frightened people.[54]

The condition of the Empire was exacerbated by bickering between the Emperors and their families, particularly between John V and his son, Andronicus IV. These internecine squabbles continued sporadically until the last decade of the fourteenth century and so degraded the participants that on occasion they called on the Sultan to mediate. No less ruinous were the struggles for ascendancy between various factions within the imperial court. Threats were met with counterthreats, accusations with recriminations: [55] "our people, decadent now for so many years," lamented the contemporary scholar, Theodore Potamios, "have become but a mere simulacrum of the nation they once were." These conditions of instability were of course propitious for the rise of opportunists and self-seekers, many of whom climbed to positions of great power and influence in the state and proceeded by illegal and unscrupulous means to amass huge fortunes.[56] Such wealth, by its very size and conspicuousness amid the general poverty, usually proclaimed its nature, thereby stirring the people to anger and providing grounds for new social disturbances.[57]

By 1394, the Byzantine capital itself began to be slowly strangled by the armies of the Sultan. Only the fear of slavery, the dread of being forced into recantation of their faith, and the prospect of the desecration of their churches gave the inhabitants courage to withstand the siege for seven years.[58] It was their good fortune that the Turks had not yet fully developed the technique of siege operations. Nevertheless, Constantinople experienced the same agonies as all those cities which subsequently suffered sustained siege by the Turk. Palaces, public buildings, churches, and monasteries were either destroyed or allowed to fall into decay.[59] The inhabitants of the city (and we may presume that this was the case in other cities and regions) continuously decamped. Most of these refugees eventually found their way to Venetian-controlled Crete, where of course they only encountered fresh difficulties.[60] Some were monks and artists who took to their new abode the conservative spirit of Orthodoxy in art; others, like the monk Athanasius,[61] were scholars who nourished Byzantine culture in this distant island by their influence as teachers of children. Indeed, they seem to have inspired a new style of painting in Crete, one characterized by its austerity; [62] simultaneously, men like John Simeonakis actively fostered Hellenic studies, at least in a small way, long before the scholars and teachers did who fled there after the fall of Constantinople.[63] Such slight evidence of these developments as we possess is important for the light it sheds on the artistic and intellectual flowering of the sixteenth century.

The desperation of the Greeks was intensified by the defeat of the Crusaders at Nicopolis (28 September 1396). This event seemed to precipitate a flight from all Greek communities. Most of the inhabitants fled towards the Danubian principalities on the coasts of the Black Sea, where remnants of ancient Greek colonies still existed, and towards the Peloponnese, where eventually a dynamic center of Hellenism was formed. Thus began a new phase in Greek history.

From the beginning, the stream of refugees included artists, intellectuals, and members of eminent families. Among them, for instance in Serbia, were a number of painters from Thessalonica whose murals presently adorned the monastery of Ravanica (built 1385–1387), the church of Sisojevac (1390–1400), and the monastery of Resava (1407–1418).[64] Others, or their descendants, achieved fame as writers in Serbia: Antonije Rafail, for example, grateful for the protection offered him by the Despot of Serbia, Stephen Lazarević, who wrote in 1419/20 an encomium in honor of the Despot's father, Lazare, a martyr and saint, who had been killed at the battle of Kosovo Polje (1389); Nikon Hierosolymites (born c. 1380), confessor of Lazare's daughter, the princess Helen, for whom he recounted his journey between 1398 and 1412 to Jerusalem, to the monastery at Sinai, and to Egypt; the poet, Demetrius Cantacuzenus, descendant of a branch of the great Byzantine family, who settled in the mining center of Novo Brdo towards the middle of the fifteenth century. Cantacuzenus wrote several books in the old Serbian language, some of them still unpublished.[65]

Certain extant sources document the settlement of many Greek refugees in the Danubian principalities from the beginning of the fifteenth century. Here they rapidly acquired honors and wealth, the more easily, perhaps, because Greek influence had preceded them. A metropolitan see for Hungary and Walachia had been established in Curtea-de-Argeş as early as 1359, during the reign of Alexander Basarab (1352–1364); its first bishops were Greeks (Hyakinthos, succeeded by Chariton, who was followed by Anthimos Kritopoulos). The Danubian rulers, in particular those of Walachia, maintained close ties with the monasteries of Mt. Athos and often invited Greek priests to their courts. The priests were followed by Greek merchants, mariners, artisans, painters, and also architects, who built churches and monasteries. The close and harmonious rapport between the principalities and Hellas brought about the introduction of popular Greek books, which affected the rudimentary beginnings of Rumanian literature.[66] Thus the Greek refugees on the Danube developed little oases of Hellenic civilization. Later, during the long period of Turkish domination, they nourished from afar the economic and intellectual development of the modern Hellenic nation by providing financial assistance, books, and other necessities.

The consequences of Greek movement to the south were no less important an influence on modern Hellenism. The populations of entire towns and districts scattered like leaves throughout the islands of the Aegean and the Peloponnese. Although definite evidence of the gradual evacuation of Thessalonica and Constantinople exists, there is no written evidence testifying to the large-scale dispersal of peasants. Thus, while the motive for flight—the hope of freedom in the still unoccupied south— seems plain enough, the origins of the refugees and the nature of their impact on their new abodes remain obscure. Only the findings of linguistic and geolinguistic research enable us to unravel a part of this historical mystery. Thus, the marked resemblances between the dialects of Andros, Tenos, Mykonos, and Syros in the Aegean Sea on the one hand and those of northern Greece on the other seem to support an hypothesis that Greeks from the north sought refuge on these islands between 1364 and 1413. Similarly, the dialectal similarities between the inhabitants of Korthion and those of Chalcidice provide some grounds for a belief that refugees from Chalcidice went to Apano Castro on Andros. The dialect of Tenos is also similar to that of Apano Castro in its distinctive tonal features as well as in the change of the nonaccented vowels ε and o into ι and ου and the dropping of the nonaccented ι and ου, which are both characteristic of northern phonetics. Apparently, the disjunction of the dialects of Mykonos and Syros from the others can be explained in terms of the settlement of southern Greeks on those particular islands after the fourteenth century.[67]

The evidence of linguistics may again be offered as proof of the northern Greek origins of certain villages in the Peloponnese—between Lacedemon and Kynouria, near Mt. Parnon, for example. It is not entirely gratuitous to suppose that Greeks from the north fled to these districts as the Turks took over their lands in the latter half of the fourteenth century.[68] From all over threatened Constantinople itself, from its borders, from places outside it, and from others much further afield, they streamed down to the Peloponnese. Lands formerly forested, wild, and uninhabited were cleared for habitation and the population multiplied. Ten thousand Albanians joined the Greeks in common exile.[69]

The Peloponnese became not only the haven but the hope of Hellas. John VI Cantacuzenus had installed his capable son Manuel as governor there in 1348 with the avowed intent of completing the expulsion of the Franks and rooting out the Catalans from their strongholds in central Hellas. Manuel's people stood solidly and loyally behind him, and the Peloponnese attracted more and more Greeks who had tasted persecution. There was a notable increase in prosperity and culture. The capital city, Mistra, became virtually the City of Hellenism. Fully cognizant of the Turkish threat, Manuel moved resolutely to ensure the security and integrity of his realm. To this end, on one occasion he entered into an alliance with Frankish lords and bishops, reinforced by a few galleys belonging to Venice and the Order of the Knights of St. John of Jerusalem. In the summer of 1364, this motley array routed the Turks at Megara, burned thirty-five Turkish ships, and pursued the remnants of the enemy force clear to the walls of Thebes. Only by claiming the protection of the Turkish ally, the Catalan Roger de Lluria, *fils*, did the Turkish forces escape total annihilation.[70]

Thus, when Thessalonica, Constantinople, and the other cities which still remained nominally free were wracked by civil strife and intermittent warfare, Mistra, under Manuel (1348–1380) [71] and Matthew (1380–1383) Cantacuzenus, in spite of the greed and factiousness of Peloponnesian lords,[72] became undisputed leader of Hellas. Unfortunately, not many clues remain as to the quality of Mistra's political and cultural pre-eminence. Apart from a few splendid examples of architecture, both sacred and profane and some evidence of distinguished ancient Greek scholarship,[73] little else remains besides this fragment written by Demetrius Kydones to the monk, Agathias, then in the Peloponnese: "You will make me happy with news of your people, which I pray you to cast in the incomparable literary style which has always been your badge but which now seems all the more beautiful for having been developed in Hellas." [74]

Finally, the Peloponnese acquired another politically important dimension, crucial in the development of modern Hellenism: a mettlesome contingent of refugee Greeks and a generous infusion of naturally warlike Albanians and Arvanito-Vlachs had been absorbed into the original population. A people with such qualities tended to inspire resistance against the Turk and afterwards formed a strong bulwark for the defense of Hellenism.

Figure 7. Monastery of Peribleptos, Mistra.

Figure 8. Palace of Mistra.

No small contributor to the terror and chaos which marked the end of the fourteenth century was the fearsome Tamerlane.[75] The fury of his invasion struck first in the East, where it drove the Christians to headlong flight in every direction, but especially towards the West. Waves of refugees, Christian and Moslem, arrived in Constantinople and spread fresh panic among the population of the city.[76]

The Christians of Asia Minor, and indeed of all those provinces conquered by Tamerlane, suffered cruelly. They incurred his full wrath in reprisal for Manuel II's letting the remnants of defeated Turkish armies cross into Europe from Asia Minor—and in Greek ships.[77]

With Tamerlane's defeat of the Turks at the battle of Ankara in 1402 and the widespread internal convulsions attendant upon it, a temporary pause occurred in the seemingly inexorable rise of the Turkish nation. Manuel II took advantage of its weakened state and succeeded in having Suleiman concede him the taxes formerly imposed on the monasteries of Mt. Athos and their lands in the region of Thessalonica. He gave two-thirds of the latter to the monks.[78] In 1403, Thessalonica itself was restored to the Byzantine Empire.[79] The defeat at Ankara brought an unexpected but welcome intermission that permitted some temporary economic resuscitation of Constantinople [80] and other cities, including Thessalonica.[81] Some, however, mistook the respite for reprieve; though the monk, Joseph Bryennios, at least did not. Bitterly, he deplored the lavishness with which the wealthy in the city spent their money on three-storied homes instead of on city walls, where the "renovations" were needed.[82]

THE CHURCH AT BAY

The Crisis of Faith

During the Turkish invasion the Orthodox clergy suffered the same trials as their flock, but because of the additional responsibilities of their vocation, they also suffered the anguish of not being able to give real comfort to their people, especially in those pastorates under Moslem rule where they faced daily the agonies of thousands of captives. "All of these people come to us," wrote the Metropolitan of Ephesus, Matthew, some time after 1325, "as though in search of a savior, and they weep as they unburden their miseries. Since we can offer them nothing but tears—nothing—we are unable to help them." Save only, of course, the most fervent prayers for the mercy and salvation of God.[1]

The ordeals and afflictions of everyday life moved the clergy to search for theological explanations. Thus, the many narratives, letters, speeches, and theological works of this period not only reflect the dolor of the people, but offer all manner of advice, consolation, and encouragement. It was at this time that the sermon became exalted, with an emphasis quite novel in Orthodoxy, as a vehicle for sustaining the faith, and it came to have enormous influence on the lives of the people. Many of the preserved texts have never been studied in any systematic way, but they provide a rich fund of information on the nature of the people's sufferings and also offer insight into the theological convolutions within the Church.

Of course the great problem confronting Orthodoxy was how to explain the decadence of the state and the accompanying atrophy of the Christian spirit. In theological terms, the answer was soon given that the decline of the state was caused by Christian sinfulness, ingratitude towards God, and deliberate infraction of God's commandments, especially the one that commands love of neighbor.[2] "Love, indeed, has completely disappeared," wrote Joseph Bryennios typically, "and brotherly harmony has vanished. No one any longer knows the meaning of human understanding. Solicitude has been forgotten. One looks in vain for Christian compassion, a tear of pity, a single prayer to Christ. Such hatred has arisen among us that we take greater delight in our neighbor's miseries than in our own well-being." [3] Or, according to another who wrote between 1365 and 1370, the estrangement of the Orthodox from God had resulted only in universal corruption: "it is not that none of us does any good, but that we are calumniators, blasphemers, prattlers, traitors. We are covetous, greedy, and treacherous towards one another. There is no pity, only contumely, suspicion, and malevolence." That was why, in the opinion of this anonymous monk, "the wrath of God is just." [4]

In the same vein, Bryennios' comments ranged over society as a whole. Nobles took part in acts of gross illegality; those in charge of civic affairs were rapacious; judges were venal; and the agents of all those in authority were cheats and frauds. If those who governed society were arrogant, selfish, avaricious, impious, unrepentant, and incorrigible, it was only to be expected that such qualities would have their counterparts among the mass of the people.[5]

The decline of religious life in both the eastern and western provinces of the Orthodox Church was an incontestable fact. The only exceptions appear to have been in Constantinople, as Bessarion pointed out in 1463, and its adjacent islands, in Thessalonica, and perhaps a few other places. Elsewhere, Christians scarcely knew even the name of the Holy Bible, much less the number or names of its books. They were quite incapable of discussing the hope which their souls sustained, and on the rare occasions when the Gospels were read to them, were merely mystified.[6] The majority of Christians, said Bryennios, no longer knew what it was to be a Christian; and even those who could make the sign of the cross disdained to do so. Many were openly profane towards that which was most holy, even denying its existence, and their blasphemy went unpunished by Christian or civil authority. All forms of religious teaching and counsel came to be looked upon as mummery and so fell upon deaf ears.[7]

The conduct of some of the clergy did not help matters.[8] Monks in Crete and other islands frequently lived in concubinage.[9] The sacerdotal life became a refuge not only for those who genuinely sought to realize a vocation but for those who merely sought mundane comforts. Most priests, indeed, lived lives of uselessness, "because they came to the priesthood not in order to work long and hard but to find escape from all work." [10] Others were no different from merchants in their involvement in the affairs of the market place.[11]

No less iniquitous were the priests whose eagerness to hear confessions was motivated more by lust for money than by concern for the remission of sin. The body and blood of Christ were sold to those who remained steadfastly impenitent. How dared they use the excuse that they were merely making a living when they extracted every possible profit from masses for the dead, donations of money and goods, endless commemorative feasts, and monastic properties? [12] It was such people as these whom Bryennios, in one of his palace speeches after 1417, held responsible for the dreadful conditions in Church and state, the depopulation of the cities, the despoliation of the provinces, the burning of churches, and the desecration of altars and sacred objects.[13]

At the root of the Christians' despair lay a sense of deep indignation: how was it possible for the Turks to conquer, prosper, and be happy while Christians suffered? [14] The question left them restless and perplexed. Gregory Palamas tells us that when he arrived in Lampsacus as a prisoner of the Turks, a crowd of men, women, and children surrounded him. "Some wished to be confessed and spiritually cleansed; others wished to have certain doubts about their faith removed; but most wanted to know why God had forsaken them." [15] The Christians agonized over this question for centuries.

The striking contrast between the rise of the Turkish nation and the decline of the Empire constituted the most potent weapon of Moslem religious propaganda. "Our faith, our God, and all our works," they would say, "are obviously much better than yours. If this were not so, such great power as our nation possesses would not be ours, nor would most Christians be our captives and slaves." [16] Many Christians at this time felt forced to admit that the intensity of the Moslem faith in God, that burning quality which formed the animus of their religion, seemed more vital and durable than their own.[17]

The defeat of Bayezid I at the battle of Ankara brought some relief to the Christians, many of whom interpreted it as a demonstration of divine mercy. Others, however, were less sanguine. Their relief was tempered by a recognition of Christian unworthiness and by a knowledge of Christian sinfulness, which, they felt, had only grown worse. When in a short time their sufferings returned, the despairing "Why" became as insistent as before. They looked for a single ray of light which might penetrate their wilderness; in all those dark years it was the feasts of the Church that alone seemed to provide any consolation. At one of these, recorded Gabriel, Archbishop of Thessalonica, "on the Sunday before the feast of the great martyr, Demetrius," they came crushed in spirit and eager for the warmth of the Church, among them the arrogant, the rapacious, and the vainglorious as well as the poverty-stricken and the slaves, the young and the old, people of every age and condition in life.[18] The religious sense was sometimes stimulated by the dutiful practice of the liturgy,[19] though often it was transformed by sheer spiritual despair into mere pietism.

Invariably, after formal worship, the congregations gathered in the churchyards to discuss the misfortunes of the Greeks. Such scenes were common throughout the world of Orthodoxy during the entire period of Turkish domination. The churches became centers of political as well as moral and religious indoctrination. Religious preaching was never divorced from the lives of the people: its content always bespoke an awareness of the contemporary condition and a continual search for the Church's relevance to life.

The monastic spirit managed to survive throughout the crisis, and many monks became paradigms of virtue in the conduct of their lives, unwavering in their efforts to comfort and counsel all Christians who lived under Moslem rule or under its threat. They strove by continual preaching to resuscitate the faith of the laity. Always cognizant of the duress under which such Christians lived, their ministrations were based upon a realistic acceptance of the *force majeure* and of the necessity of reaching some kind of accommodation with it. By persuading Christians to bend before the tempest, they hoped to protect them from its full impact and retain their devotion and loyalty. Christians were therefore adjured to obey local elders and to live by patience, hard work, purity and "with wisdom, forbearance, honesty, true love, and the guidance of the divine word and therefore to be virtuous by the power of God." [20]

The Church also looked tolerantly on frightened crypto-Christians, whose allegiance it naturally wished to retain. This phenomenon probably appeared during the period of Arab conquest, beginning in the seventh century, and later, beginning in the eleventh century, under the Seljuk conquest, though the sources remain silent as to its occurrence at those times.[21] The first recorded case of crypto-Christianity is to be found in the period when the Ottoman Turks spread into Bithynia. Two patriarchal epistles, dated 1339 and 1340 respectively, refer to Christian inhabitants of Nicaea [22] who became Moslem after its capture by the Turks in 1331. Later, full of remorse for their action, they asked Patriarch John XIV Aprenos if the Church would receive them back. This patriarch, with an expression of charity that was representative of Christianity at its best, replied that the Church would certainly consider them restored to the body of the faithful. He who was truly contrite and, moreover, had the courage to risk opprobrium and suffering for his faith could be considered a martyr like the early Christian, James the Persian.

Even towards those whose fear of torture and retribution was such as to inhibit a merely secret declaration of their faith, the Church extended its tolerance and acceptance. They would be saved as long as they made every effort to obey the commandments of God. The enemy could enslave their bodies but not their souls.[23] Thus, while the Church extolled any sacrifice "for the faith" and thereby prepared the ground for the appearance of its new martyrs (whom we shall presently discuss), it also acknowledged the duress which produced crypto-Christianity. This manifestation was not unique to the time and circumstances about which we speak, but it almost certainly led to Islam.

Since the Turks were generally tolerant, even indifferent, towards both the teachings and the internal affairs of the Christian Church, patriarchs, archbishops, and priests took advantage of this attitude to spread the word of God by every oral and written means at their disposal,[24] usually without molestation. Surprisingly enough, however, they by no means limited themselves to religious ministrations, but seized every opportunity to condemn the Turk for his tyranny. Such criticism, whether open or covert, established a tradition of Christian pertinaciousness which continued throughout the several centuries of Turkish occupation. One frequently encounters references to the "barbarian" or the "infidel," and ecclesiastical stalwarts of the fourteenth century, at a time when the Turks still looked upon Christian teaching with indifference, even dared to engage in public disputations with Moslem religious (*hodjas*).[25] Others, such as an anonymous priest of Sosandra on the Magnesia River,[26] though sorrowful at the spread of Turkish power, never resigned their faith or their hope. This devout priest and fervent patriot exhorted the Greeks to shoulder their burdens in the manner of their illustrious forebears: it was John III Vatatzes [27] whom he chose to elevate as a saintlike exemplar of courage and virtue and whom he proceeded to honor, a hundred years after his death, with a glowing manifesto of his life.[28]

Eschatological Teaching after 1204

The closer the Byzantine Empire approached final collapse, the less satisfied were the clergy with their explanation of the state of Orthodoxy. Sinfulness could not be denied, but that seemed hardly a sufficient cause for the Orthodox plight. There was no comfort in the fact that both Moslems and Catholics were using the charge as a weapon in religious proselytism. Nevertheless, it was hard to believe that the Orthodox plight was not some kind of divine omen. How illumine the darkness? How find meaning and consolation? How offer uplifting insight into the brutish conditions of life? Such questions stimulated the spirit of mysticism. It was the revival of this spirit, inspired by renewed study of the New Testament and Byzantine theological literature, that led to the proposal of an alternative explanation for the Orthodox predicament: the spread of Islam and the social injustices inflicted by the Turks were but signs of the approach of Armageddon.[29]

Thus, there was fertile ground for the vigorous reassertion of eschatological ideas after 1204.[30] All eschatological teaching was adapted to the new conditions. The Byzantine misfortune was in no sense the consequence of divine displeasure, but purely and simply because of its geographical location and perhaps the envy of Satan. It could not be otherwise "because the Greeks value self-restraint, wisdom, and prayer above all others." God had prevented neither the coming of "the false prophet," Mohammed, nor the spread of his teachings at the expense of Christianity, because the coming of the Antichrist was merely a prelude to the end of the world and the beginning of God's Kingdom. The peoples who welcomed the teachings of Mohammed would be destroyed with the Antichrist himself and would be cast "into a lake of fire where they will suffer torment for centuries." The Great Day of God, when "He who judges the whole world" would come, was therefore near at hand. Christians had to prepare themselves. God was punishing them now in order that they might later be admitted to everlasting glory. Christians should therefore strive harder than ever to withstand temptation.

"Blessed is the man that endureth temptation; for when he is tried, he shall receive the crown of life, which the Lord hath promised to them that love him" (Epistle of James I:xii). And there were certainly many other passages from Scripture which comforted the faithful masses. In it, they could find exculpation from the instinctive desire to flee before the Turkish storm, or solace for life's bitter miseries, or encouragement for the patient bearing of sorrow. "Remember the word that I said unto you, The servant is not greater than his lord. If they have persecuted me, they will also persecute you; Blessed are they which are persecuted for righteousness' sake; When they persecute you in this city, flee ye into another; but he that endureth to the end shall be saved" (John XV:xx; Matthew V:x; and X:xxii–xxiii). Bryennios considered the victims of the invaders as martyrs for the faith.[31]

This kind of eschatological teaching naturally had its greatest impact on the simple souls of the masses. The times were exceedingly favorable, as might well be imagined, for the widespread circulation of oracular prophecies, both ancient and new, which foretold the end of the Empire, the ultimate defeat of the Turks, and the second coming of Christ. Research has still to be done, however, on this coincidental phenomenon.

Those Christian virtues which had received special emphasis since the time of the Apostles, love, hope, and faith, the very crown of virtue,[32] were particularly lauded in this period. Faith was seen as the universal salve which would enable all Christians to endure their manifold miseries with fortitude and even with joy.[33] This at least was the gist of the remarks of the Metropolitan Isidore Glabas, as he attempted to assuage the sufferings of the people of Thessalonica after 1383: "Since these in a certain sense are but a trial, a catharsis of sinful corruption, so therefore you can only be purified by the insults and sufferings with which you are afflicted; in this way you stand before the glorious Christ and, having shed all blemish, commune with Him." [34] In the same manner, the Turkish occupation was regarded as an affliction designed only to test their faith; in the opinion of the Patriarch Gennadius, it was "an exercise of faith." [35] "After all," said Isidore, "so many of the saints are renowned for the ways in which they resisted temptation. Even among barbarians and foreigners there were those who not only saved themselves, but, by their example, enlightened others. That is why we need spiritual strife as well as vigilance, and everyone ought to realize this." [36] Persistence in faith is the only path to Christian salvation and the redemption of each individual soul. We have no record that a single theologian disagreed. In times of conquest and occupation, the only real danger is that the deprivation of freedom and wealth seems a greater evil than the loss of faith. But, in truth, all the physical and mental torment which slavery brings are as nothing compared with corruption of the soul. Even the loss of all worldly goods is preferable to the dereliction of duty towards God. For without God, hope itself is impossible.[37]

Far from being dissonant with Church tradition, these ideas represented an attempt to return to the original doctrines of Christianity and thus exercised a restorative influence upon religious life. The Church thereby prepared itself inwardly for the struggles and sacrifices for the faith which were still to come and tried to imbue its flock with the same resolve. The faithful were taught that they must endure everything, even the sacrifice of their own lives, for the Church: the eternal glory of the heavenly life awaited them only. Those to whom faith and devotion brought the crown of martyrdom were to be blessed and revered.[38] Indeed, the years of persecution and torture that Christians endured in Roman times had truly returned. It was not long before the conqueror, by oppression and calumny, forced many to recognize the choice that would sooner or later have to be made: to be converted or to be killed. With this realization, many prepared themselves for martyrdom.[39]

The "New" Martyrs

Converts to Islam were often fanatical devotees of their new religion and assiduous enemies of Christianity,[40] thus providing an example for those who remained Christians. Christianity was therefore continually menaced. Nevertheless, the struggles of Christians who were tortured for their faith served to inspire and to rally the faithful, and the martyrdom of the Orthodox Church bears witness to the numerous champions of the faith during the period of Turkish occupation. In the past, it has been customary to designate as "new" martyrs only those who suffered after the fall of Constantinople; to these, however, ought properly to be added the large numbers of people who met martyrdom much earlier, from the very time when the conqueror began his march.[41] Among such martyrs were the young, the simple, and the plain—monks, craftsmen, merchants, servants of both Turk and Greek. "And I still affirm," wrote the biographer of the martyr, John of Ioannina, in 1543, "that he gave strength to many then, as he will continue to do in the future. He was a source of courage for all who came after him; and just as many were brought by his example to demonstrate the same eagerness to die for their country, so others in the future will also be encouraged to become heirs of the Kingdom of Heaven. His example has constrained many Christians to reflect again upon the denial of their religion, about which they seemed to have no qualms in the past." [42] These remarks help to explain a widespread tendency among the people of particular regions to honor their martyrs as saints long before the Church accorded them official recognition. The lore of martyrs always evoked a good deal of popular interest; hymnographers often composed canticles in their praise.[43] It is clear that the "new" martyrs, by arousing the people's determination to resist the conquerors, were national heroes in a palpable sense. Thus, by maintaining religious zeal and by sustaining a popular Christian conviction of moral primacy in the contest with Islam, the Church contributed in a positive, if indirect, way to the movement of national resistance.

Yet the Church never announced a policy of official opposition to the Turks. The reasons for this become apparent after even the most cursory reflection upon the circumstances of conquest. The upper clergy knew how harsh the conqueror could be and were therefore loath to provoke him, and they also knew that the Turk, unprovoked, allowed the Church to exist in relative freedom and did not prevent the clergy from carrying out their religious duties. At the same time, the Church was not preserved "unchanged in form," as Joseph Bryennios would have us believe.[44] There were other more subtle ways in which the Turks occasionally wielded their power so as to influence Church affairs in accordance with their designs—for example, in the appointment of bishops, where, ironically enough, the opportunity to interfere was provided by Christians themselves with their process of episcopal election.[45]

In other respects, as for instance in the ecclesiastical and liturgical life of the Church, the Turkish influence, though apparent in a variety of ways, was really superficial, except in certain provinces. Where the Turkish language had taken hold, in Cappadocia, for example, the parochial priests, even some bishops, spoke Turkish and dressed in the Turkish fashion. The Gospels, Epistles, and the Mass in general were often the only things which continued to be read or sung in Greek. And in some of the provinces of the Church, where economic and intellectual decay was especially marked, priests often did not possess a whole Bible even but had to rely on fragments. "When reading texts, they merely parroted a sound which they vaguely thought to resemble Greek, but they could not understand a whit of what they were saying." [46]

There were, however, more fundamental reasons for the Church's reluctance formally to announce its opposition to the Turks. These had to do with the specific injunctions of Holy Scripture and the precepts of sacred tradition handed down by the Church Fathers. There were innumerable lessons which seemed to exalt the temporal power.[47] On the basis of such texts, Isidore Glabas, the Metropolitan of Thessalonica, in an undated letter from Constantinople, advised his flock to submit to domination by the Turk. He deplored any attempts to resist the conqueror: "It is our duty to obey our masters. We who have become servants must serve. We must carry out all those orders which relate to the affairs of the world. We must do this because so we have been taught by those who are saints, by the Apostle Peter himself who said, 'Submit yourselves to every ordinance of man for the Lord's sake'; and by Paul who commanded, 'Let every soul be subject unto the higher powers. For there is no power but of God: Whosoever therefore resisteth the power, resisteth the ordinance of God' (Epistle to the Romans XIII:i). We must therefore do that which it is clear must be done: love our masters and obey them in all temporal things." [48] The same kind of counsel was taken up by prominent officials in Thessalonica, probably priests, during the actual siege of the city (1383–1387). "To try to liberate the homeland from the Turks was to do no less than to wage war against God." [49]

What appears to have been uppermost in the minds of the clergy was the need "to keep things spiritual secure and intact." All had to be sacrificed for the sake of Orthodoxy, even life itself if necessary. Isidore's concern for the preservation of the Church was quite as explicit when he enumerated the more positive duties of Christians: "Let us be sure above all, my brothers, that with all our energy and power we keep Orthodoxy unstained, even if it be necessary to this end that our worldly wealth be dissipated, our country enslaved, our limbs mutilated, our bodies tortured, our lives violently extinguished. Let us endure all this with joy if it mean that our flawless religion be not betrayed." [50] These words, of course, carried the indirect injunction that it was incumbent on all Christians, in the interests of a higher duty, to disobey both temporal and spiritual leaders whenever Holy Law was contravened or flouted. There was no mistaking such an obligation when the Apostles themselves had laid down that "We ought to obey God rather than men."

The Church in the Latin Dominions

It was not only with Islam that the Church had to contend. The struggle for the preservation of the faith and of the Greek race had also to be carried on against Roman Catholic proselytism. Certain Greek votaries of the Union of the Orthodox and Roman Churches were a not inconsiderable element in this regard. Conditions in the Latin dominions were especially unfavorable to the Orthodox Church, and its travail in those places was bitter and protracted. In Cyprus, for example, the difficulties of the local Church were directly attributable to Roman Catholic ascendancy and the efforts of individual Roman Catholic hierarchs to subvert the integrity of the Orthodox Church. Against the persistent encroachments of Roman Catholicism (as, for example, in meetings in Cyprus at Limassol, October 1220, and Ammochostos [Famagusta], September 1222), Orthodoxy was able to maintain its position only by compromise and concession. Moreover, the number of Orthodox episcopal sees declined. Orthodox bishops were required to seek the approval of the Latin bishop in the assumption of their ecclesiastical offices; thus, formal acknowledgement of Roman Catholic primacy could not be avoided. The Orthodox clergy thought it necessary to accept such restrictions in the interests of preserving the substance of Orthodoxy, of preventing more drastic limitations, and of cushioning the inhabitants against actual persecution and conversion to the Roman Catholic doctrine. Even so, the Oecumenical Patriarchate refused to condone such submissiveness and continually exhorted the clergy to hold their ground firmly and faithfully in the defense of Orthodoxy; and in general, the people of Cyprus were united in opposing Rome's interference and oppression. True, the Cypriot Church was reduced to a position of virtual subservience by the *Bulla* or *Constitutio Cypria* of Pope Alexander IV of 3 July 1260; true, too, that with the passing of time the Cypriot Church found itself isolated from Orthodoxy and generally considered apostate to "the tradition of our ancestors' faith." Yet, from at least the beginning of the fifteenth century, the Cypriots maintained that they had never abjured the rules, customs, and traditions of Orthodoxy and indeed actively solicited the normalization of relations with the Oecumenical Patriarchate. It was in response to these overtures that the austere Joseph Bryennios was dispatched to Cyprus as an emissary of the Patriarchate, though on that occasion he recommended the rejection of the Cypriot proposals (17 March 1412).[51]

During the period of Venetian domination in Crete (1211–1669), metropolitan and archepiscopal sees were occupied by Roman Catholics, chiefly Venetians. Only the lower clergy were left in relatively untrammelled charge of their parishes, though still subject to occasional restrictions and oppression. The upper clergy, however, were forced to discontinue their ministrations,[52] with the consequence that such spiritual oversight as still remained was exercised directly by the Oecumenical Patriarch. Despite these disabilities, the Patriarch retained a spiritual hold over the masses of the faithful and sought constantly to strengthen it by means of encyclical letters and the missions of clerical ambassadors. It was with the aim of maintaining the isolation of his ungoverned Cretan flock from Roman influence [53] that Anthimos, "Archbishop of Athens and President (*Proedros*) of Crete" was sent to the island, there to suffer martyrdom, probably towards the middle of the fourteenth century.[54] He was followed in 1381 by Joseph Bryennios, who, however, was quickly removed by the Venetians [55] because of fears of a possible priest-inspired, popular movement of religious and political independence.

Various attempts to substitute Latin for Orthodox ritual invariably failed because of popular resistance. This was probably the chief reason why the authorities allowed the lower clergy, with archpriests (*protopapades*), or leaders among the lower clergy, as their only superiors, to continue their pastorates according to Orthodox rites. On the other hand, neophyte priests were required first to appear before the Latin archbishop, who demanded that they swear obedience to the Roman Catholic faith. Later, with the permission of the central authority in Herakleion (formerly Chandax) and bearing letters of credence from the Latin archbishop, they would be allowed to journey to one of the Venetian-controlled cities of the Peloponnese (principally Coron or Modon), there to be formally ordained by the Greek bishop according to Orthodox ritual.[56] Naturally in order to win this privilege many Cretan priests were prepared to be demonstratively philo-Latin in their relations with their nominal Roman archbishop.

Through archpriests and archchoristers who had demonstrated their trustworthiness in this way, Venice was able to keep fairly well apprized of the temper of her Orthodox subjects and of their relations with the

Oecumenical Patriarchate as well as of the missionary activity of exarchs and other clergy who were sent to Crete by the Patriarch. Any persons suspected of conniving at the extension of patriarchal influence in Crete were severely punished by imprisonment or banishment.[57] Yet it was also true, as we have noticed, that certain restraints were put on the Roman clergy. Venetian authority was quick to curb excessive zeal on their part or to curtail the demands of particular Roman hierarchs when it seemed that these might trespass too far on the sensibilities of the Orthodox Church.[58]

On the whole, the people of Crete remained loyal to Orthodoxy. Indeed, in one way at least they were able to advance it. During the fourteenth and fifteenth centuries, there was a veritable spate of church-building, which left its mark for posterity in the hundreds of churches to be found today in villages, big and small, in fields, inaccessible valleys, and even on the tops of mountains. The frescoes in these churches depict the spirit of the Cretans and their devotion to the traditions of their nation; they also reflect the austere Orthodox character and faithfully preserve the Byzantine tradition of iconography. They are devoid of Italian influences, for which Constantine Kalokyres offers the most probably correct explanation:

This is due to the unshakable faith of the Greek people of Crete and to their worthy priests. In the other realms of art and of the intellect (as for example in architecture and sculpture), the Cretans clearly accept the Western-oriented influences of their environment and their period. The two streams, Greek and Latin, are merged. But in every respect which touches upon the character of Orthodoxy and Orthodox doctrine, the Greek influence is rigidly preserved. The beliefs and traditions of the race which stemmed directly from the Byzantine Empire were never forgotten by the Cretans, enslaved though they were. . . . And as they looked at their frescoes throughout the whole period of Venetian and Turkish domination, the common memory of the Empire lived on. They were consoled by the unity of past and present; they received hope in the silence and mystery of their churches; they taught their children of the glories of the Empire to which they were all inseparably bound; their hearts were warmed by the thought of what lay in the future, of the time which would surely come when they gathered their strength and shook off the foreign yoke . . . Truly, as they clustered in the village churches with the darkness of slavery all about them, as they gazed upon the frescoes and together taught their children the story which these conveyed, here was a message which not only all could understand but which could simultaneously uplift their souls. For the frescoes spoke of the persecuted Founder of the Faith and of the struggles of the saints and martyrs and of the agony of the Church and the faithful in Orthodoxy—a story which only those who were enslaved could really understand.[59]

The situation in Euboea was similar. Again, the designs of the Roman Catholic clergy were circumscribed by the Venetian authorities, who, though interested in religious matters, had no hesitation in subordinating these to the interests of political expediency. Thus, considerable understanding and toleration were frequently extended towards the Orthodox Church.[60] On one occasion, for example, Theodore II, Despot of Mistra, took steps to obtain official recognition of the ordination of Cretan priests by the Orthodox bishops of his realm. With the agreement of John VIII Palaeologus and the Oecumenical Patriarch, he founded a new bishopric on the peninsula of Maina (probably in 1429) and by 1435 was successful in winning Venetian acknowledgement of the valid ordination of such priests in Venetian dominions.[61]

In regard to the conversion of the Orthodox to the Latin rite, and vice versa, the evidence is meager indeed. Nevertheless, it is known that many of the Catalans who settled in continental Greece after their victory near the Cephisus River in Attica in 1311 over the descendants of the Franks, who had originally established themselves there and who, with the Catalans, were on that occasion excommunicated by the Pope, eventually became Orthodox as a result of continual intermixing over the years with the Orthodox inhabitants. In an attempt to put an end to such apostasy (and no doubt to set them against the Turks who had settled in Thebes as allies of the Catalan brothers, Roger and John de Lluria), Pope Urban V (1362–1370), on Christmas Day, 1363, suspended the excommunication for three years. On the other hand, double abjuration of the Roman Church on the part of the Orthodox was punished by the confiscation of property. Thus, Stephen Mastrothodoros of Thebes, son of a Greek merchant, lost all his property to Michael de Gaspo when, on his death-bed, he denied Roman Catholic dogma and returned to the Orthodox fold. Again, Pope Clement XVI once bitterly complained to the Archbishop of Nicosia because he had been told by King Peter de Lusignan that large numbers of Catholic women were participating in Greek Masses and generally discharging their religious obligations according to the rites of Orthodoxy.[62]

In the case of Crete, the number of converts to Rome was considerably less than the number of Venetian settlers who made the journey to Orthodoxy. Apostasy from the Roman Church continued in spite of the severe punishments prescribed by the Roman Church. According to Hofmann, this was no mere "transient phenomenon" but a "continuous evil," which he attributed to three factors: first, the indigent condition of the Roman clergy, who lived on the domains of Venetian noblemen, but who were so poorly paid they were eventually forced to abscond; second, the absenteeism of many Latin bishops; and third, lack of education and widespread immorality on the part of the priests themselves.[63] These are cogent reasons, no doubt, but of far greater importance was the simple and inescapable fact of contiguity. Venetians, especially the nobility, gradually became accustomed to the new environment and to Greek mores; and from this familiarity grew an identification of interests, mutual understanding, and, eventually, spiritual rapprochement.

In sum, although Frankish control in the Aegean and eastern Mediterranean would seem to have provided ideal conditions for the propagation of Catholicism [64] and although Orthodoxy was constricted by the very circumstances which gave Catholicism its opportunity, it was the conversion of Catholics to Orthodoxy, rather than the reverse, which appeared to be the rule.[65]

The Question of Union of the Churches

In those Greek lands which still remained free, the question of Church reunion always loomed large and was the source of much controversy. Naturally, it was a problem which seemed to assume greater immediacy when the Turks set foot in Europe; for in the face of Turkish invasion, the Orthodox attitude towards Catholicism could only appear as a great dilemma.

The Palaeologi, believing that the security of the state depended upon assistance from the West, were disposed to proffer the Union of the Churches as an enticing *quid pro quo*—a diplomatic weapon, unfortunately, which was already blunted from too much use. Whenever they appeared to be on too friendly terms with the votaries of Union, they merely incurred the wrath of the Orthodox.[66]

Some of the reasons which motivated the desire for reunion were genuinely patriotic, but there was also the fear of a future under Turkish domination and of the loss of their wealth. In addition, many scholars, attracted to the world of antiquity, were filled with admiration for the classical revival in the West.[67] These philo-Latin scholars and theologians assiduously studied the texts of the Church Fathers, among others, and theological tradition generally. And as they analyzed those matters in dispute between the Churches, they came to the conclusion that the two opposing systems, both of which had sprung from the same source, were fundamentally not in opposition at all.

Their most eloquent spokesman at the end of the fourteenth century was Demetrius Kydones, who had translated the works of St. Augustine, St. Anselm, and St. Thomas Aquinas. He had close connections with Western clerics and scholars, even with the Pope himself, as well as with John VI Cantacuzenus, John V Palaeologus, and Manuel II Palaeologus. The last three held him in high esteem.[68] Indeed, Kydones' later conversion to Catholicism was seen as a substantial blow to Orthodoxy.[69] In one of his works, he re-examined his whole spiritual life and his *rapprochement* with Catholicism. There is no more interesting testament than this to the ideological ferment of the Byzantine scholars, the quality of the dialectic of Kydones' opponents, and the pitiful struggle between both factions, which was exacerbated by jealousies and personal rivalries within their own circles and even within the palace. He pointed to the long separation of East and West, which had estranged the people and "caused a great deal of ignorance on both sides." The Byzantine people, he went on to say, had come to lean upon these differences—differences between Greeks and "barbarians"—and utterly to despise the West. However, a study of Western literature had revealed to him a new world of ideas. It had shown him a people "who toiled ceaselessly to penetrate the fantastically complex thought of Plato and Aristotle," philosophers towards whom his own countrymen manifested a supreme disregard. After himself examining the texts of the Fathers of both the Western and the Eastern Churches, he found that there existed among them all "an admirable harmony." Finally, he maintained that the ties of New Rome (Constantinople) with its more ancient counterpart were much closer than his contemporaries believed. Everything great that New Rome possessed —empire, government, even name—was derived from antiquity, that is, ancient Rome, and that was why it owed a debt of deference towards Rome. The same position could be attributed to the clergy of both East and West. These things had to be borne carefully in mind by those who spoke as though ancient Rome were in an inferior position to New Rome. Equally interesting were the remarks he later made about the caesaropapism of the Emperor, the dependence of the Patriarchate on the temporal power.[70]

The views of Kydones on the question of Church reunion were also held by his disciple, Manuel Calecas; [71] by Theodore, Andrew,[72] and Maximus Chrysoberges; Manuel Chrysoloras; and, in the middle of the fifteenth century, by the former Archbishop of Nicaea, Bessarion. Kydones and Maximus Chrysoberges, in particular, took the Roman Catholic view that the root cause of Orthodox woes was the Photian Schism, which had occurred when a synod in Constantinople denied that the Holy Ghost proceeded from the Father and the Son: the Greeks were being enslaved and destroyed because they had strayed from the proper path of faith.[73] This explanation, however, was rejected by Joseph Bryennios: "If we suffer," he wrote to Maximus Chrysoberges, "it is not because we will not submit to your pope, as you say; on the contrary, it is because of the rise of this impure and infamous race of unbelievers, which itself is due to the righteous wrath of God, whom we have made angry. Even so, our pitiable plight is due to some extent to the sheer physical proximity of our neighbors. You are wrong to rejoice over our miseries. It is not your place to assail us, but rather to assist us as brothers. But there is no mercy in you. You attack us as though you believe our sufferings to be just." He went on to say that all who opposed reunion were proud of their unshakable faith in Orthodoxy, in spite of the heretical proclivities of many emperors and patriarchs. Lastly, he proceeded to enumerate the long list of those who would remain true to Orthodoxy until the Second Coming of Christ.

Bryennios was a determined and unrelenting apologist for Orthodoxy: "You yourselves suffer from an incurable affliction," he wrote to Maximus again, "though its causes are not external. You incite one another to war like madmen; even your Popes do battle among themselves, and you force your people to stain their hands with the blood of their brothers. You are no better than those lunatic people who cut off their own limbs . . ." Or again, "if purity of life and correctness of behavior be the touchstones, then right is clearly on our side. Nor is that all, for we have wisdom, humility, and self-restraint, we treat our churches with decency and proper vigilance, we are the true supporters of the dignity and sacred practices of the Church . . ." [74] Bryennios also greatly criticized the hypocritical stance of those who embraced the Roman Church's doctrines even though they considered "our ancestors to be much more pious," an attitude, he felt, in view of the circumstances of the time, to be transparently self-serving.[75]

Philo-Latin scholars and priests remained in a distinct minority. The air seemed to be filled with theological discord and recrimination, typified by the continual verbal onslaughts of Kydones against various patriarchs and archbishops, and vice versa,[76] but the sound and the fury were really deceptive. Most of the clergy, especially the monks, unflinchingly rejected the idea of reunion; they were merely following the body of the faithful. Thus, when the traveller Buondelmonti commented on the sparseness of the population in the capital at the beginning of the fifteenth century, he bore witness to its irreconcilable hatred of the Latins. The capital would brook no alliance or agreement with the Latins, even though it received a thousand assurances that such an agreement would be kept.[77] Brocquière wrote later of the conquered Greeks of Bithynia that they despised the Latins much more than the Turks.[78]

At the same time, the decline of the Empire brought on a crisis which rent the Eastern Church and gave impetus to the reassertion of Catholic claims. The situation was considered of sufficient gravity to warrant the persecution of eminent philo-Latins at the end of the fourteenth century.[79] Thus, division in Church and state appeared at precisely the time when unity against a redoubtable enemy was most needed. It is this internal

laceration to which Demetrius Chrysoloras no doubt refers in his remark after 1403, that "our entire people has been split in twain." [80]

In order to combat the philo-Latin predilections of certain scholars and
theologians and to reinforce the traditions of Orthodoxy, the Oecumenical
Patriarchate renewed its contacts with the sister churches of the Balkans.
Orthodox peoples, including those of Russia, were further united by
the influence of Hesychasm, its associated movements, and the body of
literature arising from them.[81] On the whole, clerical and scholarly opposition to the movement for reunion may almost be said to have been determined a priori by the pervasive influence of the Greek Orthodox tradition.
When, for example, the Emperor Manuel II Palaeologus deemed it expedient to extend toleration towards the West and to the movement for
Church reunion, though without any intention himself of renouncing Orthodoxy, the clergy prevailed upon him to reverse his policy. In the event,
he appeared satisfied to use men like Kydones and Chrysoloras, whom he
greatly esteemed, in no more vital a capacity than that of diplomatic envoys charged with seeking assistance from the West. But the powerful
states of the West in any case insisted on the Union of the Churches as
prerequisite to any negotiation.[82]

Thus, the chasm between the Eastern and Western Churches remained.
Apart from the diverse intellectual, economic, and national differences
between the two cultures, the Orthodox tradition had been further reinforced by the Photian Schism and recollections of the Fourth Crusade and
Frankish domination, which served to promote the growth of national
consciousness. For it was not long before every philo-Latin was regarded
as a kind of traitor.[83] Of course, national consciousness in its modern sense
still did not exist, but a common loyalty to Orthodoxy afforded a most
durable base.

But there was also another base. The opponents of Church reunion and
papal primacy were apprehensive that a merger of the Churches could
only mean the surrender of the traditional inheritance. This was the fear
that George Kourtesis Scholarios, then known as the monk Gennadius,
had voiced on the eve of the siege of Constantinople. The legacy of
Greece was part of the national foundation as surely and as inseparably
as Orthodoxy itself. That this was the meaning of "traditional inheritance"
seems to have been made abundantly clear by Bryennios when he stood
before the members of the Synod of Santa Sophia on 17 March 1412. As
he presented his views "on the suggested reconciliation of the Cypriot
Church with Orthodoxy," he emphasized the points which in his opinion
justified such a step: "It is the Orthodox Church we have in common; it is
our riches, it is our past glory, it is our nation . . ." [84]

The Orthodox Church, then, while it continued to be an important repository of the official Roman tradition and therefore from time to time disapproved of the use of the national appellation, Hellene, nevertheless by its inflexible attitude towards the Roman Church it contributed substantially to the growth of an Hellenic national consciousness. This trend was accentuated by certain political and social spasms within the Hellenic world which paralleled its religious upheaval.

THE CATALYST OF CONQUEST

Hellenism in the Frankish Dominions

At the end of the fourteenth century, as we have seen, the intellectual and political frontiers of Neo-Hellenism became more clearly defined. The seeds of Hellenic renascence were sown amid the debris of Byzantine ruin. As the major centers of Hellas—Constantinople, Thessalonica, western Thessaly, Epirus, Athens, and the Despotate of Morea—were engulfed by the Turkish tide, so the very extremity of the Greek people revived the sense of a common historical destiny.

However defective the documentation for the rise of modern Hellenism, enough is known to indicate its general direction. It might be thought, for example, that most of the relevant information (like the *Chronicle of Galaxidi* or the kinds of narratives which are occasionally unearthed in Greek monasteries and which have proved so useful in the illumination of Greek history) would have been lost or destroyed with the passing of time. But this is not entirely so. The continual publication of new texts and the systematic study of old ones are constantly yielding further knowledge of the essential components of Greek national consciousness.

The fact of this national awakening is confirmed, as might perhaps be expected, by a study of the Greek lands which still remained free at the end of the fourteenth and the beginning of the fifteenth centuries. It is even true of the Greek provinces which were occupied by the Franks, who held complete political dominion over the Greek people, a fact which served to stimulate Greek national resurgence. The Franks formed a tiny minority in the midst of the Greeks, and because of this they never felt their sovereignty to be secure. They sought both to understand and to cohabit peacefully with their subjects. Indeed, they went a good deal further. Henry of Flanders (1206–1216) was perhaps the first of the

Frankish emperors of Constantinople to set a precedent for his successors, which we have no reason to suppose was not subsequently followed, when "though Frankish himself, he behaved with friendliness and magnanimity towards the people of Constantinople and the Greeks as a whole. Many of those in the city became his officials and soldiers, and he always treated the masses as though they were his own people." [1]

The Frankish yoke was never so rigorous as to prevent the Greeks, especially the nobles, from seeking profit and prestige, and Greeks were able to express themselves and move about within fairly generous limits. Such freedom, though expedient for Frankish purposes, provided scope for the growth of a spirit of resistance and the more rapid maturation of national consciousness. These effects can be observed even in distant and isolated Cyprus off the coasts of Syria and Asia Minor. In 1425, the Greek peasants of Cyprus, following a piratical incursion and pillage by the Mamelukes (Saracens), rose in angry insurrection against their overlords. Under their leader, the groom Alexis, they quickly overran the center of the island and set up chieftaincies in Lefka, Limassol, Peristeronas, Morphou, and Oreine. Although the revolt was soon squashed, many Frankish nobles and Roman Catholic clergy were caught up in its fury. The revolt had obvious socioeconomic overtones, but its nationalistic character is evident in the fact that it was above all a spontaneous peasant uprising against foreign domination.[2] Leontios Machairas, though himself a Greek, described it in his *Chronicle* from a Frankish point of view, and did not, or did not wish to, comprehend this nationalistic significance. The struggles of the Greeks to extricate themselves from their servitude were later assisted by Helen, second wife of John II Lusignan and daughter of the Despot of the Peloponnese, Theodore II Palaeologus. We will note her role in another context.

In the Despotate of Morea, Theodore I Palaeologus (1382–1406), while forced to contend with his fractious nobility and forever at loggerheads with Venice and Frankish lords, constantly strove to build on the achievements of his predecessors, in particular those of Manuel Cantacuzenus. Lest his spirit flag, he was reminded of the glorious history of Sparta and Lycurgus [3] by Demetrius Kydones. The outlook in the Morea was more favorable than that in Constantinople: the Turkish threat was not yet imminent there and the Despot remained more or less independent. It was in order to ensure the continuance of this situation that Theodore I (probably when he passed through Thessalonica on his way to the Morea) and his brother devised a plan of political and military collaboration with the aim of permanently staving off Turkish invasion. The alliance was soon broadened by an agreement with the Florentine ruler of Corinth, Nerio Acciajuoli, and was directed against both the Navarrese mercenaries in the Peloponnese and the Catalans in Athens and Amphissa. In 1383, however, the two brothers were hard pressed by the Turks and invoked the assistance of Venice; but with the voluntary capitulation of Thessalonica in 1387, Theodore saw no other option than to commit a complete tactical *volte-face*. He thereupon made overtures to the fierce ghazi Evrenos Bey, ostensibly with the aim of suppressing a rebellion of his own recalcitrant nobility led by John, son of Matthew Cantacuzenus. No doubt he hoped that this new compact with one enemy, the Turk, would be just as useful for the time being in forestalling another, the Frank. However, his plan of effecting the expulsion of the Franks from the whole of the Peloponnese with Turkish aid—as a preliminary to confronting the Turks—completely misfired (1394).[4] And finally, when the armies of Evrenos Bey began to ravage the Peloponnese in 1400 and Theodore, in despair, attempted to sell Mistra to the Knights of St. John, he was foiled by his own people, who responded to the angry protests of their metropolitan.[5]

After the conquest of Crete by Venice (at the end of 1210 or the beginning of 1211), the Greek population there also remained unsubdued. Arbitrary acts of government, the usurpation of nobles' land, the proscription of the upper Orthodox clergy, and onerous taxation resulted, as we have seen, in continuous turmoil and unyielding defiance.[6] In the period 1364–1367, the rebellion of the Kallerges brothers in Crete and their attempts to re-establish contact with Constantinople were but some of the many instances of Greek tenacity. Even Venetian noblemen who had previously played a leading part in the revolt which temporarily set up the so-called Republic of St. Titus in Crete in August 1363 conspired openly with the Kallerges. This was a phenomenon which we have attempted to explain before in terms of the mutual understanding and gradual identification of interests between the Greek population and Venetian colonists in Crete. What it signified, of course, especially in the period after the Council of Florence (1439), was an increasing confluence of the two peoples and the eventual assimilation and hellenization of Venetian settlers. Characteristically, the eldest of the Kallerges brothers, John, always acted in the name of the Byzantine Empire and announced that he fought not only for the liberation of his island but for its union with the Empire.[7] The ardor with which the peoples of Crete (and indeed all the island peoples of the Aegean) proclaimed their Greek connections has been previously noted.[8] It was an attachment to an idea, both national and religious, which the historian Ducas succinctly expressed when he spoke of the Cretans as guardians of the Royal Gate (*Basilike Pyle*), later known as the Golden Gate, at Constantinople and remarked: "These faithful Cretans were always devoted to the saints and relics of the Church and to the Empire of Constantinople." Ducas described the Cretans, furious because of the treachery of a citizen in Constantinople, as addressing the Emperor thus: "O great Emperor, is it fair that we should place Constantinople before our own land and that we should be eager to spill our blood for the sake of the City when those who live in it and therefore bask in an inherited glory are no more than traitors?" [9] The national awareness of the Cretans was also reflected by the inscriptions in Orthodox churches during the period of Venetian domination which referred pointedly to the various reigning sovereigns. "It is obvious from these inscriptions," wrote Constantine Kalokyres, "that the Cretans struggled continuously against the Venetians throughout the fourteenth century and into the fifteenth; the spirit of Greek nationalism was developed from generation to generation to a point where the Cretans . . . even made provocative references to the Byzantine Emperors, declaring openly not merely that they acknowledged the Empire's supreme authority but that everything they did was directed towards bringing them into conjunction with it." [10] The Church in Crete and the lower clergy in particular were the chief protagonists in this movement of national resistance.[11]

The position of the Greeks in Messenia, Euboea, and Corfu was rather more fortunate. Corfu was surrendered in 1386–1387, but only after the islanders won Venetian acceptance of a number of demands aimed at preserving the security and integrity of the Greek community. These concessions in fact inaugurated a new form of limited political control for places under Venetian rule, and the same kind of regime was subsequently set up with only minor variations in Nauplia (1389), Tenos, and Mykonos (both in 1392). The same also occurred in Argos, which had previously fallen within the jurisdiction of the feudal "Assises of Romania." [12]

In Chios, which was occupied by Genoa for the second time between 1349 and 1566, there was a conspiracy, probably some time between 1380 and 1388, which had both national and religious undercurrents. Greeks on the island rose up against their Genoese rulers and the Roman Catholic clergy, but the uprising sputtered out because of the treachery of one of the rebels. Ten of those involved were hanged, their properties confiscated, and a portion of their lands given to the traitor as a reward.[13] If this event did in fact take place between 1380 and 1388, it was at the time when Manuel II was rallying the Greeks against the Turks in Thessalonica and eastern Macedonia.

The conditions of life in mainland Greece, Frankish-controlled as far as the Isthmus of Corinth, are almost completely unknown. The excellent researches of Antonio Rubió y Lluch, mainly in the Catalan archives, on Catalan rule (1311–1388), provide almost the only light on the subject.

In Frankish documents there is not a single mention of the Greeks of
Attica and Boeotia throughout the entire period of Frankish occupation
and only a very few during the Acciajuoli period (1388–1460). Rubió y
Lluch epitomizes the situation with the remark: "it would seem as if the
Greeks had been banished completely from the history of their own
country." [14] Fortunately, Catalan documentation is replete with information on the Greeks and filled with allusions to their gradual increase in
influence at Athens and other cities of the duchies of Athens and Neopatras, at Thebes, Levadia, and so on.[15] Yet the Catalans, like the Franks,
generally treated the Greeks as an inferior people and excluded them
from the jurisdiction of the civil law, which applied only to the conquerors—the *conquistadors* as they called themselves.[16]

Majorca seems to have achieved an especial primacy in the Catalan
sphere. Its trade flourished, and Majorcans served in a number of high
offices in Thebes, where their services were much esteemed. Nevertheless,
Athens and Levadia figured more prominently as centers of Catalan settlement and influence. As for the Greek urban dwellers—merchants, craftsmen, amanuenses—none escaped the exactions of Catalan rule. But it was
undoubtedly the peasants who fared the worst. They were scarcely more
than chattel slaves.[17] No one was permitted to engage in any legal trans-
action (the buying or selling of property, for example) unless certain
political rights had first been explicitly conferred.[18]

Rights of this kind, however, were not wholly withheld from the Greeks.
Those in Levadia were endowed with "all the rights and privileges of the
Franks," under the Great Seal of St. George,[19] as a reward for opening
the gates of their city to the victors after the Catalans defeated the Franks
of the Duchy of Athens at Cephisus in 1311. Catalan magnanimity in this
case was not altogether disinterested: Levadia was the key to the entire
Catalan military position in Greece. Not only did it lie roughly at the
center of the Catalan possessions, but its mighty castle, one of the most
beautiful survivals from Frankish occupation, strategically dominated the
crossroads which in one direction led to the narrow passes of Parnassus
and in another to the ancient route between the duchies of Athens and
Neopatras.[20] Seventy years later, in 1381, Peter III of Aragon again rewarded the inhabitants of the city, Greek and Catalan, who had successfully defended it against the Navarrese, by a bestowal of the unique right
to govern themselves according to Catalan laws and the "customs of
Barcelona." [21]

Specially favored treatment was accorded the Levadian family of
Mavronicholas. Immediately after the capture of the city in 1311, a number of the Mavronicholas family was designated Notary and assumed all
the rights of Catalan citizenship. Later, in 1366, at the instigation of

Roger de Lluria, *fils,* Frederick III of Sicily renewed these privileges for the benefit of Mavronicholas' son, Nicholas.[22] Nicholas' son, Constantine, in turn succeeded his father as Notary at the time of Peter III, who confirmed the same citizenship rights, though now with the addition of perpetual rights in chancery and the privilege of naming his successor.[23] Peter III also stipulated that Constantine's children could marry Frankish women, a right which had never previously been bestowed.

Similar substantial privileges were conferred on Nicholakes Maniakes, who had helped to extend the authority of Roger de Lluria, *fils,* in Thebes; and the Athenian, Demetrius Rentes, Notary and later Chancellor of Athens, who, with a few other Greeks, had courageously defended Megara against the Acciajuolis.[24] Another Demetrius was designated Castellan of Salona (now Amphissa).[25] Such Greeks invariably became the most influential among all leading noble families.

These illustrations of generosity towards Greeks and the fact that the Catalans recruited Greeks for their subsequent military expeditions against various enemies would seem to indicate that by the second generation the Catalans had lost their initial uncomprising bellicosity. But there was still no doubt who the masters were, for these Greeks were impressed into fighting whether they liked it or not. Of all the Greeks, the Catalans preferred to have Peloponnesians in their ranks, especially the cavalry of the Albanian settlers in the Peloponnese, whom they regarded as the most experienced in war. The constant social intercourse and the growth of mutual interests over the years brought about relatively less stringent policies on the part of the conquerors. A number of Catalans, for example, disregarding the Roman Catholic Church's specific injunction to the contrary, married Greek women and even adopted the Orthodox faith.[26] Indeed, in 1365, during the patriarchate of Philotheos, the first Orthodox Archbishop of Athens under Frankish domination was consecrated. He was "the Most Honored" and "the Exarch of all Greece." However, he died in Constantinople before assuming his charge. A provisional replacement, the monk Neophytos, was sent to Athens in the following year "pending the consecration of an Archbishop of Athens by the grace of God." This particular metropolitan was given full ecclesiastical rights over the archdiocese of Thebes and Neopatras and the patriarchal diocese of Aegina, though he never actually took up his intended post because of certain political irregularities in the Duchy of Athens at that time.[27]

The Greeks benefitted, too, from mutual antagonism between the Catalans and Navarrese during the years 1375 to 1388. As we have seen, Theodore I of the Morea and Manuel II of Thessalonica had previously entered an alliance against Catalans and Turks with the Florentine ruler of Corinth, Nerio Acciajuoli. Acciajuoli's constant preoccupation in this alliance, his obsession even, was the displacement of Catalan authority.[28] And in the general political confusion groups of brigands emerged from their mountain fastnesses in the eastern highlands and preyed on anyone they met. Once, near Bitrinitza (now Tolophon), the brigands Cuyrataci, Androni, Gostila, Pacioti, and others relieved the Archbishop of Megara of 160 ducats. "Their names," writes Rubió y Lluch, "are obviously Greek and call to mind the mountain guerrillas (*klephts*), and armatoles, the heroic fighters of the glorious war of independence." [29]

At the same time the political position of the Greeks showed marked improvement. Greeks are mentioned among the foreign members of the Council (*Consell, Universitad*) of Athens and Neopatras.[30] Very little is known of the actual method of election of these members; only that spokesmen (*sindichs, procuradors*) of the whole Council were chosen to deal with the Duke.[31] One would like to imagine that there was in existence a separate Greek authority which handled all affairs affecting the Greek community, but this hardly seems possible. Nevertheless, in its ordinary reports furnished direct to the Duke (always written in simple and artless style), the Council made many requests; they were rarely ignored. Occasionally, the members even went so far as to demand the recall of high Catalan officials when these had incurred popular displeasure.[32]

King Peter III of Aragon, an admirer of antiquity and the Greeks,[33] seemed to reflect this discernible improvement in Greco-Catalan relations when, in a letter of 1381, he thanked the Count of Neopatras and all Albanians who lived in Greece (*Allada*) because as good and faithful vassals they had defended Catalan lands against the Navarrese and other enemies. Rubió y Lluch is assuredly correct when he assumes that by *Allada* Peter III meant Phthiotis and certain other districts in the Duchy of Neopatras. In December of the following year, 1382, Peter III permitted Greeks and Albanians to settle in Attica under the generous condition of tax exemption for two years.[34]

Nerio Acciajuoli, who succeeded Peter III as ruler in Catalan Greece, also saw that the situation required delicacy and forbearance in handling the Greeks. He acknowledged the tenure and jurisdiction of the Orthodox metropolitan, accepted the official status of the Greek language in his duchy, and generally adopted a political stance calculated not to antagonize the Greeks. Like the Catalans before him, Acciajuoli acceded to the appointment of Greek officials and notaries, allowed Greek aldermen to participate in public affairs, and tolerated intermarriage between the Catalans and the indigenous Greek inhabitants.[35] The assertion of Greek influence in these diverse ways was symbolized in Athens by the restora-

tion of old churches and the foundation of new ones.[36] Similar concessions, notably in the religious field, which were extended to Greeks in the
county of Salona [37] constituted demonstrable proof that the conquerors'
grip in Hellas was growing looser.

There was a certain amount of intellectual activity during the Catalan
period. Scholarly copyists were particularly prominent: Nicholas Chrysoberges and his brother-in-law, George Protobelissenos; Demetrius Chlomos, who in 1339 entrusted the monk Kosmas Kamelos with the task of
copying the medical works of Nicholas Myrepsos and Oreibasios (fourth
century); Demetrius Peroules, who was translating the works of Theocritus in the same year; one Alfonso, of Catalan descent, who, at the
beginning of the fourteenth century, was copying various works by Galen;
and Simon Atoumanos, Archbishop of Thebes, who published the New
Testament in Greek and Latin and translated Plutarch into Latin.[38]

Hellenism in Epirus and Thessaly

At the turn of the fifteenth century, western Thessaly and southern
Epirus, which had always maintained a close cultural affinity, continued
to support the traditional values of Hellenic-Christian learning and civilization. Certain places in particular were notable for their contributions
to the Greek heritage through the long night of foreign rule, whether
Albanian, Arvanito-Vlach, Serbian, Frankish, or Turkish. There was Trikkala, for instance, with its restored monastic community of Stagai (one
of a group of monasteries known as Meteora), whose five monks, Neilos,
Makarios, Athanasius, Gregorios Stylites, and Neophytos,[39] almost contemporaries of one another in the fourteenth century, achieved lasting
renown. Athanasius, who had learned ancient Greek in the vigorous intellectual atmosphere of Thessalonica,[40] was certainly the most imposing
of the five. There was also Phanarion, near Karditsa, famed both for its
staunch nobility and its monastery of Levkousias. The monastery, which
fell within the jurisdiction of the patriarch, had as its abbot in 1383
Euthymios, who also was "superintendent of the neighboring monasteries in Vlachia [Thessaly]." [41] There were also the cities of Epirus, particularly Ioannina and Arta,[42] which clung to the strong Greek traditions
of the Despotate of Epirus and still kept "the Greek nation pure." And
everywhere there were old noble families, schools, and monasteries, both
near the cities themselves and in remote parts of the Pindus Mountains
and its spurs, which remained constant in their guardianship of the
national heritage.[43]

Places like these must surely have retained a large part of the treasure
of manuscripts that Nicephorus Blemmydes had studied some one hundred years before. At the time, he had wondered that there were so

many "books": they were "difficult to count" and "hard to get at." Some
were unknown, even to people who had spent their whole lives studying
manuscripts.[44] Indeed, it was these remote monasteries that continually
supported Christianity and Greek learning, thus maintaining a constant
source of national unity. Some of the educated and determined abbots
in these monasteries greatly influenced the course of intellectual and
political change in this troubled period.

There had always been a strong Hellenic tradition in the Despotate
of Epirus, which had never been expunged by Serbian, Albanian, or
Arvanito-Vlach rule. It should not be forgotten that in Thessaly, throughout the Frankish occupation and even after the conquest of Stephen
Dušan in 1348, a sizable class of Greek nobles had not only managed
to survive but had stubbornly clung to certain liberties and privileges.
That Dušan should have renewed these privileges was clear evidence of
the extent to which Greek influence was entrenched in Thessaly at the
time. These noble families (among the most prominent and best-known
of whom were the Melissenoi, Strategopouloi, and Gabrielopouloi) were
instrumental in introducing traditional Byzantine law and feudal customs
into the Serbian social organization.[45] Besides the more prominent families, there were many other nobles who played a similar role in places
like Phanarion (as was mentioned as early as 1295), Larissa, Trikkala,
Pharsala, Domokos, Demetrias (Volos), and the two Almyroses. In the
manner of their compeers elsewhere, they were still able through their
wealth and power to wield considerable influence in the local government of their districts, and their authority in most areas of public
activity was undeniable. According to unwritten law, the law of custom,
Notables also exercised substantial judicial powers in their communities.[46]

The prominent families of Epirus and Thessaly and the Greek population in general always tried to reassert their former predominance. Unfortunately, there is no conclusive evidence to this effect, but it can be
illustrated, for example, by the transitory triumph of Nicephorus II of
Epirus in Thessaly after the death of Stephen Dušan (1355) and his attempts to rehabilitate the scattered Greek inhabitants in their former
lands. These plans were of course thwarted by Nicephorus' death at the
hands of the Albanians in the battle of Achelous in 1359.[47] Then, during
the period from 1367 to 1383 the Serbian Despot of Epirus, Thomas
Preliumbović, sought to crush his Greek subjects forever. To this end, he
tried to extirpate the authority of the Church in Epirus by banishing
Sebastianos, the Metropolitan of Ioannina, distributing the "villages and
estates" of the Church among the Serbs, marrying Greek widows to Serbs
while providing them with dowries from the confiscated property of the

local inhabitants, and generally entering upon a campaign of outright persecution of the clergy and Notables of Ioannina.[48]

However, it was the rampaging Albanians, with their uncontrollable eagerness for pillage, who constituted the greatest danger to the regime of Preliumbović. Even those who had settled down in Ioannina he subjected to the most repressive of measures. Since he desired to be known by the soubriquet, "Slayer of the Albanians," his policies redounded indirectly to the benefit of the Greek community.[49] By the end of his reign, his obsessive hatred of the Albanians and perhaps the fact that the Turkish danger was beginning to loom ominously on the horizon led him to make overtures to Manuel Palaeologus, the ruler of Thessalonica, who had already achieved fame for his resistance against the Turks. Or perhaps Manuel initiated the *rapprochement* by sending out feelers to Preliumbović. Whatever the case, in 1383, in September of which year the Metropolitan Matthew arrived to take up his seat in Ioannina, Gabriel, the Abbot of the monastery of Archimandreion, was dispatched to Manuel in Thessalonica, whence he returned with a nobleman named Mangaphas. Both envoys were subsequently present at an imposing religious ceremony in which, with the blessings of the metropolitan, "the Despotate was vested in Thomas Preliumbović." [50] Their mutual concessions and courtesies doubtless signified close collaboration between the two. As Loenertz observes, Thomas Preliumbović acknowledged Manuel as sovereign, by whom he was in turn acknowledged despot.[51] Later, Preliumbović again expelled his metropolitan, who, like Sebastianos, retired to Arta, but left the Church's tenant-farmers undisturbed [52]—an action which was of course attributable to Manuel's diminishing usefulness after the investment of Thessalonica by the Turks (1383–1387).

The Serbian hold on Epirus (1346–1385) was irretrievably broken after Preliumbović's assassination by his personal guard in December 1384. All authority there was then assumed by the Florentine patrician, Esau de Buondelmonti, brother of the Duchess of Cephalonia and Leukas, at the invitation of both Greek and Serbian noblemen in Ioannina and Ioasaph, Abbot of Meteora, former king of Thessaly, and brother of Preliumbović's widow, Maria Angelina Ducaina Palaeologina. "Then," according to the *Chronicle*, "Esau the Despot, being well-disposed towards Christianity, ignored the demands of the Serbs that they continue to remain in possession of the Church's lands and fortune formerly bequeathed to them." [53] The Metropolitan Matthew was recalled, the properties and tenants of the Church reinstated, and the integrity of the realm secured. Palaeologus Vryones bore the insignia of the Despotate there from Constantinople, and Esau was duly invested with it in the presence

of Matthew by the bishops of Vella and Dryinoupolis. In 1387, when
Thessalonica became tributary to Murad I, Esau was forced to appear
before the Sultan and acknowledge Turkish suzerainty over the Despotate.[54]

In Thessaly, foreign rule still had indigenous support.[55] The successors
of Stephen Dušan (1331–1355), his stepbrother Symeon Uroš (1355–
1371?), and the latter's hellenized son, John, could not but acknowledge
a situation in which Slav settlers were being progressively assimilated by
the Greek inhabitants and the great Greek families still exercised preponderant control. Indeed, the fact that the Greco-Serb John Ouroš
Palaeologus, the ruler of Thessaly (1371?–1381?),[56] was succeeded by
"powerful" Greeks, who were probably his relatives [57]—Alexius Angelos
Philanthropenos (1381?–1388?), afterwards famed as Caesar of Greater
Walachia, and later Alexius' brother, Manuel Angelos Philanthropenos
(1388?–1393)—can only be interpreted as further evidence of the domi-
nance of these Greek families. These brothers were descendants of the
Epirotic-Thessalian branch of the great Byzantine family of Philanthro-
penos.[58] To another relative, Stephen Ducas, son of Radoslav Chlapen,[59]
Ouroš was in a position to grant only the districts of Domokos and
Pharsala. Yet precisely how the Philanthropenoi were able to succeed
Ouroš remains an obscure problem; [60] as obscure as it is clear, on the
other hand, that Serbian rule in Thessaly came to an end not with the
Turkish invasion in 1393, as hitherto thought,[61] but with the abdication
of John Ouroš Palaeologus in 1381(?)—the same hellenized Serbian ruler,
in fact, who finally became Abbot of Meteora with the name of Ioasaph.

Alexius Angelos Philanthropenos came into contact with Makarios
Choumnos and, later, Gabriel, abbots of the *Nea Mone* of Thessalonica,
to which Alexius bequeathed, in January 1384, the village of Kolindros
in Macedonia, for possession after his death. He also entered into relations with the brothers Theodore and Manuel Palaeologus of Thessalonica [62]—partly no doubt out of consideration of the familial ties which
joined the houses of Palaeologus and Philanthropenos,[63] but partly too
in order to help set up a common front against the new political forces
throughout Hellas. It seems unlikely that there could have been any other
purpose behind Alexius' presence in Thessalonica in January 1384, a few
months after the commencement of the Turkish siege, for Alexius, the
ruler of Thessaly, and Thomas Preliumbović of Epirus had acknowledged
Manuel as suzerain in 1382 and 1383, and negotiations were in progress
between Greek and foreign rulers for concerted opposition to the Turk.[64]

At the beginning of the fifteenth century, the Count of Cephalonia
and Zacynthus (Zante), Carlo I Tocco, laid claim to the inheritance of
his uncle, Esau de Buondelmonti. With the backing of the people of

Figure 9. John Ouroš Palaeologus as the Monk Ioasaph.

Epirus, he began a series of campaigns against Albanians and Arvanito-Vlachs in Aetolia, Acarnania, and Epirus for the re-establishment of the Despotate of Epirus. Carlo's struggles against the Albanians immediately attracted the attention of Manuel II, who, it seems, never gave up his plans for effecting an alliance between all (or at least the most powerful) Christian rulers in Hellas in order to resist the Turk.[65] The Greek nobility of Ioannina were no less diligent in prevailing upon their ruler, the Duke of Cephalonia, to effect just such an alliance and to assume the title of Despot with which his predecessors, Thomas Preliumbović and Esau de Buondelmonti, had been honored. Thus, when Manuel II went to the Peloponnese on 29 or 30 March 1415,[66] Carlo I with alacrity sent his brother, Count Leonardo, there to assist the Byzantine ruler in subduing certain refractory noblemen. Leonardo blockaded the castles of Elea-voulcos, who was among the most unruly of the nobles, forced him into submission, and was promptly honored by a grateful Manuel with the title, "Great Constable." Carlo I for his part was dignified with the accolade of "Despot of the Romans." The event was celebrated in Ioan-nina with lyrical enthusiasm:

There was great joy in Ioannina as rich and poor sang out the honor of their lord; afterwards, Carlo as Despot immediately turned his sword against Arta so as to assert his authority throughout the Despotate.[67]

With the Greek population steadfastly behind him, Carlo marched against Arta and was successful in ridding southern Epirus of the Al-banian yoke. Carlo's wife, Francesca, beloved daughter of Nerio Accia-juoli, who was well known for his philhellenic proclivities, appears to have learned well from her father. Since she was by all accounts capable and ambitious ("she dominated her husband"), it was probably due to her influence on him that the Greek archbishopric of Leukas was re-stored. Her paternal inheritance made her "sufficiently Greek and suffi-ciently proud" to subscribe her letters as "Empress of the Romans" and to affix to them a vermilion wax seal in the manner of the Byzantine Emperors.[68] Thus the court of Tocco, like others in Hellas, could be con-sidered thoroughly hellenized.[69] It had become so through the persua-sion and support of the Greek community on which it was superimposed and which thus constituted fertile ground for the growth of Greek nationalism.

Hellenism in Macedonia

Serrai and Thessalonica were the twin bases of Hellenism in Macedonia. Greeks there had held important positions in the state of Stephen Dušan; indeed, the Notables of Serrai, Prosakon, Zichna, and Hierissos were all

Figure 10. Manuel II Palaeologus, between His Father and Eldest Son.

Greeks. A supreme court, whose members were dignified with the title of superior judge,[70] was constituted from the body of Greek Notables and other nobles. Municipal councils, which also served as lower courts, were composed of aldermen and nobles, also Greek. Of course the importance of such findings is that they help us to determine the nationality of local populations.

Manuel undoubtedly had come into contact with such Notables when he entered Serrai in November 1371 (see page 77 above), though, as we have seen, his dominion there was brought to an abrupt end by the Turkish invasion in 1383.[71] After that date, Thessalonica remained the only bastion of Hellenism in Macedonia, and the future could not have looked more dismal. The enemy ravaged the countryside without let or hindrance, while in the city the disagreeable effects of Zealot rule lingered on.[72]

In defying the Turk, Manuel chose to act completely independently of the Byzantine court. For four whole years (1383–1387), while his father, John V, had opted for vassalage as the price of friendly relations with the Sultan, Manuel staunchly resisted its demands before the very walls of Thessalonica. His courageous stand had the effect of provoking enthusiastic comment from the citizenry of Constantinople and even calling forth a stream of volunteers for the defense of Thessalonica. "Freedom is a great thing," wrote Manuel's teacher, Kydones, from Constantinople, "and it is equally great to show that one does not cringe before one's inferiors. People who do not have freedom ought to direct all their energies towards getting it, and those who already have it towards keeping it." Kydones' letters to Manuel were filled with lofty sentiments about freedom and the duty of hurling defiance at one's enemies.[73]

Manuel's struggle was an unequal one, though he made every endeavor to seek allies and reinforcements. An approach to the Venetians brought the response, in April 1385, of a quantity of arms, two officers, and a regiment of excuses. Another approach to Pope Urban VI led to the dispatch in 1386 of a papal emissary to Thessalonica, who offered Church reunion as the price of assistance from the West. Manuel indicated his preparedness to pay, but the Hesychasts thought the price too high and turned against him, so the projected union never in fact occurred.[74]

The ruler of Thessalonica surrounded himself with a group of young and educated advisers who were fired by the same ideals. One of these, in continual touch with Manuel's teacher, Kydones, endlessly castigated his apathetic compatriots in his search for some means of easing Thessalonica's plight. Some of these youthful followers were considered too implacable in their patriotism and too remorseless in their antagonism towards the Turk, but with all their influence on "Manuel and the goings-on in the city," they were unable to prevent the city's eventual submission to the Turk.[75]

Thessalonica nevertheless became the core of national resistance and the pivot of various coalitions against the Turk. Manuel's contacts with other dignitaries (his brother Theodore, who ruled in the Peloponnese; the ruler of Corinth, Nerio Acciajuoli; the Greco-Serbian Despot of Epirus, Thomas Preliumbović, and his successor, Esau de Buondelmonti; the Caesar of Thessaly, Alexius Angelos Philanthropenos), all comprised, as Loenertz observes, "the warp and woof of a fabric from which a pattern slowly emerged."[76] There are still many gaps in the story, though the researches of G. T. Dennis have gone a long way towards filling them in. But it is curious that Dennis does not interpret the pattern and Manuel's part in its fabrication as a stage in the awakening of Greek nationalism.[77]

Thessalonica's leadership in continental Greece before its surrender to the Turks is incontrovertible. The city was not only a symbol of freedom for all Greeks but a center of diplomatic activity and a home of significant learning based on classical education. Examples of past courage which shone through the classical heritage were readily summoned to mind by savants and higher clergy, and were at least recollected as

Figure 11. The Walls of the Citadel of Thessalonica.

legend by most inhabitants. Indeed, the ancient Greeks were thought to be so admirable that the Metropolitan, Isidore Glabas (1380–1384), could unblushingly represent them to his Christian compatriots as "paragons of brotherly love." [78]

The adulation of antiquity was therefore universal and unreserved. Many of the writings of politicians, savants, and even clergy were filled with remembrances of the ancient Greek world: Gods, demi-gods, heroes, generals, poets, philosophers, orators, historians, all found reverent and affectionate mention.[79] To these, all contemporary officials, however lowly or distinguished, were compared with a view to offering solace or praise [80] —or to shaming them into defiance of the enemy.[81] Thus, in the middle of the fourteenth century, Demetrius Kydones compared Manuel Cantacuzenus, the Despot of the Morea, with the Athenian general, Iphicrates,[82] and later, in 1383, congratulated Manuel for his ability to metamorphose the people of Thessalonica into "heroes of Marathon." In order to combat despair and defeatism, he advised: "let us face the enemy and stand firm before the tide; let us resist the spirit of defeat and endure everything that we must. Let us do all this in full knowledge that a sense of desperation cannot possibly be of any assistance; on the contrary, it can only prevent us from utilizing one of our good characteristics—if indeed we have any left." [83]

Manuel II was equally eloquent in exhorting his people to resist the Turk: "I must remind you that we are Romans, that ours is the land of Philip and Alexander and that it has always been the destiny of their successors to triumph against any foe. No enemy has ever prevailed against them: no more than the dust against the wind or the candle against the flame." And he continued with words that were just as much a hymn to freedom as they were characteristic of the young prince's constant exhortations to his people:

With God's help, the enemy will not now, nay never, conquer us while we are capable of bearing arms and fighting for the honor with which we prefer to die . . . I know that all of us believe it better to fulfill our destiny, that is to die, than voluntarily to submit to this most profane of barbarians.

Death under such circumstances, far from being horrible, was a true release,

for it saves us from many more and much greater evils. Death is only the final evil which . . . brings a swift end to all troubles. Death is not the worst evil, as many have said before and as I believe many will say again. This is assuredly proved by the fact that all those cities which have fallen to the barbarian have, without exception, come to prefer death to slavery. Let us therefore do our utmost, let us suffer everything for freedom, for if there is nothing more vile than slavery, there can be nothing better than freedom.[84]

This period of trial for the people of Thessalonica (1383–1387), though it ended finally in submission, was, in the judgment of at least one unknown writer at the beginning of the fifteenth century, a glorious moment in their history.[85]

Manuel's historical allusions were not lost on his people. There was the cenotaph of G. Vibius Quartus, for example, a square Roman column outside Philippi which gave rise to many traditions. The column, "the rack of Alexander's mare," as the local people called it, was seen by Giovanni Maria degli Angiolello in 1470 and by the traveller, Pierre Belon, about 1550, during the darkest years of Turkish rule.[86]

This monument, a huge square monolith in the shape of an altar, four meters high, which had been erected in honor of the Roman centurion, G. Vibius Quartus, still exists today. However, the square shape at its base has become almost round because of continual scrapings over the centuries by peasants. They collect the dust of the marble and give it dissolved in water to mothers, so that their milk will produce children with the courage of Alexander.[87]

Alexander the Great had become so much a part of the popular mythology of this period that, in a fourteenth-century manuscript of the *Alexander Romance* which is preserved in the archives of the Greek community in Venice, he is depicted standing with the crown and garb of a Byzantine Emperor and holding an orb in his left hand. The barely legible inscription underneath reads: "In the name of Christ faithful King and Emperor of all the East and the whole . . ." [88]

Manuel recognized that the people of Thessalonica were descended from two nations, the Roman and the Greek. That is, like his predecessors the emperors of Nicaea, he knew that the Byzantines were Greeks who had chosen on grounds of imperial prestige and political utility not to reject their Roman traditions. Typically, in a palace speech to officials and others around 1415, Joseph Bryennios spoke of an unbroken history from Lycurgus and Themistocles through the Romans to their Byzantine successors.[89] Again, the unknown author of the *Panegyric to Manuel and John VIII Palaeologus* spoke of the commingling of the two "official nations," Greek and Roman, from which emerged "one nation, the best and most distinguished, and of whom if it be said 'Romano-Greek' [*Romellenes*] it were well said." [90] The Roman tradition, as we have previously noticed, existed chiefly in Constantinople,[91] where it derived its strength from official, imperial, and ecclesiastical sanction. Although the tradition still persisted, increasing stresses had progressively weakened it; and out

Figure 12. Cenotaph of G. Vibius Quartus.

of the weakening eventually came a formulation of the national problem, first by the Neo-Platonist philosopher, George Gemistos, and then by the historian, Laonicos Chalcocondyles, a half century later. The earlier commentaries are nonetheless important as starting points for a direct approach to the ferment of ideas that ultimately resulted in the definition of Greek nationalism.

None of the Palaeologi had been as assiduous as Manuel in disseminating the Hellenic spirit and arousing the Hellenes. His love of Hellenism was such that it expressed itself not only in unflagging opposition to the Turks but in a desire for fundamental social reform. After 1371, with the aim of bolstering the defenses of his realm, Manuel, impervious to the protests and complaints of Isidore, Archbishop of Thessalonica,[92] expropriated half the monastic properties of Mt. Athos and the district of Thessalonica and distributed them in *pronoia* to the military.[93] Manuel's social ideas and projections would make an interesting subject for more detailed study.

Curiously enough, Bayezid I and later Mohammed II embarked on similar programs of property redistribution at the expense of the class of *ulema,* or learned men. Bayezid pre-empted certain religious property endowments (*wakf*) on behalf of the state and reassigned them to the military class as a means of strengthening it.[94] It would be gratuitous to suppose that the actions of Manuel and Bayezid were unrelated to each other, though it is a matter for some conjecture as to who imitated whom. In all probability, however, the program originated with Manuel. All the lands which were found subsequently to have been distributed in *pronoia* fell within the district in which Manuel exercised effective jurisdictional control while ruler of Thessalonica. In general he never hesitated to confiscate ecclesiastical property or to arrive at a variety of other radical solutions to serve the emergency needs of his country's defense [95]—as can be concluded from a memorandum to him from Gemistos which we shall shortly discuss.

Without question, Manuel's measures strengthened the military oligarchy at the expense of the monasteries, and to this extent the system of *pronoia* benefitted the state, but it did not produce the same salutary results that the former system of small military holdings had done.[96]

So Bayezid seems to have been provided with a model for ready action when the institution of *wakf* began to fall apart. In an attempt to circumvent the law and evade taxes, certain prominent fief-holders had converted portions of their estates into *wakf,* ostensibly for philanthropic reasons. In reality, however, the big landed families continued to derive sole benefit from the lands which they had pretended to give up; thus, while the number of *wakf* increased, the fief-holdings, on which the

Ottoman military and social organization was primarily based, correspondingly decreased.[97]

Manuel II, who succeeded his father John V, reigned over the Byzantine Empire from 1391 to 1425, a most critical time. His contemporary, Manuel Calecas, postulated, "had Themistocles been alive, the chaos would make his senses reel." [98] In 1391, at the beginning of Manuel's reign, Thessalonica was taken by Bayezid I. For this most formative transitional stage in the development of Greek nationalism, Isidore, the archbishop of the city, is the most illuminating source of information on Thessalonica's internal affairs, civic organization, and social structure.[99]

Who then were the civic leaders, the "intendants" (*hoi ton koinon phrontistai*) of this city at the end of the fourteenth century? There were first of all those who had traditionally held power in the city (*hoi dynatoi*), then the middle class and clergy (*hypourgoi tou theou*).[100] Thus the authority of the lords temporal (*politeuomenoi archontes*) had not disappeared,[101] though it was now certainly diminished by the Turkish conquerors. In particular, Turkish encroachments so circumscribed the traditional authority of the "intendants" (*proïstamenoi ton koinon*) that they were no longer able, whatever their wishes may have been, to guarantee the integrity of property or the security of life and limb.[102] The people of Thessalonica, whose memory of the Zealots [103] was still vivid, tended to cast the entire blame for these conditions on their leaders, whom they accused of avarice and wanton sacrifice of the interests of the community. It was therefore hardly surprising when the city's leaders, faced with such a precipitate and bitter reaction, chose to adopt the line of least resistance by resigning their positions and dropping all interest in civic affairs. Recognizing in this abdication of responsibility an immediate danger to the city, Archbishop Isidore attempted to change their minds by emphasizing the need for responsible leadership. Only such men as they, he urged, men who possessed mental and administrative talents, could be expected to handle public affairs, while the peasants, the artisans, the tent-makers, and the shoemakers, the lower class (*hoi chydaioi*) in effect, had no hope of being able to cope with the needs of the city in such critical times. Those who formed the upper class, both by right of "reason and intellect," were not only the few but the best.[104]

Thus in an hour of crisis, the leaders of Thessalonica were brought to a recognition of their responsibilities and, with it, an understanding of the necessity to persevere against the Turk in order to preserve whatever authority they could. The institutions of the city were gradually adapted to meet both the requirements of Turkish hegemony and the exigencies of effective government. As a direct result of the personal representations of Isidore at the court of the Sultan, certain substantial privileges (*charites*) [105] were accorded the city. Although not actually enumerated, they nevertheless helped to maintain the social and religious freedom of the inhabitants, without, however, allaying the people's suspicion of their own leaders. To protect the city's institutions its leaders had to attempt to mollify the Turkish authorities by working with them.[106] Moreover, it was easy for those who were weak, ambitious, or self-interested to assume a servile role or to encourage Turkish interference in civic affairs on their own behalf. For these and other reasons many, indeed most, of the leaders were branded by the people as collaborators of the conqueror.

It is in Thessalonica in 1395 that we encounter first mention of the enforced recruitment of Christian youths who were subjects of the Ottoman Empire for service in the corps of janissaries. From the text of Isidore, who commiserated with the unfortunate parents of the boys, we learn that the fledgling janissaries were trained in the use of dogs and falcons, that they were in training through summer and winter, and that they were subjected to endless marches across mountain, river, and plain.[107] However, the actual year in which the impressment of Christian boys began is still not known.[108]

After the death of Isidore in 1396, his successor, Archbishop Gabriel, appears to have won the esteem and respect of the Turks by dint of his personable qualities, his virtue, and his high morality. At any rate, the Turks acceded to many of his wishes and thereafter behaved with unaccustomed mildness, even generosity, towards the inhabitants of Thessalonica. On two different occasions he represented his people at the court of Bayezid I and was successful in obtaining further privileges for the city, or, at least, according to his anonymous eulogizer, he was the principal cause of a "more tolerable slavery." [109]

After the surrender of Thessalonica in 1387 and its later occupation in 1391 the future seemed gloomy indeed. But Bayezid's defeat at Ankara in 1402 and the attendant convulsions over the Ottoman succession provided some ray of hope for the Greeks, however evanescent. Manuel's plans [110] to obtain support in the West were dashed by the rivalries and animosities of the Christian powers. Who will save the state and its people? was the cry of despair echoed by everyone. "Piety has vanished from the earth," wailed Joseph Bryennios, "learning has departed, wisdom has faded away. Were only the philosophers of ancient times capable of understanding? Is there no one today who can provide the answers to our problems?" Bryennios and many other clergy tried, but their answers, to say the least, tended to be discrete. It was difficult to see how the moral regeneration of the Orthodox was going to effect the kind of change which society, if it were to survive, so patently and urgently needed. Bryennios' waspish suggestion after 1415 that the wealthy in Constantinople ought to see to the repair of the city's walls certainly seemed, in the circumstances, rather more practical.[111]

GEORGE GEMISTOS

Prospectus for Reform

In the Peloponnese, remote from the influences of the capital, certain features of Greek nationalism—military, political, social—tended, because of this remoteness, to appear in clear focus. Here, in the person of George Gemistos, by all odds the most ardent devotee of Hellenic civilization in the period under consideration, Neo-Hellenism found its first true spokesman.

After a rich and variegated experience in the brisk political and religious atmosphere of Constantinople, Gemistos settled in Mistra some time before 1414. Almost in the shadow of the Taygetus Mountains, it was indeed an environment of repose and calm which contrasted strongly with that of the capital.[1] He was appointed to a superior judgeship, which we may deduce from a contemporary reference to him as *prostates tou ton Hellenon megistou dikasteriou* (president of the greatest tribunal of the Hellenes),[2] and from a play of words (*mochthon mestos*—full of pains) in the literary work *Epidemia tou Mazari en Hadou* (*The Sojourn of Mazaris in Hades*) hinting at his name, Gemistos (Full).[3] No doubt his talents had brought him to the notice of the Emperor Manuel II which thus led to his appointment as a trusted adviser to Manuel's son, Theodore II, Despot of Morea. From this influential position in Theodore's court, Gemistos must soon have become intimately acquainted with the problems of the city. Even without this opportunity, however, his judicial office provided an unparalleled vantage point from which to view the manifold social miseries of the Despotate and, in particular, the arbitrary actions of the nobility. Whatever the case, he was in a position both to study individual injustices and to observe the situation throughout the state before expounding his ideas. It is probably in terms of this comprehensiveness of outlook that the words of his pane-gyrist, the monk Gregory, in the funeral peroration, take on their full meaning: "with love of mankind his driving motivation, he appeared not so much the judge . . . as the protector and guardian, the helper, the father, the man who always held out his hand to the downtrodden, who so many times came to the aid of widows, who comforted the poor and defended everyone in need with every means at his disposal . . ." [4] Gemistos' stay in Mistra up to the time when he submitted his first memorandum to the young Theodore II seems to have had a crucial influence on the formation of his ideas.

His philosophy was Platonist in inspiration and was therefore fundamentally concerned with the reform of government and society. The reorganization of the state was the *sine qua non* of any effective solution of its economic, social, and political problems. Gemistos thus leaned heavily on the traditions of ancient Greece, and he also encountered some of the quandaries and anxieties inherent in this reliance. The past may have been sacrosanct, but it was not enough. Still, in a manner which was characteristic of so many of the scholarly votaries of Greek civilization, Gemistos [5] saw the Turks, for example, as reincarnated Persians and the struggles against them as a revival of the Persian wars. It was a notion which, interestingly enough, recurred on the eve of the great nationalist resurgence of 1821, when it actually precipitated the final achievement of nationhood.

The times seemed favorable for an attempt at reorganization. Manuel was preoccupied with his many projects to this end. As we have seen, he even expropriated ecclesiastical property in order to gain such strength as was necessary to throw back the enemy. In the middle of 1415, he was successful in apprehending and removing to Constantinople many of the Peloponnesian nobles who arrogantly pursued their own feudal interests [6] to the detriment of others and persistently defied the "Greek higher authority." It is against the backdrop of such events that Gemistos' manifestoes must be seen: first, in the wake of Manuel's moves, a letter to Manuel (before 1415) and a memorandum to Theodore (perhaps in 1415); then, later, in 1418, a second memorandum to Manuel, [7] in which he developed his ideas about the individuality of the Greek nation and the rise of Greek nationalism. Above all, improvement of the political, social, and economic situation in the Peloponnese was seen as a necessary prelude to successful confrontation with the Turk. Gemistos revealed himself not only as a theorist of Neo-Hellenism but as one who could offer concrete proposals to translate his theory into the reality of a viable nation state.

For many years, he says, he studied various means of saving the state.

He now ventures to suggest that the situation would benefit from the application of his ideas.[8] Hellenism, social justice, and determined opposition to the enemy are the three fundamentals of his thought. The state can be saved from the tyranny of the nobility and from the depredations of its enemies if the spirit of Hellenism among his compatriots is revived and strengthened and if a series of reform measures is adopted.

Gemistos was well versed in Greek history and sensible of the lessons of his nation's past.[9] The nature of his national and historical awareness was, in essence, what he tried to impart, beginning with the memorandum to Manuel. To Gemistos, the two facts which proved the Hellenic roots of the inhabitants of the Greek lands were a common culture and language.

The cradle and natural abode of the Greek nation was the Peloponnese itself, the Greek peninsula, and the surrounding islands. But the Peloponnese possessed special historical and geographical advantages which enhanced its importance to Hellenism: the fact that, as he believed, "from there, the greatest and most glorious works of the Greeks have sprung" and that its mountainous configuration, its fortresses, to say nothing of the valor of its people, all provided a singularly effective defense against its enemies. Its security should be further strengthened by building walls across the Isthmus of Corinth.

However, "bad government" had negated the natural defensive advantages of the country. Since the nobles had abdicated the responsibilities of leadership because of the degrading activities in which they engaged and because of their ruthless exploitation of the peasantry, their spheres of action ought to be severely circumscribed. Moreover, if there were merchants who had been elevated to positions of public responsibility, they ought either to cease commercial trafficking or resign from office.[10] Thus, although it was the conflict between public and private interests which Gemistos was most concerned with denouncing, his reference to merchants disclosed the fact that the middle class was already taking an active part in politics. If his proposals be read as a whole, it is clear that Gemistos' primary concern was to reinforce the position of the middle class, of which he was a member, vis-à-vis the great noble families of the Peloponnese. These latter, by opposing the concentration of power in the hands of the Despots, had prevented the necessary creation of a unified state. And the ideal state, according to Gemistos, could only be a monarchy "advised by those who were truly worthy, and with excellent and valid laws." Besides the Platonist strain, which of course is evident here, Gemistos may have been influenced by the prevailing political climate in Italy: he is known to have been interested in the forms and functions of government as seen by various rulers in that country.[11] As for the "truly worthy," where else could they be found if not among the middle class? ". . . The best advisers are the educated men of the middle class . . . those who are neither very rich nor very poor. The rich, from sheer habit of wealth and love of it, think only how to turn a profit and want nothing else; the poor, from sheer poverty, are unable to think of anything save escape from want. It is those in between who can be expected to look to the common interest." To have dared to express opinions of this kind suggests that the nobility had already suffered serious, if only temporary, reverses in the state.

Laws, he went on, had to be brought into harmony with the contemporary needs of the state and society. Above all, the laws must aspire towards political, social, and economic reform of a kind, radical if need be, that would free the people from onerous taxation, from forced labor (which was "akin to slavery"), and the other exactions of the nobility. The nobility, and the Despot in particular, ought to eschew the life of luxury and direct all their attentions and energies to military preparations for the defense of the state.[12]

The military problem was the most formidable one facing the state. There was an urgent need to organize a national army—an army composed only of citizens of the state—which would always be in top fighting trim. To accomplish this, it was essential for the military class to devote itself exclusively to military matters and to be exempt from all taxation.[13] Gemistos here offered a solution to the problem with which Theodore Kolokotrones came to grips some four hundred years later: how to figure out the number of soldiers there would be in camp next day. What chiefly caused the uncertainty, of course, was the soldiers' ever present necessity to return to their villages and farms to stave off their families' destitution. Gemistos, adapting an idea from Plato's *Republic,* suggested that the people of the Peloponnese be divided into two categories: those who were liable to military service and those who paid taxes. Those in the former group, by their exemption from taxation, could be expected to develop strong convictions of loyalty and a sense of devotion to duty.[14] Kolokotrones also thought to divide citizens into two similar classes, though with the difference that each class would alternate between stints of military service and farming every six months.[15]

Gemistos' ideas on monastic life and property, as he expounded them to Manuel II, were no less daring for his time. It is not proper, he said, for monks to lay claim to a share of the "public wealth" on the grounds that the monastic life was taken up with "meditation." [16] Nothing within the "public domain," whether property or serfs, was theirs by right. On the contrary, they ought to be content with the returns from their own properties, which were in any case already exempt from taxation. He

later went on to say that the religious had deviated from the true spirit
of the monastic life, which prescribed only such work as was necessary
to live plainly in accordance with normal monastic resources. There was
too much profit from "that which was improper" to the monastic life, in
particular the work of serfs, the toil of others.[17]

Next, Gemistos launched into a criticism of officialdom. The state's situation was deplorable because of public expenditure on projects "which
could not be justified" and because of the preposterous claims of a class
of officials who always seemed to be after privileges, exemptions, and
grants. Shamelessly indifferent to the common weal, this class was interested only in preparing itself for a life of idleness. By squandering the
wealth of the state, which was indispensable to its security, they would
deliver it into the hands of its enemies and so would be guilty of a heinous
crime. Yet they had the impertinence to claim that their properties and
offices were no more than payment due for services rendered, either by
themselves or their predecessors. They were oblivious to the impending
disaster hovering over all. They could not see that if the state were ruined
by their presumptuous demands upon it, they, too, would suffer ruin along
with it. Gemistos had no wish to dispossess those whose gain was the
result of honest service: it was parasitical service and counterfeit gain
that he reviled.[18]

He accused the nobility of regarding justice, truth, and the public good
as empty words, while measuring happiness in terms of vestments, silver,
gold, luxuries, and pleasures, to the exclusion of any thought about the
safety of themselves, their children, their country, or even freedom. There
are those who speak eloquently of "justice and truth" when the matter
at hand is barren of profit, but only let them smell personal gain and see
how their tongues become tied and their lips sealed. "When cities are
governed by men like these," he added, "even where the strongest and
best laws have previously been enacted and still are valid, they inevitably
come to ruin, for those very laws are hedged around by obfuscation and
confusion. Good laws are always needed, but they are good only while
they have force. When they do not, even the best are of little or no practical use. And it is the integrity of officials which determines whether or
not the force of law will prevail." [19]

To counterbalance the power of the great landed magnates, Gemistos
put forward a radical plan for the increase of cultivation and the reform
of the agricultural economy: complete freedom to own, to build, to plant,
and to cultivate as much land as the individual proprietor was able and
willing to cultivate. By opening up virgin lands in this way, Gemistos
thought to solve a dual agricultural and social problem. Another side of
his social program, to which we have already alluded, was his support

of the middle class—that is to say, merchants who had acquired wealth, power, and office through legitimate trade.[20] For their part, the members of the middle class were only too pleased to co-operate and indeed were able to reach positions of power and influence by allying themselves with the common people.[21] He deplored the practice of mutilating prisoners and suggested instead that they be put to useful work: "it is pitiful to see among us those who have suffered this kind of punishment; it is barbaric and quite alien to Greek custom." [22]

The thought of this singular man ranged the gamut of his society's ills. He offered a plan for restoring the currency and stabilizing public finance by a system of controls over the export and import of goods to protect local products. And he declared that, if called upon to do so, he would not hesitate to accept responsibility for the application of his ideas. For the times were so critical that no one could afford to turn his back upon them. The state had to be reorganized and modernized in order to face a new and deadly enemy, an enemy whose military organization had already proved equal to the job of conquest, however ill-equipped its society seemed in other respects. The proposed reforms, without which the enemy could not effectively be met, were not impossible or even difficult to apply. Their successful implementation waited only upon the enthusiasm and sincerity of the ruler. Indeed, no greater or nobler ideal existed, he told Theodore, than the task of securing the realm by every means in his power and thus preserving the "nation." [23]

While some of Gemistos' suggestions have a utopian flavor, the use of successive memoranda as a framework for the expression of a coherent corpus of ideas suggests that their content had sufficient immediacy to evoke responses in men like Manuel, Theodore, and perhaps others of their kind. At least, their willingness to listen encouraged Gemistos to persist further in the hope of realizing his ideas though the hope eventually proved vain.[24]

As we shall see, his ideas were discussed for many years, especially by his students, and in 1427 Theodore rewarded him with the benefice of the castle and district of Phanarion.[25] Perhaps it was only the disorderly state of society that restrained the Palaeologi from proceeding to the realization of his program.

Gemistos' discouragement at not having his program adopted can only be guessed at. No one saw more clearly than he or said with such tenacity what had to be done. But his ideas, it would seem, were too radical, and he certainly lacked the power to impose them. To this extent, he remains a tragic figure in history. The honors and rewards which the Palaeologi bestowed upon him (perhaps in a calculated effort to flatter or to appease —and thereby silence—possible ambition) could not divert him from his purpose. His later works not only continue to project the ideas of his first simple memoranda but do so in a more profound way.[26] The plans were never abandoned by him or his students, as we shall attempt to show.

Gemistos' Influence

An important piece of historical exegesis which has recently come to light is the interpretation of an ancient oracle that purports to unfold the destiny of the Peloponnese far into the future. Written by a monk named Isidore, this commentary contributed indirectly to an understanding of certain ideological cross-currents in the Peloponnese which have definite bearing on the renascence of Hellenism. Isidore addressed his commentary on the oracle (which was supposedly an oracle of the ancient Pythia's) to the Italian princess, Cleopa Malatesta (who married Theodore II in Mistra on 19 January 1421).[27] Cleopa had adopted the Hellenic way of life (probably Orthodoxy along with it)[28] and in common with her compatriots was profoundly disturbed by the Turkish peril. The oracle, which was in fact written some time before 1430 and not between 1446 and 1449 as has been hitherto believed, spoke of "a leader of the Hellenes, short of stature, crook-nosed, blond and fair" who would build a wall across the Isthmus, the third to do so. His efforts would be in vain, though, and he would be disappointed because the Turks would defeat the warlike Greeks.[29] Isidore rendered the phrase "leader of the Greeks" as "Emperor of the Hellenes" (*Basileus ton Hellenon*) and thus became the first person, so far as can be determined, to use the modern title, which is so much a part of the national consciousness.

The oracle further prophesied that the time would come, however, when the Turks would be defeated. This would occur "when the pine-tree falls upon the ground and blood is shed upon the pine" (*hotan konis pityn dexetai kai pitys lythron*), when, as Isidore explained, "fighters receive laurels and honor in war and are ready to shed their blood for these laurels." The defeat of the Turks would follow a reorganization of the army and a renewal of the determination to fight back (a rekindling of the spirit of ancient Greece, so to speak). He who fortified the Isthmus for the "fourth time" would therefore be the fortunate one.[30]

There is little doubt about the origin of the oracle. A number of clues —use of the phrase, "leader of the Hellenes," mention of the persistence of an Hellenic entity from ancient times far into the shadowy future, the archaic style of composition, the emphasis on honoring the military class, an underlying optimism for the future, all these point to the authorship of Gemistos or his circle of followers. In other words, by attempting to invest their beliefs with the authority of ancient oracular prophecy, they hoped to gain acceptance of their ideas. Just what, however, Isidore's connection with the coterie of Gemistos was and just what currency his commentary had cannot be ascertained.

All the same, Isidore tried to assist Gemistos' plans by bringing persuasion to bear on Cleopa to improve the military situation in the Peloponnese. And since Gemistos himself had previously made a direct approach to Theodore, it can only be assumed that his plans were at least well known in that quarter. Unfortunately, that is all we do know. What Theodore thought about Gemistos' plans for social reform and renewal of the Greek spirit remains hidden from us.

In 1433, Cleopa died,[31] and Gemistos seized the opportunity in her funeral panegyric to return to the political situation and to remind Theodore II of his duty to take drastic and decisive steps for the state's security: "only you have the power to accomplish what is needed. It ought to be your main, if need be, your only concern, for others will follow where you lead. God willing, we can be saved, but if you neglect your duty our danger will only be increased . . . Great deeds, not little ones, are called for; only they can ensure the safety and well-being of the people." [32]

Cleopa's reaction to Gemistos is equally unknown. But at least the behavior of her daughter, Helen, indicated a degree of national alertness among some members of the family of Theodore II Palaeologus. After Helen's marriage to John II Lusignan, the King of Cyprus, on 3 February 1442, she was able to impose her will on her weakling of a husband for sixteen years. Relentlessly, she fought against the powerful hold of the Frankish military and ecclesiastical establishment in her island, always striving to ameliorate the condition of the Greeks, to raise them to positions of political and military prominence, to enhance their influence generally, and to restore the prestige of the Orthodox Church. Naturally, these efforts met with stern opposition from the Latin element, especially the Roman Catholic Church. Then and later she was criticized and traduced for her efforts. Aeneas Sylvius Piccolomini (later Pope Pius II) recognized the deep national consciousness of this Greek princess when he denounced her as hostile to the Latin religion and an enemy of the Roman Church,[33] and it seems probable that Gemistos (whom she must have listened to on several occasions, and whose proposals she must have discussed) was instrumental in the development of this consciousness.

Notwithstanding the opposition Helen encountered, it was from this time that the hellenization of foreigners, particularly the French, gathered momentum. Greeks began to hold offices even in the Lusignan palaces, and they as well as their language eventually came into the ascendant.

Surely this trend should be attributed to a revival of national feeling.[34] The trend, however, was abruptly arrested during the period of Venetian domination from 1489 to 1571. The Venetians imposed a system of such rigid centralization in order to subordinate the interests of the colonies to those of the metropolitan power that the Cypriots came to look back nostalgically to the Lusignan period and show affection towards French travellers.[35]

There only remains for consideration an assessment of the influence of Gemistos' ideas on those regions close to Mistra, both north and south. Was there, for example, any connection between these ideas and the movement in Venetian-controlled Crete in 1415, which, instigated apparently by only a few persons, aimed at the liberation of the serfs? [36] Or, if the evidence remains inconclusive on this point, can anything more explicit be said of Gemistos' influence to the north? Gregorovius affirms the probability that Gemistos' ideas had echoes in Athens and northern Greece [37] but confesses his inability to offer definite proof.

Though neither question can be answered, at least one event may be mentioned, as much for its likely bearing on the question of Gemistos' influence as for its certain relevance to the awakening of national consciousness among the Athenians. When Antonio Acciajuoli, Duke of Athens, died without heirs in 1435, George Chalcocondyles, father of the historian, Laonicos, and relative of the Duke's widow, Maria Melissene, moved quickly to break the Frankish yoke. Maria sent him as her envoy to Murad II to obtain the Sultan's consent to the proposal that the government of the Duchy be entrusted to herself and her "most worthy" kinsman, as she fondly described Chalcocondyles. However, Chalcocondyles' rivals, who still held substantial political power in Athens (*proestesan tou demou*), managed by various stratagems to persuade Maria to abandon the citadel, whereupon they installed in it her late husband's family. They then banished Chalcocondyles' family from Athens.[38] There were apparently two opposing factions in Athens: the one, led by Maria and Chalcocondyles, claimed the succession and promoted the expulsion of all foreign rulers; the other, out of jealousy, perhaps, towards the family of Chalcocondyles, or simply for reasons of self-interest and self-preservation, followed a policy of subservience to foreign rule. The former clique also appears to have sought alliance with the chief aspirant to national leadership, Constantine Palaeologus, then Despot of Morea, who possessed kinship ties with the extensive Peloponnesian branch of the Melissenoi family. This supposition would seem to be borne out by the remarks of Sphrantzes: that at the request of Maria Melissene he had been sent by Constantine with many soldiers and "bearing his official silver seal" (*enorkon argyroboullon*) to receive Athens and Thebes in exchange for certain territories in the Peloponnese near Laconia, where the Melissenoi had their estates. But just at that time the Turkish general, Turahan, besieged and captured Thebes (while Chalcocondyles languished in the Sultan's prison as a hostage for the deliverance of Athens to the Turks). The Sultan knew Constantine's plans only too well, which accounted for Chalcocondyles' incarceration and Turkish acquiescence in the seizure of the Duchy of Athens by the relatives of Antonio Acciajuoli. Sphrantzes' mission was therefore abortive.[39] Constantine was too ambitious and too dangerous. But although Constantine's plans were foiled on this occasion he remained undaunted and, as we shall see, merely waited for a more auspicious moment to put his plans into effect.

Where now could Chalcocondyles pursue his goal if not in the Despotate of Morea? Here, indeed, he (not his son, Laonicos) next appears in 1446 as Constantine's ambassador to the court of Murad II.[40] He was guided there because in Constantine he recognized a kindred spirit whose approach to the requirements of Neo-Hellenism and to the solution of contemporary political and economic problems was consonant with his own.

THE BYZANTINE AND OTTOMAN
EMPIRES AFTER ANKARA

Some General Observations

The boundaries of the Byzantine world from the time of the battle of
Ankara (1402) to the accession of Murad II (1421) included, besides the
capital itself, a few small cities and towns along the Sea of Marmara—St.
Stephanos, Epivatae, Selymbria, Herakleia—and the Black Sea—Medea,
Agathopolis (Aktopol), Pyrgos (Burgas), Anchialus (Pomoriye), Mesembria (Nesebar), Varna (Stalin). Present-day Thrace and Eastern Rumelia,
which had only recently been occupied, were still known to travellers of
the fifteenth century as Hellas or Graecia or Grèce,[1] whereas Asia Minor
was already being called Turkey.[2] Also belonging to the Byzantine Empire
was the coastal district from the Strymon River (which included Chalcidice and Thessalonica) to the center of the Malian Gulf, along with
the coast of Thessaly and an undefined segment of its hinterland, as well
as the town and district of Lamia. The Despotate of Morea, of course,
was also part of the Byzantine Empire. In addition, Scyrus and the islands
of the northern Sporades fell within the Empire, but since they harbored
nests of pirates, Byzantine sovereignty there was scarcely more than
nominal.[3]

The Emperors still exercised a shadowy suzerainty over Thracian Ainos
(now Turkish Enos) and the islands of the Northern Aegean—Lemnos,
Imbros, Samothrace, and Thasos—though these were also tributaries of
the Genoese house of Gattilusi.[4] This was a time when the financial resources of the Empire were as meager as its social and religious problems
were great. The Byzantine gold piece (the celebrated bezant of the
Crusaders), which had for centuries broadcast its wealth and strength

throughout the markets of the world, had lost its value and practically ceased to circulate outside the Empire. This was a consequence of the Palaeologi's practice of continually debasing the coinage in order to finance their manifold projects and needs.[5]

Commerce and navigation had fallen into the hands of foreigners, Venetians and Genoese in particular, who wielded immense economic power in Constantinople and the ports of the Aegean and Black Seas.[6] They vied with one another to see who could most profitably sap the Empire. Venetian loans, which were offered to Byzantine Emperors in exchange for commercial concessions, also contributed to the economic ruin of the Empire.[7] Kydones had described the humiliation of John V at the hands of Venetian merchants: "surety having been given and the promise of a loan extracted from the moneylender, he then turns around and reneges on his pledge and thus contributes to the worsening of an already desperate economic plight," adding that "to a merchant, money is more precious than his eyes."[8] Financial exploitation of this kind was hardly less significant than fundamental religious antagonism in deepening Byzantine hostility towards the West. Therefore the Emperors cast around for new ways of meeting the financial commitments of the Empire and paying the heavy tribute demanded by the Turks (which, in 1432, was 10,000 gold pieces)[9] and could only hit upon new taxes, of which they devised a ruinous number.[10]

Certain extant descriptions of travellers shed an illuminating light on the Empire's social decay. For example, the Spaniard, Pero Tafur, a nobleman himself, remarked in 1433 that in no part of the world did the nobility enjoy so much freedom (license, of course, is what he meant) as in Greece. Nowhere else were serfs so dependent on the nobility; in effect, they were the chattel slaves of noblemen.[11] Similarly, Schiltberger, who was a captive of the Turks at the end of the fourteenth century, had written that his masters criticized wealthy Byzantines so volubly mainly because of their gross behavior towards the poor, which was why the Turks considered this to be one of the reasons God had decided to deprive Christians of their lands and give them to the Turks.[12]

The political and economic collapse of the Byzantine Empire was paralleled by its intellectual decline. "Who," Manuel Calecas had asked some time before 1390, "in the midst of this debacle would want to worry about learning when every moment one's very life is in danger?" Nor did the capital itself avoid the effects of intellectual blight. Its inhabitants could no longer form a clear picture of the purposes and meaning of learning. According to Calecas, they were no longer impressed by the ideals of the sort of teacher who was modest, dispassionate, and purposeful, but rather (and here he seems to have had a particular person in mind) by those of the gross and self-conceited blusterer whose precepts were just what might be expected from a "great, hairy, fleshy" creature.[13] The fifteenth-century traveller, Christopher Buondelmonti, also accused the people of the capital of being avaricious and totally indifferent to their past glories.[14]

The future seemed black indeed. Only the West, perhaps, could have saved the Empire. To that end, Manuel II and John VIII entered into fitful negotiations with the Pope and his curia and finally subscribed to the Union of the Churches at the Council of Florence in 1439. The decisions of the Council for many years bewildered the Orthodox in Frankish-occupied lands. The Pope lost no time in sending Catholic bishops to the islands of the Aegean and granting special privileges to those Orthodox who demonstrated their eagerness for Union.[15] In Crete, especially, the efforts to gain acceptance of Union were so sustained that a Unionist party emerged among the Orthodox.[16] Still, very few of the leaders of that society (particularly scholars and priests, among them was the bibliographer, John Plousiadenos, who was also noted for his literary and musical talents)[17] were for financial, political, and social reasons disposed to support Union. As for the people as a whole, they resisted the blandishments of foreign bishops and their Greek puppets and remained faithful to Orthodoxy.[18] They were guided by the circulars and letters of many—Marc Eugenicus and George Scholarios, to mention only two—who opposed Union and urged further resistance to the imposition of Western dogma.[19]

The struggle of Helen Palaeologina in Cyprus for the welfare of her compatriots also appears to have received definite, if unintentional, assistance from the Council of Florence. In spite of initial resentment in Greek lands under Frankish occupation at the decisions of the Council, the consequences which soon flowed from those decisions were vastly different from those the Catholic Church had anticipated. As Hackett observes, when Pope Eugenius

announced to the nations of the West that, as a result of the Conclave, the once-despised Orthodox were now not merely of one flesh and blood, but also of the same faith with themselves, it seemed to many of these Latin settlers no act of apostasy to abandon their ancestral creed for one which by their own spiritual head had been pronounced so absolutely identical with their own.

This development, entirely unforeseen, was immediately opposed by Eugene and his successor, Nicholas V, both of whom sought to reverse this drift among Franks in Greek countries. Writing to the Inquisitor and Exarch of the "province of Greece," Nicholas ordered that appropriate measures be taken to eradicate the evil, if need be with the assistance and backing of the civil arm:

The Pope, while disclaiming any idea of condemning the tenets of the Orthodox, protests that it is not permissible to thus mix up the two rites—an act neither intended, nor sanctioned, by the Council of Florence.

But so far as the Cypriots were concerned, as Hackett points out, these measures met with no success whatever.[20]

It was from this time that the area of dissension between Unionists and anti-Unionists began to resemble a battleground. "Union became division."[21] Among the Byzantine delegates to the Council were Antonios, Archbishop of Heraclea, and Dorotheos, Archbishop of Trebizond, and others who had subscribed to Union only with considerable reluctance. On their return, they were so completely taken aback by the bitter disapproval of their actions which they encountered everywhere that they disavowed their stands and repudiated their signatures.[22] The conservative spirit of Orthodoxy reasserted itself.

John VIII, who lacked the diplomatic finesse of Manuel II, found himself utterly incapable of coping with the revolt of the clergy, particularly the monks, and the opposition of an equally zealous populace. The people stayed away from Masses celebrated by Unionist priests, whom they looked upon as infamous, and Marc Eugenicus, the chief protagonist of Orthodoxy and leader of the anti-Unionist party, fought for his cause eloquently and unceasingly. After his death in 1445,[23] his disciple, George Kourtesis (Scholarios), continued the struggle. But the Empire deemed it politically expedient to support the Union cause despite its unpopularity. This attempted rapport with the West and the continued comings and goings of the Byzantines were meanwhile watched by the Turks with growing annoyance. They resolved to put a stop to the proceedings. In the opinion of Sphrantzes at least, it was indeed the Union of the Churches which was the "first and foremost" reason for the eventual capture of Constantinople.[24]

As against this state of affairs in Constantinople, the situation among the Ottomans was quite different. As an example, we may turn to the organization of the Turkish army and quote the striking description provided by Bertrandon de la Brocquière, who saw it in 1432 or 1433:

They are good-looking, of medium height and build, with long beards. I am well aware of the expression "strong as a Turk," yet I have seen many Christians who surpass the Turks in this regard . . .

They are diligent, willingly rise early, and live on little food, being satisfied with badly baked bread, raw meat dried in the sun, milk, curdled or not, honey,

Figure 13. John VIII Palaeologus.

cheese, grapes, fruit, vegetables, and a mere handful of flour, with which they make a soup—enough to sustain six or eight men for a whole day. . . . They think nothing of sleeping on the ground.

Their dress consists of two or three cotton tunics, thrown over one another, which fall to their feet. Over these they wear a robe made of felt, like a mantle, which they call a *capinat*. This garment, though light, withstands the rain, and some are very fine and handsome. They wear knee-length boots and long pantaloons, which may be of red velvet, silk, fustian, or common stuff. When on the march or in battle, they pull up their tunics and tuck them into their trousers so they can move more freely.

Their horses are good, cost little in food, gallop well and for a long time. They feed them only at night, and then only five or six handfuls of barley and double the quantity of chopped hay . . . Nearly all their horses are gelded; a few are kept as stallions, but so few that I have never seen a single stallion. . . .

Their headgear consists of a round white cap, ornamented with plates of iron on all sides to protect the whole head and the neck. It is about six inches high and ends in a point . . . They sink deeply into their saddles, as if in an armchair, and keep their knees very high in short stirrups; in this position, the least thrust from a lance is enough to unseat them.

The weapons of those who possess reasonable means are a bow, a shield, a sword, and a strong, short-handled mace spiked at one end. The last is a vicious weapon . . . I am convinced that a strong blow from it on a helmeted head would stun a man. Several of the Turks have small wooden bucklers with which they cover themselves well on horseback when they draw the bow. . . .

The soldier's obedience to his leaders is unequivocal . . . his great feats of arms and the resounding conquests which have made him master of a land more extensive than all of France are mainly due to that constant obedience.

I have been assured that, whenever Christians have taken up arms against them, the Turks have never been caught unawares. Whenever the Christians are after them, the Turkish commander selects men to spy out the enemy's march and sends his army forward two or three days' march from the place where he has decided to fight. If he considers the circumstances favorable, he falls upon the enemy suddenly, adopting a different order of march. A big drum gives the signal, and the front-line troops move forward noiselessly; those behind also follow quietly without disturbing the ranks in any way. Men and horses alike are trained to the exercise, and ten thousand Turks advancing in this fashion make less noise than a hundred armed Christians. . . . The Turks attack on the run, and since they are all lightly armed they cover a distance of three days' normal march between nightfall and dawn. Trained in these tactics, they could not possibly wear full armor like the French and the Italians. . . . Yet by the very speed of their advance, they nearly always succeed in their various battles in taking the Christians by surprise and crushing them. . . .

The manner in which they deploy for battle varies according to the circumstances. When they decide that a particular place offers favorable opportunities for attack, they separate into several corps, the actual number depending on the size of the army, and they press the attack from different sides. Since they have mastered the art of converging their various corps, wooded or hilly country presents no difficulties, and this particular technique is commonly employed in such places.

At other times, they prefer ambush. A few well-armed men are sent to search out the enemy, and, if he is reported unprepared, an immediate decision is made to take advantage of the situation. But if they find the enemy prepared and in orderly array, they surround his army at the distance of an arrow's flight and then press hit-and-run attacks continually from all sides. Backwards and forwards, punishing man and beast alike, the Turks keep up the attacks until the enemy is thrown into confusion. . . . The lightning speed with which they move enables them, almost by this alone, to inflict defeat upon the Christians almost invariably. Even when retiring from the field of battle, they use their bow with such deadly skill and accuracy as rarely to miss either horseman or horse.

Each mounted Turk has a small tabor attached to the front of his saddle. If the commander, or any officer, descries any disorderliness in an enemy advance, he beats the tabor three times, which is the signal for everyone within earshot to do the same. In a moment, every man is thus alerted to rally round his leader and, depending upon the circumstances, either to receive an attack in well-ordered array or to join his squadron in a series of sharp counterattacks on all sides.

In pitched battles, they sometimes adopt other tactics. In order to terrify the horses, fire is hurled into the midst of the opposing cavalry; or large numbers of camels or dromedaries, each chosen for his spiritedness and stoutness of heart, are driven ahead of the front-line troops.

These are some of the ways in which the Turks have been fighting the Christians until now. Certainly I do not wish to speak ill of them or to underrate them . . . nevertheless, I am quite sure that well-trained armies, properly led, could easily triumph over them. . . ." [25]

The size of these irregular armies was always fluid. Various accounts estimate them to contain as few as 50,000 men (30,000 from Anatolia and 20,000 from Rumelia) [26] and as many as 120,000. In the latter case, approximately half were mounted and well armed with shield and sword, while the remainder were poorly armed and on foot. Some of these foot soldiers carried only a sword or a bow, and many had no more than a club. Nevertheless, the Turkish infantryman was generally considered better than his Greek counterpart and, by any standards, an excellent soldier.[27] Ducas is in general agreement with Brocquière's description of Turkish infantry: "They no sooner hear the herald's call to battle, which in their language is called akın, than they advance in a seething and agitated mass, most of them without kitbag or rucksack, without spear, bow, or sword; most of them, in fact, with no more than a club and a single intent . . . to capture a Christian." [28] The jumbled appearance of an army composed of such infantry inspired Brocquière to add the indignant comment that "it is Christendom's great shame to be beaten into submission by such people, who are much less formidable than they think." [29]

In conquered territories, the sultans introduced the system of spahi feudatories to bolster their authority. Some of these, the *Hisar-eri* or *Kale-eri*, occupied castles and constituted regular fortress garrisons throughout the fifteenth century.[30]

The Turks of this period were still a folk with simple customs, imbued with the faith, fanaticism, and frenzy of newly-converted Moslems.[31] They also had the natural robustness of a people inured to the primitive hardships of a life spent in tents summer and winter [32] and raised in an heroic atmosphere of *chansons de geste*.[33] They had a lust for plunder and perhaps, too, for the incidental gain of feudal seignory. Their fiefs, of course, resembled those of the Franks and the Byzantine *pronoia*. However, the fief-holders, as we have seen, had only the temporary usufruct of their fiefs, which were always revocable at the will of the sultan. They did not form a closed class in the manner of the feudal lords of the West; neither did they behave abominably towards the common people as did their Byzantine counterparts, who had succeeded in having the transmission of *pronoia* made heritable.

Turkish moral standards and outlook were of course derived from the precepts of the Koran and the religio-ethical ideas of the *Akhis*,[34] all of which had substantive application in everyday life. Compassion and charity in particular, especially towards those of the same faith, brought everlasting rewards in paradise. These two ideals accounted for the charitable works which were characteristically prolific in Islam—the foundation of mosques, poorhouses, fountains, bridges, religious schools (*medrese*), and the like.

Many contemporary travellers provided interesting testimony to the moral virtues of the Ottoman Turks during peacetime: they were compassionate, cheerful, charitable, sincere, honest, and, when the need arose, courageous. According to Pero Tafur, "The Turks are a noble people, much given to truth. They live in their country like nobles, in their expenditure and in their actions, in the matter of food and of sports, in which latter there is much gambling. They are very merry and benevolent, and of good conversation, so much so that in those parts, when one speaks of virtue, it suffices to say one is like a Turk." [35] With their appreciation of moral values and their respect for social justice, the Turks certainly seemed to live on a higher plane than the Byzantines and other Christians.

Certainly, this was what the Turks themselves felt, and this was their principal moral weapon against the Christians. They could not stomach the Byzantines, those conceited sophisticates—men who looked upon all others as barbarians while themselves transgressing the laws of their Bible. The Turks thought that "therefore Almighty God has decreed that they should take the land from [Byzantine] Christians, because they do not conduct their affairs, spiritual or temporal, with justice, because they look to wealth and favor, and the rich treat the poor with haughtiness and do not help them either with gifts or with justice and do not hold to the doctrine which the Messiah has given them." The Turks, who were astonished at the ease with which they defeated Christians, searched for an explanation and found it precisely in their social iniquities: the Turks were the chosen instruments of God's retribution. Their conquest of Christian lands could not be explained in terms of their own strength, wisdom, or holiness, but rather in terms of the injustice, ignominy, and arrogance of Christians. The bad deportment of the Turks towards the Byzantines is probably attributable to this belief. At the same time, its corollary was that Turks and Moslems would only be successful in conquest for as long as the spiritual and temporal leaders of Christendom persisted in their unjust and corrupt ways. The Turkish books of prophecy were quite explicit on this point.[36] It was a telling augury, all the more so because it had its Greek analogues (which we shall later show), and it survived until the Greek revolution of 1821 [37] —indeed until present times.[38]

Such ideas as these not only formed the basis of the Turkish view of the world but could also be used effectively in imposing it. They could not have been unknown to the Byzantines—to the philosopher, Gemistos, for example, who had lived and studied in Bursa (Prusa) under the Jewish teacher, Elissaeus, and may well have influenced him in the formulation of his social reforms.

While the social and political ideas of Gemistos and his followers were being propounded as a solution to the critical condition of the Byzantine Empire, a ten-year struggle for supremacy between Bayezid's sons came to an end (1403–1413), and the Turks, after reorganizing their forces, resumed their advance against what remained of the Byzantine Empire.

Murad II

After the battle of Ankara in 1402, unity was restored to the Ottoman Empire during the period of Mohammed I's sole reign (1413–1421) and the reign of Murad II (1421–1451). The old passion for conquest soon revived among the Turks, along with their engagingly sung [39] epics, full of national and religious sensitivity, pride and fervor.

Murad II was short, fat, and dark-complexioned, with mongoloid features, exaggerated cheek-bones, beady eyes, a huge hooked nose, and a rounded beard. Although his predilections were for peace rather than war (which only interfered with the pleasures of sodomy, the harem, and wine-bibbing), he nevertheless exhibited formidable military and administrative abilities.[40] Among his Turkish subjects, he came to be regarded as gentle, good, just, and generous. Also, he adopted the practice of his predecessors of distributing fiefs among those whom he wished to honor. These, as we have seen, were obliged in time of war to furnish the sultan with a stipulated number of men and to accompany their lord into battle.[41]

In 1422, one year after Murad II ascended the throne, Turkish armies besieged Constantinople, laid waste the surrounding countryside, captured and forcibly removed the inhabitants living in the environs of the capital.[42] Manuel II, now an old man, watched the storm "pensively" and reflected how inert the inheritance of the past, the ancient and glorious Byzantine traditions, had become. "We no longer need an emperor," he confessed to his courtier, Sphrantzes, "but a financial wizard." [43]

On 21 July 1425, Manuel II died, to be succeeded by John VIII (1425–1448). Murad proceeded to detach Varna and the districts of the Strymon River and Zituni (Lamia) from the Empire. It was hardly more than a formal gesture, however, since the governor of Zituni had already recognized his inability to ward off the Turks: two years before, he had ceded Stylis and Avlaki to the Venetians.[44]

The capital slowly became deserted, with whole quarters uninhabited. The patriarchal Church of the Apostles, with its sumptuous, porphyry tombs of the Byzantine Emperors, had already succumbed to the ravages of time. Constantine XI (1449–1453), the last of the Palaeologi, found himself unable to restore his crumbling palace. Most of the population was in flight to the imagined security of distant places. As for those who stayed, ubiquitous poverty, beggarly attire, and uniformly low spirits spoke eloquently of the sufferings already endured and still to come.[45]

It is all the more astonishing, therefore, to watch the exhausted citizens drawing upon some untapped reservoir of strength and continuing to resist the Turks. A number of reasons of course underlay this pertinacity: we need only reiterate here their remembrance of the past—an historical consciousness which subserved national precognition. The living organism of Hellenism, that is to say, was transmuted into a new Hellenism by the stubborn will to survive. It was a will whose force was attested by Pero Tafur when he wrote that Thrace had become depopulated "because the Greeks carried the entire burden of war and were subjected to great cruelty by the Turks." [46] Or as the last Byzantine historian Critobulus pointed out, the Turks were opposed to the last by

the "forces of the Romans" on land and sea and met with much resistance and a fighting spirit.[47]

A similar fate befell Thessalonica, the capital of Macedonia. Bürak Bey,
son of Evrenos, invested it in June 1422, and then proceeded to pillage
the neighboring district of Kalamaria, to the east as far as Cassandrea
(ancient Potidaea).[48] According to a benefactress of the Mt. Athos monastery of St. Dionysius in 1420,[49] there were many inhabitants of the city
who, "in the oppressive atmosphere of this impending storm," had fallen
like herself "from wealth, glory, and prosperity" into utter poverty. Many,
indeed, were suffering from hunger. That was why about eight thousand
had abandoned their homes and left the city. In 1423, the governor of
Thessalonica, Andronicus Palaeologus, and the local nobility saw no alternative but to deliver Thessalonica into the hands of the Venetians, on
the condition that municipal autonomy, archepiscopal rights, and the
privileges of the Church would be respected.[50] The precedent for such a
move already existed in the case of Corfu (see page 107 above).

After the death of Manuel II, Murad II stepped up military activities
against Thessalonica and Lamia, and again Turkish forces ravaged the
countryside in the vicinity of both towns. But at the end of 1425 or the
beginning of 1426, after John VIII agreed to the surrender of Varna and
the districts of Strymon and Lamia, the harassment ceased.[51]

So, for a few more years, the Venetians remained in Thessalonica.
But it was not a very comfortable stay. The Turks were intent on making
their position untenable, and the Greeks accused them of breaking their
promises and violating the rights of the community.

What were these rights? It is vital to know them since, constituting
as they did a concrete system of privilege, they enabled Thessalonica to
preserve without interruption until the very end of the Turkish occupation the traditional framework of communal life that had made her a
stronghold of Hellenism. First in importance among these was the Senate
(sometimes called Council) or, as it seems to have been popularly known,
the "Twelve"; it is referred to in fourteenth-century Byzantine texts. Its
composition was predominantly aristocratic, though burghers were included in it. Intimate knowledge of the customs of the land was a necessary qualification for membership, and the institution's responsibilities
were to take charge of civic affairs and (in the absence of central authority) defense. The Venetians, however, suspended its prerogatives over
the protests of the people of Thessalonica and in spite of written guaran-
tees to the contrary. It cannot have met more than a few times during
the entire period of Venetian control. However, it is probable that the
council of twelve Notables, which functioned with broad governmental
and judicial powers until the last years of Turkish rule, was a continua-

tion of this original Council of Nobles.[52] Evidence provided by a metropolitan deed of sale, dated 1502, and signed by clerical officials and "nobles of the city" establishes this connection. Professor Stilpon Kyriakidis, who published the document, stresses the need to examine this evidence carefully for the light it can throw on the form of government of Thessalonica.[53] The first question to be asked is, what was the composition of the Senate? If their signatures are counted the riddle is resolved, for there were twelve: twelve members of a municipal council of whom a majority of seven were clergy. The deduction that the "Twelve" was a continuation of the earlier council of Notables would appear to be sound if account is taken of the various references to "ministers of God" who were members of the Council at the end of the fourteenth century (see page 124 above). As for its structure at that time, it is likely that the election of its members would have taken place "in accordance with the wealth and personal merit" of each, to use Aristotle's phrase. In these circumstances, it would have been in no way extraordinary for clergy, together with nobles, to comprise the mainstay of municipal organization. We may assume, therefore, that the structure was the same both before and during the period of Turkish rule.

Another right the Venetians had granted the people of Thessalonica was that of being tried before their own archepiscopal court in accordance with custom. Information concerning this privilege contributes to a fuller understanding of the central and continuing points of Greek law throughout the periods of Venetian and Turkish domination. The judicial authority of the archbishop, following "ancient custom," was this: "To be able to sit in judgment in every case where a person wishes to appeal to his judgment, and where a litigant seeks to establish his rights in some dispute to be able without let or hindrance to oblige the opposing party to appear before the hearing . . . the decisions and arbitraments of the archbishop to have legal validity without fear of contravention and the archbishop to be free to collect all entitlements arising from his decisions on the basis of custom . . ." Thus, the judgments of an archbishop were binding on both parties in any suit.

These privileges were not confined to the archbishops of Thessalonica. Generally speaking, all bishops had acquired extensive civil jurisdiction after the judicial reforms of Andronicus III Palaeologus and in particular from the creation of the institution of "general judges" (catholikoi kritai) in 1329. Four judges comprised a supreme court, with a bishop as the presiding member. In this way, the Church came to exercise substantial influence in civil matters. The reforms of Andronicus III thus set an important precedent for the continuation of episcopal jurisdiction during the period of Turkish rule, and the continuum was preserved. The conse-

quences of this for a captive nation were salutary indeed, for communal
life could still cohere around the traditional institution. We recognize in
the prerogatives of bishops during the Turkish period the same judicial
authority, following ancient custom, of the former archbishops of Thessalonica.[54]

To the extent then that local autonomy remained under both Venetian
and Turkish rule, the judicial privileges of archbishops and their court
assessors formed an integral part of it. In Thessalonica, certain members
of the Twelve probably themselves constituted a sort of lower court, while
the archbishop presided over a high court. The traveller Robert de Dreux
noted in 1666 that the Christians of Thessalonica, along with Jews and
Turks, possessed their own separate courts (*"y avaient aussi leur justice"*).[55] Presumably, these institutions were maintained during the
Turkish occupation not only in Thessalonica but throughout the entire
Hellenic world. That is, civic Notables, aldermen, bishops, and Church
officials continued to dispense justice indulgently according to traditional
prescription and in conformity with the main written source of law, the
Procheiron or the *Hexabiblos* of that "most respected guardian of the
law and judge of Thessalonica," Constantine Armenopoulos.

Venetian rule in Thessalonica, though of brief duration (1423–1430),
was distressing enough. Hunger persisted in spite of occasional attempts
by the Venetians to mitigate its worst effects, at least among those appointed to defend the city, by bringing in money and food. But many
had nothing at all to eat and fled to Constantinople,[56] Turkish occupied
territory,[57] or other Venetian colonies. On 29 March 1430, there was a
successful Turkish assault, and for three whole days the city was given
over to the plunder, slaughter, and imprisonment of its inhabitants.[58]
Many of the people of Thessalonica hastily adopted Islam.[59] The inci-
dence of religious abnegation in rural areas was probably far higher.
Murad II was quick to reassure the inhabitants. In an effort to populate
the city again, he invited back those who had fled and brought in others
from different parts of the Empire. A number of these were entrusted
with garrison duty, alongside Turks, in the turrets of the sea walls, and
in return were exempted from various taxes.[60]

At this time, too, the municipal council of Thessalonica would appear
to have been restored.

After capturing Thessalonica, Murad II next thrust against northern
Epirus, and quickly subdued parts of it. He then marched to the south
of Ioannina, thus transferring his military operations to the region [61] ruled
by Carlo II Tocco (1429–1448).[62] The capital of Epirus capitulated on
9 October 1430. This surrender took place, however, after the metropolitan of the city and its Greek and Serbian noblemen received a promise

from Valesi Sinan Paşa,[63] the governor of the European provinces of the Ottoman Empire that is, Rumelia, that certain rights and privileges would be reserved to the inhabitants. The Turkish general gave written assurances that the people of Ioannina "need have no fear that they will be taken captive or their children abducted, that churches will be destroyed or turned into mosques [Masgidi]. The bells of the churches will continue to ring. *The Metropolitan [of Ioannina] will retain his judicial prerogatives and all other ecclesiastical rights, and nobles will be allowed to keep their fiefs.* Ancestral rights, property and personal possessions will be guaranteed without question, and *anything else you ask for will be granted."* A great many copies of this document, which was in Greek and known as the "Order [Orismos] of Sinan Paşa," have been preserved. This document is of great importance in tracing the history of community privileges because it is not only the oldest Turkish document known to exist in a Greek center but it probably also served as a model for other subsequent "Orders." [64]

The reference to the judicial rights of the metropolitan commands our attention because these were the same kinds of rights the Venetians had accorded the people of Thessalonica. No less interesting are the reference to noblemen and the additional concession that "anything else you ask for will be granted."

The right of Christian lords to keep their fiefs is also attested in oral tradition, which speaks of the so-called Christian spahis of Epirus who were required to accompany the sultans on their military expeditions. For two centuries, whenever an order arrived from the sultan, the feudal lords of Delvino, Argyrokastron, Paramythia, Konitsa, and many other places foregathered in Ioannina, whence they would set out to war bearing aloft the banners of St. George. Only on arrival at the Pindus Mountains would they fold these away and unfurl the Turkish standards.[65]

After the conquest of Ioannina in the spring of 1432, Umur Bey, son of Sarutza Bey, was charged with recording all land titles in the official registry of the province (*sancak*) of Albania.[66] By this means, of course, Ottoman control in Epirus and Albania could be more effectively imposed. At the same time, this act immediately provoked the Albanians into determined opposition and marked the beginning of their active resistance against the Turks.[67]

From the book of registered titles of the *sancak* (which has been published by Professor Inalcik), a great deal can be learned of the manner of provincial administration in this period; the toponymy of the region (which remained Greek to a noteworthy degree); the settlement in rural areas of Moslem foreigners or Christian converts to Islam; the existence of great and petty feudal lords, chiefly Albanian and Turkish; and the

process of rapid conversion to Islam of Christian lords who were indigenous to the region. Although it is true that the records often mention
the names of Christians who were brothers or fathers of converts, the
reader of these lists would quickly form the impression, from the pre-
ponderance of Moslem, converted Moslem, and spahi feudal lords, that
Christian spahis were a tiny minority and soon disappeared altogether.
Yet this would be a misleading conclusion, for there were in fact (as we
have already noticed from the evidence of oral tradition) a large number
of Christian spahis in northern Epirus who remained faithful to Christianity. There were also many more who, after their apparent conversion
to Islam, continued for many years, even for centuries, not only to speak
Greek but secretly to practice their Christian religion.[68]

The earliest known registrations of people and economic resources in
the conquered territories (vilâyet tahriri) date from the time of Murad
II. The commissions which undertook this vital task of registration were
often headed by prominent military figures as, for example, Timurtaş
Bey, Halil Bey, Michal Oğlu Ali Bey, Tursun Bey, and others. Competent
recorders on the spot methodically assessed taxable capacity and carefully registered the names of persons and places in the book of titles.
This procedure was indispensable to the smooth functioning of the Ottoman governmental apparatus. Every twenty or thirty years, in the interests of more perfect justice, special commissions were formed to review
the original lists. Local Christians often served as recorders on these commissions—as well as local Moslem converts, when perhaps a more diligent
registration of names was required.[69]

The books themselves actually fell into two categories: the mufassal,
which registered taxation dues and also minutely detailed the economic
means of persons and places (and is therefore an invaluable guide to
nomenclature); and the icmâl, which recorded only the names of feudal
lords and the villages in their fiefs.[70] Needless to say, a full and comprehensive study of the relevant archives will one day uncover new and
vital evidence bearing upon the history of modern Hellenism.

Also dating from the period of Murad II are numerous valuable sources
which deal with the mobilization of raias for the purpose of meeting the
military needs of the Ottoman Empire.

11

IMPRESSMENT OF CHRISTIANS

Reorganization of the Janissaries

Shortly before the capture of Thessalonica, Murad II authorized the compulsory recruitment of Christian boys who were subjects of the Ottoman Empire.[1] According to Uzunçarsılı, his motives were twofold: to fill out the ranks of the janissaries, thereby creating an army in peak fighting condition capable of resuming the Ottoman conquests which had been brought to a halt in the wake of internal troubles after the battle of Ankara; and gradually to build up the number of Moslems in Rumelia, the Balkan peninsula that was in fact the place where impressment of Christian boys first took place. The first of these motives, if not altogether spurious, was certainly the less important of the two; but in any case it is much more likely that Murad II's sole concern was simply to ensure the strength of the janissaries by a regular recruitment of Christians without regard to the success of his military operations.

The reorganization was a decisive one. As Sphrantzes says, "Murad II gave the janissaries special privileges and issued instructions which gave them the institutional form they have retained to this day. Their former role was quite different, as different indeed as the very clothes they wore. Now they were ordered to forsake marriage altogether so as not to be preoccupied with the care of wives and children and thus to be able to devote all their energies solely to military pursuits. They became "the sons of the sultan." These were not Murad II's only reforms, nor indeed were they necessarily new, as Sphrantzes would have us believe. There are a number of problems associated with the practice of impressing Christian boys which may remain forever unsolved, not least that of determining the extent to which the new organization and system of recruitment of janissaries were in fact Murad's original innovations or merely the adaptation of older policies. For the moment at least, I think we must accept the fact that Murad's policies were refinements of traditional arrangements for the recruitment and education of Christian captives and that the emergence of the janissaries as the distinctive force with which we are familiar was simply the outcome of a systematic revision and consolidation of those arrangements. It is just that the extent of Murad's reorganization and the quality of his reforms left such an impression on posterity that it obscured the work of his predecessors and gave rise to the notion that it was he who had instigated the impressment of Christian children and originated the institution of janissaries.[2] For it was not long before the new organization made itself felt in a renewal of the strength and minatory disposition of the Turkish army.

Candidates for the ranks of the janissaries (called *acem oğlan*) were henceforth recruited either from among captive Christians or from among the Christian subjects of the Ottoman Empire. The latter method was much the more usual. At first, impressments were carried out every five years, though later, depending on the exigencies of warfare, these periods were reduced to every one, two, three, or four years.[3] The janissaries were the only truly organized component of the Turkish army under Murad II. The rest, the *akıntzıs,* were irregulars.

Christian Spahis

Besides the janissaries and *akıntzıs* in the armies of Murad II and those of his predecessors, Murad I and Bayezid I, there were also a number of Christian auxiliary armies. These, as previously noted, comprised the armies of tributary Christian kings as well as Christian feudal lords (*hırıstiyan timar-erleri*) or Christian spahis, the Christian livery servants, and others—all of whom were exempt from certain taxes.[4] The spahis were normally knights from the several Christian states of the Balkan peninsula who had preferred to submit to the Turks in consideration of being allowed to retain their fiefs.[5] They consisted not only of Greeks, but also of Bulgarians, Albanians, Vlachs, and Serbs, who, however much they may have detested the despotic ways of the sultans, were nonetheless required to follow them to war. "If they had only seen other Christians, and above all the French, take up arms against the Sultan," wrote Brocquière, "then I do not doubt that they would have turned their backs on him and inflicted considerable injury upon him." [6] According to J. Torzelo, the Christian spahis and their men may have numbered as many as fifty thousand.[7]

These Christian knights and landowners existed as a class only at the tolerance of the Ottoman state. The merest soupçon of suspicion that they were engaged in seditious activities against the Empire was enough to lead to the prompt sequestration of their lands. Financial self-interest therefore shackled them to the new regime. And as an auxiliary arm of the main Turkish forces they proved extraordinarily useful in the process of conquest and consolidation.[8] Without them, large numbers of Turks would have been tied down to garrison duty in the numerous fortresses of the Empire.[9]

The sultans were therefore indulgent towards "infidels" who showed themselves ready to submit and to co-operate. And yet it must still evoke our admiration that they were able not only to hold the allegiance of such a large, heterogeneous, and alien-speaking group, but to send them as military allies against people of the same religion, to enjoy the fruits of their victories, and even in the fullness of time, as we shall see, to assimilate them.

This process can be followed in the official Books of Titles of two separate years (1454–1455 and 1466–1467) during the reign of Mohammed II. It can be ascertained beyond question, for example, that certain of the local nobility—Albanian, Arvanito-Vlach, and Greek—in the Turkish districts of Trikkala, Phanarion, and Agrafa were permitted to retain their properties by agreeing to co-operate with the Turks. This situation had already come about by the time Ömer Bey, son of the provincial governor of Thessaly, Turhan or Turahan, held sway in the particular *sancak* which incorporated these districts. All told, in 1466–1467 there were twenty-three districts (*nâhiye*) in the *sancak*, including Mikira-li, Platamon, Lidorikion, Domokos, and Chatalja (Pharsala). There were 182 fiefs in the *sancak* (1454–1455), of which thirty-six were held by Christian spahis.[10] In the district of Trikkala, for instance, we find mention of a fief belonging to Demetrius, son of one of the first of the spahis (*kadîmi sipâhi*), Michael, as well as various others belonging to the many sons of Mikira(?),[11] who was apparently a powerful figure and an extensive landowner in the district. One of the largest districts in the whole province of Trikkala took its name from Mikira (Mikira-li) and another from the prominent spahi, Kravaldi(?). There is little doubt that the present name, Kravari, is derivative of this Kravaldi. The sons of Mikira, Peter, and Mustafa (whose name surely points to his conversion to Islam) were jointly seised of one of the fiefs in Mikira-li; jointly given was another fief to three other sons, Iglava, Domeniko, and Mouzeraki; a third fief went to still another son, Paul. These fiefs have probably given their names to the present-day villages of Domeniko and Mouziariko in the neighborhood of Trikkala. The names of the members of this powerful family would seem to indicate that they were of Albanian or

Arvanito-Vlach origin. Similarly, from the Book of Titles for the year 1466–1467, we learn that there were twenty-four shepherd holdings in Levadia held by Albanians and thirty-four in the district of Thebes (Istifa). By this time, there were only twenty Christians among the 343 spahis in the district, a mere four of whom were fief-holders—proof enough of the inexorable, if gradual, conversion to Islam of feudal lords. Apart from the twenty Christian spahis, another nineteen whose fathers had been Christian were recent converts.[12]

The Albanians and Arvanito-Vlachs who had settled in the rugged province of Trikkala and generally throughout western Thessaly and Epirus lived nomadic lives in the manner of other mountain peoples. They had intermixed with the Vlachs of the Pindus Mountains and probably also with Slavs who still remained from early migrations and from the more recent incursions of Stephen Dušan.[13] It is only in these terms, I think, that we can explain the existence in Trikkala in 1454–1455 of Christian feudal lords with the names Boga and Pelegrin, whose father was called Bogoslav.[14] This conclusion would seem to be borne out by a reference in the *Chronicle of Proklos and Comnenus* to one Bouges (*Bouges*) or Bogoes (*Bogkoes*), which is certainly the same name as Boga in the Turkish sources. This Bogoes is described as "Serbo-Arvanito-Bulgaro-Vlach" in the *Chronicle*.[15]

In 1466–1467, the Bogoslav's fief became for a time the inheritance of his sons, Ali and Mustafa, both of whom were Moslem converts (*nev-müsülman*). Mustafa continued to manage half the fief, while the other eventually reverted to the sons of Pelegrin, Gön and Girgor. In the district of Trikkala in 1454–1455, mention was also made of the fief of Klazinos(?), which was jointly held by the sons of Mihos, Ostoya, and Miraş, together with Ahmed, converted son of one Gin.[16]

These examples, of course, point to the rapidity with which Christian lords were converted to Islam.[17] There are many instances of one son's becoming a Moslem while the other remained a Christian.[18] They probably hoped by this means to ensure that their property would remain in the bosom of the family,[19] for converts immediately took the title of Bey and were thereby entitled to aspire to the highest offices in the Empire.[20] Such conversions must have had an unsettling effect on the Christian peasants who worked their lands.

The fief-holders of western Thessaly and central Hellas who became converts to Islam were mainly of Albanian origin. Inalcik calls this to our attention and even attempts to trace their ancestry.[21] Of course the presence of many Albanians, or to be more precise, Arvanito-Vlachs, in these parts during the middle of the fifteenth century is to be expected from the remarks we have made *passim* about their settlement in the mountainous regions of Thessaly. A number of Greek lords were also to be found there: Demetrius, son of Theodore, for example; and in 1466–1467, Ilandari (Leondaris ?), cannoneer of the fortress of Zituni (Lamia). Both of these were fief-holders. So, too was Peter, among the first of the spahis, whose three sons in turn rendered military service to the sultan; they jointly inherited their father's fief in 1466–1467. Other lords, Moslem converts, appear to have had ancestors who were Greeks—Mustafa, son of Filatrino,[22] for instance, who was assuredly descended from the great Philanthropenos family.

Besides Christian spahis in the district of Trikkala, there is also mention of 103 Christian livery servants (*voynuklar*);[23] Christian livery servants served in the Turkish army until the sixteenth century.[24] The suitability of the open plain of Thessaly for the grazing of horses probably accounts for such a large number of such servants.

An Order of 1520 (that is, some fifty-four years later) affecting Trikkala mentions the existence of Albanian, Greek, and Vlach raias, but makes no mention whatsoever of Slavs.[25] Since Slav and Albanian foreigners had previously inundated this region, how are we to explain the sudden reappearance of Greeks and disappearance of Slavs? The fact that the Greeks are mentioned *after* the Albanians in this context is of course no indication that they were a minority in western Thessaly. Where then did they live? Perhaps we should recall that Trikkala, Phanarion, and Karditsa, with their neighboring villages and purlieus, were ancient centers of Hellenism. As for the Slavs, we can only assume that they had become assimilated by the end of the fifteenth century.

On the other hand, the explicit reference to Albanians attests to the extensive nature of their settlement. The fact that they intermixed, as did the Vlachs, with the Slav population probably supports the contention already advanced that they had also become bearers of Slav place-names. At the time of Murad II's reign, we observe, too, in Macedonia— in Kastoria, Nevrokop, Serrai, and Veles—a number of Christian lords of Slav and Greek origin. Again, some of their descendants became converts to Islam—Musa, son of Petko; Bayezid, son of Augustus; Umur, son of Theodore—to mention a few.[26]

There remains the problem of when the Christian spahis first appeared in Thessaly. If we attempt to deduce the event from the fact that the fief of Demetrius was inherited from his father, Michael, one of the first spahis, we arrive at the reign of Murad II or perhaps Mohammed I (1413–1421)—possibly even earlier, at the time of Bayezid I. For it is quite probable that immediately following Bayezid's conquest of Thessaly, Christian landowners who declared their fealty and willingness to co-operate were left unmolested, with the sole obligation to render military service to the sultan. This supposition would seem to be strength-ened by the fact that the practice of granting fiefs had begun as soon as the first Turkish armies of Bayezid occupied Thessaly. Of the 182 fiefs in the *sancak* of Trikkala, thirty-six were known to be Christian. The re-mainder had been apportioned among the military commanders of Evrenos and Turahan after the first Turkish invasion (and later among those who accompanied Turahan when he settled there permanently), as well as among the relatives and retainers of the Beys (*gulâm-i mîr*), the janissaries and other "slaves of the Porte" (*kapı-kulları*). Another, though less significant, category of fiefs consisted of those bestowed upon the Christian relatives of the converted palace retainers of Beys and civil functionaries (*gulâm-i mîr*). Still others were granted to the volunteer soldiers (*gönüllü*) and military heroes of renown (*garip yiğit*).[27]

Thus, the Albanian, Slav, Vlach, and Greek nobility of Thessaly sub-mitted to the Turks in order to avoid an imagined reign of terror if they refused. They chose to become vassals of the Turkish Empire in order to save their lives and their fortunes. Most of the nobles, it would seem, were converted to Islam in short shrift—by the second generation. In the following centuries, many local Moslem Beys and Agas were descended from them. And yet, it would also appear that the overwhelming majority of Vlach- and Greek-speaking people, together with other Albanian or Arvanito-Vlach settlers, simply withdrew into the mountain villages of the Pindus and its spurs. Here, notably in the district of Agrafa, but generally throughout Epirus and the west, they found the ideal refuge from persecution; and here, aided by the natural advantages which the region afforded, they staked new claims to life, liberty, and fortune. Here, too, the Albanians eventually became assimilated by Vlachs or Greeks, or else they finally emerged as Moslems. Only the Arvanito-Vlachs, as we have seen, preserved their former identity.

In sum, except for the large class of Turkish fief-holders, the possession of fiefs was limited to the small groups of *gulâm-i mîr*, *gönüllü*, and *garip yiğit*, or to the remnants of the Byzantine military oligarchy that had been absorbed into the class of Turkish feudal lords. On the whole, Christian raias were excluded from the official Ottoman hierarchy and military class. Indeed the Ottoman Empire, always mindful of its eco-nomic welfare, saw that the raias (*haracgüzâr re'âya*) were the chief productive element in the Empire and therefore could not lightly be released from payment of taxes by being allowed access to the military class. This was a fundamental principle enshrined in the codes of law (*Kanunname*), whose violation was expressly forbidden.[28]

Nevertheless, certain Christian raias came to perform duties of a military nature which exempted them from some taxes, in particular those of a supplemental kind (*avarizi divaniye*).[29] These duties usually involved the guarding of fortresses, narrow passes, and the like, and exemptions were granted by extraordinary decree. Those exempted were called *mu'âf ve müsellem,* meaning exempt from taxation, especially supplementary taxation. Even so, Christians who acted as garrison troops in fortresses in the interests of security came under the constant surveillance of Turkish soldiers.[30] In some cases, whole villages guarding narrow passes (*Dervenochoria*) were granted additional immunities besides total, or partial, exemption from taxation [31] in order to secure transportation and communication routes along which the official mails passed. Thus unruly peoples were won over and Turkish forces were freed for more urgent military commitments elsewhere.

The Greek Armatoles

A widespread institution under Turkish rule was that of the Christian Armatoles, a sort of militia entrusted with certain defensive and police duties. The question instantly arises: was there any connection between the Armatoles on the one hand and the system of Christian spahis or those other Christians exempt from taxes (*mu'âf ve müsellem*) on the other? Or did the Armatoles perhaps evolve from one or the other of these contemporary institutions? It must be admitted at the outset that the likelihood of there being any relationship between the Armatoles and the Christian spahis is remote indeed. The latter resembled the Byzantine military caste, from whose remnants it was to a large extent composed. Furthermore, there is no suggestion anywhere to be found that the duties of the spahis were similar to those of the Armatoles. This was not the case with the *mu'âf ve müsellem,* many of whom indeed served under the name Armatoles in various parts of the Balkan peninsula.[32]

But the Armatoles, at least of Greece, appear to have been a distinctive institution. Although first mentioned as auxiliaries of the Turkish armies at the time of Mohammed II,[33] certain coincidental evidence exists which fixes their origins in the reign of Mohammed's father, Murad II. In the valuable introduction, written in 1824, to his two-volume work on Greek folk songs, Fauriel noted that the institution of Armatoles first appeared in Thessaly. According to oral tradition among very old Greeks, the warlike and unsubdued people of the mountains used to come down into the plains, entering villages and towns and robbing Turks and raias with impunity.[34] The attackers assuredly emerged from the mountain range which bisects Greece, the Pindus. Here, especially in the Vlach-speaking district of Agrafa, the very remoteness of their abode provided perfect shelter and security.[35]

These western regions were not only far away from Constantinople and the main Turkish centers, but were also oriented towards the Venetian colonies of the Ionian Sea. Since arms could be replenished and help requested from these sources, the sultans had good reason to feel concerned about the disposition of their inhabitants. We may therefore give credence to the hitherto unverified evidence (probably based on Turkish sources), of the Phanariote, Rizos Neroulos, that the original seat of the Armatoles—the first *armatoliki*—was in Agrafa and that the Turks extended recognition to them in the reign of Murad II.[36] This evidence is borne out by another, much later, source to the effect that the Turks imposed only minimal imposts on these people, which were only rarely paid.[37]

If final proof be needed, we may turn to the comments of the traveller, Urquhart, who visited Tyrnavos in Thessaly in 1830. The Turkish commandant there, who was himself descended from the first Turkish provincial governor of Thessaly, Turahan Bey, told him that Murad II had established the system of Greek Armatoles after Turahan proposed it. This information was contained in an old Arabic manuscript from the library of Tyrnavos which set forth the life of Turahan. According to it, so Urquhart was told, Turahan had sanctioned the Armatoles in order to pacify Thessaly and to be rid of the nuisance of wild mountain people.[38] Thus, long before the capture of Constantinople, the first elements of a national fighting force took shape.

The system of Armatoles proved an effective device for controlling mountain people. In the western part of Greece, the densely forested mountains and ravines, the torrential rivers, the thick and generally rugged terrain provided extremely effective means of defense. By the same token, it was an advantageous base for guerrilla operations. And second to none as a place of refuge in these parts was the wilderness of Agrafa, a veritable labyrinth of peaks, ravines, valleys, and forests. Other similar places were Valtos and Xeromero, where the Tocco family still held sway. From Agrafa the inhabitants could easily pour down into the plain of Thessaly. In fact, it was in these places that those who did not follow the Toccos to Leukas and Cephalonia found refuge.[39] This untamed and self-willed people continued to exist in a semi-wild and semi-independent state until the 1821 revolution, controlling narrow mountain passes, harassing or halting transportation, and pillaging Turkish settlements in the plains.[40]

The Turks therefore found themselves among a hostile people. It could only have been a waste of time and manpower to attempt to penetrate and neutralize these mountain fastnesses far from the major centers of population. Moreover, their conquests in the region generally could not then be regarded as permanent; there were still formidable enemies in the West awaiting an auspicious moment to strike.[41] Rather than set a course which would only arouse the bellicose instincts of the mountain people, the sultans sought to win them over with privileges in return for garrisoning strategic points in their mountain region. They thus served to supplement the insufficient Turkish military force. From being an internal enemy of the Empire to be reckoned with, they were transformed into a useful regional militia. Of course these nomads, mainly Pindus Vlachs, were by no means oblivious of the advantages attendant upon maintaining their semi-independent status. With the coming of winter, they were free to go down with their flocks to the Turkish-controlled parts of Thessaly and Macedonia. The sultans had shrewdly completed the job of conquest.

A lack of documentary material prevents us from tracing the history of these mountain regions and ascertaining how they were governed. The scanty information which is relevant mostly dates from a much later period. However, it can be presumed from the little we do know that, just as towns and districts which capitulated without resistance were granted privileged status, so the mountain peoples who surrendered were spared the humiliating obligations of compulsory labor. They were required to pay very few taxes and were granted a certain amount of autonomy. The details of these written agreements varied, but the spirit in which they were contracted was everywhere the same.[42] One common provision, for example, was that Turkish armies and military detachments were not allowed to billet in, or even to enter, the places concerned. However, military exigencies constrained the Turks to proceed cautiously in some districts. Trikkala, therefore, in fact became the seat of a large *sancak* comprising in 1466–1467, as we have seen, no fewer than twenty-three districts (*nahiye*).[43]

In regard to the Armatoles, only one further consideration remains: that perhaps, after all, they did not appear for the first time during the reign of Murad II and that what seemed to be the institution of Armatoles in that period was merely a revival of the old system of frontier guards, which stretched back beyond the Byzantine era to Roman times— even, as some at least would say, to the period of the Macedonian kings.[44] There is no simple answer to this suggestion, though the continuous existence of the old system of frontier guards into the Turkish period would appear to be ruled out by the fact that the Armatoles first appeared in Greece in the Agrafa. Since it was here that the Turks first encountered a serious obstacle to their conquest, it is reasonable to suppose that they attempted to surmount it by founding the institution of Armatoles. But precisely what the position of the Armatoles in the Ottoman Empire was cannot be ascertained. Nor is it possible to determine the nature and extent of their responsibilities and regional jurisdiction. Hitherto, the practice has been merely to ascribe to the past the image of the Armatoles which the institution had on the eve of the revolution of 1821. But this approach is patently inadequate. Even in the most isolated districts where the institution survived in a form which was perhaps closest to its original type, it was subject to change and it must have assumed forms which varied not only from time to time but from place to place. The task of the historian is to project himself into these places and times. Only in this way will he have any hope of tracing the evolution of the Armatoli themselves and defining the boundaries of their *armatolikia.*

TURKISH COLONIZATION
AND ECONOMIC RECONSTRUCTION

While on the one hand the sultans pacified the Greeks and other Balkan peoples by a series of wise concessions, on the other the *akıncıs* continued to spread destruction and devastation from Thrace to the Adriatic.[1] Joseph Bryennios observed, in an account of the ecclesiastical provinces of the Oecumenical Patriarchate at the beginning of the fifteenth century, that, five hundred years before, almost every province had a hundred flourishing cities, whereas in his own time scarcely more than two or three, and those poverty-stricken, survived. Three hundred years before, each archbishopric had within its jurisdiction a thousand villages, but now there were no more than twenty. Two hundred years before, villages were healthily populated by as many as a hundred or more prosperous families, whereas in his day there were never more than ten, and these reduced to penury.[2]

This description, which has gone unnoticed until now, may be exaggerated, but it does contain a lot of information which accurately depicts prevailing conditions. It is incontrovertibly true that the vitality of urban life throughout the Byzantine Empire had been slowly sapped. City populations had thinned out and homes were everywhere abandoned. Formerly populous villages fared no better.

The rate of urban and rural decline was due not only to decrease in trade with the East and the steady accretion of land by big landowners at the expense of small ones, but above all to repeated invasion by the Turks. As we have seen, the Turkish rulers rewarded their military commanders and heroes with fiefs in Christian lands. In order to secure their conquests, they also adopted the practice of settling their own colonists in fertile areas and establishing villages exclusively inhabited by Turks.

Turkish colonization in Thrace was begun in the middle of the four-teenth century during the reign of Orchan. By the end of that century, that is to say during the reigns of Murad I and Bayezid I, it had been extended into Macedonia, Thessaly, and the northern regions of the Balkan peninsula.[3] In northern Greece, mass colonization by the Turcoman peoples began at the end of the fourteenth century, usually following peaceful infiltration and settlement by individual families or small groups. The invasion of Tamerlane may well have swollen this stream of Turkish immigrants into Europe.[4] It ought to be stressed, however, that the fact that acculturation took place in certain districts where no organized colonization ever occurred was a consequence not so much of the ingress of Turkish peoples as of the religious conversion of the local inhabitants.

Although it is difficult to determine the exact numbers of Turks who settled in the north of Greece, an early sixteenth-century census provides us with a probably fairly reliable guide. A hundred or so years after the initial colonization took place, this census listed in Macedonia and Thes-saly 4,574 Yuruk families, who were broken up into groups and organized after a military fashion.[5]

The center of Yuruk settlement, for which a separate legal code, the *Selanik Yürükler Kanunname,* was later promulgated, was Thessalonica. From the official Register of Titles for the year 1543, we are able to present for the first time an accurate analysis of the distribution of the companies (*ortas*) of Yuruk colonists: 36 in Phlorina, 33 in Servia, 23 in Phanarion, 5 in Hypate (Neopatras), 60 in Pharsala, 117 in Larissa, 35 in Kalamaria, 8 in Pournar Dağı, 2 in Genitsa (now Giannitsa), 47 in Avret Hisar, 28 in Strumica, and 8 in Siderokastron. The number of *ortas* in the more northern districts, apart from 13 in Prilep, 10 in Philippopolis (Plovdiv) and 26 in Silistra, was less significant. The largest concentra-tion of Yuruks was in Phlorina, Servia, Phanarion, Larissa, and Pharsala—precisely those places close to mountain districts which were the rallying points of resistance to the Turk.[6]

Turkish colonization in Thrace really got under way on the initiative of Suleiman, son of Orchan. Here, it was the Gallipoli peninsula which was first settled by Arab nomads brought in from Karasi in Asia Minor. There settlements eventually spread out from Gallipoli and survived for a very long time. A number of prominent Christian families in the area, chiefly those engaged in military pursuits, were obliged to leave the pen-insula fortresses of Tzympe and Aya Silonya and move to Karasi. This expulsion was undoubtedly caused by considerations of military secu-rity. According to the testimony of the Grand Mufti, *Haïroullah effendi* (a much later source, and probably exaggerated), the number of Moslems who moved into Thrace from Biga, Karasi, and Aydin during Orchan's reign amounted to no fewer than ten thousand souls.[7] From Gallipoli, the Turkish settlers colonized the fertile valley of the middle and lower Hebrus, where a number of Turkish warlords were known to have been granted extensive fiefs.[8] In this district, soldiers, *yaya* and *müsellem*, continued thereafter to comprise a high percentage of the Turkish population. Nesri records that in 1387 Sarutza Bey, in his capacity as commander of Rumelia's *yayas*, led an expedition against Karaman. He played an important part in the Bulgarian campaign of 1388 and in the battles of Kosovo Polje (1389) and Ankara (1402). No less prominent a military figure was Sarutza's son, Umer Bey, who bore the honorific titles, *Iftihâr ül-mucâhidîn* (Pride of the Warriors of Islam) and *Seref ül-guzzât* (Glory of the Ghazis), both of which were customarily bestowed upon the ghazi beys of the marches of the Empire. Sarutza is also remembered for the mosque which he built in Çirmen. His son followed this example by building a refuge for paupers.[9]

The colonization of present-day Greek Macedonia occurred during the reigns of Murad I and Bayezid I, when a large number of Yuruk farmers and shepherds settled around Serrai (1385),[10] Thessalonica, and the Axios. These people occupied the mountainous region north of Lake Koroneia, extending from Serrai to Drama, and formed the largest Yuruk community in the Balkans.[11] They brought to the north of Greece the simple and primitive customs of their Turcoman ancestors.[12] In the sixteenth-century census rolls, these Yuruks of central Macedonia were referred to as the "Yuruks of Evrenos," probably because they had accompanied Evrenos, Bürak, and Umur (father, son, and grandson) on their conquests and indeed belonged to the same tribe of the district of Saruhan (now Manisa), whence they had originally set out. By all accounts these nomads (who considered Yenice Vardar—Genitsa—a holy place, since it was there that Evrenos' tomb and other Yuruk monuments were to be found) settled in Macedonia after 1385.[13] Local tradition names six Turkish villages as being settled by the "men of Evrenos": Asiklar, Kisalar, Asarbey, Nidir, Yayakioï, and Karamtza.[14] At least in the case of Yayakioï ("Village of the *Yaya*"), the tradition would appear to be an authentic one.

The census rolls [15] also disclose that other Yuruk nomads, whom Boué believed to be Konyar Yuruks (from Konya, Latin Iconium) [16] settled in northwestern Macedonia in 1390, principally in the districts of Kozane, Sarigöl, and Kailar (Ptolemais). These were probably kin to the warlord Pasha Yiğit Bey, father of Turahan Bey of Thessaly, and were probably also moved there from Saruhan.[17] When Evliya Tschelebi visited them in the latter part of the seventeenth century, they still retained their old military duties, which were to serve as reservists (*eşkinci*) and to support military operations.[18] By the twentieth century, their descendants had become peaceable farmers and carpetmakers, with Ioannina, apart from a few neighboring small towns, their only trading center.[19] Very soon these nomadic people accustomed themselves to a settled agricultural existence and eventually adopted it entirely.

Turcoman peoples remained in Macedonia until the population exchange of 1923 returned them to Turkey. Up to the very moment of their departure, they recalled keenly and with pride that they were the "children of the conquerors" (Evlâd-ı Fâtihân).

It is known that Turkish colonization of Thessaly took place at the time of Bayezid I.[20] However, Urquhart has advanced apparently conflicting evidence, based on an Arabic manuscript on the life of Turahan, which was reported to him by a descendant of Turahan, the Turkish commandant (*Kaymakam*) of Tyrnavos (see page 158 above). This suggested that around 1423 Murad II settled in the northern part of Thessaly five or six thousand industrious peasants from Konya, all of them skilled in the arts of war. There he built for them twelve villages: Tatar, Kazaklar, Çayır, Misalar, Koufala, Karatsoğlan, Delir, Ligara, Rantgoun, Karademilli, Derili, and Balamout, of which only three or four were still standing at the beginning of the nineteenth century.[21] The rest had disappeared, according to tradition, because of successive epidemics, particularly a plague in the middle of the eighteenth century.[22] Urquhart's informant also said that Murad II originally established these settlements as a shield against the Bulgarians who inhabited neighboring mountain districts. When Turahan took Larissa with five thousand men, the Bulgarians retreated before him, and their ruler retired to Meteora, where he founded a monastery.[23]

Now it is quite apparent that the Turkish commandant (if indeed Urquhart himself recounted the conversation faithfully) was guilty of gross inaccuracies in his reportage of names and events from 1381 to 1423. The facts are that in 1381 the hellenized Serbian (not Bulgarian) ruler, John Ouroš Palaeologus, abdicated and withdrew to Meteora; and that in 1393 the Turkish invasion of Thessaly commenced, and fighting immediately broke out, as we have previously noticed, between the Turks and the conglomerate mountain population of Thessaly, mainly Vlachs.[24] However, other information, such as the names of the original Turkish villages, the reference to Murad II and his purpose in effecting the colonization, would appear to be sound. It is therefore likely that Turkish settlement was not systematized until the time of Murad II, though it began in the reign of Bayezid I.

When the bulk of Larissa's inhabitants abandoned the city in the shock of the Turkish advance, it was probably Bayezid I who repopulated it. This would explain the official Turkish name of the city—"Yeni Sehir" (New City). Yet it must also be noted that the Turkish settlers in Thessaly were not recorded in the census rolls as Konyars, but simply as "Yuruks of Yeni Sehir" or Yuruk Tatars.[25] These were the militant nomads who, with the passing of time and under the influence of a more settled Turkish farming population, were eventually transformed into industrious farmers.

Oral tradition also mentions Turkish settlement in the district of Almyros, centered upon the village of Yenitzek in the northwestern part of the plain of Krokion at the foot of Mount Othrys. Here, the Turks chased off the local inhabitants and took over their village, whose original Christian name has been lost.[26]

With the Turkish capture of Trikkala in 1395,[27] the former capital of the Greco-Serbian state of western Thessaly acquired even greater importance as a forward military base and the most advanced stronghold from which the unsubjugated people of Agrafa and the Pindus could be contained.

The conquest of the plains of Thessaly and their subsequent settlement by Turkish colonists was accomplished peacefully and with the compliance of lay and ecclesiastical nobility, who were extensive landowners there. There is consequently no mention by any of the Byzantine historians of resistance encountered in these areas. But this was in any case subject to easy conquest. Unstable conditions prevailed throughout the whole of the fourteenth century, when a succession of rulers—Greek, Serbian, and Albanian—exercised dominion there. Various forms of oppression, including heavy taxation, afflicted the free farmers and serfs. Large areas of common land, together with derelict property (*mahlûl*) formerly belonging to big landowners who had fled to free or to Frankish-controlled territory, either reverted with their serfs to the Turkish public domain or were usurped outright by Turahan and other lesser feudal lords. By these means, the first Turkish estates (*çiftliks*) were founded. Even those lords who chose to remain behind soon succumbed to the harsh and exigent conditions of life and were forced to relinquish their properties or acknowledge Islam. A good deal of monastic property was similarly confiscated. The property of Turkish feudal lords was increased further by the appropriation of many small holdings and villages, Christian and Turkish, which had become derelict as a result of poverty, disease, famine, or debt.[28] Such conditions could only have led to the flight of many of the people of Thessaly to the mountain wildernesses of the Pindus [29] and Olympus,[30] and even perhaps to the Peloponnese, where a remarkable confluence of peoples could be observed at this time. Never-

theless, small, free peasant holdings continued to exist in certain mountainous and infertile places of Thessaly throughout the Turkish occupation. These constituted the *kephalophoria* (villages of free peasants) as
opposed to the *çiftliks* of the Turkish period.[31] But the survival of these
villages was due not so much to Turkish respect for the rights of Christians to hold property as to their sheer geographical isolation and the
stubborn hostility with which their inhabitants resisted Turkish encroachments.

The sultans were determined to prevent the mass flight of their subjects. They realized the need to stabilize economic activity after a protracted period of chaos and decomposition. Accordingly, the capture of
cities and provinces was invariably followed by reconstruction. Encouragement was given to those who had survived the Turkish onslaught,
and enticements were held out to lure back those inhabitants who had
fled. New settlers, Greek and Turkish, were also invited (or compelled)
to change abode in order to complete the task of repopulation. The
sultans clearly saw that the raias, peasants, craftsmen, and laborers alike,
were indispensable to economic life everywhere and therefore to the
maintenance of imperial viability.

It was also natural that the great Turkish provincial governors, once
having acquired vast estates by the dispossession of the raias, should
nevertheless wish to enhance the productivity of their properties with a
view to organizing and strengthening the economies of their various
governances. Typical of these were Lala Sahin Paşa in the province of
Philippopolis (to whom is accredited the introduction of rice in that district),[32] Ghazi Evrenos Bey in Macedonia, and Turahan in Thessaly. The
achievements of these men and their descendants fixed their families'
names in the memories of local inhabitants until the very end of the
Turkish occupation.

Evrenos, for example, whose properties stretched across the fertile
plains of Macedonia to the very foothills of the ridge of Mount Vermion,
resettled the unruly inhabitants of that district (probably from Palionaousta on the lower summits of that range) in present-day Naousa and
promptly conciliated them by gaining the Sultan's agreement to the grant
of various immunities. These included the payment of limited taxes only
and the exclusion of all Turks from the town except the judge and military commandant. They permitted the establishment of various handicrafts, industrial arts, weapons' manufacture, and weaving and dyeing
industries. Some of these crafts have survived down to the present.[33]

Similarly, Turahan, who had appropriated to his own use a vast amount
of property in the urban and rural centers of Thessaly,[34] devoted himself
unstintingly to the economic stability and growth of his province. He

first established a military cordon of Turkish villages; inside it he repopulated Tyrnavos,[35] which possessed unrivalled geographical advantages, especially in regard to its lines of communication with Larissa and Sarantaporos. His efforts to obtain immunities for the town were successful and Tyrnavos was declared a *wakf* (a religious foundation) belonging, that is, through the *Kızlar ağa* to the Sherif of Mecca and therefore outside the jurisdiction of the provincial governor. The inhabitants of the town were thus exempt from all taxes save the *haraç* (which all non-Moslems were obliged to pay) and the tithe (a compulsory levy of one-tenth of every person's income or produce). In addition, there were the usual privileges of exemption from compulsory labor, the prohibition of any Turkish military presence, and the like.[36] All were preserved almost inviolate until as late as the Greek revolution and the reforms of Mahmud II (1808–1839).[37] Turahan was notably munificent with his public benefactions. In Trikkala, Yenisehir (Larissa), Chatalja (Pharsala) and many nearby villages he endowed mosques, monasteries, theological seminaries, schools, caravanseries, poorhouses, bridges, baths, bazaars, and other institutions for the welfare of the public.[38]

To Turahan has also been attributed the introduction of the art of dyeing, as well as the development of the silk, cotton, and woollen industries, which were the mainstays of Thessaly's economy under Turkish occupation. If the attribution is correct, the Turks also introduced into Tyrnavos at the same time yellow berries and madder as well as the kali plant, from which potash was made. These then came into general use in the dye industry throughout European Turkey and many parts of Western Europe. An inscription on a reservoir in the village of Makrynitsa on Mount Pelion which was used for the washing of dyed fabrics and which remained in use until 1830 reveals that it too was the work of Turahan.[39]

Unfortunately, the trustworthiness of some of these sources is doubtful. The exaggerated praise which Fallmerayer, for example, has lavished upon Turahan (with whom Byzantine statesmen are invidiously compared as no more than "silly prattlers") [40] is surely inflated; Fallmerayer seems also to have put inordinate trust in every word that reflects handsomely upon the peaceful accomplishments of Turahan. It is, however, a verifiable fact that economic development was well begun in Byzantine times. We have already seen, for example, that Thessaly was famous for its weaving and silk-making as early as the middle of the thirteenth century (see p. 39 above). Even then, thousands of liters of silk were being exported to Apulia by the "Duke" of Neopatras.[41] Indeed, the technique of weaving and silk-making in Thessaly may have had its origins in antiquity. Only in this way does it seem possible to explain the incomparable skill in spinning of the people of Thessaly, their traditional proficiency in tending silk-worms, and their meticulous care for the softness and perfection of their product—which even Fallmerayer recognized as unsurpassed anywhere else.[42] Turahan, we may presume, merely found these industries in a flourishing state, preserved them, and encouraged them.

Thus, from the very beginning of the Turkish occupation, economic development was sustained, the more smoothly no doubt because conquest was effected peacefully. The centuries'-old roots of a vigorous economy were only more deeply cultivated and continued to bring forth their fruit until the very end of Turkish rule. Even in so modest a way, we have yet another illustration of the continuity of Hellenic history.

THE LAST PROTAGONISTS
OF NEO-HELLENISM

The Morea under Constantine Palaeologus

Murad II, as we have seen, accomplished and consolidated his conquests by a dexterous combination of military and political means. In doing so, however, he raised up two new champions of Neo-Hellenism—Constantine Palaeologus, Despot of the Morea (1443–1449), and Cardinal Bessarion of Trebizond. Dismayed at the continuing spread of Turkish power and fired by the reforming zeal of Gemistos, both attempted to remodel the Despotate into a dynamic new Hellenic state.

Constantine personified the spirit of the nation. Having inflicted final defeat on the Franks in the Peloponnese, he then overcame successive obstacles in his path. Gemistos' statement that the Peloponnese was the strategical pivot of the Hellenic world and the source of its *élan* rang constantly in his ears. It was in his court, as we have seen, that the Athenian, George Chalcocondyles, took refuge after his abortive move to detach Athens from Turkish rule (see p. 45 above).

Although formidable difficulties at first prevented him from bringing his plans to fruition—strife with his brother, Theodore II, Despot of Morea, the unending struggles with Frankish rulers, and, most importantly, the efforts of Turahan Bey to frustrate him—his reputation as a brilliant military leader was already established when he assumed the Despotate of the Morea. By 1437 his reputation in Constantinople was that of an "exceptional, prudent, wise, sensible, and courageous man." [1] The years 1437–1443 found him in Constantinople and the Greek cities along the west coast of the Black Sea; then, in 1443, by arrangement with his brother, Theodore II, he assumed control over the latter's dominions in the Peloponnese and its capital Mistra, while Theodore was installed in the cities of the Black Sea and Selymbria on the Propontis.[2]

The intellectual life of the Morea at this time is described by Francesco Filelfo, a Hellenist. In a letter in 1441, he advised a friend, whom he addresses simply as Saxolo, to pursue his studies in Constantinople and not in the Peloponnese, because "the repeated invasions of the barbarians and the apathy of the people have left the country destitute of anything good; save for one person, George Gemistos, truly a wise man, in whose words and decorum we find our only consolation, you will find no one here worthy of the faintest praise. The Palaeologi themselves have become stricken by their needs and consequently behave towards one another in the most reprehensible and selfish of ways. The language of the people has become vulgar, and their customs 'more barbaric than those of the barbarians.' In Constantinople, on the other hand, there are still educated people whose language is pure and whose mores are above reproach." [3]

This account was not completely accurate, for the Morea, small and isolated though it was, still retained some vital elements of its former high civilization. In 1444, to give just one example, the classicist Cyriacus of Ancona discovered a large library in Kalavryta owned by George Cantacuzenus, from which he borrowed Herodotus' history.[4] Scholars and librarians had not vanished completely.[5] And of course Gemistos was still there, a figure of singular intellectual prominence. While research has bridged a number of gaps in our knowledge, it is still not possible to plot the full progress of his thought or to discern what its goal was and whether it was reached. If Gemistos' ultimate philosophical position remains hidden from us, so, too, do many of its links with the thought of his various disciples. We do know that at the time of the Council of Florence (1439), Gemistos wrote an essay, *Peri hon Aristoteles pros Platona diapheretai* (*How Aristotle Differs from Plato*), in which he attempted to liberate the thought of his contemporaries, the humanists of the West in particular, from the static philosophical and ideological conceptions of the Middle Ages. These of course were based on Aristotle's system, which, however, had suffered frequent mutilation in the process of Arabic translation and annotation. By elevating Plato to a higher plane than that of Aristotle, he awakened, as we shall see, a new interest in Platonic studies and thereby exercised a profound influence on human thought. Thoroughly disenchanted by the situation in his homeland and despairing of the ability of either the Orthodox Church or the Byzantine state to do anything about it, he cast around for some new force in the free firmament of his own philosophizing. He gradually became absorbed in a form of Neo-Platonism which was both ideal and mystical and which therefore segregated him from the realities of contemporary Greek life.

Gemistos possessed an inordinate faith in the power of the ancient Hellenic culture and especially in the system of Platonism which he revived in a new guise. "For him," writes Knös, "Platonism or Neo-Platonism was a declaration of independence not only for his people but for the whole of mankind; it was at once Neo-Hellenism and humanism."[6] He probably made the first public declaration of his mystical Neo-Platonism at the time of the Council of Florence.[7] In his *Nomoi* (*Laws*), which he was then composing, he moved beyond traditional belief and the tenets of the Church to a new kind of polytheism, pantheism perhaps—to a new religion, in effect, which reflected the influence of ancient Greek mythology and Platonic conceptions of the universe.

Moslem ideas also exerted a deep influence upon him. He sought to impress on Christians the need for a vital faith in providence and fate, the kind of faith, that is, that so impelled the Turks.[8] While Gemistos' profound concern for the problems of his time and his people was attributable in part to the influence of his old Jewish teacher, Elissaeus, nevertheless his awareness of Moslem religion and society, apparent in the *Nomoi,* was also plain. To be sure, the precise identification of these influences still presents many problems for research.[9] But such evidence as we already have clearly establishes Gemistos as a visionary, if perplexed, figure, who represents the awakening of a new and modern spirit, as much European as Hellenic.[10]

While he was still alive, however, Gemistos' philosophy remained almost obscure to contemporary scholars. This was due in the main to the fact that Gemistos himself made no attempt to put his *Nomoi* into circulation. Only a limited currency was given to his ideas by the publication separately of the first three chapters and, it would seem, their relatively widespread dissemination by his students. It was not until later, with his *Pros tas hyper tou Aristotelous Georgiou Scholariou antilepseis* (*The Views of George Scholarios in His Defense of Aristotle*), a disquisition against Aristotle's most ardent defender, George Scholarios, and with the *Pros to hyper tou latinikou dogmatos biblion* (*Concerning the Book in Favor of the Latin Dogma*) addressed to Johannes Bessarion, that Gemistos revealed at least some facets of his intellectual inclination to the theological elements of ancient Greek thought. At any rate by about 1450 George Scholarios felt that he knew enough of Gemistos' philosophy to make a specific riposte to the philosopher's recent criticisms. In a tract entitled *Kata Hellenon* (*Against the Hellenes*) he accused Gemistos of pagan inclinations and warned darkly that the author of such ideas "was deserving only of fire." He then pleaded with Gemistos to return to the bosom of the Church or at least to cease propagating his ideas.[11]

Later, when George Scholarios was patriarch, he called the then-deceased Gemistos a "new Julian" and again excoriated that particular work for its unsupported arguments, its obscurantism, and its disorderly arrangement of ideas.[12] History must find it difficult to express an opinion on such charges since they were made by Gemistos' most violent ideological opponent, who took care to destroy the manuscript on which they were based. Only fragments of it are still extant.

Meanwhile, Constantine succeeded in reorganizing his state both militarily and politically. His reign was distinguished by a definite Hellenic style, which was early revealed by his enclosure in stone of space for annual athletic competitions, held in emulation of the ancient Hellenic spirit, with money prizes awarded to the champions. According to the traveller Cyriacus of Ancona in 1447, the plains and valleys of the realm were cultivated with fruit-bearing trees, vineyards, and olive-trees, which suggests a practical concern on the part of Constantine for the encouragement of agriculture and the welfare of his farmers.[13]

In March 1444, Constantine built a wall across the Isthmus of Corinth.[14] Was he the "fortunate" one who would fortify the Isthmus for the "fourth time" and bring about the destruction of the Turks? After all, were there not many who were predicting that 1451 was the year when the oracle would be fulfilled [15] and the Turks annihilated? And did not the rumors of actual military preparations by powerful rulers in the West who would soon confront the implacable foe of Christendom actually presage his overthrow?

Bessarion

There was one whose enthusiasm for the fortification of the Isthmus was unlimited—George Bessarion, one of Gemistos' former students. In a letter which has been brought to light by Lambros, Bessarion, in Italy, congratulated Constantine, as well as "the nation and all Greeks." As a virtual blueprint for the social and political development of the nation, the letter is a landmark in the awakening of the Greek national consciousness. It was the third letter Bessarion wrote to Constantine after the fortification of the Isthmus, an event which had gratified him immensely. The first two letters have never been found, but the contents of all three, in the words of Bessarion himself, were substantially the same. According to Lambros, the third letter was written sometime between 1443 and 1446. However, if we take into account the actual date of the fortification of the Isthmus, together with a reference in the letter to the crusade which was known to have ended in the battle of Varna, 10 November 1444, it can probably be dated in the year 1444 (p. 17).[16]

Moved by a strong national awareness (p. 27),[17] Bessarion expatiated at length on conditions in society. He exposed mercilessly the existing state of affairs in the Byzantine Empire, especially the Peloponnese. He spared the nobility least of all, castigating them for their incompetence and for oppressing the people. His views on the nobility derived from the time when he had first studied under Gemistos and discussed the philosopher's ideas with his circle of students. Bessarion realized that the problem of the nobility was most acute in the Peloponnese and that urgent action was needed there. For him, as for his mentor, the problem was not only social but political; he therefore appealed to Constantine to institute significant reforms. The reorganization of the Despotate would provide the key to the recapture of occupied Greek lands and the restoration of the Byzantine imperium.

Bessarion's proposals were rather more specific than those of Gemistos, no doubt partly because they came later and matters had grown steadily worse since the time of Gemistos' memoranda. Also, Bessarion had a more reasoned and temperate outlook. Since he had had considerable experience in other European countries, his proposals benefitted from a thorough knowledge of their social and economic organization. And because he was actually living in Italy when he wrote, he could express his ideas without prejudice or self-interest and free from any interference or restraint by the nobility, whereas Gemistos was to a large extent the prisoner of his environment. Bessarion put Greece's problems in sharp focus and felt it his duty to expose them with complete candor.

It is apparent from the very beginning of the letter that Bessarion, like all Greeks then, saw in Constantine the only hope for the salvation of the nation. The completion of the wall across the Isthmus had further enhanced the Despot's repute. Constantine is the unquestioned leader of the nation: "not only have you not disappointed our expectations, but in truth you have exceeded them; and for this I congratulate you." (P. 15.) He went on to praise Constantine for his attachment to the ideals of ancient Greece and the vigor with which he pursued his enterprise: "I know only too well how eagerly your heart is set upon imitating our forebears, who accomplished so much with so little." And again: "Do not think I am ignorant of those things which exercise your mind each day, that I do not know what you want, what you are thinking, all the ideas you have and how you devise every possible way of putting them into effect." (Pp. 15–16.) Bessarion evidently was well informed about events in the Peloponnese and at Constantine's court in Mistra, in view of his claim that he knew "each day" what the Despot was thinking. He must have had an informant living in close proximity to Constantine, and that person may well have been either Gemistos himself or one of his close disciples. Perhaps Gemistos had ascertained Constantine's intentions in discussion with him and thought it judicious to have those intentions reinforced by some respected outside authority, a function Bessarion was obviously well qualified to perform. It is therefore probably unreal to consider Bessarion's letter apart from Gemistos' memoranda.

Bessarion next urged Constantine to build a city at the Isthmus, to garrison it, and reside in it. Such a city would come to "preside over all others." Following earlier precedents, he should also increase the population by allowing any who wished to do so to take up residence in the Peloponnese. Even prisoners of war should be treated not as slaves but as immigrants and settlers possessing the same rights as other citizens. (Pp. 16–17.)

The present inhabitants of the Peloponnese, he said, were robust and courageous, though untrained and unarmed. If their morale was low, this was because of the oppressive conduct of the nobility, the burden of taxation, and the malevolence of the tax collectors as well as the "flabby indifference and crassness which everywhere prevails." Thus he castigated the arch stupidity of nobles and despots, who did not seem to realize that the present external danger threatened their own interests first. He reiterated Gemistos' plea that the military should be separated from the peasantry and that each class should confine itself solely to its respective concerns. Only by total release from economic obligations could morale be restored to the military; only by this means could the "ancient nobility of soul" (an expression redolent of the attachment to antiquity which characterized Greek leaders) be recaptured. (Pp. 17–18.)

In the meantime, however, it behooved Constantine to train the men and instruct them in the tactics of war. He reminded Constantine that the great military exploits of Spartan generals offered innumerable examples of what could be done. If his soldiers were properly trained, he would succeed in that greatest of all enterprises—the liberation of the Greek lands of Europe. After that, like Agesilaos at the head of the new Lacedemonians, he will reform them and then cross into Asia and take back the entire national patrimony. (Pp. 18–19.)

This exhortation reveals the same spirit that animates all the popular traditions and oracles with which the Greeks tried to console themselves during the long and difficult years of occupation. It is the recurrent national dream, an expression of the popular yearning for "restoration."

On the whole, we must agree with H. G. Beck that Constantine's own politics was based on the European politics of the period,[18] while emphasizing, however, that *Reichspolitik* at this time and also in subsequent centuries corresponded with the growth of a national political consciousness among the Greeks aimed at the liberation of the entire Greek territorial inheritance, not only in Europe but in Asia Minor. A "national policy" aimed at the creation of a separate Greek state in the southern Greek lands not only never existed but was unthinkable to the Greeks. What happened was simply this, that the consciousness of being "Roman" gradually faded and was supplanted by a sense of "Greekness," though without any obvious break with historical tradition or the immediate past. The Hellenes merely adopted the political and cultural heritage of both ancient Greece and the Eastern Roman Empire (in ways already attempted by John III Ducas Vatatzes, as we have seen above, pp. 63–64), which over the centuries a Greek tradition eventually encompassed.

Bessarion's many references to Greek antiquity signified more than a sentimental attachment to the classical past: they also revealed a keen national pride. Thus Constantine, he wrote, ought not to despair at the limited size of his forces in the Peloponnese. On the contrary, the diverse examples of Alexander the Great, Cyrus, Rome, Sparta, Tamerlane, and, most recently, the Turks themselves (whose numbers were so small at first but whose power and extensive authority were now evident), all showed what greatness might flow from the most inauspicious of beginnings—of course given sound and determined organization.

There were, he went on, a number of great nobles who deplored conditions within the state and even felt a sense of contrition at the part they themselves might have played in contributing to this decline; but more to blame, they said, were appalling conditions within the state which obliged them to do what they did not really want to do (p. 23). In other words, there were those who saw a need for reform and might even have supported it—except that they found it more convenient to regard themselves as prisoners of the regime than actively to participate in its reform. Bessarion saw scant cause to trust the intentions and motives of such men. There was no panacea for overcoming the state's ills, but the essential prerequisite was the thorough overhaul of government and law in the light of actual circumstances and pressing social and political needs. (This became Bessarion's dominant idea.) There were illuminating examples of what could be accomplished in the cities of ancient Greece and contemporary Italy. Ancient Lacedemonian society was a vital model. (Pp. 20, 23.)

There was also a need, Bessarion continued, for the honors of public office to be distributed on the basis of personal distinction rather than personal means. The nobility ought to be constituted "in accordance with merit," not "according to wealth." Neither money nor position should be permitted to determine social differences and inequalities. Certain pernicious habits which threatened to erode public morality should be got rid of. For example, expensive jewelry, luxurious gilded fabrics, silken finery imported for feasts, and undue expenditures on marriages, funerals, and the adornment of "servant girls" represented conspicuous extravagance which could no longer be afforded. The voracious appetites of the avaricious led to injustice, deprivation, and want. Even when the people are scarcely distinguishable from slaves in their poverty, the avaricious continue on their greedy and stupid ways. It was Constantine's duty to see that the multitude was freed from penury and public morality restored. (Pp. 20–22.) [19]

Bessarion's comment that those bowed down by poverty were "scarcely distinguishable from slaves" showed that a distinction between peasant and slave could still be made in the Peloponnese. But nothing less was needed, he said, than a reorganization of the entire economy. It was absurd, for instance, to permit the exportation of grain when large segments of the population were starving. (P. 24.)

There were a number of pertinent lessons which Constantine could learn from the ancient law-givers Solon, Lycurgus, and Numa. "You know what they are better than I do. They are a veritable treasure locked in your mind. Draw upon this treasure. Do not hesitate to copy that which you esteem nor to apply that which you admire." (P. 22.)

Even if Constantine should fail in the end to build a disciplined and real state, a sustained effort would result at least in the partial fulfillment of his aims. For the Greeks would be behind him. And although as a race (*to ton Hellenon genos*) they are by nature easy-going, proud, courageous, concerned about virtue and morality, and lovers of knowledge, they nevertheless need good leaders and governors like Constantine. If, on the other hand, the people have lost their probity and behave in ways which belie their true nature, it is because some evil has insinuated itself into the life and social organization of the state, thereby debasing the "nation" to the level of this evil. (Pp. 22–23.)

Despite the seemingly inevitable retrogression which characterizes this period, what emerges from Bessarion's letter, even more unmistakably than from Gemistos' letters, is a genuine confidence in the qualities and capabilities of the people and a pervasive note of optimism. Whereas Gemistos' inspiration derived from a profound faith in the revivifying influence of the spirit of ancient Greece, Bessarion was no less moved by the example of contemporary Western Europe. Bessarion is the archetype of the modern Hellene who feels as much bound by the intellectual tradition of the West as by that of ancient Greece. The superiority of the West wounded his national *amour-propre*. Who were these foreigners who looked upon the Greeks as their mental servitors when it was they who had learned the very rudiments of civilization from the ancestors of the present-day Greeks? (Pp. 24–25.)

His advice to Constantine was to have young Peloponnesians—"youth neither too young nor too old"—trained in Italy, not merely in classical studies, which were almost moribund in Greece, but also in the mechanical arts, which had all but disappeared. In this way science and the arts could be restored to Greece, for there was no doubt that the young people of the day possessed ample resources of intelligence and wit. A sense of shame was no good reason for the Greeks to turn their backs on "the pursuit of the good" because, if the Franks had been slow in taking that which was not even properly theirs, they would never have attained their present level of knowledge. After all, the Greeks would be merely repossessing what really belonged to them.

Bessarion especially urged the advancement of practical education. He was convinced of the need to strike a rational balance between theory and practice and therefore of the importance in education of developing a parallel stream of technical training—a concern all the more interesting because only today is it at last fully appreciated by the Greeks. It was not sufficient merely to adopt a worshipful attitude towards the accomplishments of one's forebears. Some of the young Greeks sent to Italy should be trained in iron-working especially (since there were many iron mines in the Peloponnese, even around Mistra itself), in the manufacture of arms, and in ship-building. Four other crafts in which Italy excelled were glass-making (the splendid tradition of Murano, of course, surviving to this day), the manufacture of silk, once a flourishing industry around Corinth, the woollen industry, and dyeing. These were no longer indispensable in Greece. (Pp. 25–27.)

These remarks, like those made by Gemistos some thirty years before, showed that the Peloponnese had lost a significant part of its industry.[20] Indeed, for several centuries afterwards, the Greeks had to rely on the handicrafts and industrial manufactures of the West. On the whole, Bessarion placed far greater emphasis than Gemistos had done on the need for technical education and specialization, whether of craftsmen, farmers, or soldiers. The call for "more specialized knowledge by leaders and manufacturers" recurs throughout his letter.

Finally, Bessarion maintained that the application of his ideas would usher in a period of happiness for the Greek people. He added that he felt a sense of profound obligation towards Constantine (for what reason or reasons can only remain a subject of conjecture) and dared only to hope that the advice tendered might serve to repay part of his debt. He doubted that it would, for he was also aware not only that Constantine had held the same ideas "for a very long time," but that he had reflected upon them a great deal, had found them unexceptionable, and would put them into effect as soon as the right opportunity presented itself. Beyond that, Bessarion could only wish Constantine power and long life in order to bring them to fruition. (P. 27.) [21]

What was the precise nature of Constantine's relationship with Gemistos and with the circle of Gemistos' followers? To what extent was Constantine influenced by Gemistos' general philosophy and by his specific proposals for social and political reform? Perhaps these questions will never be answered or perhaps some future discovery of Bessarion's first two letters to Constantine and a careful sifting of the contents of all three will at last throw light on this problem of Greek history. Any full understanding of the nature of Mistra's social and intellectual impact must await its solution.

But this much at least can be said: that Gemistos, Constantine, and Bessarion were in unanimous accord on the question of instituting substantial reforms and on the need for fearless action in surmounting the grave perils of their time. All three struggled to light the way through the thickening darkness. The glow thus shed shines like a beacon in the history of the Hellenic nation. For the spirit of freedom which it symbolized was the same which ultimately led to the dispersal of external enemies, deliverance from internal petty tyrants, and the redemption of the Greek nation.

Constantine and the Turkish Peril

In his effort to realize the aspirations of Bessarion, Constantine sought to agitate the Christian conscience and to take advantage of actual war preparations in the West against the Turk. Like his brother, John VIII, he was in continual touch with some of the most powerful forces in Europe, among them Pope Eugenius IV, the Hungarian King Ladislaus, and the government of Venice. In April 1444, emissaries of John VIII passed through Ragusa (now Dubrovnik) on their way to Hungary.[22] With the winds of crusade again blowing strong in Europe, Constantine was inspired to renewed confidence and optimism. He believed that the right moment had at last arrived to carry his plans to a favorable conclusion. Exactly as Bessarion had advised, the Byzantine territories would be liberated and his rightful patrimony restored. So even before the armies of the King of Hungary and John Corvinus Hunyadi of Transylvania began to move (the latter to be destroyed at the battle of Varna in November 1444), Constantine had gathered together an army, invaded Attica, and exacted tribute from Nerio II Acciajuoli. Afterwards, he advanced to the north, conquering Thebes and all of Boeotia. Meanwhile, too, the Vlachs of the Pindus, mostly from the highland fastnesses of Agrafa (who, as we have seen, had their own leaders and maintained a semi-independent existence), watched Constantine's progress with more than casual interest. Envoys were in fact dispatched to swear Vlach allegiance to his cause. In return, Constantine provided them with a military commander and they promptly undertook military operations against the warlike Yuruks of Thessaly. No doubt the Greek-speaking population of Thessaly and western central Hellas also actively partici- pated in this campaign. Lidorikion received one of Constantine's lieuten- ants and thereby pledged its loyalty to him. Finally, even the Albanians (*Arabaioi Albanoi*) who lived in the mountains north of Naupactos and who possessed a privileged autonomy accorded by the Sultan also went over to the Greek side.[23] Thus, Constantine's first attempts to organize a national resistance movement were generally aimed at the unsubdued peoples of the Pindus and its spurs. It is also very likely that he had concluded an alliance with his brother-in-law, Carlo II Tocco (1429– 1448), who rebelled against the Turks in 1443. Although initially success- ful, the rebellion collapsed in 1444 when Carlo was captured in battle and had to buy his life with vassalage.[24] Greek and Turkish sources in this and the period immediately subsequent are scarce and unreliable,[25] but it would seem to be about 1443 that Constantine formally requested aid from his powerful contacts in the West. In 1444 a detachment of three hundred men was dispatched from Burgundy; it arrived in the Peloponnese in March or April of the following year, after the battle of Varna.[26]

Constantine meanwhile attempted to hold the Turk at the wall of Hexamilion on the Isthmus. However, in 1446 the torrent could no longer be contained. His defenders on that occasion, according to Ducas, were both Albanians and Greeks.[27] These, still poorly organized as they were, eventually took off in panic-stricken flight. The ensuing pillage, cruelty, and destruction throughout the entire Peloponnese were fearful.[28] A later source placed the number of people killed at twenty-two thousand,[29] and more than sixty thousand people were enslaved by the invader.[30] It was largely as a result of this defeat that George Scholarios again accused the Peloponnesians of cowardice,[31] an accusation that Bessarion had re- jected two or three years previously.

After the defeat of the Peloponnesians at the Isthmus, all of the lands north of the Hexamilion that had previously adhered to Constantine were compelled to revert to the Sultan's suzerainty. Even the district of the Pindus followed suit, no doubt in order to retain its semi-independent status. The Despotate of Morea similarly capitulated and became tribu- tary to the Sultan.[32] How Constantine, Gemistos, and Bessarion reacted to this series of disasters and how, if at all, their relationships were affected by it are not known. Only this much seems reasonably certain: that Gemistos withdrew more closely into himself and into his circle of

students and that his thought tended more strongly towards Neo-Platonism and pantheism. Constantine, for his part, merely bided his time.
Evidently unsympathetic towards the kind of mystical solutions in which
Gemistos found increasing solace, he merely held on to his plans and
awaited the time when conditions would again seem ripe for their implementation.

The situation in the Pindus was confused, though it was probably at
this time that the Vlachs finally submitted. According to Aravantinos,
however, Vlach resistance did not come to an end until 1479. His claim
is based on a vague oral tradition which asserts that the Vlachs who
inhabited the mountainous marches of Epirus and Thessaly lost their
autonomy then because they saw that continued resistance would end
only in annihilation. They therefore acknowledged the nominal sovereignty of the Sultan after first extracting the guarantee of specified rights
of self-government. Their lowland neighbors suffered untold hardships.
And this was the political situation which obtained in the Vlach villages
until the time of Ali Pasha of Ioannina at the end of the eighteenth and
the beginning of the nineteenth centuries, when the introduction of a
rigorous centralized system of government eventually put an end to all
Vlach privileges.[33]

Constantine as Emperor

The Turks meanwhile were strengthening their position throughout the
conquered territories. On 19 October 1448, they crushed a new army
which had been raised by Hunyadi. A few days later, on 31 October,
John VIII Palaeologus died. Murad II immediately seized this opportunity to demand the cession of Herakleia, the most important port on the
Sea of Marmara. The Byzantines could only yield to the *force majeure*.[34]

The universal dismay caused by this new crisis was portrayed by the
contemporary Unionist scholar, John Argyropoulos. In a panegyric to the
late "Sun King of Greece," he said: "With this death, Time, ruler of us
all, has dealt the deadliest blow . . . there can be now no deliverance
. . . he who was glory and perfection to the Greeks is no more. . . .
Hope has fled. Aidos and Nemesis have departed for Olympus. Only the
bitter cup remains to be quaffed. Our enemies and all barbarians rejoice,
while we are enshrouded in gloom and shriveled up by fear. . . . The
walls of our Grecian cities quake and seem about to fall and admit the
barbarians." [35]

Immediately on the death of John VIII, the capital was thrown into
confusion by a dispute over the imperial succession. Taking advantage
of the absence of the lawful successor Constantine, his ambitious brother
Demetrius schemed to seize the throne. His designs were foiled only by

the combined opposition of his mother, the chancellors (*mesazontes*) Cantacuzenus and Lucas Notaras—the latter in particular—and other powerful members of the court.[36] Those who abetted Demetrius were most likely fanatical anti-Unionists, egged on by their leader, George Scholarios, who distrusted Constantine's Unionist propensities, as indeed he confessed later on.[37]

Meanwhile, Constantine, who had been crowned Emperor in Mistra (6 January 1449), arrived in Constantinople on board a foreign vessel [38] and at once saw the extent of the Turkish danger for the capital. There was even less freedom of movement and action than in the Peloponnese. Thereupon he divided the Despotate of Morea between his two brothers, Thomas and Demetrius. After protracted negotiations, the new boundaries were defined so as to rule out, it was hoped, the possibility of friction between them of a kind which might provoke Turkish intervention. Thomas' domain took in the northwestern part of the Peloponnese, with his capital probably in Glarentza (now Kyllene); Demetrius held sway in the southeast and in Mistra. However, the two brothers possessed none of the strategic acumen of Constantine and also seemed totally oblivious of the social and political problems which beset them. Where they might have been expected at least to master the situation in their respective states, they were content to become the puppets of powerful nobles. Otherwise, each acted as though his only concern was to dislodge the other and thereby control the entire Peloponnese. It was therefore not long before they came into conflict with each other, as well as with Venice, which produced disastrous consequences for the economy and internal stability of the region.[39]

Gemistos died on 26 July 1452.[40] His student and protégé, the monk Gregory, described him in his funeral peroration as: "this transcendent mind, so fertile . . . the most brilliant and precious jewel in the crown of ill-starred Greece." [41] The panegyric of yet another of his students, Jerome Charitonymos of Mistra, was equally filled with economiums. Above all, he praised the breadth of Gemistos' knowledge and referred to him as "the greatest, the noblest, the pride of the nation." With his death, "Sparta can no longer be famous, or Lacedemonia fortunate, or the Peloponnese enviable." [42] Referring to Gemistos' polemic against Aristotle, he said: "By exhaustive analysis he showed the philosophy of Aristotle, which some in olden times had revered as though divine, to be insubstantial." His death was a greater loss by far than that of emperors, for most of them were beneath contempt and often "more responsible than anyone else for the many miseries of their subjects who, for that reason, only wanted their deaths." Gemistos' courage and forbearance towards others was always remarkable, and he had become noticeably

Figure 14. Constantine XI Palaeologus.

even more restrained towards the end, though he never stopped advocating certain of his ideas. Of course the reason for this reticence might have been advancing age, but—and here the panegyrist makes plain his own interpretation of Gemistos' changed attitude—it might also have been due to "the strictures of those who bore ill will towards him." This comment, which has gone unnoticed until now, suggests that powerful landed magnates coerced Gemistos into remaining silent on some subjects. These probably include many of his plans for reform as well as his religious views.[43]

Charitonymos also spoke of the special duty incumbent on Gemistos' disciples to bear their grief with fortitude. Since it was they who most valued his wisdom, who had found happiness each day merely in conversing with him, who were therefore "men of true learning, righteous nature, and resolute conviction," it was also they who should continue to work for the rebirth of the nation. These were the enlightened and reform-minded men who, with the loss of their spiritual leader, would now go out to the ends of the earth and perhaps know manifold sorrows "in spreading their gospel of truth." [44]

This might be construed as a warning of probable persecution, such as occurred in the case of the monk, Juvenal, a follower of Gemistos. (See page 184.)

The new emperor did not abandon his plans of reconstruction and expansion. He was "Constantine the Hellene" of the demotic song, who is seen as the first emperor of the Hellenes to incarnate the new spirit of the nation.[45]

It is unfortunately not possible today to trace the various ways in which the new national consciousness became diffused throughout the Hellenic world. Its features still remained amorphous; and even the assimilation of alien races (notably the Albanians) was not yet complete. Nevertheless there is one certain element in the picture. From the beginning of the fifteenth century, and certainly by the middle of the century during the reign of Constantine XI Palaeologus, the use of the word Hellene in place of Roman became not only general but almost official. And this was no mere coincidence. Scholars, those of Unionist sentiment in particular, responded eagerly to the new ideas of their emperor.[46] John Argyropoulos, for instance, who referred to Constantine as "Emperor of the Hellenes," considered him the defender of "the freedom of the Hellenes." That time of freedom, he hoped, would shortly arrive.[47] Constantine was obviously the sort of person who could arouse the hopes of his people—at any rate the Unionists among them.

To the followers of Gemistos it seemed that the only solution to the problems of the time lay in a change of existing political and religious attitudes, and upon just such a course as this they determinedly embarked. The monk Gennadius (George Scholarios) later made this comment on the results of their efforts: "unhappily, in the process of becoming lost, the faith was also deliberately scorned; there was a terrible ungodliness on all sides; some became pagan worshippers of ancient Greek culture, others were either ignorant of the faith or indifferent towards it, and everywhere there was a tergiversation from traditional institutions and religion."

Gemistos' views on the failure of Church and state to deal with the vital issues of the time made headway in the north, in the capital itself, and in Thracian Ainos. There they were made public by the monk Juvenal, among others, one of Gemistos' foremost protagonists; and when he continued to propagate them just as earnestly on his return to the Peloponnese, he was apprehended and put to death by a local lord, Manuel Raul Oises. That event gladdened the heart of Gemistos' most uncompromising opponent, Gennadius. Although Juvenal died a martyr for his beliefs he was probably the first and last of Gemistos' disciples to do so: his execution had the intended effect of intimidating Gemistos' followers. Gennadius praised Oises' action and deemed it worthy of imitation by other nobles, great and small; he added the warning that failure to take concrete steps against the spread of Gemistos' ideas could only be regarded as actual connivance. "Either they are trying to conceal the fact that they are indeed worshippers of ancient Greek culture or they should be judged as such by God and men." [48]

It is easy to understand the fear and haste with which one young initiate into Gemistos' circle, the scholar Michael Apostolis, addressed himself to Constantine Palaeologus, imploring his intervention. He had been accused by the Church, by Gennadius principally, of course, of adherence "to the beliefs of the ancient Greeks and of other pagan and ungodly worship." He believed in Zeus, Poseidon, and Hercules, worshipped before their statues and idols—so the accusation ran—and was therefore a follower of Gemistos. Apostolis was at pains to impress upon the Emperor (who of course was well acquainted with Gemistos and his movement, and perhaps also with Apostolis' place in it) the genuineness of his Orthodox profession. He denounced vigorously what was being said against him.[49]

What in particular had Apostolis done to incur the wrath and hostility of the Church? Some light is thrown on the matter by a letter Apostolis had written to Gemistos. In this, after first introducing himself, Apostolis declared his admiration and devotion, begging Gemistos to regard him as one of his followers. Apostolis then identified himself as the one who had secured a copy of Gennadius' Aristotelian polemic, *Kata tou Ple-*

thonos aporion ep' Aristotelei (*Against the Doubts of Plethon about Aristotle*), and sent Darius the Cretan with it to Gemistos.[50] This suggests that the literary dispute between Aristotelians and Platonists which took so many Byzantine scholars to the West was already raging in Constantinople. Obviously, it was this action which Gennadius never forgave, quite apart from Apostolis' ideas. The Church's accusation against Apostolis is explicable in terms of an identification in the minds of the clergy of those of Gemistos' circle, whose pagan inclinations were plain, with those who were merely devotees of ancient Greek culture. The Church had never forgotten Julian the Apostate's attempted revival of paganism.

That there were admirers of Julian among Gemistos' followers who lapsed into pagan heresy cannot be denied. For instance, there is the commentary (full of misspellings) on Julian's oration, *On the Sovereign Sun* (Oratio IV), written by Gemistos' devoted student and friend, Demetrius Ralles Kavakes. In it Kavakes confessed to the same veneration for the sun as the Emperor Julian; his adoration, which had begun when he was seventeen years old, continued to grow though he was then seventy-four years old.[51]

Despite the unrelenting opposition of the Church, the use of the word Hellene was increasingly adopted, even by some of the most distinguished apologists of Orthodoxy and those who remained anti-Unionist in outlook. These were men like Joseph Bryennios and George Scholarios, the latter of course none other than Gennadius himself.[52] Thus, in 1450, in a speech of "condolence" to Constantine, later written down "in commemoration of the death" of the Emperor's mother, Helen, Gennadius used the words Hellene and Roman more or less interchangeably. In addressing Demetrius Palaeologus, he used Hellene and Hellenic exclusively.[53] In this light, Voyatzidis is probably mistaken when he says that Scholarios intended the word Roman to apply only to the people of Constantinople and those who still remained under imperial rule, while by the word Hellene he referred to the Peloponnesians.

We can only conclude that the presence of Constantine Palaeologus in the capital, his commanding stature, his love of Greek culture, his constancy in regard to policies both pursued and projected, all conspired to bring about a change in attitude towards the use of the term Hellene, even to the extent that the leaders of the anti-Unionist party came generally to accept it. The word had come to signify the Greek people wherever they lived. It is clear from a letter George Scholarios wrote to the Emperor of Trebizond, John IV, in 1449 or 1450 that Scholarios used it with this meaning only. Here he referred to the brilliance and nobility of John IV's reign, which embellished "the whole nation of the Hellenes." [54] It was also clear from this letter that the name Hellene was known and understood in the region of the Pontus, a point we will refer to again. And it was clear finally that the clergy had adopted the word Hellene, however hesitantly, as an alternative to Roman.

It was during this period that the word seems to have acquired in the popular mind the additional connotation, preserved in contemporary tradition, of a supernatural being with a gigantic body and tremendous strength.[55] Merely to have survived the dark centuries of Turkish rule,[56] these local traditions of the courageous Greeks and popular memories of old Greek castles [57] must have been extraordinarily deep-seated.

Is there perhaps some connection between the flowering of such traditions at the popular level and the revival of the word Hellene among scholars? Were there, that is to say, at least some scholars and statesmen cognizant of those traditions who then deliberately employed them for a purpose—using the word Hellene, for example, as a means of reinforcing the morale of the people? The probability that they did is a strong one, though it is admittedly beyond proof. Only for the Pontus, through the evidence of popular songs which have survived, is it possible to offer some verification of this assumption identifying the Greeks of that region with the race of "courageous" Greeks of old.[58]

THE TURKS AT THE GATES
OF CONSTANTINOPLE

Preparations for War and the Union Controversy

Constantine's vigorous pursuit of his religious policies had resulted in intensification of the religious controversy. The anti-Unionists had made definite gains at their opponents' expense as a result of the Turkish success at the battle of Varna in 1444 and the follow-up victory at Kosovo Polje on 19 October 1448.[1] Constantine and the Unionist Patriarch Gregory III Mammas found themselves in an uncomfortable position. In the same year as Kosovo Polje, Jonah, the Metropolitan of Moscow, distrustful of the Patriarch and fearful lest the Orthodox faith become tainted, proclaimed the autonomy of the Russian Church. Gregory was dethroned in 1450, no successor was elected in his place, and a Church synod of 1450–1451 denounced the Union dictum of the Council of Florence.[2]

It seems that George Scholarios was an active participant in these events. Therefore, Constantine, who apparently had not forgotten Scholarios' attempts to prevent his ascending the throne, had banished him from the court. So the Emperor was still surrounded at court by the pro-Unionist enemies of Scholarios. Bitterly disappointed, Scholarios had retired to the monastery of Charsianeites as the monk Gennadius.[3]

There were echoes of the conflict even as far away as Rome. The Unionist scholar, T. Gazes, evinced thorough disgust with his compatriots in Constantinople, who, he said, spent all their time bickering with Italians about theological issues. "I am afraid," he remarked, "they will still be engaged in religious arguments and penning diatribes against the Roman Church while the few cities that are left are being taken and their wives and children sold into slavery." [4]

These developments in the controversy prompted Pope Nicholas V to write to Constantine in the autumn of 1451 urging him to take the sort of resolute action once and for all that would bring about the Union of the Churches. The Pope pointed to the misfortune of the once great and glorious Greek people and suggested, in line with the opinion prevalent throughout the West, that the Photian Schism was its cause. Union was the only hope of salvation. The Greeks, he went on, always deferred the issue with the same pretexts and excuses, but they should not think that the Pope and the Western Church could go on forever suffering this vacillation. On the contrary, there was already in Rome a large group of Catholics vehemently opposed to the dispatch of any assistance at all to Constantinople.[5]

In addition to the religious quarrel, Constantine also had to contend with economic difficulties. He was in constant need of money and as a consequence tried to restrict the privileges which the mercantile republics sought or enjoyed. In negotiations with the emissary from Ragusa (Dubrovnik), Vuk Bobaljević, in 1451, he refused to exempt its citizens from payment of all taxes in Constantinople, but agreed to a 2 per cent impost.[6] His attempts to increase the taxes payable by Venetian merchants and brokers failed, however, because of outright threats that they would leave the capital altogether.[7] On another occasion he agreed to an arranged marriage with the daughter of the King of Iberia, whose dowry would consist of 56,000 gold pieces and an additional 3,000 per annum for charities for the poor.[8]

This was the situation in Constantinople when, in February 1451, Mohammed II came to the Ottoman throne for the second time. He was barely nineteen years of age.[9] He was convinced that the Turkish conquests could only be secured by the conquest of Constantinople. His father, Murad II, had felt a similar need when Turkish armies had to be ferried across from Asia Minor to Europe in order to meet the Hungarians in 1444. With the young Sultan it became an obsession.[10] None of the Greek rulers, however—neither Constantine XI nor John IV of Trebizond[11]—had yet had occasion to notice this ambition of Mohammed's or his military ability and relentless determination.

The first year of his reign was marked by frenetic activity. He readied his army, put his finances in order, swore to live in peace with Constantine (and even restored Herakleia to him), maintained friendly relations with the Despot of Serbia, George Branković, extended the terms of his treaty of peace with Hunyadi, and reaffirmed peaceful relations with Venice.[12]

It was actually Constantine who gave the signal for the beginning of hostilities. When Ibrahim Bey, ruler of Karaman, invaded Turkish soil,

Figure 15. Mohammed II the Conqueror.

Constantine was quick to perceive his advantage. Ambassadors were sent to Mohammed's encampment demanding a double ransom for the Sultan's relative, Prince Orchan, who had sought asylum in Constantinople. Unless the ransom were paid, Orchan would be set free to harass the Sultan. This feint was reminiscent of Constantine's moves ten years before, when he had sought to exploit the central-European Crusade and had advanced victoriously, though only temporarily, as far as Thessaly. He now saw Ibrahim Bey's incursion (and no doubt the extreme youth of the Sultan) as providing him with a unique opportunity to strengthen his position vis-à-vis Mohammed. But his hopes were dashed. Mohammed accepted the challenge, hurriedly made peace with the ruler of Karaman, and turned on Constantine.[13]

This unexpected reversal forced Constantine to request immediate assistance from his brothers as well as from Hunyadi and the West.[14] But the times could scarcely have been less propitious for the organization of a crusade in the West or for the dispatch of any significant aid to the dying Byzantine Empire. The only positive indications of interest came from Pope Nicholas V, Alfonso V, the ambitious King of Aragon and Naples, and the cities of Venice and Genoa, who saw Turkish domination as a manifest threat to their substantial economic interests in Constantinople and the Black Sea. But, by the time this concern was translated into proposals for effective action, it was too late.[15]

Mohammed instituted systematic military operations. The fortress of Rumeli Hisar was built on the European coast [16] opposite that of Anadolu Hisar on the Asia Minor side, and the narrow straits of the Bosphorus were thus expertly controlled. He ordered Ak-Tsaïrli Oğlu Mohammed Bey to lay waste the environs of Constantinople and, having achieved that, to proceed to Adrianople.[17] In the winter of 1452–1453, Turahan and the other Yuruk Beys of Thessaly and Macedonia led a large force of the army of European Turkey against the Palaeologus brothers and put them *hors de combat*. Bayezid I had followed the same strategy once before.[18]

But Constantine was not found unprepared. Several months before he had had the foresight to make sure that the fields were harvested, the grain threshed, and the castles in the vicinity of the capital thoroughly provisioned; peasants from the city's surrounding districts had been brought to safety inside the wall.[19] Constantine had taken one further precaution: he had purchased oil, wheat, legumes, and other foods from the Aegean islands as well as from the republics of Genoa and Venice and the Kingdom of Naples. When the supplies from these countries came, small military detachments arrived with them, led by exemplary officers—John Longo Giustiniani, the Genoese (who arrived in January

1453), and John Grant, the German engineer, figuring most prominently among them. The Greek cardinal Isidore, formerly Archbishop of Kiev, also came in November 1452. As a representative of the Pope, his task was to reconcile the opposing religious factions and to ensure Greek observance of the Florentine dictum.[20]

In Constantinople the controversy had grown worse, with the monk, Gennadius, inciting anti-Unionist mobs to riot.[21] Threats against Gennadius' life were being made openly by the Unionist faction, which consisted chiefly of palace officials, who considered that the monk's leadership and fiery harangues were alone responsible for the increasingly fanatical attitude of the hyper-orthodox masses. On 1 November Gennadius nailed this fervent declamation to the door of his cell: "Ah, benighted souls, not only have you lost everything, but you now infamously and perfidiously turn your backs on that which is most holy. Instead of finding solace in God during these iniquitous times, is it rather separation from God that you seek? As for me, I have right on my side; as God, the saints, and you yourselves are my witnesses, I have been negligent in nothing. Now I bear witness before God that this Union of yours is evil; you are finished. Do you curse me and threaten me? Kill me if you will, for I am ready even for that . . . No, dear Orthodoxy, cherished faith of our fathers, I shall neither forswear you nor betray you while there remains breath in my body." [22]

The arrival of Isidore that same month was the signal for renewed outbursts of theological disputation and a sharpening of religious tensions.[23] Gennadius remained quite unconvinced and determined to maintain his stand against Union. He did not take part in the first official discussions following Isidore's arrival at the Xylalas Palace. On 15 November 1452, he merely reaffirmed in a letter to the "ecclesiastics and others" assembled there that he would not change his mind. At the same time, Gennadius was sensible of the menace which grew greater each day and of the heavy burden of responsibility which he bore towards his country, his compatriots, and his emperor. Since the intensity of the Unionist tirade against him lessened not a whit, he finally bent before the storm and on 27 November declared his intention at least to desist from further polemics. These were "insidious" times and although "there are many who believe in what I have so often and in so many words shown to be disadvantageous . . . nevertheless faith is free and unforced, and either you must therefore restrain me or I you; but I have failed to restrain you even though I have tried to place every obstacle in your path, and that is why I will no longer embarrass you. Yet I will no more take part in your Union now than I could have in the past—nor will I in the future." [24] It was in this atmosphere that Cardinal Isidore officiated on 12 December at the first Catholic and Orthodox concelebration of Mass ever held in Hagia Sophia. Pope Nicholas and the exiled Patriarch Gregory were commemorated in the "diptychs" of that Mass.[25]

If Gennadius had shown himself less intransigent in this exchange than formerly, his views regarding the outcome of the siege remained unalterably pessimistic. The morale of the defenders could not have been helped by the utterance of these views. Everyone, he wrote after the fall of the city, who had watched the inexorable growth of the enemy's forces and the simultaneous paralysis of the city, had long before arrived at the conclusion that freedom would soon be lost. Most people, however, lulled both by false hopes and the very staleness of their fears, were reluctant to believe even in their most fearful imaginings that the end would come within a year. Then he made the following comment, which obviously included a reference to himself: "There were a few, though, who foresaw it clearly and said so with unshrinking frankness, even to the unfortunate Emperor himself [26] and the Notables of the city. And these few, having searched for reasons, pointed to certain divine portents which foretold (and also explained) 'God's judgment'; they also discovered, paradoxically enough, what could have been done to prevent it and obtain the city's reprieve." [27] These were strange remarks, and one wonders what purpose he hoped to serve by making them, especially to the Emperor. After all, predictions of imminent catastrophe would seem hardly a restorative tonic to a people already tortured by fear, hardship, privation, and religious conflict. In view of the injurious effects they must have had, it was ironic that Gennadius, after the capture of the city, should accuse his compatriots of showing less courage than the magnitude of the danger required; or that he should criticize them for committing a gross blunder in entrusting the defense of the wall to foreigners.[28] What had he himself done to meet the Turkish threat more effectively?

The one other leader of the anti-Unionist faction whose name stood out was the Grand Duke Lucas Notaras, more powerful than anyone else in Constantinople save only the Emperor himself. Early in life his sensibility and intellectual acuity had attracted the attention, first, it would seem, of Manuel II, then later of John VIII. In the last years of John VIII's reign it was largely Notaras who had shaped the Empire's external relations.[29] The Grand Duke's religious views were not nearly as inflexible as they were usually made out to be. It is necessary to revise previous opinions about Notaras' attitude in the religious dispute.[30] The celebrated remark usually attributed to him—"better to see the Moslem turban in the city than the Latin miter" [31]—was in fact an imputation by his Unionist rivals.[32] Notaras was above all a realist who well understood the dire peril the Empire faced; and only if the populace maintained the pretense of upholding papal primacy and supporting Union could it possibly be averted. Gennadius, who usually reserved for him only the most adulatory expressions of esteem, yet found this fault: "He proposes what has been put forward many times before, that, for instance, if we wish to show real reverence towards God, we should proclaim in our churches that the Pope does not err but that we are still Orthodox, even though we believe precisely the opposite of that which the Pope believes and could never believe otherwise." [33] Notaras' ideas nevertheless gained ground. There were even some extreme Unionists and a few in the West who believed that Constantine himself harbored anti-Unionist views of this sort. Be that as it may, they were views which signified the emergence of an anti-Unionist splinter group that was prepared to be conciliatory in its attitudes and opportunist in its aims: "Let's see first," they said, "whether God will deliver us from this enemy who stands before us, this ugly serpent that boasts it will swallow Constantinople. Then you will see whether we will have Union with the Latins." [34] Of course these views disappeared with the capture of the city.

Siege of the City

The religious dissensions continued even when the Turkish armies were outside the very walls of the city. At the beginning of 1453, the Turkish vanguard under the generalship of Rumeli Valesi Karatza Bey, commander of the European army, on the Sultan's orders moved from Adrianople, conquered the last free strongholds in Thrace and its neighboring districts, and carried the invasion to the gates of the capital. St. Stephanos, Epivatae, and Herakleia (Eregli) on the Sea of Marmara were the first to fall; Vizye, Pyrgos, Anchialus, and Mesembria along the Black Sea coast followed soon afterwards. [35] At the beginning of April, the Sultan arrived before Constantinople with his main force, pitched his tent facing the St. Romanos Gate, and commenced siege operations. [36] A large number of Greeks, Franks, Germans, Hungarians, and others [37] in the Turkish army contributed in no small part to the ultimate success of the besieging force. [38] Descriptions of the first encounters suggest that the initial size of this force was not large. At first there were the regular levies only, all exceedingly well equipped and supplied; [39] but their ranks were swollen daily by large numbers of irregulars, young and old, [40] for whom the promise of plunder proved even more alluring than the Holy War. Ever since the first Arab invasions the riches of Constantinople had been fabled throughout Islam.

The defenders numbered about eight thousand Greeks and two thousand foreigners; and they eventually faced a host of 250,000. [41] The entire hopes of the city therefore rested on the impregnability of the land walls, which stretched from the Sea of Marmara to the Golden Horn. There were in fact two walls, originally built by the Emperor Theodosius II (the Little) (408–450); the Emperor Heraclius (610–641) pulled down part of the fortification from the Palace of Evdomon to the Golden Horn so as to take in the quarter of Blachernae; he replaced it by a single rampart. Theodosius' walls were about 4,950 meters long and were capped by ninety-four large towers and eighty smaller ones. The inner line of defense, known as the Great Wall, was from 10 to 20 meters high and about 2½ meters in width. It stood about 17.8 meters from the Outer Wall, which subtended the plain outside the city. Since any enemy faced virtually insurmountable difficulties in gaining access to the area between the walls, and since the area itself was unconscionably exposed to any attacking force, this enclosure was an equally vital part of the city's defenses. In normal circumstances, however, the defense would have been conducted from behind the lower and narrower Outer Wall. Towers were spaced at intervals of 48 meters along the Great Wall, but each was a self-contained structure without any communication with the wall itself. Together with the enclosure, the inner wall formed the last line of defense. The single wall built by Heraclius was thicker than the Great Wall—3.7 meters wide and 20 meters high. Since its fortified towers were integrated with the wall in a single defensive system, the defenders generally had greater mobility here than on the Great Wall. Finally, at a distance of 17.2 meters from the Outer Wall there was a moat, which also ran, though with occasional breaks, from the Sea of Marmara almost to the Golden Horn. Its width varied from 19.2 meters to 21.15 meters; its depth was nearly a uniform 10 meters. The sides of the moat were properly constructed, and a low wall of breastwork surmounted the inside rim of the moat. This outwork, built in 1341 by the Grand Duke Alexius Apocaucus,[42] formed with the moat itself the first line of defense.

On 7 April, the Sultan began the deployment of his batteries—a task which occupied several days.[43] Bombardments and successive assaults at various points along the wall immediately followed, and considerable damage was inflicted on the palace and the houses of nobles which abutted the wall. The defenders retaliated as best they could, and so continuous salvos from both sides, emitted by small guns, big guns, bows, and other engines of war, steadily decimated the opposing ranks. Though Turkish superiority in artillery had already determined the outcome of the siege, the inhabitants of the city resisted with singular courage and devised a thousand stratagems to ward off the inevitable. They repaired breaches in the wall with earth, caissons, and fascines. The Turks would fill in the moat in order to get closer to the wall; under cover of night

Figure 16. View of Walls of Constantinople.

the defenders would clear it.[44] The Genoese found themselves in an almost untenable position in Galata and could easily have turned into unreliable allies, but they defiantly cast in their lot with the Greeks and
brought them what assistance they could by secretly crossing the Golden
Horn Bay.[45] The Sultan concentrated his attacks on the St. Romanos Gate,
where the Emperor himself fought shoulder to shoulder with the valiant
John Giustiniani.[46]

On 20 April a naval battle in front of the sea wall between the Turkish
fleet and four Christian ships which had arrived from Chios (three Genoese and one Byzantine under the command of Captain Flandanelas),
provided a stirring spectacle. Leaving considerable damage in their wake,
the four ships ran the gauntlet of the Turkish fleet and fought their way
inside the boom which guarded the entrance to the Golden Horn Bay.
The Turkish admiral, Balta Oğlu, found himself discredited; his entire
fortune was confiscated by the irate Sultan and distributed among the
janissaries.[47] Two days later, however, under cover of night, the Turkish
fleet gained entry to the Golden Horn by means of a slipway of wooden
rollers leading from a point near present-day Tophane to the naval
caserns.[48] The besieged garrison then had to be thinned out along the
single wall facing the Bay, which had previously been left undefended.[49]
A Venetian attempt on 28 April to set fire to the Turkish fleet riding in
the Golden Horn failed dismally.[50]

By dint of fanatical persistence the invading force succeeded in filling
in the moat, thus forcing the defenders at last to abandon the breastwork
and retreat behind the Outer Wall. Simultaneously, a furious bombardment was concentrated on the most vulnerable section of the wall and a
length stretching through four towers was practically demolished. The
Great Wall was thereby exposed, and it, too, sustained serious damage.
However, Turkish attempts to storm the wall were repeatedly repulsed
by the defenders under Giustiniani's command.[51] On 18 May the Sultan
was disappointed by the failure of an assault—an "immense battering
ram" on wheels surmounted by "towers and escutcheons." [52] In vain the
Turks attempted to force an entry into the city by a network of under-
ground mines; the last of these was destroyed on 25 May by countermin-
ing activity directed by the German engineer, John Grant.[53] By 24 May
there had been rumors in the city that the Turk would launch his final
attack on 29 May.[54] Outside the walls, ladders and wooden towers were
being placed in position.[55] The Sultan demanded the surrender of the
city and received a characteristic reply from Constantine: "It were better
that you do not count on myself or on any of the inhabitants of the city
to deliver Constantinople into your hands, for we are all of like mind in
preferring to die rather than do so, without so much as a single regret."

In the meantime continuous artillery bombardment had performed its task with such devastating effect that by 27 May the Sultan was able to suspend all ancillary operations. In the vicinity of the St. Romanos Gate the damage was appalling: its tower had collapsed and the adversaries were visible to one another through the gaping breach.[56] The way was then open for a final massive assault by land and sea.[57]

During these last days, the forces of the defenders were redeployed, each man being assigned his final defensive position on the wall.[58] The beleaguered garrison withdrew finally to the Great Wall; that this occurred is evident from the fact that small parties began to infiltrate the enclosure between the Outer Wall and the Great Wall. The purpose of these sorties was not, as Ducas suggests, to harass the Turk, but to effect repairs to the Great Wall and to dig ditches in front of its most indefensible sections. But, when the presence of these parties was detected, the besieged requested that they be allowed egress through a small gate, the Kercoporta. Apparently the Turks had not yet stationed themselves in the enclosure, presumably because its narrow confines inhibited proper deployment and freedom of movement.[59]

The failure of the Venetian attempt to set fire to the Turkish fleet in the Golden Horn, the disagreements between the Venetians and the Genoese, the continuing religious dispute, the fatigue and the inferior discipline of the Greek defenders, continual desertions, the paucity of food and spiralling prices, and the refusal of the wealthy to lend financial aid to the Emperor,[60] all served to undermine the morale of the besieged. These woes seemed the more terrible amid the persistent circulation of old oracles, divinations, and rumors [61] to the sporadic accompaniment of flashes in the sky, earthquakes, dark clouds, spring downpours, "horrific" thunder, and other coincidental phenomena of nature. The nerves of a superstitious and overcredulous populace were strained almost to the breaking point. Thus, during the course of a solemn litany three or four days before the final assault, an icon of the Madonna slipped out of the hands of priests and fell to the ground; whereupon, instantaneously, a quasi-biblical deluge poured from the heavens and flash torrents swept through the streets with such force as almost to carry away small children. At this, there were hysterical outbursts on all sides because it was feared that "a flood of waters would carry away everything that is in the earth." [62]

By now the Emperor had lost all touch with the multitude and their priests. The anti-Unionists openly rebuked him since it seemed that he could no longer protect Orthodoxy. Although Sphrantzes was generally reticent in his history about the religious dispute (perhaps because his pro-Unionist sympathies at the time of the siege could not easily be reconciled with his monastic vocation when the history was written), nevertheless he spoke circumspectly about everyday attitudes characterized by "oaths and abuse in the squares and streets of the city against the unfortunate Emperor and noblemen. But thrice blessed Constantine was a second David; I, as a deaf man, heard not; and I was as a dumb man that openeth not his mouth." [63]

The Emperor continually sought the advice of the noblemen and did everything possible to save the city. But the wealthy still refused to place their wealth at his disposal.[64] Constantine was forced to melt down ecclesiastical plate to obtain money; he promised to repay to the institutions concerned after the city was saved an amount four times as great as that borrowed. He also ordered his prefects to register all men, clergy and laymen alike, who wished to fight and were capable of doing so and took various other steps to strengthen the defenses of the city and to secure food for his soldiers and their families.[65]

Capture of the City

In vain the Constantinopolitans had waited for help from the West. Their ranks had been continually depleted by defections during the course of the siege;[66] probably not more than about fifty thousand people remained in the city.[67] God was now their only hope.[68] As Critobulus says, Constantinople survived in name only: "as for the rest, it seemed to be little more than an enclosure containing cultivable earth, plants, vines, and disused buildings and walls which were not only uninhabited but in ruins." Each tower was manned by no more than two or three men, with about the same number between towers; and almost without exception they were inexperienced fighters and pitifully armed.[69] The Great Wall had taken a terrific pounding. There were now three complete sections which had been practically razed and which offered no serious obstacle even to cavalry charges. Ducas affirms that many of the defenders were standing quite exposed on the ruins of the walls.[70]

On the night of Sunday, 27 May, the Sultan ordered his men to make the necessary religious observances, light fires and festive lanterns, and prepare themselves for the final assault and pillage of the city. On the "grievous evening of Monday," after a moving litany for the people in the streets of the city, Constantine took communion in Hagia Sophia, returned to the palace, and begged forgiveness of all. "How to describe at that hour," writes Sphrantzes, "the weeping and lamentation in the palace? If a man had been made of wood or stone, he must have wept at the scene." [71] The attack was launched by sea and land about two hours before dawn on Tuesday, 29 May. Wave after wave of the attackers were swept back by the defenders. As the day drew on, the battle raged back and forth in the enclosure before the Great Wall. Between 8 a.m. and 9 a.m.[72] John Giustiniani was wounded in the chest by an arrow and retired to one of the ships. Immediately, the line of defense near the St. Romanos Gate from which he withdrew showed signs of wavering. Quickly perceiving his advantage the Sultan sent in his janissaries. Ladders were thrown up and the attackers began to scale the wall. A huge janissary from Olubad (Lopadion) named Hassan was the first to reach the battlements and cut down the defenders. Others followed him, and a savage fight ensued on the Wall. At that moment, the Turks broke into the city by way of the Kercoporta—Critobulus' "Gate of Giustinus [Giustiniani]" [73] —and other breaches in the Wall threw the entire defensive line facing the enclosure into utter confusion. While trying to stem the torrent of invaders in one of these breaches, on a ruined section of the Great Wall facing the Church of St. Romanos, Constantine met his death.[74] "And the whole life of this memorable and dignified martyr-emperor counted but forty-nine years, three months and twenty days." John Dalmates, Theophilus Palaeologus, and several other elite officers died by his side.[75] The initial breaches immediately paralyzed the defense along the remaining parts of the wall. And so, with the enemy behind them and fearful of the fate which might befall their wives and children, the defenders laid down their arms. Some, rather than surrender, threw themselves to their deaths from the top of the wall.[76] Then the pillage began. All who continued to resist were slaughtered. Old people were butchered and infants thrown outside their homes, which were then sacked; women were raped and many made captive. The resplendent capital had become a purgatory.[77] A few hours were enough to transform it into "a field of destruction," just as Joseph Bryennios had foreseen in a vision almost half a century before. Everything was lost: "Church, Empire, state and all that was noble and worthy, purity, charity, sanctity, tradition, freedom, the honor and glory of our race, all that was good was gone forever." [78] A large group of men, women and children that had taken refuge in Hagia Sophia surrendered conditionally,[79] perhaps after putting up at least a token resistance. Evliya Tshelebi has preserved some recollections of that particular pocket of resistance.[80] Even more memorable was the resistance offered by a defiant contingent of Cretans in the towers of Basil, Leo, and Alexius; they abandoned their positions only after the Sultan offered certain terms of surrender and then only with the greatest reluctance.[81] It was probably from such isolated incidents as these that the legend grew, supported by latter-day testimony (if it is not totally false) that as much as half the city surrendered only conditionally. According to the patriarchs Theoleptos I (in 1519) and Jeremiah I (in 1539) during the reigns of Selim I and Suleiman I respectively, these conditions were to ensure the inviolability of the Christian churches.[82]

At about 2 p.m. on the afternoon of the capture, the Sultan entered

Constantinople in the company of a large escort and went straight to Hagia Sophia to pray. Immediately afterwards, he inquired about Constantine and ascertained with some relief that the Emperor had met his end.[83] The evidence concerning the fate of Constantine's body is conflicting. Paspatis believes that the body was never found.[84] Evliya Tschelebi says that it was found and eventually buried in the monastery of Peribleptos (Sulu Manastir) in Hypsomatheia.[85] X. A. Siderides suggests that Tschelebi really meant the Turkish Balıklı (Zoödochos Pege) and not the Sulu Manastir; he then goes on to develop an interesting thesis which rejects various opinions and supports the view that Constantine's body was buried in the Church of the Holy Apostles. Later, Siderides insists, when the architect, Christodoulos, built the Mosque of the Conqueror on the site of the Church of the Holy Apostles, he took care to see that the remains were disinterred and transferred to the Church of St. Theodosia.[86]

The Turkish prince, Orchan, tried to escape from the city disguised as a monk but was betrayed and immediately done to death.[87] Others captured were the Grand Duke Lucas Notaras, his wife and two sons; a certain Cantacuzenus, identified only as the son of the sometime chancellor[88] and fiancé of the Duke's eldest daughter, Anna; and nine other Notables and their families. At first, Mohammed II treated them with due deference, but a few days later all except the women and children were killed. The comelier of these boys and girls he gave into the custody of his chief eunuch. At the same time the officials among the Venetian prisoners were also put to death. Especially tragic was the execution of Lucas Notaras. His eldest son and son-in-law were beheaded before his very eyes "so that he himself might see that their faith remained stronger than their fear of death." His own execution followed. Notaras, who displayed great nobility during the whole terrible ordeal, may be considered as the first of the martyrs of Neo-Hellenism after the capture of the city. His youngest son, Jacob, was confined in the Sultan's palace in Adrianople. One reason for this mass execution was Notaras' staunch refusal to deliver up his son to the debauched Sultan. Another reason was that the Sultan bowed to the wishes of powerful Turkish nobles, who insisted that the Byzantine nobility could never be trusted and would therefore have to be exterminated to a man.[89] No doubt they expected to benefit from the forfeiture of Byzantine property.

Notaras saved his daughters, Anna, Theodora, and Euphrosyne, by sending them to Italy with a large fortune before the fall of the city. A few years later (some time between 1458 and 1464, though exactly when is not known), these daughters were reunited with their younger brother Jacob, who had succeeded in escaping (how is not known) from the Sultan's seraglio.[90] Jacob found his way to Rome and was sheltered by Bessarion and Pope Pius II.[91] In 1475, Anna Notaras was in Venice and patroness of a large Greek community, not of scholars only, which had gravitated towards that city. The port of Venice became a sort of "window on the East," through which the survivors of the Greek nation looked towards their Turkish-dominated homeland. In Venice, Anna Notaras and Evdokia Cantacuzenus,[92] another noblewoman, were granted the privilege of worshipping in their own chapel according to the rites of Orthodoxy.[93] Anna, a bereaved fiancée, remained Orthodox and unmarried up to her death in 1507.[94]

Following ancient Turkish custom, Mohammed confined in his seraglio not only Notaras' son Jacob but the sons of other Byzantine noblemen. Some of these were destined to attain the highest offices in the Ottoman Empire and to wield enormous power. Among these were Murad of the house of Palaeologus and Mohammed, son of Mandrominos, who became Bey of the *sancak* of Ankara.[95] While still children their future careers in the civil service were mapped out. Known as *iç oğlan,* they were subjected to a rigorous regimen of training and instruction in a special school of the seraglio and eventually filled some of the most important posts in the Sultan's government. Together with the janissaries they comprised the separate class of *kapı kulları,* slaves of the Porte. Mohammed II used them to reinforce his own position as sultan and, contrary to previous custom, increasingly appointed men from this class to the office of Grand Vizier. In consequence, the power of the old Turkish noble families underwent a progressive diminution.[96] Mohammed II gradually took over the reins of power until he became absolute monarch.

It used to be believed, mistakenly, that none of the Greek military dignitaries survived the capture of Constantinople.[97] But there are a great many Hellenic traditions, as well as documentary proof, testifying to the escape of many Byzantine officials and their families to the islands of the Aegean and other Greek lands.[98] A Venetian source, for instance, records that a galley belonging to a Genoese, Zorzi Doria, slipped away from the tormented city on the very night of the capture. Besides Genoese, there were a number of Greek families on board: Theodore and Andronicus Palaeologus; Emmanuel, Thomas, and Demetrius Palaeologus; John and Demetrius Cantacuzenus; Theodore and Emmanuel Lascaris; Constantine and Isaac Comnenus; Vlasios and Matthew Notaras; Michael and Jacob Kalaphatis; Jacob, John, and George Katallactis; Stamatis, Emmanuel, Leo, and John Vardas; Leo and Andrea Thalassinos; Andronicus and Emmanuel Phocas; Philippe Scarlatos; Leo and Antony Mousouros; Sergius, Antony, and Nicholas Metaxas; one Marianos; and the Achilles family, Demetrius and Theodore Bozikis of Albanian descent. These nobles and their families initially took refuge on Chios and later moved to Canea, Crete. Some of them remained permanently in Crete—the Kalaphatis, Mousouros, and Vardas families, for instance—and subsequently scattered throughout the towns of the island; others went to the Despotate of Morea and to Zacynthus; the Metaxas and Phocas families settled in Cephalonia; the Lascaris family found its way to Corfu; and still others went to Rome, where they sought the protection of the Pope. It is extremely likely that many present-day families of the same name are descended from these Byzantine officials, especially those from places to which their forebears had fled. A few of these nobles—some from the Lascaris and Palaeologus families—later enlisted as officers in the Venetian corps of light horse known as *Stradioti*.[99]

Besides the foreign ships, four Cretan vessels and their crews also escaped from the city. Sorrowfully they put out into the Aegean and took their melancholy news from island to island. This struck terror into the hearts of the island people: surely their turn was next. What else to do but flee? [100]

On 1 June, the Genoese governor of Galata surrendered the keys of the castle to Mohammed.[101] This voluntary submission predisposed the Sultan towards granting the Genoese community a number of significant privileges: they would have self-government, their religious observances would be respected, free trade concessions throughout the Ottoman Empire would be granted, and their children would be exempt from the customary military impressment of Christians.[102] According to Amantos, the treaty thus framed was used as a model for the subsequent extension of similar rights to other Christian communities under Ottoman dominion.[103]

The siege, capture, and three days' pillage of Constantinople cost the lives of about four thousand men, women, and children, both Greek and foreign. About fifty thousand captives were enslaved.[104] Not a soul was permitted to remain in the city, whether Greek, Frank, Armenian, or Jew.[105] On the fourth day, Mohammed allowed his soldiers to return to their provinces with captives and booty. Immediately after the fall of the capital, Selymbria, the last oasis of freedom in Thrace, also surrendered.[106] Scyrus and other islands of the northern Sporades were occupied by the Venetians in the following year.[107]

Echoes of the Fall in Legend and Tradition

Thus was effaced "the hearth of all the Greeks, the home of the muses, the seat of all learning, the queen of cities." [108] Its fall had world-wide historical significance because Constantinople was regarded as the common property of Christianity and European civilization. All European peoples—Slavs, Rumanians, Hungarians, Germans, French, Italians, Spaniards, and the rest—were acutely conscious of the loss, and of course from that time to this a concourse of poets, artists, and savants has been moved by the tragedy. But although at the time its end produced genuine reactions of sorrow, pessimism, and concern, these were not sufficient to submerge the conflicting interests of powerful forces which might otherwise have launched a crusade for reconquest.[109]

The event gave rise to harrowing inquests. Generally speaking, clerical circles and the super-orthodox masses in West and East adhered rigidly to the traditional explanations of the fall: in the West, the capture was no more than divine retribution for the sins of the Orthodox, particularly the Photian Schism; in the East, this was no question of schismatic "illegality," but rather of a "certain torment" which God had visited upon the Orthodox and which ennobled them because the saints had suffered the same "agony." [110]

Many Greeks had had sure presentiments of the capture, though naturally they had tried to shut such thoughts out of their minds and secretly hoped that something would happen at the last moment to avert it. Prophecies circulated which held out some hope for reprieve; and where no comfort was taken in these there was a belief in ultimate intervention by God, Who surely would never allow the "queen of cities" to fall defenseless into the hands of the infidel. Thus fear and impotence only made the masses more blind in their faith than before. As long as Constantinople held out, it was felt, there was always some hope that one day their enslaved brothers would be free. But of course with the fall of the city the last glimmer of hope disappeared. The event was so shocking that the Orthodox were driven to ask themselves whether or not it could indeed be God's retribution as the Catholics claimed. Could the Orthodox really be heretics? Was Islam, perhaps, the only true religion? The crisis shook the beliefs of the faithful and the Orthodox Church to their foundations.

The severity of the blow and the great depths of despondency into which the Greeks were plunged can only be gauged from the large number of prose and verse laments,[111] both erudite and popular, and the even more numerous oracles, legends, and traditions which have remained part of the popular heritage to this day.[112]

The heroic figure of Constantine and the conflicting evidence as to the disposition of his body obsessed the imagination of the Greeks.[113] Some of the rumors and legends that sprang up and later spread to every corner of the Greek world had their origin in those first hours of confusion and uncertainty after his death. Some of the older traditions were also modified or distorted later on by the interpolation of additional material. There was one, for example, that "The Turks would enter Constantinople in great force and slaughter the 'Romans' until they got as far as the column of Constantine the Great. Then an angel of the Lord would descend from heaven and present a mighty sword, and with it the Empire, to a simple and poorly dressed stranger who would be standing near the column. [Here, the words 'poorly dressed' recall that most persistent of Byzantine traditions regarding the 'unfortunate Emperor.'] The angel would then say to him, 'take this sword and avenge God's people,' whereupon the 'Romans' would turn upon the Turks, put them to flight and cast them out of Constantinople; nor would pursuit end until the very boundaries of Persia had been reached—at Kokkini Melia [Red Apple Tree] in the place called Monodendrion [Only One Tree]." [114] (These were legendary places in Asia Minor.) In essence, the tradition was in circulation many years before the capture, but the reference to Kokkini Melia was an embellishment added by later Hellenic tradition. Its significance and that of its Turkish equivalent, *kızıl elma* (red apple), however, remain uncertain.[115]

Another of the older oracles prophesying the downfall of the Turks concerned a "fair-haired race" [116] and was commonly attributed to Emperor Leo the Wise. The oracle was later amended to conform to the reality of the capture, and it appeared as a consoling appendage to the Russian "Narrative concerning the Fall of Constantinople." The original text was written before 1460,[117] probably by a Greek from somewhere outside the capital. In the Russian version, the "fair-haired race" was identified as the Franks; [118] and these, with the assistance of the former inhabitants of Constantinople, would defeat the "Ishmaelites," the Turks, and reconquer New Rome. By the sixteenth century, however, the "fair-haired race" had for the Greeks come to signify the Russians, probably through a copyist's error in transcribing the Russian text: the addition of the single letter *k* to the phrase *rusij rod* (fair-haired race) changed it into *ruskij rod* (Russian race).[119]

The Byzantine legend of the angel who would present a mighty sword to a stranger, interwoven, it would seem, with the rumors that Constantine's body was not found, apparently also gave rise to two further legends: the first told of the dead Emperor, who would be awakened after a long sleep and again take up his scepter. The second told of the "Emperor who had been turned into marble" and of an angel of the Lord who would "change him back into a living person" and restore to him the sword he had used during the battle, a sword with which he would then smite the Turks and chase them as far as Kokkini Melia.[120] This is the most poetic and moving of all the Greek national legends. Just as Bessarion and all those who still remained in what was left of the Byzantine Empire had anticipated great deeds from Constantine during his lifetime, so throughout the long years of Turkish rule Constantine was expected miraculously to restore freedom to the Greeks. Thus, Constantine became a symbol of the national will to be free. There was really a prophetic tone in Bessarion's letter to Constantine: "and your immortal name will be handed down by posterity; and death, which extinguishes the fame of most kings and nobles, will in your case only glorify it." [121]

Other legends which later spread throughout Christendom concerned the rape of Constantine's empress and her daughters by Mohammed II and their death (the Empress, of course, had died long before the city's capture); [122] the Emperor's murder while trying to escape; and the mockery made of his severed head.[123]

All of these traditions emanating from the capture, in particular those nebulous oracles predicting the downfall of the Turks and the recapture of Constantinople, which were mainly attributed to Leo the Wise, generally had widespread currency. Many extant manuscripts attest their circulation throughout Russia and Western Europe.[124] This oracular literature conveys a sense of the profound disquiet which afflicted Christian consciences everywhere after the fall, while at the same time marking the persistence of Greek faith in the ultimate restoration of their nation. We shall remark elsewhere on the appearance and influence of these oracles.

The capture of Constantinople, of course, predetermined the fate of the remaining fragments of the medieval Greek Empire. Yet a few remnants managed to survive unconquered by the Turks for a few more years, the Despotate of Morea and the Empire of Trebizond, to take the two most notable examples. And there were other Greek lands which remained under the dominion of individual Frankish rulers or Western states—for instance Crete under the Venetians.

But Constantinople was no longer the pre-eminent center of civilization and cultural diffusion in Europe, East or West. Its cultural and economic ties even with neighboring Orthodox peoples such as Georgians and Russians [125] were effectively severed.

Its capture also led to a deterioration of the plight of Greek raias in lands already occupied by the Turks. They were treated as a people without a country and therefore powerless and of no account. An examination of their predicament and the changing attitude of the Turks has to rely on posterior sources, the only ones available, or on the evidence of oral tradition and legend.[126]

15

COMPLETION OF THE
TURKISH CONQUEST

Structure of Ottoman Empire after 1453

With the capture of Constantinople the Ottoman Empire acquired a central capital which was the natural pivot of all those countries stretching from the Euphrates to the Adriatic Sea—"the key to all Romania," in the words of an anonymous post-Byzantine poet.[1]

Laonicos Chalcocondyles' description of the imperial structure at this time discloses that the European territory was divided into thirty-six *sancaks,* and that of Asia Minor forty. The *sancak* chiefs were paid direct from the Sultan's treasury, and their salaries ranged from various levels to a maximum of twenty thousand gold pieces. Some of the larger cities such as Thessalonica, Skoplje (Üsküb) and Philippopolis were governed by pashas, but these were still required to follow the *sancak* chiefs in time of war. Both the pashas and the *sancak* chiefs in Europe were responsible to the *beylerbey,* or governor-general of Europe (*Rumeli Valesi*); those of Asia Minor and rulers with varying degrees of autonomy in the Ottoman Empire were responsible to the *beylerbey* of Asia. However, great power became concentrated in the hands of the chief palace officials, who were not only paid huge salaries from the Sultan's purse, but also received gifts from the *sancak* chiefs and pashas of particular districts. Other palace retainers were also powerful—couriers, advisers, financial administrators, the treasurer, and a multitude of clerks responsible for the compilation of the Sultan's decrees and other official documents.

The Sultan's revenue was derived from a variety of sources. A total of 900,000 gold pieces per annum came from the tax on European raias, the tithe (which, from the time of Mohammed II, was also levied on Turks) and a tax on sheep. Other revenue which found its way into the Sultan's treasury included taxes on horses, camels, mules, and cattle (approximately 300,000 gold pieces), rents (250,000), and income from the forage of camels and mules (50,000). There were also customs duties, as well as taxes on mines, rice, copper, alum, and an extensive array of other products and activities. The overall income of the Sultan and his palace officials from all sources in the Empire was estimated at 14,000,000 Venetian gold pieces. The salaries of the janissaries and other "slaves of the Porte" were paid every three months and depleted the Sultan's treasury by nine million gold pieces annually.[2]

After the fall of Constantinople, the Ottoman Empire thus acquired cohesion as well as strength. If a new period of conquest were inaugurated, it would clearly be only a matter of time before the remaining Greek lands also fell.

Fall of the Despotate of Morea

The capture of the city was preceded in October 1452 by Turahan's invasion of the Peloponnese as far as the Gulf of Messenia, and because of the rapidity with which the one event followed the other the Palaeologus brothers, Thomas and Demetrius, and their nobles were already preparing to leave for Italy. For the time being, however, reassured by the pacific disposition of the Sultan, they elected instead to remain as his tributaries. But the Despots' fears did not go unnoticed by the local Albanian settlers, who immediately sought to exploit these weaknesses by means of a rebellion under the leadership of the unscrupulous but clever Peter Cholos (the Crippled).[3] They were no doubt goaded into doing so by the onerous taxation and numberless other economic grievances with which they were burdened.[4] An additional incitement may well have been the very powerlessness of the Greek population of the Peloponnese. Successive invasions by Turahan Bey in Thessaly and the Peloponnese during 1423, 1431, 1446, and 1452 [5] were attended by widespread devastation and chaos and had thinned out the population, especially in those cities and villages which lay across the path of the invaders; Corinth, for example, was virtually a city without people in 1436.[6] The Albanians, on the other hand, suffered much less, since they lived a nomadic life and nowhere maintained permanent settlements.[7]

Chalcocondyles suggests that the rebellion had certain nationalistic overtones. If the rebel leaders did make a nationalist appeal of sorts, the eagerness of the majority to reach an understanding with the Despots shows that it remained largely ineffectual. Nonetheless, the rebellion spread because the Albanian leaders and Greek noblemen had no interest in finding such an accommodation and did everything possible to prevent it. Greek nobles, ever eager to assert their independence and shake off the sovereignty of the Palaeologi, actually brought in Manuel Cantacuzenus to be their ruler. The insurrection caused great havoc throughout the country.[8]

In a short while, the Albanians and the unruly Greek nobles controlled the greater part of the Peloponnese. The Palaeologus brothers thus found themselves in a mortifying position, which was not alleviated by the Sultan's intervention. Undoubtedly fearing that Albanian ascendancy would only create fresh problems—similar perhaps to those which Mohammed's father had faced when fighting Scanderbeg, otherwise known as George Castriota, the famous Albanian leader who carried on an heroic war against the Turks—Mohammed chose to aid the weaker party. In December 1453, Ömer, son of Turahan, was sent to the Peloponnese and was followed a year later by the old bey himself. There they co-operated with the forces of the Palaeologi and after hard fighting succeeded in re-establishing the sovereignty of the Despots.[9] In December 1454, the Sultan, anxious to restore peace in the Peloponnese, prevailed upon certain Greek and Albanian noblemen who had taken refuge in the Venetian colonies to return to their homes, where he promised them a better life. Among these were Manuel Raul, one Sophianos, Demetrius Lascaris, members of the Diplovatatzes, Kavakes, Pagomenos, and Petrobouas families, and others.[10]

But the peace was evanescent. Insufficient evidence prevents us from knowing exactly what happened, but it is clear that political and economic confusion continued to reign. The invasions had exacerbated the already miserable plight of the Greek and Albanian populace, and the nobles continued to brawl with one another. The people announced that they would henceforth refuse to pay taxes unless "a certain person" (by whom they undoubtedly meant the Sultan) agreed to divide the country between the Greeks and Albanians and ratify such division by formal rescript. However, these protests were of no avail.[11]

The behavior of the Palaeologus brothers did nothing to improve matters. Each continued to win over (or to try to win over) by flattery individual Greek and Albanian nobles, and also to cajole certain refugees from Constantinople into joining him.[12] Each aimed at becoming supreme in the Peloponnese, if necessary by seeking assistance from the West. Accordingly, in 1455 each of the brothers separately sent envoys to the courts of Pope Callixtus III, Duke Francesco Sforza of Milan, and King Charles VII of France. Thomas' emissary was the celebrated scholar and votary of Church Union, John Argyropoulous, while Demetrius sent Frangoulios Servopoulos. Their mission was to inveigle the Western rulers into organizing a crusade.[13] As we shall see, Cardinal Bessarion had already aroused the keen interest of the Pope in such a project.

The Despots' reluctance to honor their obligations as vassals, the internal disturbances in the Peloponnese, and the diplomatic rapprochement with the West at first perturbed the Sultan, then enraged him. Accordingly, in the winter of 1457 he made overt military preparations to invade the Peloponnese.[14]

In the spring of 1458 the Sultan set out from Adrianople, crossed the Greek peninsula, and on 15 May arrived at the Peloponnese. He encountered his first resistance at Acrocorinth, which was defended by Lucanis Nicephorus. Leaving there his cannon and the army of the East, he advanced into the interior, pillaging as he went, and everywhere crushing the Greeks and Albanians, who had finally united in order to confront the common danger. Within two months he had conquered the mighty fortresses of Polyphengon, Tarsos, and Mouchlion, which were strategically situated between the Parthenion and Artemision ranges straddling the present-day road from Argos to Tripolis; then, turning to the northwest and skirting the mountainous and virtually impenetrable district of Mainalon and the Erymanthos Mountains, he arrived by a series of forced marches at the Gulf of Patras. The inhabitants of Patras had already fled either to the Venetian colonies or to Naupactus, and only the citadel was garrisoned. After plundering the city, he laid siege to the fortress, which surrendered conditionally after a few days. The Sultan was enormously impressed by both the strategic advantages which the city offered and the general fertility of the district, and he lingered there for a while. Indeed, he made it his business to repopulate Patras and sent couriers to those who had fled, offering them substantial inducements to return: they would be permitted to live unmolested; they would receive land and would be exempt from taxes for several years. Mohammed then resumed his march along the shore of the Gulf of Corinth, accepted the conditional surrender of Aigion (Vostitsa) and sweeping aside everything that stood in his way returned to Acrocorinth after an absence of four months.[15] Since the citadel there had still not fallen, he immediately suspended further operations until it could be taken. His army was redeployed in more advantageous positions around the castle to wait until hunger and privation should force the defenders to surrender. However, Demetrius dispatched his brother-in-law, Asanes Matthew, to reconnoiter the situation, gain entry to the citadel, attempt to boost the morale of the defenders, and negotiate with the Sultan terms of surrender, which, if possible, would not sacrifice the Greek position in Corinth. Under cover of night Asanes Matthew and seventy men, all carrying supplies of grain, succeeded in slipping through the Turkish lines and entering the fortress

Figure 17. Acrocorinth.

of Acrocorinth. No sooner had he accomplished this much than he came to the conclusion that the defenders' position was hopeless and accepted the Sultan's harsh conditions of surrender. These stipulated the surrender of all that territory previously conquered by the Sultan which was bounded by a rough triangle whose apex was Mouchlion and whose base was the northern shore of the Peloponnese. Most of this territory belonged to Thomas Palaeologus and comprised about one-third of the total area of the Peloponnese. Thomas and Demetrius Palaeologus were restricted to the remainder, and in addition were obliged to pay an annual tribute of three thousand gold pieces and request aid from the Sultan if ever they were attacked.[16]

It was remarkable of course that, in acceding to these terms, Asanes and the commander of the Acrocorinth garrison, Lucanis Nicephorus, had completely discounted the wishes of Thomas. When Thomas eventually met them—"The architects of such meritorious deeds," as Sphrantzes sarcastically called them—he found himself presented with a *fait accompli;* however, he seemed convinced that the only practicable course had been taken, and hastily confirming the action of his subordinates gave away his territory "as though it were a vegetable plot." These precipitate and ill-considered moves aroused universal indignation—at least so we infer from Sphrantzes' derisory comments, as well as from additional evidence supplied by Critobulus. What was specially condemned was the surrender of Acrocorinth to the Turks: no castle in the entire Peloponnese was more strategically placed, and since whoever occupied it controlled the Peloponnese the Sultan had now an established bridgehead from which future operations against the Palaeologus brothers could be conducted. As governor of his newly acquired territories the Sultan appointed Ömer, son of Turahan, the governor of Thessaly.[17] Thus ended Mohammed's first campaign in the Peloponnese.

Mohammed interrupted his return journey to Adrianople the following autumn with a four-day visit to Athens. The city had previously been delivered over to Ömer by the last of the Frankish rulers in Attica, Francesco Acciajuoli.[18] The Sultan, a great admirer of antiquity, doted on the ancient monuments which still stood, particularly those of the Acropolis; and moved by their former glory he acted in a most generous manner towards the inhabitants of the city, bestowing many privileges and acceding to most of their requests.[19] Athens retained these privileges throughout the entire period of Turkish domination.

Immediately after their arrival in Athens, the Turks began construction of the Mosque of the Conqueror in the middle of the city, as it then was— the part which was later known as the Marketplace (*Pazar*).[20]

In the Peloponnese Demetrius continued to strengthen his rapport with the Turks, while Thomas was leaning more and more towards association with the West. In order to consolidate his position in the Peloponnese and simultaneously neutralize the opposing forces of the Despots, the Sultan made overtures to Demetrius to marry his daughter. However, in January 1459, the Peloponnesian nobility, believing that any situation in which intrigue and suspicion were fostered could only enhance their independence, urged Thomas to move against his brother and the Sultan's dependencies. Among these nobles there were some who had disavowed the sovereignty of both Despots and were already indiscriminately looting and destroying property. Moreover, Turkish garrisons in the Peloponnesian castles instituted military operations against Thomas.

The inhabitants were finally so appalled at the extent of destruction and so disgusted with the misgovernment inflicted on them that they at last bestirred themselves. The Palaeologus brothers were, of course, primarily responsible for this state of affairs and were accordingly despised by the Turks. An outburst of unfavorable public opinion forced the brothers to meet in Kastritsi, a fortress in central Peloponnesus, in an attempt to settle their differences. But the respite was a brief one: the following winter Demetrius violated the terms of their agreement and recommenced hostilities. However, he was eventually forced to take refuge in Monemvasia, whence he requested direct intervention by the Sultan.[21]

The Sultan, angered by the anarchy which continued to rend the Peloponnese and fearful that others might cast covetous eyes on so tempting a prey, decided to incorporate the Peloponnese in the Ottoman Empire. So in April 1460, for the second time, he set out from Adrianople with a large army; he reached Corinth in twenty-seven days. From there, instead of moving, as expected, against Thomas, he turned south and marched into Demetrius' territory without encountering any resistance.[22] It may have been at this time (though according to the oral tradition of a much later period, it was earlier) that the Sultan granted the inhabitants of the Dervenochoria, mountain villages south of Corinth, a number of privileges in return for their acceptance of responsibility for the security of the Turkish mails.[23] These included payment of nominal taxes only, exemption from forced labor and from the requisitioning and billeting of Turkish troops. Continuing his march, Mohammed went around Argos towards the center of the Peloponnese and Mistra. By a quirk of fate, that city fell on 29 May, the anniversary of the capture of Constantinople. Demetrius offered no resistance: his reward was the Sultan's promise of a princely living in the future. Indeed, after his return to Adrianople and his marriage to Demetrius' daughter, Mohammed bestowed on his father-in-law the entire revenues of the islands of the northeastern Aegean (Imbros, Lemnos, Thasos, and Samothrace), together with those of Thracian Ainos, which had recently belonged to the Genoese house of Gattilusi.[24]

Mohammed next turned against certain strongholds held by Thomas in the central and southwestern Peloponnese—against Kastritsi and later against Gardiki near Leondari. He gave no quarter to the gallant Greek and Albanian defenders, seeking to quell all resistance by terrorizing his opponents.[25] The garrisons were slaughtered to a man. The memory of this massacre is still preserved in the traditions of the people of Gardiki and in the toponym Kokkala (bones), signifying the place of martyrdom.[26]

With the fall of these two castles the way was open for an invasion of Messenia and the end of the war was in sight. Resistance simply melted away on all sides. Thomas' lieutenants abandoned their posts in towns and castles, and, followed by the local nobles, fled to the Venetian colonies of Korone, Methone, and Pylos (then Navarino). The various fortresses were occupied one after the other. Those the Sultan judged unsuitable were pulled down to preclude their use as future pockets of resistance. Local residents were generally permitted to remain in their homes, though some were removed in order to assist in the repopulation of Constantinople. By the time he reached Pylos, Mohammed was undisputed master of Messenia: to escape battle, Thomas Palaeologus, last Despot of Morea, and a few nobles had already sailed away to Corfu. Thomas had finally abandoned all hope that some castles would hold out and that refuge might be found somewhere in the Peloponnese.[27]

Simultaneously, the fortresses of Chlomoutsi and Santameri in the northwestern Peloponnese capitulated, and they were soon followed by the remaining castles in Achaia and Elis. The last scene of this drama was set in Achaia, where by a strange coincidence the curtain would go up in the Greek war of independence in 1821. After an heroic defense, the last castle, Salmenico, accepted honorable terms of surrender late in July 1461. According to Mahmud, Master of the Sultanic Household,[28] its defender, Constantine Palaeologus, known as Graetzas, was the only man left in the entire Peloponnese.[29] Isolated and sporadic resistance by elements of Thomas Palaeologus' army was probably all that remained— at least so Thomas himself claimed in one of his communications to the Venetian Senate the following year.[30]

All of the Peloponnese except the Venetian colonies and Monemvasia had by then passed into Mohammed's hands. It is likely, too, that Maina accepted terms of surrender at this time, though its inhospitable shores and mountainous hinterland no doubt continued to provide shelter for large numbers of refugees. Indeed, an early seventeenth-century source suggests that the Turks had still not forced Maina [31] and that many noble

Figure 18. Castle of Modon (Methone).

families, among them the hellenized descendants of the Florentine Medicis, who had settled in Athens at the time of the Acciajuoli Duchy,[32] lived there in perfect security alongside the Greek inhabitants and the Albanian settlers.[33] Thus, the district of Maina was one of the wellsprings of Greek nationalism—the Peloponnesian counterpart of the Pindus district in western Greece. Both of them appear to have preserved the same autonomous privileges and semi-independence that they had enjoyed during the Byzantine period, and both remained the most restive parts of Hellas under Turkish dominion. Maina's form of government and the precise nature of its privileges, at least during the first centuries of Turkish domination, remain unknown.

Mohammed brought with him on his return to Adrianople not only Demetrius himself but his courtiers and various nobles and officials from Achaia, Laconia, and the other provinces. He killed any Albanian notables who did not manage to escape.[34] This reflected Mohammed's Draconian treatment of the Albanians in general. A later legend told of Albanians who fled to the desolate islands of Hydra and Spetsai in order to escape the Sultan's unrelenting persecution and whose descendants in 1821 burst out of their islands to avenge their ancestors.[35] However, since the traveller André Thevet reported in 1550 that Hydra was uninhabited, the legend was probably a highly romanticized version of actual events.[36]

In November 1460, after leaving his family in Corfu, Thomas set out for Rome in the hope of finding new resources and inciting the powerful forces of the West against the Turks. As a gift to the Pope he took the head of St. Andrew, which had previously reposed in Patras. (Pope Paul VI returned the head to Patras in September 1964.) The Pope, the cardinals, and Venice each granted Thomas annual subsidies of three hundred, two hundred, and five hundred ducats respectively.[37] Although there were insuperable obstacles in the way of successfully organizing a crusade, Thomas' hopes were raised in 1463 by the beginning of protracted hostilities between Venice and the Ottoman Empire. He died, however, in May 1465 while negotiating with the princely courts of Europe for an extension of that war.[38] Cardinal Bessarion assumed the guardianship of his children, Andrew, Emmanuel, and Zoë, and had them brought up in accordance with the provisions of the Florentine agreement.[39]

Meanwhile the nobles, assembled in Corfu, had been awaiting the outcome of Thomas' representations. When the failure of his first attempts dashed their hopes of obtaining any kind of aid from the West, they regretfully dispersed.[40] A Venetian document of 27 April 1461 notes the presence of many Greek noblemen and clerics in Crete, which would seem to indicate that some at least took refuge in Candia and other towns and villages on the island. Venice, discovering evidence of a conspiracy against her, became alarmed at the persistent congregation of these Greeks and instructed the local authorities to exercise extreme caution in dealing with them and to banish those engaged in suspicious activities.[41] On the other hand, some of the nobles appear to have remained permanently in Corfu—among them Constantine XI Palaeologus' chamberlain, George Sphrantzes, who spent his last days as a monk. Here, in 1486, moved by his memories and inspired by discussions with the nobles of Corfu (and begged by them to set down all that he had seen, heard, and lived), the aging Sphrantzes set about the writing of his *Chronicle*.[42] Tradition has it that he was buried in front of the ancient Church of the Prophet Elijah.[43]

The fate of Demetrius Palaeologus was bound up with that of the islands of the northeastern Aegean, as will be seen below.

Seizure of the Gattilusi Possessions

The islands of the northeastern Aegean (Thasos, Samothrace, Imbros, Lemnos, and Lesbos) had been attached as fiefs to the house of Gattilusi by the Emperors Manuel II (1391–1425) and John VIII Palaeologus (1425–1448). Although they continued to acknowledge the suzerainty of the Emperors, the imperial functionaries on the islands, who were descended from aristocratic families, were in fact no more than ineffectual figureheads.[44] By the time of the fall of Constantinople virtually full authority had devolved upon members of the house of Gattilusi, in particular on Dorino I, who ruled in Lesbos, and his younger brother Palamedes, who ruled in Thracian Ainos. Dorino I's fief also included Lemnos and Thasos, and that of his brother Imbros and Samothrace. When Genoese ships brought the news of the city's capture, Constantine XI Palaeologus' governors on Lemnos and Imbros, believing that all was lost, departed on the very ships that carried the news, leaving their territories ungoverned.

The likelihood of imminent invasion by a Turkish fleet was uppermost in the minds of the islanders. Consequently their chief concern was to escape. Two hundred men from Lemnos, among them most of the wealthy and prominent citizens, sailed away with their families to Crete, Chios, and Euboea.

In the midst of this turmoil, Critobulus of Imbros, one of the most powerful landowners there and later renowned as an historian of the Byzantine Empire's last years, appeared on the scene for the first time. He attempted to hold the invader at bay by opening negotiations with the Sultan, an initiative which he took on behalf of the neighboring islands of Lemnos and Thasos, as well as of his own Imbros. Critobulus succeeded in restoring the courage of the island inhabitants and in stopping their headlong flight. He had quietly sent a trusted envoy to Hamza, the admiral of the Turkish fleet and the governor of Gallipoli, and this official, having had gifts lavished upon him, was persuaded to hold off his fleet. Soon afterwards, Hamza interceded with the Sultan on Critobulus' behalf, and Mohammed received another deputation, again laden with gifts, in Adrianople. On this occasion, Critobulus offered to place the islands under the Sultan's sovereignty, though at the same time entreating him to grant them their previous status and to "allow them to pay the annual tribute which is your due and to have a governor if you so order."

At the same time, Palamedes of Ainos also sent a "paramount and trusty" noble to the Sultan's court with the request that he be allowed to retain Imbros and that his authority over the island already enfeoffed to him be legally vouchsafed. Similarly, his elder brother Dorino I, the aging ruler of Lesbos, had dispatched his own eldest son and co-ruler, Domenico, to press the same suit on behalf of the islands of Lemnos and Thasos. The envoys of these petty Genoese rulers met Critobulus' deputation in Adrianople, and since all were in complete accord as to what the future of the islands should be, they decided to act in concert before the Sultan in order to ensure the preservation of the political and social *status quo*. Their joint efforts were crowned with success when Mohammed, as Critobulus wrote, "set aside the islands under the same conditions which obtained at the time of the late Emperor [Constantine]." Lemnos and Thasos went to Dorino and Imbros and Palamedes, and an annual tribute from the former was fixed at 3,000 gold pieces for Lesbos and 2,325 for Lemnos. Palamedes was required to furnish 1,200 gold pieces for Imbros.

This solution was satisfactory to the Sultan because of considerations of political expediency, not because his generosity and magnanimity got the better of him, as Critobulus would have us believe. The Genoese rulers maintained close ties with their compatriots in the Christian West and the danger still existed that their incessant pleas for the organization of a crusade might not always fall on deaf ears. By refraining from the immediate incorporation of these islands in his vast empire, Mohammed hoped to avoid unnecessary provocation.

Nevertheless, Mohammed's conciliatory attitude did not long suffice those Christian rulers whose propinquity to the Turkish might made them most vulnerable. After recovering from the initial shock of the capture of Constantinople, they began to look to the defense of their territories and lost little time in establishing close contact with the West. Their chief protagonist was Jean de Lastiq, the Commander of the Knights of

Rhodes, who began to send letters to all rulers in the West, adjuring them to avenge the Christian blood which had flowed in Constantinople and especially to support Christianity's strongest bastion in the East— Rhodes itself. These appeals struck some chords of sympathetic response in the West and aroused a degree of indignation against the "infidels," but not enough to induce Pope Nicholas V to launch a new crusade. The Pope died in March 1455, however, and his successor, Callixtus III, reacting more favorably to Bessarion's persuasions, worked tirelessly for a common understanding among all Christian rulers and for a united front against the Turk. Europe was crisscrossed by an army of preachers appealing to Christian consciences and offering indulgences to those who provided money or personal services for the success of the cause. But the West was torn by the rivalries and disputes of individual European rulers, and only scant interest was kindled. Pope Callixtus raised a force of but twenty-five ships, five thousand soldiers, and one thousand sailors, at the head of which he placed Lodovico Scarampi, Patriarch of Aquileia in Italy.[45]

In the face of the Crusade, the Sultan obviously could no longer ignore the Frankish rulers of the Aegean, whose territories formed potential naval bases. He therefore abruptly reversed his Aegean policies. First, he demanded that Rhodes pay tribute as Chios, Lesbos, Lemnos, and Imbros did. "From now on," envoys of the Knights Hospitalers were brusquely informed by the viziers, "the Sultan is master of all the islands of the Aegean." When the Knights refused to comply with the Sultan's demand, hostilities began, but the Sultan's forces found the island's fortifications impregnable.

Mohammed was therefore obliged to adopt an alternative ploy. The small Genoese possessions of the Gattilusi at the entrance to the Hellespont were easier prey. The death on 30 June 1455 of Dorino I of Lesbos and the succession of his son and heir, Domenico, provided a favorable opportunity. On 1 August, Domenico's emissary, Michael Ducas, later noted as an historian, arrived in Adrianople with the annual tribute and found himself in an atmosphere of grim foreboding. The Sultan's viziers, Mahmoud and Seïdi Ahmet, icily informed him that Domenico would not be recognized as ruler unless he appeared in person to receive that authority from the Sultan. Accordingly, Domenico started out from Mytilene with an escort composed of Ducas and some Greek and Frankish nobles and in due course arrived in Adrianople, only to find that a pestilence which had killed many people in Thrace was still raging and that the Sultan had left the city. Domenico went in search of the Sultan first to Philippopolis, then to Sofia, and at length found him in the Bulgarian village of Izlati. After leaving Domenico to cool his heels for three days, two of the Sultan's viziers told him that the Sultan wanted Thasos as a gift. The Frankish ruler acceded to the Sultan's demand. Domenico left Izlati wearing a golden robe and with his entourage attired in silken raiments, all gifts from the Sultan, and reached Mytilene in thirteen days. There he thanked God for having delivered him out of the clutches of the "Knave"; for despite the Sultan's presents, Domenico suspected that the Sultan's demands were a foretaste of worse to come.

And so they were. All of the Gattilusi possessions fell one by one to the Turk. On Christmas Eve, 1455, Mohammed captured Palaea Phocaea, Domenico's possession in Asia Minor.[46] Then, on 24 January 1456, provoked by suspicious undertakings on the part of Dorino II, the new ruler of the fiefdom of Ainos (who had succeeded his father, Palamedes), Mohammed captured Ainos. The last trace of Frankish rule in Thrace thus disappeared. Samothrace and Imbros, which formed part of the fiefdom of Ainos, were similarly taken over. Finally, he captured Lemnos at the invitation of its inhabitants, who were discontented with their governor, Nicholas, Domenico's brother. The first phase of Mohammed's operations in the northeastern Aegean thus ended in his absolute dominion.

The final phase of the Sultan's Aegean campaign involving the Crusade organized by Pope Callixtus was inaugurated at the beginning of 1457. The Christian fleet anchored first in Rhodes and then proceeded to Chios and Lesbos. However, the Genoese rulers of these islands, members of the Giustiniani and Gattilusi families, respectively, refused to take part in the Crusade against the Sultan. Of course they had learned to respect the Turk, but perhaps more importantly they were reluctant to assist the spread of Venetian influence in the Aegean: it had not escaped their notice that of all the West Europeans it was the Venetians who commanded the fleet. The Venetians had already cast covetous eyes on the Gattilusi possessions of Ainos, Lemnos, and Imbros. In November 1456, they had entered into secret negotiations with George Palaeologus, also known as Dromakaïtis or Comnenus, a powerful landholder on Lemnos, who offered to capture them in Venice's name on condition that they be recognized as his fiefs. Possibly these surreptitious moves became known to the Genoese rulers of Chios and Lesbos; and, if so, they were no doubt sufficient to predispose the Genoese against participation in the Venetian venture. On the other hand, the fleet itself looked completely inadequate to protect the Frankish possessions in the East, and this, too, may have been a factor in persuading the Genoese to adopt a policy of benevolent neutrality.

The Crusaders therefore put in to Mytilene for provisions and began to use Domenico's harbors as bases for armed forays against Turkish merchantmen and the opposite shores of Asia Minor. Presently, the Crusaders' fleet of forty ships—privateers and other assorted vessels, some Venetian, some Catalan—sallied forth from Mytilene and carried the invasion to the islands of the northeast Aegean. Lemnos, the first to be singled out, fell quickly: at the very approach of the fleet the inhabitants surrendered the island, and the Turkish garrison of one hundred men capitulated. Thasos was next, but this time the garrison put up a fight; in a spirited assault, however, a landing party overwhelmed the defenders and the "fortress of the harbor" was taken. This operation was accomplished with such speed that the remaining castles on the island quickly surrendered. Within fifteen days the Christian force had taken the whole island, and their leaders had installed a new regime. Samothrace also fell after a brief skirmish.

After returning to Lemnos for four days, Lodovico Scarampi, the commander of the fleet, left for Rhodes with the Turkish prisoners taken at Lemnos, Thasos, and Samothrace. While in Lemnos, he dispatched ten ships, probably under the command of a Count Anguillara of Rome, to offer terms of surrender to Critobulus' islands. With diplomatic guile, Critobulus extended the Count the warmest of welcomes and convinced him that he was really dealing with a friend and ally. Anguillara was so disarmed that he almost forgot the purpose of his mission—at least he seemed loath to recall it. Still, the islands of the northeast Aegean were again in the hands of the Christians, mainly of course in the hands of the Venetians.

Only money, however, could properly secure these newly acquired interests, and in Venice at the time no other commodity was in shorter supply. Accordingly, in May 1457, the Venetians left Scarampi to defend this area as best he could with whatever assistance the Knights of Rhodes might give him. For the remainder of 1457 the Crusaders continued to dominate the Aegean and even defeated a Turkish naval force near Mytilene in August. Twenty-five Turkish ships were captured in the battle.[47] But by the spring of 1458 and especially after the Pope died in early August 1458, the crusading frenzy whipped up by Pope Callixtus III had definitely died down. The good will of the new Pope, Pius II, was not in itself sufficient to revive flagging interests,[48] and the protection offered by the Christian fleet was virtually nonexistent.

In this situation the Notables of Lemnos, fearful that the Turkish fleet would launch a surprise attack to castigate them for surrendering to the Crusaders, found themselves in complete agreement with Critobulus that they should again come to terms with the Turk. The astute Critobulus saw only too clearly that the balance of power in the Aegean had tipped in favor of the Turks and that the time was never more opportune to demonstrate his loyalty to the Sultan. He therefore interceded with the Sultan and persuaded him to transfer Lemnos and Imbros to the jurisdiction of

Demetrius Palaeologus, the pro-Turkish Despot of the Morea. An annual tribute of three thousand gold pieces sealed the bargain.

As soon as these negotiations at the Sultan's court in Adrianople were concluded, Critobulus returned to Imbros, where he stayed only one day before leaving for Lemnos to ensure that island's adherence to the terms of the new agreement. The nobles and people of the island rallied to Critobulus' side. Italian captives were apparently allowed to remain as permanent settlers or to leave the island in peace. Immediately afterwards, he sent two Notables from Lemnos to inform Demetrius of the new arrangements and to request that governors be installed in the islands. Whether or not these actually took up residence at this time has never been definitely ascertained.

Since these events followed hard upon Mohammed's first expedition to the Peloponnese (spring–autumn 1458), they may be presumed to have taken place in the winter of 1458–1459 and the spring of 1459. Shortly after that, the new admiral of the Turkish fleet, Ismail, officially took possession of the islands. Ismail's part in this operation ceased when he sent the unfortunate Italian prisoners to the Sultan in Philippopolis, where they were forthwith executed. In October 1459, his successor, the assiduous Zaganos, led an expedition of forty ships to the other islands of the northeast Aegean, Samothrace and Thasos, where Frankish garrisons were still entrenched. Zaganos crushed all resistance and, probably in pursuance of Mohammed's orders, transferred most of the inhabitants of the islands to Constantinople.

During the autumn of 1460, after the second Turkish invasion of the Peloponnese and the overthrow of the Despotate of Morea, the Sultan returned to Adrianople with Demetrius, whose family and entourage were virtual prisoners. He nevertheless offered Demetrius the islands of Imbros, Lemnos, Thasos, and Samothrace as well as Thracian Ainos. Demetrius' revenues from these territories amounted in all to 700,000 silver pieces, including 100,000 that he received from the mint in Adrianople.

Demetrius resided in Adrianople and governed Ainos and the islands through his plenipotentiaries, but he lived to enjoy the income from his territories for only a few years. Shortly after the death of his wife's brother, Asanes Matthew, in 1467, he fell out of favor with the Sultan and was exiled to Didymoteikhon. He died as a monk in Adrianople in 1470, a rather more fortunate fate than that which befell the royal family of David Comnenus in the Empire of Trebizond.

Overthrow of the Empire of Trebizond (1461)

Although the early history of the Empire of Trebizond is shrouded in mystery, it is known that it was founded by Alexius Comnenus, grandson of the Byzantine Emperor Andronicus I Comnenus. In the anarchy which attended the Frankish rape of the Byzantine Empire in 1204, Alexius, at the head of an army of Georgian mercenaries placed at his disposal by his aunt, Thamar of Georgia, captured the city of Trebizond and its adjacent region. The new Greek state of Trebizond, taking its name from the capital city, thereafter maintained an independent existence analogous to that of the other remaining states of the Empire and, after 1261, of the restored Byzantine Empire under the Palaeologian dynasty.[49] From the time of its inception, the Empire of Trebizond preserved close intellectual and artistic links with Constantinople. Byzantine art, the most pervasive influence, strikingly affected the ecclesiastical architecture of Trebizond until its fall in 1461.[50]

At the time of the capture of Constantinople, the spruce and elegant town of Trebizond had four thousand inhabitants [51] and was an important center of trade for the whole of the East. This population was soon swollen by a flood of refugees from Constantinople. Moreover, Trebizond, the seat of the "Grand Comnenus," was the only independent polity which still remained legally Greek, and it therefore assumed the status of a second Constantinople.[52] Mohammed II perfectly understood its attraction for all Greeks as a free enclave of Hellenism; and he was also aware of its key location on the trade routes between Europe and the Far East.[53]

The dominion of the "Grand Comnenus" hugged the southern shore of the Black Sea. According to the description of the traveller Clavijo at the beginning of the fifteenth century, its terrain was rugged and densely forested, and the trees were choked with wild vines and climbing plants. Until the exchange of population between Greece and Turkey in 1923, the Greek population mostly lived in small settlements called *choria*, consisting of a sprinkling of solidly constructed peasant houses. The countryside could be traversed via a network of paths, but these were so rough and precipitous as to cost Clavijo the lives of all his pack animals. The interior, known as the Mesochaldion, was mountainous and barren, dotted with castles, and inhabited by a poverty-stricken population. These people, under the leadership of a member of the Kavazitis family, were constantly defending themselves against the attacks of Turks from across the border. Apparently their indigence also drove them into predatory attacks on their foes and into exacting tolls and tribute from merchants who passed through their strongholds.[54] No environment could have been better suited to guerrilla operations.

Mohammed therefore had a number of reasons for proceeding against the Trapezuntines. Three years after the capture of Constantinople and as soon as Turkish hegemony in the Peloponnese and the northern Aegean had been successfully established, he accordingly ordered Hitir, Pasha of Amasya, to reduce this last independent outpost of Hellenism. Hitir marched through the undefended passes of the Pontic Alps and descended on Trebizond with such extraordinary expedition that Emperor John IV ("the Good") was unaware of his approach almost until he began setting up his encampment on the outskirts of the city. In the meantime, a Turkish fleet had set out from Samsun (Amisus) to plunder the coast of Trebizond. Since John found himself faced with a critical food shortage and a plague which had already taken a huge human toll both inside and outside the capital, he felt impelled to come to immediate terms with Hitir. For his part, the Turkish commander was only too pleased to accommodate John: he had no wish to have his forces pinned down outside the heavily fortified town while the Sultan was fighting the Hungarians before Belgrade in 1456. Hitir offered to let Trebizond alone as soon as John agreed to pay an annual tribute of two thousand gold pieces to the Sultan. These terms were substantially confirmed by the Sultan on his return from his first expedition to the Peloponnese in the autumn of 1458, though he raised the tribute to three thousand gold pieces.

In an attempt to avert complete political subjugation [55] John made overtures of friendship towards the ruler of the Ak Koyunlu (White Shepherds) Turcomans of Mesopotamia, Uzun Hassan, whose capital was in Diyarbakir. In consideration of an arranged marriage with John's daughter Catherine, who was famed for her beauty throughout the entire East, and with Cappadocia—which nominally belonged to the Grand Comnenus—as dowry, Uzun Hassan agreed to enter into a defensive alliance with John.

John signed a treaty embodying acceptance of Uzun Hassan's conditions and then turned to the fulfillment of a much larger ambition, the extension of the treaty to include the Christian princes of Georgia and Mingrelia, as well as the Moslem prince of Kastamonu, Isfendiaroglou Ismaïl Bey, the Sultan's brother-in-law, and the Moslem prince, Ibrahim Bey, of Karaman. For many years the last two princes had nursed hostile feelings towards the Ottoman state: in the case of Ibrahim Bey, because Mohammed II's father, Murad II, had confiscated part of his lands. It was intended that the treaty serve not only as a guarantee of the territorial integrity of those countries that subscribed to it, but also as a means of effecting the expulsion of the Ottoman Turks from the whole of Anatolia. However, John died in 1458 without realizing his scheme.[56]

Since the legal heir, John V, was only four years old, he was at once brushed aside by his uncle, David Comnenus, with the support of the noble Kavazitis family from the Mesochaldion.[57] Nonetheless, David Comnenus sought to implement and expand his brother's plans. On 22 April 1459 he wrote to Philip, Duke of Burgundy, outlining the action he had taken to form an aggressive alliance against the Turks and deliberately exaggerating the size of the combined forces of Georgia, Mingrelia, and Armenia. Michael Alighieri, the bearer of the letter, called on Pope Pius II, who gave him another letter for the Duke (13 January 1460). In this, Pius pointed out that he had already sent a delegation to Trebizond and the other courts of the East for the specific purpose of organizing a holy alliance against the Turks; and he urged Philip of Burgundy to follow the example of the Eastern princes. However, the leader of this delegation, Fra Lodovico da Bologna, was a treacherous Franciscan monk, who had prevailed upon the Pope to allow him to take charge of the negotiations.[58] As a consequence, the only result of David's diplomatic initiative was that Mohammed learned of the plans.[59]

At a critical stage in these proceedings, David made an imprudent move that angered the Sultan even more. He asked Uzun Hassan, his niece's husband, to request exemption from the tribute Trebizond was then paying the Sultan. With singular lack of diplomatic finesse, Uzun Hassan hastened the dissolution of the Anatolian alliance by agreeing to intercede and making an importunate request of his own. He instructed his envoys to ask for the restitution of the annual subsidy which Mohammed's grandfather had formerly paid him but which had been suspended some fifty years before. The Sultan's reply was charged with an ominous double meaning: "Go in peace and I will come next year myself and settle this debt." [60]

Mohammed spent the whole of that winter preparing for an expedition against the states of northeast Asia Minor. By the following spring of 1461, three hundred warships with auxiliary transports were ready. Individual crew members were specially selected for physical size and seasoning in battle, and each was well armed. Two highly competent admirals were placed in charge of the expedition, Kassim, governor of Gallipoli, and Yakoub, "a man who was not only a sailor of vast experience but a superlative naval commander as well." This superb fleet put out from the shores of the Bosphorus in an almost jocund mood, the martial roars of its crews echoing the exultant slapping of the oars.[61] It was an impressive array of Turkish naval might.

Soon afterwards, in June 1461, the Sultan crossed the Straits with his European army and arrived at Bursa (then Prusa), where he had given orders for the Asian army to assemble. It was a formidable host by the standards of the day—sixty thousand cavalry and eighty thousand infantry, all eagerly awaiting news of the purpose of the Sultan's expedition.[62] The inhabitants of the Aegean islands and the free cities of the Black Sea —Kaffa (now Feodosiya), Trebizond, and Sinope—were overawed by the assemblage. The Sultan's first objective, which so far he had not disclosed to anyone, was Sinope.[63] This rich and lovely city, especially famous as a port for the export of copper from the mines of its hinterland, was an "important entrepôt not only for its adjacent regions, but also for a large part of Asia Minor." [64]

To fool his enemies, however, the Sultan made a feint towards the southeast and camped at Ankara. From there he announced to Isfendi-aroglu Ismaïl Bey that if Sinope were surrendered, he would gladly, by way of exchange, recognize Ismaïl's authority in Philippopolis and its suburbs. Mohammed then marched straight towards Sinope and secured the narrow isthmus of the peninsula on which the city was built. Simultaneously, the Turkish fleet blockaded its shores. Although Ismaïl commanded an ideal defensive position and both the size of his garrison and the number of his cannon were more than adequate to repulse the combined attacks of the Turkish land and naval forces for a protracted period, not a single clash took place. Ismaïl left the city to pay homage to the Sultan. Then, after accepting the exchange which Mohammed had previously offered, he surrendered Sinope.[65]

The Turkish fleet was ordered to Trebizond, and Mohammed led his army into the interior of Armenia. By a forced march, which was remarkable for the endurance of his troops, Mohammed brought his entire army over the undefended tracks of the Anti-Taurus Mountains through wild, dangerous terrain covered with dense forest and thicket.[66] His descent followed the road leading from Amasya and Sivas (ancient Sebastia) to Erzurum; along the way a stop was made to reduce the castle of Koïnlu, or Koyunlu Hisar. This castle was situated east of Tokat and was Uzun Hassan's westernmost stronghold. Continuing in an easterly direction, Mohammed presently encountered Sara Hatun, the mother of Uzun Hassan, who had come to meet him, bearing gifts, to assure him of the friendship and loyalty of her son. The Sultan was inclined to accept her protestations, but requested as proof of their sincerity that Uzun Hassan immediately cease his hostile operations against Turkish territory and abrogate his alliance with David Comnenus. As additional insurance against the future disposition of Uzun Hassan, Mohammed also insisted that Sara Hatun accompany him on his expedition. Only the forbidding Pontic Alps separated him from his prize; and, setting an example to his troops,[67] who were exhausted by the rigors of the march and depleted food supplies,[68] Mohammed, on foot most of the time, led them on the climb over this last formidable obstacle.

Meanwhile, the Turkish fleet from Sinope had arrived suddenly before Trebizond. David Comnenus, taken thoroughly by surprise, found himself with harvest not gathered from the fields and the full complement of his garrison inside the walls. The Turks were able to land about ten thousand well-armed men virtually without opposition, and these proceeded to burn and loot in the suburbs and lay waste the fields.[69] At first, the Trapezuntines tried to put up some resistance outside the walls, but the superiority of the Turkish force compelled them to immure themselves in the city. The capital was cut off from all communication with the outside. Still, for twenty-eight consecutive days the besieged resorted to surprise sorties against the enemy. "In these forays," says Critobulus, "they showed themselves in no way inferior to the enemy."[70] All the while, too, Pontic peasants from the surrounding heights descended on the enemy, and their attacks resulted in significant Turkish losses. Since the people of Trebizond still believed that the main Turkish force was engaged against the Ak Koyunlu Turcomans, they by no means regarded their fortune as irretrievable.[71]

Their hopes were abruptly dashed, however, by the appearance of the Sultan and his army on the Trapezuntine side of the Pontic Alps. The news of his successful crossing spread alarm, confusion, and defeatism in the town. Mahmud, the Grand Vizier of Greco-Serbian descent, who commanded the vanguard of the Turkish army, demanded, as soon as he arrived outside its walls, the surrender of the city and set up camp in a place known as Skylolimni. Since destruction and pillage were the only other alternatives offered, David Comnenus capitulated. This sudden *volte-face* on the part of David can only be explained in terms of a defeatist state of mind, the seeds of which were apparently sown in no small measure by his own chamberlain, the philosopher George Amiroukes or Amiroutses. A man of handsome and imposing aspect, Amiroukes was yet another of the opportunists who appeared in these unsettled times—men who preferred to appease the Sultan rather than to oppose him. It was Amiroukes who took charge of the negotiations for the surrender of Trebizond. A little later, he attempted to vindicate his actions in a feeble explanation to Bessarion, his compatriot: the people were already demoralized by the sight of the enemy's huge war machines and by lack of food and water, "which had never before been known to occur." All resistance was thus paralyzed and the people were bent upon surrender.[72] And so, in the middle of August 1461 the last independent outpost of Hellenism ceased to exist:[73] in the words of the melancholy Pontic folk song, "Romania is gone, Romania was taken."[74]

News of the success of Mohammed's campaign reached Venice in October, whence it rapidly spread to other major European countries. As usual, the feelings of anger and sorrow it aroused did not last long.[75]

It was Amiroukes who pointed out that, despite the voluntary capitulation of the city, its royal house and inhabitants were subjected to the same reprisals, pillaging, and attendant sufferings as if there had been a forcible conquest.[76] David Comnenus and the royal family, together with a few servants and some of the more prominent officials and wealthy families, were ordered aboard Turkish galleys and transported to Constantinople. David Comnenus, stripped of all wealth and honors except the few personal treasures that he had been able to take with him, after a brief but difficult sojourn in the city, was moved to Adrianople, where that other fallen ruler, Demetrius Palaeologus, also had his residence. While there, however, the Sultan granted David the income from certain estates in the vicinity of the Strymon, near Serrai, amounting to 300,000 pieces of silver annually.

But the life of the Grand Comnenus was cut short within two years of the capture of Trebizond. On 23 March 1463, he and other members of the royal family were incarcerated in the "tower" of Adrianople and then transferred to the Fortress of Heptapyrgion (Seven Towers) in Constantinople. There, during the night of 1 November 1463, Comnenus, three of his children, and his nephew Alexius were beheaded and their bodies cast outside the walls. The only members of his family spared were his wife, Helen, his youngest son, three-year-old George, and his daughter, Anna. Anna went to the Sultan's harem, and George was brought up a Moslem. The widowed queen, like Antigone, to prevent the corpses of her family from being devoured by scavenging dogs and birds of prey, buried them in graves she scraped in the earth with her bare hands. She became a nun and spent the rest of her days in a cottage made of straw.

The explanation for these murders is to be found in a letter allegedly written by Catherine, the wife of Uzun Hassan, in which she requested David Comnenus to send her one of his sons or his nephew Alexius, son of Alexander Comnenus, to be brought up in her court. This letter was entrusted to George Amiroukes, who, out of fear of the Sultan, delivered it instead to Mohammed. Infuriated at the time by the failure of his Bosnian campaign, Mohammed gave vent to his rage upon seeing the letter by ordering the execution of David Comnenus and his family.[77] Mohammed evidently did not want any of the Comneni to be brought up in another court and later prove to be troublesome. Thus, the very man who, less than a year and a half befc.e, had been mainly responsible for his country's downfall was now instrumental in the betrayal of his emperor. It was probably this event which led many Trapezuntine noblemen finally to leave Adrianople for Constantinople, where they later figured prominently in the internal affairs of the patriarchate and the development of post-Byzantine society.

According to certain oral traditions, some Comneni managed to escape to Maina. This has never been proven, although there is some evidence to suggest that a number of nobles from Trebizond dispersed throughout the islands of the Aegean, the Peloponnese, Italy, and several other places.[78] Indeed, as early as 1414, 880 Trapezuntine families, seeking to escape Turkish enslavement, were permitted by the Venetians to settle in Crete.[79]

Immediately after the capture of Trebizond, some fifteen hundred of the strongest and most handsome young men of the town and adjacent areas, principally from noble and wealthy families, were impressed for service in the corps of janissaries and in the palaces of the Sultan and other grandees. Amiroukes bewailed the temporary conscription of his own son and young son-in-law. In addition, large numbers were transported to Constantinople as "colonists"—as elements in the repopulation of the city.[80] As for those who remained behind, the Turks allowed them to live only outside the walls of the city in suburbs which had been reduced to ashes.[81] A source in the Turkish archives records that Kassim and Umur Bey were responsible for the removal of many inhabitants of the new *sancak* of Trebizond to Rumelia (that is, the European regions of the Ottoman Empire) and for the conversion of their former vineyards into Turkish fiefs.[82]

Mohammed stayed only a few days in Trebizond while the necessary arrangements were effected. His admiral, Kassim, was appointed governor of the region as a *sancak* chief. Four hundred elite janissaries from the Sultan's personal guard were selected to garrison the citadel and *azaps* (irregular infantry) were assigned as guards in the rest of the city. Since only the city itself and its immediate environs had thus far surrendered, Hitir was charged with the task of subjugating the remainder of the Empire of Trebizond. Mohammed then left for Constantinople, almost exactly retracing his steps [83] through the wild and mountainous district of Tzapnides.[84] Nearing the territory of Uzun Hassan, he released Sara Hatun, giving her great honors and valuable gifts plundered from the House of Comnenus. Emissaries were also dispatched to assure Uzun Hassan of the Sultan's desire to renew their friendship and alliance. By a forced march which "took him safely across the Taurus mountains," he reached Bursa in twenty-eight days and crossed to Constantinople.[85] The word "safely" in this context suggests that the Empire of Trebizond had not yet been entirely subjugated. This assumption is further supported by the fact that he had deliberately bypassed numerous Greek castles and strongholds during his rapid advance against David Comnenus.[86]

Chalcocondyles states that Hitir did not have to resort to force in the pacification of certain districts around Trebizond and the Mesochaldion (variously known as Ardasa or Torul). The two strategic fortresses of Trebizond and Ardasa, together with several others anchored by these two, capitulated voluntarily. These latter, along with Ardasa itself, belonged to the Kavazitis family—the "most honorable" father and his son—though they were erstwhile supporters of David Comnenus and his claims to the throne.[87] Merne(?),[88] surely a member of the Kavazitis family, surrendered his castle in Ardasa (the ruins of which can be seen today above Ardasa),[89] apparently on the condition that he be allowed to retain his estates in fief. Barkan, who discovered the name "Merne" some five hundred years later in a book of land titles from the official registry of the *sancak* of Trebizond, expresses some doubt as to whether it is a correct transcription. From this source we learn that nine out of twelve "soldiers," that is, *pronoiarioi,* of David Comnenus betrayed him so that they might keep their fiefs.[90] At least the popular muse was not prepared to overlook this betrayal: there is a Pontic folk song which refers to the treasonable surrender of a castle, no doubt a particular castle, since both the name of the traitor and the universal opprobrium which his actions incurred are vividly recalled:

> O fortress, my fortress, my Palaeocastron so solid:
> Old and strong were you—then how were you surrendered?
> You had a cunning guard, a cowardly master:
> Marthas the dog was the traitor within your walls.[91]

It is likely that "Palaeocastron" refers to the principal fortress in the interior, the castle of Ardasa, and that the name "Marthas" is the same "Merne" concerning whose correct spelling Barkan expressed some doubt. The latter conclusion is based on an assumption that the similarity between the Arabic letters corresponding to *t* and *n* could easily have led to the confusion of the two characters. Thus, the word could be read as either "Merne" (as Barkan read it) or "Merte"; but equally, too, it might be "Marna" or "Marta." Since this last form resembles the Greek name "Marthas" it may be presumed to be the correct one.

The Kavazitises were probably successful in securing a measure of independence for their region in return for some payment of tribute. Virtual freedom was also assured by the inaccessibility and mountainous nature of this region. The fact that Christian monuments in the area survived the usual ravages of war suggests that this was the case.[92]

Other traditions and folk songs, Greek and Turkish, attest that a number of key fortresses along the coast and in the interior refused to follow the example of David Comnenus and the Kavazitises. According to these traditions, the Turks turned first to the capture of fortresses along the coast such as Kordyle (Aldja Kale) and Platana; these were taken only after the most heroic defense on the part of the inhabitants. Others surrendered willingly or succumbed to treachery.

Thus, the coastal areas and parts of the interior were gradually subdued. Most villages were destroyed and the castles themselves razed.
Their skeletal outlines are still to be seen today, mute witnesses of their
past. Of the inhabitants, some were killed outright, some apostatized to
Islam in order to escape their sufferings, some fled to Iberia and Georgia,
and others found temporary refuge in remote inland fastnesses where
privation and hardship seemed lesser enemies. Many nobles from the
coastal regions, suddenly bereft of wealth, honors, and office, took refuge
in the mountainous interior of "Romania" and resumed their struggle
against the Turk.[93] A Pontic song tells of the resistance the Turks encountered there:

> The evil Turk came and occupied the land
>   And overflowed the plains,
> But the mountains—these were filled with
>   Brave and handsome men.[94]

These "brave and handsome men" (leventoi) were Hellenes (drakoi
Hellenoi, "brave Hellenes") in "Hellenic castles" who grasped their
"Hellenic spears" and fought gallantly on mountain peaks and in narrow
ravines until the earth was soaked with their own and the enemy's blood.
The invaders were too numerous to be counted; it was as though God
had rained them upon the earth. So the last of the heroes eventually fell
and each died with a tragic question on his lips: "Why, O God, hast thou
painted the earth with our blood?" The castles themselves, the song goes
on, reverberated with the noise of battle until they, too, no longer stood
and only the plaintive singing of birds disturbed the silence of their
lonely ruins.[95]

Just when these flickering flames of resistance in the Pontus finally
died down is not known,[96] though they cannot have lasted very long. All
that can be said with any certainty is that, as the Turks penetrated further and further inland, more villages were levelled, more killings took
place, more conversions to Islam followed, and more escapes were made
to havens even more remote and wild. The destruction of life was such
as to leave an indelible imprint on the memories of the people, which
not even the passing of centuries has been able to expunge:

> Woe unto us! Romania has fallen
> The churches grieve, the monasteries lament,
> St. John Chrysostom weeps and tears his hair.[97]

At length the entire country was conquered and divided up into fiefs,
which were distributed among the Turkish spahis. Only then was a modicum of order restored and the sufferings of the inhabitants partially

alleviated. The spahis issued new land titles (*hocet* and *tapı*), which recognized small tenant holdings, and then proceeded to collect the rents from their estates.[98]

The decimation of the Greek population in the Pontus resulted in the atrophy of the Church there. Where once sixteen bishoprics had flourished, only two, Ophis (Chaldia) and Kanis (Cheroiana) remained; and Ophis had become defunct by the middle of the seventeenth century. Many churches were converted into mosques, among them the cathedral of Panagia Chrysokephalos, which was called the Mosque of Fatih (the Conqueror) in honor of Mohammed II. Archbishop Dorotheos was forced to transfer his seat outside the walls of Trebizond to the Church of St. Philip, which remained in Christian hands till 1665.[99]

All the Greek lands except Cyprus, the Ionian islands, and the Aegean islands south of Lemnos were united under the dominion of the Sultan in 1461. They were also united by the common bond of Orthodoxy. This situation was by no means wholly inimical to the Greeks: not only was economic and intellectual intercourse among them facilitated, but a consciousness of national unity was thereby able to develop. Resentment against the common oppressor was nurtured and eventually expressed in common action.[100]

However, the economic, cultural, and social development of the Hellenes did not proceed in any uniform manner. The years of Frankish and Turkish domination prevented that, and economic, political, cultural, and geographical disparities characterized every stage of growth.

A Greek Historian Looks to the Restoration of His Nation

With the fall of Trebizond, the last independent Greek polity had vanished, and the development of the Hellenic nation can thereafter be traced only through its Church and small separate communities in cities, towns, and villages. The centuries-old tradition of Greek historical writing linking antiquity with the current era also came to an abrupt end. Virtually all that remained was the Greek people's thirst for knowledge of past and contemporary events. Of course, there were Greek chroniclers of the Ottoman Empire, but since their chronicles or narrations have not yet been subjected to systematic study, particularly in regard to their consistency with one another and the reliability of their sources, they are of indeterminate value. In addition to these, a number of valuable "Brief Chronicles" or memoirs and a corpus of hagiographical and other religious literature provide a modicum of historical information. But all these are outside the mainstream of traditional historiography. More and more, the historical consciousness of the Greek raias was expressed in the form of oral traditions, legends, folk songs, and other lore; these are what mirror the lives of the people and provide an outlet for their feelings and aspirations.

The last traditional historian was Laonicos Chalcocondyles. Born after 1430, Chalcocondyles spent his youth in Mistra, but later, after the fall of the Duchy of Athens, he returned to his native city and there wrote his history of the origins and evolution of the Greek nation.[101] Chalcocondyles viewed the events of his time from the same philosophical vantage point as his father George, as Bessarion, Constantine XI Palaeologus, and Gemistos and his circle had done.

Chalcocondyles demonstrated a surer knowledge of history than any other scholar of his time. The Hellenes and Romans (the names themselves are always differentiated with scrupulous exactness) were different peoples; the Romans conquered the East and thereby came into contact with the Greeks who, however, *being far more numerous than their conquerors, preserved their language, manners and customs, though not their name,* because the Byzantine Emperors were proud to call themselves "Emperors of the Romans" rather than "Emperors of the Hellenes."[102] Similar assertions have been made here and there throughout this work and may be asserted as historical fact. The Greeks, that is, retained the title "King and Emperor of the Romans" out of respect for the great Roman tradition. The converse of this tradition might also be affirmed (in the same unequivocal manner in which John III Ducas Vatatzes had once addressed Pope Gregory IX): that the inheritance of Constantine the Great's empire gradually passed over into the "nation" of the Greeks (see pages 37–38 above). If Greek emperors not only adopted the official title but never abandoned it, this was because they were loath to reject a brilliant inheritance.

Unlike Gemistos, Chalcocondyles was not rigidly attached to the idea that the Hellenes of his day were descended exclusively from the ancient Greeks: on the contrary, his explanation that the Byzantine Emperors adopted the title "Roman" instead of "Greek" is made precisely in order to stress in the most positive terms the existence of a palpable Greco-Roman affinity. At the same time, there was no doubt in his mind as to the essential differences between Romans and Greeks: the former were Latins and Franks or Westerners in general. Having established to his own satisfaction the predominant stock of the inhabitants of mainland Greece and Asia Minor, he did not hesitate to substitute the word Hellene for Roman where appropriate, or even to call the last Byzantine Emperors "Emperors of the Hellenes." Since it was no especial veneration of antiquity which led him to make this distinction, one may assume that it was due to a recognition of the actual growth of Hellenism during that period.

Chalcocondyles also seems to have diagnosed the social malaise which led to the demise of the Byzantine Empire. At least he hints at this while speculating upon the future of the nation: the Greeks would eventually form themselves into a state which mainly lack of cohesion had hitherto prevented. His confidence in the future resurrection of a kingdom in which Greeks would govern themselves "very happily" according to their customs remained unshakable.[103]

Chalcocondyles was in part merely reflecting the popular faith in national rehabilitation, and his optimism was partly based on the renaissance of Greek studies. Chalcocondyles watched delightedly as Greek language and culture spread throughout the West. Prominent among its torchbearers was his cousin, the renowned Hellenist, Demetrius Chalcocondyles. Would the humanist revival lead to a hellenization of the European spirit or at least arouse Hellenist sympathies on the part of powerful forces in the West?

GREEK SCHOLARS IN THE WEST

Italy as a Greek Refuge

Escape, escape: the same monotonous refrain was taken up by the people of Constantinople again and again from the time of the fall of Gallipoli in 1354. "Everyone wished to leave hurriedly for Italy and Cádiz and for the ocean beyond the Pillars of Hercules, thinking that only there would they be safe from enslavement." [1] That safety could only be found in flight was an idea made more palatable by the knowledge that death through hunger or the like was possibly the only alternative. [2] Scholars in particular found the situation in Greece the more insufferable since "education and the pursuit of letters could only with difficulty be cultivated in the absence of freedom." Thus, scholars too gave themselves up to thoughts of escape. But where could refuge be found? There were in fact a number of places readily accessible by ship, wrote Demetrius Kydones in 1387, any of which would provide safe haven for those who did not care to live through the last tragic moments of the Byzantine capital. "From afar, they will then see those who stay and drown; while if they stay themselves and attempt to go to the aid of those who are drowning, not only will their efforts be futile, but they too will drown." [3]

Of course philo-Latin scholars frequently exhibited a yearning for the West,[4] and Rome, especially, had a considerable attraction for men of letters. Ever since Kydones had accompanied Emperor John V on his trip to Italy (1369–1371) and visited Venice, Milan, Florence, and Rome, he had strongly urged collaboration with the scholars of the West. Only the West could possibly aid the Byzantine Empire.[5] Therefore, the people ought to re-establish their former connections with Rome—with their own metropolis in fact—for "who are closer allies of the 'Romans' than the Romans themselves? Who more trustworthy as allies than those who are Roman? In truth, their metropolis is just as much ours." This expressed need for a closer relationship with Rome appears to have been prompted in part by an oracle (probably attributable to the Unionists) which predicted that allies would indeed come to the assistance of Constantinople and they would come from across the sea and over the Alps.[6]

The new effulgence of the European spirit also served as a magnet to many scholars. As scholars, their search for new centers of learning where the intellect could be stimulated and enriched in secure and liberal surroundings never ceased. A steady stream of such travellers, making their way through the southern and western parts of Greece, the Peloponnese, Crete, and the Ionian islands (especially Corfu, which also served as a stepping-stone for the rest), went via Ragusa [7] (Dubrovnik) to Ancona and Venice. Venice, the first major city in the West they encountered, was where most of them stayed. Its commercial dealings with the Byzantines were of long standing, and its people, its situation, even its buildings, were by no means unfamiliar to them. The ties between Venice and Crete were particularly close, Crete having been under Venetian domination since 1211.

When these Greeks began to arrive in the West, the Renaissance was flowering and the study of ancient Greek and Latin writers (*humanitatis studia*) was thought of as the only ideal education for men.

Classical learning in Italy had not entirely died out during the Middle Ages, but had been chiefly limited to a number of Greek monasteries in Apulia and Calabria, as well as in Sicily. Nardò was perhaps the most outstanding center of Greek studies. The monastery of San Nicola di Casola possessed a rich library of Greek manuscripts and also became a mecca of Greek ecclesiastics, many of them well educated, who sought to perpetuate the Greek literary and cultural tradition.[8] We are indebted to the work of early researchers, supplemented more recently by that of Rohlfs and Caratzas, for the knowledge that this region was inhabited not only by Byzantine colonists, but also by Greek-speaking settlers who were descended from the original inhabitants of Magna Graecia. Even today, no fewer than thirty thousand Greek-speaking villagers live in the south.[9]

It is therefore not surprising that a revival of Greek learning in Italy should be inspired by two scholars from the south. They were the monk Barlaam (Bernardo), of Greek descent, from Seminara in Calabria (the same Barlaam who was the chief rival of Gregory Palamas, Archbishop of Thessalonica, during the Hesychast controversy), who gave lessons to Petrarch; and the uncouth and mulish Leonzio Pilato who, like his teacher Barlaam, had lived for many years in Greece. In 1360, Pilato was in Florence at the invitation of Boccaccio, who created for him a special

chair of ancient Greek literature in the university there—the first such
chair in the West—and extended to him the hospitality of his home.
Pilato's translations gave two of his students, Boccaccio and Petrarch,
access to the works of Homer and Plato and thus to the fountainhead
of the classical spirit. Petrarch, though continuing to honor Aristotle,
became a disciple of Plato.[10]

Two fourteenth-century Greeks, Paul, Archbishop of Smyrna, and
Simon Atoumanos, Archbishop of Thebes, both Roman Catholic converts,
may also be said to have made a contribution of sorts to the development of humanistic studies. On their visits to Italy they established contacts with other ecclesiastics and humanists, and gave Greek lessons to
various prominent personages, thereby helping to effect a reconciliation
between the Eastern and Western worlds. Unfortunately, however, very
little else is known about the activities of these two.[11]

By the end of the fourteenth century, the evidence of intellectual ferment in the West was unmistakable. In the autumn of 1375, Kydones
wrote that there were many in Italy from whom a great deal could profitably be learned. Whereas in Thessalonica, he went on, there was no place
at all for philosophers (he refers here, of course, to the period after the
triumph of Hesychasm), in Rome they were not only welcomed but
showered with laurels and honors. Indeed, it was the very warmth of
the welcome that made them think seriously of taking up permanent
residence there.[12]

Still, the cultivation of Greek studies in the West was only beginning.
Petrarch's comment that in all Italy there hardly existed ten people who
could understand Homer in Latin, let alone in Greek,[13] was probably not
a great exaggeration. At the very end of the fourteenth century and in
the beginning of the fifteenth, Italy drew to her shores a small group
of Byzantine scholars, chief among whom were the ageing Demetrius
Kydones himself, Manuel Calecas, and Manuel Chrysoloras,[14] all of philo-
Latin sentiment. To these must also be added the three scholarly brothers,
Theodore, Andrew, and Maximus Chrysoberges, all Roman Catholic converts in the Dominican Order.[15]

The political situation in Italy was anything but auspicious: petty
states everywhere warred with one another, and widespread banditry
made any journey a most hazardous undertaking.[16] Notwithstanding this,
the Greek scholars sought to establish contacts with humanists and with
Italian society in general in the hope of imparting a thorough knowledge
of the ancient Greek language—a task in which they met with some
success, at least among the more ardent lovers of antiquity. The letters
of the Greek scholars are filled with admiration for the attainments of
the Western world. Without exception, they decried the Byzantines'

amour propre, which led them to underestimate the quality of Western erudition; [17] and whenever they returned to Constantinople, or "New Rome," they took with them the most vivid memories of the "older" Rome. Kydones, for example, felt equally at home in both places.[18]

Although the publication of a variety of special and general studies has thrown considerable light on the renaissance of humanistic studies in the West,[19] there has been no complete study of the Greek contribution to this movement. As yet, the number of detailed monographs based on published and unpublished material is deficient.[20] But according to Martinus Crusius there were four scholars to whom the Latins and Germans owed the origin of Greek studies in their countries during the Renaissance: Manuel Chrysoloras, John Argyropoulos, Demetrius Chalcocondyles, and Janus Lascaris.[21] To these we must add George Gemistos and Cardinal Bessarion, who, though not teachers of Greek, contributed a great deal to its dissemination.

Manuel Chrysoloras

It was Chrysoloras who gave the first serious impetus to the growth of Greek studies in Italy. As the Turkish siege at the end of the fourteenth century and the continual and growing animosity of the inhabitants towards the Unionists made life in Constantinople more unbearable, Chrysoloras reluctantly accepted, on 23 February 1396, an invitation from Coluccio Salutati,[22] a patron of the arts, to take the honorary post of Professor of Greek at the University of Florence. A man of medium height, with a ruddy complexion set off by a ginger beard, this foreigner in Italy was by all accounts a man of dignified bearing with a calm, amiable, and kindly disposition, deeply religious, knowledgeable, magnanimous, wise, and just. Though he held his chair only until the end of 1399, he captivated the citizens of Florence and exercised a profound influence on its youth.

Soon after he came to Italy, Chrysoloras began to represent his country in a diplomatic capacity. In 1404, 1406, from 1408 till the middle of 1410, and from the end of 1410 till 1415, he was sent by Emperor Manuel II Palaeologus on missions to secure and expedite aid from the West. Guarino da Verona studied under him during the intervening periods in Constantinople.[23]

Chrysoloras worked indefatigably for a rapprochement between East and West. His frequent advocacy of Greek studies for Italians was intended to make the point that through such studies they would become better versed in philosophy and better scholars in general.[24] In Constantinople he talked about the Italian scholars he had met, the beauty of Italian cities, the warmth of welcome and hospitality that had been extended

Figure 19. Manuel Chrysoloras.

to him, and the honors that had been bestowed upon him. The picture he drew no doubt differed considerably from that familiar to the haughty and tradition-minded Byzantines. Unlike so many others, Chrysoloras refused to look upon the East as the religious, cultural, and commercial antithesis of the West. As another Unionist, Kydones, had done before him, he tried to stress those elements which the peoples and civilizations of Rome and Constantinople had in common.[25] It was therefore not only personal religious conviction, but also the facts of history which led him to believe in the uniqueness of the Romano-Byzantine tradition and the need for a resumption of contacts between the two worlds.

His *Old and New Romes: A Comparison,* written in the form of a letter to John VIII Palaeologus, underlines these similarities. He described the relationship between the two civilizations as being as intimate as that between a mother and her daughter. The contributions which each had made to humanity were homologous. His prime purpose in expressing these ideas was to strengthen the ideological bonds between the two peoples.[26] Chrysoloras erected a signpost, as it were, whose directions Byzantine scholars were soon to follow, when all other roads led only to enslavement.[27]

During his final sojourn in Italy, Chrysoloras identified himself closely with Roman Catholicism.[28] His absorption in Roman Catholic doctrine apparently proceeded from an increasing preoccupation with religion as a whole. By the middle of 1413, Chrysoloras, along with two cardinals, was entrusted by the Pope with the preparatory work for the convocation of the Council of Constance.[29] This was the first time the Germans had an opportunity to meet the noted Byzantine scholar and such Italian humanists as Leonardo Bruni, Poggio Bracciolini, and Pier-Paolo Vergerio.[30]

Scholars of renown like Leonardo Bruni, Ambrogio Traversari, and Carlo Marsuppini were in the same literary tradition that Chrysoloras established in Florence. Greek culture was a vital element in Florentine humanism and the Florentine Renaissance in general.[31] The fame of Florence soon spread to Constantinople, and her admirers there, Nicholas Calecas, for instance, hoped that Florence would continue to sponsor Greek as well as Latin learning. "And in this respect fortune smiled upon you, sending you the literary treasures of our ancestors so that they might be preserved for us all. Life-giving waters thus continue to flow from the fountainhead of all literature." [32] Indeed, the brilliance of the humanists, poets, and artists of Florence assured that city's place in the forefront of the Renaissance movement at a time when Rome, for example, was only just beginning to stir.[33]

Even in Florence, however, Chrysoloras had to surmount the difficulties inherent in teaching foreigners quite ignorant of ancient Greek, and he had to serve rather as a patient school-teacher than as a professor. He taught elementary grammar, syntax, and vocabulary and led his students through simple exercises in translation. He prepared a basic grammar and translated ancient Greek authors specifically to serve the needs of these students. The grammar, entitled *Questions* (*Erotemata*) because of its question-and-answer technique, proved to be an invaluable aid to all students of ancient Greek in Italy and elsewhere. Originally published in Venice in 1484, it was subsequently used by such men as Erasmus and Reuchlin.

Chrysoloras' approach to the problem of translation was summed up by him in the prescribed method: *transferre ad sententiam.* His advice to students was that they should first study the text with love and attention, discuss its precise meaning, and then try faithfully to render the sense of the text in their own words.[34] They should eschew a literal translation except when this best conveyed the sense. This approach, of course, was in tune with new humanistic conceptions and humanist opposition to the earlier methods of translating word by word.[35]

Chrysoloras can scarcely be regarded as a great man of letters according to modern standards of scholarship, but he exerted an immense influence on his students. Guarino da Verona called him "a supernatural being, a divine messenger, an instrument of Providence who was sent from Heaven out of divine compassion for Italy's pitiable condition in order to dispel the darkness of her ignorance." The extant letters of Guarino are replete with recollections of his wise and beneficent teacher.[36]

On 15 April 1415, while the Council of Constance was in session, Chrysoloras died of a malignant fever. He was buried in the chapel of a Dominican monastery which ceased to function in 1784 and was converted towards the end of the nineteenth century into the spacious Hôtel de l'Ile. The visitor may still read today his epitaph in the dome of the chapel.[37] A year after Chrysoloras' death Guarino da Verona saluted his teacher in these words: *quidquid graecorum hodie studiorum ad nostrates derivatum est homines* ("whatever our scholars possess of Greek studies today comes from him").[38]

At the time of Chrysoloras' death, Constantinople, despite continued economic and intellectual decline, was still the principal center of civilization in the world. In Guarino's words, *orbis terrarum Europa, Europae Graecia, Graeciae regina urbs Byzantii est* ("Europe is the orb of the world; Greece of Europe; the city of Byzantium the queen of Greece").[39] But in the period following Chrysoloras' death Constantinople's former "centers of letters," her so-called Museums—the superior schools where once the teaching of grammar, rhetoric, philosophy, and theology had flourished—preserved little more than their names, or else they had truly become museums in which only the fossilized remains of classical studies were displayed. Italy had by now become the new center for classical studies.[40]

Gemistos and Bessarion

The arrival in Italy of Greek delegates, mainly clerics, to the Councils of Ferrara and Florence in 1439 brought about a vigorous confrontation of the Byzantine spirit with that of Western Europe and stimulated and enriched Greek scholarship in Italy. The progress in Western thought and philosophy was undeniable. George Scholarios remarked that "those with whom we contested [at the Councils] were true savants, which is why they returned polemic for polemic." [41] The Greeks were not worsted in these debates at Florence, but they were forced into an area of final agreement with the Italians; "there were good reasons, which we all know," Gemistos pointedly observed, "why they should have so agreed." [42] This was, then, a tactical retreat. Despite the overall debasement of the Byzantine intellect, a number of Greek savants made an impression on the Italian humanists, particularly because of their eagerness and energy in arguing for a revival of ancient Greek studies. One Italian humanist, Lapo da Castiglionchio, compared them with the ancient Greeks and added that in his discussions with a few he felt as though he were in the Academy or the Lyceum. These Greek scholars had with them numerous copies of ancient texts, notably those of the Church Fathers, many of which thus became known in Italy for the very first time.[43]

Among the more brilliant in this company were George Gemistos and his disciple, Ioannis Bessarion, then Archbishop of Nicaea. In his discussions with the Florentine humanists, Gemistos expatiated on his reasons for placing Plato on a higher plane than Aristotle. It was the doubts and queries of his audience which prompted his treatise, *Peri hon Aristoteles pros Platona diaphere tai,* and its publication stimulated further interest in Platonist studies.[44]

Gemistos' ideas were the more readily received because the Italians had already been introduced to Plato's works by the translations of Palla Strozzi, Manuel Chrysoloras, and Leonardo Bruni. These Platonic studies later led Marsiglio Ficino to establish the Academia Platonica.

Platonists turned to Gemistos' treatise for ideas and arguments with which to attack the Aristotelians. Around 1462, the mild and scholarly Theodore Gazes of Thessalonica wrote his *Rebuttal (Antirretikos)* in order to defend Aristotle against Gemistos, which provided the occasion for bitter philosophical warfare and the polarization of scholarly allegiances, including an acrimonious response from Michael Apostolis, the young and noisy Platonist.[45]

Figure 20. Cardinal Bessarion, Kneeling before a Reliquary of the Holy Cross.

Gemistos' ideas found another opponent in the testy and irascible George Trapezountios. His treatise, *Comparationes philosophorum Aristotelis et Platonis* (*Comparison of the Philosophies of Aristotle and Plato*), again drew an eloquent reply from Bessarion, *In calumniatorem Platonis* (*Against Plato's Calumniator*, 1469). This work is a lengthy and dispassionate analysis of the life, work, and philosophy of Plato with a balanced appraisal of Plato's ideal world. Bessarion's analysis made a profound impression on Greek, Italian, and other scholars, among whom it was generally treated as a justification of Plato's philosophy.[46] Bessarion exercised a stabilizing influence in the development of intellectual affinity between the West and the Byzantine East.

Bessarion's personal reasons for conversion to Roman Catholicism are not known, but it is probable that he found that the extreme unpopularity of the Florentine accords among the Byzantine masses made his position as an Orthodox prelate untenable. Whatever the case, he was elected to the cardinalate of the Catholic Church on 18 December 1439, and about a year later settled permanently in Italy. There he gathered around him a circle of scholars—the so-called Bessarion Academy—where they produced a number of literary works. He translated into Latin Xenophon's *Memorabilia*, Aristotle's *Metaphysics*, and Theophrastus's work of the same title; after 1455, he occupied himself with problems of Platonist literary exegesis. He tried to reconcile the teachings of both Aristotle and Plato, just as he did the two worlds of East and West. For a time, after 1457, as Permanent Trustee of the monastery of San Salvatore in Messina, he became interested in the teaching of Greek; he installed there as teacher Andronicus Galesiotes (1461–1467) and, following the latter's death, Constantine Lascaris (1468–1501).[47] According to Apostolis' encomium,[48] Bessarion's encouragement was responsible for the founding of a number of schools of Greek all over Italy. In one of Bessarion's letters, probably to Michael Apostolis, he exhorted his correspondent to search for manuscripts in Adrianople, Athens, Thessalonica, Ainos, Gallipoli, and various other places,[49] and he sent the humanist Niccolò Perotti, his secretary, to Trebizond to gather Greek manuscripts for the Pope.[50] Particularly after the capture, Bessarion interested himself more and more in the purchase and collection of literary treasures and their preservation: "as long as there are Greeks somewhere, they are capable of achieving greatness in the future. Many things can happen over a long period, and the Greeks will be aided in attaining their goal if they can find in a safe place everything that has been written in their language—at least what has been written until now. For having found it, they will augment it." This was the consideration which led him shortly before his death to bequeath his personal library to Venice.[51] When Pope Nicholas V died in 1455, he left

824 Latin manuscripts, all beautifully bound, which came to form the nucleus of the Vatican Library; Bessarion at the end of his life gave Venice a collection of from eight to nine hundred manuscripts, more than six hundred of them in Greek, which became the most substantial intellectual resource of the La Marciana Library. A few years later, Bessarion's manuscripts were put to good use by the Hellenist Aldus Manutius, the noted publisher of ancient texts.[52]

Among those in Bessarion's circle were George Trapezountios, whose reputation was tarnished by the misguided literary quarrels in which he persistently engaged in Constantinople and Italy and by his hasty and maladroit translations; [53] Theodore Gazes, a member of the Greek delegation in 1438 to the Councils of Ferrara and Florence,[54] professor in Ferrara from 1441 to 1450,[55] and translator of Greek writers at the court of Pope Nicholas V; [56] and Andronicus Callistus of Constantinople.[57] In 1452 Trapezountios and in 1455 Gazes were invited by King Alfonso I of Naples to become translators of certain ancient Greek works at his court, where he had assembled a number of Italian humanists. In 1444, Alfonso had inaugurated the teaching of Greek at Catania in Sicily and had attracted the attention of Pope Eugenius IV, who wanted to bring educated Greeks to Orthodox monasteries in Calabria, Apulia, and Sicily.[58]

If the Italians at the Councils of Ferrara and Florence became acquainted at first hand with some of the most distinguished exemplars of the Hellenic spirit, the Greeks for their part can have been no less dazzled by the civilization with which they were suddenly confronted and the excellence of the Italians' attainments in all fields of science and the arts. Increasingly the Greek intellectuals looked upon the West as the true heir of ancient Greece and the preceptor of mankind. As we have already observed, Bessarion suggested that young Greeks of talent be sent to Italy from the Peloponnese to learn the latest techniques in engineering, shipbuilding, and the like, and even to study ancient Greek literature under Italian Hellenists. They would then return to impart the newly acquired knowledge to their own compatriots.[59] This was indeed a complete reversal: no Westerner previously was thought to have received a sound classical education unless he had studied for a time in Constantinople.[60]

Thus the Byzantine intellectual inheritance passed into the safekeeping of worthy foreign successors. Contemplating this *bouleversement,* the anti-Unionist George Scholarios had the grace to acknowledge that "the Italian race, which we once ranked among the barbarians, now not only turns its attention to the arts but creates new intellectual edifices beside the old ones." Before long, the Italians were cultivating scholarship in ancient Greek while the Byzantines could scarcely understand it.[61] The Greeks had frittered away their great inheritance until it was they who were in danger of becoming barbarians.

Argyropoulos and Chalcocondyles

The capture of Constantinople caused the rapid dispersion of the few intellectual nuclei that remained in Greece. Some scholars journeyed to the West by sea; others followed an overland route, despite generally unsettled conditions which prevailed throughout the interior.[62] Some passed through Ragusa (Dubrovnik) and even stayed there for varying lengths of time.[63] Manuel Maroullos, the physician, for instance—undoubtedly the father of the poet, Michael Maroullos Tarhaniotes, who had spent his childhood days in that city [64]—stayed from 1465 to 1470.[65] The fall of the city was lamented by those who had already migrated: "What will you do now, miserable one," cried Andronicus Callistus, "where will you go, to which city, under which ruler, among which of your relatives and friends? Who now would you have as your teacher? O unhappy life, O bitter exile, O fickle times, to what abyss have you brought me and then cast me in? O beloved family and friends who have guided me, how can you bear to abandon one of your own? Take me, take me with you quickly. Do not delay, for I can no longer endure the light, the air, even life itself. O death, death, I await your visitation . . ."[66]

Among the refugee scholars who came to Italy after the fall of Constantinople, the most important was John Argyropoulos (c. 1415–1487), of a distinguished Byzantine family. Argyropoulos was a participant at the Councils of Ferrara and Florence, where he made the acquaintance of various Italian scholars, one of whom, Francesco Filelfo, entrusted his son, Gian Mario, to Argyropoulos' tutelage when the latter returned to Constantinople. In 1441, he was in Italy again, this time at Padua, where Chrysoloras' student, Pier-Paolo Vergerio, had inaugurated Greek studies at the beginning of the century. Apparently, Argyropoulos gave private lessons in Padua while studying Latin in the university there. A degree from an Italian university could have proved useful if the Turkish storm had forced him to find shelter in the West. Exactly when he returned to Constantinople from this visit is not known, though he immediately began to revive the city's educational facilities. With the support of John VIII Palaeologus, he founded a school which was housed in the guest chambers (xenon) of Stephen II Uroš (1282–1320). Both Constantine Lascaris and Michael Apostolis were among his students.

In October 1456, with the backing of a group of young Florentine humanists, especially Donato Acciajuoli, Argyropoulos was appointed Professor of Ancient Greek at the University of Florence, where he worked productively for fourteen years. Although he devoted most of

Figure 21. John Argyropoulos.

his time to the exposition of Aristotle's works, Argyropoulos, like Bessarion, tried to synthesize the intellectual contributions of both Aristotle and Plato.[67]

Following a pedagogical method that had also been used by Chrysoloras, Argyropoulos supplemented his university lectures with lively discussions in his own home. The only difference in their approaches was that Chrysoloras relied exclusively on the technique of the seminar, as we would call it today, in which both instruction and discussion were integrated within the formal hour of teaching; Argyropoulos' students were expected to take notes from a piece of pure academic exposition and to discuss the material of the lecture afterwards in his home. Argyropoulos' fame as a teacher brought many new students to the old Florentine Academy, and he received numerous honors and privileges from the Medici. The deaths of two or three of his children between 1467 and 1469 drove him from the city sometime before July 1471, and his life after that was disoriented. At first, it appeared that he would accept the invitation of Matthew Corvinus, the King of Hungary, a noted patron of the arts, to settle in that country; but he turned instead towards Rome and the company of his good friend Bessarion and the new Pope Sixtus IV, his former fellow student at the University of Padua. But since his stipend in Rome was too small (the needs of war had forced the Pope to reduce professorial salaries and increase taxes), and the troubles of the papal curia and the work of translation he had been engaged to do drained both the time and energy he wished to expend on teaching, he returned to Florence. At the time the chair in ancient Greek at the university there was occupied by Andronicus Callistus, after 1475, by Demetrius Chalcocondyles. Argyropoulos probably resorted to private teaching; at least he was doing that in August 1477. Having returned to Rome in 1481, he died in that city on 26 July 1487 in straitened circumstances. The economies which reasons of state had forced Sixtus IV to introduce brought about a decline of letters in Rome that was not arrested until the pontificate of Leo X (1513–1521). Argyropoulos' renown, like that of Chrysoloras, rested more on his teaching than his writing, the latter consisting mainly of translations of Aristotle, the introductory remarks to Argyropoulos' lectures, his letters, and sundry theological studies.[68]

Demetrius Chalcocondyles taught from the chair in Florence longer than Argyropoulos or any other Greek incumbent. Member of an old Athenian family and cousin of the historian Laonicos Chalcocondyles, Demetrius was born in Athens in August 1423 and came to Rome in 1449. When Theodore Gazes arrived from Ferrara early in 1450, Demetrius Chalcocondyles became his student and eventually his intimate and devoted friend. Later, Chalcocondyles taught at the University of Padua,

Figure 22. Demetrius Chalcocondyles.

where Janus Lascaris was one of his students, and in 1475, on the recommendation of his friend, Francesco Filelfo, he was appointed to a chair at the University of Florence. Both Aristotelian and Platonist studies had been pursued in Florence at the same time—the former in the old Academy, the latter in the Platonist Academy more recently established by Marsiglio Ficino. The appointment of the Platonist Chalcocondyles to succeed the Aristotelians Chrysoloras and Argyropoulos, apparently led to the rapid advancement and eventual ascendancy of the Platonist viewpoint. Lorenzo de' Medici himself, ruler of Florence, while maintaining his support of the old Academy, eagerly encouraged the new studies. Chalcocondyles' students included two Englishmen, William Grocin and Thomas Linacre, who instituted Greek studies in England, as well as the German, Johann Reuchlin, in 1490.

In December 1488, towards the end of his stay in Florence, Chalco-condyles' fame was enhanced by his edition of the texts of the *Iliad* and the *Odyssey*. Those last years were spoiled, however, by personal rancor and professional friction involving Angelo Poliziano, a colleague and erstwhile student in the University, who, in addition to teaching Latin literature, which was his special competence, began to interpret the works of Hesiod, Homer, and finally in 1490 Aristotle. Chalcocondyles felt himself to have been placed in a most invidious position in the University and accordingly accepted a proposition put to him by Lodovico Sforza (*Il Moro*, "The Moor") that he come to teach in Milan. A number of distinguished Hellenists had preceded him there as teachers, Manuel Chrysoloras, Demetrius Kastrinos, Andronicus Callistus, and Constantine Lascaris, though none had stayed long, and their influence, consequently, was not overly apparent. Therefore, classical studies were nowhere near as well advanced in Milan as they were in Florence.

Nevertheless, Chalcocondyles' students in Milan were numerous and distinguished. Among the best were the Italians, Baldassar Castiglione and Gian Giorgio Trissino; the German, Johann Reuchlin, who followed Chalcocondyles there from Florence; and the Frenchman, Guillaume Budé, who had previously studied under Janus Lascaris in France. Chalcocondyles throve amid the economic security and intellectual tranquility of so civilized a community as Milan, whither, incidentally, so many other notable men of the period—Leonardo da Vinci and Donato Bramante, for example—had also been attracted by the generosity of the Grand Duke. His teaching flourished as did his writing. In 1493 came his edition of the works of Isocrates, in the following year his grammar, and in 1499 his edition of Suidas (Suda). The sudden deaths of his three children, however—in particular that of Theophilus, his last, who was extremely gifted—brought him to his grave on 9 January 1511. His library eventually wound up in the monastery of San Giovanni di Carbonara in Naples. Chalcocondyles had taught in the various universities of Italy longer than any other Greek scholar—at least nine years in Padua, sixteen in Florence, and almost twenty in Milan.[69]

Greek scholarship did not thrive in meridional Italy, though it is true that the Greco-Byzantine tradition there never completely disappeared. Until the arrival of Constantine Lascaris in Naples in 1465, humanistic studies were generally limited to Latin studies in the grammar schools. Even after Lascaris settled in Naples, most young people showed a far greater interest in the study of law than in the study of Greek. After only a year in that city, disillusioned, no doubt, by the political and intellectual climate which prevailed in Naples, Lascaris went to Rome to be at Bessarion's side. A little later, in 1466, he left for Messina with the intention of returning to Greece, though on encountering a friendly reception at Messina he decided to stay. At the beginning of 1468, he succeeded Andronicus Galesiotes as teacher of ancient Greek in the monastery of San Salvatore and successfully taught many students until his death in August 1501.[70]

Greek Scholars outside Italy

Little is known of the activities of Greek scholars in Western countries outside Italy. A number of refugees from Constantinople and the Peloponnese seem to have crossed the Alps in search of better fortunes in France, but few of them were scholars.

One scholar who went to France was Andronicus Callistus of Constantinople, who had received a fine education in literature and philosophy. Hoping to improve his condition in life, he went from Padua to Bologna; then to Rome; to Florence, where he stayed from 1471 to 1475; and finally to Milan, where he sold his folios, celebrated for their elegant calligraphy; and on the proceeds made the long journey to France. The very brief nature of his stay there, however, suggests that he never became a teacher of Greek at the University of Paris; for by March 1476 he was already in London, where he eventually died.[71] Nicholas Secundinus of Euboea, who served Venice as a diplomatic emissary on various occasions from 1434 till his death in 1464,[72] said, speaking of Callistus' classical erudition: "Thanks to you, the glory of Greece lives on and the children of the Greeks continue to emulate their fathers; through your voice, something which is supernally beautiful and infinitely precious to myself continues to be preserved in its pristine form." [73]

There was also George Hermonymos, a Spartan, who taught at the Sorbonne in 1476. A man whose knowledge of Greek deserved no acclaim whatever, this rather pedestrian Hellenist nevertheless had the good fortune to count among his students three who served as heralds of Greek letters among their own peoples—the German, Johann Reuchlin (or Kapnion, as Ermolao Barbaro, the Venetian, hellenized his name); the Dutchman, Erasmus; and the Frenchman, Guillaume Budé, who became for France what Aldus Manutius was for Italy.[74] George Hermonymos copied a large number of books, and many of his manuscripts are still extant; they consist of grammars, dictionaries, texts of Hesiod, Phocylides, Aeschylus, Euripides, Thucydides, Xenophon, Demosthenes, Aeschines, Aristotle, Plutarch, the Church Fathers, and the Gospels.[75]

In France, the work of Hermonymos was completely outdistanced in terms of importance by that of Janus Lascaris (1445–1535), the last of the great Greek scholars and a tireless advocate of ancient Greek studies in the West. After a period of study in Padua, he supported himself by giving private lessons in ancient Greek literature in Florence; finally, upon the recommendation of his former teacher, Demetrius Chalcocondyles, he became librarian to Lorenzo de' Medici. At his patron's behest, he made two trips to Greece between 1489 and 1492 to track down Greek manuscripts. A record of the places and peoples he visited on these travels is preserved in his notebook. His first stop was Corfu, where a kinsman, George Eparchos, lent him considerable assistance. From there he went to Arta, then through Acarnania and Thessaly to Meteora and Thessalonica. In Thessalonica, he purchased manuscripts from relatives of the recently deceased Matthew Lascaris, as well as from Manuel Lascaris (both probably his own distant relatives), Demetrius Sgouropoulos, and others. Resuming his journey across plains burned bare by the summer sun, Lascaris experienced the same emotions as all those pilgrims from afar when the walls, towers, and palaces of Constantinople gradually came into sight. He arrived too late to see Matthew Kamariotes, first director of the Patriarchate School (whose death had occurred a year before), but he was fortunate to meet such other prominent scholars as Manuel Corinthios and Demetrius Kastrinos—the latter Lascaris described as "a philosopher in words and deeds." The ravaged state of Constantinople's libraries appalled him. He extended his search to Adrianople, Sozopolis, Serrai, Mt. Athos (where some rare and valuable finds were made), and Crete. He returned to Florence with no fewer than two hundred manuscripts. It was at this time that Aldus Manutius first began to publish the works of ancient authors in Venice.[76]

On 3 September 1492, upon his return to Italy from this undertaking, Lascaris recounted the fruits of his mission to Sergio Stiso: "I have come back from lengthy travels in Greece and thereabouts, having survived with God's help no little danger and hardship. I have brought back many useful books, among them a few of whose very existence until now we have been unaware. I will send you the names of the most rare of these—it would be difficult to send them all—so that you too can rejoice at the incalculable profit which this trip has yielded. Not, God forbid, monetary profit or any profit in base and worthless things, but genuine profit of the kind that is most needed—by which of course I mean knowledge and wisdom, those two noble things of the Greeks, the superior and only virtues upon which all others, indeed all good, are dependent." [77]

Lascaris succeeded Chalcocondyles in his chair on 2 October 1492.[78] It was at this time, apparently, that his most distinguished student, Marcos Mousouros (1470–1517) of Candia, came to him for instruction. Between 1494 and 1496, Lascaris edited the hymns of Callimachus, the tragedies of Euripides, the *Argonautica* of Apollonius of Rhodes, and various other works.

These literary pursuits were interrupted towards the end of 1494, when Charles VIII of France, among whose aims was the destruction of the Ottoman Empire, invaded Italy at the head of a large army. No undertaking could have been better calculated to capture Lascaris' imagination. Accordingly, when Charles VIII passed through Florence, we may presume that this fervent Greek patriot gave the French king the full benefit of the knowledge he had obtained from his recent experiences in the East. Charles' venture was abortive, but it occasioned Lascaris' departure for France, where his close association with the French royal court continued throughout the reigns of Louis XII and Francis I.

The French capital, with its splendid university, was renowned for its intellectual prowess in humanistic studies. Lascaris could not have arrived at a more propitious time. Unlike George Hermonymos, however, he did not exert his influence in a formal academic way, but rather as a librarian and intellectual adviser to French kings. In this capacity, he came in touch with various coteries of noted humanists, including Guillaume Budé, and thus contributed to the advancement of learning through informal discussion.

From time to time, the French kings entrusted him with various diplomatic missions to Venice, Rome, and other Italian cities. He was Louis XII's ambassador to Venice from July 1503 to January 1509. Humanism was still flourishing in Venice because of the city's continuing economic prosperity, the presence there of many Greek refugees, and the salutary influence of various printing establishments like that of Manutius. The perquisites of his office enabled Lascaris to offer economic help to many of his compatriots and to assist young people in the purchase of books or payment of fees. While in Venice he became a member of the Aldus Academy and met many Italian, French, and other foreign Hellenists, Erasmus among them.[79]

No less rewarding in terms of acquaintances made and work accomplished was his sojourn in Rome (April 1513–autumn 1518), where the election of Pope Leo X, a descendant of the Medicis and an enthusiastic philhellene, had taken place a month before his arrival. Lascaris persuaded the Pope to found a Greek college on the Quirinal, where young people from all European countries, but especially from Greece, could study Greek and Latin. Classes began in February 1514. Very little is known about the organization and operation of the college except that it had its own printing press. Its first professor was a Cretan of the noble family of Kallierges or Kallerges named Zachary, who was formerly a calligrapher and publisher of Greek books in Venice. Kallierges continued to work as a publisher while he was in Rome. Both Lascaris and Marcos

Mousouros (1515–1517) later taught Greek at the college, and Lampridio di Cremona Latin.[80]

Lascaris also continued to publish new editions of ancient texts. Mousouros described him as the "ambassador of the Greeks": "to those recently arrived he often gave assistance far beyond his means; to those who were not there he gave his every solicitude; he introduced all his friends to the ruling circle." When Lascaris left Rome at the end of 1518, the college, which had drawn so much inspiration from him, began to decline. It came to an end with the death of its original founder, Leo X, in 1521.[81]

Lascaris, revered as a patriarch of Greek letters, divided his last years between Paris, where he lived from 1525 to 1529 or 1530, and Rome, where he died on 7 December 1534. A large part of his library can be found today in the Bibliothèque Nationale of Paris. His burial in the Church of Sant'Agata di Goti extinguished "the last flickering flame of ancient Greece." [82]

The foundation of the Greek college in Rome made a considerable impression on Western Europe. It may very well have been with this model in mind that Erasmus gave his moral support to the foundation in 1518 at Louvain in Flanders of the Busleiden Collège des Trois Langues for the study of Latin, Greek, and Hebrew. The Flemish example led the advisers of Francis I to urge upon their king the foundation of the Collège de France in honor of his people.[83]

It would be a mistake to assume from the prominence of some of the more notable Greek scholars and the praise heaped upon them by both contemporary and later admirers that all Greek scholars in the West were equally fortunate. Most of them, even those who found it expedient to acknowledge papal primacy [84] and to profess the Roman Catholic faith, toiled long and hard as teachers, copyists, and translators, except perhaps during the pontificate of Nicholas V, the great patron of the *litterae humaniores,* a period generally remembered as a heyday for scholars. "His death," wrote Filelfo to Theodore Gazes, "was the death of all savants." [85] Neither Callixtus III nor even Pius II showed an equivalent interest in scholarly activity.[86] The death of Bessarion deprived the scholars of yet another patron and friend. "From whom else now," lamented Demetrius Kastrinos, "can we draw courage and inspiration; in whom else take pride—we who have suffered so much? He was for all of us the voice of our nation—nay, more than that, its life-blood." [87] In the south of Italy, after the death of Alfonso I of Naples, scholars suffered under a reign of frugality.[88] There (according to Constantine Lascaris,[89] in a letter he wrote from Messina sometime after 1478 to Giovanni Pardo in

Milan, the Spanish philosopher and poet), the Greco-Byzantine tradition was still alive, but only barely. Calling his friend's attention to the fate which had befallen many distinguished scholars, the letter continued: "The spirit of parsimony which prevails among the rulers has driven Theodore, a man who had arrived at the very summit of wisdom, to Calabria, where, alas, at Policastro he lies in a common grave; Andronicus Callistus died friendless in the British Isles; Frangoulios [Servopoulos], a true scholar, has gone to some other place in Italy, I know not where; Demetrius has been forced to return to the homeland and there serves the barbarians. My own great teacher, John Argyropoulos, wanders the streets of the city destitute and poor, each day having to sell more of his books." [90]

The consciousness of exile, the daily struggle for bread and other material hardships, memories of their country and its past, pride of background, all tended to make these scholars oversensitive, hypercritical, and generally incapable of adjusting to new conditions or settling down in one place, like the uprooted of every age. They quarreled with the Italian humanists on fundamental grounds, and this conflict resulted in a kind of competition between Italian and Greek intellectuals. The Italians felt that they had hewn a rough and steep path to the summit of knowledge, that they had reached their goal, and that the vista was theirs to enjoy.[91] Thus, Giovanni Pontano, humanist and founder of the Academy Pontaniana in Naples, pointed out that he had learned Greek from Gregorio da Tiferno in Italy, because now in Greece one learned Turkish rather than Greek.[92] Conversely, Constantine Lascaris, noting in the preface to his grammar the flourishing state of Greek studies in Italy, had to apologize for their decline in Greece.[93] Apostolis, who claimed rather vaingloriously just after the capture that "everywhere in Italy now, as before, the Greeks teach the Westerners about Romans [Byzantines]," was finally forced to admit that the Italians, equally with others in the West, had become "heirs not only to the achievements of Greece, but also to those of Rome." [94]

What was the connection between the work of Greek scholars and the Renaissance? What was the nature of the Greek scholars' contribution to it? These questions have of course been endlessly discussed. Some have so overestimated the Greek contribution as to judge it the principal cause of the Renaissance, while some have gone to the other extreme of all but disregarding it.[95] Much still remains to be learned before the extent of this contribution can be measured, and there is much to be learned from a systematic study of the literary and philosophical works of the Greek scholars and their successors. However, it can be said with certainty that the fifteenth-century Greek scholars preserved the Greco-

Byzantine heritage and transmitted it to the West at the most auspicious moment for its reception. The point is not that the Renaissance would not have occurred without this transmission, but that it would not have assumed the aspect of a universal intellectual movement that it did.

Cammelli has acutely observed that a successful grafting of Greek and Roman cultures had already occurred in Italy in ancient times. After that, "it was destined to flourish again in the same soil, cultivated by the same people who were awakening brisk and refreshed after one thousand years of the Middle Ages, which, however, was not given over entirely to slumber. The soil was the same and the miracle was accomplished by the hard work and inexhaustible energy of the same Italian people. And the seed, too, was the same, for we know that it had been carefully husbanded for those one thousand years in the soil of Greece. When at last the West awoke out of her long torpor, she immediately perceived its life-sustaining properties, and for the second time received it back gratefully as a gift." [96]

Such was the contribution of the Byzantine scholars to mankind. Were they able to do as much for their own unfortunate country?

THE QUESTION OF NATIONAL LIBERATION

Since these wandering Greek scholars no longer had a country they could call their own, it was important to their pride that they at least be known throughout the West as "remnants of the Greeks," as they were generally acknowledged to be.[1] They were keenly aware of their nationality at a time when national consciousness in Europe was still inchoate. An important element in that awareness, of course, was their implacable hatred of the Turk.

Charitonymos Hermonymos, the bibliographer, who had studied under Gemistos, when completing a codex to the works of Aristotle in Rome in 1467 (Biblioteca Marciana, Cod. No. CCVI), remarked: "My country, once happy but now downtrodden, is still Lacedemonia." Demetrius Trivolis sedulously recorded in his manuscripts not only the places he visited on his perambulations but also the years that had passed since his "country's capture." Demetrius Ralles Kavakes, also one of Gemistos' former students and his close friend, possessed the same sentiments. "Though no scribe," he "came from the aristocratic senatorial class" and considered himself a "Spartan and Byzantine" or, as he also wrote, "a Greek and a Thracian." [2] Kavakes was a devoted disciple of Gemistos and apparently shared the philosopher's pagan propensities. Despite the threat of excommunication, he once dared to collate a series of extracts from Gemistos' On Law (Peri nomon), which Gennadius, the first Patriarch after the capture of Constantinople, had once consigned to flames.[3] His every moment seemed to be consumed by Gemistos' vision for Greece.[4] At the end of the fifteenth century, Michael Souliardos of Argos said that he copied "not for reward but for nation." [5] Theodore Gazes seized every opportunity to give vent to his patriotic feelings.[6]

Very few of the exiled scholars besides Demetrius Kastrinos were so overcome by privation or nostalgia for their homeland as actually to return to it and attempt to find some manner of accommodation with the conqueror. George Trapezountios provides an interesting case in point for, although he sought to conciliate the conqueror of the Greek lands, he had a clear motive for doing so—the desire to mitigate his country's plight. Barely two months after the capture he sent a tract to Mohammed II, *The Truth of the Christian Faith,* which praised the Sultan fulsomely and suggested a closer and more fraternal relationship between the two peoples. The only obstacle to this was religious division, which, he said, had been brought about mainly by the Jews. The difference between Greek and Turk would be seen as unreal if only the truth about their respective religions were properly understood. Hostility would then be replaced by amity.[7]

Much later, when he was seventy years old, Trapezountios again acclaimed Mohammed and his conquests. On this occasion, he had been sent to Greece and the East by Pope Paul II (November 1465—18 March 1466) to observe and report on the condition of the inhabitants and the situation which generally obtained throughout the area. He secretly sent two letters to the Sultan, one from Galata (25 February 1466) and the other from Rome, which were replete with unctuous salutations (referring to the Sultan as "unique," "self-made," "greater than Caesar and Alexander the Great") and which provided the Sultan with valuable information about the West. Finally, he called Mohammed "Emperor of the Romans" and of the world, and urged him to lose no time in launching his projected enterprise against Italy. "The august throne of Constantine the Great has been given to you, which is a sure sign that the Almighty has chosen Your Majesty for this task." Trapezountios' machinations almost cost him his life in Rome; he was saved only by the intervention of the Pope himself, who had once studied under him.[8]

Although Bessarion had managed to fire with crusading zeal the old but mettlesome Pope Callixtus III, and later Pius II,[9] who convened the Congress of Mantua in order that the Christian rulers of the West might be brought to commit themselves at last to a definite course of action, both Pius II and Bessarion became thoroughly disheartened at what appeared to be the insuperable barrier of political discord in the West. After Mantua, Germany seemed the last remaining hope. Accordingly, in February 1460, despite inclement weather and his failing health, Bessarion set out as legate at large to visit Nuremberg, Worms, and Vienna. Any participation by the German rulers in a future crusade proved to be contingent on the peaceful resolution of a multiplicity of conflicting interests and raging antagonisms which then rent the German states. The failure of Bessarion's mission was further preordained by the beginnings of ideological ferment which ended in the Reformation. He returned to Rome on 20 November 1461,[10] a disappointed man.

Meanwhile, the overthrow of the Despotate of Morea and the Empire of Trebizond increased his despair. As we have seen, he assumed the guardianship of the children of Thomas Palaeologus, the last despot of Morea, and brought them up in the Catholic faith; he was likewise solicitous of the welfare of the Greek scholars still flocking to Italy, one of whom was Constantine Lascaris.[11]

Bessarion's hopes were raised when relations between the Venetians and the Turks became strained and a war party came to the fore in Venice. On 22 July 1463, he arrived in Venice as a papal legate, and on the night of 28 July, after six days of negotiations, "the most serene republic" declared war on the Porte. However, the Pope's death on 15 August 1464 and the subsequent dislocation which preceded the election of his successor frustrated Bessarion's efforts for the extension of the war. The new Pope, Paul II, was a man whose indifference towards humanistic studies was entirely consistent with his general indolence of disposition, and he was totally unsuited to the task of arousing the Christian world for a crusade against the Turks, even if the overall situation at the time had been more favorable, which, of course, was not the case. Bessarion's mission therefore miscarried, as did his final one in France during the pontificate of Sixtus IV.[12]

After the fall of Euboea in 1470, Bessarion tried in a succession of impassioned speeches to convince the rulers of the West that the military might of the Turks was not nearly so overwhelming as was generally believed in the West. Except for the permanent corps of janissaries, which was in any case a substantial burden on the Ottoman economy, the remainder of the Ottoman army was hardly more than an undisciplined horde of irregulars. Bessarion was puzzled, he said, as to how the Turks had managed to become masters of Asia Minor and the Balkans and even to threaten central and Western Europe. The disconsolate Bessarion eventually died in Ravenna on 18 November 1472—"not only the glory of Greece, but a pillar of the Roman Church and a lustrous star in the Italian firmament"—at least in the estimation of the Bishop of Parma.[13]

A patriot and protégé of Bessarion's was Janus Lascaris, whose travels in the East were motivated at least as much by his eagerness to gather information about the military disposition of the Turks and Ottoman imperial organization generally as by his desire to collect Greek manuscripts. He was the first person to make any study in depth of the new situation in the East. Not only did he visit and carefully observe all the provinces of European Turkey, but he endeavored to establish contacts with many Greeks and came to realize the assistance they would be able to offer the rulers of the West if ever an attack were launched on the Turks. He made many appeals to the rulers of the West—Charles VIII of France, Maximilian I of Germany, Pope Julius II, Pope Leo X—for the organization of a crusade against the Turks. At the age of eighty, as an emissary of Pope Clement VII, he renewed that appeal to the powerful Holy Roman Emperor, Charles V, after Charles' victory over Francis I of France at Pavia (24 February 1525). His exhortation began by emphasizing that his one concern in life had been the freedom of Greece, and it concluded with the plea: "Those who represent the last remnants of ancient Greece fall at your feet and beg you to free them from the misery which now oppresses them, a misery which consists in their having to watch children torn from mothers' breasts and in being forced to renounce their religion, in being used for God knows what nefarious purposes, and in being obliged to take up arms against their own families. These aggrieved people, though with scarcely the opportunity to do so, have secretly sent messages imploring you to sympathize with the predicament of a Christian people, promising to expose themselves to every kind of danger in the interests of winning your support. Their lot is not so desperate as to prevent them from assisting you significantly with arms and provisions, which they possess, in the execution and completion of any enterprise you might be pleased to undertake on their behalf. These are the proposals, Your Majesty, which Greece has charged me with placing before you. Speaking now for the faithful as a whole, I can assure you that the disputes which rage among your vassal kings and the other monarchs of the West can only lead ultimately to the misfortune of your subjects and the discord of your Church."

Lascaris' efforts, however, were in vain. His epitaph, composed by himself, reads: "Lascaris lies buried here in an alien land, though with not a single complaint, O foreigner, against that land. He found it friendly. But what pain that there was no longer any free earth in his homeland where an Achaian could be buried." [14]

There were other trustees of Hellenism, of course, who, though lacking the personal contacts of Bessarion and Lascaris, tried to sway the leaders of European nations with "laments," prefaces to their literary works, other addresses and appeals, and poems.[15] In his *Ode on Constantinople's Misfortune*, for example, Andronicus Callistus entreated both the Pope and Venice for assistance: "O divine Rome, what will you do now that your daughter is a helot? O Holy Father [to the Pope] can you bear to behold such a terrible thing? And you Blessed Father [to the Patriarch], white-haired, infinitely wise, shepherd of a stolen flock, what will you do? O great and peerless Venice, will you accept the loss of your sister and friends? Where will your galleys go now when they venture to the Black Sea? Who will receive them in a fit and proper manner? Will you be chased from Constantinople, even caught between Scylla and Charybdis?" [16]

Michael Apostolis, having settled in Crete after the capture, was urged by two obscure Greeks, Aristonymos Byzantios and John Stavrakios, to turn to the Emperor of Germany, Frederick III.[17] Apostolis became convinced that Frederick could defeat the Sultan and reconquer all the lands that had formerly belonged to the Byzantine Empire: the fluctuating fortunes of mankind told him so.[18] Also, the oracles themselves provided grounds even more substantial for such a belief. Indeed, according to these, the moment had already arrived when speeches would be replaced by action and war; that is, according to prophecies delivered by those "who possessed an esoteric knowledge vouchsafed by God," "the legendary year" had come and a "sleeping serpent" [Frederick] would bestir himself, "strike at the youthful one" [the Sultan], free the Greeks, and subdue the barbarians. (This consultation of oracles was to be a feature of the entire period of Turkish occupation.) Apostolis therefore beseeched Frederick to appoint his son, Maximilian, as Emperor of Byzantium, and to restore Greece to the Greek race, "once proud and learned, but now weak and humiliated and scattered all over the earth." It was not just the Byzantine people who made this appeal; the spirit of the Emperor Constantine itself called upon Frederick to avenge all those who had died in war. Exactly when Apostolis made this entreaty is uncertain, but it was probably written around 1470, when Frederick's son, Maximilian, was only eleven years old! [19]

Standing before the ancient monuments of the Hierapetra, Apostolis wrote ecstatically to his student, Emmanuel Atramyttenos, "O Greek race, O hands of Daedalus and Phidias and Praxiteles and all who shaped and sculpted this marble, I think that they were not born like to us mortals. I think only divine beings could have fashioned the like of those men who could create such wondrous things. O my son, I swear by my faith and on the Bible itself that it seemed to me I was looking not so much at stones and statues as at men who talked, and that it was not so much stone my fingers touched as flesh! O what exquisite statuary depicting all manner of divine creatures; O how straight and slender the columns; O how symmetrical and luminous this marble; O what marvellous art and handiwork . . ." [20]

Michael Maroullos Tarhaniotes (1453/54–1500), a poet and a soldier, was another exile well known in Greek and Italian humanist circles during the Renaissance.[21] His descriptions of the expatriates' feelings were especially sensitive. As a small child with his refugee parents in Ragusa

(Dubrovnik)—his "sweet former friend"—he experienced the first pangs of grief. In a poem dedicated to Charles VIII of France, he wrote that, as "the erstwhile homeland of heroes and the arts, the true hearth of religion and the gods, now mortified by her shame as a ravished and dishonored Christian land," Greece calls for him. And he continues, "If you remain unmoved by Greece's glory, her fame and her magnificent works, which belong to all people for all time, will you be moved by the piteous condition of so many exiles who throw themselves at your feet, or by the bleaching bones and devout tears of so many Christians, or by the plight of Christ's religion polluted in so many shameful ways . . ." [22]

In a poem dedicated to Greece, a country he never saw, Maroullos called her the "light of all countries, star of all nations." Yet she had become a "pathetic corpse," "an atrocity perpetrated against Heaven." "O miserable and unhappy race," he wrote, "where was your happiness lost?" In another poem, "On the Bravery of a Constantinopolitan Woman," he evoked an image of the Constantinopolitan mother as a celestial being, a symbol not only of the nation but of freedom itself. [23]

His aimless travels with all the attendant troubles and hardships reinforced his longing for Greece, as indicated in his poem, "On His Exile"— "although absent from my homeland in a Scythian country, I have still to endure the haughty dictates of Bessus and tolerate the arbitrary exercise of power by a tyrannical ruler, and my freedom is no more than sham. . . . It is surely better to be among the ashes and relics of one's own people, even though the authority of one's forebears has been supplanted by a new authority; it is surely better to enjoy one's own country while one has air to breathe than to be a mere nothing in a foreign land. All honor, both of race and family, vanishes once one steps in exile onto an unknown shore . . ."

Tarhaniotes reflected how different his reputation abroad would have been had he only come from a country that was free. How much more preferable was death in battle than slavery, a truth he professed to have learned from bitter experience: "Then we should have died, youngsters and elders, not surviving only to suffer such manifold and great misfortunes. We ought to have remembered the courage of our fathers, the ancestral virtue which made men run with noble wounds to meet their death, or else to preserve their freedom by fighting. There lies the only certain road to freedom. . . .

"O, let us put out of our minds forever that we must first count those who will stand up," he said; "the number will never be inadequate if confidence is there. If the soldier wields his ancestral arms with ardor; if he charges intrepidly into the thick of the fray; if he receives encouragement, now from his wife, now from his family, now from his relatives, now from his father who remains behind to take care of the house—then that is enough. What kind of madness is it to fortify one's country against hostile attack and then to entrust its defense to foreigners? To have the standards of one's country held aloft by unknown hands is to bring contempt on Greeks as lacking confidence in the success of their own arms." [24]

Occasionally, Tarhaniotes sought forgetfulness in hedonism. He advised another exile, Manuel Ralles, to do the same: "turn your back on these senseless cares, my good Ralles, you have already shown enough concern for what remains of your country . . . Why should we unfortunate ones grieve each day and fritter away the little time we have? . . . Come, child Hyllus, bring the jar of wine, let us banish sadness and despair . . ." In another poem addressed to Ralles, he appears to have entertained the hope that the Emperor of Germany would come to Greece's aid: "We, Manuel, have had our time of family greatness in our native land. What could be more noble now than to accept the vicissitudes of exile with all its cruel exactions? Thus inexorable fate destroyed Croesus; thus old Priam was reduced to a supplicant for the body of Hector; but thus, too, the Shepherd of Latium [Romulus] overthrew emperors. The years, of course, which triumph over all, in time brought to perdition the Shepherd, for whom at least a similar threnody can be sung. Who knows if a better fate does not await us? True, we must live among whatever lares the gods please; but for myself, I do not worry about the paternal care they can provide as long as Caesar [the Emperor of Germany] is my augur." [25]

Tarhaniotes' hymns were often dedicated to the sun, the moon, the air, and sundry ancient divinities, and are imbued with the pagan spirit of ancient Greece. His ideas were even more daring than those of the Italian Renaissance scholars, among whom they were well known, but they seem to be self-conscious literary expressions rather than manifestations of religious belief,[26] just as the Italian scholars on the whole remained faithful to the Christian tradition while their pagan literary inclinations sprang mainly from a veneration of antiquity. Yet Erasmus, himself an ardent lover of antiquity, found Tarhaniotes' poems unconscionably idolatrous. Professor D. Zakythinos has noted that Tarhaniotes "did not praise the beautiful symbols of Olympus and ancient religion merely for their beauty and serenity, which was usual, but rather as living symbols of a force in whose renewal he apparently believed." In ancient religion, "he could find not so much religion itself as a means of the rebirth of his occupied homeland." [27] Thus, Tarhaniotes went beyond the conventional forms of classical adulation, identifying ancient Greek religion and the Greek spirit in general with the political renascence of Hellenism. His work has not yet been subjected to sufficient critical scrutiny, but his views will probably be found to come closest to those of Gemistos and his circle.

An exhaustive treatment of the ideas and activities of the Greek scholars concerning the question of national liberation cannot be given in a single chapter, especially since all the relevant material is not available. It is evident that their literary and political earnestness, as well as the impact of their everyday discussions with foreigners, contributed to the gradual growth of a philhellenic sentiment in the West, notably from the beginning of the sixteenth century.

The lessons of enslavement, though painful, were most salutary for the scholars and ultimately for the entire nation. Through all the vicissitudes of a difficult and turbulent life, these scholars clung to the belief that freedom was a supreme and transcendental good. Those who had it were blessed: "there is nothing better or sweeter than freedom," wrote Constantine Lascaris to his Italian friend Andrea of Cremona, "so rejoice now that you live amongst your own." [28]

Another truth the Greeks had learned most dearly was the pernicious consequences of discord and civil war. Urging the rulers of Italy to bury their quarrels and unite against the Turks, Bessarion had counselled: "Believe one who has had the experience and suffered. There is one thing, and one thing only, that has destroyed unfortunate Greece and that is discord. Not only in recent years, but in ancient times as well, civil war has brought the downfall of the Greeks."

Anxious that his words should carry conviction, he continued: "When the Greeks were persuaded by the benefits of entente, they defeated Xerxes though their forces were vastly inferior. What could you not achieve, with the help of Divine Providence, when in numbers you are on a par with the enemy and in valor you outstrip him—if only you acted in amity among yourselves and in concert against the enemy? O would that that day could dawn when, having quashed all hatreds, you will strike the enemy in unison! I would have no doubt about the outcome: the battle would already have been won." [29]

NOTES

Every reference is given in full the first time it appears in a chapter of the Notes. Because so many languages are involved, foreign language titles, unless the meaning is generally obvious, have also been given in translation the first time the title appears in the Notes. The number in parentheses immediately following the title is the number of the note in the same chapter where the full citation occurs; in the case of translated titles, if there is an additional number preceding a colon, that is the number of the chapter where both the translation and a full citation may be found.

Chapter 1

1. Regarding the man and his work, see the recent monograph, Herbert Seidler, *Jakob Philipp Fallmerayers geistige Entwicklung: Ein Beitrag zur deutschen Geistesgeschichte des 19. Jahrhunderts* [*Jakob Philipp Fallmerayer's Intellectual Development: A Contribution to German Intellectual History of the Nineteenth Century*] (Munich, 1947). For an analysis of his theory, see pp. 28, 43–48, 94–95. Fallmerayer has made some general comments on this theory in *Schriften und Tagebücher* [*Writings and Diaries*] (Munich-Leipzig, 1913), II, 196–203. A certain animus against the modern Greeks can be detected in these writings.

2. The Viennese Slavist Bartholomäus Kopitar was apparently the father of Fallmerayer's theory (Alexander Vasiliev, *History of the Byzantine Empire* [Madison, Wis., 1961], I, 179), though he does not accept the extreme views propounded by the latter: "Die Griechen also, die nicht nur griechisch *glauben*, sondern auch neugriechisch *sprechen*, können wir mit gutem Gewissen auch ferner für Nachkommen der Griechen gelten lassen [Therefore, the Greeks who not only have Greek *beliefs* but also *speak* modern Greek we might with good conscience allow to pass, moreover, as descendants of the Greeks]" (Polychronis Enepekides, "Kopitar und die Griechen [Kopitar and the Greeks]," *Wiener Slavistisches Jahrbuch,* III [1953], 67).

3. See Denis Zakythinos, Οἱ Σλάβοι ἐν Ἑλλάδι [*The Slavs in Greece*] (Athens, 1945), pp. 22 ff.; Max Vasmer, *Die Slaven in Griechenland* (Berlin, 1941), pp. 1 ff., for a brief critical survey of the works written before 1940; and Antoine Bon, *Le Péloponnèse byzantin jusqu'en 1204* (Paris, 1951), pp. 27 ff., which also annotates the basic bibliography on this subject. Besides objective observations, the study offers a brief, critical survey of the problem as a whole, and presents the texts of the known Byzantine sources. A recent study of the *Chronicle of Monemvasia* is that of Paul Lemerle, "La Chronique improprement dite de Monemvasie: Le Contexte historique et légendaire," REB, xxi (1963), 5–49.

4. See Franjo Barišić, *The Miracles of Saint Demetrius of Thessalonica as a Historical Source* (Serbocroatian) (Belgrade, 1953), which contains the older bibliography; Paul Lemerle, "Invasions et migrations dans les Balkans depuis la fin de l'époque romaine jusqu'au VIIIᵉ siècle," *Revue historique*, ccxi (1954), 265–308; and Peter Charanis, "Ethnic Changes in the Byzantine Empire in the Seventh Century," DOP, xiii (1959), 13 ff., for the most recent bibliography.

5. See Demetrios Pallas, "Τά ἀρχαιολογικά τεκμήρια τῆς καθόδου τῶν βαρβάρων εἰς τήν Ἑλλάδα [The Archaeological Evidence for the Descent of the Barbarians into Greece]," Ἑλληνικά, xiv (1955), 87–105, for the relevant bibliography.

6. George Ostrogorsky, *History of the Byzantine State*, 2nd Eng. ed. (New Brunswick, N.J., 1969), pp. 80–81. See Epaminondas Chrysanthopoulos, "Τά βιβλία τῶν θαυμάτων τοῦ Ἁγίου Δημητρίου, τό Χρονικόν τῆς Μονεμβασίας καί αἱ σλαβικαί ἐπιδρομαί εἰς τήν Ἑλλάδα [The Books of the Miracles of Saint Demetrius, the Chronicle of Monemvasia, and the Slavic Incursions into Greece]," Θεολογία, xxvi (1955), 106 ff.

7. See Wilhelm Ensslin, "Slaveneinfälle [Slavic Invasions]," in RE, Zweite Reihe [R-Z] Fünfter Halbband (Stuttgart, 1927), cols. 697–706.

8. Peter Charanis is of the opinion that the Avaro-Slav invaders of 578 not only penetrated as far as, but also settled in, the western and central Peloponnese. Thus, only the eastern Peloponnese and Corinth managed to maintain their communications with the Byzantine Empire ("On the Slavic Settlement in the Peloponnese," BZ, xlvi (1953), 100),

9. See A. Pertusi, ed., *Constantino Porfirogenito, De thematibus* (Vatican, 1952), p. 91. Denis Zakythinos, *Le Despotat grec de Morée* (Athens, 1953), ii, 20–21; Stilpon Kyriakidis, "Οἱ Σλάβοι ἐν Πελοποννήσῳ [The Slavs in the Peloponnese]," Βυζαντιναί Μελέται (Thessalonica, 1947), vi, 95; and Epaminondas Chrysanthopoulos, "Τά βιβλία [The Books]," Θεολογία, xxvii (1956), 87 ff. Regarding the peaceful penetration of the Slavs and the explanation of many Slav toponyms, see Constantine Amantos, Ἱστορία τοῦ Βυζαντινοῦ κράτους [*History of the Byzantine Rule*], 2nd ed. (Athens, 1939), i, 348–349. See also Kirsten's attempt to trace the route of the Slavs and Vlachs from Epirus to Thessaly and Achaia, and from Olympus to Pelion (Alfred Philippson and Ernst Kirsten, *Die griechischen Landschaften* [*The Greek Territories*] [Frankfort-on-the-Main, 1950], i, 1. 277–278).

10. See Georg Stadtmüller, "Τά προβλήματα τῆς ἱστορικῆς διερευνήσεως τῆς Ἠπείρου [The Problems of the Historical Investigation of Epirus]," HX, IX (1934), 160, 161; and Vasmer, *Die Slaven* (3), pp. 322–324.

11. Charanis, "On the Slavic Settlement" (8), p. 42.

12. Francis Dvornik, *The Slavs: Their Early History and Civilization* (Boston, 1956), pp. 116–117, which contains the relevant bibliography.

13. *Ibid.*, p. 117.

14. For the relevant bibliography, see Zakythinos, Οἱ Σλάβοι (3), pp. 48–51.

15. See Spyridon Lambros, " Ὀλίγαι λέξεις περί Σλάβων ἐν Πελοποννήσῳ καί περί τῶν κληθέντων σλαβικῶν κτιρίων τῆς Ὀλυμπίας [A Few Words concerning Slavs in the Peloponnese and the So-Called Slavic Buildings of Olympia]," Ὥρα, May 5, 1874, pp. 5–6; in Zakythinos, Οἱ Σλάβοι (3), p. 95.

16. Vasmer, *Die Slaven* (3), pp. 324–325. Antoine Bon mentions two large centers in particular, Athens and Corinth, and extols Corinth's role after 783 in the reconquest and hellenization of the Peloponnese (see his report to the Xe Congrès international des études byzantines, *Tebliğleri-Actes* (Istanbul, 1957), p. 207).

17. Nikos Bees, "Zum macedonischen Bistum Kaesareia [On the Macedonian Diocese of Caesarea]," BNJ, x (1934), 346–348. Antonios Keramopoullos saw the remains of such castles in western Macedonia; his Τί εἶναι οἱ Κουτσόβλαχοι; [*Who Are the Koutsovlachs?*] (Athens, 1939), pp. 141–142, contains much interesting information.

18. For some interesting findings about the origins and bases of Hellenism in eastern Thessaly, see Philippson and Kirsten, *Die griechischen Landschaften* (9), I, 1. 278, 279, 280, 293, 295. One such castle in western Sterea Hellas must have been Naupactus (*ibid.*, II, 2, 616: "Danach ist anzunehmen, dass vom Altertum her in dem verödeten Festlandsraum West-Mittelgriechenlands nur die Festung Naupaktos bestand, als die Slaven einwanderten. Von ihr ging dann die Graecisierung dieser Gebirgsbevölkerung aus, die offenbar ihre Herden zu den Seen und Sümpfen auf Winterweide trieb wie heute die Aromunen und daher den Seen die Namen gab [Wherefore we might assume that from antiquity only the stronghold of Naupactus existed in the deserted land of west middle Greece when the Slavs came in. From this point spread out the hellenization of this mountain people, which openly drove its herds to the lakes and marshes for winter pasture, as do today the Aromuni, and thereby gave to the lakes their names]." See also Charanis, "On the Slavic Settlement" (8), pp. 40–41, where some other, older works are mentioned).

19. G. Da Costa-Louillet, "Saints de Grèce aux VIIIe, IXe, et Xe siècles," *Byzantion*, XXXI (1961), 331.

20. See George Kremos, Φωκικά (Athens, 1874), I, 38, 148, 165.

21. Esprit Cousinéry, *Voyage dans la Macedoine* (Paris, 1831), II, 140; I, 53; cf. p. 68: "Il est à remarquer que les Bulgares n'ont jamais pénétré dans ces bois. La population y est toute grecque, ainsi que dans la Piérie, jusqu'à Caraféria et à Gniaousta. Il paraît que c'est dans l'épaisseur de ces remparts naturels que les Grecs, pendant l'invasion des Bulgares, trouvèrent un refuge

[One must observe that the Bulgars never penetrated into these forests. The population there is entirely Greek, just as in Pieria, up to Caraveria and Gniaousta. It seems that it is in the denseness of these natural bulwarks that the Greeks, during the invasions of the Bulgars, found a refuge]." This refuge became both more extensive and more permanent at the time of the Turkish invasions.

22. See Stilpon Kyriakidis, Θεσσαλονίκια μελετήματα [*Thessalonian Studies*] (Thessalonica, 1939), pp. 9, 11, 12, 15.

23. See Epaminondas Chrysanthopoulos, Τά βιβλία (6), in Θεολογία, xxvii (1956), 115–117, 132–133.

24. See Constantine Sathas, Χρονικόν ἀνέκδοτον Γαλαξειδίου [*Chronicle of Galaxidi*] (Athens, 1865), pp. 192 ff., and pp. 122 ff. For the chronology of the Bulgar invasions given in the *Chronicle*, see Nikos Bees, "Αἱ ἐπιδρομαί τῶν Βουλγάρων ὑπό τόν τζάρον Συμεών καί τά σχετικά σχόλια τοῦ Ἀρέθα Καισαρείας [The Incursions of the Bulgars under the Tsar Symeos and the Relevant Comments of Arethas of Caesarea]," Ἑλληνικά, ι (1928), 350 ff. On the reliability of the manuscript, see Bees's "Τό χειρόγραφον τοῦ Χρονικοῦ τοῦ Γαλαξειδίου καί νέαι αὐτοῦ ἀναγνώσεις [The Manuscript of the Chronicle of Galaxidi and New Readings of It]," ΠΑΑ, xix (1944), 347–356.

25. See Kyriakidis, Θεσσαλονίκια (22), pp. 94–95.

26. See Zakythinos, *Le Despotat grec de Morée* (9), ii, 29.

27. Spyridon Lambros, "Κανανός Λάσκαρις καί Βασίλειος Βατάτζης. Δύο Ἕλληνες περιηγηταί τοῦ ΙΕ' καί ΙΗ' αἰῶνος [Kananos Laskaris and Basileios Vatatzes. Two Greek Travellers of the Fifteenth and Eighteenth Centuries]," Παρνασσός, v (1881), 707, 710–713.

28. See Zakythinos, Οἱ Σλάβοι (3), p. 65.

29. Socrates Kougeas, Περί τῶν Μελιγκῶν τοῦ Ταϋγέτου ἐξ ἀφορμῆς ἀνεκδότου βυζαντινῆς ἐπιγραφῆς ἐκ Λακωνίας [*Concerning the Melingi of Taygetus, from an Unpublished Byzantine Inscription from Laconia*] (Athens, 1950), pp. 30–31.

30. See J. B. Bury, *A History of the Eastern Roman Empire from the Fall of Irene to the Accession of Basil I (802–867)* (London, 1912), pp. 379–380, and Bon, *Le Péloponnèse byzantin* (3), pp. 31 ff., which contains the relevant bibliography.

31. See Apostolos Vacalopoulos, *Thasos, son histoire, son administration de 1453 à 1912* (Paris, 1953), pp. 59, 60. This book contains the relevant bibliography.

32. See Keramopoullos, Τί εἶναι οἱ Κουτσόβλαχοι; (17), p. 56, and Stilpon Kyriakidis, *The Northern Ethnological Boundaries of Hellenism* (Thessalonica, 1955), pp. 46, 51 ff., 54 ff. Cf. also the recent case of the Greek-speaking Kataphygion Macedonians who, after settling in Klisura (between 56 and 66 miles from Thessalonica on the international railway), subsequently lost their mother tongue and became Bulgar-speaking (see A. K. O., "Κλεισούρα," in Μακεδονικόν 'ημερολόγιον, ιι [1909], 261).

33. See Demetrius Georgakas, "Beiträge zur Deutung als slavisch erklärter Ortsnamen [Contributions to the Interpretation of Place-Names Said to Be Slavic]," BZ, xli (1941), 353, for the opinions of the specialists.

34. Gustav Meyer, *Neugriechische Studien* [*Studies in Modern Greek*], II (Vienna, 1894), 6 ff. Cf. Franz Miklosich, "Die slavischen Elemente des Neugriechischen [The Slavic Elements of Modern Greek]," *Wiener Sitzungsberichte*, LXIII (1869), 529–566.

35. Veselin Beshevliev, "Βούλγαροι καί ῞Ελληνες στίς ἀμοιβαῖες τούς ἐπιδράσεις ἀνάμεσα στούς αἰῶνες [The Bulgars and Greeks in Their Mutual Influences through the Centuries]," tr. Nikolaos Andriotis, Ἑστία, XXVIII (1940), 1072 ff.; and Andriotis, "Τά ἑλληνικά στοιχεῖα τῆς βουλγαρικῆς γλώσσης [The Greek Elements of the Bulgarian Language]," ΑΘΓΛΘ, XVII (1952), 33–100.

36. See Vasmer, *Die Slaven* (3), p. 316.

37. See Alexander Vasiliev, *Justin the First* (Cambridge, Mass., 1950), pp. 303–304, for the most recent historical bibliography.

38. Ares Poulianos, Ἡ προέλευση τῶν Ἑλλήνων [*The Origin of the Greeks*] (Athens, 1960), pp. 16, 18. See also pp. 109–110, 111.

39. Thomas Gordon, *History of the Greek Revolution* (London, 1844), I, 34n.

40. Léon Heuzey, *Excursion dans la Thessalie turque en 1858* (Paris, 1927), pp. 171–172: "il ne faut pas voir en eux de véritables Albanais, mais des Arvanito-vlaques comme ils sont encore appelés dans la Grèce du nord, c'est-à-dire des populations roumaines émigrées anciennement de l'Albanie et parlant couramment la langue albanaise en même temps que leur langue maternelle [It is not necessary to see in them real Albanians, but Arvanito-Vlachs (as they are still called in the north of Greece), that is to say Rumanian populations which emigrated in ancient times from Albania and speak fluently both the Albanian language and their mother tongue]."

41. See the opinion of Peter Kanellidis ("Μάνη καί Μανιᾶται [Maina and Maniotes]," Ἑβδομάς, IV [1887], nos. 37–38) that the Albanians of the Peloponnese had settled there since at least the eighth century. This theory is also advanced by Constantine Biris, Ἀρβανίτες, οἱ Δωριεῖς τοῦ νεωτέρου ἑλληνισμοῦ [Albanians, the Dorians of Modern Greece] (Athens, 1960), pp. 63 ff.

42. The opinion that the Albanians settled in Thessaly in the twelfth century is put forward by Ioannis K. Voyatzidis in his study, "Τό χρονικόν τῶν Μετεώρων [The Chronicle of Meteora]," ΕΕΒΣ, II (1925), 155. Peter A. Phourikis is also of the opinion that the Albanians came into Greece several centuries before 1300 ("Γάμος καί γαμήλια σύμβολα παρά τοῖς ἀλβανοφώνοις τῆς Σαλαμῖνος [Marriage Wedding Symbols among the Albanian-Speaking Population of Salamis]" [Athens, 1927], reprinted from Λαογραφία, IX, 3. See his other studies, "Παρατηρήσεις εἰς τά τοπωνύμια τῶν Χρονικῶν τοῦ Μορέως [Observations on the Place-Names of the *Chronicles of Morea*]," Ἀθηνᾶ, XL [1928], 59, and "Συμβολή εἰς τό τοπωνυμικόν τῆς Ἀττικῆς [A Contribution to the Toponymy of Attica]" [Athens, 1929], pp. 128–129), though he was not able to develop his theory. For other similar theories, see Ioannis K. Poulos, "Ἡ ἐποίκησις τῶν Ἀλβανῶν εἰς Κορινθίαν [The Settlement of the Albanians in the Area of Corinth]," ΕΜΑ, III (1950), 40–42.

43. See Franz Miklosich and Joseph Müller, *Acta et diplomata graeca medii aevi sacra et profana* [*Greek Acts and Documents, Sacred and Secular, of the Middle Ages*] (Vienna, 1860–1887), v, 260–261.

44. See Antonio Rubió y Lluch, "Els Governs de Matheu de Moncada y Roger de Lluria en la Grecia catalana (1359–1370)," *Anuari de l'Institut d'estudis catalans* (Barcelona, 1901, 1912), pp. 19–20; also the same author's "La Població dels Ducats de Grecia [The Population of the Dukedoms of Greece]," *Institut d'estudis catalans* (*Mémoires de la secció histórico-arqueológica*), iv (Barcelona, 1933), 26. I was able to consult the works of Rubió y Lluch in a handwritten French version by my friend, G. P. Tzitzelis, who kindly placed it at my disposal. See also Zakythinos, *Le Despotat grec de Morée* (9), i, 103; ii, 30–31.

45. See Athanase Gegaj, *L'Albanie et l'invasion turque au XVe siècle* [*Albania and the Turkish Invasion of the Fifteenth Century*] (Paris, 1937), pp. 25–30, and George Soulis, "Περί τῶν μεσαιωνικῶν ἀλβανικῶν φυλῶν τῶν Μαλακασίων, Μπουίων καί Μεσαριτῶν [Concerning the Medieval Albanian Tribes of the Malakasioi, the Bouïoi, and the Mesaritai]," ΕΕΒΣ, xxiii (1953), 213–216. Contrary to the opinion of many scholars, Soulis believes these to have been Albanian tribes.

46. Regarding the Karagounides, see G. M., "Περί Καραγυούνιδων [On the Karagounides]," Πανδώρα, xviii (1868), 140–142, and Panagiotes Aravantinos, Χρονογραφία τῆς Ἠπείρου [*The Annals of Epirus*] (Athens, 1856), p. 147. On the Arvanito-Vlachs of Acarnania, see Léon Heuzey, *Le Mont Olympe et l'Acarnanie* (Paris, 1860), pp. 267–268. The descent of the Arvanito-Vlachs is traced in Apostolos Vacalopoulos, "'Ιστορικαί ἔρευναι ἐν Σαμαρίνῃ τῆς Δυτ. Μακεδονίας [Historical Investigations in Samarina in Western Macedonia]," Γρηγόριος ὁ Παλαμᾶς, xxi (1937), 13 (of the reprint).

47. See John Cantacuzenus, *Historiarum libri IV* ['Ιστοριῶν βιβλία Δ, *Four Books of Histories*], ed. L. Schopen, 3 vols. (Bonn, 1828–1832), i, 474. See also Ioannis K. Voyatzidis, "Τό χρονικόν τῶν Μετεώρων" (42), ΕΕΒΣ, i (1924), 155.

48. See George Soulis, "'Η πρώτη περίοδος τῆς Σερβοκρατίας ἐν Θεσσαλίᾳ (1348–1356) [The First Period of Serbian Rule in Thessaly (1348–1356)]," ΕΕΒΣ, xx (1950), 56–73.

49. Cantacuzenus, *Historiarum* (47), iii, 147.

50. Constantin Jireček, *Geschichte der Serben* [*History of the Serbs*] (Gotha, Germ., 1911), i, 394.

51. Constantin Jireček, "Die Witwe und die Söhne des Despoten Esau von Epirus [The Widow and Sons of the Despot Esau of Epirus]," BNJ, i (1920), 1–2; and Karl Hopf, *Griechenland im Mittelalter und in der Neuzeit* [*Greece in the Middle Ages and in Modern Times*] (Leipzig, 1867–1868), ii, 32 ff. See also Poulos, 'Η ἐποίκησις (42), pp. 36, 45, where the relevant bibliography will be found. For mention of the Albanians, Serbs, and Bulgars, see Andreas Moustoxydis, ed., "'Ιστορικόν Κομνηνοῦ μοναχοῦ καί Προκλου μοναχοῦ [The

History of the Monks Comnenus and Proclus]," Ἑλληνομνήμων, ι (1843–1853), *passim*, and a recent work, edited by Sebastián Ciràc Estopañán, entitled *Bizancio y España* (Barcelona, 1943), vols. 1–2. As to the incorrect title Ἱστορικόν, see Leander Vranoussis, "Deux Historiens qui n'ont jamais existés: Comnenos et Proclos," EMA, xii (1962), 23–29.

52. Note the fourteenth-century expression, "τῆς ἁγιωτάτης ἐπισκοπῆς τῆς ἐν τῇ Ἀκαρνανίᾳ Ἄρτης [the most holy bishopric of Arta in Acarnania]." (See Germanos, Archbishop of Sardes, "Ἐπισκοπικοί κατάλογοι τῶν ἐν Ἠπείρῳ καί Ἀλβανίᾳ ἐπαρχιῶν τοῦ πατριαρχείου Κωνσταντινουπόλεως [Episcopal Catalogues of the Epirote and Albanian Districts of the Patriarchate of Constantinople]," HX, xii [1937], 12.) See Laonicos Chalcocondyles, *Historiarum demonstrationes* [Ἀπόδειξις ἱστοριῶν], ed. Eugene Darkó, 2 vols. (Budapest, 1922–1927), ι, 197.

53. See Moustoxydis, "Ἱστορικόν" (51), p. 496. (This document is also published in Ciràc Estopañán, *Bizancio y España*, ιι, 37 ff.)

54. See Moustoxydis, "Ἱστορικόν" (51), pp. 491–492. Moustoxydis deduces that Achelous is the ancient Ambracia (p. 504, n. 24). More likely is the view held by Philippson and Kirsten, *Die griechischen Landschaften* (9), ι, 1. 616, 617. See also George E. Papatrechas, "Ἐπισκοπή Ἀχελώου καί ἡ ὁμώνυμη βυζαντινή πόλη [The Diocese of Achelous and the Byzantine city of the same name]," ΑΕΑΣ, ι (1958), 173–177. On the date of Nicephorus II Ducas Orsini's death, see Raymond Loenertz, "Notes sur le regne de Manuel II à Thessalonique, 1381/82–1387," BZ, ʟ (1957), 393.

55. Rubió y Lluch, "La Poblaciò" (44), p. 20.

56. On the extent of Vagenitia, see Michael Lascaris, "Vagenitia," *Revue historique du Sud-Est Européen*, xix (1942), ιι, 423–437. See also the map of northern Epirus and Albania in Halil Inalcik, *Hicrî 835 tarihli sûret-i defteri Sancak-i Arvanid* [*A Copy of the Notebooks of the Province of Arvanid, Dated Hegira 835*] (Ankara, 1954).

57. See Moustoxydis, "Ἱστορικόν" (51), pp. 504–505.

58. See George P. Anagnostopoulos, "Γλωσσικά ἀνάλεκτα [Linguistic Analects]," Ἀθηνᾶ, xxxvi (1924), 62–63.

59. Note Symeon Uroš Palaeologus' edict regarding Thessaly: "καί πάντα μέν τά μοναστήρια καί τάς ἁγίας τοῦ Θεοῦ ἐκκλησίας εὑροῦσα ἐρημωμένας ἀπό τῆς τοῦ καιροῦ ἐπιθέσεως [and having found all of the monasteries and the holy churches of God ruined by the adversary circumstances]." (Nikos Bees, "Σερβικά καί βυζαντιακά γράμματα Μετεώρου [The Serbian and Byzantine Documents of Meteora]," Βυζαντίς, ιι (1911–1912), 81.

60. *Ibid.*, pp. 80, 84, for titles.

61. On the date of Symeon's death, see the observations of Michael Lascaris, "Byzantinoserbica saeculi XIV [Byzantine-Serbian Affairs of the Fourteenth Century]," *Byzantion*, xxv–xxvii (1955–1957), 278 ff.

62. See Moustoxydis, "Ἱστορικόν" (51), pp. 503–505; and William Miller, *The Latins in the Levant: A History of Frankish Greece (1204–1566)* (New York-Cambridge, Eng., 1964), p. 294.

63. Hopf, *Griechenland* (16), II, 40.

64. See Moustoxydis, "Ἱστορικόν" (51), pp. 526, 532 ff.

65. Rubió y Lluch, "La Poblaciò" (44), p. 23. See Poulos, Ἡ ἐποίκησις (42), which contains the relevant bibliography; Frederick Hasluck, "Albanian Settlements in the Aegean Islands," BSA, xv (1908–1909), 224–225; and Biris, Ἀρβανίτες (41), pp. 240–245.

66. Spyridon Lambros, Παλαιολόγεια καί Πελοποννησιακά [*Palaeologian and Peloponnesian Affairs*] (Athens, 1926), III, 41; and Zakythinos, *Le Despotat grec de Morée* (9), II, 31–32. Poulos correctly mentions a second colonization of the Peloponnese by the Albanians after 1418, that is, after Albanian domination in Aetolia and Acarnania was brought to an end by Carlo I Tocco (Ἡ ἐποίκησις (42), pp. 52 ff., especially pp. 76, 78–79, and elsewhere). On Albanian penetration into Greece, see also Jakob Fallmerayer, *Das Albanesische Element in Griechenland* [*The Albanian Element in Greece*], vols. 1–3 (Munich, 1857–1860); and Eulogios Kourilas, Πανεπιστημιακά. Τό κράτος τῆς ἀληθείας [University Affairs. The Power of Truth] (Athens, 1944). On the colonization, see especially pp. 294–304; and Biris, Ἀρβανίτες (41), pp. 273–285.

67. Cousinéry, *Voyage* (21), I, 18. See also the important evidence of Peter Kanellidis, "Αἱ σλαβικαί ἐποικίσεις [The Slavic Colonizations]," Ἑβδομάς, IV (1887), no. 39, 1.

68. See Ioannis K. Voyatzidis, "Συμβολή εἰς τήν μεσαιωνικήν ἱστορίαν τῆς Ἠπείρου [A Contribution to the History of Epirus in the Middle Ages]," HX, I (1926), 74.

69. See Hopf, *Griechenland* (16), II, 105; and Philippson and Kirsten, *Die griechischen Landschaften* (9), II, 2. 596.

70. Lambros, Παλαιολόγεια (66), III, 194–195.

71. See Voyatzidis, "Συμβολή" (68), pp. 77–78.

72. See Heuzey, *Le Mont Olympe* (46), *passim*. He says on p. 241, "Tout ce pays, depuis le golfe d'Arta jusqu'aux bouches de l'Aspropotamo, est entièrement peuplé de Grecs. La race grecque est restée ici plus libre et, par conséquent, plus pure que partout ailleurs; mais elle ne l'a pu qu'à la condition de se faire barbare et misérable. [All of this land, from the bay of Arta to the estuary of the Aspropotamos, is populated entirely with Greeks. The Greek race has there been left freer and, consequently, purer than anywhere else. But it has been able to remain so only by making itself uncivilized and wretched]."

73. See Spyridon Lambros, "Ἡ ὀνοματολογία τῆς Ἀττικῆς καί ἡ εἰς τήν χώρα ἐποίκησις τῶν Ἀλβανῶν [The Nomenclature of Attica and the Albanians' Settlement in the Country]," Ἐπετηρίς Παρνασσοῦ, I (1897), 167–192, which contains also the relevant bibliography. See Giuseppe Schirò, "Una Cronaca in versi inedita del secolo XV; 'Sui Duchi e I Conti di Cefalonia' [An Unpublished Chronicle in Verse from the Fifteenth Century, 'On the Dukes and Counts of Cephalonia']," XIᵉ Congrès international des études byzantines, Munich, 1958, *Akten* (1966), p. 535.

74. See Constantine Mertzios, "Μία ἀνέκδοτος ἐπιστολή τοῦ Καρόλου Α΄ τοῦ Τόκκου πρός τόν δόγην Βενετίας γραφεῖσα ἐξ Ἰωαννίνων τό 1425 [One

Unpublished Letter from Carlo I Tocco to the Doge of Venice Written at Ioannina in 1425]," in Πεπραγμένα τοῦ Θ′ Διεθνοῦς Βυζαντινολογικοῦ Συνεδρίου, ιι (Thessalonica, 1956) (Περιοδικόν " Ἑλληνικά," Παράρτημα, Αριϑ. 9), 556–559, and Hopf, *Griechenland* (16), ιι, 106.

75. In Demetrius G. Kambouroglou, Μνημεῖα τῆς ἱστορίας τῶν Ἀθηναίων, Τουρκοκρατία [*Monuments of the History of the Athenians; Turkish Domination*] (Athens, 1891), ι, 338. For the communication of Tassos D. Neroutsos, "Περί τῆς ἐν Ἑλλάδι ἐποικήσεως τῶν Ἀλβανῶν ὑπερμεσοῦντος ΙΔ′ αἰῶνος [Concerning the Settlement of the Albanians in Greece in the Latter Half of the Fourteenth Century]," see pp. 341–345. Cf. Biris, Ἀρβανίτες (41), p. 107. On the Albanianization which took place in the district of Karystia and on the same process in Attica, see pp. 107, 109, 322–326.

76. See Vasmer, *Die Slaven* (3), pp. 5–7, 9, 313–315.

77. See Constantine Amantos, Μακεδονία. Συμβολή εἰς τήν μεσαιωνικήν ἱστορίαν καί ἐθνολογίαν τῆς Μακεδονίας [*Macedonia; A Contribution to the Medieval History and Ethnology of Macedonia*] (Athens, 1920), p. 23.

78. See the rare and bizarre book which George C. Rozias wrote in Greek and German on alternate pages. Its Greek title is Ἐξετάσεις περί τῶν Ρωμαίων ἤ τῶν ὀνομαζομένων Βλάχων ὅσοι κατοικοῦσιν ἀντιπέραν τοῦ Δουνάβεως, ἐπί παλαιῶν μαρτυριῶν τεθεμελιωμέναι [Investigations, Founded on Ancient Testimonies, concerning the Romans, or So-called Vlachs, Who Dwell on the Other Side of the Danube] (Pesth, Hung., 1808), pp. 81–89.

79. *Ibid.*, p. 99.

80. Constantine Koumas, Ἱστορίαι τῶν ἀνθρωπίνων πράξεων [*Histories of Human Deeds*] (Vienna, 1832), xιι, 520–521. The eighteenth-century Vlach scholar Nikolaos Tzartzoulis believed that his countrymen were descended from the ancient Greeks. See Μετέωρα, March 12, 1951, p. 68. See also the interesting study (which, however, must be used with caution) by the poet Constantine Krystallis, in his ῝Απαντα [*Complete Works*], ed. George Valetas (Athens, 1959), ιι, 457–657. In the development of his final theory regarding the essential "Greekness" of the Vlachs of Greece, Keramopoullos (Τί εἶναι οἱ Κουτσόβλαχοι; [17]) owes a great deal to Michael Chrysochoou, Βλάχοι καί Κουτσόβλαχοι [*Vlachs and Koutsovlachs*] (Athens, 1909). According to Keramopoullos' theory, the Vlachs are the latinized descendants of poor indigenous Greek peoples who, following Macedonia's submission to the Romans in 168 b.c., served in the Roman army as frontier guards or as guards of the mountain passes which bordered on their homelands.

81. See John Lydus, Περί ἀρχῶν τῆς Ρωμαίων πολιτείας [*Concerning the Offices of the Roman State*], ed. Richard Wuensch (Leipzig, 1903), ιιι, 68. On the process of latinization by Diocletian, see Ernst Stein, *Geschichte des spätrömischen Reiches* [*History of the Late Roman Empire*] (Vienna, 1928–1949), ι, 113–114. There were other similar tendencies much later, during the third and fourth centuries a.d. (*ibid.*, pp. 443–444).

82. See the relevant extract in the *Acta* of St. Demetrius (PG, cxvι, col. 1337); and Oreste Tafrali, *Thessalonique des origines au XIVe siècle* (Paris,

1919), pp. 128 ff., where the relevant bibliography will be found; also Chrysanthopoulos, "Τά 6ι6λία" (16), pp. 617–619.

83. Nicephoros Moschopoulos, "Ἡ Ἑλλάς κατά τόν Ἐλ6ιά Τσελεμπῆ [Greece according to Evliya Tshelebi]," ΕΕΒΣ, xiv (1938), 503.

84. It would seem that the following characteristic comment belongs to the tenth century, at the time of the great Bulgarian conquests of Symeon and Samuel: "Καί νῦν δέ πᾶσαν ῎Ηπειρον καί Ἑλλάδα σχεδόν καί Πελοπόννησον καί Μακεδονίαν Σκύθαι Σκλά6οι νέμονται [And now Scythian Slavs enjoy the land of all Epirus and nearly all of Greece, and the Peloponnese and Macedonia]" (Geographi graeci minores [The Lesser Greek Geographers], ed. Karl Müller, ii (Paris, 1882), 574 [= Στρά6ωνος Χρηστομάθεια, vii, 47]). See William Miller, Essays on the Latin Orient (Cambridge, Eng., 1921), p. 39. In this extract from an abridged geography of his, Strabo means that the existence of a Greek population was not precluded since the Slavs came to enjoy the lands through which they wandered.

85. See Stadtmüller, "Τά προ6λήματα" (10), p. 162.

86. See Nikolaos Kasomoulis, Ἐνθυμήματα στρατιωτικά τῆς ἐπαναστάσεως τῶν Ἑλλήνων, 1821–1833 [Military Reminiscences of the Greek Revolution, 1821–1833] (Athens, 1939), i, 104 ff.; and Koumas, Ἱστορίαι (80), xii, 530, 531.

87. See Demetrius Georgakas, "Περί τῆς καταγωγῆς τῶν Σαρακατσαναίων καί τοῦ ὀνόματος αὐτῶν [Concerning the Origin of the Sarakatsans and of Their Name]," ΑΘΓΛΘ, xii (1945–1946), 65–128; xiv (1948–1949), 65–151, which has the relevant bibliography. On their art and culture, see Angeliki Chazimichali, Σαρακατσάνοι [The Sarakatsans], vol. i, parts A–B (Athens, 1957).

88. See Ioannis K. Voyatzidis, "Οἱ ῎Ελληνες καθολικοί [The Catholic Greeks]," HME, 1924, pp. 175–176, and "Γλῶσσα καί λαογραφία τῆς νήσου ῎Ανδρου [The Language and the Folklore of the Island of Andros]," ΑΧ, ix (1960), 131–132, 136–139. See also Antonios Sigalas, "Die griechische Insel Syros in ethnischer und religiöser Hinsicht in der byzantinischen und neueren Zeit [The Ethnic and Religious Aspects of the Greek Island of Syros in the Byzantine and Modern Periods]," Ostkirchliche Studien, vii (1958), 85–92. The same article was published in Greek in greater detail and in a more popular vein under the title "Ἡ Ἑλληνική καταγωγή τῶν καθολικῶν τῆς Σύρου [The Greek Origin of the Catholics of Syros]," Κυκλάδες, i (1956), 293–299.

89. For cases of the christianization of young Turks (in the thirteenth and fourteenth centuries) and the Gagauz in general, their settlement in the Dobruja and the districts of Veroia and Zichna, and the obscure historical problems connected with these events, see Paul Wittek, "Yazijioghlu 'Ali on the Christian Turks of the Dobruja," BSOAS, xiv (1952), 639–688, where the relevant bibliography will be found. Missing from this bibliography, however, is the study by Athanasios Manof, "Ποῖοι εἶναι οἱ Γκαγκαοῦζοι [Who the Gagauz Are]," ΕΕΒΣ, x (1933), 383–400. For the descent of the Gagauz from the district of Varna in western Thrace after the anti-Greek persecutions of 1906, see Maximos Maravelakis and Apostolos Vacalopoulos, Αἱ προσφυγικαί

ἐγκαταστάσεις ἐν τῇ περιοχῇ Θεσσαλονίκης [*The Refugee Settlements in the Area of Thessalonica*] (Thessalonica, 1953), p. 13.

90. See, for instance, Gordon, *History of the Greek Revolution* (39), I, 32; and the elementary, but probably first, comparative study of the relationship between ancient and modern Greece, that of Friedrich Kruse, *Fragen über mehrere für das höhere Alterthum wichtige Verhältnisse im heutigen Griechenland beantwortet von einem Philhellenen* [*Questions on Several Conditions of Modern Greece Important for Antiquity, Answered by a Philhellene*] (Berlin, 1827). The subject is approached in a systematic way by Bernard Schmidt, *Das Volksleben der Neugriechen und das hellenische Altertum* [*The Life of the Modern Greeks and Greek Antiquity*], vol. I (Leipzig, 1871). See also William Miller, *Essays on the Latin Orient* (Cambridge, Eng., 1921), p. 35: "No one who has been in Greece can fail to have been struck by the similarity between the character of the modern and ancient Greeks."

91. See Guillaume Lejean, *Ethnographie de la Turquie d'Europe, Petermanns geographische Mitteilungen*, Ergänzungsheft 4 (Gotha, Germ., 1861), pp. 13–14.

92. See Stadtmüller, "Τά προβλήματα" (10), pp. 140–169.

Chapter 2

1. See Ioannis K. Voyatzidis, "Ἡ θέσις τῆς κυρίως Ἑλλάδος ἐντός τοῦ βυζαντινοῦ κράτους [*The Position of Greece Proper within the Byzantine State*]," ΕΕΒΣ, xix (1949), 252–258.

2. See Ferdinand Gregorovius, *Geschichte der Stadt Athen im Mittelalter, von der Zeit Justinians bis zur türkischen Eroberung* [*History of the City of Athens in the Middle Ages, from the Time of Justinian to the Turkish Conquest*] (Stuttgart, 1889), Greek translation (with emendations and additions) by Spyridon Lambros (Athens, 1904–1906), I, 89.

3. *Ibid.*, 91 ff.

4. See Procopius' use of the word, in Kilian Lechner, *Hellenen und Barbaren im Weltbild der Byzantiner* [*Greeks and Barbarians in the View of the Byzantines*] (Munich, 1955), pp. 5, 10.

5. Peter Charanis, "The Term *Helladikoi* in Byzantine Texts of the Sixth, Seventh, and Eighth Centuries," ΕΕΒΣ, xxiii (1953), 619.

6. See Nikolaos Politis, Μελέται περί τοῦ βίου καί τῆς γλώσσης τοῦ ἑλληνικοῦ λαοῦ, Παραδόσεις [*Studies in the Life and Language of the Hellenic People; Traditions*], I (Athens, 1904), 52 ff., 729 ff. For those traditions relating to the ancient Greeks, see Léon Heuzey, *Le Mont Olympe et l'Acarnanie* (Paris, 1860), *passim*, his *Excursion dans la Thessalie turque en 1858* (Paris, 1927), *passim*, and Alexander Chatzigakis, "Οἱ Ἕλληνοι [The Greeks]," Μετέωρα, March 12, 1951, pp. 28–30. .

7. See Stilpon Kyriakidis, Αἱ ἱστορικαί ἀρχαί τῆς δημώδους νεοελληνικῆς ποιήσεως [*The Historical Origins of Popular Neohellenic Poetry*], 2nd ed. (Thessalonica, 1934), pp. 10–19, 27 ff.; and George I. Theocharidis, *Beiträge zur Geschichte des byzantinischen Profantheaters im IV. und V. Jahrhundert, hauptsächlich auf Grund der Predigten des Johannes Chrysostomos, Patriarchen*

von Konstantinopel [*Contributions to the History of the Byzantine Profane Theater in the Fourth and Fifth Centuries, Principally on the Basis of the Sermons of John Chrysostom, Patriarch of Constantinople*] (Thessalonica, 1940).

8. See Gregorovius, *Geschichte der Stadt Athen* (2), Greek tr., ɪ, 97 ff.

9. *Ibid.*, 98–121, 126.

10. I say "almost" because most of the place-names mentioned by Max Vasmer remain doubtful (*Die Slaven in Griechenland* (Berlin, 1941), pp. 120–123). See Gregorovius, *Geschichte der Stadt Athen* (2), Greek tr., ɪ, 184–191, 218.

11. *Ibid.*, ɪɪ, 478. Cf. also ɪ, 165, n. 3 and 4. Gregorovius believes the evidence regarding St. Gislenus' studies in Athens to be of dubious worth.

12. Karl Hopf, *Griechenland im Mittelalter und in der Neuzeit* (1:51) (Leipzig, 1867–1868), ɪ, 113.

13. See Kenneth Setton, "The Byzantine Background to the Italian Renaissance," *Proceedings of the American Philosophical Society*, C, no. 1, February, 1956, p. 5, for the relevant bibliography.

14. Vasily Vasilevsky, *Russovizantijskija isledovanija* [*Russian-Byzantine Studies*], ɪɪ (St. Petersburg, 1893), 75. I borrowed this information from Peter Charanis, "Ethnic Changes in the Byzantine Empire in the Seventh Century," DOP, xɪɪɪ (1959), 41.

15. Georgius Cedrenus, Σύνοψις ἱστοριῶν [*A Summary of Histories*], ed. Immanuel Bekker (Bonn, 1838–1839), ɪɪ, 170. On the point that Leo's teacher was in fact called Michael Psellus, see Demetrios Paschalis, Ἡ ᾽Ανδρος (Athens, 1925–1927), ɪ, 654–663. Compare this, however, with Ioannis K. Voyatzidis' persuasive view ("Γλῶσσα καί λαογραφία τῆς νήσου ᾽Ανδρου" [1:88], ΑΧ, ɪx (1960), pp. 108 ff.) that a philosopher named Michael Psellus in Andros who was born before the known Michael Psellus of Constantinople never existed.

16. See Charles Diehl, *Byzantium: Greatness and Decline*, tr. Naomi Walford (New Brunswick, N.J., 1957), pp. 112–121, and Charanis, "Ethnic Changes" (14), pp. 25–36, 42, where the relevant bibliography will be found.

17. See Ernst Stein, *Geschichte das spatrömischen Reiches* (1:81) (Vienna, 1928–1949), ɪ, 5. In connection with the composition of the population, see Peter Charanis, "On the Ethnic Composition of Byzantine Asia Minor in the Thirteenth Century," Προσφορά εἰς Στίλπ. Κυριακίδην (Thessalonica, 1953), pp. 140–147.

18. See Stilpon Kyriakidis, Ἑλληνικά λαογραφία, Μερ. Α´ Μνημεῖα τοῦ λόγου [*Greek Folklore, Part I, Records of the Speech*] (Athens, 1923), pp. 20 ff. and *Two Studies on Modern Greek Folklore*, tr. by Robert A. Georges and Aristotle A. Katzanides (Thessalonica, 1968), pp. 56 ff.

19. For this point of view, see the monumental work by Phaidon Koukoules, Βυζαντινῶν βίος καί πολιτισμός [*The Life and Civilization of the Byzantines*], ɪ–v (Athens, 1952), and especially that part of volume v which is entitled " Ἡ νέα ἑλληνική γλῶσσα καί τά βυζαντινά καί τά μεταβυζαντινά

ἔθιμα [The Modern Greek Language and the Byzantine and Post-Byzantine Customs]." See also Demetrius Petropoulos, "Συμβολή εἰς τήν ἔρευναν τῶν λαϊκῶν μέτρων καί σταθμῶν [Contribution to the Investigation of the People's Weights and Measures]," ΛΑ, vii (1952), 101.

20. See Demetrius Petropoulos, "Θεοκρίτου εἰδύλλια ὑπό λαογραφικήν ἔποψιν ἑρμηνευόμενα [The *Idylls* of Theocritus Interpreted from the Point of View of Folklore]," Λαογραφία, xviii (1959), 90–91.

21. For some characteristic examples, see Phaidon Koukoules, Θεσσαλονίκης Εὐσταθίου τά λαογραφικά [*Folklore Elements in the Works of Eustathius of Thessalonica*], i–ii (Athens, 1950).

22. Some of the superstitions and beliefs which have survived over the centuries, for example, include those concerning fairies, ghosts, the fires of St. John, as well as the attributions of good or evil which accompany itching palms, itching noses, or twitching eyelids. Christmas carols are of similarly ancient lineage. (*Ibid.*, vol. ii.) See Joseph Bryennios, Τά παραλειπόμενα [The Remaining Works], ed. Thomas Mandakasis (Leipzig, 1784), iii, 120–122; and George Megas, Ἑλληνικαί ἑορταί καί ἔθιμα τῆς λαϊκῆς λατρείας [*Greek Festivals and Customs of the Popular Religion*] (Athens, 1956). On the continuity between ancient and modern Hellenism, see John Lawson, *Modern Greek Folklore and Ancient Greek Religion: a Study in Survivals* (Cambridge, Eng., 1910; Photostatic Reprint, 1964).

23. See Constantine Sathas, Μεσαιωνική βιβλιοθήκη [*Library of the Middle Ages*] (Venice, 1872–1874), vii, x, xi–xiii.

24. See Spyridon Lambros, "Περί τῆς βιβλιοθήκης τοῦ μητροπολίτου Ἀθηνῶν Μιχαήλ Ἀκομινάτου (1182–1205) [Concerning the Library of Michael Akominatos, Archbishop of Athens (1182–1205)]," Ἀθήναιον, vi (1887), 354–367; and Nikolaos Tomadakis, " Ἦσαν βάρβαροι αἱ Ἀθῆναι ἐπί Μιχαήλ Χωνιάτου; [Was Athens Barbarian at the Time of Michael Choniates?]," ΕΕΦΣΠΑ, Period 2, vii (1956–1957), 88–109, where the relevant bibliography will be found.

25. Gregorovius, *Geschichte der Stadt Athens* (2), Greek tr., i, 302 ff., ii, 506, 599 ff., believes this to be mere legend, while both William Miller (*Essays on the Latin Orient* (Cambridge, Eng., 1921), p. 66) and, more recently, Setton (*The Byzantine Background* [13], pp. 61–62) have found a certain significance in it.

26. Kyrkiakidis, Αἱ ἱστορικαί ἀρχαί (7), pp. 6 ff.

27. Sathas, Μεσαιωνική βιβλιοθήκη (23), p. xiii. In connection with the Danishmend dynasty, see J. Laurent, "Sur les Émirs Danischmendites jusqu'en 1104," *Mélanges à Nicolae Jorga* (Paris, 1933), pp. 503–504, and p. 499 for the relevant bibliography. There is a more recent study by Irène Mélikoff, *La Geste de Melik Danişmend* [*The Acts of Melik Danishmend*] (Paris, 1960), i, 71–101.

28. The song of Armouris will be found in Stilpon Kyriakidis, Ὁ Διγενῆς Ἀκρίτας [*Digenis Akritas*] (Athens, 1926), p. 121.

29. Mélikoff, *La Geste* (27), pp. 46 ff.

30. See Stilpon Kyriakidis, Αἱ ἱστορικαί ἀρχαί (7), p. 5, and his *Forschungsbericht zum Akritas-epos* [*Researches on the Akritas Epic*] (Munich, 1958), p. 8.

31. See Kyriakidis, *Forschungsbericht* (30), pp. 17, 19, 21–22, where various problems associated with the song are examined and the relevant bibliography is given.

32. See Demetrius Petropoulos, "Ἀκριτικά τραγούδια στήν Πελοπόννησο [The Akritic Songs in the Peloponnese]," Πελοποννησιακά, ΙΙ (1957), 358, where the relevant bibliography will be found; and Nikos Bees, "Τό Ἀνδρονικόπουλλο τοῦ ἀκριτικοῦ κύκλου ἐκ Μονεμβασιακοῦ χειρογράφου [The Song of Andronikos of the Akritic Cycle, from a Manuscript in Monemvasia]," Ἀκρίτας, Ι (1904), 23–26. Cf. Nikolaos Politis, "Τό ᾆσμα τῶν υἱῶν τοῦ Ἀνδρονίκου [The Song of the Sons of Andronikos]," Ἀκρίτας, Ι (1904), 98–103.

33. See Demetrius G. Kambouroglou, "Περί τοῦ ἑλληνικοῦ κώδικος 202 τῆς βιβλιοθήκης Πετρουπόλεως [On Greek Codex 202 of the Leningrad Library]," ΠΑΑ, VII (1932), part III, 285–286. This entry contains an unknown versicle of Armouris. See also Samuel Baud-Bovy, "Le Chant d'Armouris et sa tradition," *Byzantion*, XIII (1938), 249–251.

34. See their songs in Demetrius Petropoulos, Ἑλληνικά δημοτικά τραγούδια [*Greek Popular Songs*] (Athens, 1958), Ι, 3–65.

35. See Hubert Pernot, *Chansons populaires grecques des XVᵉ et XVIᵉ siècles* (Paris, 1931), 8, where he writes: "Il y'a des chances pour que, sous ce qui se présente ainsi à nous, se trouve une couche plus ancienne, que malheureusement nous sommes dans l'impossibilité de sonder [There is a chance that, underneath that which presents itself to us in this way, there is a more ancient layer, which, unhappily, we are unable to fathom]." See also Spyridon Lambros, "Ein Byzantinisches Volklied [A Byzantine Folksong]," BZ, III (1894), 165–166.

36. Antoine Gidel, *Études sur la littérature grecque moderne* (Paris, 1866), pp. 123–124. See Constantine Sathas, "La Tradition hellénique et la légende de Phidias, de Praxitèle et de la fille d'Hippocrate au moyen âge," AAEEG, XVI (1882), 123; also his "Le Roman d'Achille. Texte inédit en grec vulgaire," AAEEG, XIII (1879), 129, n. 2.

37. See the extract from the criticism of Gidel's *Études* (36), p. v.

38. See the *Alexander the Great Romance*, ed. Alexander Pallis (Athens, 1935), p. 21. For the various Byzantine and post-Byzantine publications, see p. 70. On Pseudo-Callisthenes, see Karl Müller, *Arriani Anabasis et Indica* (Paris, 1846). For the demotic version in metric verse, see Wilhelm Wagner, *Trois Poèmes grecs du moyen âge* (Berlin, 1881), pp. 56–241. For the Armenian translation, see P. N. Akinian, "Die handschriftliche Überlieferung der armenischen Übersetzung des Alexanderromans von Pseudokallisthenes [The Manuscript Tradition of the Armenian Translation of the Alexander Romance of Pseudo-Callisthenes]," *Byzantion*, XIII (1938), 201–206. On the Byzantines' knowledge of history and the Alexander Romance, see the specialized study

of Friedrich Pfister, "Alexander der Grosse in der byzantinischen Literatur und in neugriechischen Volksbüchern [Alexander the Great in Byzantine Literature and in Modern Greek Popular Books]," *Probleme der neugriechischen Literatur,* III, *Berliner byzantinische Arbeiten,* XVI (1960), 112–130.

39. See Pallis, *Alexander the Great* (38), p. 32, for the relevant bibliography.

40. See Stilpon Kyriakidis, " Ὁ Μ. Ἀλέξανδρος εἰς τούς μύθους καί τάς παραδόσεις [Alexander the Great in Myth and Tradition]," ΜΕΕ, III, 660–664, which contains also the relevant bibliography. Cf. also George Spyridakis, "Συμβολή εἰς τήν μελέτην τῶν δημωδῶν παραδόσεων καί δοξασιῶν περί τοῦ Μεγάλου Ἀλεξάνδρου [A Contribution to the Study of the Popular Traditions and Beliefs Concerning Alexander the Great]," Γέρας Αντ. Κεραμοπούλλου (Athens, 1953), pp. 385–419, where there is a supplemental bibliography.

41. See Andreas Xyngopoulos, " Ὁ Μ. Ἀλέξανδρος ἐν τῇ βυζαντινῇ ἀγγειογραφίᾳ [Alexander the Great in Byzantine Pottery Painting]," ΕΕΒΣ, XIV (1938), 275–276; and Pallis, *Alexander the Great* (38), p. 32.

42. Sathas, *La Tradition hellénique* (36), p. 123, on Vinsauf's *Itinerarium regis Anglorum Ricardi [The Itinerary of Richard, King of England]* (Oxford, 1687), p. 261.

43. Michael Glykas, Βίβλος χρονική [*Chronicle*], ed. Immanuel Bekker (Bonn, 1836), p. 599.

44. Kurt Weitzmann, *Greek Mythology in Byzantine Art* (Princeton, 1951), p. 194.

45. See Andreas Xyngopoulos, "Παραστάσεις ἐκ τοῦ μυθιστορήματος τοῦ Μ. Ἀλεξάνδρου ἐπί βυζαντινῶν ἀγγείων [Representations from the Alexander Romance on Byzantine Vases]," AE, 1937, pp. 192–202; and " Ὁ Μ. Ἀλέξανδρος" (41), pp. 267–276. Cf. also Weitzmann, *Greek Mythology* (44), especially pp. 104, 186–188, 194, 197–198.

46. Anastasios Orlandos, "Νέον ἀνάγλυφον τῆς ἀναλήψεως τοῦ Ἀλεξάνδρου [A New Bas-Relief of the Ascension of Alexander]," ΕΕΦΣΠΑ, II (1954–1955), 281–289, where there is an excellent bibliography; and "Γλυπτά τοῦ μουσείου Θηβῶν [Sculptures in the Museum at Thebes]," Ἀρχεῖον τῶν βυζαντινῶν μνημείων τῆς Ἑλλάδος, V (1939–1940), 134–136; also with a bibliography.

47. See Tomadakis, " Ἦσαν βάρβαροι αἱ Ἀθῆναι" (24), pp. 88–109. On the relationship between Eustathius and Michael Choniates, see Spyridon Lambros, Μιχαήλ Ἀκομινάτου τά σωζόμενα [*What Remains of Michael Akominatos*] (Athens, 1879), I, xvi, xxxvi–xxxvii, xxxviii, 283–306.

48. Lambros, Μιχαήλ Ακομινάτου (47), p. xxxviii.

Chapter 3

1. Spyridon Zambelios, Ἄσματα δημοτικά τῆς Ἑλλάδος ἐκδοθέντα μετά μελέτης ἱστορικῆς περί μεσαιωνικοῦ ἑλληνισμοῦ [*Popular Songs of Greece, Published with an Historical Study of Medieval Hellenism*] (Athens, 1852). See especially pp. 462 ff., and the same author's Βυζαντιναί μελέται. Περί

πηγῶν ἑλληνικῆς ἐθνότητος ἀπό η' ἄχρι ι' ἑκατονταετηρίδος [Byzantine Studies. Concerning the Sources of Greek Nationality, from the Eighth to the Tenth Century] (Athens, 1857).

2. Constantine Paparrhegopoulos, Ἱστορία τοῦ ἑλληνικοῦ ἔθνους [History of the Greek Nation] (Athens, 1932), v. part 1, v, 3, 5, 8–9, 15.

3. Constantine Sathas, Μεσαιωνική βιβλιοθήκη (2:23) (Venice, 1872–1874), vii (1894), x ff.

4. Constantine Amantos, Ἱστορία τοῦ βυζαντινοῦ κράτους (1:9) (Athens, 1939), ι, 7–8.

5. Ioannis K. Voyatzidis, "Ἱστορικαί μελέται [Historical Studies]," ΕΕΦΣΠΘ, ιι (1932), 302. See also Ioannis Mamalakis, "Προβλήματα τῆς νεοελληνικῆς ἱστορίας [Problems of Modern Greek History]," Χρονικά τοῦ Πειραματικοῦ Σχολείου Πανεπιστημίου Θεσσαλονίκης, v (1951), 72 ff.

6. For descriptive information, see Constantine Dyovouniotis, "Αἱ ἀνέκδοτοι κατηχήσεις τοῦ μητροπολίτου Ἀθηνῶν Μιχαήλ Ἀκομινάτου [The Unpublished Catechisms of Michael Akominatos, Metropolite of Athens]," ΠΑΑ, ιιι (1928), 312–314.

7. See Geoffroy de Villehardouin, La Conquête de Constantinople, ed. Edmond Faral (Paris, 1939), ιι (1203–1204), 88–89; and Oreste Tafrali, Thessalonique au quatorzième siècle (Paris, 1913), p. 67, where the relevant bibliography will be found. The tendency on the part of Greek cities and countries to hang on to their autonomy was pronounced. However, I am not aware of the sources on which Neroutsos based his assertion that the inhabitants of Athens, Megara, Thebes, Levadia, and Atalante submitted to the Franks in exchange for the retention of their local independence (Tassos Neroutsos, "Χριστιανικαί Ἀθῆναι [Christian Athens]," ΔΙΕΕ, ιν (1892–1895), 53.

8. On the question of the voluntary servitude of certain nobles, see Sathas, Μεσαιωνική βιβλιοθήκη (2:23), ι, 109–110.

9. Nicetas Choniates, Χρονική διήγησις [Historical Narration], ed. Immanuel Bekker (Bonn, 1835), pp. 840–844.

10. See Sathas, Μεσαιωνική βιβλιοθήκη (2:23), ι, 104; Athanasios Papadopoulos-Kerameus, "Περί συνοικισμοῦ τῶν Ἰωαννίνων μετά τήν φραγκικήν κατάκτησιν τῆς Κωνσταντινουπόλεως [Concerning the Settlement of Ioannina after the Frankish Capture of Constantinople]," ΔΙΕΕ, ιιι (1889), 454; the description in Choniates, Χρονική διήγησις (9), pp. 837 ff.; and Spyridon Lambros, Μιχαήλ Ἀκομινάτου τά σωζόμενα (2:47), ιι (1880), 292.

11. See Papadopoulos-Kerameus, Περί συνοικισμοῦ (10), pp. 451–455. For the correct name of Michael I, see Lucien Stiernon, "Les Origines du despotat d'Epire. À propos d'un livre récent," REB, xvιι (1959), 91–126. Cf. the communication to the XIIᵉ Congrès international des études byzantines, Ochrida, 1961: "Les Origines du despotat d'Epire—problèmes de titulature et de chronologie," Résumés des communications (Belgrade-Ochrida, 1961), pp. 100–101.

12. See Donald Nicol, The Despotate of Epirus (Oxford, 1957), p. 16.

13. Choniates, Χρονική διήγησις (9), pp. 767–768. After the fall of Constantinople (1204), Bishop Theodore of Alania wrote his younger brother:

"Ἑάλω μέν ἡ πατρίς, αλλ' ἀνδρί σοφῷ πᾶς τόπος Ἑλλάς [Our country has been taken, but to the wise man any place is Greece]" (PG, cxl, col. 414).

14. See Louis Halphen, "Le Rôle des 'Latins' dans l'histoire intérieure de Constantinople à la fin du XIIᵉ siècle," *Mélanges Charles Diehl* (1930), i, 140–145.

15. See Ioannis B. Papadopoulos, "Γρηγορίου Χιονιάδου τοῦ ἀστρονόμου ἐπιστολαί [The Letters of Gregorios Chioniades the Astronomer]," ΕΕΦΣΠΘ, i (1927), 151–203.

16. See William Miller, *Trebizond. The Last Greek Empire* (London, 1926), pp. 15 ff.

17. See Nicol, *The Despotate of Epirus* (12), p. x.

18. See Sathas, Μεσαιωνική βιβλιοθήκη (2:23), vii, 460–461, 468–469.

19. See Mathias Wellnhofer, *Johannes Apokaukos, Metropolit von Naupaktos in Aetolien (c. 1155–1223)* [*Ioannis Apocaucus, Metropolite of Naupactus in Aetolia (ca. 1155–1223)*] (Freising, Germ., 1913), pp. 31 ff.

20. Parthenios Polakis, Ἰωάννης Ἀπόκαυκος, μητροπολίτης Ναυπάκτου [*Ioannis Apocaucus, Metropolite of Naupactus*] (Jerusalem, 1923), pp. 5, 21 ff., 37 ff. On the opposition between the churches of Epirus and Nicaea and the attendant controversies, see Wellnhofer's comments in *Johannes Apokaukos* (19), pp. 46–64, 67–68. Cf. also Nicol, *The Despotate of Epirus* (12), pp. 76–102.

21. Vasily Vasilevsky, "Epirotica saeculi XIII [Affairs of Epirus in the Thirteenth Century]," Viz. Vrem., iii (1896), 246, 265. See also Wellnhofer, *Johannes Apokaukos* (19), pp. 6–30, and, for Apocaucus' position in the hierarchy of the Church of Epirus, pp. 44–45. On the actual date of the capture of Thessalonica, see Jean Longnon, "La Reprise de Salonique par les Grecs en 1224 [The Recapture of Thessalonica by the Greeks in 1224]," VIᵉ Congrès international des études byzantines, Paris, 1948, *Actes*, i (1950), 141–146; and B. Sinogowitz, "Zur Eroberung Thessalonikes im Herbst 1224 [On the Conquest of Thessalonica in the Autumn of 1224]," BZ, xlv (1952), 28.

22. See Nikolaos Tomadakis, "Οἱ λόγιοι τοῦ δεσποτάτου τῆς Ἠπείρου [The Intellectuals of the Despotate of Epirus]," ΕΕΒΣ, xxvii (1957), 13. See also Wellnhofer, *Johannes Apokaukos* (19), p. 47; Polakis, Ἰωάννης Ἀπόκαυκος (20), p. 36.

23. See Polakis, Ἰωάννης Ἀπόκαυκος (20), p. 66.

24. Tomadakis, Οἱ λόγιοι (22), pp. 24–25.

25. See Athanasios Papadopoulos-Kerameus, "Συνοδικά γράμματα Ἰωάννου τοῦ Ἀποκαύκου μητροπολίτου Ναυπάκτου [The Synodic Letters of Ioannis Apocaucus, Metropolite of Naupactus]," Βυζαντίς, i (1909), 10.

26. See Eduard Kurtz, "Georgios Bardanes, Metropolit von Kerkyra [George Vardanis, Metropolite of Corcyra]," BZ, xv (1906), 603–613. Cf. also Wellnhofer, *Johannes Apokaukos* (19), pp. 38–39.

27. See Lambros, Μιχαήλ Ἀκομινάτου (2:47), ii, 350.

28. See Panagiotis Aravantinos, Χρονογραφία τῆς Ἠπείρου (1:46) (Athens, 1856–1857), ii, 34–35.

29. Vasilevsky, *Epirotica* (21), p. 252. Cf. also Wellnhofer, *Johannes Apokaukos* (19), pp. 41–42.

30. See Apocaucus' letter to Vardanis (Vasilevsky, *Epirotica* [21], pp. 250–252). Cf. Tomadakis, Οἱ λόγιοι (22), p. 18, and Polakis, 'Ιωάννης 'Απόκαυκος (20), p. 29.

31. Papadopoulos-Kerameus, Συνοδικά γράμματα (25), p. 21.

32. The monograph announced by Michael Dendias more than forty years ago, on Michael II Comnenus Ducas and his contribution to the renascence of the Greek nation (see " Έλένη 'Αγγελίνα Δούκαινα, βασίλισσα Σικελίας καί Νεαπόλεως [Helene Angelina Ducaina, Queen of Sicily and Naples]," HX, I [1926], 219–220) has not yet been published.

33. See Demetrius Mavrophrydis, 'Εκλογή μνημείων τῆς νεωτέρας ἑλληνικῆς γλώσσης [*A Selection of the Monuments of the Modern Greek Language*] (Athens, 1866), I, vii–x, 73–182, and Karl Hopf, *Griechenland im Mittelalter und in der Neuzeit* (1:51) (Leipzig, 1867–1868), I, 429.

34. Franz Miklosich and Joseph Müller, *Acta et diplomata graeca medii aevi sacra et profana* (1:43) (Vienna, 1860–1887), v, 260–261.

35. Regarding the brief reign of Constantine Lascaris, see B. Sinogowitz, "Über das byzantinische Kaisertum nach dem IV Kreuzzuge (1204–1205) [Concerning the Byzantine Empire after the Fourth Crusade (1204–1205)]," BZ, XLV (1952), 353–356.

36. See Jean Pappadopoulos, *Théodore II Lascaris, empereur de Nicée* (Paris, 1908), p. 24, fn.

37. See Villehardouin, *La Conquête* (7), II, 267 ff.

38. See Sathas, Μεσαιωνική βιβλιοθήκη (2:23), I, 112.

39. *Ibid.*, VII, xxi. On Nicaea as a focal point of Greek studies, see Pappadopoulos, *Théodore* (36), pp. 9–14.

40. An expression which would seem to correspond with that used by the Metropolitan of Neopatras, Euthymios Malakis: "λαοσυναξίαι τε καί συσκευαί [gatherings and assemblies of the people]" (Athanasios Papadopoulos-Kerameus, Εὐθύμιος Μαλάκης, μητροπολίτης Νέων Πατρῶν [Euthymios Malakis, Metropolite of Nea Patras]," 'Επετηρίς Παρνασσοῦ, VII [1903], 22).

41. Sathas, Μεσαιωνική βιβλιοθήκη (2:23), I, 110.

42. See Hélène Glykatzi-Ahrweiler, "La Politique agraire des empereurs de Nicée," *Byzantion*, XXVIII (1958), 51–66.

43. Sathas, Μεσαιωνική βιβλιοθήκη (2:23), I, 106–107, 110, 112, 113, 115, 122, 129, 131 ff.

44. See Stilpon Kyriakidis, *Forschungsbericht zum Akritas-epos* (2:30) (Munich, 1958), p. 23, also p. 9; and Nicephoros Gregoras, Ρωμαϊκή ἱστορία [*Roman History*], ed. Ludwig Schopen, I (Bonn, 1829), 377.

45. See Kyriakidis, *Forschungsbericht* (230), p. 25.

46. Herbert Hunger, "Von Wissenschaft und Kunst der frühen Palaiologenzeit [On Science and Art in Early Palaeologian Times]," JÖBG, VIII (1959), 126–127.

47. See Pappadopoulos, *Théodore* (36), p. 23.

48. Stephanos Xanthoudidis, Ἡ ἐνετοκρατία ἐν Κρήτῃ καί οἱ κατά τῶν Ἐνετῶν ἀγῶνες τῶν Κρητῶν [Venetian Rule in Crete and the Struggles of the Cretans against the Venetians] (Athens, 1939), pp. 37–43. Cf. also Freddy Thiriet, La Romanie vénitienne au moyen âge (Paris, 1959), pp. 97–99.

49.   καί ἡ 6άτος ἀπό πέρα
             ἤπλωσεν κ' ἔπιασεν τόπον
             τό λεγόμενον Σκουτάριν
             ἔχων ῥόδον λασκαράτον
             μέ τ' ἀρμένικον ἀκάνθιν.

["And the bramble from afar spread and pressed upon the place called Scutari, having a scarlet rose and Armenian thorn."] In August Heisenberg, "Kaiser Johannes Batatzes der Burmherzige. Eine mittelgriechische Legende [Emperor Johannes Batatzes the Charitable. A Middle-Greek Legend]," BZ, XIV (1905), 176; see also Cyril Mango, "The Legend of Leo the Wise," Zbornik Radova (Recueil de travaux of the Institute of Byzantine Studies of Belgrade), LXV (1960), no. 6, 66–67.

50. Mango, "The Legend of Leo" (49), pp. 71–72.

51. Heisenberg, "Kaiser Johannes Batatzes" (49), p. 160.

52. See Glykatzi-Ahrweiler, "La Politique" (42), p. 66.

53. Only Jean Pappadopoulos, in various parts of his monograph Théodore (36), speaks about the cultivation of Greek studies in Nicaea and Theodore II's love of antiquity. See Nicetas Choniates, Ῥωμαϊκή ἱστορία [Roman History], ed. Immanuel Bekker (Bonn, 1835), p. 794: "καί Λαρίσης αὐτῆς ἐπιβῆναι καί δι' Ἑλλάδος ἐλάσαι καί χειρώσασθαι τήν τοῦ Πέλοπος [to attack Larissa itself and to march through Greece and seize the Peloponnese]." Cf. p. 860: "ἐν Ἀκτίῳ, ὅ ἔστιν ἡ καθ' Ἑλλάδα Νικόπολις [in Actium, which the Greeks call Nikopolis]." See also Spyridon Lambros, Μιχαήλ Ἀκομινάτου τά σωζόμενα (2:47) (Athens, 1879), I–II, passim.

54. See Ioannis Sakellion, " 'Ἀνέκδοτος ἐπιστολή τοῦ αὐτοκράτορος Ἰωάννου Δούκα Βατάτση πρός τόν πάπαν Γρηγόριον, ἀνευρεθεῖσα ἐν Πάτμῳ [An Unpublished Letter from the Emperor Ioannis Ducas Vatatzes to Pope Gregory, Discovered in Patmos]," Ἀθήναιον, I (1872), 369–378 (wrongly numbered).

55. Pappadopoulos, Théodore (36), p. 13.

56. Nicola Festa, Theodori Ducae Lascaris epistulae CCXVII [217 Letters of Theodore Ducas Lascaris] (Florence, 1898), pp. 165, 176: "ὁπόταν δέ ὁ πανιερώτατος μητροπολίτης Σάρδεων ἐκ τῆς Εὐρώπης ἐπανέλθῃ πρός τό ἑλληνικόν [when the most reverend metropolite of Sardes comes from Europe to Greece]." See his letter to Phocas, the metropolitan of Sardes: "Σύ δέ πότ' ἄν ἐκ τῆς Εὐρώπης ἀνέλθῃς εἰς τήν Ἑλλάδα· πότ' ἄν δέ καί τήν Θρᾴκην διελθών τόν Ἑλλήσποντον διαπεράσῃς καί τήν ἔσω Ἀσίαν κατίδῃς; [And when will you come to Greece from Europe, and when, passing through Thrace and crossing the Hellespont, will you look upon Asia on the opposite side?]"

57. On the extent of Theodore II's state, see Pappadopoulos, Théodore (36), pp. 56–57.

58. Festa, *Theodori* (56), pp. 58, 62–63, 252–253: "πρός τήν Φιλίππου κεκατηντήκαμεν καί γῆν ἐθεασάμεθα, ἄριστε, τήν Ἀλεξάνδρου ποτέ σκυλευομένην καί παιζομένην παρά Βουλγάρων ὀλιγοστῶν ἀσθενῶν [we came to the land of Philip and Alexander and looked upon it, O noblest, that which was ravished from very few and powerless Bulgarians]," and p. 268.

59. *Ibid.*, p. 107. For some literary reflections on his letter to George Acropolitis, see Sophie Antoniadis, "Sur une lettre de Théodore II Lascaris," Hell. contemp., 1954, pp. 356–361.

60. Sathas, Μεσαιωνική βιβλιοθήκη (2:23), vii, 507, 535–536.

61. For details, see Pappadopoulos, *Théodore* (36), pp. 85–89. For Theodore II's avowal, see Festa, *Theodori* (56), p. 272.

62. For extracts from Theodore II's praise, see Pappadopoulos, *Théodore* (36), p. 86. On the question of the reconciliation between classical learning and Christian theology, see Hunger, "Von Wissenschaft" (46), pp. 136–138. Theodore's encomium was published by Ludwig Bachmann in *Theodori Ducae Lascaris imperatoris in laudem Nicaeae urbis oratio* [*The Emperor Theodore Ducas Lascaris' Speech in Praise of the City of Nicaea*] (Rostock, 1847).

63. See Hunger, "Von Wissenschaft" (46), p. 137, where the relevant extracts will be found.

64. See Johannes Dräseke, "Theodoros Lascaris," BZ, iii (1894), 500.

65. Festa, *Theodori* (56), p. 8.

66. *Ibid.*, pp. 201–211, for his letters to Pope Alexander IV and the cardinals Ricardo, Octaviano, and Peter the Capuzzo.

67. *Ibid.*, p. 52, for his letter to his teacher, Blemmydes.

68. See Pappadopoulos, *Théodore* (36), pp. 79–89, and Festa, *Theodori* (56), p. 58.

69. George Pachymeres, Συγγραφικαὶ ἱστορίαι [*Histories*], ed. Immanuel Bekker (Bonn, 1835), i, 37–38. Cf. pp. 24, 33; and George Acropolitis, *Opera*, ed. August Heisenberg (Leipzig, 1903), i, 123–124; and Pappadopoulos, *Théodore* (36), pp. 79, 81.

70. See Ioannis K. Voyatzidis, "Ἡ Μεγάλη Ἰδέα [The Great Idea]," Hell. contemp., commemorative volumes, 1453–1953 (Athens, 1953), pp. 307 ff.; and his older study, "Ἡ ἀρχή καί ἡ ἐξέλιξις τῆς Μεγάλης Ἰδέας [The Origin and Evolution of the Great Idea]," HME, 1923, pp. 161–171. In connection with the double-headed eagle, see Giuseppe Gerola, "L'Aquila bizantina imperiale a due teste [The Byzantine Imperial Eagle with Two Heads]," *Felix Ravenna*, 1943, fasc. i, pp. 7–36, where the early bibliography will also be found.

71. After a while, the liberated part of the Peloponnese with its capital at Mistra became an important center of Greek resistance against the Frankish conquerors and a bright beacon of civilization. The Church of Sts. Theodore was built there between 1290 and 1295 (see Anastasios Orlandos, "Δανιήλ ὁ πρῶτος κτίτωρ τῶν Ἀγ. Θεοδώρων τοῦ Μυστρᾶ [Daniel, the First Founder of the Church of Sts. Theodore of Mistra]," ΕΕΒΣ, xii [1936], 443–448). In 1291–1292 the Church of St. Demetrios was built by Nicephoros Moschopoulos, Metropolitan of Lacedemonia (see Manoussos Manoussacas, "Ἡ

χρονολογία τῆς κτιτορικῆς ἐπιγραφῆς τοῦ 'Αγ. Δημητρίου τοῦ Μυστρᾶ [The Date of the Dedicatory Inscription of the Church of Saint Demetrios of Mistra]," ΔΧΑΕ, ιν, 1 [1959], 72–79). While in Mistra at the end of the thirteenth century and the beginning of the fourteenth century, this latter Church hierarch and scholar, Metropolitan of Lacedemonia and πρόεδρος of Crete, also made artistic copies of ancient Greek and Christian manuscripts or commissioned their copying by others. His annotated codices, which have survived to this day, bear witness to the richness of his own library (Manoussacas, "Νικηφόρου Μοσχοπούλου ἐπιγράμματα σέ χειρόγραφα τῆς βιβλιοθήκης του [The Epigrams of Nicephoros Moschopoulos in the Manuscripts of His Library]," Ἑλληνικά, xv [1957], 232–246). In 1310 the Church of Panagia Hodegetria ('Αφεντικοῦ) was also built (see Manolis Chatzidakis, Μυστρᾶς [Athens, 1948], p. 15).

72. See Thiriet, La Romanie (48), pp. 145–146, for the relevant bibliography.

73. Ibid., pp. 152–153. For details, see Stephanos Xanthoudidis, Ἡ ἐνετοκρατία ἐν Κρήτῃ (48), pp. 45–74.

74. Ibid., pp. 134, 149–150, 152. Of course, Venice relinquished her plans to re-establish the Latin control of the Near East only after a long time (see pp. 155 ff.).

75. See Pachymeres, Συγγραφικαὶ ἱστορίαι (69), ιι, 209: "οὕς Κρήτηθεν προσχωρήσαντας βασιλεῖ ὡς μή καταδεχομένους τήν ἐκ τῶν 'Ιταλῶν ἐπικράτειαν [who, going over to the king, from Crete, as if not accepting the dominion of the Italians]." Regarding their leader, George Chortatzes, see pp. 221 ff.

76. See Karl Hopf, Griechenland im Mittelalter und in der Neuzeit (1:51) (Leipzig, 1867–1868), ι, 464; and Thiriet, La Romanie (48), p. 161. On Sanudo, see the article by Giovanni B. Picotti, "Sanudo, Marin, il vecchio," in Enciclopedia italiana, xxx (Rome, 1936), 801–802.

77. See Steven Runciman, "Byzantine and Hellene in the Fourteenth Century," Τόμος Κωνσταντίνου 'Αρμενοπούλου ἐπί τή ἑξακοσιετηρίδι τῆς 'Εξαβίβλου αὐτοῦ, νι (Thessalonica, 1952) (= Νομ. Σχ. Πανεπιστημίου Θεσσαλονίκης, ἐπιστημονική ἐπετηρίς, τόμος ς'), 29; and Tafrali, Thessalonique (7), p. 157. Since he meant Lesbos when he wrote to Manuel Chrysoloras in 1404, Manuel Calecas used the word Hellas with its present-day connotation (Raymond Loenertz, Correspondance de Manuel Calecas [Rome, 1950], p. 300). Cf. Kilian Lechner, Hellenen und Barbaren im Weltbild der Byzantiner (2:4) (Munich, 1955), pp. 64–72.

78. See Raymond Loenertz, Démétrius Cydonès, correspondance (Vatican City, 1956), ι, 3, 12, 20, 96, 100, 115; ιι (1960), 56, 57, 62, 66 ff., passim.

79. Giovanni Mercati, Notizie di Procoro e Demetrio Cidone, Manuele Caleca e Theodoro Meliteniota ed altri appunti per la storia della teologia e della letteratura bizantina del secolo XIV [Notes concerning Procorus, Demetrius Kydones, Manuel Calecas, Theodore Meliteniota, and Other Remarks on the History of Byzantine Theology and Literature in the Fourteenth Century] (Vatican City, 1931), p. 365: "Οἱ γάρ ἡμέτεροι πρότερον μέν τῆς παλαιᾶς διαιρέσεως εἴχοντο καί πάντας ἀνθρώπους εἰς Ἕλληνας καί βαρβάρους

διχοτομοῦντες τό παρ' αὐτούς πᾶν ἀνόητον ᾤοντο καί σκαιόν, ὄνων ἤ βοῶν τούς λοιπούς οὐδαμῇ βελτίους ἡγούμενοι [Since formerly our people held to the ancient division and, separating all men into Hellenes and barbarians, considered everything beyond themselves senseless and rude, thinking the rest no better than donkeys or oxen]."

80. See, for example, Geoffroy de Villehardouin, *La Conquête* (7), *passim*. According to an old tradition, the word Γραικός was used in the Greek language at that time (Vasily Vasilevsky, "Epirotica saeculi XIII [3:21]," Viz. Vrem., III (1896), p. 252). See also Joseph Bryennios, Τά παραλειπόμενα (2:22), ed. Thomas Mandakassis (Leipzig, 1784), III, 148, and *passim*. Cf. Panagiotis Christou, Αἱ περιπέτειαι τῶν ἐθνικῶν ὀνομάτων τῶν Ἑλλήνων [*The Vicissitudes of the National Names of the Greeks*] (Thessalonica, 1960), pp. 37–39.

81. Bertrandon de la Brocquière, *Voyage d'outremer et retour de Jérusalem en France par la voie de terre, pendant le cours des années 1432 et 1433*, ed. Pierre Legrand D'Aussy, in *Mémoires de l'Institut national des sciences et arts; sciences morales et politiques*, v (Paris, fructidor an XII), p. 569: (Andrenoply) . . . la plus forte de toutes celles que le Turc possède dans la Grèce [the strongest of all those which the Turk possesses in Greece]." See Pero Tafur, *Travels and Adventures, 1435–1439*, tr. Malcolm Letts (New York-London, 1926), p. 128.

82. See Giannis Tozis, " Ὁ ἑλληνικός κόσμος κατά τόν ΙΔ' αἰῶνα, ὅπως τόν εἶδεν ἕνας Ἰσπανός περιηγητής [The Greek World in the Fourteenth Century; How a Spanish Traveler Viewed It]," ΑΘΓΛΘ, XXII (1957), p. 150: "ἦρθα στή Μεσημβρία κι' ἀπό κεῖ στή Βάρνα. Ἐδῶ εἶναι ἡ ἀληθινή Ἑλλάδα [I went to Mesembria, and from there to Varna. Here is the real Greece]."

83. Festa, *Theodori* (56), p. 176. This use of *Hellas* was retained from the time of the church historian, Evagrius, in the sixth century, which circumstance, as Tozis attempts to convince us, at least helps to explain the obscure sentence, "οἱ Ἄραβες . . . Ἀγχίαλον τε καί τήν Ἑλλάδαν πᾶσαν [The Arabs . . . Anchialos and all of Hellas]" (Tozis, " Ὁ Ἑλληνικός (82), p. 150, n. 2). See also Constantine Amantos, "Παρατηρήσεις εἰς τήν μεσαιωνικήν γεωγραφίαν [Observations on Medieval Geography]," ΕΕΒΣ, ι (1924), 42. Did Theodore's love of Greece lead to its revival?

84. *Chronicle of Morea*, ed. John Schmitt (London, 1904), verse 794 ff.; and ed. Peter P. Kalonaros (Athens, 1940), verse 794 ff.

85. See Nikolaos Tomadakis, Ὁ Ἰωσήφ Βρυέννιος καί ἡ Κρήτη κατά τό 1400 [Joseph Bryennios and Crete around 1400] (Athens, 1947), pp. 73–74.

86. Karl Hopf, *Chroniques gréco-romanes* (Berlin, 1873), p. 143. See also Michael Dendias, "Sur les rapports entre les Grecs et les Francs en Orient après 1204," ΕΕΒΣ, XXIII (1953), p. 377. This study, as the author says (p. 371), is extracted from the introduction to his unpublished monograph on the Greek despotate of Epirus.

87. See Mavrophrydis, Ἐκλογή μνημείων (33), ι, 183–211; and Antoine Gidel, *Études sur la littérature grecque moderne* (Paris, 1866), pp. 63–64, 197–229.

88. See Dirk Hesseling, *L'Achilléide byzantine* (Amsterdam, 1919), p. 15.

89. Constantine Sathas, "Le Roman d'Achille," AAEEG, xiii (1879); and Paolo Stomeo, "*Achilleide,* poema bizantino anonimo," *Studi salentini,* Lecce-Galatina, vii (1959), 156–157. Stomeo places its origins somewhere between the twelfth century and the beginning of the fifteenth. See also Börje Knös, *L'Histoire de la littérature néogrecque* (Stockholm-Göteborg-Uppsala, 1962), pp. 133–137.

90. See Hesseling, *L'Achilléide* (88), pp. 9, 11.

91. Paolo Stomeo, *Osservazioni sull'Achilleide bizantina* (Lecce-Galatina, 1958), pp. 5–6.

92. See Manoussos Manoussacas, "Les Romans byzantines de chevalerie et l'état présent des études les concernant," REB, x (1952), pp. 70–83; and Emmanuel Kriaras, "Die zeitliche Einreihung des 'Phlorios und Platzia-Phlora' Romans im Hinblick auf den 'Imberios und Margarona' Roman [The Chronological Place of the 'Phlorios and Platzia-Phlora' Romance in regard to the Imberios and Margarona Romance]," XIᵉ Congrès international des études byzantines, Munich, 1958, *Akten* (Munich, 1960), pp. 269–272. For an opposing view, see Hugo Schreiner, "Der älteste Imberiostext [The Oldest Imberios Text]," XIᵉ Congrès international des études byzantines, Munich, 1958, *Akten* (Munich, 1960), pp. 556–562. A more comprehensive analysis of the novels and the various problems associated with them will be found in Knös, *L'Histoire* (89), i, 104 ff.

93. See Ioannis Romanos, Ἱστορικά ἔργα [*Historical Works*] (Corfu, 1959), pp. 173–175, where the relevant bibliography will also be found.

Chapter 4

1. See Herbert Hunger's comments in "Von Wissenschaft und Kunst in der frühen Palaiologenzeit" (3:46), JÖBG, viii (1959), 139–144.

2. *Ibid.,* pp. 145, 147. See Wilamowitz' comparison: "D.T. ist in der Wahrheit eher als der erste moderne Tragiker-kritiker zu führen [D.T. is, indeed, to be considered rather the first modern tragedian-critic]."

3. See Basileios Laourdas, "Βυζαντινά καί μεταβυζαντινά ἐγκώμια εἰς τόν ῞Αγ. Δημήτριον [Byzantine and Post-Byzantine Encomia of St. Demetrius]," Μακεδονικά, iv (1955–1960), 84 ff., 142–143.

4. See Polychronis Enepekides, "Der Briefwechsel des Mystikers Nikolaos Kabasilas [The Correspondence of the Mystic Nicholas Kavasilas]," BZ, xlvi (1953), 31.

5. See Basileios Laourdas, Ἡ κλασσική φιλολογία εἰς τήν Θεσσαλονίκην κατά τόν δέκατον τέταρτον αἰῶνα [Classical Philology in Thessalonica in the Fourteenth Century] (Thessalonica, 1960), 13–15, where there is also a special bibliography.

6. Hunger, "Von Wissenschaft" (3:46), pp. 148–149, 150–151.

7. For the date of his birth, his life, and his education, see Herbert Hunger, "Theodoros Metochites als Vorläufer des Humanismus in Byzanz [Theodore Metochites as the Forerunner of Humanism in Byzantium]," BZ, xlv (1952), 4–19. See also Hans-Georg Beck, *Theodoros Metochites* (Munich, 1952), 1 ff.

8. Beck, *Theodoros* (7), pp. 92–95, 100–114, especially p. 116: "das ererbte, klassische byzantinische Weltbild ist bei Metochites in eine deutlich wahrnehmbare Krise getreten [the inherited, classical Byzantine world-outlook has in Metochites clearly come to a noticeable crisis]"; and Herbert Hunger, "Der Ἠθικός des Theodoros Metochites [The 'Ethic' of Theodore Metochites]," IXᵉ Congrès international des études byzantines, Thessalonica, 1953, Πεπραγμένα (Athens, 1955–1958), ιιι, 157.

9. See S. Radojčić, "Die Entstehung des Paläologenstils in der Malerei [The Origin of the Palaeologian Style in Painting]," in the *Korreferate* of the XIᵉ Congrès international des études byzantines (Munich, 1958), pp. 29 ff. and 32.

10. See George Sotiriou, "Die byzantinische Malerei des XIV. Jahrhunderts in Griechenland [Byzantine Painting of the Fourteenth Century in Greece]," Ἑλληνικά, ι (1928), 95–117. A concise exposition of the subject and various associated problems appear in Otto Demus, *Die Entstehung des Paläologenstils in der Malerei* [*The Origin of the Palaeologian Style in Painting*] (Munich, 1958), also the relevant bibliography.

11. Demus, *Die Entstehung* (10), p. 59.

12. *Ibid.*, p. 54. Ioannis K. Voyatzidis expressed the opinion that the Greek racial consciousness, that is, the sense of Greek nationality, contributed to the Renaissance ("Τό ἱστορικόν φαινόμενον 'ἡ ἀνάκτησις τοῦ ἀπολεσθέντος' [The Historical Phenomenon 'the Recovery of the Lost']," ΠΑΑ, xxxiii [1958], 372).

13. Constantine Sathas, Μεσαιωνική βιβλιοθήκη (2:23) (Venice, 1872–1874), ι, 151, 152.

14. Apostolos Vacalopoulos, "Συμβολή στήν ἱστορία τῆς Θεσσαλονίκης ἐπί Βενετοκρατίας (1423–1430) [A Contribution to the History of Thessalonica under Venetian Rule (1423–1430)]," in Τόμος Ἀρμενοπούλου (Thessalonica, 1952), pp. 128–130. This article contains the relevant bibliography.

15. See Oreste Tafrali, *Thessalonique au quatorzième siècle* (Paris, 1913), pp. 157–161, 165–168.

16. See Andreas Xyngopoulos, "Die Entstehung des Paläologenstils in der Malerie [The Origin of the Palaeologian Style in Painting]," XIᵉ Congrès international des études byzantines, *Korreferate* (Munich, 1958), p. 34.

17. See Andreas Xyngopoulos, *Thessalonique et la peinture macédonienne* (Athens, 1965); and George I. Theocharidis, " Ὁ βυζαντινός ζωγράφος Καλλιέργης [The Byzantine painter Kallierges]," Μακεδονικά, ιν (1960), 541–543. For Yugoslavian points of view, see the publication, D. Bosković-K. Tomorski, "L'Architecture médiévale d'Ochrid," *Recueil de Travaux*, Edition spéciale du Musée national d'Ochrid, publiée de l'occasion du Xᵉ anniversaire de le fondation du Musée et dediée au XIIᵉ Congrés internationale des études byzantines (Ochrida, 1961), pp. 71–100, 101–148; and Vojislav Djurić, *Icônes de Yougoslavie* (Belgrade, 1961), pp. 23–24, 27, 34, 36, which also contains the relevant Slav bibliography. Cf. Demus, *Die Entstehung* (10), p. 51; and Xyngopoulos, "Nouveau témoignages de l'activité des peintres macédoniens

au Mont-Athos [New Evidence of the Activity of Macedonian Painters at Mount Athos]," BZ, LII (1959), 61–67.

18. See Bariša Krekić, *Dubrovnik (Raguse) et le Levant au moyen âge* (Paris, 1961), pp. 128, 137, 150.

19. See Tafrali, *Thessalonique au quatorzième siècle* (15), p. 156; and Theodore Metochites' "Π ρεσβευτικόν [The Embassy]," in Sathas, Μεσαιωνικὴ βιβλιοθήκη (2:23), I, 163–164.

20. Raymond Loenertz, *Démétrius Cydonès, correspondance* (Vatican City, 1956), II, 60.

21. Tafrali, *Thessalonique au quatorzième siècle* (15), pp. 150, n. 1, 157.

22. See Constantine Triantaphyllopoulos, Ἡ Ἑξάβιβλος τοῦ Ἀρμενοπούλου καί ἡ νομικὴ σκέψις ἐν Θεσσαλονίκῃ κατά τόν δέκατον τέταρτον αἰῶνα [*Armenopoulos' Hexabiblos and Thessalonian Legal Thought in the Fourteenth Century*] (Thessalonica, 1960).

23. Tafrali, *Thessalonique au quatorzième siècle* (15), pp. 149–152, 161–165.

24. See S. Salaville, "Quelques Précisions sur la biographie de Nicolas Cabasilas," IXᵉ International Congress of Byzantine Studies, Thessalonica, 1953, Πεπραγμένα (Athens, 1955–1958), III, 215–226.

25. See the lecture by Laourdas, Ἡ κλασσικὴ φιλολογία (5), pp. 6, 8.

26. See Alexander Solov'ev, "L'Oeuvre juridique de Mathieu Blastarès," *Studi bizantini e neoellenici*, V (1939), 698–707; and "Der Einfluss des byzantinischen Rechts auf die Völker Osteuropas [The Influence of Byzantine Law on the Peoples of East Europe]," *Zeitschrift der Savigny-Stiftung für Rechtsgeschichte*, LXXVI (1959), Romantische Abteilung, 432–479.

27. Raymond Loenertz, *Correspondance de Manuel Calecas* (Rome, 1950), p. 233.

28. See Rodolphe Guilland, "Le Traité inédit 'Sur l'usure' de Nicolas Cabasilas [The Unpublished Treatise 'On Usury' by Nicholas Kavasilas]," in Εἰς μνήμην Σπυρίδωνος Λάμπρου (Athens, 1935), pp. 269–277, which also refers to the works of other contemporary scholars on the bad social situation.

29. Tafrali, *Thessalonique au quatorzième siècle* (15), pp. 157–161.

30. Loenertz, *Démétrius Cydonès* (20), I, 23. See pp. 14–20, where the influence of ancient Greek writers is obvious.

31. See Peter Charanis, "On the Social Structure and Economic Organization of the Byzantine Empire in the Thirteenth Century and Later," Byz.-Sl., XII (1951), 97; and George Ostrogorsky, *Pour l'histoire de la féodalité byzantine* (Brussels, 1954), pp. 9, 16, 26 ff.

32. B. T. Gorianov, "Крупное феодальное землевладение в Византии в XIII–XV вв. [Great Feudal Landownership in Byzantium from the Thirteenth to the Fifteenth Centuries]," Viz. Vrem., X (1956), 116. The main Russian works (A. P. Každan, Zinaida Vladimirova Udalcova, *et al.*) and those of Bulgarian historians (Dimitar Angelov, *et al.*) may be found in the journals Viz. Vrem. and *Istoričeski Pregled*.

33. Gorianov, "Great Feudal Landownership" (32), p. 116.

34. Nicetas Choniates, Χρονική διήγησις (3:9), ed. Immanuel Bekker (Bonn, 1835), pp. 272–274.

35. See Franz Dölger, "Politische und geistige Strömungen im sterbendem Byzanz [Political and Intellectual Currents in Declining Byzantium]," JÖBG, III (1954), 5 ff.; and his "Der Feudalismus in Byzanz," Vorträge und Forschungen, v (1960), 186, 191–192.

36. See E. Francès, "La Féodalité et les villes byzantines au XIIIe et au XIVe siècles," Byz.-Sl., XVI (1955), 85–86, 87: "la ville apparaît comme le centre nécessaire qui polarise toute la vie économique de la féodalité dans la région." For an interpretation of Balkan feudalism in Marxist terms, see Dimitar Angelov, "Zur Frage des Feudalismus auf dem Balkan im XIII. bis zum XIV. Jahrhundert [On the Question of Feudalism in the Balkans in the Thirteenth and Fourteenth Centuries]," Études historiques à l'occasion du XIe Congrès international des sciences historiques, Stockholm, 1960 (Sofia, 1960), pp. 107–131.

37. See Germaine Rouillard, La Vie rurale dans l'empire byzantin (Paris, 1953), p. 147: "Plus d'un grand propriétaire a bien pu adopter les modes occidentales déjà en vogue à la cour des Comnènes, mais les paysans qui cultivent ses terres ou celles de quelque grand seigneur latin n'en ont point été touchés. Bien plus, ce sont au contraire les conquérants qui adoptent les termes même usités par les Byzantines à propos de l'organisation agraire [More than one great overlord could adopt the Western manners already in fashion at the court of the Comneni, but the peasants who tilled their lands or those of some great Latin lord were not touched by them. On the contrary, the conquerors adopted the same terms used by the Byzantines in the matter of agrarian organization]." Cf. Panagiotis Zepos, "Τό δίκαιον εἰς τό Χρονικόν τοῦ Μορέως [Law in the Chronicle of Morea]," ΕΕΒΣ, XVIII (1948), 212 ff. See also the observations of Freddy Thiriet, La Romanie vénitienne au moyen âge (Paris, 1959), pp. 110–113.

38. See John Danstrup, "The State and Landed Property to c. 1250," Classica et Mediaevalia, VIII (1946), 229.

39. See Charanis, "On the Social Structure" (31), pp. 94 ff., 105 ff.; Ostrogorsky, Pour l'histoire (31), pp. 93 ff.; and Rouillard, La Vie rurale (37), pp. 155–156.

40. George Ostrogorsky, "Mémoires et documents pour l'histoire de l'immunité à Byzance [Reports and Documents on the History of the Exemption at Byzantium]," Byzantion, XXVIII (1958), 205 ff.

41. Charanis, "On the Social Structure" (31), p. 108.

42. See Alexander Diomedis, Βυζαντιναί μελέται [Byzantine Studies] (Athens, 1951), I, 88–102.

43. Rouillard, La Vie rurale (37), p. 170. This writer considers a certain Theodore Karavas, vineyard-owner and proprietor in Macedonia, as a characteristic representative of this rural middle class.

44. See Chronicle of Aşik paşa Zade, tr. Richard Kreutel (Vienna, (1959), pp. 39, 40.

45. See Charanis, "On the Social Structure" (31), p. 131, and pp. 132–133 for this writer's views on the differences between the old and new classes of military landowners.

46. The following are interesting studies of the situation of tenants: Franz Dölger, *Sechs byzantinische Praktika des 14. Jahrhunderts für das Athoskloster Iberon* [*Six Byzantine Records of the Fourteenth Century for the Athos-monastery of Iberon*] (Munich, 1949). On the difficulty of defining the position of these tenants, see Charanis, "On the Social Structure" (31), pp. 134 ff. For Dölger's interpretation of their position, see his *Ein Fall slavischer Einsiedlung im Hinterland von Thessaloniki im 10. Jahrhundert* [*The Case of a Slavic Settlement in the Hinterland of Thessalonica in the Tenth Century*] (Munich, 1952), p. 27. The latter may be contrasted with the views of George Ostrogorsky, *Quelques Problèmes d'histoire de la paysannerie byzantine* [*Certain Problems concerning the History of the Byzantine Peasantry*] (Brussels, 1956), which are summarized on pp. 66–74.

47. See Rouillard, *La Vie rurale* (37), pp. 156–157, 158, 159–160, 163 ff.; Charanis, "On the Social Structure" (31), pp. 119 ff., 122–126, and "The Monastic Properties and the State in the Byzantine Empire," DOP, ɪv (1948), 97–118.

48. See Charanis, "The Monastic Properties" (47), pp. 108 ff.

49. For an interpretation of the condition, see Denis Zakythinos, *Le Despotat grec de Morée* (Athens, 1953), ɪɪ, 185–187.

50. See Constantine G. Zisiou, "Ἐπιγραφαί χριστιανικῶν χρόνων τῆς Ἑλλάδος. Αʹ Λακεδαίμονος [Greek Inscriptions of the Christian Period. 1. From Sparta]," Βυζαντίς, ɪ (1909), 433, 435.

51. See Nikos Bees, "Σερβικά καί βυζαντιακά γράμματα Μετεώρου [Serbian and Byzantine Letters of Meteoron]," Βυζαντίς, ɪɪ (1911–1912), 59–62.

52. Jean Meyendorff, *Introduction à l'étude de Grégoire Palamas* (Paris, 1959), pp. 45 ff.; see Hans-Georg Beck, *Kirche und theologische Literatur im byzantinischen Reich* [*The Church and Theological Literature in the Byzantine Empire*] (Munich, 1959), pp. 712 ff.; Giuseppe Schirò, Ὁ Βαρλαάμ καί ἡ φιλολογία εἰς τήν Θεσσαλονίκην κατά τόν δέκατον τέταρτον αἰῶνα [*Barlaam and Philosophy in Thessalonica in the Fourteenth Century*] (Thessalonica, 1959); the studies relating to Hesychast teaching in Πανηγυρικός τόμος ἑορτασμοῦ τῆς ἑξακοσιοστῆς ἐπετείου τοῦ θανάτου τοῦ Ἁγ. Γρηγορίου Παλαμᾶ, ἀρχιεπισκόπου Θεσσαλονίκης, 1359–1959 [*Festive Volume for the Celebration of the Six Hundredth Anniversary of the Death of St. Gregory Palamas, Archbishop of Thessalonica, 1359–1959*] (Thessalonica, 1960); and the recently published texts of Gregory Palamas, ed. Panagiotis Christou (vol. ɪ, Thessalonica, 1962; vol. ɪɪ, Thessalonica, 1966).

53. Schirò, Ὁ Βαρλαάμ (52), p. 11.

54. Loenertz, *Démétrius Cydonès* (20), ɪɪ, 51. Cf. Giuseppe Cammelli, *Démétrius Cydonès, correspondance* (Paris, 1930), p. 116.

55. See Konrad Onasch, "Renaissance und Vorreformation in der byzantinischen-slavischen Orthodoxie [Renaissance and Pre-Reformation in Byzan-

tine-Slavic Orthodoxy]," *Berliner byzantinischen Arbeiten,* v (1957), part 9, 288–302; and Antonios Tachiaos, Ἐπιδράσεις τοῦ ἡσυχασμοῦ εἰς τήν ἐκκλησιαστικήν πολιτικήν ἐν Ρωσία, 1328–1406 [*The Effects of Hesychasm on Church Policy in Russia, 1328–1406*] (Thessalonica, 1962). Regarding the activity of the painter Theophanes in Russia in the second half of the fourteenth century, see V. N. Lazarev, "Этюды о Феофане Греке [Studies on Theophanes the Greek]," Viz. Vrem., vii (1953), 244–258, viii (1956), 143–165, ix (1956), 193–210.

56. See Andreas Xyngopoulos, "L'Activité des peintres macédoniens," BZ, lii (1959), 61–67.

57. See Tafrali, *Thessalonique au quatorzième siècle* (15), pp. 25 ff.; and Freddy Thiriet, "Les Vénitiens à Thessalonique dans la première moitié du XIVe siècle," *Byzantion,* xx (1952), 323–332. There is some interesting information on the attitude of the Zealots and the social character of the movement in Guiseppe Cammelli, "Demetrii Cydonii orationes tres, adhuc ineditae [Three Orations by Demetrius Kydones, Hitherto Unpublished]," BNJ, iii (1922), 70 ff.; and Loenertz, *Démétrius Cydonès* (20), i, 4, 5. The most recent studies are Ernst Werner, "Народная ересь или движение за социально-политические реформы? Проблемы революционного движения в Солуни в 1342–1349 гг. [National Absurdity or Agitation for Sociopolitical Reforms? Problems of the Revolutionary Movement in Thessalonica, 1342–1349]," Viz. Vrem., xvii (1960), 155–200; and V. Hrochová, "La Révolte des Zélotes à Salonique et les communes italiennes," Byz.-Sl., xxii (1961), 1–15.

58. See Loenertz, *Démétrius Cydonès* (20), i, 110.

59. See the judgment of the Arab Muhammed b. Mängli, in the second half of the fourteenth century: "Kämpfen sie bloss um des reinen Siegens und Überwindens Willen, nicht um einen Glauben oder eine Religion zu verteidigen, als ob sie ihre Lust hätten am Blutvergiessen und Zerstören . . . wenn sie aber in gesittete Länder verpflanzt werden und die muhammedanische Religion annehmen, wird ihre Lebensführung gut und ihre Natur bessert sich [They fight merely for the desire of overpowering and of victory, not in order to defend a belief or a religion—as if they had a lust for bloodshed and destruction . . . but when they are transplanted into civilized lands and take up the Mohammedan religion, their manner of living becomes good and their nature improves]." (See H. Ritter, "Werke über Taktik und Kriegswesen [Works on Tactics and Military Affairs]," *Der Islam,* xviii [1929], 147.) On the Turkish method of fighting, see also Ibn Khaldûn, *The Muquaddimah* (London, 1958), ii, 81.

Chapter 5

1. See İbrahim Kafesoğlu, "Doğu Anadoluya ilk Selçuklu akini (1015–1021) ve tarihî ehemmieyti [The First Invasion of the Seljuks in Eastern Asia Minor (1015–1021) and Its Historical Importance]" in *Fuad Köprülü Armağani* (Istanbul, 1953), pp. 259–274.

2. Cf. Claude Cahen, "La Première Pénétration turque en Asie Mineure," *Byzantion,* xviii (1948), 5–67.

3. See the brief study by J. Laurent, "Byzance et les Turcs Seldjoucides en Asie Mineure. Leurs Traités anterieurs à Alexis Comnène," Βυζαντίς, ιι (1911–1912), 101–126.

4. See Sir John Maundeville, *The Voiage and Travaile of Sir J. Maundeville, Which Treateth of the Way to Hierusalem* (London, 1887), p. 20.

5. See Franz Miklosich and Joseph Müller, *Acta et diplomata graeca medii aevi sacra et profana* (1:43) (Vienna, 1860–1887), vol. ι.

6. See Heinrich Gelzer, *Ungedruckte und ungenügend veröffentlichte Texte der Notitiae Episcopatuum; ein Beitrag zur byzantinischen Kirchen- und Verwaltungsgeschichte* [*Unprinted and Insufficiently Publicized Texts of the Notitiae Episcopatuum; a Contribution to Byzantine Church- and Administrative History*], Abhandlungen der königlichen bayerischen Akademie der Wissenschaften, 1. Klasse, Band XXI, Abt. 3 (Munich, 1900), 613 ff.; and Manuel Gedeon, Πατριαρχικοί πίνακες (xxxvι, 1884) [*Patriarchal Tables* (xxxvι, 1884)] (Constantinople, 1885–1890), *passim*.

7. Albert Wächter, *Der Verfall des Griechentums in Kleinasien im XIV. Jahrhundert* [*The Decline of Hellenism in Asia Minor in the Fourteenth Century*] (Leipzig, 1903), pp. 38–39, 60.

8. Georgius Pachymeres, Συγγραφικαὶ ἱστορίαι (3:69), ed. Immanuel Bekker (Bonn, 1835), ι, 310–311.

9. *Ibid.*, 502.

10. Friedrich Giese, *Die Altosmanischen anonymen Chroniken* [*The Old Ottoman Anonymous Chronicles*] (Leipzig, 1925), ιι, 16.

11. See George Georgiadis-Arnakis, "Ἡ περιήγησις τοῦ ἴμπν Μπατούτα ἀνά τήν Μ. Ἀσίαν καί ἡ κατάστασις τῶν ἑλληνικῶν καί τουρκικῶν πληθυσμῶν κατά τόν ΙΔ´ αἰῶνα [The Tour of Ibn Batouta through Asia Minor and the Condition of the Hellenic and Turkish Populations in the Fourteenth Century]," ΕΕΒΣ, xxιι (1952), 135–149. On the cities of Bithynia during the period of Turkish domination, see Johannes Sölch, "Historisch-geographische Studien über bithynische Siedlungen [Historical and Geographic Studies of Bithynian Settlements], BNJ, ι (1920), 296 ff.

12. See Bertrandon de la Brocquière, *Voyage d'outremer et retour de Jérusalem en France par la voie de terre, pendant le cours des années 1432 et 1433*, ed. Pierre Legrand D'Aussy, in *Mémoires de l'Institut national des sciences et arts; sciences morales et politiques*, v (Paris, fructidor an XII), pp. 520–521, 526; and Nompar II, Seigneur de Caumont, *Voyage d'outremer en Jhérusalem l'an 1418* (Paris, 1858), p. 45.

13. Wächter, *Der Verfall* (7), pp. 9–10. The district of Neocaesarea fared better (p. 9). Cf. Pericles Triantaphyllidis, Οἱ φυγάδες [*The Fugitives*], a play about the Pontus, in five acts with lengthy prologues (Athens, 1870), pp. 51–52.

14. On this colonization, see Maximos Maravelakis and Apostolos Vacalopoulos, Αἱ προσφυγικαί ἐγκαταστάσεις ἐν τῇ περιοχῇ Θεσσαλονίκης (1:89) (Thessalonica, 1953), p. 30; and Anastasios S. Alektoridis, "Λεξιλόγιον τοῦ ἐν Φερτακαίνοις τῆς Καππαδοκίας γλωσσικοῦ ἰδιώματος [Vocabulary of the

Dialect spoken in Phertakaina in Cappadocia]," ΔIEE, ι (1883–1884), 482–483, 483–484, 485.

15. Karl Hopf, *Chroniques gréco-romanes* (Berlin, 1873), p. 143. See also Jacques Gassot, *Le Discours du voyage de Venise à Constantinople* (Paris, 1550), p. 18b.

16. See Wächter, *Der Verfall* (7), p. 29.

17. See Hopf, *Chroniques* (15), p. 143: "Anco l'Armenia che si chiamava anticamente Cilicia, è abitata da Greci [Armenia also, which was formerly known as Cilicia, was inhabited by Greeks]."

18. See Wächter, *Der Verfall* (7), pp. 20 ff., *passim*.

19. Regarding the Turkish-speaking population of Pontoherakleia (Zongouldak), for instance, see Panagiotis Makris, Ἡράκλεια τοῦ Πόντου [Herakleia on the Pontus] (Athens, 1903), p. 33; and Wächter, *Der Verfall* (7), p. 26.

20. See Karl Dieterich, *Das Griechentum Kleinasiens* [*The Hellenism of Asia Minor*] (Leipzig, 1915), pp. 10–12, which contains the relevant bibliography. On the Armenian presence, see Savvas Ioannidis, Ἱστορία καί στατιστική Τραπεζοῦντος καί τῆς περί ταύτην χώρας ὡς καί τά περί τῆς ἐνταῦθα ἑλληνικῆς γλώσσης [*The History and Statistics of Trebizond and of the Region around It; and on the Greek Language of the Area*] (Constantinople, 1870), p. 134; and Speros Vryonis, "Byzantium: the Social Basis of Decline in the Eleventh Century," *Greek, Roman, and Byzantine Studies*, ιι (1959), 169 ff.

21. See Pachymeres, Συγγραφικαὶ ἱστορίαι (3:69), ι, 16 ff.

22. Pierre Belon, *Les Observations de plusieurs singularitez et choses mémorables, trouvées en Grèce* (Paris, 1553), p. 164a.

23. See Apostolos Vacalopoulos, "Ἱστορικές παραδόσεις τῶν Ἑλλήνων προσφύγων τοῦ Σογιούτ [Historical Traditions of the Greek Refugees of Sogut]," in Προσφορά εἰς Στίλπωνα Κυριακίδην (Thessalonica, 1953), pp. 78 ff., which contains the relevant bibliography.

24. See Theodor Nöldeke, "Auszüge aus Nešri's Geschichte des osmanischen Hauses [Extracts from Nesri's History of the Ottoman House]," ZDMG, xiii (1859), 192–193. On the Domanits villages and the beauty of the district, see Andreas Mordtmann, *Anatolien, Skizzen und Reisebriefe aus Kleinasien (1850–1859)* [*Anatolia; Sketches and Travel Correspondence from Asia Minor (1850–1859)*] (Hannover, 1925), p. 61.

25. See Franz Taeschner, "Anatolische Forschungen [Anatolian Researches]," ZDMG, n. F. vii (1928), 93.

26. On the part played by the ghazis in Turkish history, see Paul Wittek, "Deux Chapitres de l'histoire des Turcs de Roum," *Byzantion*, xi (1936), 302–319, and his *The Rise of the Ottoman Empire* (London, 1938), pp. 14, 17–20, 31–32, 45.

27. On the date of Orchan's ascent to the throne, see Ismail Hakki Uzunçarşılı, "Gazi Orhan beğin hükümdar olduğu tarih ve ilk sikkesi [When Gazi Orchan Bey Became Ruler and His First Coin]," *Belleten*, ix (1945), 207–211. On the date of Orchan's death, see Peter Charanis, "Les Βραχέα

χρονικά comme source historique [The *Short Chronicles* as a Historical Source]," *Byzantion*, XIII (1938), 349–351.

28. See Julian Palmer, "The Origin of the Janissaries," *Bulletin of the John Rylands Library*, XXV (1953), 453–454. On the distribution of fiefs by Orchan, see Giese, *Die Altomanischen* (10), II, 21–22.

29. See Sir Hamilton Gibb and Harold Bowen, *Islamic Society and the West* (London–New York–Toronto, 1951), I, part 1, 46, 48 ff., which contains the relevant bibliography.

30. See George Georgiadis-Arnakis, Οἱ πρῶτοι ᾿Οθωμανοί [The First Ottomans] (Athens, 1947), pp. 99 ff.

31. Nicephoros Gregoras, Ρωμαϊκή ἱστορία (3:44), ed. Ludwig Schopen, I, 458.

32. P. A. Vaphiadis, Τό Ρύσιον (᾿Αρετσοῦ) [*The Village of Rysion (Aretsou)*] (Athens, 1924), p. 9.

33. Pachymeres, Συγγραφικαὶ ἱστορίαι (3:69), II, 318–319, 335–336.

34. Georgiadis-Arnakis, Οἱ πρῶτοι ᾿Οθωμανοί (30), p. 99.

35. Constantine I. Dyovouniotis, Γρηγορίου Παλαμᾶ ἐπιστολή πρός Θεσσαλονικεῖς [A Letter of Gregorios Palamas to the Thessalonians]," NE, XVI (1922), 11–12. On the participation of the Christian governor of Harmankaya, Köse Michal, in the enterprises of Osman, see *Chronicle Aşik paşa Zade*, tr. Richard Kreutel (Vienna, 1959), pp. 31–46. According to a Turkish source of 1467, Michal Bey possessed Harmankaya and its surrounding villages as his property or fief (*mülk*) (see Halil Inalcik, "Ottoman Methods of Conquest," *Studia islamica*, II [1954], 121, fn. 1).

36. See examples in Halil Inalcik, "Stefan Dušan'dan Osmanli imparatorluğunda XV asirda Rumeli' de hıristiyan sipahiler ve menşeleri [Christian Spahis in Rumelia during the XVth Century from Stephan Dušan to the Ottoman Empire: Their Origin]," in *Fuad Köprülü Armağani* (Istanbul, 1953), pp. 211 ff. See also Vacalopoulos, ᾿Ιστορικές παραδόσεις (23), pp. 85–87, and contrast Stilpon Kyriakidis' opinion on the interpretation of the passage from George Pachymeres mentioned by Vacalopoulos (Stilpon Kyriakidis, "Διόρθωσις εἰς χωρίον τοῦ Παχυμέρους [Correction of a Passage in Pachymeres]," ᾿Ελληνικά, XIV [1955], 174–176.

37. See *Chronicle Aşik paşa Zade* (35), p. 46, which mentions Köse Michal's conversion to Islam at the time of Osman.

38. See Max Treu, *Matthaios, Metropolit von Ephesos; ueber sein Leben und seine Schriften* [*Matthaios, Metropolite of Ephesus; on His Life and Writings*] (Potsdam, 1901), pp. 53, 54, 55.

39. Theodor Seif, "Der Abschnitt über die Osmanen in Šükrüllāh's persischer Universalgeschichte [The Section on the Ottomans in Šükrüllāh's Persian Universal History]," MOG, II (1923–1925), 67, 83. See further: "Da kam ihm in den Sinn, dass er die Ungläubigen jener Länder ebenfalls zum Glauben rufen müsse. Wenn sie nicht annähmen, müsse es Kampf und Tötung geben [Then it occurred to him that he must likewise call to belief the unbelievers of those lands. If they should not accept this, there must be war and death]."

40. See the letter from the captured Gregory Palamas to the Thessalonians
in NE, xvi (1922), 12. This terror is certainly attested by the widespread
currency among them of a tradition that the Turks cut out the tongues of
those they conquered so that they would forget their language and their
religion. Cf. Nikolaos Politis, Μελέται περί τοῦ βίου καί τῆς γλώσσης τοῦ
ἑλληνικοῦ λαοῦ, Παραδόσεις (2:6) (Athens, 1904), ι, 16. The same tradition
persisted in the district of Zichna in Macedonia (Natalis E. Petrovits,
" Ἐξισλαμισμοί [Conversions to Islam]," Σερραϊκά χρονικά, ιι [1957], 163).

41. See Giese, Die Altosmanischen (10), ιι, 18–19, and p. 23 regarding the
memories in certain districts of the good government of Suleiman, the son
of Orchan: "Alle Ungläubigen in diesem Gebiete [Taraklijenidschesi, Göjnük,
and Modreni] sahen die Gerechtigkeit Süleman Paschas und wurden all
Muslime) [All the unbelievers in this area saw the righteousness of the pasha
Suleiman, and all became Moslems]."

42. See Ömer Lûtfi Barkan, "Osmanlı imperatorluğunda bir iskân ve kolonizasyon metodu olarak vakıflar ve temlikler. I Istilâ devirlerinin kolonizatör
Türk dervişleri ve Zâviyeler [Use of Wakfs and Temliks in the Settlement and
Colonization of the Turkish Empire. I: Turkish Dervishes and Monasteries
as Colonizers during the Invasion Periods]," Vakıflar Dergisi, ιι (1942), 279–
286; and the résumé in the French section of this journal, pp. 59–65. For the
different meanings of the word ribât, see the article under this title by Fuad
Köprülü in the same journal, pp. 267–278.

43. See Seif, "Der Abschnitt" (39), p. 83; Basileios Delighiannis, "Τό ἐν
τῇ περιφερείᾳ Προύσης χωρίον Κουβούκλια [The Village of Kouvouklia in the
District of Prousa]," Μικρ. χρονικά, ι (1938), 291, fn. 1; and Vacalopoulos,
" Ἱστορικές Παραδόσεις" (23), pp. 80 ff. On crypto-Christianity among the
inhabitants of Nicaea, see pp. 89–90 of the present work.

44. Fuad Köprülü, Alcune osservazioni intorno all' influenza della istituzioni
bizantine sulle istituzioni ottomane [Some Observations on the Influence of
Byzantine Institutions on Ottoman Institutions] (Rome, 1953). Köprülü supports the view that Ottoman institutions underwent no change as a result of
Byzantine influence, though an influence was previously discernible during the
Seljuk period (see especially pp. 135–140). Compare, however, the criticism
of Hans Kissling, in BZ, xlviii (1955), 399–401, where he makes a number
of interesting observations of a general nature: "das Renegatentum, insonder-
heit das griechische Renegatentum, bei der Weiterentwicklung des osmanischen Staates eine entscheidende Rolle wohl auch in der besprochenen Hinsicht gespielt haben dürfte [the apostasy, and in particular the Greek apostasy,
during the further development of the Ottoman state, probably played a decisive role also in this regard]" (p. 401). This opinion is now accepted by
modern Turkish historians, Enver Z. Karal, for example. See his study "La
Transformation de la Turquie d'un empire oriental en un état moderne et
national," in Cahiers d'histoire mondiale, iv (1958), 426, where the relevant
bibliography may be found. Cf. Georgiadis-Arnakis, Οἱ πρῶτοι Ὀθωμανοί
(30), pp. 101 ff. Regarding the nature of Greek influence, particularly on the
religious beliefs and traditions of the Turks, and vice versa, a body of re-

vealing historiographical material has been gathered by Frederick Hasluck (*Christianity and Islam under the Sultans* [Oxford, 1929], vols. I–II). Although Hasluck's comments on this material are interesting, it remains yet to be properly studied and employed.

45. Mordtmann, *Anatolien* (24), pp. 123–124. On the conversion to Islam of the Greek population of Galatia, see also George K. Skalieris, Λαοί καί φυλαί τῆς Μικρᾶς 'Ασίας [*Peoples and Tribes of Asia Minor*] (Athens, 1922), pp. 157–158; and Moses Moÿsidis, "Συμβολή εἰς τήν ἱστορίαν τῆς ἀνθυπατικῆς Γαλατίας. Μονογραφία περί 'Αγκύρας [Contribution to the Study of the Proconsular Galatia. Ankyra Monograph]," Ξενοφάνης, II (1904–1905), 436.

46. See Heinrich Gelzer, *Pergamon unter Byzantinern und Osmanen* [*Pergamum under the Byzantines and the Ottomans*] (Berlin, 1903), pp. 95–97; Karl Krumbacher, *Griechische Reise* [*Travels in Greece*] (Berlin, 1886), pp. 264–265; and Panteles Kontogiannis, 'Η ἑλληνικότης τῶν νομῶν Προύσης καί Σμύρνης [*The Hellenic Character of the Provinces of Prousa and Smyrna*] (Athens, 1919), pp. 20–21, 29.

47. See the journal Μικρασιατικά χρονικά, vols. I–V (1938–1952).

48. Raymond Loenertz, *Démétrius Cydonès, correspondance* (Vatican City, 1956), II, 390; and Halil Inalcik, "The Ottoman Record-Books as a Source of Place-Names," *Proceedings and Transactions of the Fifth International Congress of Onomastic Sciences* (Salamanca, 1958), II, p. 5 of the reprint.

49. Demetrius Kydones, "Ρωμαίοις συμβουλευτικός [Counsels to the Romans]," PG, CLIV, col. 965.

Chapter 6

1. Vasily Vasilevsky, "Epirotica saeculi XIII" (3:21), Viz. Vrem., III (1896), 242. The Metropolite of Naupactus, John Apocaucus, provides us with a graphic description of the terror of the people in one of his letters to the "powerful Ducaina," wife of the Despot of Epirus, Theodore Comnenus Ducas, at the beginning of the thirteenth century. See also the description by his contemporary, Michael Choniates, in Constantine I. Dyovouniotis, "Αἱ ἀνέκδοτοι κατηχήσεις τοῦ μητροπολίτου 'Αθηνῶν, Μιχαήλ 'Ακομινάτου [The Unpublished Catechisms of Michael Akominatos, Metropolite of Athens]," ΠΑΑ, III (1928), 315.

2. See Paul Wittek, *Das Fürstentum Mentesche* [*The Principality of Menteše*] (Istanbul, 1934), pp. 45 ff., 58 ff.

3. Ruy Gonzales de Clavijo, *A Diary of the Journey to the Court of Timur, 1403–1406*, tr. (from the Spanish) Guy Le Strange (London, 1928), p. 47. Regarding the measures taken by the interested Christian powers against Turkish pirates in the fourteenth century, see Spyridon Theotokis, " 'Η πρώτη συμμαχία τῶν κυριάρχων κρατῶν τοῦ Αἰγαίου κατά τῆς καθόδου τῶν Τούρκων ἀρχομένου τοῦ ΙΔ' αἰῶνος [The First Alliance of the Sovereign Powers of the Aegean against the Descent of the Turks at the Beginning of the Fourteenth Century]," ΕΕΒΣ, VII (1930), 283–289.

4. For the relevant bibliography, see Nikos Bees, "Geschichtliche Forschungsresultate und Mönchs- und Volkssagen über die Gründer der Meteoren-

klöster [The Results of Historical Investigations, and Monks' Tales and Folktales concerning the Founders of the Meteora Monasteries]," BNJ, III (1922), 366, fn. 4.

5. Peter Charanis, "Piracy in the Aegean During the Reign of Michael VIII Palaeologus," *Annuaire de l'Institut de philologie et d'histoire orientales et slaves*, x (1950), 127–136.

6. See Irène Mélikoff, Le Destân d'Umur pacha (Düstürname-i Enverî) [*The Ballad of Umur Pasha*] (Paris, 1954). Cf. Nicephoros Gregoras, Ῥωμαϊκή ἱστορία (3:44), ed. Ludwig Schopen, II (Bonn, 1830), 683; Spyridon Lambros, Παλαιολόγεια καί Πελοποννησιακά (1:66) (Athens, 1926), III, 37; and Antonio Rubió y Lluch, "Els Governs de Matheu de Moncada y Roger de Lluria en la Grecia catalana (1359–1370)," *Anuari de l'Institut d'estudis catalans* (Barcelona, 1901, 1912), pp. 29–30. There is yet need for a systematic study of the pillage of the Aegean and Ionian islands and of the consequences generally of piratical enterprise.

7. William Miller, *Essays on the Latin Orient* (Cambridge, Eng., 1921), p. 61.

8. See Clavijo, A Diary (3), pp. 54–55. The Venetians transferred the 4,000 inhabitants of the island to Bourgos in Chandax, which from that time came to be known as τά Τενέδια (Stephanos Xanthoudidis, Ἡ ἐνετοκρατία ἐν Κρήτῃ καί οἱ κατά τῶν Ἐνετῶν ἀγῶνες τῶν Κρητῶν [3:48] [Athens, 1939], p. 111), and to Karystos, near Chalcis, and to Cythera (see Freddy Thiriet, *La Romanie vénitienne au moyen âge* [Paris, 1959], p. 264). On the devastation of Tenedos at the beginning of the fifteenth century, see Christopher Buondelmonti, *Description des îles de l'Archipel. Version grecque par un anonyme, publiée d'après le manuscrit du sérail, avec une traduction française et un commentaire par Émile Legrand* [*A Description of the Islands of the Aegean. Greek Version by an Unknown Author, after the Manuscript of the Seraglio, with a French Translation and Commentary by Émile Legrand*], première partie (Paris, 1897), p. 79.

9. Buondelmonti, *Description des îles* (8), p. 33.

10. Clavijo, A Diary (3), pp. 40, 46–47, 48, 49.

11. Nompar II, Seigneur de Caumont, *Voyage d'outremer en Jhérusalem l'an 1418* (Paris, 1858), pp. 41, 85 ff. See also Clavijo, A Diary (3), p. 4.

12. Buondelmonti, *Descriptions des îles* (8), pp. 6, 35, 36–37, 40, 53, 54, 58, 59, 61, 67, 68, 69–70, 72, etc.

13. Rubió y Lluch, "Els Governs" (6), pp. 13–14.

14. For details of the activities of the Serbs and Bulgarians before 1369, see Demetrius Kydones, Ῥωμαίοις συμβουλευτικός, PG, CLIV, cols. 973–974.

15. See Georgius Phrantzes, Χρονικόν [*Chronicle*], ed. Immanuel Bekker (Bonn, 1838), p. 43.

16. Raymond Loenertz, *Démétrius Cydonès, correspondance* (Vatican City, 1956), I, 85, 98. See also pp. 95–96.

17. For some characteristic examples, see Manuel Gedeon, Πατριαρχικαί Ἐφημερίδες [*Patriarchal Journals*] (Athens, 1936), p. 48.

18. Constantine I. Dyovouniotis, "Γρηγορίου Παλαμᾶ ἐπιστολή πρός Θεσσαλονικεῖς" (5:35), NE, xvi (1922), pp. 8, 9.

19. See the study by Ihor Ševčenko, "The Decline of Byzantium Seen through the Eyes of Its Intellectuals," DOP, xv (1961), 169–186.

20. The events surrounding the conquest of Thrace are still clouded. See, however, the informative study by Franz Babinger, *Beiträge zur Frühgeschichte der Türkenherrschaft in Rumelien (14.–15. Jahrhundert)* [*Contributions to the Early History of the Turkish Dominion in Rumelia (fourteenth to fifteenth century)*] (Munich, 1944), pp. 41 ff.

21. Maximos Maravelakis and Apostolos Vacalopoulos, Αἱ προσφυγικαί ἐγκαταστάσεις ἐν τῇ περιοχῇ Θεσσαλονίκης (1:89) (Thessalonica, 1953), pp. 378, 427. See also p. 428. A Turkish source testifies to the rebelliousness of the Greek-speaking districts of Saros at the time of the Greek revolution in 1821—Ioannis K. Vasdranellis, Οἱ Μακεδόνες κατά τήν ἐπανάστασιν τοῦ 1821 [*The Macedonians in the Revolution of 1821*], 3rd ed. (Thessalonica, 1967), p. 262.

22. See Theodor Seif, "Der Abschnitt über die Osmanen in Šükrüllāh's persischer Universalgeschichte" (5:39), MOG, ii (1923–1925), 87–88, 89.

23. Julian Palmer, "The Origin of the Janissaries," *Bulletin of the John Rylands Library*, xxv (1953), 458–462, 473. The infantry and cavalry corps ceased to exist in 1592 (Tayyib Gökbilgin, *Rumeli'de Yürükler, Tatarlar ve Evlâd-i Fatihân* [*Yuruks, Tatars, and the Sons of the Conquerors in the Balkans*] [Istanbul, 1957], p. 21).

24. Seif, "Der Abschnitt" (5:39), p. 89.

25. Maximilian Braun, *Lebensbeschreibung des Despoten Stefan Lazarević von Konstantin dem Philosophen* [*Biography of the Despot Stefan Lazarević by Constantine the Philosopher*] (Wiesbaden, 1956), p. 6.

26. I consider the date given by Athanasius Ypsilantis (Τά μετά τήν "Αλωσιν 1453–1789 [*History of Affairs after the Conquest (1453–1789)*] [Constantinople, 1870], p. 761) to be correct, even though he lived several centuries later. His education and position were such as to make him *au fait* with most Turkish matters.

27. It is quite likely that the application of this unpopular measure, at least in the early years, can be attributed in large part to the *Kadiasker* (the highest judge of the army) Kara Chalil of Tsantarlı (Franz Taeschner and Paul Wittek, "Die Vezirfamilie der Candarlyzāde (14.–15. Jahrhundert) und ihre Denkmäler [The Family of Viziers of Tsantarlizade and Their Monuments]," *Islam*, xviii (1925, 691).

28. See Apostolos Vacalopoulos, "Προβλήματα τῆς ἱστορίας τοῦ παιδομαζώματος [Problems of the History of the Recruitment of Youths]," Ἑλληνικά, xiii (1954), 274–293. The subject has been investigated anew and a complete bibliography compiled by Basilike Papoulia, *Ursprung und Wesen der "Knabenlese" im osmanischen Reiche* [*The Origin and Nature of the Recruitment of Youths in the Ottoman Empire*] (Munich, 1963). Papoulia concludes that the impressment of children and the founding of the janissaries took place at the

time of Orchan, while the conscription of one fifth of the prisoners of war (*pencik*) was introduced by Murad I.

29. See Jacovaky Rizos Neroulos, *Analyse raisonnée de l'ouvrage intitulé "Charte turque,"* fols. 9, 27, 90. This manuscript, in the Public Library of Geneva, should be examined by a specialist in Turkish studies.

30. Halil Inalcik, "Ottoman Methods of Conquest," *Studia islamica*, II (1954), 120–121.

31. August Heisenberg, "Kaiser Johannes Batatzes der Barmherzige; eine mittelgriechische Legende" (3:49), BZ, XIV (1905), 194, 228.

32. Demetrius Kydones, Ῥωμαίοις συμβουλευτικός (5:49), PG, CLIV, cols. 1004–1005. See also Raymond Loenertz, "Manuel Paleologue, épitre à Cabasilas," Μακεδονικά, IV (1960), 38–39; and Kydones' similar indictments around 1373 (Loenertz, *Démétrius Cydonès* (16), I, 81, 156).

33. Halil Inalcik, *Edirne'nin fethi "Edirne" Armağan, Türk Tarih Kurumu Basimevi [The Capture of Adrianople, "Gift to Adrianople," Turkish Historical Association Press]* (Ankara, 1964), pp. 137–159.

34. See Laonicos Chalcocondyles, *Historiarum demonstrationes* (1:52), ed. Eugene Darkó (Budapest, 1922–1927), I, 30. Cf. Babinger, *Beiträge* (20), pp. 46 ff.

35. See Charles Schefer, ed., *Le Voyage d'outremer de Bertrandon de la Broquière* (Paris, 1892), p. 272.

36. Nicephoros Moschopoulos, "Ἡ Ἑλλάς κατά τόν Ἐλβιᾶ Τσελεμπῆ" (1:83), ΕΕΒΣ, XIV (1938), 504.

37. Loenertz, *Démétrius Cydonès* (16), I, 127–128.

38. See Polychronis Enepekides, "Der Briefwechsel des Mystikers Nikolaos Kabasilas" (4:4), BZ, XLVI (1953), 41: "Τό δέ κεφάλαιον οἶσθα, τάς ψήφους, τήν δικαιοσύνην, τούς δικαστάς καί ὅσου πωλοῦνται· σφόδρα δέ ἄρα ὀλίγου [And, in short, you know of the votes, of the 'justice,' and of the judges and what it takes to buy them—indeed it is very little]." Kavasilas was writing in 1363.

39. See Loenertz, *Démétrius Cydonès* (16), I, 30: "εἶτ' ἀπῆγον ἐπί τόν δικαστήν . . . δῆλον δ' ὅτι ἐφ' ἕτερον ἦλθεν ὁ δυστυχής ἐκεῖνος ληστήν [and then they led him away to the judge, and it was obvious that that unfortunate man was coming before another robber]."

40. See Rubió y Lluch, "La Grecia catalana de 1370 a 1377," *Anuari de l'Institut d'estudis catalans*, 1913–1914 (Barcelona, 1914), pp. 47–48.

41. See Raymond Loenertz, "Manuel Paléologue et Démétrius Cydonès; remarques sur leurs correspondances," *Échos d'Orient*, XXXVI (1937), 278, where the relevant bibliography will also be found.

42. *Ibid.*, pp. 476–477. See Loenertz's *Démétrius Cydonès* (16), II, 147–148, 150–152, and I, 175, on the Turkish invasion as far as Thessalonica at the beginning of April, 1372, when Manuel Palaeologus sailed from the city.

43. Taeschner and Wittek, "Die Vezirfamilie" (27), 71 ff.

44. Peter Papageorgiou, "Αἱ Σέρραι καί τά προάστεια, τά περί τάς Σέρρας καί ἡ μονή Ἰωάννου τοῦ Προδρόμου (συμβολή ἱστορική καί ἀρχαιολογική) [Serrai and Its Suburbs and the Monastery of John of Prodromos (an Historic

and Archaeological Contribution]," BZ, III (1894), 292, 294. The Eski Mosque was restored in 1719 and again in 1836.

45. See Taeschner and Wittek, "Die Vezirfamilie" (27), pp. 71 ff. On the date of the capture of Christoupolis, see Raymond Loenertz, "Pour l'histoire du Péloponnèse au XIVᵉ siècle (1352–1404)," REB, I (1944), 167. On the descent of the Turks into Epirus, Aetolia, and Acarnania, see Andreas Moustoxydis, ed., Ἱστορικόν μοναχοῦ Κομνηνοῦ καί Προόκλου (1:51) Ἑλληνομνήμων, I (1843–1853), passim, and on events leading up to the battle of Ankara, see Peter Charanis, "The Strife among the Palaeologi and the Ottoman Turks, 1370–1402," Byzantion, XVI (1942–1943), 287–314; Apostolos Vacalopoulos, "Οἱ δημοσιευμένες ὁμιλίες τοῦ ἀρχιεπισκόπου Θεσσαλονίκης Ἰσιδώρου ὡς ἱστορική πηγή γιά τήν γνώση τῆς πρώτης τουρκοκρατίας στήν Θεσσαλονίκη (1387–1402) [The Published Homilies of Isidorus, Archbishop of Thessalonica, as an Historical Source for Knowledge of the First Turkish Dominion in Thessalonica (1387–1402)]," Μακεδονικά, IV (1960), 31, 32–33; and Loenertz, Démétrius Cydonès (16), II, 121: "νῦν τάς πρός Ἰονίῳ κόλπῳ κατατρέχουσι πόλεις. Ἔναγχός δέ τοσαύτην ἐκ Πελοποννήσου λέγονται λείαν ἐλάσαι [Now (1380–1381) they (the Turks) are persecuting the cities on the Ionian gulf. And recently they are said to have taken just as much booty from the Peloponnese]." On the importance of Eer Baba, the conqueror of Almyros, see Δελτίον τῆς ἐν Ἀλμυρῷ φιλαρχαίου Ἑταιρείας τῆς Ὄρθρυος [A List of Donors to the Museum of Almyros], τεῦχ. 1 (1899), 8 (author unknown). His standard was preserved in the Greek museum of Almyros until 1898.

46. See Arkadios Vatopedinos, "Ἁγιορειτικά ἀνάλεκτα—15—Βασιλική διαταγή πρός Δημήτριον τόν Βουλιωτήν περί Ἁγ. Ὄρους [Monastic Selections, 15—the Royal Mandate to Demetrius Bouliotes concerning the Holy Mountain]," Γρηγόριος ὁ Παλαμᾶς, II (1918), 452.

47. Johann H. Mordtmann, "Die erste Eroberung von Athen durch die Türken zu Ende des 14. Jahrhunderts [The First Conquest of Athens by the Turks at the End of the Fourteenth Century]," BNJ, IV (1924), 346–350, and especially p. 350.

48. Athanasius Petridis, "Χρονικόν Δρυοπίδος [The Chronicle of Dryopis]," Νεοελληνικά ἀνάλεκτα, II (1871), 4–6, 24. On the position of the spahi villages, see p. 32. Most of the villages are noted in the text of the Turkish land register of the district and on the map published by Inalcik, Hicrî 835 tarihli sûret-i defter-i Sancak-i Arvanid (1:56) (Ankara, 1954). For mention of the Turkish invasion of northern Epirus, see the codex of Delvino in Themistocles Bamichas, "Κῶδιξ τοῦ ναοῦ τῆς πόλεως Δελβίνου [The Codex of the Church of the City of Delvino]," HX, V (1930), 58.

49. See Inalcik, Hicrî 835 tarihli sûret-i defter-i (1:56), p. xv; and the article "Arnawutluk" in the Encyclopaedia of Islam I (1960), 651–658.

50. Loenertz, Démétrius Cydonès (16), II, 121.

51. Basileios Laourdas, Ἰσιδώρου ἀρχιεπισκόπου ὁμιλίαι εἰς τάς ἑορτάς τοῦ Ἁγ. Δημητρίου [The Addresses of Archbishop Isidorus on the Holidays of Saint Demetrius] (Thessalonica, 1954), p. 58. Cf. Loenertz, Démétrius Cydonès (16), 116.

52. Franz Miklosich and Joseph Müller, *Acta et diplomata graeca medii aevi sacra et profana* (1:44) (Vienna, 1860–1887), II, 130, 131.

53. Giovanni Mercati, *Notizie di Procoro e Demetrio Cidone, Manuele Caleca e Theodoro Meliteniota ed altri appunti per la storia della theologia e della letteratura bizantina del secolo XIV* (3:79) (Vatican City, 1931), p. 374. I think Kydones refers not to the conquest of new lands, but to the conquest of the soul, by conversion to Islam: "ὅτι καί καθ' ἡμέραν τό πλεῖστον ἐπί τήν ἀσέβειαν ὥσπερ ρεῦμα ἀποχετεύεται [that even daily, for the most part, upon impiety, as a stream is drained]." This interpretation depends upon the phrase "upon impiety."

54. See Ioannis Vasdravellis, " Ἱστορικά περί Ναούσης ἐξ ἀνεκδότου χειρογράφου [Histories on Naousa, from an Unpublished Manuscript]," Μακεδονικά, III (1953–1955), 132–133; and Halil Inalcik, "The Ottoman Record-Books as a Source for Place-Names," *Proceedings and Transactions of the Fifth International Congress of Onomastic Sciences* (Salamanca, 1958), II, p. 7 of the reprint.

55. Loenertz, *Démétrius Cydonès* (16), II, 407: "καί ὡς ἑκάστῳ (τῶν μεγίστων) σπουδή εἰ δύναιτο μόνῳ πάντα καταφαγεῖν καί ὡς εἰ μή τοῦτο λάβοι ἀπειλεῖν πρός τούς πολεμίους αὐτομολήσειν, καί μετ' ἐκείνων τήν τε πατρίδα καί τούς φίλους πολιορκήσειν [and as each (of the greatest ones) was eager to devour everything by himself, and, if he could not get this, to threaten to go over to the enemy and with him assault their fatherland and their friends]."

56. See Spyridon Lambros, "Θεόδωρος ὁ Ποτάμιος καί ἡ εἰς Ἰωάννην τόν Παλαιολόγον μονῳδία αὐτοῦ [Theodoros Potamios and His Monody to Ioannis Palaeologus]," ΔΙΕΕ, II (1885–1886), 58, 59. Cf. Mercati, *Notizie* (3:79), p. 374: "ἡμεῖς δέ ὀλίγοι πάνυ καί ὅσοι λοιπόν μηδ' ἐν προσθήκης μέρει νομίζεσθαι· καί τοῦτο δέ τό μικρόν δουλεύει τήν πασῶν αἰσχίστην καί ἐπιπονωτάτην δουλείαν [And we very few are a remnant not large enough to be considered an adjunct, which, small though it is, labors under the most disgraceful and burdensome slavery of all]" (Kydones' words).

57. Mercati, *Notizie* (3:79), pp. 374–375. On the question of Manuel II's participation in the Turkish expeditions in Asia Minor, see Kydones' letters in Loenertz, *Démétrius Cydonès* (16), II, 386–396, and 407–408. The dating of these letters is, however, in my opinion, incorrect.

58. Ducas, ed. Immanuel Bekker (Bonn, 1834), p. 53 (ed. Basile Grecu [Bucharest, 1958], pp. 81–82). Cf. Spyridon Lambros, Παλαιολόγεια καί Πελοποννησιακά (1:66) (Athens, 1926), III, x–xi, 159. For the bibliography on the duration of the siege, see Babinger, *Beiträge* (20), p. 62, fn. 96. The siege did not, as Mercati says (*Notizie* [3:79], pp. 112–115), last about six years, but rather seven years, as a hitherto unexamined source observes (Johann Schiltberger, *The Bondage and Travels of Johann Schiltberger, a Native of Bavaria, in Europe, Asia, and Africa, 1396–1427*, tr. Commander J. Buchan Telfer [London, 1879], p. 80). Although the patriarchal document on which Mercati bases his assertion speaks of a six years' siege, it does not say that the siege was not continuous and in fact ended. Even shortly before

the Battle of Varna (1396) the Turks had already turned against Galata, though little success attended their efforts (Braun, *Lebensbeschreibung* [25], p. 94). Taking Schiltberger's statement as correct, we may roughly place the beginning of the siege in 1394, which is the date generally accepted. Cf. George Ostrogorsky, *History of the Byzantine State*, 2nd ed. (New Brunswick, N.J., 1969), pp. 549–550; and John Barker, *Manuel II Palaeologus (1391–1425); A Study in Late Byzantine Statesmanship* (New Brunswick, N.J., 1969), app. 10, pp. 479–481.

59. Clavijo, *A Diary* (3), pp. 88, 90.

60. Raymond Loenertz, *Correspondance de Manuel Calecas* (Rome, 1950), *passim*, but especially pp. 264–265. Other inhabitants of Constantinople and Thessalonica fled at a later time (Neculai Iorga, *Notes et extraits pour servir à l'histoire des Croisades au XVe siècle* [*Observations and Extracts Pertaining to the History of the Crusades in the Fifteenth Century*], vol. I, series 1 [Paris, 1899], pp. 240, 258–259).

61. Loenertz, *Démétrius Cydonès* (16), II, 364.

62. Manoussos Manoussacas, " Ἡ διαθήκη τοῦ Ἀγγέλου Ἀκοτάντου (1436), ἀγνώστου Κρητικοῦ ζωγράφου [The Testament of Angelos Akotantos (1436), an Unknown Cretan Painter]," ΔΧΑΕ, IV, 2 (1960), 139; contains also a bibliography on the arrival in Crete of Constantinopolitan painters at the end of the fourteenth century and the beginning of the fifteenth century.

63. Silvio Mercati, "Di Giovanni Simeonakis, protopapa di Candia [On Giovanni Simeonakis, Protopope of Candia]," *Miscellanea Giovanni Mercati*, III (1946), 312–341. Cf. Basileios Laourdas, "Κρητικά παλαιογραφικά [Cretan Palaeographs]," KX, II (1948), 539–543. Laourdas' article contains the relevant bibliography.

64. See Vojislav Djurić, "Solunsko poreklo Resavskog živopisa [The Thessalonian Origin of the Frescoes of the Monastery of Resava]," *Zbornik Radova*, Vizantološkog Instituta (Belgrade, 1960), LXV, no. 6, 111–128.

65. Djordje Radojičić, "Drei Byzantiner, alt-serbische Schriftsteller des 15. Jahrhunderts [Three Byzantines—Early Serbian Authors of the Fifteenth Century]," XIe Congrès international des études byzantines, Munich, 1958, *Akten* (Munich, 1960), pp. 504–507. See also the study by the same author, "Un Byzantin, écrivain serbe: Démétrius Cantacuzène," *Byzantion*, XXIX–XXX (1959–1960), 77–87.

66. See Demostene Russo, *Studii istorice greco-române* [*Greco-Roman Historical Studies*] (Bucharest, 1939), II, 489–521, especially pp. 518–521. Cf. Emanuel Turczyński, *Die deutsch-griechische Kulturbeziehungen bis zur Berufung König Ottos* [*Greco-German Cultural Relations up to the Appointment of King Otto*] (Munich, 1959), p. 31, which contains the relevant bibliography.

67. Ioannis K. Voyatzidis deals with this subject extensively in his "Γλῶσσα καί λαογραφία τῆς νήσου Ἄνδρου" (1:88), ΑΧ, IV (1949), 51–56.

68. Phaidon Koukoules, Οἰνουντιακά [*On Oinous*] (Canea, 1908), pp. 50–51, 72–73.

69. Lambros, Παλαιολόγεια καί Πελοποννησιακά (1:66), III, 40–41. Therefore, they were not all Albanians, as Ioannis K. Poulos believes ('Η ἐποίκησις τῶν 'Αλβανῶν εἰς Κορινθίαν [1:42], ΕΜΑ, III [1950], 62).

70. See Rubió y Lluch, "Els Governs" (6), pp. 35–36.

71. See the laudatory characterization by Demetrius Kydones in Loenertz, *Démétrius Cydonès* (16), II, 117.

72. They are accurately characterized in John Cantacuzenus, *Historiarum libri IV* (1:47), ed. Ludwig Schopen (Bonn, 1828–1832), III, 86–87. Cf. Kydones' letter to George the philosopher in Loenertz, *Démétrius Cydonès* (16), I, 63. In a letter to Kydones George entered a plea in behalf of the known δυνατός [magnate] of Monemvasia, and in another he gave a description of τήν τῶν Κυκλώπων ἀγοράν [the market of the Cyclopes] which undoubtedly referred to the unreasonable δυνατοί of the Peloponnese.

73. See William Miller, *The Latins in the Levant: A History of Frankish Greece (1204–1566)* (New York–Cambridge, Eng., 1964), pp. 379–384. Denis Zakythinos, *Le Despotat grec de Morée* (Athens, 1953), I, 94–118; Spyridon Lambros, "Λακεδαιμόνιοι βιβλιογράφοι καί κτήτορες κωδίκων κατά τούς μέσους αἰῶνας καί ἐπί τουρκοκρατίας [Lacedemonian Bibliographers and Book Owners in the Middle Ages and under Turkish Rule]," NE, IV (1907), 160–187, 303–312; and François Masai, *Pléthon et le Platonisme de Mistra* (Paris, 1956), p. 49. Kydones made some flattering remarks about John VI Cantacuzenus and his sons (see Loenertz, *Démétrius Cydonès* [16], I, 31–32: "οὐρανομήκης στήλη οὐκ ἐν Πελοποννήσῳ κατ' 'Ιφικράτην [A sky-high pillar not in the Peloponnese as Iphicrates said]." See Alexandre Oleroff, "Démétrius Trivolis, copiste et bibliophile," *Scriptorium*, IV (1950), 261–262.

74. Loenertz, *Démétrius Cydonès* (16), I, 26.

75. Joseph Bryennios, Τά παραλειπόμενα (2:22), ed. Thomas Mandakasis (Leipzig, 1784), III, 116. Cf. p. 117.

76. See Loenertz, *Démétrius Cydonès* (16), I, 175; and Braun, *Lebensbeschreibung* (10), p. 20.

77. Clavijo, *A Diary* (3), p. 49.

78. Vatopedinos, " 'Αγιορειτικά ἀνάλεκτα" (46), pp. 449–452.

79. See Apostolos Vacalopoulos, " 'Ο ἀρχιεπίσκοπος Γαβριήλ καί ἡ πρώτη τουρκική κατοχή τῆς Θεσσαλονίκης [The Archbishop Gabriel and the First Turkish Occupation of Thessalonica]," Μακεδονικά, IV (1960), 371–373.

80. See Bryennios, Τά παραλειπόμενα (2:22), III, 179–180; Nikolaos Tomadakis, 'Ο 'Ιωσήφ Βρυέννιος καί ἡ Κρήτη κατά τό 1400 (3:85) (Athens, 1947), pp. 129–130; and Lambros, Παλαιολόγεια καί Πελοποννησιακά (1:66), III, 163–164.

81. On Thessalonica, see Basileios Laourdas, "Τό ἐγκώμιον τοῦ Δημητρίου Χρυσολωρᾶ εἰς τόν 'Αγ. Δημήτριον [The Encomium of Demetrius Chrysoloras on Saint Demetrius]," Γρηγόριος ὁ Παλαμᾶς, XL (1957), 349. Cf. pp. 351–352.

82. Joseph Bryennios, Τά εὑρεθέντα [*Works Found*] (Leipzig, 1768), II, 280.

Chapter 7

1. Max Treu, *Matthaios, Metropolit von Ephesos; Ueber sein Leben und seine Schriften* (5:38) (Potsdam, 1901), p. 56, and, for this sort of prayer, pp. 51–52.

2. Constantine I. Dyovouniotis, "Γρηγορίου Παλαμᾶ ἐπιστολή πρός Θεσσαλονικεῖς" (5:35), ΝΕ, xvi (1922), 8. See also Spyridon Lambros, " 'Ισιδώρου Μητροπολίτου Θεσσαλονίκης ὀκτώ ἐπιστολαί ἀνέκδοτοι [Eight Unpublished Letters of Isidorus, Metropolite of Thessalonica]," ΝΕ, ix (1912), 349–350, 382 ff.; and Basileios Laourdas, 'Ισιδώρου ἀρχιεπισκόπου ὁμιλίαι εἰς τάς ἑορτάς τοῦ 'Αγ. Δημητρίου (6:51) (Thessalonica, 1954), pp. 56–57.

3. Joseph Bryennios, Τά εὐρεθέντα (6:82) (Leipzig, 1768), ii, 245–246. Cf. Lambros, " 'Ισιδώρου" (2), pp. 413–414.

4. August Heisenberg, "Kaiser Johannes Batatzes der Barmherzige; eine mittelgriechische Legende" (3:49), BZ, xiv (1905), 199.

5. Bryennios, Τά εὐρεθέντα (6:82), ii, 246. Cf. iii, 122–123.

6. See Cardinal Bessarion, 'Επιστολή καθολική, PG, clxi, col. 460.

7. Bryennios, Τά εὐρεθέντα (6:82), iii, 120, 122. Cf. the patriarchal advice to the clergy of Crete in Franz Miklosich and Joseph Müller, *Acta et diplomata graeca medii aevi sacra et profana* (1:43) (Vienna, 1860–1887), ii, 477–481.

8. Laourdas, 'Ισιδώρου ἀρχιεπισκόπου ὁμιλίαι (6:51), pp. 35 ff.

9. See Nikolaos Tomadakis, "Μελετήματα περί 'Ιωσήφ Βρυεννίου [Studies on Joseph Bryennios]," ΕΕΒΣ, xxix (1959), 1–12.

10. Bryennios, Τά εὐρεθέντα (6:82), iii, 107–108. See also p. 120.

11. Johann Schiltberger, *The Bondage and Travels of Johann Schiltberger, a Native of Bavaria, in Europe, Asia, and Africa, 1396–1427*, tr. Commander J. Buchan Telfer (London, 1879), p. 83.

12. Bryennios, Τά εὐρεθέντα (6:82), ii, 252–253, 266. Cf. ii, 256, 259, and iii, 108–109.

13. Nikolaos Tomadakis, 'Ο 'Ιωσήφ Βρυέννιος καί ἡ Κρήτη κατά τό 1400 (3:85) (Athens, 1947), p. 28.

14. Bryennios, Τά εὐρεθέντα (6:82), ii, 103.

15. Dyovouniotis, "Γρηγορίου Παλαμᾶ" (2), p. 11. See also Basilike Papoulia, *Ursprung und Wesen der "Knabenlese" im osmanischen Reiche* (6:28) (Munich, 1963), pp. 102 ff.

16. See Basileios Laourdas, "Γαβριήλ Θεσσαλονίκης ὁμιλίαι [The Homilies of Gabriel of Thessalonica]," 'Αθηνᾶ, lvii (1953), 165. Cf. Dyovouniotis, "Γρηγορίου Παλαμᾶ" (2), pp. 10, 17.

17. George Gemistos, Πρός τό ὑπέρ τοῦ λατινικοῦ δόγματος βιβλίον [On the Book concerning the Latin Doctrine], PG, clx, col. 980.

18. Laourdas, "Γαβριήλ" (16), pp. 164–165, 169–170. Even though destitute and miserable by the end of the fourteenth century, the poor were still clearly distinguishable from the slaves.

19. Bryennios, Τά εὐρεθέντα (6:82), ii, 103–104. For Demetrius Chrysoloras' invocations to Saint Demetrius, see Basileios Laourdas, "Τό ἐγκώμιον

τοῦ Δημητρίου Χρυσολωρᾶ εἰς τόν "Άγιον Δημήτριον" (6:81), Γρηγόριος ὁ
Παλαμᾶς, xl (1957), 350–351, where Chrysoloras is brief but impressive.
Cf. Ioannis Anagnostes, Διήγησις περί τῆς τελευταίας ἁλώσεως τῆς Θεσσα-
λονίκης [Account of the Last Capture of Thessalonica], ed. Immanuel Bekker
(Bonn, 1838), pp. 526–527.

20. Lambros, "Ἰσιδώρου" (2), pp. 35 ff.

21. See Ioannis K. Voyatzidis, Ἱστορικαί μελέται (3:5), ΕΕΦΣΠΘ, ιι
(1932), 149.

22. Most of the Greek population of the city stayed, even most of the
stratiotai (see the Chronicle of Aşik paşa Zade, tr. Richard Kreutel [Vienna,
1959], p. 68).

23. Miklosich and Müller, Acta et diplomata (1:44), ι, 183–184, 197–198.

24. Ibid., ιι, 87, for the letter of Patriarch Neilos to Pope Urban VI, written in September 1384. Cf. Spyridon Lambros, "Ὑπόμνημα περί τῶν ἑλληνικῶν χωρῶν καί ἐκκλησιῶν κατά τόν 15 αἰῶνα [Notes on Greek Regions and
Churches in the Fifteenth Century]," NE, vιι (1910), 362.

25. See Treu, Matthaios (1), p. 57.

26. Regarding this monastery, see Tryphon Evangelidis, "Ἡ μονή τῶν
Σωσάνδρων [The Monastery of Sosandroi]," Ξενοφάνης, ι (1896), 474–478.

27. Heisenberg, "Kaiser Johannes Batatzes" (2:49), p. 178. In Magnesia
on the right aisle of Saint Athanasius' (the archepiscopal seat) there existed
until 1922 a small chapel of Saint John Vatatzes (Olga Vatidou, Ἡ χριστιανι-
κότητα τῶν Τούρκων καί οἱ Έλληνες τῆς Μικρασίας [The Attitude of the
Turks towards Christianity and the Greeks of Asia Minor] (Athens, 1956),
p. 39).

28. See Heisenberg, "Kaiser Johannes Batatzes" (2:49), pp. 161–162, 167,
192. The king's remains are in the monastery (p. 171).

29. On these eschatological ideas before 1204 and after 1453, see Alexander
Vasiliev, "Medieval Ideas of the End of the World: West and East," Byzantion,
xvι (1942–1943), 462 ff.

30. Parisinus Graecus 2661, of the year 1365, folios 208–209, contains "the
most holy Andritzopoulos' prediction to Michael Zorianos . . . about the Antichrist and the overthrow of the Byzantine state." Cf. George Sotiriadis,
"Βυζαντιναί ἐπιγραφαί ἐξ Αἰτωλίας [Byzantine Inscriptions from Aetolia],"
Ἐπετηρίς Παρνασσοῦ, vιι (1903), 213–215. These persons were alive at the
end of the thirteenth century and the beginning of the fourteenth century
(Spyridon Lambros, "Πρόχειρον σημείωμα περί Μιχαήλ Ζωριανοῦ [Extem-
poraneous Note on Michael Zorianos]," Ἐπετηρίς Παρνασσοῦ, vιι [1903],
221).

31. Bryennios, Τά εὑρεθέντα (6:82), ιι, 47, 103–104, 109–111, and ιιι,
153, 154.

32. St. Paul, I Thessalonians 5:8: "νήφωμεν ἐνδυσάμενοι θώρακα πίστεως
καί ἀγάπης καί περικεφαλαίαν ἐλπίδα σωτηρίας [let us be sober and put on
the breastplate of faith and love and for a helmet the hope of salvation]."

33. Laourdas, "Γαβριήλ" (16), p. 148.

34. See Lambros, " Ἰσιδώρου" (2), p. 388.

35. Louis Petit, Xenophon A. Siderides, and Martin Jugie, Γεωργίου Σχολαρίου ἅπαντα [The Complete Works of George Scholarios] (Paris, 1930), III, 290.

36. Lambros, " Ἰσιδώρου" (2), p. 391.

37. Demetrius Kydones, Ῥωμαίοις συμβουλευτικός (5:49), PG, CLIV, col. 968.

38. See above, pp. 89–90, for an analysis of the epistles of Patriarch John XIV Calecas. See also Lambros, " Ἰσιδώρου" (2), pp. 390–391; and Matthew Kamariotes, Θρῆνος [Lamentation], PG, CLX, col. 1061.

39. See Chrysostomos Papadopoulos, Οἱ νεομάρτυρες [The New Martyrs], 2nd ed. (Athens, 1934), 6 ff.; and Constantine Amantos, Σχέσεις Ἑλλήνων καί Τούρκων ἀπό τοῦ ἐνδεκάτου αἰῶνος μέχρι τοῦ 1821, vol. I: Οἱ πόλεμοι τῶν Τούρκων πρός κατάληψιν τῶν ἑλληνικῶν χωρῶν, 1071–1571 [The Relations of the Greeks and the Turks from the Eleventh Century to 1821, vol. I: The Wars of the Turks for the Conquest of the Greek Areas, 1071–1571] (Athens, 1955), 190–193.

40. Cf. Bryennios, Τά εὑρεθέντα (6:82), III, 149.

41. The Virgin of Edessa, who was betrayed by her father, Kell Petros (i.e., "Scald-headed Peter"), after the Turks captured her country, and who then suffered martyrdom, has for this reason been most properly classified as a modern Martyr (see Dionysios, Metropolite of Edessa and Pella, Ἀκολουθία τῆς Ἁγίας ἐνδόξου νεομάρτυρος Παρθένας τῆς Ἐδεσσαίας [The Office of the Famous Saint and New Martyr, the Virgin of Edessa] [Athens, 1958]). Her biography and the historical records pertaining to her life have yet to be studied in a scholarly fashion.

42. Spyridon Lambros, "Συμβολαί εἰς τήν ἱστορίαν τῶν Μετεώρων [Contributions to the History of Meteora]," NE, II (1905), 143.

43. See Papadopoulos, Οἱ νεομάρτυρες (39), pp. 6 ff., which contains also the relevant bibliography. For a more complete bibliography, see Constantine Amantos, "Νεομάρτυρες [The New Martyrs]," ΕΕΦΣΠΑ, II, 4 (1953–1954), 162.

44. Lambros, " Ὑπόμνημα" (24), 366.

45. See Laourdas, "Γαβριήλ" (16), p. 206; Joseph Bryennios, Τά παραλειπόμενα (2:22), ed. Thomas Mandakasis (Leipzig, 1784), III, 152; and the patriarchal letter of 1387 to Bishop Myron, Miklosich and Müller, Acta et diplomata (1:43), II, 95.

46. Cardinal Bessarion, Ἐπιστολή καθολική (6), PG, CLXI, col. 460.

47. The relevant texts are in Constantine Kyriazis, "Τό δίκαιον τῆς ἀντιστάσεως ἐξ ἐπόψεως ὀρθοδόξου [The Justice of the Opposition from the Orthodox Point of View]," ΕΕΘΣΠΘ, IV (1959), 160 ff. Kyriazis eschews an examination of the specific historical problem of the attitude of the Church towards the Turks—such as I have attempted here—in favor of a more theoretical treatment.

48. Lambros, " Ἰσιδώρου" (2), p. 390. See also Ioannis Anagnostes, Διήγησις (19), p. 497.

49. Raymond Loenertz, *Démétrius Cydonès, correspondance* (Vatican City, 1956), II, 254, and 249 on similar ideas in Constantinople.

50. See Lambros, "Ἰσιδώρου" (2), pp. 389, 390.

51. See the brilliant study by John Hackett, *A History of the Orthodox Church of Cyprus from the Coming of the Apostles Paul and Barnabas to the Commencement of the British Occupation* (A.D. 45–A.D. 1878) *together with Some Account of the Latin and Other Churches Existing in the Island* (London, 1901), pp. 74–149; and Sir George Francis Hill, *A History of Cyprus* (Cambridge, Eng., 1948), III, 1041–1088.

52. See Stephanos Xanthoudidis, Ἡ ἐνετοκρατία ἐν Κρήτῃ καί οἱ κατά τῶν Ἐνετῶν ἀγῶνες τῶν Κρητῶν (3:48) (Athens, 1939), p. 19.

53. See Nikolaos Tomadakis, "Ὀρθόδοξοι ἀρχιερεῖς ἐν Κρήτῃ ἐπί ἐνετοκρατίας [Orthodox Prelates in Crete under the Venetian Rule]," Ὀρθοδοξία, XXVII (1952), 63–65, which contains the relevant bibliography; and the same author's Ὁ Ἰωσήφ Βρυέννιος (3:85), 83 ff.

54. See Constantine I. Dyovouniotis, "Ὁ Ἀθηνῶν Ἄνθιμος καί Πρόεδρος Κρήτης ὁ Ὁμολογητής [Anthimos of Athens, the Confessor, and President of Crete]," ΕΕΒΣ, IX (1932), 47–79.

55. See Tomadakis, Ὁ Ἰωσήφ Βρυέννιος (3:85), pp. 106 ff.; and Raymond Loenertz, *Correspondance de Manuel Calecas* (Rome, 1950), pp. 99–100.

56. See Georg Hofmann, "Nuove Fonti per la storia profana ed ecclesiastica di Creta nella prima metà del secolo XV [New Sources for the History, Secular and Ecclesiastic, of Crete in the First Half of the Fifteenth Century]," IXth International Congress of Byzantine Studies, Thessalonica, 1953, Πεπραγμένα, II (Athens, 1956), 465 ff.; and Nikolaos Tomadakis, "Οἱ ὀρθοδόξοι παπάδες ἐπί ἐνετοκρατίας καί ἡ χειροτονία αὐτῶν [The Orthodox Priests under Venetian Rule and Their Ordination]," KX, XIII (1959), 46 ff., 61 ff.

57. For typical convictions in 1418 and 1419, see Manoussos Manoussacas, "Μέτρα τῆς Βενετίας ἔναντι τῆς ἐν Κρήτῃ ἐπιρροῆς τοῦ πατριαρχείου Κωνσταντινουπόλεως κατ' ἀνέκδοτα βενετικά ἔγγραφα (1418–1419) [Venetian Measures against the Influence in Crete of the Patriarchate of Constantinople, according to Unpublished Venetian Documents (1418–1419)]," ΕΕΒΣ, XXX (1960), 85–144.

58. Manoussos Manoussacas, "Βενετικά ἔγγραφα ἀναφερόμενα εἰς τήν ἐκκλησιαστικήν ἱστορίαν τῆς Κρήτης τοῦ 14–16 αἰῶνος (Πρωτοπαπάδες καί πρωτοψάλται Χάνδακος) [Venetian Documents Relating to the Ecclesiastical History of Crete from the Fourteenth to the Sixteenth Century (the Chief Priests and Choir Leaders of Chandax)]," ΔΙΕΕ, XV (1961), 154–160.

59. Constantine Kalokyris, Αἱ Βυζαντιναί τοιχογραφίαι τῆς Κρήτης [The Byzantine Frescoes of Crete] (Athens, 1957), pp. 181, 184–185.

60. See Freddy Thiriet, *La Romanie vénitienne au moyen âge* (Paris, 1959), 289–290; and Freddy Thiriet and Peter Wirth, "La Politique religieuse de Venise à Negrepont à la fin du XIVe siècle [The Religious Policy of Venice in Euboea at the End of the Fourteenth Century]," BZ, LVI (1963), 297–303.

61. Thiriet, *La Romanie* (60), p. 405.

62. Antonio Rubió y Lluch, "Els Governs de Matheu de Moncada y Roger de Lluria en la Grecia catalana (1359–1370)," *Anuari de l'Institut d'Estudis Catalans* (Barcelona, 1901, 1912), pp. 33–34. See also his "La Grecia catalana de 1370 á 1377," *Anuari de l'Institut d'estudis catalans, 1913–1914* (Barcelona, 1914), pp. 44, 45; and William Miller, *The Latins in the Levant: A History of Frankish Greece (1204–1566)* (New York–Cambridge, Eng., 1964), p. 242.

63. For details on converts to Rome, see Georg Hofmann, "Wie stand es mit der Frage der Kircheneinheit auf Kreta im XV. Jahrhundert? [What Was the State of the Question of Church Unity in Crete in the Fifteenth Century?]," OCP, x (1944), 93, 111, 112, and pp. 102–104 for the condition of the clergy.

64. Loenertz, *Correspondance de Manuel Calecas* (55), pp. 62–63; and "Pour la chronologie des oeuvres de J. Bryennios," REB, vii (1949), 21, fns. 21–22, where Loenertz notes that in 1398 M. Chrysoberges obtained permission to found a Dominican monastery in Crete.

65. See the resolution of the Venetian Senate on May 18, 1425: "Cum in terris et partibus nostris Levantis fides catholica multum diminuatur, et schismatici de die in diem multiplicentur [Since in the land and in our parts of the Levant the Catholic faith is much diminished, and schismatics increase from day to day]." (Hofmann, "Wie stand" [63], p. 103.)

66. See Loenertz, *Démétrius Cydonès* (49), i, 19, for Kydones' letter to John V Palaeologus in the autumn of 1371.

67. Cf., for example, the letter of T. Gazes to his brothers George and Demetrius, written about two years before the capture, Spyridon Lambros, Παλαιολόγεια καί Πελοποννησιακά (1:66) (Athens, 1926), iv, 46 ff.

68. See Loenertz, *Démétrius Cydonès* (49), i, *passim*.

69. The letter will be found in Bryennios, Τά παραλειπόμενα (2:22), iii, 133–135. Cf. Loenertz, "Pour la chronologie" (64), 15–16; and Tomadakis, "Μελετήματα" (9), pp. 20 ff.

70. See Giovanni Mercati, *Notizie di Procoro e Demetrio Cidone, Manuele Caleca e Theodoro Meliteniota ed altri appunti per la storia della teologia e della letteratura bizantina del secolo XIV* (6:53) (Vatican City, 1931), pp. 365–366, 367, 370–371, 372, 374. Kydones' work has been translated by Hans-Georg Beck into German, "Die 'Apologia pro vita sua' des Demetrios Kydones," *Ostkirchliche Studien*, i (1952), 208–225, 264–282. Cf. the opinions of Sir John Maundeville in *The Voiage and Travaile of Sir John Maundeville, Which Treateth of the Way to Hierusalem* (London, 1887), pp. 18–19.

71. For some interesting comments on the ideological standpoint of Demetrius Cydones, Manuel Calecas, and others in relation to this matter, see Mercati, *Notizie* (6:53), *passim*.

72. See Raymond Loenertz, "Les Dominicains byzantins Théodore et André Chrysobergès et les negotiations pour l'union des églises grecque et latine de 1415 à 1430," *Archivum fratrum praedicatorum*, ix (1939), 5–60.

73. See Tomadakis, 'Ο 'Ιωσήφ Βρυέννιος (3:85), pp. 96, 103, 105; and Loenertz, *Démétrius Cydonès* (49), i, 22, 23. Elsewhere Kydones expresses the opinion that Roman domination also must eventually come to an end

(Giuseppe Cammelli, "Demetrii Cydonii orationes tres, adhuc ineditae" (4:57), BNJ, III, 1922, 70).

74. Bryennios, Τά παραλειπόμενα (2:22), III, 118, 150, 153, 154, and Τά εὐρεθέντα (6:82), I, 453.

75. Gemistos, Πρός τό ὑπέρ τοῦ λατινικοῦ δόγματος βιβλίον (17), col. 980.

76. See Loenertz, Démétrius Cydonès (49), I, 164–168.

77. Christopher Buondelmonti, Description des îles de l'Archipel. Version grecque par un anonyme, publiée d'après le manuscrit du sérail, avec une traduction française et un commentaire par Émile Legrand (6:8), première partie (Paris, 1897), p. 89.

78. Bertrandon de la Brocquière, Voyage d'outremer et retour de Jérusalem en France par la voie de terre, pendant le cours des années 1432 et 1433, ed. Pierre Legrand D'Aussy, in Mémoires de l'Institut national des sciences et arts; sciences morales et politiques, V (Paris, fructidor an XII), p. 554.

79. Loenertz, Correspondance de Manuel Calecas (55), pp. 232–233, 314 ff. Cf. George T. Dennis, The Reign of Manuel II Palaeologus in Thessalonica, 1382–1387 (Rome, 1960), p. 36, where he refers to Pope Gregory XI's complaints to John V over the punishment of proselytes to Catholicism.

80. See Laourdas, "Τό ἐγκώμιον" (6:81), p. 349.

81. See M. Şesan, "La Chute de Constantinople et les peuples orthodoxes [The Fall of Constantinople and the Orthodox Peoples]," Byzantinoslavica, XIV (1953), 272–274.

82. See Guillebert de Lannoy, Gilbert de Lannoy i jego Podróże przez Joachima Lelewela [Gilbert de Lannoy and His Travels, according to J. Lelewel] (Brussels-Poznan, 1844), I, 82.

83. See Kydones, Ρωμαίοις συμβουλευτικός (5:49), col. 1221; and Loenertz, Correspondance de Manuel Calecas (55), p. 81.

84. See Bryennios, Τά εὐρεθέντα (6:82), II, 16.

Chapter 8

1. George Acropolitis, Opera, ed. August Heisenberg (Leipzig, 1903), I, 28.

2. See Neculai Iorga, France de Chypre [The France of Cyprus] (Paris, 1931), pp. 181, 195 ff.; Leontios Machairas, Χρονικόν Κύπρου [A Chronicle of Cyprus], ed. Richard Dawkins (under the title Recital concerning the Sweet Land of Cyprus Entitled 'Chronicle') (Oxford, 1932), I, 672–674; and Constantine Spyridakis, "Ὁ χαρακτήρ τῆς Κυπριακῆς ἐπαναστάσεως τοῦ 1426 καί ὁ Λεόντιος Μαχαιρᾶς [The Nature of the Cypriote Uprising of 1426 and Leontios Machairas]," Εἰς μνήμην Ἀμάντου (Athens, 1960), pp. 71–75.

3. Raymond Loenertz, Démétrius Cydonès, correspondance (Vatican City, 1956), II, 157.

4. Raymond Loenertz, "Pour l'histoire du Peloponnese," REB, I (1944), 152–181. For details, see George T. Dennis, The Reign of Manuel II Palaeologus in Thessalonica, 1382–1387 (Rome, 1960), pp. 114 ff.

5. See Georgius Phrantzes, Χρονικόν (6:15), ed. Immanuel Bekker (Bonn, 1838), pp. 63–64; Laonicos Chalcocondyles, Historiarum demonstrationes

(1:52), ed. Eugene Darkó (Budapest, 1922–1927), ι, 91–92; and Denis Zakythinos, *Le despotat grec de Morée* (Athens, 1953), ι, 158–160.

6. See Stephanos Xanthoudidis, Ἡ ἐνετοκρατία ἐν Κρήτῃ καί οἱ κατά τῶν Ἐνετῶν ἀγῶνες τῶν Κρητῶν (3:48) (Athens, 1939), pp. 37 ff.; and Nikolaos Zoudianos, Ἱστορία τῆς Κρήτης ἐπί ἐνετοκρατίας [*History of Crete under Venetian Rule*] (Athens, 1960), ι, 60 ff.

7. See Agathangelos Xerouchakis, Ἡ ἐν Κρήτῃ ἐπανάστασις τοῦ 1363–1366 [The Cretan Uprising of 1363–1366] (Alexandria, 1932), pp. 29–30. Compare Zoudianos, Ἱστορία (6), ι, 176–189; and Xanthoudidis Ἡ ἐνετοκρατία (3:48), pp. 81 ff., 99–110.

8. The Cretans' will to be free is also demonstrated by the conspiracy of Rethemniot Sephes Vlastos some one hundred years later (1453–1454), that is, at the time of the fall of Constantinople. See the special study by Manoussos Manoussacas, Ἡ ἐν Κρήτῃ συνωμοσία τοῦ Σήφη Βλαστοῦ (1453–1454) καί ἡ νέα συνωμοτική κίνησις τοῦ 1460–1462 [*The Conspiracy in Crete of Sephes Vlastos (1453–1454) and the New Conspiratorical Movement of 1460–1462*] (Athens, 1960).

9. Ducas, ed. Immanuel Bekker (Bonn, 1834), p. 185 (ed. Basile Grecu [Bucharest, 1958], p. 233).

10. See Constantine Kalokyris, Αἱ Βυζαντιναί τοιχογραφίαι τῆς Κρήτης (7:59) (Athens, 1957), pp. 184, 191–192.

11. The relevant material is on pp. 048 ff. of the appendix to the documents in Vladimir Lamansky's *Secrets d'État de Venise; documents, extraits, notices et études servant à éclaircir les rapports de la Seigneurie avec les Grecs, les Slaves et la Porte Ottomane à la fin du XVᵉ et au XVIᵉ siècles* (St. Petersburg, 1884). See pp. 055–056 for the document of the Council of Ten in 1487 which characterizes the Orthodox priests as follows: "papates non catholici, quos semper recognovimus primos auctores et compulsores et fautores contra statum nostrum [non-Catholic priests, whom we always acknowledge as the first authors, movers, and promoters against our state]."

12. See Freddy Thiriet, *La Romanie vénitienne au moyen âge* (Paris, 1959), pp. 395–398, 399–401.

13. See Aimilia Sarou, Τό Κάστρον τῆς Χίου [*The Fortress of Chios*] (Athens, 1916), pp. 59–68; George Zolotas, Ἱστορία τῆς Χίου [History of Chios] (Athens, 1924), ιι, 484–495; and Philip Argentis, *The Occupation of Chios by the Genoese and Their Administration of the Island, 1346–1566* (Cambridge, Eng., 1958), ι, 651–658.

14. Antonio Rubió y Lluch, "Els Governs de Matheu de Moncada y Roger de Lluria en la Grecia catalana (1359–1370)," *Anuari de l'Institut d'estudis catalans* (Barcelona, 1901, 1912), pp. 48–49.

15. For some interesting details on the Greek presence and influence during the period of Catalan domination, see Rubió y Lluch, "La Poblaciò dels Ducats de Grecia" (1:44), *Institut d'estudis catalans* (*Mémoires de la seccio histórico-arqueológica*), ιν (Barcelona, 1933), 25 ff.

16. William Miller, *The Latins in the Levant: A History of Frankish Greece (1204–1566)* (New York–Cambridge, Eng.), p. 240.

17. Rubió y Lluch, "La Poblaciò" (1:44), pp. 11–12, 26.

18. See Kenneth Setton, *Catalan Domination of Athens, 1311–1388* (Cambridge, Mass., 1948), p. 251: "Without having acquired a patent of freedom and Frankish status." The cruel treatment of the Greeks by the conquerors is revealed in a number of popular adages which are still extant among the people of Thrace, Euboea, Thessaly, Acarnania, Athens, and the Peloponnese (pp. 247–248).

19. See Ferdinand Gregorovius, *Geschichte der Stadt Athen im Mittelalter, von der Zeit Justinians bis zur türkischen Eroberung* (2:2) (Stuttgart, 1889), Greek tr. by Spyridon Lambros (1904–1906), iii, 399. Cf. Miller, *The Latins in the Levant* (16), pp. 229–230.

20. Antonio Rubió y Lluch, "La Grecia catalana de 1370 á 1377," *Anuari de l'Institut d'Estudis Catalans,* 1913–1914 (Barcelona, 1914), pp. 24–25.

21. Rubió y Lluch, "La Poblaciò" (1:44), p. 27.

22. Rubió y Lluch, "La Grecia catalana" (20), p. 41.

23. Rubió y Lluch, "La Poblaciò" (1:44), p. 27.

24. Rubió y Lluch, "Els Governs" (14), pp. 48–49; see also his "Chanceliers et notaires dans la Grèce catalane," in Εἰς μνήμην Λάμπρου (Athens, 1935), pp. 153–154. Regarding the services and remuneration of Demetrius Rentis, see Rubió y Lluch, "La Poblaciò" (1:44), pp. 37–38; and his "Atenes en temps dels Catalans," *Anuari de l'Institut d'estudis catalans,* i (Barcelona, 1907), 14–15.

25. See Rubió y Lluch, "La Poblaciò" (1:44), p. 27. Rubió y Lluch mentions two different persons, Demetrius and Metros, but it is likely that they were in fact one and the same person. Cf. Miller, *The Latins in the Levant* (16), p. 240.

26. Rubió y Lluch, "La Poblaciò" (1:44), pp. 25–27, 29–30. See Miller, *The Latins in the Levant* (16), p. 240.

27. Franz Miklosich and Joseph Müller, *Acta et diplomata graeca medii aevi sacra et profana* (1:43) (Vienna, 1860–1887), i, 483–484, 564. See Tassos Neroutsos, "Χριστιανικαί 'Αθῆναι" (3:7), ΔΙΕΕ, iv (1892–1895), 198–199.

28. See Miller, *The Latins in the Levant* (16), pp. 311–330; and Dennis, *The Reign of Manuel II* (4), pp. 119 ff.

29. Rubió y Lluch, "La Poblaciò" (1:44), p. 32.

30. See Antonio Rubió y Lluch, "Περί τῆς ἐποχῆς καθ' ἥν οἱ Καταλάνοι ἀπώλεσαν τάς 'Αθήνας [On the Period in Which the Catalans Lost Athens]," ΔΙΕΕ, iv (1892–1895), 540.

31. See Rubió y Lluch, "La Poblaciò" (1:44), p. 29; and Setton, *Catalan Domination* (18), p. 85.

32. Miller, *The Latins in the Levant* (16), p. 238.

33. See Setton, *Catalan Domination* (18), pp. 17, 187–188, 200, 257. On Athens during the Catalan period, see also Rubió y Lluch, "Atenes en temps dels Catalans" (24). Compare the note on the Parthenon as a church of the Virgin Mary in Antonio Rubió y Lluch, *La Acrópolis de Atenas en la época catalana* (Barcelona, 1908), p. 27. On Athens and the Acropolis generally

during the period of Catalan domination, see Rubió y Lluch, "La Grecia catalana" (20), pp. 29–37.

34. Rubió y Lluch, "La Poblaciò" (1:44), pp. 21–22. For some bibliographical material on the geographical term "Hellas" within the confines of the district of Sperchios-Lamia in medieval and modern times, see Giannis Kordatos, Ἱστορία τῆς ἐπαρχίας Βόλου καί ᾿Αγιᾶς [A History of the Province of Volos and Agia] (Athens, 1960), p. 171, fn. 1.

35. Miller, The Latins in the Levant (16), pp. 334–338, 403–406. See his Essays on the Latin Orient (Cambridge, Eng., 1921), pp. 135–136, 146. Compare Gregorovius, Geschichte der Stadt Athen (2:2), Greek tr., II, 322–323, and 328–329, 347 ff. For further information on the rise of the Greek element, see Alfred Philippson and Ernst Kirsten, Die Griechischen Landschaften (1:9) (Frankfurt, 1950), I, 3. 1024–1026, which contains the relevant bibliography. On Nerios Acciajuoli's settlement in the Peloponnese and the gradual growth of his power until he was able to impose his will on the Catalans, see Rubió y Lluch, "La Grecia catalana" (20), pp. 67–71. Cf. Rubió y Lluch, "Chanceliers" (24), p. 154; and Setton, Catalan Domination (18), pp. 161, 166–173, 218 ff., for a note on the Greeks mentioned in the Catalan archives, especially the notary John Rentis.

36. See Ioannis Travlos, Πολεοδομική ἐξέλιξις τῶν ᾿Αθηνῶν ἀπό τῶν προϊστορικῶν χρόνων μέχρι τῶν ἀρχῶν τοῦ 19ου αἰῶνος [The Evolution of the Athenian City Plan, from Prehistoric Times up to the Beginning of the Nineteenth Century] (Athens, 1960), pp. 170–171.

37. See Rubió y Lluch, "Περί τῆς ἐποχῆς" (30), pp. 541, 542; and Setton, Catalan Domination (18), p. 218.

38. See Rubió y Lluch, "La Poblaciò" (1:44), p. 31; and "La Grecia catalana" (20), p. 88.

39. On the history of Stagoi, see Ioannis K. Voyatzidis, Τό χρονικόν τῶν Μετεώρων (1:42), ΕΕΒΣ, II (1925), 153 ff., especially pp. 169 ff.

40. On the life of this saint, see Spyridon Lambros, "Συμβολαί εἰς τήν ἱστορίαν τῶν μονῶν τῶν Μετεώρων" (7:42), NE, II (1905), 65–66. Cf. Nikos Bees, "Συμβολή εἰς τήν ἱστορίαν τῶν μονῶν τῶν Μετεώρων [A Contribution to the History of the Monasteries of Meteora]," Βυζαντίς, I (1909), 212, 230.

41. See Spyridon Lambros, "Νείλου Κωνσταντινουπόλεως σιγίλλιον περί τῆς μονῆς Λευκουσιάδος [The Seal of Neilos of Constantinople, Concerning the Monastery of Levkousias]," NE, VI (1909), 174–178. Although there must have been an important reason for Patriarch Neilos' designation of Archimandrite Euthymios as πρωτοσύγκελλος (superintendent) of the Vlachia (Thessaly) monasteries, I do not agree with Lambros that his intention was to counteract increasing Serb influence in Meteora.

42. See Spyridon Lambros, Παλαιολόγεια καί Πελοποννησιακά (1:66) (Athens, 1926), III, 194.

43. See Spyridon Lambros, " ᾿Ηπειρωτικά [The Affairs of Epirus]," NE, XI (1914), 3 ff.; and Athenagoras, " ῾Η ἐν τῷ φρουρίῳ τῶν ᾿Ιωαννίνων σχολή τῶν Δεσποτῶν (ἱστορικαί ἐπανορθώσεις) [The School of Despots in the Fortress of Ioannina (Historical Rectifications)]," ΔΙΕΕ, VIII (1922),

557–565, where the older bibliography will be found. The Varlaam monastery in Meteora was built in 1542 by the monks Nectarius and Theophanes, members of the house of Apsarades in Ioannina (Lambros, "Συμβολαί εἰς τήν ἱστορίαν" (7:42), pp. 93 ff.).

44. *Nicephori Blemmydae curriculum vitae et carmina*, ed. August Heisenberg (Leipzig, 1896), p. 36.

45. Alexander Solov'ev, "Θεσσαλійскіе Архонты в XIV вѣкѣ [The Archons of Thessaly in the Fourteenth Century]," Byz.-Sl., IV (1932), 159–174.

46. See D. K. Tsopotos, Γῆ καί γεωργοί τῆς Θεσσαλίας κατά τήν Τουρκοκρατίαν ἐπί τῇ βάσει ἱστορικῶν πηγῶν [*The Land and Farmers of Thessaly during Turkish Rule, according to Historical Sources*] (Volos, 1912), pp. 6, 10–11, which contains the appropriate references.

47. See p. 8 above. The Orthodox Church in the Serb-dominated regions of mainland Greece suffered a good deal between 1352 and 1371 as a result of the disruption brought about by Stephen Dušan. Schism followed when Dušan placed the Church under the jurisdiction of the Archbishop of "Peć and Serbia." These troubles came to an end only in May 1371, when John Ugliesa, "Despot of Serbia," consented to restore the Church in the Serb-dominated lands to the Ecumenical Patriarchate. The restitution was ratified by a Synodic letter. See Miklosich and Müller, *Acta et diplomata* (1:43), I, 553–555, and 560–564. The Metropolitan of Larissa, "ὑπέρτιμος καί ἔξαρχος δευτέρας Θετταλίας καί πάσης Ἑλλάδος [the very honorable exarch of the second Thessaly and of all of Greece]," although he was able to establish himself in his seat, complained to Patriarch Philotheos that many bishoprics within his jurisdiction were in places "under the control of barbarians and people of other races" (that is, Albanians, Arvanito-Vlachs, and Catalans) and that therefore it was not possible to visit them or to take care of his flock. The inhabitants of these areas either did not know that they belonged to the diocese of Larissa or, feigning ignorance, disregarded the Metropolitan who visited them for the purpose of attending to certain matters, consecrating bishops, or merely asserting his rights. Having been apprised of these difficulties, the Patriarch, in September of the same year, definitely delineated the extent of the diocese of Larissa to include the bishoprics of Demetrias, Pharsala, Thavmakos, Zitounion, Ezeros, Lidorikion, Mountinitza, Stami, Triki, Domeniko, Katria (Krania?), Gardiki, Peristera, Radovisdi, Patsouna, and Vesaini. See Miklosich and Müller, *Acta et diplomata* (1:44), I, 587–589; and Neroutsos, "Χριστιανικαί Ἀθῆναι" (2:7), pp. 202–203.

48. See Ἱστορικόν Κομνηνοῦ μοναχοῦ καί Προκλου μοναχοῦ (1:51), ed. Andreas Moustoxydis in Ἑλληνομνήμων I (1843–1853), 494–496, 510, 527, and *Bizancio y España*, ed. Sebastián Cirác Estopañán (Barcelona, 1943), II, 40 ff. The first known Metropolitan of Ioannina was Sebastian. Regarding his activities and the Church in Ioannina in general, see Athenagoras, "Ἡ Ἐκκλησία τῶν Ἰωαννίνων [The Church of Ioannina]," HX, III (1928), 11 ff.

49. Cf. Michael Lascaris, "Byzantinoserbica saeculi XIV" (1:61), *Byzantion*, XXV–XXVII (1955–1957), 314.

50. Ἱστορικόν Κομνηνοῦ καί Π ρόκλου (1:51), ed. Moustoxydis, pp. 534–535 (*Bizancio y España,* ed. Estopañán, p. 48).

51. See Raymond Loenertz, "Un Prostagma perdu de Théodore Iᵉʳ Paléologue regardant Thessalonique (1380/82?) [A Lost Order of Theodoros I Palaeologus concerning Thessalonica (1380/82?)]," ΕΕΒΣ, xxv (1955), 171.

52. Ἱστορικόν Κομνηνοῦ καί Π ρόκλου (1:51), ed. Moustoxydis, p. 535 (*Bizancio y España,* ed. Estopañán, p. 48).

53. Ἱστορικόν Κομνηνοῦ καί Π ρόκλου (1:51), ed. Moustoxydis, pp. 536–551 (*Bizancio y España,* ed. Estopañán, II, 48–51).

54. Karl Hopf, *Griechenland im Mittelalter und in der Neuzeit* (1:51) (Leipzig, 1867–1868), II, 39–40.

55. Cf. the opinions of Léon Heuzey, *Excursion dans la Thessalie turque en 1858* (Paris, 1927), pp. 187, 189, 191; and the pertinent documents in Nikos Bees, "Σερβικά καί βυζαντιακά ἔγγραφα Μετεώρων" (1:59), Βυζαντίς, I (1909), 73 ff.

56. On the dates, see Lascaris, "Byzantinoserbica" (1:61), pp. 4 ff. John Uroš was a Palaeologus on his mother's side (Averkios Papadopoulos, *Versuch einer Genealogie der Palaeologen, 1259–1453* [*An Attempt at a Genealogy of the Palaeologi 1259–1453*] [Munich, 1938], p. 25).

57. Lascaris has made the rather convincing speculation that the wife of Alexius Philanthropenos, Maria Radoslava Angelina, was the daughter of Radoslav Chlapen (Lascaris, "Byzantinoserbica" (1:61), xxv–xxvii, 321–322).

58. Ioannis K. Voyatzidis describes these events in "Τό χρονικόν τῶν Μετεώρων" (1:42), ΕΕΒΣ, I (1924), 175. On the Philanthropenos family, see Athenagoras, "Συμβολαί εἰς τήν ἱστορίαν τοῦ βυζαντινοῦ οἴκου τῶν Φιλανθρωπηνῶν [Contributions to the History of the Byzantine House of the Philanthropeni]," ΔΙΕΕ, XI (1928–1929), no. 4, 61–74.

59. Hopf, *Griechenland* (1:51), II, 40.

60. See Raymond Loenertz, "Notes sur le règne de Manuel II à Thessalonique, 1381/82–1387," BZ, L (1957), 390–394.

61. See Voyatzidis, "Τό χρονικόν τῶν Μετεώρων" (1:47), p. 175.

62. See George Theocharidis, "Δύο νέα ἔγγραφα ἀφορῶντα εἰς τήν Νέαν Μονήν Θεσσαλονίκης [Two New Documents Relating to the *Nea Mone* of Thessalonica]," Μακεδονικά, IV (1960), 320–322; and Dennis, *The Reign of Manuel II* (4), pp. 100–101.

63. See Papadopoulos, *Versuch* (56), *passim;* and Athenagoras, "Συμβολαί εἰς τήν ἱστορίαν" (58), pp. 61–74.

64. See Loenertz, "Notes sur le règne de Manuel II" (60), pp. 392–394; and "Un Prostagma perdu" (51), pp. 170–172.

65. Hopf, *Griechenland* (1:51), II, 106; and Miller, *The Latins in the Levant* (16), pp. 370–373. The publication of the verse chronicle of Carlo's deeds will throw considerable light on his character and achievements, if one may judge from the fragments already published: Giuseppe Schirò, "Una Cronaca in versi inediti del secolo XV; 'Sui Duchi e Conti di Cefalonia,'" XIᵉ Congrès international des études byzantines, Munich, 1958, *Akten* (Munich, 1960), pp. 531–538. See also Schirò's "Manuele Paleologo incorona Carlo Tocco

Despota di Gianina [Manuel Palaeologus Crowns Carlo Tocco the Despot of Ioannina]," *Byzantion,* XXIX–XXX (1959–1960), 209–230.

66. John Barker, "On the Chronology of the Activities of Manuel II Palaeologus in 1415," BZ, LV (1962), 43.

67. Schirò, "Manuele Paleologo incorona Carlo Tocco" (65), pp. 228–230.

68. Hopf, *Griechenland* (1:51), II, 106; and Miller, *The Latins in the Levant* (16), pp. 337–338, 370–373. Documents concerning Francesca may be found in Gregorovius, *Geschichte der Stadt Athen* (2:2), Greek tr., II, 743–746.

69. Neculai Iorga, *Byzance après Byzance* (Bucharest, 1935), p. 59.

70. Alexander Solov'ev, "Греческіе Архонты в Сербском Царствѣ XIV вѣка [The Greek Archons in the Serbian Empire]," Byz.-Sl., II (1930), 275–287.

71. See Spyridon Lambros and Constantine Amantos, Βραχέα χρονικά [Brief Chronicles] in the series Μνημεῖα τῆς ἑλληνικῆς ἱστορίας, I, part 1 (Athens, 1932), 33, 38, 41, 61.

72. See Loenertz, *Démétrius Cydonès* (3), I, 110.

73. *Ibid.,* II, 220, 226–227, 238; and Dennis, *The Reign of Manuel II* (4), pp. 71–73, 108–109.

74. Loenertz, *Démétrius Cydonès* (3), II, 220, 258; Thiriet, *La Romanie* (12), p. 357; and Dennis, *The Reign of Manuel II* (4), pp. 123–126, 136–150, 163–164.

75. Giuseppe Cammelli, *Démétrius Cydonès, correspondance* (Paris, 1930), pp. 90–91: "τῆς περί τά βελτίω σπουδῆς μεμνημένος [Remembering his zeal for better things]." For the attitude of the people of Thessalonica, see Dennis, *The Reign of Manuel II* (4), pp. 85–88.

76. Loenertz, "Un Prostagma" (51), p. 171.

77. Although Dennis should have taken note of the revival of the word "Hellene" at that time, he does not mention it. His research is based principally on the letters of Kydones published by Loenertz in the second volume of his *Démétrius Cydonès* (3).

78. See Oreste Tafrali, *Thessalonique au quatorzième siècle* (Paris, 1913), p. 157.

79. There are examples in Émile Legrand, *Lettres de l'empereur Manuel Paléologue* (Paris, 1893).

80. Raymond Loenertz, *Correspondance de Manuel Calecas* (Rome, 1950), pp. 200, 329; and *Démétrius Cydonès* (3), I, 146.

81. See Demetrius Kydones, Ρωμαίοις συμβουλευτικός (5:49), PG, CLIV, col. 968.

82. Cammelli, *Démétrius Cydonès* (75), p. 8.

83. Raymond Loenertz, "Paléologue et Cydonès," *Échos d'Orient,* XXXVI (1937), 476–477. Cf. Loenertz's *Démétrius Cydonès* (3), II, 217, 238. On the date, see Dennis, *The Reign of Manuel II* (4), p. 73.

84. Apostolos Vacalopoulos, Ἡ ἱστορική συνείδηση καί τό ἀγωνιστικό πνεῦμα τοῦ νέου ἑλληνισμοῦ [The Historic Conscience and Competitive Spirit of the New Hellenism] (Thessalonica, 1957), p. 9.

85. See Basileios Laourdas, "Ὁ Γαβριήλ Θεσσαλονίκης, ὁμιλίαι" (7:16), Ἀθηνᾶ, LVI (1952), 203.

86. See Constantine Mertzios, Μνημεῖα μακεδονικῆς ἱστορίας [*Monuments of Macedonian History*] (Thessalonica, 1947), p. 203; and Pierre Belon, *Les Observations de plusieurs singularitéz et choses mémorables, trouvées en Grèce* (Paris, 1553), pp. 58b–59a. For a bibliography concerning travellers who saw the monument, see Paul Collart, *Phillipes, ville de Macédoine, depuis ses origines jusqu' à la fin de l'époque romaine* (Paris, 1937), pp. 326–327.

87. George Bakalakis, "Ἀπό τήν ζωντανή φυλλάδα τοῦ Μεγάλου Ἀλεξάνδρου [From the Lively Novel of Alexander the Great]," Μακεδονικόν Ἡμερολόγιον, 1939, pp. 97–98.

88. Andreas Xyngopoulos, "Παραστάσεις ἐκ τοῦ μυθιστορήματος τοῦ Μ. Ἀλεξάνδρου [Representations from the Romance of Alexander the Great]," AE, 1938, p. 199. Cf. pp. 23–24 of the present work.

89. Joseph Bryennios, Τά εὑρεθέντα (6:82) (Leipzig, 1768), II, 278. For the classical education (θύραθεν παιδεία) of the monk of Thessalonica, Makarios Makris, and that of some of his contemporaries, see Athanasios Papadopoulos-Kerameus, "Μακάριος Μακρῆς," ΔΙΕΕ, III (1889), 463, 464.

90. Lambros, Παλαιολόγεια (1:66), III, 152. The word Ῥωμέλληνες has been found in the exegesis of an oracle, relating to the Isthmus of Corinth, written by Isidore, later Metropolitan of Kiev. See Denis Zakythinos, "Μανουήλ Β΄ Παλαιολόγος καί ὁ καρδινάλιος Ἰσίδωρος ἐν Πελοποννήσῳ [Manuel II Palaeologus and Cardinal Isidore in the Peloponnese]," *Mélanges Merlier*, III (1957), 61. Does this word betray also the identity of the anonymous author of the panegyric "Εἰς Μανουήλ καί Ἰωάννην Η΄ Παλαιολόγους [On Manuel and John II Palaeologus]" in Lambros, III, 194?

91. See Manuel Chrysoloras, Σύγκρισις τῆς παλαιᾶς καί νέας Ῥώμης [*Comparison of the Old and the New Rome*], PG, CLVI, col. 40. Cf. Denis Zakythinos, Βυζάντιον. Κράτος καί κοινωνία, ἱστορική ἐπισκόπησις [*Byzantium. The State and Society; an Historical Survey*] (Athens, 1951), pp. 30–31.

92. Dennis, *The Reign of Manuel II* (4), p. 89, fn. 25; and Spyridon Lambros, "Ἰσιδώρου Μητροπολίτου Θεσσαλονίκης ὀκτώ ἐπιστολαί ἀνέκδοτοι" (7:2), NE, IX (1912), 350. See similar textual extracts in Ihor Ševčenko, "A Postscript on Nicholas Cabasilas' 'Anti-Zealot' Discourse," DOP, XVI (1962), 406, fn. 24a.

93. See George Ostrogorsky, *Pour l'histoire de la féodalité byzantine* (Brussels, 1954), pp. 161 ff., 172 ff.

94. See Halil Inalcik, "Osmanlı hukuna giriş [Introduction to Ottoman Law]," *Siyasal bilgiler fakültesi dergisi*, XIII (1958), p. 8 of the reprint.

95. Similar proposals made by him in 1383 and 1390 may be found in Dennis, *The Reign of Manuel II* (4), pp. 90–91, which also contains the relevant bibliography.

96. Ostrogorsky, *Pour l'histoire de la féodalité* (93), pp. 173–175.

97. See Fuad Köprülü, "Vakıf müessesessinin hukuk mahiyeti ve tarihî tekâmülü [The Legal Character of the Wakf Institution and Its Historical

Evolution]," *Vakıflar dergisi*, ɪɪ (1942), 26–32 (pp. 36–44 of the French section).

98. Loenertz, *Correspondance de Manuel Calecas* (80), p. 200.

99. See Apostolos Vacalopoulos, "Οἱ δημοσιευμένες ὁμιλίες τοῦ ἀρχιεπισκόπου Θεσσαλονίκης Ἰσιδώρου ὡς ἱστορική πηγή γιά τήν γνώση τῆς πρώτης τουρκοκρατίας στήν Θεσσαλονίκη (1387–1402)" (6:45), Μακεδονικά, ɪv (1960), 23 ff.

100. See Basileios Laourdas, Ἰσιδώρου ἀρχιεπισκόπου ὁμιλίαι εἰς τάς ἑορτάς τοῦ Ἁγ. Δημητρίου (6:51) (Thessalonica, 1954), p. 57.

101. See Laourdas, " Ὁ Γαβριήλ" (85), p. 206.

102. Cf. Laourdas, Ἰσιδώρου ἀρχιεπισκόπου ὁμιλίαι (6:51), p. 62.

103. Regarding these memories in 1372, see Loenertz, *Démétrius Cydonès* (3), ɪ, 110.

104. Laourdas, Ἰσιδώρου ἀρχιεπισκόπου ὁμιλίαι (6:51), p. 63. See Vacalopoulos, "Οἱ δημοσιευμένες ὁμιλίες" (6:45), pp. 20–34.

105. The word χάριτες, with the meaning *pronoia*, was used also by the Venetians (*gratie*). See Spyridon Theotokis, " Ἀποφάσεις Μείζονος Συμβουλίου Βενετίας, 1255–1669 [Resolutions of the Greater Council of Venice, 1255–1669]," Μνημεῖα τῆς ἑλληνικῆς ἱστορίας (Athens, 1932–1933), ɪ, part 2, 51.

106. See Vacalopoulos, "Οἱ δημοσιευμένες ὁμιλίες" (6:45), pp. 25, 31–32; and Laourdas, Ἰσιδώρου ἀρχιεπισκόπου ὁμιλίαι (6:51), p. 61.

107. Basileios Laourdas, " Ἰσιδώρου ἀρχιεπισκόπου ὁμιλίαν περί τῆς ἁρπαγῆς τῶν παίδων καί περί τῆς μελλούσης κρίσεως [The Homilies of Archbishop Isidore on the Seizure of Children, and on the Last Judgment]," Ἑλληνικά, appendix 4, presented to S. P. Kyriakidis (Thessalonica, 1953), pp. 389–398.

108. Speros Vryonis attempts to show that the institution of both the janissaries and the impressment of children were inspired by Kara Halil Tsantarlı, and that they were begun simultaneously during the reign of Murad I ("Isidore Glabas and the Turkish 'devshirme,'" *Speculum*, xxxɪ [1956], 438, 442). On the spread of the conscription of janissaries among the subjects of the Ottoman state, see the hypotheses advanced by Paul Wittek, "Devshirme and shārī'a," BSOAS, xvɪɪ (1955), 271–278. Wittek's suppositions, however, on matters pertaining to the Greeks are quite groundless. Basilike Papoulia has recently supported the view that the impressment of children was introduced at the time of Orchan (*Ursprung und Wesen der "Knabenlese" im osmanischen Reiche* [6:28] [Munich, 1963], pp. 62 ff.).

109. See Louisa Syndika-Laourda, " Ἐγκώμιον εἰς τόν ἀρχιεπίσκοπον Θεσσαλονίκης Γαβριήλ [Encomium on Gabriel, Archbishop of Thessalonica]," Μακεδονικά, ɪv (1960), 366 ff.

110. See Neculai Iorga, *Notes et extraits pour servir à l'histoire des Croisades au XVᵉ siècle*, ɪ, first series (Paris, 1899), 179–180, 258–259, 300–301. Cf. the successive journeys made by Manuel Chrysoloras to the West (chapter 16 of the present work).

111. Bryennios, Τά εὑρεθέντα (6:82), ɪɪ, 246–247.

Chapter 9

1. As to the date of Gemistos' arrival in the Peloponnese, I think that the view of Ioannis Mamalakis in Γεώργιος Γεμιστός—Πλήθων [George Gemistos–Pletho] (Athens, 1939), pp. 60–64, is closest to the truth. François Masai, however, believes that Gemistos arrived in Mistra shortly after Theodore II ascended the throne of the despotate (*Pléthon et le Platonisme de Mistra* [Paris, 1956], pp. 67, 386–387).

2. Gregory the monk, Μονῳδία τῷ σοφῷ διδασκάλῳ Γεωργίῳ τῷ Γεμιστῷ [*Monody for the Learned Teacher George Gemistos*], PG, CLX, col. 817. Cf. Hieronymos Charitonymos, Ὑμνῳδία τῷ σοφωτάτῳ διδασκάλῳ κυρίῳ Γεωργίῳ τῷ Γεμιστῷ [*Hymns for the Most Learned Teacher, Lord George Gemistos*], PG, CLX, col. 808.

3. See George I. Theocharidis, "Τέσσαρες βυζαντινοί καθολικοί κριταί λανθάνοντες ἐν βυζαντινῷ γνωστῷ κειμένῳ [Four Catholic Byzantine Judges, Unnoticed in a Familiar Byzantine Text]," Μακεδονικά, ιν (1960), 497–498.

4. Gregory, Μονῳδία τῷ σοφῷ (2), col. 817.

5. Συμβουλευτικός πρός δεσπότην Θεόδωρον περί τῆς Πελοποννήσου [Advisory Speech to the Despot Theodore concerning the Peloponnese] (Spyridon Lambros, Παλαιολόγεια καί Πελοποννησιακά [1:66] [Athens, 1926], ιν, 114, 116); see Basileios Laourdas, "Ὁ Γαβριήλ Θεσσαλονίκης" (7:16) Ἀθηνᾶ, LVI (1952), 205, 206, 207.

6. See Laonicos Chalcocondyles, *Historiarum demonstrationes* (1:52), ed. Eugene Darkó (Budapest, 1922–1927), ι, 173, and 202–203. However, the power of the nobility did not disappear. We do not know precisely what happened after the removal of the nobles to Constantinople, but it is likely that a certain compromise was reached with Manuel.

7. On the chronology of the memoranda, see Mamalakis, Γεώργιος Γεμιστός (1), pp. 387–388. A German translation of the memoranda appears in Adolf Ellissen, *Analekten der mittel- und neugriechischen Literatur* [*Analects of Medieval and Modern Greek Literature*] (Leipzig, 1860), ιν, part 2, 85–130.

8. See Εἰς Μανουήλ Παλαιολόγον περί τῶν ἐν Πελοποννήσῳ πραγμάτων [To Manuel Palaeologus, concerning Matters in the Peloponnese] (Lambros, Παλαιολόγεια [1:66], ιιι, 247).

9. See Mamalakis, Γεώργιος Γεμιστός (1), pp. 49–51.

10. Lambros, Παλαιολόγεια (1:66), ιιι, 247–249, 309–310; ιν, 121, 131–132.

11. Masai, *Pléthon* (1), pp. 67–68: "Pléthon s'intéressait même au fonctionnement des états contemporains: j'ai notamment retrouvé à Venise une copie de la *Constitution de Florence*, opuscule grec de Leonardo Bruni, portant des corrections autographes de Pléthon."

12. Lambros, Παλαιολόγεια (1:66), ιν, 116, 119.

13. *Ibid.*, ιιι, 249–265, ιν, 119–122. Cf. ιιι, 310–312.

14. *Ibid.*, ιν, 131–133.

15. See Apostolos Vacalopoulos, Τά ἑλληνικά στρατεύματα τοῦ 1821 [*The Greek Troops in 1821*] (Thessalonica, 1948), pp. 107–108.

16. On the meaning of the word φιλοσοφῶ, see the observations of Ellissen in *Analekten* (7), IV, 142.

17. Lambros, Παλαιολόγεια (1:66), III, 257–259.

18. *Ibid.*, III, 258–259.

19. *Ibid.*, IV, 128–129.

20. *Ibid.*, III, 260, 261, IV, 131–132. Cf. Denis Zakythinos, *Le Despotat grec de Morée* (Athens, 1953), I, 179–180.

21. On the granting of immunities in Monemvasia, see Franz Miklosich and Joseph Müller, *Acta et diplomata graeca medii aevi sacra et profana* (1:43) (Vienna, 1860–1887), II, 154–155, 165–168, 172. Cf. E. Francès, "La Féodalité et les villes byzantines au XIIIe et au XIVe siècles," Byz.-Sl., XVI (1955), 90–91, 95.

22. Lambros, Παλαιολόγεια (1:66), III, 261–262. Cf. IV, 124–125. The Spanish traveller Pero Tafur mentions mutilations of hands and eyes in Constantinople in 1438 (*Travels and Adventures, 1435–1439*, tr. Malcolm Letts [New York-London, 1926], pp. 146, 147), and notes: "I enquired why they did not put him to death, and they replied that the Emperor could not order his soul to be destroyed."

23. Lambros, Παλαιολόγεια (1:66), III, 262–265, 310; IV, 130.

24. Dräseke believes that the main reason that Gemistos' proposals were not put into effect consisted "in den vielfach überspannten geistigen Voraussetzungen, von Seiten des Platonischen-Philosophen [in the much exaggerated spiritual presuppositions on the part of the Platonic philosopher]" (Johannes Dräseke, "Plethons und Bessarions Denkschriften 'Über die Angelegenheiten in Peloponnes' [Pletho's and Bessarion's Memoirs 'On the Affairs in the Peloponnese']," NJKA, XXVII [1911], 114). His study is based on Spyridon Lambros, "Ὑπόμνημα τοῦ καρδιναλίου Βησσαρίωνος εἰς Κωνσταντῖνον τόν Παλαιολόγον [A Memorandum from Cardinal Bessarion to Constantine Palaeologus]," NE, III (1906), 12–50.

25. Miklosich and Müller, *Acta et diplomata* (1:43), III, 173 ff. On the nature of the benefice, see George Ostrogorsky, *Pour l'histoire de la féodalité byzantine* (Brussels, 1954), pp. 180 ff.; and "Pour l'histoire de l'immunité byzantine," *Byzantion*, XXVIII (1958), 232–234.

26. Cf. Mamalakis, Γεώργιος Γεμιστός (1), p. 213.

27. See Denis Zakythinos, "Μανουήλ Β′ Παλαιολόγος καί ὁ καρδινάλιος Ἰσίδωρος ἐν Πελοποννήσῳ" (8:90), *Mélanges Merlier*, III (1957), 61.

28. See Zakythinos, *Le Despotat* (20), I, 188–191, 299–302. Compare with this Gemistos' testimony, Μονῳδία ἐπί τῇ ἀοιδίμῳ βασιλίδι Κλεόπῃ [*Monody on the Renowned Queen Cleopa*], in Lambros, Παλαιολόγεια (1:66), IV, 167: "Σωφροσύνης δ' ἐκεῖνο μέγα τεκμήριον, ἡ ἐκ τῆς ἰταλικῆς ἀνέσεώς τε καί ῥαστώνης ἐπί τό κατεσταλμένον τε, καί κόσμον τοῦ ἡμετέρου τρόπου μεταβολή ἀκριβεστάτη. . . . Εὐσεβείας δέ ἀπόδειξις ἡ τοῦ θεοῦ λατρεία, ἥν προσευχαῖς τε καί ἀσιτίαις ἐνδελεχέσι τόν ἡμέτερον νόμον ἐπεδείκνυτο [And that great token of prudence, the most exact change from Italian relaxation and indolence to the restraint and order of our manner. . . . And the

worship of God is evidence of piety, which it displays by prayers and by constant fasting, according to our custom]."

29. See Zakythinos, "Μανουήλ Β′′′" (8:90), p. 61; and Spyridon Lambros, "Τά τείχη τοῦ Ἰσθμοῦ τῆς Κορίνθου κατά τούς μέσους αἰῶνας [The Walls of the Isthmus of Corinth in the Middle Ages]," NE, ΙΙ (1905), 472 ff. Cf. Lambros, "Προσθήκη εἰς τά περί τῶν τειχῶν τοῦ Ἰσθμοῦ τῆς Κορίνθου κατά τούς μέσους αἰῶνας [Supplement to the Study 'The Walls of the Isthmus of Corinth in the Middle Ages']," NE, ΙV (1907), 21–22, 240–243.

30. Zakythinos, "Μανουήλ Β′′′" (8:90), p. 61.

31. Georgius Phrantzes, Χρονικόν (6:15), ed. Immanuel Bekker (Bonn, 1838), p. 158.

32. Lambros, Παλαιολόγεια (1:66), ΙV, 174–175.

33. "Regnum ipsa gubernavit, magistratus veteres deposuit, novos instituit, sacerdotia pro suo arbitrio ordinavit, et, eliminato Latinorum ritu, Graecanicum superinduxit, belli pacisque leges dixit. Viro satis fuit convivari, deliciisque affluere, atque in hunc modum universa insula in potestatem Graecorum rediit [she herself governed, removed old magistrates, installed new ones, arranged the priesthoods according to her own judgment, did away with the Latin rite and replaced it with the Greek, and made laws concerning war and peace. It sufficed her husband to feast and to be surrounded with delights. It was in this fashion that the entire island returned to the domination of the Greeks]." (See Sir George Francis Hill, A History of Cyprus, ΙΙΙ [Cambridge, Eng., 1948], 527 ff.)

34. See John Hackett, A History of the Orthodox Church of Cyprus from the Coming of the Apostles Paul and Barnabas to the Commencement of the British Occupation (A.D. 45–A.D. 1878) together with Some Account of the Latin and Other Churches Existing in the Island (London, 1901), p. 155. Hill's protestations and reservations (A History of Cyprus [33], ΙΙΙ, 754–756) in regard to the character of Cypriot national beliefs reveal a certain political bias. When Hill's book appeared, the Cypriots had resumed their vigorous struggle for union with Greece, and his basic intention appears to have been to denigrate the national zeal of the Cypriots. Only in these terms is it possible to explain his conclusion: "It is impossible to avoid the conclusion that long centuries of foreign domination had left in the people nothing of the stuff of which a nation could be made."

35. Jean de Belesta, Voyage à Jérusalem de Philippe de Voisins, Seigneur de Montaut (Paris, 1883), p. 25: "et seroient volountiers ez mains des François, car ilz en ayment naturellement la nation [and they would willingly be in the hands of the Franks, for they naturally love their nation]."

36. For an account of this movement, see Freddy Thiriet, La Romanie vénitienne au moyen âge (Paris, 1959), p. 297.

37. See Ferdinand Gregorovius, Geschichte der Stadt Athen im Mittelalter, von der Zeit Justinians bis zur turkischen Eroberung (Stuttgart, 1889), Greek trans. by Spyridon Lambros (Athens, 1904–1906), ΙΙ, 323.

38. Chalcocondyles, Historiarum demonstrationes (1:52), ΙΙ, 93. On the question of the name of the historian's father, see Giuseppe Cammelli, I Dotti

bizantini e le origini dell' umanesimo [*The Byzantine Scholars and the Origins of the Renaissance*], III, Dem. Calcondila (Florence, 1941–1954), pp. 4–5.

39. See Phrantzes, Χρονικόν (6:15), p. 159, and pp. 130–133; also Chalcocondyles, *Historiarum demonstrationes* (1:52), II, 94.

40. Chalcocondyles, *Historiarum demonstrationes* (1:52), II, 113–114. Cf. William Miller, "The Last Athenian Historian: Laonicos Chalkokondyles," *JHS*, XLII (1922), 37.

Chapter 10

1. See Christopher Buondelmonti, *Description des îles de l'Archipel. Version grecque par un anonyme, publiée d'après le manuscrit du sérail avec une traduction française et un commentaire par Émile Legrand* (6:8) (Paris, 1897); Bertrandon de la Brocquière, *Voyage d'outremer et retour de Jérusalem en France par la voie de terre, pendant le cours des années 1432 et 1433,* ed. Pierre Legrand D'Aussy, in *Mémoires de l'Institut national des sciences et arts; sciences morales et politiques,* v (Paris, fructidor an XII); and Pero Tafur, *Travels and Adventures, 1435–1439,* tr. Malcolm Letts (New York-London, 1926).

2. See Ruy Gonzales de Clavijo, *A Diary of the Journey to the Court of Timur, 1403–1406,* tr. Guy Le Strange (London, 1928), p. 48; and Buondelmonti, *Description des îles* (6:8), p. 78.

3. Apostolos Vacalopoulos, "Les Limites de l'empire byzantin depuis la fin du XIVe siècle jusqu'à sa chute (1453)," *BZ,* LV (1962), 56–65, which contains the relevant bibliography.

4. Laonicos Chalcocondyles, *Historiarum demonstrationes* (1:52), ed. Eugene Darkó (Budapest, 1922–1927), I, 6–7.

5. Regarding these illegitimate acts, see Georgius Pachymeres, Συγγραφικαί ἱστορίαι (3:69), ed. Immanuel Bekker (Bonn, 1835), II, 494. See also Denis Zakythinos, *Crise monétaire et crise économique à Byzance du XIIIe au XVe siècle.* Reprint from Hell. Contemp. (Athens, 1948), *passim.*

6. The book of accounts for the period 1436–1440 belonging to the merchant Giacomo Badoer is typical. See Umberto Dorini and Tommaso Bertelè, eds., *Il Libro dei conti di Giacomo Badoer, Constantinopoli, 1436–1440* (Rome, 1956). There were many foreigners in the capital (Castilians, Venetians, etc.), either as merchants or as soldiers in the service of John VIII (Tafur, *Travels* (1), p. 123).

7. See Louis Brehier, *Les Institutions de l'empire byzantin* (Paris, 1949), pp. 278–280.

8. Raymond Loenertz, *Démétrius Cydonès, correspondance* (Vatican City, 1956), I, 103.

9. Bertrandon de la Brocquière, *Voyage d'outremer* (1), p. 566.

10. Raymond Loenertz, *Correspondance de Manuel Calecas* (Rome, 1950), p. 330.

11. Tafur, *Travels* (1), p. 120.

12. Johann Schiltberger, *The Bondage and Travels of Johann Schiltberger, a Native of Bavaria, in Europe, Asia, and Africa, 1396–1427,* tr. Commander J. Buchan Telfer (London, 1879), p. 77.

13. Loenertz, *Correspondance de Manuel Calecas* (10), p. 168.

14. Buondelmonti, *Descriptions des îles* (1), p. 89.

15. See Neculai Iorga, *Notes et extraits pour servir à l'histoire des Croisades au XVe siècle,* I, 2nd series (Paris, 1899), 365–367, 397.

16. On the activities of Pope Eugenius IV in connection with the enforcement of the Union of the Churches in Crete, see Georg Hofmann, "Wie stand es mit der Frage der Kircheneinheit auf Kreta?" (7:63), OCP, x (1944), 95–96, 112–113.

17. See Manoussos Manoussacas, "Recherches sur la vie de Jean Plousiadénos (Joseph de Methone), 1429?–1500," REB, XVII (1959), 28–51, which contains the relevant bibliography.

18. See Hofmann, "Wie stand" (7:63), p. 114; Nikolaos Tomadakis, "Μιχαήλ Καλοφρενᾶς Κρής, Μητροφάνης Β´ καί ἡ πρός τήν ἔνωσιν τῆς Φλωρεντίας ἀντίθεσις τῶν Κρητῶν [Michael Calophrenas of Crete, Metrophanes II, and the Opposition of the Cretans to the Union with Florence]," ΕΕΒΣ, XXI (1951), 110–114, especially pp. 124–130; and Basileios Laourdas, "Κρητικά παλαιογραφικά" (7:15), ΚΧ, v (1951), 245–252. Cf. Constantine Kalokyris, Αἱ βυζαντιναί τοιχογραφίαι τῆς Κρήτης (8:59) (Athens, 1957), pp. 181–182.

19. See Tomadakis, "Μιχαήλ Καλοφρενᾶς" (18), pp. 126–130.

20. See John Hackett, *A History of the Orthodox Church of Cyprus from the Coming of the Apostles Paul and Barnabas to the Commencement of the British Occupation (A.D. 45–A.D. 1878) together with Some Account of the Latin and Other Churches Existing in the Island* (London, 1901), pp. 152–153.

21. Anonymous, Ἱστορία πολιτική Κωνσταντινουπόλεως [*Political History of Constantinople*] (Bonn, 1849), p. 9.

22. See Ducas, ed. Immanuel Bekker (Bonn, 1834), p. 216 (ed. Basile Grecu [Bucharest, 1958], pp. 270–271); and Ludwig Mohler, *Kardinal Bessarion als Theologe, Humanist und Staatsmann,* I (Paderborn, 1923), 31 ff., 36, 37, which contains the relevant bibliography.

23. See Joseph Gill, "The Year of the Death of Marc Eugenicus," BZ, LII (1959), 23–31.

24. Georgius Phrantzes, Χρονικόν (6:15), ed. Immanuel Bekker (Bonn, 1838), pp. 178, 179. Cf. Ducas, ed Bekker (22), p. 215 (ed. Grecu, p. 269).

25. Bertrandon de la Brocquière, *Voyage d'outremer* (1), pp. 602–610. For the Turkish method of waging war, see chapter 4, fn. 59, of the present work. According to Tafur, *Travels* (1), p. 127: "The Turks have the custom to carry in the saddle an iron staff and a tambourine with their bows and quivers. This is the whole of their fighting outfit."

26. Charles Schefer, ed., *Le Voyage d'outremer de Bertrandon de la Brocquière* (Paris, 1892), pp. 263–264, 265, 266, where other pertinent information about Johannes Torzelo and about the campaign plans of the Christian forces is given.

27. Bertrandon de la Brocquière, *Voyage d'outremer* (1), p. 579. Cf. p. 592.

28. Ducas, ed. Bekker (22), p. 135, and p. 136 (ed. Grecu, pp. 177–179).

29. Bertrandon de la Brocquière, *Voyage d'outremer* (1), p. 592.

30. Halil Inalcik, "Ottoman Methods of Conquest," *Studia islamica,* ii (1954), 107.

31. Loenertz, *Démétrius Cydonès* (8), ii, 240: "τοῖς μή πειθομένοις ἀδιάλλακτα πολεμοῦσι, καί λατρείαν θεῷ προσφέρειν τήν ἐκείνων σφαγήν [they fight without mercy against those who do not obey and slaughtering them worship their god]."

32. See Tafur, *Travels* (1), p. 127: "The Grand Turk and his people are always in the field in tents, both in winter and summer, and although the city is close at hand, he never enters it unless it is to go with women to the bath."

33. Bertrandon de la Brocquière, *Voyage d'outremer* (1), p. 527: "sont gens de fatigue, d'une vie dure, et à qui il ne coûte rien, ainsi que je l'ai vu tout le long de la route, de dormir sur la terre comme les animaux [they are people of hardship, of a harsh life, and it means nothing to them. I have even seen them all along the way, sleeping on the ground like animals]." For the epics of the Turks, see M. Canard, "Delhemma. Sayyid Battâl et 'Omar Al-No 'mân," *Byzantion,* xii (1937), 183–188.

34. On these ideas, see George Georgiadis-Arnakis, Οἱ πρῶτοι 'Οθωμανοί (5:30) (Athens, 1947), pp. 110 ff.; and "Futtuwa Traditions in the Ottoman Empire. Akhis, Bektachi Dervishes, and Craftsmen," *Journal of Near Eastern Studies,* xii (1953), 232–247.

35. Bertrandon de la Brocquière, *Voyage d'outremer* (1), pp. 527–528, 610: "J'ay veu bien souvent, quant nous mengions, que s'il passoit ung povre homme auprès d'eulx, ils le faisoient venir mengier avec nous *ce que nous, ne fésiesmes point* [Many times when we were eating I have seen them invite a poor man passing by to eat with us, something we never do]" (p. 528). However, in the middle of Asia Minor, and especially in Karamania, the inhabitants were cruel and of marauding habits, and foreigners were in danger of being killed if they went out at night, pp. 540 ff. See Tafur, *Travels* (1), p. 128.

36. Schiltberger, *The Bondage and Travels* (12), pp. 54–55, 77: "that the Christians will yet expel them out of the country and will again possess the country" (p. 77).

37. See Photios Chrysanthopoulos, 'Απομνημονεύματα περί τῆς ἑλληνικῆς ἐπαναστάσεως [*Memoirs on the Greek Revolution*] (Athens, 1899), i, 135–136.

38. See B. K., 'Από τήν αἰχμαλωσία [From Captivity] (Athens, 1923), p. 61.

39. Bertrandon de la Brocquière, *Voyage d'outremer* (1), p. 257.

40. *Ibid.,* pp. 575, 576, 577, 578.

41. Murad II did not impose a land tax or personal tax (*taille*)—by which Broquière means the poll tax, *harac*—on his subject compatriots, nor did he take money by force or extortion (Bertrandon de la Brocquière, *Voyage*

d'outremer [1], p. 578). A similar assessment of Murad—and, of course, a flattering one—is made by his own adviser, Šükrüllāh (Theodor Seif, "Der Abschnitt über die Osmanen in Šükrüllāh's persischer Universalgeschichte" (5:39), MOG, II [1923–1925], 115–116).

42. See the narrative of Ioannis Kananos, Διήγησις περὶ τοῦ ἐν Κωνσταντινουπόλει γεγονότος πολέμου τὸ 6930 (1422) ἔτος [*Account of the War in Constantinople in the Year 6930 (1422)*], ed. Immanuel Bekker (Bonn, 1838). Compare the additional information in Spyridon Lambros, Παλαιολόγεια καί Πελοποννησιακά (1:66) (Athens, 1926), III, xvi ff., 215.

43. Phrantzes, Χρονικόν (6:15), p. 179.

44. Apostolos Vacalopoulos, "Les Limites de l'empire byzantin" (3), p. 62.

45. See Christopher Buondelmonti, *Description des îles* (6:8), pp. 88–89; Bertrandon de la Brocquière, *Voyage d'outremer* (1), p. 559; and Tafur, *Travels* (1), pp. 145–146, and p. 123: "the city is badly populated."

46. Tafur, *Travels* (1), p. 128.

47. Kritoboulos of Imbros, Ἱστοριῶν συγγραφή [*Histories*], ed. Karl Müller, in *Fragmenta historicorum graecorum* (Paris, 1883), v, 40–161: I, xiv (3)–(9).

48. Socrates Kougeas, "Notizbuch eines Beamten der Metropolis in Thessalonike aus dem Anfang des XV. Jahrhunderts [Notebook of an Official of the Metropolis in Thessalonica, from the Beginning of the Fifteenth Century]," BZ, XXIII (1914–1920), 148. The "Μπαράκος(?) τοῦ Βρανέως(?)" of the chronicle is Bürak, son of Evrenos.

49. See George I. Theocharidis, " Ἄγνωστα τοπογραφικά τῆς Θεσσαλονίκης ἐξ ἀνεκδότου ἐγγράφου τῆς ἐν Ἀγ. Ὄρει Μονῆς Διονυσίου [Unknown *Topographica* of Thessalonica from an Unpublished Document of the Dionysios Monastery on Mt. Athos]," Μακεδονικά, v (1960), 4.

50. See Apostolos Vacalopoulos, *A History of Thessaloniki*, tr. T. F. Carney (Thessalonica, 1963), pp. 62–70; and Camillo Manfroni, "La Marina veneziana alla diffesa di Salonicco (1423–1430) [The Venetian Navy in the Defense of Thessalonica (1423–1430)]," *Nuovo Archivio veneto*, n.s. (1910), 5–68.

51. Vacalopoulos, "Les Limites de l'empire byzantin" (3), p. 62.

52. See Apostolos Vacalopoulos, "Συμβολή στήν ἱστορία τῆς Θεσσαλονίκης ἐπί βενετοκρατίας" (4:14), Τόμος Ἀρμενοπούλου, pp. 137–141. The document of Bishop Meletios of Campania, dated April 14, 1421, also mentions the "nobles of the Senate" (see Franz Dölger, *Aus den Schatzkammern des Heiligen Berges* [*From the Treasuries of the Holy Mount*] [Munich, 1948], p. 266).

53. Euthymios Dionysiatis and Stilpon Kyriakidis, " Ἔγγραφα τῆς ἱερᾶς μονῆς τοῦ Ἀγ. Διονυσίου ἀφορῶντα εἰς ἀγνώστους ναούς τῆς Θεσσαλονίκης [Documents of the Monastery of Saint Dionysios Pertaining to Unknown Churches of Thessalonica]," Μακεδονικά, III (1953–1955), 375.

54. See Vacalopoulos, "Συμβολή στήν ἱστορία τῆς Θεσσαλονίκης" (4:14), pp. 143–146.

55. Robert de Dreux, *Voyage en Turquie et en Grèce*, publié et annoté par Hubert Pernot (Paris, 1925), p. 103.

56. Kougeas, "Notizbuch eines Beamten" (48), p. 152.

57. See Constantine Mertzios, Μνημεῖα Μακεδονικῆς Ἱστορίας (8:86) (Thessalonica, 1947), pp. 49–53.

58. See Vacalopoulos, *A History of Thessaloniki* (49), pp. 71–75.

59. Bertrandon de la Brocquière, *Voyage d'outremer* (1), p. 557.

60. Ioannis Vasdravellis, Ἱστορικά ᾽αρχεῖα Μακεδονίας, Α΄. ᾽Αρχεῖον Θεσσαλονίκης, 1695–1912 [*Historical Archives of Macedonia. I: Archive of Thessalonica, 1695–1912*] (Thessalonica, 1952), pp. 2–3.

61. See Constantin Jireček, "Die Witwe und die Söhne des Despoten Esau von Epirus" (1:51), BNJ, ɪ (1920), 11, 16.

62. See Karl Hopf, *Griechenland im Mittelalter und in der Neuzeit* (1:51) (Leipzig, 1867–1868), ɪɪ, 107.

63. On the question of the nationality of the Slav nobles, see Sebastián Cirác Estopañán, *Bizancio y España* (Barcelona, 1943), ɪɪ, 218.

64. See Constantine Amantos, " Ἡ ἀναγνώρισις ὑπό τῶν Μωαμεθανῶν θρησκευτικῶν καί πολιτικῶν δικαιωμάτων τῶν χριστιανῶν καί ὁ ὁρισμός τοῦ Σινάν πασᾶ [The Recognition by the Mohammedans of the Religious and Political Rights of the Christians, and the Order of Sinan Paşa]," HX, v (1930), 207 ff.

65. See Anonymous, " Ἱστορικόν κατά παράδοσιν τοῦ μακαρίτου Κ. Κοσμᾶ Μπαλάνου, διδασκάλου τῶν ᾽Ιωαννίνων [A History according to the Tradition of the Late K. Kosmas Balanos, Teacher of Ioannina]," ᾽Αθηνᾶ, ɪ (1831), 99–103; and Panagiotis Aravantinos, Χρονογραφία τῆς ᾽Ηπείρου (1:46) (Athens, 1856), ɪ, 225–226. See also, on the Epirotic chronicle, in Aravantinos' vol. ɪ, by an unknown author, " Ἱστορία πολιτική Κωνσταντινουπόλεως [Political History of Constantinople]," ed. by B. G. Niebuhr (Bonn, 1849), pp. 242–244.

66. Halil Inalcik, *Hicrî 835 tarihli sûret-i defteri Sancak-i Arvanid* (1:56) (Ankara, 1954), p. xv.

67. See the article "Arnavutluk" by Halil Inalcik in the *Encyclopaedia of Islam* (1960), ɪ, 654.

68. Baron de Tott, *Mémoires de Baron de Tott sur les Turcs et les Tartares* (Amsterdam, 1784), ɪɪ, 208–209.

69. For full details, see Inalcik, *Sancak-i Arvanid* (1:56), pp. xvii ff.; also his "The Ottoman Record-Books as a Source of Place-Names," Fifth International Congress of Onomastic Sciences, *Proceedings and Transactions* (Salamanca, 1958), ɪɪ, p. 4 of the reprint. Further details on the functions of the commissioners may be found in Inalcik, "Ottoman Methods of Conquest," *Studia islamica*, ɪɪ (1954), 110–111. See also Ömer Lûtfi Barkan, "Essai sur les données statistiques des registres de recensement dans l'empire ottoman aux XVᵉ et XVIᵉ siècles [Essay on the Statistical Data of the Registers of the Census in the Ottoman Empire, in the Fifteenth and Sixteenth Centuries]," *Journal of Economic and Social History of the Orient*, ɪ (1957), 11 ff.

70. See Inalcik, "Ottoman Methods of Conquest" (69), p. 5.

Chapter 11

1. Apostolos Vacalopoulos, "Προβλήματα τῆς ἱστορίας τοῦ παιδομαζώματος" (6:28), Ἑλληνικά, xiii (1954), 281; and İsmail Hakkı Uzunçarşılı, *Kapukulu ocaklari* [The Corps of the "Slaves of the Porte"] (Ankara, 1943), i, 13. Cf. Uzunçarşılı's article "Devsirme" in *Islâm Ansiklopedisi* (Istanbul, 1940–1960). He accepts and combines the separate opinions of William Langer and Robert Blake, "The Rise of the Ottoman Empire and Its Historical Background," *The American Historical Review*, xxxvii (1932), 504, and Herbert Gibbons, *The Rise of the Ottoman Empire* (New York, 1916), pp. 117–118.

2. Vacalopoulos, "Προβλήματα" (6:28), pp. 281–282.

3. See *ibid.*, pp. 281–283, which also includes a bibliography.

4. See Halil Inalcik, "Stefan Dušan 'dan Osmanli imparatorluğuna XV asirda Rumeli' de hıristiyan sipahiler ve menşeleri," in *Fuad Köprülü Armağani* (5:36) (Istanbul, 1953), pp. 213–214, 228–229, 246–247.

5. B. A. Cvetkova, "Новые данные о христианах-спахиях на Балканском полуострове в период турецкого господства [New Evidence on Christian Spahis in the Balkan Peninsula during Turkish Domination]," Viz. Vrem., xiii (1958), 184–197.

6. Bertrandon de la Brocquière, *Voyage d'outremer et retour de Jérusalem en France par la voie de terre, pendant le cours des années 1432 et 1433*, ed. Pierre Legrand D'Aussy, in *Mémoires de l'Institut national des sciences et arts; sciences morales et politiques*, v (Paris, fructidor an XII), pp. 579, 610.

7. See Charles Schefer, ed., *Le Voyage d'outremer de Bertrandon de la Broquière* (Paris, 1892), p. 265.

8. For a similar situation in Albania, see Halil Inalcik, "Timariotes chrétiens en Albanie au XV siècle [Christian Timariots in Albania in the Fifteenth Century]," *Mitteilungen des österreichischen Staatsarchivs*, iv (1951), 122, 123, 124, 128.

9. See Halil Inalcik, "Ottoman Methods of Conquest," *Studia islamica*, ii (1954), 107, 114.

10. Inalcik, "Stefan Dušan" (5:36), pp. 214–216.

11. Very probably this reference was to the descendant of the great πριμμικήριος [Byzantine official] Miekra, of the same district, who was mentioned in a letter by Antonios, Metropolitan of Larissa (probably mid-fourteenth century). See Nikos Bees, "Σερβικά καί βυζαντιακά ἔγγραφα Μετεώρου [Serbian and Byzantine Documents of Meteora]," Βυζαντίς, ii (1911–1912), 71.

12. Inalcik, "Stefan Dušan" (5:36), pp. 214–216.

13. Regarding the Bulgarians of this district, compare the similar view of Sebastián Cirác Estopañán, *Bizancio y España* (Barcelona, 1943), ii, 218: these Bulgars "quizás deban ser considerandos como un resto de las invasiones primitivas en Epeiros o como un resto de los búlgaros que ayudaron a Esteban Dusan en la conquista del despotado, y que deben ser tenidos como pastores

o colonos y esclavos lo mismo que los blachoi [may be considered as remnants of the primitive invaders in Epirus or of the Bulgars who aided Stephen Dušan during the conquest of the despotate and, like the Vlachs, must be thought of as shepherds or farmers or slaves]." See also p. 147.

14. Inalcik, "Stefan Dušan" (5:36), p. 217.

15. Ἱστορικόν Κομνηνοῦ μοναχοῦ καί Πρόκλου μοναχοῦ in *Bizancio y España* (1:51), ed. Sebastián Ciráe Estopañán (Barcelona, 1943), pp. 560–561. Cf. the "Bulgaro-Arvanito-Vlach" philosopher, Neophytus of John Katranis (ed. Pietro Matranga, *Anecdota graeca* [Rome, 1850], II, pp. 676–677, in George Soulis, "Περί τῶν μεσαιωνικῶν ἀλβανικῶν φυλῶν τῶν Μαλακασίων, Μπουίων καί Μεσαριτῶν" (1:45), ΕΕΒΣ, xxiii [1953], 216).

16. Inalcik, "Stefan Dušan" (5:36), p. 217.

17. For examples in Albania as well, see Halil Inalcik, "Timariotes chrétiens" (8), p. 126; and his "Stefan Dušan" (5:36), p. 217.

18. Inalcik, "Timariotes chrétiens" (8), pp. 126, 130.

19. A similar event occurred about two centuries later with the conversion to Islam of the spahis of Epirus (Anonymous, "Ἱστορικόν κατά παράδοσιν τοῦ μακαρίτου Κ. Κοσμᾶ Μπαλάνου, διδασκάλου τῶν Ἰωαννίνων" [10:65], Ἀθηνᾶ, ι [1831], 101).

20. Inalcik, "Ottoman Methods of Conquest" (9), p. 115.

21. Inalcik, "Stefan Dušan" (5:36), pp. 216–217. It is therefore remarkable that Beldiceanu, who was acquainted with Inalcik's study, should still prefer to regard them all as Vlachs, or rather Rumanians (Nicoara Beldiceanu, "Les Roumains à la bataille d'Ankara," *Südost-forschungen*, xiv [1955], 441–454).

22. Inalcik, "Stefan Dušan" (5:36), p. 216.

23. *Ibid.*, p. 215. See also the Albanian *voynuklar* (Inalcik, "Timariotes chrétiens" (8), pp. 136–137).

24. Inalcik, "Ottoman Methods of Conquest" (9), p. 114.

25. Ömer Lûtfi Barkan, *XV ve XVI inci asırlarda osmanlı imparatorluğunda ziraî econominin hukukî ve malî esaslari* [The Legal and Fiscal Principles of the Agrarian Economy in the Ottoman Empire during the XVth and XVIth Centuries] (Istanbul, 1945), I, 289.

26. See Inalcik, "Stefan Dušan" (5:36), p. 218.

27. *Ibid.*, p. 215. Cf. the ancient (kadîmî) Christian *timariotes* in Albania (Inalcik, "Timariotes chrétiens" (8), pp. 120, 128, 132–133).

28. See Inalcik, "Timariotes chrétiens" (8), pp. 132–133.

29. *Ibid.*, pp. 133–135, 136. The Christians of Thessalonica who garrisoned the twenty-four coastal castles were exempt from certain taxes from the time of the city's capture in 1430 until 1605. In the latter year the *beylerbey* and *başdefterdar* of Rumelia, Ahmed Pasha, dispensed with their services on the grounds that "it is impossible to continue the garrisoning of the castle by a collection of infidels, just as it is inconceivable to imagine that they could be trusted." See Ioannis Vasdravellis, Ἱστορικά Ἀρχεῖα Μακεδονίας, Α΄. Ἀρχεῖον Θεσσαλονίκης, 1695–1912 (10:60) (Thessalonica, 1952), pp. 1–3.

Regarding those who were exempt from payment of the *avarizi divaniye*, see "Avâriz" by Ömer Lûtfi Barkan, in *Islam ansiklopedisi* (Istanbul, 1940–1960), II, 73–79.

30. Inalcik, "Ottoman Methods of Conquest" (9), p. 108.

31. See Apostolos Vacalopoulos, Νεοελληνική παράδοσις διά τά ἐπί τουρκοκρατίας προνόμια τῶν Δερβενοχωρίων Κορίνθου [*Modern Greek Tradition on the Privileges of the Dervenochoria of Corinth under the Turkish Rule*] (Thessalonica, 1941), for further details and the relevant bibliography.

32. See Inalcik, "Ottoman Methods of Conquest" (9), pp. 135–136. For the various meanings of the word *Martolos* in Balkan and other European languages (which one must constantly bear in mind in the interpretation of foreign sources), see Robert Anhegger, "Martoloslar hakkında [On *Martolos*]," *Türkiyat mecmuasi*, VII–VIII (1942), no. 1, 283–285.

33. Anhegger, "Martoloslar hakkında" (32), pp. 286–287.

34. Claude Fauriel, *Chants populaires de la Grèce moderne* (Paris, 1824), I, xlvij–xlviij.

35. See Laonicos Chalcocondyles, *Historiarum demonstrationes* (1:52), ed. Eugene Darkó (Budapest, 1922–1927), I, 31; II, 92.

36. Jacovaky Rizo Neroulos, *Histoire moderne de la Grèce* (Geneva, 1828), p. 49.

37. Eugène Yemeniz, *Scènes et récits des guerres de l'indépendance—Grèce moderne* (Paris, 1869), p. 6. Consider also, by way of elaboration, the characteristic remarks of Panagiotes Aravantinos, Χρονογραφία τῆς Ἠπείρου (1:46) (Athens, 1856), II, 4, in relation to the etymology of the word *Agrafa*. This etymology is still part of the popular heritage. See Sophronios Eustratiadis, "Ἐπιστολαί Εὐγενίου Ἰωαννουλίου τοῦ Αἰτωλοῦ [Letters of Eugenios Ioannoulios the Aetolian]," Ἑλληνικά, VIII (1935), 273.

38. David Urquhart, *The Spirit of the East* (London, 1839), I, 319–320.

39. See Léon Heuzey, *Le Mont Olympe et l'Acarnanie* (Paris, 1860), pp. 223–267, especially pp. 257–258. Cf. the description by Yéméniz, *Scènes et récits* (38), pp. 2, 4–5.

40. See Demetrius Aenian, "Ἀρματωλοί καί κλέφτες [Armatoli and *klephtes*]," Βιβλιοθήκη τοῦ λαοῦ (Athens, 1852), p. 272.

41. *Ibid.*, p. 272.

42. *Ibid.*, pp. 273–274.

43. Inalcik, "Stefan Dušan" (5:36), pp. 215–216.

44. See Antonios Keramopoullos, Τί εἶναι οἱ Κουτσόβλαχοι (1:17) (Athens, 1939), fn., p. 96, for the bibliography; also pp. 125, 129 ff., 136–138, 138–139, 142–144. Cf. Socrates Liakos, "Μακεδονικός ἀρματωλισμός [Macedonian Armatolism]," Ἀριστοτέλης, Phlorina, nos. 3, 4, 5 (May–August, 1957).

Chapter 12

1. Ducas, ed. Immanuel Bekker (Bonn, 1834), pp. 136–137 (ed. Basile Grecu [Bucharest, 1958], pp. 175–176); and Pero Tafur, *Travels and Adventures, 1435–1439*, tr. Malcolm Letts (New York-London, 1926), p. 128. Regarding the devastation in Thrace and throughout the West, see Bertrandon

de la Brocquière, *Voyage d'outremer et retour de Jérusalem en France par la voie de terre, pendant le cours des années 1432 et 1433*, ed. Pierre Legrand D'Aussy, in *Mémoires de l'Institut national des sciences et arts; sciences morales et politiques*, v (Paris, fructidor an XII), 569, 570, 571, 573–574, 591, and *passim*. Broquière mentions that in 1432 he saw in Adrianopolis, in chains, Christians whom the Turks had captured in order to sell and who were then begging in the streets (p. 589). Cf. Dimitar Angelov, "Certains Aspects de la conquête des peuples balkaniques par les Turcs," Byz.-Sl., xvii (1956), 237 ff.

2. Joseph Bryennios, Τά εὑρεθέντα (6:82) (Leipzig, 1768), ii, 217.

3. See Laonicos Chalcocondyles, *Historiarum demonstrationes* (1:52), ed. Eugene Darkó (Budapest, 1922–1927), i, 94; and *Chronicle of Aşik paşa Zade*, tr. Richard Kreutel (Vienna, 1959), pp. 39, 40.

4. See Dionysios' note in Raymond Loenertz, *Démétrius Cydonès, correspondance* (Vatican City, 1956), i, 175; Ruy Gonzales de Clavijo, *A Diary of the Journey to the Court of Timur, 1403–1406*, tr. Guy Le Strange (London, 1928), p. 49; and Ömer Lûtfi Barkan, "Les Déportations comme méthode de peuplement et de colonisation dans l'empire ottoman," extrait de la *Revue de la faculté des sciences économiques de l'université d'Istanbul*, 11e année, nos. 1–4 (Istanbul, 1953), pp. 54, 60, which contains the relevant bibliography.

5. See Barkan, "Les Déportations" (4), p. 50.

6. See Ćiro Truhelka, "Über die Balkan-Yürüken [On the Balkan Yuruks]," *Revue internationale des études balkaniques*, i (1934), 91; and Tayyib Gökbilgin, *Rumeli'de Yürükler, Tatarlar ve Evlâd-i Fatihan* (6:23) (Istanbul, 1957), pp. 74 ff.

7. See Barkan, "Les Déportations" (4), pp. 38, 39, 40 ff., which contains the relevant bibliography.

8. See Halil Inalcik, "The Ottoman Record-Books as a Source of Place-Names," Fifth International Congress of Onomastic Sciences, *Proceedings and Transactions* (Salamanca, 1958), ii, pp. 6–7 of the reprint; and "Ottoman Methods of Conquest," *Studia islamica*, ii (1954), 125–126.

9. See Halil Inalcik, *Hicrî 835 tarihli sûret-i defteri Sancak-i Arvanid* (1:56) (Ankara, 1954), pp. xv–xvii. On the *wakf*, freehold properties and fiefs of the districts of Didymoteichon, Gumuljina (Komotine), etc., which were held by the Yuruks who had settled there between 1456 and 1467, see Gökbilgin, *Rumeli'de Yürükler* (6:23), p. 21, and p. 70 for the number of *ortas* in Didymoteichon and Gumuljina in 1453, 1584, 1586, 1591, and 1642.

10. Gökbilgin, *Rumeli'de Yürükler* (6:23), p. 14. Cf. pp. 12, 69, 70, where the number of *ortas* in Demir Hisar, Kalamaria, Drama, Kavala, Sarı Saban, and Çağlayık during the years 1543, 1584, 1586, 1591, and 1642 is noted.

11. Chalcocondyles, *Historiarum demonstrationes* (1:52), i, 94. Concerning these settlers, see the brief study by P. Traeger, "Die Jürüken und Koniaren in Makedonien [The Yuruks and Koniari in Macedonia]," *Zeitschrift für Ethnologie*, xxxvii (1905), 198–206.

12. See Félix de Beaujour, *Tableau du commerce de la Grèce* (Paris, 1800), I, 325–326.

13. See Barkan, "Les Déportations" (4), pp. 44–45, 50–51.

14. See Demetrius Salamangas, Γιαννιώτικα ἱστοριοδιφικά μελετήματα: Τρεῖς εὐθυμήσεις τῶν ἐτῶν 1584, 1597 καί 1630 [*Historical Studies on Ioannina: Three Brief Chronicles of 1584, 1597, and 1630*] (Ioannina, 1958), pp. 89–91.

15. Barkan, "Les Déportations" (4), p. 50.

16. On the confusion surrounding the use of the names Yuruk, Koniar, Tatar Yuruk, and Tatar, see the detailed treatment by Gökbilgin, *Rumeli'de Yürükler* (6:23), pp. 1 ff. Gökbilgin also examines the ethnology of these peoples, as well as the problem of their settlement in various parts of Europe. See also the recent study by Ernst Werner, "Yürüken und Wlachen," *Wissenschaftliche Zeitschrift der Karl-Marx-Universität, Gesellschaft und sprachwissenschaftliche Reihe*, xv (1966), 471–478, which contains a good bibliography.

17. Barkan, "Les Déportations" (4), p. 50. Cf. Traeger, "Die Jürüken" (11), p. 205.

18. Gökbilgin, *Rumeli'de Yürükler* (6:23), pp. 76–77.

19. See Traeger, "Die Jürüken" (11), pp. 205–206.

20. See Chalcocondyles, *Historiarum demonstrationes* (1:52), I, 94.

21. David Urquhart, *The Spirit of the East* (London, 1839), I, 319–320.

22. Jakob Fallmerayer, *Schriften und Tagebücher* (1:1) (Munich-Leipzig, 1913), II, 194–195.

23. Urquhart, *The Spirit of the East* (21), I, 320.

24. Besides Vlachs and Albanians, there are also references to remnants of Slav peoples who were sometimes called Bulgarians and sometimes Serbs. See Léon Heuzey, *Excursion dans la Thessalie turque en 1858* (Paris, 1927), pp. 91, 128.

25. See Barkan, "Les Déportations" (4), p. 50. Besides Yuruks, there is also a reference to eight different *ortas* of Tatars in Yeni Sehir and four in Tsataltza, all of which performed the same duties as the Yuruks. See Gökbilgin, *Rumeli'de Yürükler* (6:23), p. 87.

26. See Nikolaos I. Giannopoulos, "Οἱ δύο μεσαιωνικοί Ἁλμυροί καί ὁ νῦν [The Two Almyroses of the Middle Ages and the Present]," Ἐπετηρίς Παρνασσοῦ, VIII (1904), 82, fn. 1.

27. On the Turkish conquest and its monuments, see Franz Babinger, "Moschee und Grabmal des Osmân Schâch zu Trikkala [The Mosque and Tomb of Osman Shach at Trikkala]," ΠΑΑ, IV (1929), 15–18.

28. See Demetrius K. Tsopotos, Γῆ καί γεωργοί τῆς Θεσσαλίας κατά τήν Τουρκοκρατίαν ἐπί τῇ βάσει ἱστορικῶν πηγῶν (8:46) (Volos, 1912), pp. 1 ff., 11 ff., 20, 21, 25, 29, 35, 36–37, 38, 42, 43, 44–45.

29. See Alfred Philippson and Ernst Kirsten, *Die griechischen Landschaften* (1:9) (Frankfurt, 1950), I, 1. 281.

30. Gustav Weigand, *Die Sprache der Olympo-Wallachen nebst einer Einleitung über Land und Leute* [*The Language of the Olympos Vlachs, To-*

gether with an Introduction on the Land and Its People] (Leipzig, 1888), pp. 11–12.

31. See Tsopotos, Γῆ καί γεωργοί (8:46), pp. 17, 18, 19.

32. See Franz Babinger, *Beiträge zur Frühgeschichte der Türkenherrschaft in Rumelien (14.–15. Jahrhundert)* (6:20) (Munich, 1944), p. 48, fn. 51.

33. See Eustathios Stougiannakis, Ἰστορία τῆς πόλεως Ναούσης [*History of the City of Naousa*], part 1 (Edessa, 1924), pp. 36 ff.; and Ioannis Vasdravellis, "Ἰστορικά περί Ναούσης ἐξ ἀνεκδότου χειρογράφου [Histories concerning Naousa, from an Unpublished Manuscript]," Μακεδονικά, ΙΙΙ (1953–1955), 128 ff. For legends about the Evrenos family, see Beaujour, *Tableau du commerce* (12), I, 111–116. They are based on a Turkish manuscript.

34. See Epaminondas G. Pharmakidis, Ἡ Λάρισα [*Larissa*] (Volos, 1926), pp. 161, 280 ff.

35. For an oral tradition connected with the settlement of Tyrnavos, see Fallmerayer, *Schriften und Tagebücher* (1:1), II, 188.

36. Urquhart, *The Spirit of the East* (22), I, 320–321.

37. Fallmerayer, *Schriften und Tagebücher* (1:1), II, 189, 193.

38. See Barkan, "Les Déportations" (4), p. 49. Barkan has done research on the returns of population and taxation compiled from the great census of Suleiman I's reign. See also Urquhart, *The Spirit of the East* (22), I, 322; and Nikolaos Giannopoulos, "Ἡ μεσαιωνική Φθιῶτις καί τά ἐν αὐτῇ μνημεῖα [Medieval Phthiotis and Its Monuments]," ΔΙΕΕ, VIII (1922), 73, which contains the relevant bibliography.

39. Urquhart, *The Spirit of the East* (22), I, 321–323. On the introduction into Montpellier of the Greek method of dyeing cotton red during the middle of the eighteenth century, see Beaujour, *Tableau du commerce* (12), I, 285–289.

40. Fallmerayer, *Schriften und Tagebücher* (1:1), II, 189–190.

41. William Miller, *The Latins in the Levant: A History of Frankish Greece (1204–1566)* (New York–Cambridge, Eng., 1964), pp. 150–151.

42. Fallmerayer, *Schriften und Tagebücher* (1:1), II, 190.

Chapter 13

1. See Socrates Kougeas, "Notizbuch eines Beamten der Metropolis in Thessalonike aus dem Anfang des XV. Jahrhunderts" (10:48), BZ, XXIII (1914–1920), 153.

2. See Denis Zakythinos, *Le Despotat grec de Morée* (Athens, 1953), I, 213, 216–217.

3. See Andreas Moustoxydis, "Ἰωάννης, Γεώργιος καί Δημήτριος Μόσχοι [Ioannes, Georgios, and Demetrios Moschos]," Ἑλληνομνήμων, I (1843–1853), 387–388.

4. See William Miller, *Essays on the Latin Orient* (Cambridge, Eng., 1921), p. 149; and Vitalien Laurent, "Le Vaticanus latinus 4789. Alliances et filia-

tions des Cantacuzènes au XVᵉ siècle," REB, ɪx (1951), 78 ff., which contains the relevant bibliography.

5. See Alexandre Oleroff, "Démétrius Trivolis, copiste et bibliophile," *Scriptorium*, ɪv (1950), 260–263.

6. Börje Knös, "Gémiste Pléthon et son souvenir," *Lettres d'humanité*, ɪx (1950), 131.

7. See François Masai, *Pléthon et le Platonisme de Mistra* (Paris, 1956), pp. 380–381: "Aussi, lorsque Georges de Trebizonte l'interrogea sur l'issue qu'il entrevoyait à la lutte qui opposait alors l'Islam et le christianisme, le philosophe proclama sa foi dans la disparition prochaine des religions en conflit et dans le triomphe des conceptions païennes. Ses Lois devaient révéler la pensée antique à un monde enfin prêt à la recevoir [Therefore, when George of Trebizond asked him about the outcome which he foresaw in the struggle in which Islam and Christianity were at that time involved, the philosopher proclaimed his confidence in the forthcoming disappearance of the religions which were in conflict and in the triumph of pagan ideas. His *Laws* would reveal ancient thought to a world which was at last ready to receive it]."

8. George Gemistos, Πρός τό ὑπέρ τοῦ λατινικοῦ δόγματος βιβλίον (7:17), PG, ᴄʟx, col. 980. Cf. E. Stephanou, "Ἡ εἱμαρμένη ἐν τῷ φιλοσοφικῷ συστήματι τοῦ Πλήθωνος [Fate in the Philosophical System of Pletho]," Εἰς μνήμην Σπυρίδωνος Λάμπρου (Athens, 1935), pp. 315–320.

9. See Franz Taeschner, "G. Gemistos Plethon, ein Vermittler zwischen Morgenland und Abendland zu Beginn der Renaissance [George Gemistos Pletho, an Intercessor between East and West at the Beginning of the Renaissance]," BNJ, vɪɪɪ (1931), 100–113. Ioannis Mamalakis pursues this problem in "Ἡ ἐπίδραση τῶν σύγχρονων γεγονότων στίς ἰδέες τοῦ Γεμιστοῦ [The Influence of Contemporary Events on the Ideas of Gemistos]," IXth International Congress of Byzantine Studies, Thessalonica, 1953, Πεπραγμένα (Athens, 1955–1958), ɪɪ, 498–532. See also Masai, *Pléthon et le Platonisme* (7), pp. 55–65, 102 ff., for a lengthy analysis of Gemistos' philosophical ideas as well as the relevant bibliography.

10. For some interesting thoughts on Gemistos and his work, see Demosthenes I. Danielidis, Ἡ νεοελληνική κοινωνία καί οἰκονομία [*The Modern Greek Society and Economy*] (Athens, 1934), pp. 79–103; and Ioannis Mamalakis' monograph, Γεώργιος Γεμιστός–Πλήθων (10:1) (Athens, 1939).

11. Mamalakis, Γεώργιος Γεμιστός (10:1), pp. 182–214, especially pp. 195–196, 200, 204, and pp. 214–220. Cf. Martin Jugie, "La Polemique de Georges Scholarios contre Pléthon," *Byzantion*, x (1935), 517–530.

12. Spyridon Lambros, Παλαιολόγεια καί Πελοποννησιακά (1:66) (Athens, 1926), ɪɪ, 19–23. Cf. pp. 24–27.

13. See Zakythinos, *Le Despotat* (2), ɪ, 226, 229–230.

14. *Ibid.*, pp. 204–226. On the wall across the Isthmus, see Spyridon Lambros, "Τά τείχη τοῦ Ἰσθμοῦ τῆς Κορίνθου κατά τούς μέσους αἰῶνας" (9:29), ΝΕ, ɪɪ (1905), 471 ff. Cf. Spyridon Lambros and Constantine Amantos, Βραχέα χρονικά (8:71), series Μνημεῖα τῆς ἑλληνικῆς ἱστορίας, ɪ, part 1 (Athens, 1932), p. 48.

15. For the interpretation of the oracle, see Denis Zakythinos, "Μανουήλ Β΄ Παλαιολόγος καί ὁ καρδινάλιος Ἰσίδωρος ἐν Πελοποννήσῳ (8:90), *Mélanges Merlier*, III (1957), 17, and especially p. 19.

16. See Spyridon Lambros, " Ὑπόμνημα τοῦ καρδιναλίου Βησσαρίωνος εἰς Κωνσταντῖνον τόν Παλαιολόγον" (9:25), NE, III (1906), 15. Page references in parentheses in this chapter refer to the reproduction of the letter given in this issue of NE. Lambros also reproduces it in Παλαιολόγεια καί Πελοποννησιακά (1:66), IV, 32–45.

17. "Πάντων μέν ἄν ἀνθρώπων ἐβουλόμην αὐτό [τό γένος] βασιλεύειν, πάντων δέ πάσαις ἀρεταῖς ὑπερέχειν [I wanted this same race to reign over the whole of mankind, and to excel all in virtue]."

18. Hans-Georg Beck, "Reichsidee und nationale Politik im spätbyzantinischen Staat [The Conception of Empire and National Politics in the Late Byzantine State]," BZ, LIII (1960), 89–90.

19. Bessarion's predecessor, Joseph Bryennios, vividly portrayed the injustices of the nobility (Bryennios, Τά εὑρεθέντα [7:34] [Leipzig, 1768], I, 96–97).

20. See one of Bessarion's letters to the Minorite monk, Jacob Pincens, in which he lists the raw materials of the Peloponnese (Lambros, " Ὑπόμνημα" [9:25], 32).

21. The last line of this text reads as follows: ὅτι δέ καί αὐτός ταῦτα ἐγκρίνεις καί πολλάκις ἀναλογίσω καί ἥδιστα ἄν πράξειας καιροῦ λαβόμενος, οὐδείς ἀγνοεῖ τῶν εἰδότων σου τά φρονήματα [and no one who knows your sentiments is unaware that you yourself sanction this and, having often considered it, would do it most willingly if the opportunity offered itself]."

22. Bariša Krekić, *Dubrovnik (Raguse) et le Levant au moyen âge* (Paris, 1960), pp. 55, 56–57.

23. Laonicos Chalcocondyles, *Historiarum demonstrationes* (1:52), ed. Eugene Darkó (Budapest, 1922–1927), II, 91–92. Cf. p. 341. It is not true, as Denis Zakythinos asserts (*Le Despotat grec de Morée* [Athens, 1953], I, 231), that Constantine Palaeologus delegated the government of the Vlachs and Albanians to a Vlach leader. Constantine Biris, in Ἀρβανίτες, οἱ Δωριεῖς τοῦ νεωτέρου ἑλληνισμοῦ (1:41) (Athens, 1960), pp. 65–66, does not interpret the passage about the "Arvanoi" (Albanians) correctly.

24. See Karl Hopf, *Griechenland im Mittelalter und in der Neuzeit* (1:51) (Leipzig, 1867–1868), II, 119–120.

25. See Franz Babinger, "Beiträge zur Geschichte von Karl-eli, vornehmlich aus osmanischen Quellen [Contributions to the History of Karl-eli, Primarily from the Ottoman Sources]," Εἰς μνήμην Σπυρίδωνος Λάμπρου (Athens, 1935), pp. 140–149.

26. Karl Hopf, *Chroniques gréco-romanes* (Berlin, 1873), p. 195.

27. Ducas, ed. Immanuel Bekker (Bonn, 1834), p. 223 (ed. Basile Grecu [Bucharest, 1958], p. 279).

28. Chalcocondyles, *Historiarum demonstrationes* (1:52), II, 114 ff.; Ducas, ed. Bekker (27), p. 223.

29. Meletios of Ioannina, Γεωγραφία παλαιά τε καί νέα συλλεχθεῖσα ἐκ διαφόρων συγγραφέων παλαιῶν τε καί νέων [A Geography, Ancient and Modern, Gathered from Different Writers, Old and New], 2nd ed. (Venice, 1807), ΙΙ, 365. Cf. Spyridon Lambros, "Προσθήκη εἰς τά περί τῶν τειχῶν τοῦ Ἰσθμοῦ τῆς Κορίνθου κατά τούς μέσους αἰῶνας" (9:29), ΝΕ, ιν (1907), 25–26.

30. Ducas, ed. Bekker (27), p. 223.

31. Lambros, "Προσθήκη" (9:30), pp. 23–24.

32. Chalcocondyles, *Historiarum demonstrationes* (1:52), ΙΙ, 118–120.

33. Panagiotis Aravantinos, Χρονογραφία Ἠπείρου (12:29) (Athens, 1856), Ι, 186. Cf. Ioannis Lambridis, "Πολιτική ἐξάρτησις καί διοίκησις Μαλακασίου [The Political Dependence and Administration of Malakasi]," Παρνασσός, χ (1886), 377.

34. See Ubertini Pusculi Brixiensis, *Constantinopoleos libri IV*, in Adolf Ellissen, *Analekten der mittel- und neugriechischen Literatur* (Leipzig, 1857), ΙΙΙ (Anhang), 27.

35. See Spyridon Lambros, Ἀργυροπούλεια [On the Byzantine Argyropoulos Family] (Athens, 1910), pp. 2–3; and Παλαιολόγεια καί Πελοποννησιακά (1:66), ΙΙΙ, 314–316. Cf. Pusculus, *Constantinopoleos libri IV* (34), p. 55.

36. Georgius Phrantzes, Χρονικόν (6:15), ed. Immanuel Bekker (Bonn, 1838), p. 204; and Chalcocondyles, *Historiarum demonstrationes* (1:52), ΙΙ, 140–141. Cf. Émile Legrand, "Ἰωάννου τοῦ Μόσχου λόγος ἐπιτάφιος ἐπί τῷ Λουκᾷ Νοταρᾷ [Ioannis Moschos's Funeral Speech on Lucas Notaras]," ΔΙΕΕ, ΙΙ (1885–1886), 420.

37. See Georgios Scholarios, Ἅπαντα τά εὑρισκόμενα [*The Complete Works*] (Paris, 1935), ιν, 464 ff.

38. See Phrantzes, Χρονικόν (6:15), p. 205; and Georg Hofmann, "Nuove Fonti per la storia profana ed ecclesiastica di Creta nella prima metà del secolo XV" (7:56), IXth International Congress of Byzantine Studies, Thessalonica, 1953, Πεπραγμένα (Athens, 1956), ΙΙ, 462 ff.

39. See Chalcocondyles, *Historiarum demonstrationes* (1:52), ΙΙ, 141; Phrantzes, Χρονικόν (6:15), pp. 206 ff.; and Zakythinos, *Le Despotat* (23), Ι, 241 ff.

40. See Mamalakis, Γεώργιος Γεμιστός (9:1), pp. 224–225.

41. PG, CLX, col. 814.

42. Hieronymus Charitonymus, Ὑμνῳδία τῷ Γεμιστῷ [Hymn to Gemistos], PG, col. 807. Cf. col. 810.

43. *Ibid.*, cols. 808, 810, 812, for quotations in this paragraph. The text in col. 812 reads, in part: Εἰ καί αὐτός ἴσως ἐσίγας, γῆρας δή μόνον προβαλλόμενος, καί τοι γε ἐν ἄλλοις ἰσχυρότατά γε ἀντέχων [and if you were perhaps yourself silent, only putting forward your old age, but in other things holding out most powerfully]."

44. *Ibid.*, cols. 809, 812, where the text reads: "Καί πολλῶν ἴσως πειρασόμεθα δεινῶν, λόγους διώκοντες, ὧν καί αὐτός πολλά ἐμνήσθην πρός σέ, ἵνα μή ταῦθ' ὑποσταίην [And we may experience many adversities employing

ourselves in philosophy, which I have often mentioned to you, in order not to undergo them]."

45. Savvas Ioannidis, Ἱστορία καί στατιστική Τραπεζοῦντος καί τῆς περί ταύτην χώρας ὡς καί τά περί τῆς ἐνταῦθα ἑλληνικῆς γλώσσης (5:20) (Constantinople, 1870), pp. 292–294. See also Lambros, Παλαιολόγεια καί Πελοποννησιακά (1:66), ι, iii–iv: "ὁ πρῶτος ἐπί τοῦ θρόνου ἀντιπρόσωπος τῆς νέας ἑλληνικῆς ἰδέας [the first representative of the new Greek idea on the throne]."

46. On the advocacy of the Unionist cause by John Argyropoulos and Michael Apostolis, see Pusculus, Constantinopoleos libri IV (34), p. 55.

47. Lambros, Ἀργυροπούλεια (35), pp. 45, 46, 47, 49. John Argyropoulos addressed the inhabitants of the Greek lands thus: "ὦ ἄνδρες Ἕλληνες [O men of Hellas]"—that is, using the word Hellenes (Lambros, Παλαιολόγεια καί Πελοποννησιακά [1:66], ιν, 67 ff.). The work referred to in the fourth volume of Παλαιολόγεια καί Πελοποννησιακά is not that of Michael Apostolis (cf. pp. ix–xi), but rather that of John Argyropoulos (see Christos G. Patrinelis, "Νόθα, ἀνύπαρκτα καί συγχεόμενα πρός ἄλληλα ἔργα τοῦ Μιχ. Ἀποστόλη [Spurious, Nonexistent, and Confused Works of Michael Apostolis]," ΕΕΒΣ, xxx [1960], 204–205).

48. Scholarios, Ἅπαντα (37), ιν, 476–489.

49. Lambros, Παλαιολόγεια καί Πελοποννησιακά (1:66), ιν, 83–87. Contrast with this Apostolis' use of Hellene in a classical, pagan sense at the funeral panegyrics of Andrew Kallerges, following the capture of Crete (see Basileios Laourdas, "Κρητικά παλαιογραφικά" (7:15), ΚΧ, χιι [1958], 384). On the character of Michael Apostolis, see also Deno Geanakoplos, Greek Scholars in Venice (Cambridge, Mass., 1962), pp. 73–110.

50. See Émile Legrand, Bibliographie hellénique ou description raisonnée des ouvrages publiés en grec par des Grecs au XVᵉ et XVIᵉ siècles (Paris, 1885), ιι, 233–234. Concerning this person, see Franz Babinger, Johannes Darius (1414–1494). Sachwalter Venedigs im Morgenland, und sein griechischer Umkreis [Ioannes Darius (1414–1494), Venice's Attorney in the East, and His Greek Circuit] (Munich, 1961), pp. 71–117.

51. See Henri Grégoire, "Les Manuscrits de Julien et le mouvement néopaïen de Mistra: Démétrius Rhallis et Gémiste Pléthon," Byzantion, v (1929), 733–734.

52. See Apostolos Vacalopoulos, Ἡ ἱστορική συνείδηση καί τό ἀγωνιστικό πνεῦμα τοῦ νέου ἑλληνισμοῦ (8:84) (Thessalonica, 1957), p. 11, which contains the relevant bibliography; and Scholarios, Ἅπαντα (37), p. 114.

53. Lambros, Παλαιολόγεια καί Πελοποννησιακά (1:66), ιι, 40: "καί ὅσοι τῶν Ρωμαίων ἤ τῶν Ἑλλήνων τοῦ πράγματος ὕστερον συναισθήσονται [and as many Romans or Greeks as will later be conscious of the fact]." See also p. 44: "οὕτω δέ ὠφελιμωτάτη τῷ κοινῷ τῶν Ἑλλήνων καί χωρίς ἑκάστῳ τῶν ἐντυγχανόντων γεγενημένη [in that way she has become most useful both to the Greek commonwealth and to each individual person]"; Gennadius' words to Demetrius Palaeologus (p. 61): "οὐ γάρ περί τῶν σῶν δικαίων ἠγώνισαι μόνον, ἀλλ' ὑπέρ τοῦ δυστυχοῦς τούτου τῶν Ἑλλήνων λειψάνου, ὅ θᾶττον ἄν ἀπόλοιτο ταῖς ὑμετέραις διαφοραῖς [you had striven not only for

your rights, but on behalf of this unfortunate remnant of the Greeks, which might more swiftly be destroyed by your disputes]"; and p. 62: "καί τῇ τῶν ἑλληνικῶν πραγμάτων στενότητι [and by the closeness of the Greek affairs]."

54. Scholarios, "Απαντα (37), p. 453.

55. For the relevant tradition, see the recent study by Johannes T. Kakridis, "Neugriechische Sagen über die alten Griechen [Modern Greek Stories about the Ancient Greeks]," Živa antika, ix (1959), 3–14, which contains the older bibliography.

56. See Léon Heuzey, Le Mont Olympe et l'Acarnanie (Paris, 1860), pp. 263–264. Characteristically, as late as a century ago, the historical memory of the people of the district of Xeromero placed the Franks before the Turks and the Greeks (who possessed supernatural faculties) before the Franks. This popular memory characterized the various historical periods as Turkish, Frankish, and Greek, rather than Byzantine, Roman, and ancient Greek.

57. See Pierre Belon, Les Observations de plusieurs singularitéz et choses mémorables, trouvées en Grèce (Paris, 1553), p. 8a, concerning the ruins near Kissamos in Crete: "les habitans la nomment Paleo Helenico Castro [the inhabitants call it the Ancient Hellenic Castle]."

58. See Vacalopoulos, Ἡ ἱστορική συνείδηση (8:84), pp. 11–12, which contains the relevant bibliography. Note in the song of Porphyris the expression "υἱόν τραντέλλενον," meaning "thirty times a Greek." See also Ioannidis, Ἱστορία καί στατιστική (5:20), p. 288. For the word Hellene in Pontic songs, see George Soumelidis, " Ἀκριτικά ᾄσματα [Akritic Songs]," ΑΠ, ι (1928), 49 ff. It is a fact, as Wagner observes in his notes to Demetrius Bikelas, Die Griechen des Mittelalters und ihr Einfluss auf die europäische Cultur [The Greeks of the Middle Ages and Their Influence on the Culture of Europe], tr. Wilhelm Wagner (Gütersloch, 1878), p. 108, that the word Ἕλλενος denoted to the Trapezuntines a strong and heroic person.

Chapter 14

1. See Ludwig Mohler, Kardinal Bessarion als Theologe, Humanist und Staatsmann, ι (Paderborn, 1923), 186–191, which contains the relevant bibliography. For the people's impression of the event, see Spyridon Lambros, Ἀργυροπούλεια (13:35) (Athens, 1910), pp. 46–47.

2. See M. Şesan, "La Chute de Constantinople et les peuples orthodoxes," Byz.-Sl., xiv (1953), 275.

3. Georgios Scholarios, "Απαντα τὰ εὑρισκόμενα (13:37) (Paris, 1935), iv, 463–473. Cf. ι, xi–xii.

4. Spyridon Lambros, Παλαιολόγεια καί Πελοποννησιακά (1:66) (Athens, 1926), iv, 46–47.

5. Ibid., pp. 49–63. Cf. Ubertini Pusculi Brixiensis, Constantinopoleos libri IV, in Adolf Ellissen, Analekten der mittel- und neugriechischen Literatur (Leipzig, 1857), iii (Anhang), 34–36; and Baron Ludwig von Pastor, Geschichte der Päpste seit dem Ausgang des Mittelalters [A History of the Popes Since the Close of the Middle Ages] (Freiburg im Breisgau, 1955), ι, 601–603, 605–608.

6. Bariša Krekić, *Dubrovnik (Raguse) et le Levant au moyen âge* (Paris, 1960), p. 60. Note also Bobaljević's negotiations in the Despotate of Morea and the granting of total exemption by Demetrius Palaeologus throughout his realm (pp. 60–61).

7. See Freddy Thiriet, *La Romanie vénitienne au moyen âge* (Paris, 1959), p. 380.

8. Georgius Phrantzes, Χρονικόν (6:15), ed. Immanuel Bekker (Bonn, 1838), pp. 217–219.

9. See Franz Babinger, "Ein Freibrief Mehmeds II des Eroberers, für das Kloster Hagia Sophia zu Saloniki, Eigentum der Sultanin Mara (1451) [A Charter of Mohammed II the Conqueror for the Monastery of Saint Sophia at Salonica, the Property of the Sultana Mara (1451)]," BZ, xliv (1951), 11, which contains the relevant bibliography. Cf. Babinger's *Aufsätze und Abhandlungen zur Geschichte Südosteuropas und der Levante* [*Essays and Treatises on the History of Southeast Europe and the Levant*], i (Munich, 1962), 97. For a Turkish historian's view of the events between 1444 and 1452, see Halil Inalcik, *Fatih devrinde üzerinde tetkikler ve vesikalar* [*Researches and Documents on the Period of the Conqueror Mohammed II*] (Ankara, 1954), pp. 1–136. In his *Belagerung und Eroberung Konstantinopels durch die Türken im Jahre 1453* [*The Siege and Conquest of Constantinople by the Turks in the Year 1453*] (Stuttgart-Augsburg, 1858) Andreas Mordtmann observes that educated Turks used the name Mohammed only for their prophet, but applied the name Mehmed to others—even to the Conqueror himself. This observation is supported by other Greek and Turkish sources.

10. See Mohammed II's speeches in Adrianopolis to Constantine's emissaries, in Ducas, ed. Immanuel Bekker (Bonn, 1834), pp. 238–240 (ed. Basile Grecu [Bucharest, 1958], pp. 297–299).

11. See Phrantzes, Χρονικόν (6:15), pp. 210–211.

12. See Neculai Iorga, *Geschichte des osmanischen Reiches* [*History of the Ottoman Empire*] (Gotha, 1908–1913), ii, 8–9; Pusculus, *Constantinopoleos libri IV* (5), pp. 33–34; and Franz Babinger, *Mehmed der Eroberer und seine Zeit* [*Mohammed the Conqueror and His Times*] (Munich, 1953), pp. 69–70, 73.

13. Ducas (10), ed. Bekker, pp. 233–237 (ed. Grecu, pp. 293–295). Mordtmann, in *Belagerung* (9), p. 7, refers to Orchan as Mohammed's nephew. The wife of Ibrahim of Karamania, a cruel ruler, was a sister of Murad II's (see Bertrandon de la Brocquière, *Voyage d'outremer et retour de Jérusalem en France par la voie de terre, pendant le cours des années 1432 et 1433*, ed. Pierre Legrand D'Aussy, *Mémoires de l'Institut national des sciences et arts; sciences morales et politiques*, v [Paris, fructidor an XII], 540).

14. Ducas (10), ed. Bekker, p. 252 (ed. Grecu, p. 315); Phrantzes, Χρονικόν (6:15), p. 327; Kritoboulos of Imbros, Ἱστοριῶν συγγραφή (10:47), in *Fragmenta historicorum graecorum*, ed. Karl Müller (Paris, 1883), v, 40–161; i, xviii, 8–20. Cf. Constantin Marinescu, "Notes sur quelques ambassadeurs byzantins en Occident à la veille de la chute de Constantinople sous les Turcs [Observations on Some Byzantine Ambassadors in the West on the Eve

of the Fall of Constantinople to the Turks]," *Annuaire de l'Institut de philologie et d'histoire orientales et slaves*, x (1950), 419–428.

15. See Rodolphe Guilland, "Αἱ πρός τήν Δύσιν ἐκκλήσεις Κωνσταντίνου ΙΑ' τοῦ Δραγάτση πρός σωτηρίαν τῆς Κωνσταντινουπόλεως [The Appeals of Constantine XI Dragases to the West for the Saving of Constantinople]," ΕΕΒΣ, xxii (1952), 60–74. For Alfonso V's relations with Byzantium, see Constantin Marinescu, "Contribution à l'histoire des relations économiques entre l'Empire byzantin, la Sicile et le royaume de Naples de 1419 à 1453," SBN, v (1939), 218–219. For the attitude of Nicholas V, see von Pastor, *Geschichte der Päpste* (5), i, 611–613. For that of Venice, see Thiriet, *La Romanie* (7), pp. 381–383, and his *Régestes des délibérations du sénat de Vénise concernant la Romanie*, iii (1431–1463) (Paris, 1961), 173 ff. For the attitude of Philip the Good of Burgundy, see Armand Grunzweig, "Philippe le Bon et Constantinople," *Byzantion*, xxiv (1954), 47–61.

16. Kritoboulos of Imbros, Ἱστοριῶν (10:47), i, vi ff.

17. See the relevant reference by Aşik paşa Zade in Abraham Papazoglou, "Μωάμεθ Β' ὁ πορθητής κατά τόν Τοῦρκον ἱστορικόν 'Ασίκ πασᾶ ζαντέ [Mohammed II the Conqueror in the Turkish History Aşik paşa Zade]," ΕΕΒΣ, xvi (1940), 220; and by Saad-ed-din in Nicephoros Moschopoulos, "'Η ἅλωσις τῆς Κωνσταντινουπόλεως κατά τάς τουρκικάς πηγάς [The Capture of Constantinople according to Turkish Sources]," Hell. Contemp., 1953, p. 30.

18. Laonicos Chalcocondyles, *Historiarum demonstrationes* (1:52), ed. Eugene Darkó (Budapest, 1922–1927), i, 90; ii, 148.

19. Ducas (10), ed. Bekker, p. 246 (ed. Grecu, p. 307).

20. Ducas (10), ed. Bekker, pp. 252, 257, 265 (ed. Grecu, pp. 315, 321, 329–330); Kritoboulos of Imbros, Ἱστοριῶν (10:47), i, xxv; Guilland, "Αἱ πρός τήν Δύσιν" (15), pp. 60 ff.; and Marinescu, "Contribution à l'histoire" (15), pp. 218–219.

21. See Pusculus, *Constantinopoleos libri IV* (5), pp. 37–38, for some interesting information about the riots in Constantinople and the participation in them of an anti-Unionist Bohemian, who was incited by Gennadius.

22. Lambros, Παλαιολόγεια καί Πελοποννησιακά (1:66), ii, 120–121. Note the fashion in which Ducas (10) preserves this declamation—with changes, of course (ed. Bekker, pp. 253–254; ed. Grecu, p. 319). He places it in time after Isidore's arrival, when, in fact, it was written before.

23. Ducas (10), ed. Bekker, pp. 252–253 (ed. Grecu, pp. 315–316). Isidore was also accompanied by Leonard of Chios, Bishop of Mytilene, who has left a vivid narrative of the commotion. See von Pastor, *Geschichte der Päpste* (5), i, 608. In the opinion of Ioannis Papadopoulos ("'Η περί ἁλώσεως τῆς Κωνσταντινουπόλεως 'Ιστορία Λεονάρδου τοῦ Χίου [The History of Leonard of Chios concerning the Capture of Constantinople]," ΕΕΒΣ, xv [1939], 85–95), Makarios Melissinos (sixteenth century), who corrupted Phrantzes' text, also used Leonard in order to complete the Μέγα χρονικόν. For a bibliography on this subject, see Gyula Moravcsik, *Byzantinoturcica*, 2nd ed. (Berlin, 1958), i, 282–288.

24. See Lambros, Παλαιολόγεια καί Πελοποννησιακά (1:66), ιι, 123: "Ἐγώ ἄλλο παρ' ὃ λέγω ἀεί οὐκ ἐρῶ ποτέ [I shall never say anything other than what I am now continually saying]"; and pp. 131–135.

25. Ducas (10), ed. Bekker, p. 255 (ed. Grecu, pp. 317–319).

26. In the expression "πένητος ἐκείνου βασιλέως [that poor king]" I would suggest that Gennadius uses the word "poor" not only in its present-day connotation of "unfortunate," but also hints at Byzantine traditions about the "πένης βασιλεύς [poor king]" (see Nikolaos Politis, Μελέται περί τοῦ βίου καί τῆς γλώσσης τοῦ ἑλληνικοῦ λαοῦ, Παραδόσεις (2:6), ι [Athens, 1904], 664–666).

27. Scholarios, Ἅπαντα (13:37), ιν, 213, 214. Sathas blames Gennadius for assuming this attitude and accuses him of having himself fabricated these pessimistic oracles (Constantine Sathas, Μεσαιωνική βιβλιοθήκη (2:23) [Venice, 1872–1874], νιι, ν').

28. "Οὐδέν τι προσῆκον τῷ μεγέθει τῶν κινδύνων ἀνδρισαμένους [showing a courage not at all commensurate with the magnitude of the dangers]" (Scholarios, Ἅπαντα (13:37), ιν, 216). Cf. ibid., ι, 279, regarding the defenders of the land walls: "φυγῇ προδεδωκότων τῶν φυλάξειν ὑποσχομένων [those who had undertaken to stand guard abandoned them in flight]."

29. See Émile Legrand, "Ἰωάννου τοῦ Μόσχου λόγος ἐπιτάφιος ἐπί τῷ Λουκᾷ Νοταρᾷ" (13:36), ΔΙΕΕ, ιι (1885–1886), 416, 417.

30. Lambros, Παλαιολόγεια καί Πελοποννησιακά (1:66), ιι, 201. Cf. the characterization in Kritoboulos of Imbros, Ἱστοριῶν (10:47), ι, lxxiii, 12. See Constantine Bonis, "Γεώργιος-Γεννάδιος Κουρτέσης ὁ Σχολάριος [Georgios Gennadios Kourtesis, Scholarios]," Νέα Ἑστία, λιιι (1953), 845; and Constantine Amantos, Σχέσεις Ἑλλήνων καί Τούρκων ἀπό τοῦ ἑνδεκάτου αἰῶνος μέχρι τοῦ 1821, τ. Α'. Οἱ πόλεμοι τῶν Τούρκων πρός κατάληψιν τῶν ἑλληνικῶν χωρῶν 1071–1571 [The Relations of the Greeks and the Turks from the Eleventh Century until 1821, vol. 1: The Wars of the Turks to Capture the Greek Lands, 1071–1571] (Athens, 1955), pp. 105–106.

31. Ducas (10), ed. Bekker, p. 264 (ed. Grecu, p. 329).

32. See Apostolos Vacalopoulos, "Die Frage der Glaubwürdigkeit der 'Leichenrede auf L. Notaras' von J. Moschos (15. Jh.) [The Question of the Authenticity of the Funeral Oration for Lucas Notaras of Ioannis Moschos (Fifteenth Century)]," BZ, λιι (1959), 16–17.

33. Scholarios, Ἅπαντα (13:37), ιν, 496. On the conciliatory attitude of Notaras, see also Lambros, Παλαιολόγεια καί Πελοποννησιακά (1:66), ιι, 125, 127: "Μάτην κοπιᾷς, πάτερ, ὅτι τό μνημόσυνον τοῦ πάπα περιέστη νά δοθῇ, καί ἀδύνατον ἄλλως γενέσθαι [you labor in vain, father; for it happens that the Pope must be mentioned by the Orthodox Church, and it cannot be otherwise]." Cf. Adamantios N. Diamantopoulos, "Γεννάδιος ὁ Σχολάριος ὡς ἱστορική πηγή τῶν περί τήν Ἅλωσιν χρόνων [Gennadios Scholarios as an Historical Source for the Period of the Capture]," Ἑλληνικά, ιχ (1936), 285, 298.

34. Leonardus Chiensis, Historia constantinopolitana, PG, clix, cols. 929–930. Cf. Ducas (10), ed. Bekker, pp. 253–255, 256 (ed. Grecu, pp. 315, 319); and Pusculus, Constantinopoleos libri IV (5), pp. 36–37.

35. Kritoboulos of Imbros, Ἱστοριῶν (10:47), ι, xvii, 3; Ducas (10), ed. Bekker, pp. 258–259 (ed. Grecu, p. 321); and Phrantzes, Χρονικόν (6:15), pp. 236–237. Pyrgos could not have fallen after the capture, as Ypsilantis later claimed (Athanasius Ypsilantis, Τά μετά τήν ῞Αλωσιν 1453–1789 [6:26] [Constantinople, 1870], p. 4). The traditions mentioned in Polydoros Papachristodoulou, "Παραδόσεις [Traditions]," ΑΘΛΓΘ, ι (1934–1935), 60, that Herakleia held on for seven years after the capture, and, in Kall. Chourmouziadis, " Ἐπαρχία Μετρῶν καί ᾽Αθύρων. Πετροχώρι [Province of Metrai and Athyran. Petrochori]," ΑΘΛΓΘ, ιv (1937–1938), 107–108, that Selymbria fell before it, are also spurious.

36. Mordtmann, Belagerung (9), p. 49.

37. Leonardus Chiensis, Historia (34), col. 927.

38. See Babinger, Mehmed der Eroberer (12), p. 88.

39. Chalcocondyles, Historiarum demonstrationes (1:52), ιι, 149–150.

40. Ducas (10), ed. Bekker, p. 262 (ed. Grecu, pp. 325–327).

41. Phrantzes, Χρονικόν (6:15), p. 240. Apparently quite a number of foreign officers (Spaniards and others) served under John VIII Palaeologus during the last years of the Empire. See Pero Tafur, Travels and Adventures, 1435–1439, tr. Malcolm Letts (New York–London, 1926), p. 123; and Kritoboulos of Imbros, Ἱστοριῶν (10:47), ι, xxiii, 3. Phrantzes (p. 240) gives the number as 258,000, and Ducas (10), ed. Bekker (p. 267), as 400,000. Cf. Maximilian Braun and Alfons Schneider, Bericht über die Eroberung Konstantinopels nach der Nikon-Chronik [Report on the Conquest of Constantinople, according to the Nikon Chronicle] (Göttingen, 1940), p. 6. Iacopo de Promontorio de Campis places the number of Turks at 70,000 (Franz Babinger, Die Aufzeichnungen des Genuesen Iacopo de Promontorio de Campis über den Osmanenstaat um 1475 [The Notes of the Genoese Iacopo de Promontorio de Campis on the Ottoman State about 1475] [Munich, 1957]). Basing his own estimate on that of Promontorio de Campis, Babinger contends that there were more than 80,000 (Mehmed der Eroberer (12), p. 91).

42. See Mordtmann, Belagerung (9), pp. 31 ff.; Scarlatos Byzantios, ῾Η Κωνσταντινούπολις [Constantinople] (Athens, 1851), ι, 105, 106; and Alexandros Paspatis, Βυζαντιναί μελέται, τοπογραφικαί καί ἱστορικαί [Byzantine Studies, Topographical and Historical] (Constantinople, 1877), pp. 5, 7, 13, 15, 17, 20.

43. Mordtmann, Belagerung (9), p. 49.

44. Phrantzes, Χρονικόν (6:15), pp. 239, 242–244.

45. Ducas (10), ed. Bekker, pp. 267, 275 (ed. Grecu, pp. 333, 343–345); and Leonardus Chiensis, Historia (34), col. 929C.

46. See Phrantzes, Χρονικόν (6:15), pp. 244–247.

47. Ibid., pp. 247–250. Cf. p. 338; and Ducas (10), ed. Bekker, pp. 268–269 (ed. Grecu, pp. 335–337).

48. Kritoboulos of Imbros, Ἱστοριῶν (10:47), ι, xlii; and Ducas (10), ed. Bekker, pp. 270–271 (ed. Grecu, pp. 337–339). Cf. Gustave Schlumberger, Le Siège, la prise et le sac de Constantinople par les Turcs en 1453 (Paris, 1922), pp. 160–164.

49. Kritoboulos of Imbros, Ἱστοριῶν (10:47), ι, xlvii, 1–2. Cf. Rodolphe Guilland, "La Chaîne de la Corne d'Or [The Bondage of the Golden Horn]," ΕΕΒΣ, xxv (1955), 103 ff.

50. Ducas (10), ed. Bekker, pp. 277–279 (ed. Grecu, pp. 347–349).

51. See Kritoboulos of Imbros, Ἱστοριῶν (10:47), ι, xxv–xxvi, xxxi–xxxii, xxxiv, xlii; and cf. xlvii, 1: "τό τε γὰρ τεῖχος τό τε ἐντός τό τε ἐκτός ταῖς μηχαναῖς κατήρριπτο μέχρις ἐδάφους [for the wall both inside and out fell to the ground under the machines]." On the problem of defense as a whole, and the actual performance of the besieged, see Leonardus Chiensis, Historia (34), cols. 927 ff., 936B; and Chalcocondyles, Historiarum demonstrationes (1:52), ιι, 151–152, 153–154.

52. Phrantzes, Χρονικόν (6:15), pp. 244–247. See also Mordtmann, Belagerung (9), pp. 71–72.

53. Kritoboulos of Imbros, Ἱστοριῶν (10:47), ι, xxxi. See also the summaries from the diary of Nicolò Barbaro in Ellissen, Analekten (5), ιιι (Nachtrag), 97 ff.; and Mordtmann, Belagerung (9), p. 80.

54. Phrantzes, Χρονικόν (6:15), p. 260.

55. See Kritoboulos of Imbros, Ἱστοριῶν (10:47), ι, xlvii, 1–2.

56. Ducas (10), ed. Bekker, pp. 275, 279–280 (ed. Grecu, pp. 343, 349–351). Cf. Braun and Schneider, Bericht über die Eroberung (41), p. 15.

57. Mordtmann, Belagerung (9), p. 80.

58. Phrantzes, Χρονικόν (6:15), pp. 252–256.

59. Ducas (10), ed. Bekker, pp. 281–282 (ed. Grecu, p. 353).

60. Kritoboulos of Imbros, Ἱστοριῶν (10:47), ι, xliv; Phrantzes, Χρονικόν (6:15), pp. 257, 260–261; and Leonardus Chiensis, Historia (34), cols. 934A, 935. Cf. Pusculus, Constantinopoleos libri IV (5), p. 78; and the testimony of Evliya Tshelebi (Mordtmann, Belagerung (9), p. 122).

61. Scholarios, Ἅπαντα (13:37), ιv, 214; and Ducas (10), ed. Bekker, p. 318 (ed. Grecu, pp. 399–401). Cf. Anonymous, Ἱστορία πολιτική Κωνσταντινουπόλεως (10:65), ed. B. G. Niebuhr (Bonn, 1849), p. 10; and Braun and Schneider, Bericht über die Eroberung (41), p. 16 (fn. 31 for the relevant bibliography).

62. Phrantzes, Χρονικόν (6:15), pp. 264–265, 277; and Braun and Schneider, Bericht über die Eroberung (41), pp. 20, 21. Cf. Kritoboulos of Imbros, Ἱστοριῶν (10:47), ι, xlv, xlvi; and Pusculus, Constantinopoleos libri IV (5), pp. 78–79.

63. Phrantzes, Χρονικόν (6:15), p. 261. For general reminiscences about the outcry against Constantine, see Evliya Tshelebi in Mordtmann, Belagerung (9), p. 116.

64. Leonardus Chiensis, Historia (34), col. 934B. Gennadius insisted shortly before that the rich should contribute money (Lambros, Παλαιολόγεια καί Πελοποννησιακά (1:66), ιι, 96).

65. Phrantzes, Χρονικόν (6:15), p. 256. Cf. pp. 260–261; and Scholarios, Ἅπαντα (13:37), ιv, 221.

66. See Scholarios, Ἅπαντα (13:37), pp. 501–502; Phrantzes, Χρονικόν (6:15), p. 241; and Evliya Tshelebi, in Mordtmann, Belagerung (9), pp. 30,

116, 117, 122, for reminiscences of the defection of the inhabitants to the Turkish camp, and their conversion to Islam.

67. See Alfons Schneider, "Die Bevölkerung Konstantinopels im XV. Jahrhundert [The Population of Constantinople in the Fifteenth Century]," *Nachrichten der Akademie der Wissenschaften in Göttingen, phil.-hist. Klasse*, 1949, pp. 236–237.

68. Leonardus Chiensis, *Historia* (34), col. 929D.

69. Kritoboulos of Imbros, Ἱστοριῶν (10:47), I, xiv, 13–15; xlix, 1–2.

70. See Ducas (10), ed. Bekker, pp. 275, 282 (ed. Grecu, pp. 343, 353); and Kritoboulos of Imbros, Ἱστοριῶν (10:47), I, xlviii, 7.

71. Phrantzes, Χρονικόν (6:15), pp. 269–279. See also Leonardus Chiensis, *Historia* (34), cols. 938C ff.; and Georgios Zoras, "Αἱ τελευταῖαι πρό τῆς ἁλώσεως δημηγορίαι Κωνσταντίνου τοῦ Παλαιολόγου καί Μωάμεθ τοῦ Πορθητοῦ [The Final Speeches of Constantine Palaeologus and Mohammed the Conqueror before the Capture]," ΕΕΦΣΠΑ, II, 9 (1958–1959), 510–538.

72. See Linos Politis, "Μιά ἐνθύμηση γιά τήν Ἅλωση [One Memoir on the Capture]," Ἑλληνικά, XVI (1958–1959), 231–232.

73. Pavlos Karolidis, Ἱστορία τῆς Ἑλλάδος, 1453–1862 [*History of Greece, 1453–1862*] (Athens, 1925), p. 30.

74. For the attack on the ruined walls and the first breaches, see Leonardus Chiensis, *Historia* (34), cols. 940B, 941 ff. See also the relevant notes in Lambros, Παλαιολόγεια καί Πελοποννησιακά (1:66), IV, 91–93, according to which Constantine met his death "ἐν τῇ γενομένῃ χαλάστρᾳ [in the breach that took place]" and "τόν Ἅγιον Ρωμανόν ἔμπροσθεν [in front of Saint Romanos']." Cf. Kritoboulos of Imbros, Ἱστοριῶν (10:47), I, lxxii, 2; Pusculus, *Constantinopoleos libri IV* (5), pp. 80–81; and the diary of Nicolò Barbaro, in Ellissen, *Analekten* (5), III (Nachtrag), 103–104.

75. Phrantzes, Χρονικόν (6:15), pp. 280 ff., 291. Cf. Ducas (10), ed. Bekker, p. 283 (ed. Grecu, p. 355). On the various portrayals of Constantine, see Spyridon Lambros, "Αἱ εἰκόνες τοῦ Κωνσταντίνου τοῦ Παλαιολόγου [The Portrayals of Constantine Palaeologus]," NE, III (1906), 229–242; and "Νέαι εἰκόνες Κωνσταντίνου Παλαιολόγου [New Portrayals of Constantine Palaeologus]," NE, IV (1907), 238–240. See also Lambros' "Καί ἄλλαι εἰκόνες Ἰωάννου καί Κωνσταντίνου τῶν Παλαιολόγων [Yet Other Portrayals of John and Constantine Palaeologus]," NE, VI (1909), 399–408.

76. Kritoboulos of Imbros, Ἱστοριῶν (10:47), I, lxiii; Ducas (10), ed. Bekker, pp. 285–286, 294 (ed. Grecu, pp. 359, 369–371).

77. Phrantzes, Χρονικόν (6:15), pp. 288–291; Ducas (10), ed. Bekker, pp. 287 ff. (ed. Grecu, pp. 361 ff.); Kritoboulos of Imbros, Ἱστοριῶν (10:47), I, li–liii; and Braun and Schneider, *Bericht über die Eroberung* (41), p. 31.

78. Joseph Bryennios, Τά εὑρεθέντα (6:82) (Leipzig, 1768), II, 280–281. Cf. the lament in Kritoboulos of Imbros, Ἱστοριῶν (10:47), I, lxix, 2.

79. Kritoboulos of Imbros, Ἱστοριῶν (10:47), I, lvi, 2. Cf. Chalcocondyles, *Historiarum demonstrationes* (1:52), II, 161.

80. Mordtmann, *Belagerung* (9), p. 126.

81. Phrantzes, Χρονικόν (6:15), pp. 287–288. Cf. Alexandros Paspatis, Πολιορκία καί ἅλωσις τῆς Κωνσταντινουπόλεως ὑπό τῶν 'Οθωμανῶν ἐν ἔτει 1453 [*The Siege and Capture of Constantinople by the Ottomans in the Year 1453*] (Athens, 1890), p. 61.

82. Ypsilantis, Τά μετά τήν ἅλωσιν (6:26), pp. 50–53, 62. Cf. Anonymous, Πατριαρχική ἱστορία Κωνσταντινουπόλεως [*Patriarchal History of Constantinople*], ed. Immanuel Bekker (Bonn, 1849), pp. 158 ff.; the contradictory remarks of Paspatis, Βυζαντιναί μελέται (42), p. 300; J. H. Mordtmann, "Die Kapitulation von Konstantinopel im Jahre 1453," BZ, xxi (1912), 129–144; Karolidis, 'Ιστορία τῆς 'Ελλάδος (73), p. 34; and the view of Turkish-speaking John Chotzis in Pericles K. Vizoukidis, "'Ηπειρωτικῶν θεσμίων ἔρευνα [An Investigation of Epirote Customs]," HX, ιι (1927), 3, fn. 2.

83. Ducas (10), ed. Bekker, pp. 298–299 (ed. Grecu, pp. 375, 377); Phrantzes, Χρονικόν (6:15), pp. 290–291; and Braun and Schneider, *Bericht über die Eroberung* (41), pp. 32–33.

84. Paspatis, Πολιορκία (81), pp. 187, 200.

85. Mordtmann, *Belagerung* (9), p. 125.

86. Xenophon A. Siderides, "Κωνσταντίνου Παλαιολόγου θάνατος, τάφος καί σπάθη [The Death, Grave, and Sword of Constantine Palaeologus]," Μελέτη, 1908, pp. 142–143. Cf. Braun and Schneider, *Bericht über die Eroberung* (41), pp. 32–33, fn. 72. There is a recent comparison and discussion of the various opinions relating to Constantine's fate and the whereabouts of his grave in Karolidis, 'Ιστορία τῆς 'Ελλάδος (73), pp. 48–61. A much later version of the events, which accords with popular belief, is that a certain Christian (who was later executed) placed Constantine's head in a silver container under the altar of Hagia Sophia and buried his body in a corner of the Imperial Palace. See Neculai Iorga, "Istanbul'un zaptı hakkında ihmal edilmis bir kaynak [A Neglected Source on the Capture of Constantinople]," tr. Fazıl Işıközlü and Adnan S. Erzi, *Belleten,* xiii (1949), 146. As for the Christian who was executed, it would seem that this popular story refers to the Greek architect Christodoulos. See also Feridum Dirimtekin's review of Babinger's *Mehmed der Eroberer und seine Zeit* (12), in *Istanbul enstitüsü dergisi,* ι (1955), 129; cf. p. 140.

87. Phrantzes, Χρονικόν (6:15), p. 301.

88. See Vacalopoulos, "Die Frage" (32), pp. 19–20.

89. See Kritoboulos of Imbros, 'Ιστοριῶν (10:47), ι, lxxiii; Leonardus Chiensis, *Historia* (34), col. 943; Phrantzes, Χρονικόν (6:15), p. 293; Ducas (10), ed. Bekker, pp. 303–306 (ed. Grecu, pp. 379–385); Pusculus, *Constantinopoleos libri IV* (5), p. 82; and Anonymous, 'Ιστορία πολιτική Κωνσταντινουπόλεως (10:65), pp. 23–24, which provides considerable information unobtainable from other sources. See also Vacalopoulos, "Die Frage" (32), pp. 19–20. On the nobleman's murder, see Theodore Spandugino, "De la origine deli imperatori ottomani" in Constantine Sathas, *Documents inédits relatifs à l'histoire de la Grèce au moyen âge* (Paris, 1890), ιx, 154–155.

90. See Spyridon Lambros, "'Ο Κωνσταντῖνος Παλαιολόγος ὡς σύζυγος ἐν τῇ ἱστορίᾳ καί τοῖς θρύλοις [Constantine Palaeologus as Consort in History

and in Legends]," NE, ιν (1907), 454–466; and Konstantinos Mertzios, "Ἡ διαθήκη τῆς ᾿Ἄννας Παλαιολογίνας Νοταρᾶ [The Will of Anna Palaeologina Notaras]," ᾿Ἀθηνᾶ, LIII (1949), 17–21.

91. Giovanni Cecchini, "Anna Notara Palaeologa: Una Principessa greca in Italia e la politica senese di ripopolamento delle Maremma [Anna Notara Palaeologa: A Greek Princess in Italy, and the Politics in Siena concerning the Repopulation of the Maremma]," *Bolletino senese di storia patria*, n.s. IX (1938), 6, 21–22, 26–27. That part of Cecchini's study which examines the relationship between Anna Notara and Constantine Palaeologus has no basis in fact.

92. Wife of Matthew Spandounis and niece of Catherine, daughter of the Despot of Serbia, George Branković, and Irene Cantacuzena (according to Michael Lascaris). On Irene, see Michael Lascaris, Византиске принцезе у средњевековној Србији [*Byzantine Princesses in Medieval Serbia*] (Belgrade, 1926), pp. 97 ff.

93. See Lambros, "῾Ο Κωνσταντῖνος Παλαιολόγος" (90), p. 461.

94. See Vacalopoulos, "Die Frage" (32), p. 20.

95. Chalcocondyles, *Historiarum demonstrationes* (1:52), II, 196–197. Some interesting comments on this forcible confinement appear in Kritoboulos of Imbros, ᾿Ἱστοριῶν (10:47), I, lxxiv, 3.

96. See Halil Inalcik, "Ottoman Methods of Conquest," *Studia islamica*, II (1954), 123.

97. Konstantinos Paparrhegopoulos, ᾿Ἱστορία τοῦ ἑλληνικοῦ ἔθνους (3:2) (Athens, 1932), v, part 1, 377; part 2, 27.

98. See Olfert Dapper, *Description exacte des isles de l'Archipel* (Amsterdam, 1703), p. 17; Apostolos Vacalopoulos, *Thasos, son histoire, son administration de 1453 à 1912* (Paris, 1953), p. 16; Margaritis Constantinidis, ῾Η Μεσημβρία τοῦ Εὐξείνου [*Mesembria on the Euxine*] (Athens, 1945), I, 48; and Margaritis Constantinidis, "῾Η Μεσημβρία παρ᾿ Εὐξείνῳ [Mesembria on the Euxine]," ΑΘΓΛΘ, XXI (1956), 19–20.

99. Konstantinos Mertzios, "Περὶ Παλαιολόγων καί ἄλλων εὐγενῶν Κωνσταντινουπολιτῶν [On the Palaeologi and Other Noble Constantinopolitans]," Γέρας Κεραμοπούλλου, pp. 355–372. Cf. Andreas Moustoxydis, "᾿Ἰωάννης Παλαιολόγος καί οἱ ἄλλοι τοῦ αὐτοῦ ἐπωνύμου [Ioannis Palaeologus and Others of the Same Family Name]," ᾿Ἑλληνομνήμων, I (1843), 295–302; and G. E. Typaldos, "Οἱ ἀπόγονοι τῶν Παλαιολόγων μετά τήν ἄλωσιν [The Descendants of the Palaeologi after the Capture]," ΔΙΕΕ, VIII (1922), 129–157. On officers named Lascaris in the *Stradioti*, see Börje Knös, *Un Ambassadeur de l'hellénisme—Janus Lascaris—et la tradition gréco-byzantine dans l'humanisme français* (Uppsala-Stockholm-Paris, 1945), pp. 66–67, which contains the relevant bibliography. Cf. the supplementary bibliography in Manoussos Manoussacas, ῾Η ἐν Κρήτῃ συνωμοσία τοῦ Σήφη Βλαστοῦ (1453–1454) καί ἡ νέα συνωμοτική κίνησις τοῦ 1460–1462 (8:8) (Athens, 1960), p. 38, fn. 1.

100. Gennadios Arambatzoglou, Φωτίειος βιβλιοθήκη [*Photian Library*], part 1 (Constantinople, 1933), 108, fn. 3. Cf. Manoussos Manoussacas, "Les

Derniers Défenseurs de Constantinople d'après les documents vénitiens," XIᵉ Congrès international des études byzantines, Munich, 1958, *Akten* (Munich, 1960), 331–340; Ducas (10), ed. Bekker, p. 297 (ed. Grecu, p. 373); Chalcocondyles, *Historiarum demonstrationes* (1:52), ii, 163; and Robert Browning, "The Capture of Constantinople in 1453," *Byzantion*, xxii (1952), 379–387. Browning's note had previously appeared in Arambatzoglou, Φωτίειος, i, 108.

101. Ducas (10), ed. Bekker, p. 297 (ed. Grecu, p. 391).

102. See E. Dallegio D'Alessio, "Le Texte grec du traité conclu par les Génois de Galata avec Mehmet II le 1ᵉʳ juin 1453," Ἑλληνικά, xi (1938), 115–124, which contains the early bibliography.

103. See Constantine Amantos, " Ἡ Ἅλωσις τῆς Κωνσταντινουπόλεως [The Capture of Constantinople]," Hell. Contemp., Commemorative Volume, 1953, p. 18.

104. Kritoboulos of Imbros, Ἱστοριῶν (10:47), i, lvii, 3.

105. Cardinal Isidore, *Universis christefidelibus* [*To All Christians*], PG, clix, col. 955.

106. Ducas (10), ed. Bekker, pp. 258, 312 (ed. Grecu, pp. 321, 391–392; Kritoboulos of Imbros, Ἱστοριῶν (10:47), i, xvii, 3.

107. Apostolos Vacalopoulos, "Les Limites de l'empire byzantin depuis la fin du XIVᵉ siècle jusqu'à sa chute (1453)," BZ, lv (1962), 63–64; Thiriet, *Régestes* (15), iii, 198, 200.

108. Andronicus Callistus, Μονῳδία ἐπί τῇ δυστυχεῖ Κωνσταντινουπόλει [Monody on Unfortunate Constantinople], PG, clxi, col. 1131.

109. See the commemorative issues of the following journals on the occasion of the 500th anniversary of the capture: Hell. Contemp., Byz.-Slav., Viz. Vrem., vii (1953), School of Oriental and African Studies, *Bulletin* ("The Fall of Constantinople").

110. Phrantzes, Χρονικόν (6:15), pp. 310, 314. It is curious that the Spaniards do not hold the same opinion as other Roman Catholics (Sebastián Cirác Estopañán, " Ἡ πτῶσις τῆς Κωνσταντινουπόλεως ἐν ἔτει 1453 καί οἱ Ἰσπανοί [The Spaniards and the Fall of Constantinople in 1453]," IXth International Congress of Byzantine Studies, Thessalonica, 1953, Πρακτικά, ii (1956), 304–324, and especially p. 321.

111. Besides the bibliography in Amantos, Σχέσεις Ἑλλήνων καί Τούρκων (30), pp. 119–121, see Spyridon Lambros, "Καί ἄλλαι μονῳδίαι εἰς τήν ἅλωσιν τῆς Κωνσταντινουπόλεως [Other Monodies on the Capture of Constantinople]," NE, viii (1911), 93; Lambros, " Ὁ ἐν τῷ Χρησμολογίῳ τοῦ Λιγαρίδου θρῆνος τῆς Κωνσταντινουπόλεως [The Lamentation on Constantinople's Capture in the Oracle Book of Ligaridis]," NE, xv (1921), 292; Emmanuel Kriaras, Τό ἀνακάλημα τῆς Κωνσταντινόπολης [*Monody on the Capture of Constantinople*] (Thessalonica, 1956); Georgios Zoras, Περί τήν ἅλωσιν τῆς Κωνσταντινουπόλεως [*On the Capture of Constantinople*] (Athens, 1959), pp. 213–253, 269–283. There is only one demotic song, so far as I know, which refers to the extinction of the Notaras family. See Argyrios Ghisas, "Τραγούδια Κοζάνης [Songs of Kozane]." Ἡμερολόγιον δυτικῆς Μακεδονίας, 1938, pp. 43–44.

112. Besides the bibliography given in n. 115 below, see Spyridon Lambros, "Προσθήκη εἰς τὰ περί τῶν τειχῶν τοῦ Ἰσθμοῦ τῆς Κορίνθου κατά τούς μέσους αἰῶνας" (9:29), NE, ιv (1907), 21–22; "Ὁ Κωνσταντῖνος" (90), NE, ιv, 446–454; "Ἡ ἐξήγησις εἰς τήν Ἀποκάλυψιν τοῦ Ζαχαρίου Γεργανοῦ [Interpretation of the Apocalypse of Zacharias Gerganos]," NE, ιv (1907), 486–487; and "Στίχοι εἰς τό μέλλον ἔσεσθαι τῇ πόλει [Verses on the Future of Constantinople]," NE, xv (1921), 294. For the modern traditions, see Polydoros Papachristodoulou, Παραδόσεις (14:35), ΑΘΓΛΘ, ι (1934–1935), 60–62; Symeon Manaseides, Λαογραφικά Μαδύτου [Folklore Material from Madytos], ΑΘΓΛΘ, ιιι (1936–1937), 117–118. Basileios Deligiannis, Λαογραφικά Μαλγάρων [Folklore Material from Malgara], ΑΘΓΛΘ, ιιι (1936–1937), 209.

113. See Siderides, Κωνσταντίνου Παλαιολόγου (86), p. 71, which contains the relevant bibliography.

114. Ducas (10), ed. Bekker, pp. 289–290 (ed. Grecu, p. 365). See V. A. Vasil'ev, Anecdota graeco-byzantina (Moscow, 1893), ι, 33, for the relevant prophecy. This Byzantine tradition had so influenced the masses that, after the Turkish entry into Constantinople, the garrison of the sea walls threw the keys to the gates into the sea in anticipation of the fulfillment of the oracle (Chalcocondyles, Historiarum demonstrationes (1:52), ιι, 160–161.

115. For these traditions, see Bartholomaeus Georgieviz, De Turcarum moribus epitome [A Summary of Turkish Customs] (Lyons, 1558), pp. 109 ff., together with the commentaries; Martinus Crusius, Turcograeciae libri octo [Eight Books on Turkish Greece] (Basel, 1584), p. 494; Frederick Hasluck, "The Prophecy of the Red Apple," reprinted in his Christianity and Islam under the Sultans (Oxford, 1929), ιι, 736–740; Franz Babinger, "Quizil Elma [The Red Apple]," in Islam, xιι (1922), 109–111; Ettore Rossi, "La Legenda turco-bizantina del Pomo Rosso [The Turkish-Byzantine Legend of the Red Apple]," SBN, v (1939), 542–553; and Richard M. Dawkins, "The Red Apple," ΑΘΓΛΘ, vι (1941), 401–406, which contains the relevant bibliography. For the modern Hellenic tradition about the duration of the Turkish occupation of Constantinople, see Deligiannis, "Λαογραφικά Μαλγάρων" (112), p. 209; and Constantine Romaios, "Ἡ Ἀοκκίνη Μηλιά' τῶν ἐθνικῶν μας θρύλων. Προβλήματα σχετιζόμενα μέ τήν καταγωγή της [The 'Red Apple' in Our National Legends. Problems Connected with Its Origin]," ΕΕΒΣ, xxιιι (1953), 676–688. The bibliography in Romaios' article is insufficient. There are various traditions about the μῆλα as a symbol. Johann Schiltberger (The Bondage and Travels of Johann Schiltberger, a Native of Bavaria, in Europe, Asia, and Africa, 1396–1427, tr. Commander J. Buchan Telfer [London, 1879], p. 80) wrote at the beginning of the fifteenth century concerning the sphere in the left hand of the statue of Justinian: "At one time the statue had a golden apple in the hand, and that meant that he had been a mighty emperor over Christians and Infidels; but now he has no longer that power, so the apple has disappeared." Cf. the traditions cited in Tafur, Travels (41), pp. 140–141, 144–145.

116. See PG, cvii, col. 1150.

117. See Braun and Schneider, *Bericht über die Eroberung* (41), pp. 33, 34–35.

118. See Michael Lascaris, Τό ἀνατολικόν ζήτημα, 1800–1923 [*The Eastern Question, 1800–1923*] (Thessalonica, 1948), ι, 233, fn. 2; and Cyril Mango, "The Legend of Leo the Wise," *Zbornik radova* (Recueil de travaux), Institute of Byzantine Studies, Belgrade, lxv (1960), no. 6, p. 67, fn. 38. For mention of "ξανθόν γένος [fair-haired race]" in Turkish sources, see Bertold Spuler's, review of Braun's and Schneider's *Bericht über die Eroberung* in *Islam*, xxix (1949–1950), 255–256.

119. Lascaris, Τό ἀνατολικόν ζήτημα (118), pp. 231–232; and Braun and Schneider, *Bericht über die Eroberung* (41), p. 33, fn. 75.

120. See Politis, Μελέται (2:6), ι, 22, 667 ff.; and Mango, "The Legend of Leo" (118), pp. 60–61.

121. See Spyridon Lambros, " Ὑπόμνημα τοῦ καρδιναλίου Βησσαρίωνος εἰς Κωνσταντῖνον τόν Παλαιολόγον" (9:24), NE, ιιι (1906), 23.

122. Georgios Zoras, " Ἡ ἅλωσις τῆς Κωνσταντινουπόλεως καί ἡ βασιλεία τοῦ Μωάμεθ Β΄ τοῦ κατακτητοῦ (κατά τόν ἀνέκδοτον ἑλληνικόν βαρβερινόν κώδικα 111 τῆς Βατικανῆς βιβλιοθήκης [The Capture of Constantinople, and the Kingdom of Mohammed II the Conqueror, According to an Uupublished Codex, Graecus Barberinus 111, in the Vatican Library]," ΕΕΒΣ, xxii (1952), 253–254. Cf. Sathas, Μεσαιωνική βιβλιοθήκη (2:23), ι, 267; and Lambros, " Ὁ Κωνσταντῖνος Παλαιολόγος" (90), 446–466.

123. See Nicolas de Nicolay, *Les Navigations, pérégrinations et voyages, faicts en la Turquie* (Anvers, 1577), pp. 90, 91; and Isidorus, *Notitia*, PG, clix, col. 951. There are some interesting comments on an investigation into the problem of suppositious narratives in Braun and Schneider, *Bericht über die Eroberung* (41), p. 6, fn. 8.

124. See Mango, "The Legend of Leo" (118), pp. 78–93. Cf. Lascaris, Τό 'ἀνατολικόν ζήτημα (118), pp. 230–236; Börje Knös, "Les Oracles de Léon le Sage (d'après un livre d'oracles byzantins illustrés récemment découvert)," Ἀφιέρωμα στή μνήμη τοῦ Μ. Τριανταφυλλίδη (Athens, 1960), pp. 155–188; and Athanasios Kominis, "Παρατηρήσεις εἰς τούς χρησμούς Λέοντος τοῦ Σοφοῦ [Observations on the Oracles of Leo the Wise]," ΕΕΒΣ, xxx (1960), 398–412.

125. See M. B. Levtchenko, "Завоевание турками Константинополя в 1453 г. и исторические последствия этого соыытия. [The Capture of Constantinople by the Turks and the Historical Results of That Event]," Viz. Vrem., vii (1953), 3–8.

126. Note the information given on Epirus by a later text in Athanasios Petridis, "Χρονικόν Δρυοπίδος" (6:48), Νεοελληνικά ἀνάλεκτα, ιι (1871), 24. Cf. Sophronios Sophroniadis, Ἡ Σινασός τῆς Καππαδοκίας καί τά δημοτικά της τραγούδια [Sinasos of Cappadocia and Its Popular Songs] (Athens, 1958), pp. 145–146.

Chapter 15

1. In Adolf Ellissen, *Analekten der mittel- und neugriechischen Literatur* (9:8) (Leipzig, 1860), III, 190.

2. See Laonicos Chalcocondyles, *Historiarum demonstrationes* (1:52), ed. Eugene Darkó (Budapest, 1922–1927), II, 197–201. On fiefs at the time of Mohammed II, see Serif Bastav, *Ordo Portae. Description grecque de la Porte et de l'armée du Sultan Mehmed II, éditée, traduite et commentée* [*The Order of the Gate. A Greek Description of the Gate and of the Army of Sultan Mohammed II, Edited, Translated, and Annotated*] (Budapest, 1947), p. 10.

3. Chalcocondyles, *Historiarum demonstrationes* (1:52), II, 148, 169–170, 406. Cf. Kritoboulos of Imbros, Ἱστοριῶν συγγραφή (10:47), in *Fragmenta historicorum graecorum*, ed. Karl Müller (Paris, 1883), V, 40–161: I, lxxiv (1)–(3).

4. See Franz Dölger, "Politische und geistige Strömungen im sterbenden Byzanz," JÖBG, III (1954), 9.

5. See Denis Zakythinos, *Le Despotat grec de Morée* (Athens, 1953), I, 196–198, 212, 233–234.

6. Pero Tafur, *Travels and Adventures, 1435–1439*, tr. Malcolm Letts (New York–London, 1926), p. 49.

7. Chalcocondyles, *Historiarum demonstrationes* (1:52), II, 170.

8. *Ibid.*, p. 170. Thus I believe his phrase "καὶ ὥρμηντο μέν ὡς ξυμβήσοντες τοῖς ἡγεμόσι, μετὰ δέ διεκωλύθησαν [and they were roused as if to come to an agreement with the leaders, but afterwards were prevented]" must be interpreted. His Latin translation is incorrect.

9. Chalcocondyles, *Historiarum demonstrationes* (1:52), II, 170–175. See Georgius Phrantzes, Χρονικόν (6:15), ed. Immanuel Bekker (Bonn, 1838), pp. 383, 385. On the conflicts between Albanians and Greeks, see Freddy Thiriet, *Régestes des délibérations du sénat de Vénise concernant la Romanie*, III (1431–1463), (Paris, 1961), 199 ff.

10. Franz Miklosich and Joseph Müller, *Acta et diplomata graeca medii aevi sacra et profana* (1:43) (Vienna, 1860–1887), III, 290.

11. Chalcocondyles, *Historiarum demonstrationes* (1:52), II, 176. The relevant passage in Chalcocondyles is both brief and obscure. Cf. p. 202.

12. *Ibid.*, pp. 175–176.

13. See Spyridon Lambros, Ἀργυροπούλεια (13:35) (Athens, 1910), pp. xxxix–xl; and Παλαιολόγεια καί Πελοποννησιακά (1:66) (Athens, 1926), IV, 196–197, 205–206.

14. Chalcocondyles, *Historiarum demonstrationes* (1:52), II, 202.

15. See *ibid.*, 203 ff.; Phrantzes, Χρονικόν (6:15), p. 387; Kritoboulos of Imbros, Ἱστοριῶν (10:47), III, iii ff.; Eugene Darkó, "Περὶ τῆς ἱστορίας καί τῶν μνημείων τοῦ Μουχλίου [On the History and the Monuments of Mouchlion]," ΠΑΑ, VI (1931), 22–29; and Darkó's "Ἡ ἱστορική σημασία καί τά σπουδαιότερα ἐρείπια τοῦ Μουχλίου [The Historical Significance and the More Important Ruins of Mouchlion]," ΕΕΒΣ, X (1933), 454–482. The

Turks destroyed just enough monuments of ancient Corinth to make projectiles for their canon (Chalcocondyles, *Historiarum demonstrationes*, II, 207).

16. Kritoboulos of Imbros, Ἱστοριῶν (10:47), III, vi (3)–(8). Cf. Chalcocondyles, *Historiarum demonstrationes* (1:52), II, 207–211.

17. See Kritoboulos of Imbros, Ἱστοριῶν (10:47), III, vii–ix; Phrantzes, Χρονικόν (6:15), pp. 337–338; and Apostolos Vacalopoulos, Νεοελληνική παράδοσις διά τά ἐπί τουρκοκρατίας προνόμια τῶν Δερβενοχωριτῶν Κορίνθου (11:31) (Thessalonica, 1941), *passim*.

18. Ferdinand Gregorovius, *Geschichte der Stadt Athen im Mittelalter, von der Zeit Justinians bis zur türkischen Eroberung* (2:2) (Stuttgart, 1889), Greek translation by Spyridon Lambros (Athens, 1904–1906), II, 384–390.

19. Kritoboulos of Imbros, Ἱστοριῶν (10:47), III, ix (4)–(7).

20. Ioannis Travlos, Πολεοδομική ἐξέλιξις τῶν Ἀθηνῶν ἀπό τῶν προϊστορικῶν χρόνων μέχρι τῶν ἀρχῶν τοῦ 19. αἰῶνος (8:36) (Athens, 1960), p. 182.

21. See Kritoboulos of Imbros, Ἱστοριῶν (10:47), III, xix; Chalcocondyles, *Historiarum demonstrationes* (1:52), II, 213–216, 224–227; and Phrantzes, Χρονικόν (6:15), pp. 388–395. For Bessarion's view of the situation in the Peloponnese, and his attempt to influence the West, see Spyridon Lambros, " Ὑπόμνημα τοῦ καρδιναλίου Βησσαρίωνος εἰς Κωνσταντῖνον τόν Παλαιολόγον" (9:24), NE, III (1906), 32–33; and Georg Voigt, *Enea Silvio de'Piccolomini, als Papst Pius der Zweite und sein Zeitalter* [*Enea Silvio de'Piccolomini as Pope Pius II, and His Age*] (Berlin, 1863), III, 56–58.

22. Kritoboulos of Imbros, Ἱστοριῶν (10:47), III, i–v.

23. See Photios Chrysanthopoulos, Ἀπομνημονεύματα περί τῆς ἑλληνικῆς ἐπαναστάσεως (10:37) (Athens, 1899), I, 139–140; and Vacalopoulos, Νεοελληνική παράδοσις (11:31), pp. 1–2.

24. Kritoboulos of Imbros, Ἱστοριῶν (10:47), III, xx; and Chalcocondyles, *Historiarum demonstrationes* (1:52), II, 227–229. For the date of the fall of Mistra, see Meletios E. Galanopoulos, " Ὁ Λακεδαιμόνιος βιβλιογράφος ἐπίσκοπος Βρεσθένης Παρθένιος [The Lacedemonian Bibliographer, Bishop of Brestheni Parthenios]," ΕΕΒΣ, XII (1936), 252. One of Demetrius' cities, Monemvasia, besought the protection of Pope Pius II and gave herself over to him (Bariša Krekić, "Monemvasie sous la protection papale," *Zbornik radova*, VI [1960], 129–135).

25. Kritoboulos of Imbros, Ἱστοριῶν (10:47), III, xxiv.

26. See Demetrius Petropoulos, "Λαϊκή παράδοση καί ἱστορία [Popular Tradition and History]," Πελοποννησιακή πρωτοχρονιά, 1958, pp. 77–78, which contains the relevant bibliography. There is some dispute as to whether the medieval Gardiki was situated in the same place as its present-day counterpart, or at Kokkala. See Alfred Philippson and Ernst Kirsten, *Die griechischen Landschaften* (1:9) (Frankfurt, 1950), III, 1. 293.

27. Kritoboulos of Imbros, Ἱστοριῶν (10:47), III, xxii (6), xxiii.

28. On the ancestry of Mahmud (that his mother was a Serb and his father a Greek), and his elevation to high office, see Chalcocondyles, *Historiarum demonstrationes* (1:52), II, 196.

29. *Ibid.*, pp. 229–239; and Spyridon Lambros, "Κωνσταντῖνος Παλαιολόγος Γραίτζας, ὁ ἀμύντωρ τοῦ Σαλμενίκου [Constantine Palaeologus Graetzas, the Defender of Salmenico]," ΝΕ, xi (1914), 260–288.

30. See Thiriet, *Régestes* (14:15), iii, 241.

31. See Michael Lascaris, "Ὁ κερκυραῖος Πέτρος Λάντζας (Συμπληρωματικά) [The Corfiote Petros Lantzas (Supplementary Materials)]," in Ἀφιέρωμα εἰς τήν Ἤπειρον εἰς μνήμην Χρ. Σούλη (Athens, 1956), p. 251.

32. Marinos P. Vrettos, "Ἀπόπειρα ἀναστατώσεως τῆς Μάνης κατά τόν ΙΖ΄ αἰῶνα [The Attempt at Disorder in Maina in the Seventeenth Century]," Ἐθνικόν ἡμερολόγιον, vi (1866), 199. Who they were, and from what countries they came, remain problematical.

33. Carlier de Pinon, *Voyage en Orient* (Paris, 1920), p. 52: "Le 6ᵉ (juin) vismes, a gauche le port delle Quaïe, ainsy appellé a raison du nombre de cailles, qui se trouvent en ladicte contrée. Ce port est pres du susdict, Capo di Matapan, auquel endroit le pays est nommé Brazzo di Maina, et les habitants Maïnati, lesquelz jusques a present se sont guarantis du joug du Turc; ils parlent albanois, et demeurent dans des cavernes ça et la par les montaignes, ayant le bruict d'estre fort belliqueux [The 6th (of June) we saw to the left the Port delle Quaïe, so called on account of the number of quails in the above-mentioned area. This port is near the said Capo di Matapan, at which spot the country is called Brazzo di Maina and the inhabitants Maïnati, who to this date have been exempted from the Turkish yoke; they speak Albanian and live in caverns here and there among the mountains, and they have the repute of being very warlike]."

34. Ducas, ed. Immanuel Bekker (Bonn, 1834), p. 340 (ed. Basile Grecu [Bucharest, 1958], pp. 425–427).

35. See Antonios Lignos, Ἱστορία τῆς νήσου Ὕδρας [*History of the Island of Hydra*] (Athens, 1946), i, 5, 10–16.

36. Frederick Hasluck, "Albanian Settlements in the Aegean Islands," BSA, xv (1908–1909), 224.

37. See Spyridon Lambros, "Ἡ ἐκ Πατρῶν εἰς Ρώμην ἀνακομιδή τῆς κάρας τοῦ Ἁγίου Ἀνδρέου [The Removal from Patras to Rome of the Head of Saint Andrew]," ΝΕ, x (1913), 33 ff.; and "Ἀλεξίου ἐπισκόπου Κλουσίου Ἀνδρεῖς [Poem on St. Andrew by Alexios, Bishop of Clusium]," ΝΕ, x (1913), 81–112. On Thomas' journey through Ragusa and the attitude of the people there toward him, see Bariša Krekić, *Dubrovnik (Raguse) et le Levant au moyen âge* (Paris, 1960), pp. 62–65.

38. Zakythinos, *Le Despotat* (5), i, 260 ff.

39. Cf. Lambros, Παλαιολόγεια καί Πελοποννησιακά (1:66), iv, 284 ff.

40. Phrantzes, Χρονικόν (6:15), p. 412.

41. Vladimir Lamansky, *Secrets d'État de Vénise; documents, extraits, notices et études servant à éclaircir les rapports de la Seigneurie avec les Grecs, les Slaves et la Porte Ottomane à la fin du XVᵉ et au XVIᵉ siècles* (St. Petersburg, 1884), p. 046. For details, see Manoussos Manoussacas, Ἡ ἐν Κρήτῃ συνωμοσία τοῦ Σήφη Βλαστοῦ (1453–1454) καί ἡ νέα συνωμοτική κίνησις τοῦ 1460–1462 (8:8) (Athens, 1960), pp. 71 ff.

42. Phrantzes, Χρονικόν (6:15), pp. 452–453.

43. See Spyridon Sakellaropoulos, "Ὁ τάφος τοῦ Γεωργίου Φραντζῆ [The Grave of Georgius Phrantzes]," Μελέτη, 1908, pp. 513–522.

44. I have treated the substance of this section in greater detail in my book, *Thasos, son histoire, son administration de 1453 à 1912* (Paris, 1953), which also contains the relevant bibliography. I have included here only a supplementary bibliography.

See Spyridon Lambros, "Ἐπιστολή Πίου Β' πρός Ἀλέξανδρον Ἀσάνην περί καταλήψεως τῆς Ἴμβρου [A Letter from Pius II to Alexander Asanes concerning the Capture of Imbros]," NE, x (1913), 118. The governors, or ἄρχοντες, as Kritoboulos called them, represented the Emperor and not the Gattilusi as Lambros believed.

45. Baron Ludwig von Pastor, *Geschichte der Päpste seit dem Ausgang des Mittelalters* (14:5) (Freiburg im Breisgau, 1955), I, 696 ff.

46. A little later, the Turks apparently removed ninety-six Christian families to Phocaea (probably Palaea Phocaea) and settled them in one of its suburbs (see Ömer Lûtfi Barkan, "Les Déportations comme méthode de peuplement et de colonisation dans l'empire ottoman," extrait de la *Revue de la Faculté des sciences économiques de l'université d'Istanbul*, 11ᵉ année, nos. 1–4 [Istanbul, 1953], p. 41).

47. Von Pastor, *Geschichte der Päpste* (14:5), I, 751–752.

48. Alexander Asanes, perhaps a son or a relative of Michael Asanes, governor of the island in 1442, during the reign of John VIII Palaeologus, then showed his interest in the liberation and occupation of Imbros by soliciting the support of the Pope. See Lambros, "Ἐπιστολή Πίου Β'" (44), p. 126.

49. Virtually the only source for these years is in Spyridon Lambros, "Τό τραπεζουντιακόν χρονικόν τοῦ πρωτοσεβάστου καί πρωτονοταρίου Μιχαήλ Παναρέτου [The Trapezuntine Chronicle of the *Protosebastos* and *Protonotarios*, Michael Panaretos]," NE, IV (1907), 257–295. On the question of the authenticity of the last part of the Chronicle, see Odysseus Lampsidis, "Ὁ γάμος Δαβίδ τοῦ Μεγάλου Κομνηνοῦ καί τό χρονικόν τοῦ Παναρέτου [The Marriage of David the Great Comnenus, and the Chronicle of Panaretos]," Ἀθήνα, LVII (1953), 365–368, which gives the early bibliography; Jakob Fallmerayer, *Geschichte des Kaisertums von Trapezunt* [*History of the Empire of Trebizond*] (Munich, 1827), pp. 29 ff.; Savvas Ioannidis, Ἱστορία καί στατιστική Τραπεζοῦντος καί τῆς περί ταύτην χώρας ὡς καί τά περί τῆς ἐνταῦθα ἑλληνικῆς γλώσσης (5:20) (Constantinople, 1870), pp. 48 ff.; Pavlos Karolidis, Ἱστορία τῆς Ἑλλάδος (14:73), 1453–1862 (Athens, 1925), pp. 160 ff.; William Miller, *Trebizond. The Last Greek Empire* (London, 1926), pp. 14–15; Alexander Vasiliev, "The Foundation of the Empire of Trebizond," *Speculum*, II (1936), 3–37; and Vasiliev's excellent critical analysis of the bibliography relating to Trebizond up to 1940, in his "The Empire of Trebizond in History and Literature," *Byzantion*, xv (1940–1941), 316–377. On the various problems associated with the chronicle, as well as some objections to Vasiliev's view of the origins of the Empire, see Odysseus Lampsidis, Μιχαήλ τοῦ Παναρέτου περί τῶν Μεγάλων Κομνηνῶν—Εἰσαγωγή-ἔκδοσις-σχόλια

[*Michael Panaretos' Work on the Great Comneni—Introduction, Text, and Commentary*] (Athens, 1958), *passim*.

50. See Gabriel Millet and D. Talbot Rice, *Byzantine Painting at Trebizond* (London, 1936), pp. 174, 177.

51. Tafur, *Travels* (6), p. 131.

52. See Pericles Triantaphyllidis, Οἱ φυγάδες (5:13) (Athens, 1870), p. 58; and Miller, *Trebizond* (49), p. 87.

53. On the topography, products, commerce, and military organization of the Empire, see Spyridon Lambros, "Βησσαρίωνος ἐγκώμιον εἰς Τραπεζοῦντα [Bessarion's Encomium on Trebizond]," NE, XIII (1916), 145–204.

54. Ruy Gonzales de Clavijo, *A Diary of the Journey to the Court of Timur, 1403–1406*, tr. Guy Le Strange (London, 1928), pp. 117, 121, 336.

55. See Chalcocondyles, *Historiarum demonstrationes* (1:52), II, 178, 222–223; Fallmerayer, *Geschichte des Kaisertums* (49), pp. 254–257; Ioannidis, Ἱστορία καί στατιστική (5:20), pp. 102–106; Karolidis, Ἱστορία τῆς Ἑλλάδος (14:73), pp. 148–179; and Franz Babinger, *Mehmed der Eroberer und seine Zeit* (14:12) (Munich, 1953), p. 201.

56. Fallmerayer, *Geschichte des Kaisertums* (49), pp. 258–261. There is an interesting article on Uzun Hassan by Vladimir Minorsky, in the *Encyclopedia of Islam*, IV (1924), 1065–1069. In Σχέσεις Ἑλλήνων καί Τούρκων ἀπό τοῦ ἑνδεκάτου αἰῶνος μέχρι τοῦ 1821, τ. Α΄. Οἱ πόλεμοι τῶν Τούρκων πρός κατάληψιν τῶν ἑλληνικῶν χωρῶν 1071–1571 (14:30) (Athens, 1955), I, 145, Constantine Amantos refers to the daughter of John the Good as Theodora (not Catherine). On the hostile disposition of Ibrahim Bey, see Bertrandon de la Brocquière, *Voyage d'outremer et retour de Jérusalem en France par la voie de terre, pendant le cours des années 1432 et 1433*, ed. Pierre Legrand D'Aussy, *Mémoires de l'Institut national des sciences et arts; sciences morales et politiques*, V (Paris, fructidor an XII), 541.

57. Chalcocondyles, *Historiarum demonstrationes* (1:52), II, 246.

58. Miller, *Trebizond* (49), pp. 97–99. For further details on the strange history of the deceiver, Fra Lodovico da Bologna, see Babinger, *Mehmed der Eroberer* (14:12), pp. 196–200.

59. Kritoboulos of Imbros, Ἱστοριῶν (10:47), IV, i (7).

60. Ducas (34), ed. Bekker, p. 339 (ed. Grecu, p. 425); and Chalcocondyles, *Historiarum demonstrationes* (1:52), II, 243.

61. Kritoboulos of Imbros, Ἱστοριῶν (10:47), IV, ii (1)–(3).

62. *Ibid.*, IV, iii (1)–(2). On the date of Mohammed II's departure, see Miller, *Trebizond* (49), p. 105.

63. Ducas (34), ed. Bekker, p. 341 (ed. Grecu, p. 427).

64. Kritoboulos of Imbros, Ἱστοριῶν (10:47), IV, iii (3).

65. *Ibid.* (4)–(8); Ducas (34), ed. Bekker, pp. 341–342 (ed. Grecu, p. 429); Miller, *Trebizond* (49), pp. 101–102; and Babinger, *Mehmed der Eroberer* (14:12), pp. 204–205.

66. Kritoboulos of Imbros, Ἱστοριῶν (10:47), IV, iv–v (1).

67. *Ibid.*, IV, vi; Miller, *Trebizond* (49), pp. 101–102; and Babinger, *Mehmed der Eroberer* (14:12), pp. 205–206.

68. Ducas (34), ed. Bekker, p. 342 (ed. Grecu, p. 429).

69. Jean François Boissonade, 'Ανέκδοτα [*Unpublished Works*] (Paris, 1883), v, 392–393.

70. Kritoboulos of Imbros, 'Ιστοριῶν (10:47), ιν, vii (1)–(3).

71. Boissonade, 'Ανέκδοτα (69), v, 393.

72. *Ibid.*, v, 394–395.

73. Kritoboulos of Imbros, 'Ιστοριῶν (10:47), ιν, vii (4)–(8) Chalcocondyles, *Historiarum demonstrationes* (1:52), ιι, 246–249; Ducas (34), ed. Bekker, pp. 342–343 (ed. Grecu, pp. 429–431); and Anonymous, 'Ιστορία πολιτική Κωνσταντινουπόλεως (10:65), ed. B. G. Niebuhr (Bonn, 1849), pp. 37–38. Cf. Fallmerayer, *Geschichte des Kaisertums* (49), pp. 275–277 for the bibliography; Spyridon Lambros, "'Η περί ἁλώσεως Τραπεζοῦντος ἐπιστολή τοῦ 'Αμηρούτζη [The Letter of Ameroutzes on the Capture of Trebizond]," NE, xii (1915), 476–477; Chrysanthos Philippidis, "'Η ἐκκλησία Τραπεζοῦντος [The Church of Trebizond]," ΑΠ, ιν–v (1936), 319–322; and Babinger, *Mehmed der Eroberer* (14:12), pp. 207–208. On the date of the capture, see Franz Babinger, "La Date de la prise de Trébizonde par les Turcs (1461)," REB, vii (1949), 205–207, which contains the relevant bibliography. Since the coincidence of the event with such an important feast of Orthodoxy as that of the Assumption appears to be nowhere mentioned in Greek sources, August 15 would seem not to be an entirely convincing date.

74. Triantaphyllidis, Οἱ φυγάδες (5:13), p. 51.

75. See Spyridon Lambros, "'Η ἅλωσις τῆς Τραπεζοῦντος καί ἡ Βενετία [Venice and the Capture of Trebizond]," NE, ιι (1905), 324–333; and Babinger, "La Date de la prise" (73), pp. 210–211.

76. Boissonade, 'Ανέκδοτα (69), v, 390.

77. See Philippidis, "'Η ἐκκλησία" (73), pp. 520–522, which contains the relevant bibliography. For the bibliography dealing with the "Brief Chronicles" on the fate of David, see Odysseus Lampsidis, Πῶς ἡλώθη ἡ Τραπεζοῦς. 'Αντιγραφή καί διερεύνησις τῶν πηγῶν [How Trebizond Was Captured. Transcription and Investigation of the Sources]," ΑΠ, xvii (1952), 54; Phrantzes, Χρονικόν (6:15), pp. 413–414; Kritoboulos of Imbros, 'Ιστοριῶν (10:47), ιν, ix (1); and Babinger, *Mehmed der Eroberer* (14:12), pp. 207–210, 231–232, 246–247. For information on the fate of the members of David's family, see Vitalien Laurent, "Le Vaticanus latinus 4789," REB, ιx (1951), 88–89. See Amiroukes' verses dedicated to the Sultan—which were flattering to the point of sycophancy—in Spyridon Lambros, "Ποιήματα Γεωργίου τοῦ 'Αμοιρούτζη [The Poems of Georgios Amiroukes]," ΔΙΕΕ, ιι (1885–1886), 275–282.

78. See Miller, *Trebizond* (49), pp. 113, 114, which contains the relevant bibliography; and Ioannidis, 'Ιστορία καί στατιστική (49), p. 119.

79. See Hippolyte Noiret, *Documents inédits pour servir à l'histoire de la domination vénitienne en Crete de 1380 à 1485* [*Unpublished Documents Pertaining to the History of Venetian Domination in Crete from 1380 to 1485*] (Paris, 1892), p. 225.

80. Kritoboulos of Imbros, Ἰστοριῶν (10:47), ιν, viii (2); Boissonade, Ἀνέκδοτα (69), v, 396 ff.; Chalcocondyles, *Historiarum demonstrationes* (1:52), ιι, 248; and Phrantzes, Χρονικόν (6:15), p. 308. See also Anonymous, Πολιτική ἱστορία (10:65), p. 37.

81. Barkan, "Les Déportations" (46), p. 41: "plusieurs habitants du Sandjak de Trébizonde, possesseurs de 'vignobles seigneuriaux' furent déportés en Roumélie par Umur et Kasim bey et leurs propriétés reduites en timars [several inhabitants of the Sancak of Trebizond, possessors of 'lordly vineyards,' were removed to Rumelia by Umur and Kasim Bey, and their properties were reduced to fiefs]." Cf. Ömer Lûtfi Barkan, "Osmanlı imparatorluğunda bir iskân, ve kolonizasyon metodu olarak sürgünler [Deportation as a Method of Settlement and Colonization in the Ottoman Empire]," *Iktisat Fakultesi Mecmuasi*, vol. 15, nos. 1–4, pp. 10, 11, fn. 90, of the reprint [n.d.].

82. See Anonymous, Πολιτική ἱστορία (10:65), p. 37.

83. Kritoboulos of Imbros, Ἰστοριῶν (10:47), ιν, viii (3)–(4). See also the *Chronicle of Aşik paşa Zade*, tr. Richard Kreutel (Vienna, 1959), p. 226: "Die Gazi hatten inzwischen mehrere Gegenden des Landes heimgesucht und gute Beute gemacht [The Ghazis had in the meantime devastated several areas of the countryside, and found good spoils]."

84. Chalcocondyles, *Historiarum demonstrationes* (1:52), ιι, 248. The district of Tzapnides is identifiable as that inhabited by the Kizilbashs. See Franz Babinger, "Der Islam in Kleinasien [Islam in Asia Minor]," in his *Aufsätze und Abhandlungen zur Geschichte Sudösteuropas und der Levante*, ι (Munich, 1962), 65–66, which contains the relevant bibliography.

85. Kritoboulos of Imbros, Ἰστοριῶν (10:47), ιν, viii (2), (4); *Chronicle of Aşik paşa Zade* (83), tr. Kreutel, p. 226; and Abraham Papazoglou, "Μωάμεθ Β΄ ὁ πορθητής κατά τόν Τοῦρκον ἱστορικόν Ἀσίκ πασᾶ ζαντέ" (14:17), ΕΕΒΣ, xvι (1940), 234.

86. Ducas (34), ed. Bekker, p. 342 (ed. Grecu, p. 429).

87. Chalcocondyles, *Historiarum demonstrationes* (1:52), ιι, 248. Cf. the later source " Ἔκθεσις χρονική [A Chronological Description]" in Constantine Sathas, Μεσαιωνική βιβλιοθήκη (2:23) (Venice, 1872–1874), vιι, 578.

88. See Barkan, Osmanlı imparatorluğunda (81), p. 11, fn. 88: "Timar-ı Merne(?) nâm zimmî ki Torul kal'asını ol vermiş [The fief of the subject named Merne (?), who handed over the Castle of Torul]."

89. See the entry entitled "Ardasa," by Demosthenes Oikonomidis, in Ἐγκυκλοπαιδικον λεξικόν Ἐλευθερουδάκη (Athens, 1927), ιι, 415.

90. See Barkan, Osmanlı imparatorluğunda (81), p. 12: "12 kayıtda mülk sahibinin Tekür'le (imparatorla) beraber giden sipahi kâfirler olduğu, 9 *unun hain olub kaçan* kâfirlere âid bulunduğu anlaşılmaktadır [at the twelfth recording it becomes evident that it belongs to nine non-Moslems, who were infidel spahis following the Emperor, the master of the property, and who became treacherous to him and abandoned him]."

91. Triantaphyllidis, Οἱ φυγάδες (5:13), p. 47. Cf. Émile Legrand, *Recueil de chansons populaires grecques* (Paris, 1874), p. 78. See Apostolos Vacalo-

poulos, "Zur Datierung zwier griechischer Volkslieder [On the Date of Two Popular Greek Songs]," *Zeitschrift für Balkanologie*, III (1965), 4–11.

92. See the view of Triantaphyllidis, Οἱ φυγάδες (5:13), pp. 40–41.

93. See Pericles Triantaphyllidis, Ἡ ἐν Πόντῳ ἑλληνικὴ φυλή ἤτοι τά Ποντικά. Ἡ προσετέθησαν καί λόγοι τινές ἐν Τραπεζοῦντι ἐκφωνηθέντες [*The Greek Tribe on the Pontus, That Is, the Pontica. To Which Are Added Certain Speeches Delivered in Trebizond*] (Athens, 1866), pp. 66–76, 80–81. For a note on the resistance, and mention of ruined castles and other buildings, see Triantaphyllidis, Οἱ φυγάδες (5:13), pp. 9, 18–35, 39–40, 42–44, 47–49. Ioannidis, Ἱστορία καί στατιστική (5:20), p. 113, disputes the fact of resistance. Cf. Philip Cheimonidis, Ἱστορία καί στατιστική Σάντας [*History and Statistics of Santa*] (Athens, 1902), pp. vii, viii, 16, 18, 27–28, 30, 32–33, 33–39; Spyridon Lambros, "Ὁ τελευταῖος Ἕλλην αὐτοκράτωρ (Δαβίδ Κομνηνός αὐτοκράτωρ Τραπεζοῦντος) [The Last Greek Emperor—David Comnenus, Emperor of Trebizond]," NE, XIV (1917), 291–292; Demetrius Apostolidis, Ἱστορία τοῦ ἑλληνισμοῦ τοῦ Πόντου [*A History of the Hellenism of the Pontus*] (Thessalonica, 1935), pp. 50–51; and Agathangelos Phosteropoulos, Ἡ Ἵμερα τοῦ Πόντου [*Himera on the Pontus*] (Thessalonica, 1939), p. 5. Also relevant is the published lecture of Philon Ktenides, "Ἡ ἀντίστασις τῶν Ἑλλήνων τοῦ Πόντου μετά τήν ἅλωσιν τῆς Τραπεζοῦντος [The Resistance of the Greeks of the Pontus after the Capture of Trebizond]," in the newspaper Μακεδονικός ἀγών, 283/58 (May 8, 1949), which, however, I have not myself seen.

94. Triantaphyllidis, Οἱ φυγάδες (5:13), p. 31.

95. "Ντ' ἐποίκαμέ σε, νέ Θεέ μ', στά αἵματα βαμμένοι;
Σαράντα χρόνια χτέσκουντουν τοῦ ξένου μου ὁ κάστρον
Καί ἀτώρα νά χαλάγεται μέ τό βαρύν τήν σπάθην;
Ἐκεῖ πουλία κελαϊδοῦν μέ φλιβερόν λαλίαν·
ἐκεῖ Ἕλλενοι ἀπέθαναν μύριοι παλληκάρια.

[What have we done to you, my God, that we are dipped in blood?
It took forty years for my host's castle to be built
And now to be demolished by the heavy sword?
There birds sing with a sad utterance:
There Hellenes were killed, a thousand brave men]".

(See Ioannidis, Ἱστορία καί στατιστική [5:20], p. 287.) There is another song in Triantaphyllidis, Ἡ ἐν Πόντῳ ἑλληνικὴ φυλή (93), p. 170, which, along with other pertinent folk songs, Anthimos A. Papadopoulos analyzes in his "Ὁ Πόντος διά τῶν αἰώνων [The Pontus through the Ages]," ΑΠ, I (1928), 27–32. Cf. the song "Ὁ αἰχμάλωτος [The Captive]," in George Soumelidis, "Ἀκριτικά ᾄσματα [Akritic Songs]," ΑΠ, I (1928), 89–91.

96. According to tradition, the resistance of the inhabitants of the district of Kromme (that is, the Mesochaldion) was very weak. See Athanasios Parcharidis, Ἱστορία τῆς Κρώμνης [*History of Kromne*] (Trebizond, 1911), pp. 37–38. Indeed, as we have seen above, Hitir Pasha took over this district peacefully.

97. Legrand, *Recueil de chansons* (91), p. 76.

98. Cheimonidis, Ἱστορία καί στατιστική τῆς Σάντας (93), pp. 41–42.

99. Philippidis, " Ἡ Ἐκκλησία Τραπεζοῦντος" (73), pp. 374, 440, 529–530, 531.

100. Cf. Gustav Hertzberg, *Geschichte Griechenlands* [*History of Greece*], II (Gotha, 1877), 548–549.

101. See Apostolos Vacalopoulos, "Les Limites de l'empire byzantin depuis la fin de XIVᵉ siècle jusqu'à sa chute (1453)," *BZ*, LV (1962), 62–63. On July 30, 1447, Ciriaco de Pizzicolli of Ancona met Laonicos Chalcocondyles, "juvenem ingenuum [a noble youth]" in Mistra. See Remigio Sabbadini, "Ciriaco d'Ancona e la sua descrizione autografa del Peloponnesso trasmessa da Leonardo Botta," *Miscellanea Ceriani* (Milan, 1910), p. 203; and Denis Zakythinos, Οἱ Σλάβοι ἐν Ἑλλάδι (1:3) (Athens, 1945), p. 65. Apparently Laonicos returned to Athens after its capture by the Turks, and lived there. See Giuseppe Cammelli, *I Dotti bizantini e le origini dell' umanesimo* (9:39), III, *Dem. Calcondila* (Florence, 1941–1954), 5.

102. Chalcocondyles, *Historiarum demonstrationes* (1:52), I, 4.

103. *Ibid.*, I, 2.

Chapter 16

1. Demetrius Kydones, Συμβουλευτικός ἕτερος περί Καλλιπόλεως [*Another Advisory Speech on Callipolis*], PG, CLIV, col. 1013.

2. See Raymond Loenertz, *Correspondance de Manuel Calecas* (Rome, 1950), p. 168.

3. Giuseppe Cammelli, *Démétrius Cydonès, correspondance* (Paris, 1930), pp. 90, 91, 126, 128. Cf. p. 92.

4. See Loenertz, *Correspondance de Manuel Calecas* (2), *passim*.

5. See Raymond Loenertz, "Paléologue et Cydonès," *Échos d'Orient*, XXXVI (1937), 275–276, 485.

6. Demetrius Kydones, Ῥωμαίοις συμβουλευτικός (5:49), PG, CLIV, cols. 977, 1008. See Giovanni Mercati, *Notizie di Procoro e Demetrio Cidone, Manuele Caleca e Teodoro Meliteniota ed altri appunti per la storia della teologia e della letteratura bizantina del secolo XIV* (3:79) (Vatican City, 1931), pp. 370–372.

7. Some interesting information about a Greek settlement in Ragusa appears in Bariša Krekić, *Dubrovnik (Raguse) et le Levant au moyen âge* (Paris, 1960), pp. 125, 127, 129 ff. See the list of Greek names on pp. 135–144.

8. For a brief survey of medieval Greek studies in Italy, see Kenneth Setton, "The Byzantine Background to the Italian Renaissance," *Proceedings of the American Philosophical Society*, C, no. 1, February, 1956, 1–76. Cf. Carlo de Frede, *I Lettori di umanità nello Studio di Napoli durante il rinascimento* [*The Professors of Humanities at the University of Naples in the Renaissance*] (Naples, 1960), pp. 84–85, 98–99, which contains the relevant bibliography; and Giuseppe Schirò, " Ἡ βυζαντινή λογοτεχνία τῆς Σικελίας καί τῆς Κάτω Ἰταλίας [The Byzantine Literature of Sicily and of Southern Italy]," Ἑλληνικά, XVII (1962), 170–187. On Greek monasticism in Calabria during the fifteenth

century, see M. H. Laurent and André Guillou, *Le 'Liber visitationis' d'Athanase Chalkéopoulos (1457–1458)* (Vatican City, 1960), *passim*.

9. In the Italian view, advanced mainly by scholars from Morosi to Parlangeli, these ancient Greek peoples had been completely absorbed, and the present-day Greek-speaking pockets are the remnants of medieval Byzantine colonization. See Michael Dendias, "'Απουλία καί Χιμάρα [Apulia and Chimara]," 'Αθηνᾶ, xxxviii (1926), 72–109; and Stamatis Caratzas, *L'Origine des dialectes néo-grecs de l'Italie méridionale* (Paris, 1958), especially p. 17.

10. Ambroise Firmin Didot, *Alde Manuce et l'hellénisme à Venise* (Paris, 1875), pp. 18–19. See Émile Legrand, *Bibliographie hellénique ou description raisonnée des ouvrages publiés en grec par des Grecs au XVᵉ et XVIᵉ siècles* (Paris, 1885), i, xvii–xxviii, which contains the relevant bibliography; and Giovanni Pesenti, "La Scuola di Greco a Firenze nel primo Rinascimento," *Atene e Roma*, xii (1931), 84, 85. On Petrarch's search for Greek manuscripts and his relations with Greek writers, see Pierre de Nolhac, *Pétrarque et l'humanisme* (Paris, 1907), i, 67, 118, 126–188.

11. See Setton, "The Byzantine Background" (8), pp. 40–41, 45–52.

12. See Raymond Loenertz, *Démétrius Cydonès, correspondance* (Vatican City, 1956), i, 22; ii, 51, 122, and ii, 409, for the impressions of his journey of 1391. See also Cammelli, *Démétrius Cydonès* (3), p. 116.

13. See Didot, *Alduce Manuce* (10), pp. 19–20.

14. See Loenertz, *Correspondance de Manuel Calecas* (2), pp. 40–41, and *passim*.

15. See Setton, "The Byzantine Background" (8), p. 60.

16. Loenertz, *Démétrius Cydonès* (12), ii, 396, 406, 409–410.

17. See, for example, a letter written by Manuel Calecas to one of his friends, Loenertz, *Correspondance de Manuel Calecas* (2), p. 270.

18. See Loenertz, *Démétrius Cydonès* (12), ii, 122: "τῷ τε γάρ μεγέθει καί τῷ κάλλει καί τῇ λοιπῇ περιφανείᾳ τῆς πόλεως ἥσθην, ὅτ' αὐτοῦ διετρί-6ομεν [I was pleased by the size, the beauty, and the other aspects of the city when we stayed there]."

19. The classic work on the subject remains Georg Voigt's *Die Wiederbelebung des classischen Altertums* [*The Rebirth of Classical Antiquity*], 4th ed. (Berlin, 1960), in two volumes.

20. See Spyridon Lambros, 'Αργυροπούλεια (13:35) (Athens, 1910), pp. v–vi; and Giuseppe Cammelli, *I Dotti bizantini e le origini dell' umanesimo* (9:39), i, *Manuele Crisolora* (Florence, 1941–1954), pp. 17, 19: "e poco più sapiammo . . . di Teodoro Gaza dopo le ricerche dello Stein e del Gercke. Giorgio di Trebizonda, Andronico Callisto, i due Lascaris, Demetrio Castreno e molti altri di minor fama, aspettano ancora l'onore di una trattazione particolare [and we know a little more of Theodore Gazis, after the research of (Ernst) Stein and (Alfred) Gercke. Georgius of Trebizond, Andronicus Callistus, the two Lascarises, Demetrius Castrenus, and many others of less note still await the honor of a special treatment]." Basileios Mystakidis singles out the *Collectio camerariana codicum latinorum 10351– 10478* in the Public Library of Munich (where, among many Latin letters,

are those by Mitrophanes Kritopoulos and Cyril Loucaris) as being the most useful for a compilation of a history of letter-writing during the Renaissance (Constantine I. Dyovouniotis, "'Εκ τῶν καταλοίπων τοῦ Β. Μυστακίδου τά ὑπ' ἀριθμόν 16 καί 17 [From the Rest of the Books of B. Mystakidis, Those under the Numbers 16 and 17]," ΕΕΒΣ, xvii [1941], 276). Of course the older works, by Umfredo Hody, Émile Legrand, and Theodor Klette, also have their worth, but they are poor and dull (see Cammelli, I Dotti bizantini, i, 18). The works of Legrand, notable for their almost overpunctilious exactness, nevertheless deserve special attention for their criticisms of the methodology, inaccuracies, and carelessness of his forerunners, Greek historians of modern Hellenic literature. See Legrand, Bibliographie hellénique (10), i, 1 ff. The more recent works by Ludwig Mohler (on Bessarion) and Cammelli (on Manuel Chrysoloras, John Argyropoulos, Andronicus Callistus, and Demetrius Chalcocondyles) treat their subjects in a methodical and exhaustive fashion. The pertinent sections of this chapter are mainly based upon these works. Cammelli's works, despite the verbosity in certain places, remain models of critical historical analysis.

21. Martinus Crusius, Turcograeciae libri octo (Basel, 1584), p. 449. Cf. Cammelli, I Dotti bizantini (9:39), i, p. 19.

22. Loenertz, Correspondance de Manuel Calecas (2), pp. 65–66.

23. Cammelli, I Dotti bizantini (9:39), i, pp. 29 ff. For a more authentic portrait of Chrysoloras, see Henri Omont, "Note sur un portrait de Manuel Chrysoloras," REG, iv (1891), 176–177.

24. Remigio Sabbadini, Epistolario di Guarino Veronese [A Collection of the Letters of Guarino of Verona] (Venice, 1915), i, 99.

25. See Manuel Chrysoloras, Epistolae, PG, clvi, cols. 53–56, on the comparison of the old Rome with the new.

26. Ibid., cols. 23–53.

27. Cammelli, I Dotti bizantini (9:39), i, 130. On the narratives of Byzantine scholars and officials who travelled to the West, see the letter written by the monk Isidore in Denis Zakythinos, "Μανουήλ ὁ Β' καί ὁ καρδινάλιος 'Ισίδωρος ἐν Πελοποννήσῳ" (8:90), Mélanges Merlier, iii (1957), 8–9.

28. See Loenertz, Correspondance de Manuel Calecas (2), p. 68.

29. Cammelli, I Dotti bizantini (9:39), i, 161 ff.

30. See Conrad Bursian, Geschichte der classischen Philologie in Deutschland von den Anfängen bis zur Gegenwart [The History of Classical Philology in Germany, from Its Beginnings to the Present] (Munich-Leipzig, 1883), 91–93.

31. See Pesenti, "La Scuola di Greco" (10), pp. 84–101.

32. Loenertz, Correspondance de Manuel Calecas (2), pp. 257–258.

33. See Ludwig Mohler, Kardinal Bessarion als Theologe, Humanist und Staatsmann, i (Paderborn, 1923), 325.

34. Cammelli, I Dotti bizantini (9:39), i, 77–98, and iii, 91, on the publication of Questions.

35. For a comparison of the two methods, see Francesco Lo Parco, "Niccolò da Reggia," in the Atti R. Accademia di archeologia, lettere e belle arti di

Napoli, new series, II, 268 ff., 1910 (cited by Setton, "The Byzantine Background" (8), pp. 50–51).

36. On Guarino's visit to Constantinople, see Cammelli, *I Dotti bizantini* (9:39), I, 131–142. For the letters, see Sabbadini, *Epistolario di Guarino* (24), I, especially p. 21—Guarino's letter to Manuel Chrysoloras, written in October 1411: "maximas gratias non vilissimae urbi sed augustae dignitatis civitatis debeamus, tibi vero in primis, qui altissimis dudum demersos tenebris Italos admota demum veluti solis lampade illuminasti. Hoc dicit Italia, hoc cunctarum artium fatentur litterae, hoc clara testantur voce [We owe the greatest thanks, not to the lowliest of cities, but to a state exalted in its worthiness—and especially to you, who, just as if you had at last brought the light of the sun closer, have enlightened the Italians who were before plunged in the deepest darkness. Italy declares this, and this does the literature of all the arts confess, testifying with a clear voice]."

37. Legrand, *Bibliographie hellénique* (10), I, xxvi–xxix.

38. See Sabbadini, *Epistolario di Guarino* (24), I, 99.

39. *Ibid.*, I, 113. Guarino's letter to the jurist Iacopo de Fabris eulogizes Manuel unreservedly.

40. See Spyridon Lambros, Παλαιολόγεια καί Πελοποννησιακά (1:66) (Athens, 1926), II, 275, where George Scholarios characteristically writes: " Ἐπεί δέ ᾤχετο φυγών τήν Κωνσταντινούπολιν ὁ πλοῦτος ἅπας τῶν ἀγαθῶν, οἷς τόν πρόσθεν χρόνον ἐκόμα, καί τό τῶν λόγων καλόν παραμένειν οὐκ ἠνέσχετο [And, when Constantinople was fled by the entire wealth of goods and chattels, upon which it once prided itself, even the comeliness of letters was not suffered to remain]." Ioannis K. Voyatzidis furnishes an analysis of this letter in his " Ἱστορικαί μελέται [Historical Studies]," ΕΕΦΣΠΘ, II (1932), 242–244. Cf. Martin Jugie, "Georges Scholarios, professeur de philosophie," SBN, V (1939), 484.

41. Georgios Scholarios, Ἅπαντα τὰ εὑρισκόμενα (13:37) (Paris, 1935), III, 288. Cf. Jugie, "Georges Scholarios" (40), 483–484.

42. George Gemistos, Πρός τό ὑπέρ τοῦ λατινικοῦ δόγματος βιβλίον, PG, CLX, col. 979.

43. See Mohler, *Kardinal Bessarion* (33), I, 113–114, 325.

44. See Arnaldo della Torre, *Storia dell'Academia Platonica di Firenze* (Florence, 1902), pp. 436–441. On the first intellectual impulses generated by Gemistos' teaching, see the letters of Francesco Filelfo, in Émile Legrand, *Cent-dix Lettres grecques de François Filelfe* (Paris, 1892), pp. 31–34, 48.

45. See Giuseppe Cammelli, "Andronico Callisto" in *Rinascita* (Florence, 1942), pp. 117–121; and *I Dotti bizantini* (9:39), III, 20–25, which contains the relevant bibliography. The text of Michael Apostolis is in J. Enoch Powell, "Michael Apostolios gegen Theodoros Gaza [Michael Apostolis against Theodore Gazis]," BZ, XXXVIII (1938), 71–86.

46. See Mohler, *Kardinal Bessarion* (33), I, 113, 325–326, 339, 347–350, 351 ff.; and Ioannis Mamalakis, Γεώργιος Γεμιστός—Πλήθων (9:1) (Athens, 1939), pp. 156–174. On his influence in the West, see Börje Knös, "Gemiste

Pléthon et son souvenir," *Lettres d'humanité,* IX (1950), 132–184. On the influence of his work, see Andronicus Byzantios' epigram, Εἰς τό Βησσαρίωνος ὑπέρ Πλάτωνος βιβλίον [*On Bessarion's Book concerning Plato*], in Legrand, *Cent-dix Lettres* (44), pp. 220–221. See the correspondence between Bessarion and Guillaume Fichet on pp. 223 ff., for the intellectual discussions and controversy that the quarrel between the Aristotelians and Platonists aroused.

47. Mohler, *Kardinal Bessarion* (33), I, 178–208, 252–256, 258–265, 265–266, 325–326. For a criticism of the translations, see p. 341. On the renewal of the activity of the Academy after the death of Nicholas V, see pp. 331–335. Most of Bessarion's theological works belong to this period (see pp. 336 ff.). Other relevant information may be found in Raymond Loenertz, "Pour la biographie du cardinal Bessarion," OCP, X (1944), 116–149. On the teaching of C. Lascaris, at the monastery of San Salvatore, see Antonino de Rosalia, "La Vita di C. Lascaris," *Archivio storico siciliano,* series III, vol. IX (1959), 35, which contains the relevant bibliography.

48. Christos G. Patrinellis, "Μιχαήλ ᾿Αποστόλη προσφώνημα ἀνέκδοτον εἰς τόν καρδινάλιον Βησσαρίωνα [Michael Apostolis' Unpublished Address to Cardinal Bessarion]," ᾿Αθηνᾶ, LXV (1961), 134, 136.

49. Spyridon Lambros, "᾿Ανέκδοτος ἐπιστολή τοῦ Βησσαρίωνος [An Unpublished Letter by Bessarion]," NE, VI (1909), 393–398; and "Οἱ ταχυγράφοι τοῦ Βησσαρίωνος [Bessarion's Stenographers]," NE, II (1905), 334–336.

50. Mohler, *Kardinal Bessarion* (33), I, 266.

51. *Ibid.,* I, 330. Cf. p. 414; and Bessarion's letter in 1469 to the Doge, in which he announced his gift, in PG, CLXI, col. 701.

52. On Nicholas V's and Bessarion's libraries, see Eugène Müntz and Paul Fabre, *La Bibliothèque du Vatican au XVᵉ siècle d'après des documents inédits* (Paris, 1887), pp. iv, 34–114. On Bessarion's library, see also Spyridon Theotokis, "Κατάλογος χειρογράφων τοῦ ᾿Αγ. Μάρκου ἐν Βενετίᾳ [A Catalogue of Manuscripts of St. Mark's in Venice]," ᾿Ελληνικά, III (1930), 90 ff.; and Mohler, *Kardinal Bessarion* (33), I, 408. On Aldus Manutius, see Didot, *Alde Manuce* (10), pp. xlv ff., 25–26.

53. On George Trapezountios' sojourn in Florence before March, 1443, and his teaching there, see Giuseppe Cammelli, *I Dotti bizantini* (9:39), II, *Giovanni Argiropulo,* 54, and 33–34 on Trapezountios' differences with John Argyropoulos; see also Lambros, ᾿Αργυροπούλεια (13:35), pp. xxvii–xxix.

54. Cammelli, *I Dotti bizantini* (9:39), III, 18, fn. 3.

55. Legrand, *Bibliographie hellénique* (10), I, xxi–xxiv.

56. Constantine Sathas, Νεοελληνική φιλολογία (1453–1821) [*Modern Greek Philology, 1453–1821*] (Athens, 1868), p. 38.

57. See Cammelli, "Andronico Callisto" (45), pp. 104–121, 172–214.

58. De Frede, *I Lettori* (8), pp. 85, 86–87.

59. Spyridon Lambros, "῾Υπόμνημα τοῦ καρδιναλίου Βησσαρίωνος εἰς Παλαιολόγον" (9:24), NE, III (1906), 25.

60. Crusius, *Turcograeciae* (21), p, 101.

61. See Voyatzidis, 'Ιστορικαί μελέται (40), 245, 251–255; and Scholarios, "Απαντα (13:37), III, 115, where, in 1443, he contemplates Bessarion's good fortune: "Νῦν δ' ὁ μέν τήν 'Ιταλίαν κοσμεῖ, ἡμεῖς δέ πολίταις μέν ἀγαθοῖς, ἀμαθέσι δέ ἄλλως πλήν ὀλίγων καί λόγων ἀνέραστοι ἐνδιαιτώμεθα, οὐδέ δυνάμενοί τι τῶν ὑπαρχόντων ἐπιδείξασθαι σφίσι, καί δόξης τινος ἤ χάριτος ἐπί τούτῳ τυχεῖν [And now he adorns Italy, while we, deprived of the joys of culture, live among citizens who are good, but, except for a few, are without learning. Nor are we able to display any of our faculties to them, and thereby gain any repute or any favor]."

62. Krekić, *Dubrovnik* (7), pp. 69, 70.

63. Among the scholars who passed through Ragusa to Ancona were Janus Lascaris and Demetrius Chalcocondyles. See Cammelli, *I Dotti bizantini* (9:39), III, 19. The tradition that scholars also went to Moschopolis, which was on the way to Ragusa, and that they there instigated the Greek studies which later raised Moschopolis to a position of intellectual pre-eminence (see Johann von Hahn, *Albanesische Studien* [Jena, 1954], I, 296) is without foundation. It is doubtful whether Moschopolis in fact existed at that time.

64. Denis Zakythinos, "Μιχαήλ Μάρουλλος Ταρχανιώτης [Michael Maroullos Tarchaniotes]," ΕΕΒΣ, v (1928), 202.

65. Krekić, *Dubrovnik* (7), pp. 132–135.

66. Andronicus Callistus, Μονῳδία ἐπί τῇ δυστυχεῖ Κωνσταντινουπόλει (14:108), PG, CLXI, cols. 1138–1139.

67. Masai considers Argyropoulos a Platonist, a protagonist of Gemistos' ideas, and an initiate into the "μυστήρια [mysteries]" of his circle (François Masai, *Pléthon et le Platonisme de Mistra* [Paris, 1956], pp. 313, 328–329, 339). This is, however, by no means proven.

68. See Cammelli, *I Dotti bizantini* (9:39), II, *passim*. In Lambros' 'Αργυροπούλεια (13:35), there are not only gaps, but a number of serious errors—attributable in the main to Lambros' failure to examine the environment in which Argyropoulos lived, his relations with others, the nature of his influence, and other factors. See the criticism by Cammelli in *I Dotti bizantini* (9:39), I, 18. On Argyropoulos' replacement in the Florentine chair by Callistus, see Cammelli, "Andronico Callisto" (45), pp. 179–189.

69. See Cammelli, *I Dotti bizantini* (9:39), III, 135–141, which has the early bibliography.

70. See de Frede, *I Lettori* (8), pp. 13 ff. 81 ff., 92–93, 95, 109; and de Rosalia, "La Vita di C. Lascaris" (47), pp. 32–50.

71. Cammelli, "Andronico Callisto" (45), pp. 104–121, 172–214; and Legrand, *Bibliographie hellénique* (10), I, l–lvii. On Callistus' stay in Florence, see "Andronico Callisto," pp. 189 ff.; and *I Dotti bizantini* (9:39), II, 128, fn. 2, and p. 151. Before 1462, Callistus stayed in Padua as the guest of Palla Strozzi (*I Dotti bizantini*, III, 30). On humanistic studies in England during the fourteenth and fifteenth centuries, see Setton, "The Byzantine Background" (8), pp. 62–64; and Robert Weiss, *Humanism in England During the Fifteenth Century* (Oxford, 1941).

72. On Nicholas Secundinos and his work, see Panagiotis D. Mastrodimitris, "Νικολάου Σεκουνδινοῦ ἀνέκδοτος ἐπιστολή [An Unpublished Letter of Nicholas Secundinos]," ΕΕΒΣ, xxxiv (1956), 203–207; and Franz Babinger, "Nikolaos Segoundinos, ein griechisch-venedischer Humanist des 15. Jahrhunderts [Nicholas Secundinos, a Greco-Venetian Humanist of the Fifteenth Century]," Χαριστήριον εἰς 'Αν. 'Ορλάνδον, ι (1965), 198–212.

73. Cardinal Bessarion, Epistolae, PG, clxi, col. 695. (See fn. 1, cols. 691–696, for Nicholas Secundinos' letter.)

74. See Bursian, Geschichte der classischen Philologie (30), pp. 120, and 121, fn. 1; and the biographies of Hermonymos in Émile Egger, L'Hellénisme en France (Paris, 1869), ι, 146–147; in Sathas, Νεοελληνική φιλολογία (56), pp. 67–70; and Knös, "Gemiste Pléthon" (46), 166–167.

75. See Spyridon Lambros, "Λακεδαιμόνιοι βιβλιογράφοι καί κτήτορες κωδίκων κατά τούς μέσους αἰῶνας καί ἐπί τουρκοκρατίας" (6:73), ΝΕ, ιν (1907), 325–331, for some interesting details.

76. See Legrand, Bibliographie hellénique (10), ι, cxxxii–cxxxvi, cliii–clvi; and Börje Knös, Un Ambassadeur de l'hellénisme—Janus Lascaris—et la tradition gréco-byzantine dans l'humanisme français (Uppsala-Stockholm-Paris, 1945), pp. 30–51, which contains the relevant bibliography.

77. Legrand, Cent-dix Lettres (44), p. 361.

78. See Cammelli, I Dotti bizantini (9:39), iii, 31, fn. 3.

79. See Knös, Un Ambassadeur de l'hellénisme (77), pp. 17–133.

80. See Manoussos Manoussacas, " 'Η παρουσίαση ἀπό τόν 'Ιανό Λάσκαρι τῶν πρώτων μαθητῶν τοῦ ἑλληνικοῦ γυμνασίου τῆς Ρώμης στόν πάπα Λέοντα Ι' (15 Φεβρουαρίου 1514) [The Presentation by Janus Lascaris of the First Students of the Greek Gymnasium at Rome to Pope Leo IX (February 15, 1514)]" in 'Ο 'Ερανιστής, ι (1963), 161–172, which contains the earlier bibliography; Knös, Un Ambassadeur de l'hellénisme (77), pp. 137–152; and Vittorio Fanelli, "Il Ginnasio Greco di Leone X a Roma," Studi romani, ix (1961), 379–389.

81. Knös, Un Ambassadeur de l'hellénisme (77), pp. 152–158. On the school at Rome, see Andreas Moustoxydis, "Τό ἐν Ρώμη ἑλληνικόν γυμνάσιον [Rome's Greek Gymnasium]," 'Ελληνομνήμων, ι (1843–1853), 231–235; and on pp. 328–336 his "Ζαχαρίας Καλλιέργης." On Kallierges and the printing shop, see Deno Geanakoplos, Greek Scholars in Venice (Cambridge, Mass., 1962), pp. 122–125, 128, 159.

82. Knös, Un Ambassadeur de l'hellénisme (77), pp. 158–217; and Fanelli, "Il Ginnasio greco" (81), pp. 389–390. For proof of the exact date of his death, see Giovanni Mercati, "Quando morì G. Lascaris? [When did Janus Lascaris die?]," Rheinisches Museum, lxv (1910), 318.

83. Egger, L'Hellénisme en France (74), ι, 164.

84. See Bessarion's letter to the tutor of the children of Thomas Palaeologus, with the strict injunction that the nobles who accompanied the children to church should not be allowed to leave when the moment arrived for reference to the Pope: "διότι ἄν φεύγωσιν ἀπό τήν ἐκκλησίαν, εἶναι χρεία νά φεύγωσιν

καί ἀπό τήν Φραγγίαν [because if they leave the church they should also leave Italy]" (PG, CLXI, cols. 680–681).

85. Legrand, *Cent-dix Lettres* (44), p. 79. Cf. pp. 119, 133, 175.

86. See Georg Voigt, *Enea Silvio de'Piccolomini, als Papst Pius der Zweite und sein Zeitalter* (15:21) (Berlin, 1863), III, 606 ff.

87. Othon Riemann, "Une Lettre d'un Grec du quinzième siècle," AAEEG, XIII (1879), 125.

88. See de Frede, *I Lettori* (8), p. 95.

89. De Rosalia, "La Vita di C. Lascaris" (47), p. 38.

90. Lambros, 'Αργυροπούλεια (13:35), pp. 305–306; and Constantine Lascaris, *Epistolae quatuordecim familiares*, PG, CLXI, cols. 957–958. Demetrius is probably Demetrius Kastrenos. See Legrand, *Bibliographie hellénique* (10), I, clxiii; Spyridon Lambros, "Δημητρίου Καστρηνοῦ ἀνέκδοτος ἐπιστολή πρός Σοφιανόν [An Unpublished Letter by Demetrius Kastrenos to Sophianos]," NE, XIII (1916), 408–413; and Cammelli, "Andronico Callisto" (45), p. 205, fn. 1. On Constantine Lascaris, see Legrand, *Bibliographie hellénique*, I, lxxi–lxxxvii. See also Constantine Lascaris' letter to I. Gato, Bishop of Catania: "φάνηθι τῶν λόγων σωτήρ, καί τάς ἐν Κατάνῃ κατερρηκυίας σπουδάς, πολλῷ σεμνοτέρας τῶν Ἰταλῶν ἀπόφηνον [show that you are the savior of education and that the decadent studies in Catania are much worthier than those in Italy]," PG, CLXI, col. 916.

91. See Cammelli, *I Dotti bizantini* (9:39), II, 174–175, 181. Cf. p. 133, and his "Andronico Callisto" (45), pp. 199–200. Manuel Chrysoloras and Theodore Gazes, with their Olympian characters, may be said to constitute exceptions (see *I Dotti bizantini*, I, 104), as Andronicus Callistus perhaps may also ("Andronico Callisto," p. 200).

92. De Frede, *I Lettori* (8), p. 88.

93. Constantine Lascaris, *Proemium ad libros suos de grammatica*, PG, CLXI, cols. 933–936.

94. Basileios Laourdas, "Μιχαήλ 'Αποστόλη, Λόγος περί 'Ελλάδος καί Εὐρώπης [Michael Apostolis' Address concerning Greece and Europe]," EEBΣ, XIX (1949), 243, and 235–236 for the bibliography on Apostolis, and Hippolyte Noiret, *Lettres inédites de Michael Apostolis* (Paris, 1889), p. 148. For an analysis of Apostolis' speech, see Deno Geanakoplos, "A Byzantine View of the Renaissance. The Attitude of M. Apostolis toward the Rise of Italy to Cultural Eminence," *Greek and Byzantine Studies*, I (1958), 157–162.

95. See Denis Zakythinos, "Τό πρόβλημα τῆς ἑλληνικῆς συμβολῆς εἰς τήν 'Αναγέννησιν [The Problem of the Hellenic Contribution to the Renaissance]," EEΦΣΠΑ, II, 5 (1954–1955), 126–138.

96. Cammelli, *I Dotti bizantini* (9:39), I, 11.

Chapter 17

1. See Basileios Laourdas, "Μιχαήλ 'Αποστόλη, Λόγος περί 'Ελλάδος καί Εὐρώπης" (16:95), EEBΣ, XIX (1949), 243.

2. Spyridon Lambros, "Λακεδαιμόνιοι βιβλιογράφοι καί κτήτορες κωδίκων" (6:73), NE, IV (1907), 311, 316–317, 331, 332, 337.

3. Henri Grégoire, "Les Manuscrits de Julien et le mouvement néo-païen de Mistra: Démétrius Rhallis et Gemiste Pléthon," *Byzantion*, v (1929), 733–734.

4. Lambros, "Λακεδαιμόνιοι" (6:73), 336.

5. Marie Vogel and Viktor Gardthausen, *Die griechischen Schreiber des Mittelalters und der Renaissance* [*The Greek Scribes of the Middle Ages and Renaissance*] (Leipzig, 1909), pp. 318, 319. On Michael Souliardos, see Spyridon Lambros, "Ναυπλιακόν ἔγγραφον τοῦ οἴκου Πουλομμάτη ἐν ἔτει 1509 καί ὁ βιβλιογράφος Μιχαήλ Σουλιάρδος [A Nauplian Document of the House of Poulommates in the Year 1509, and the Bibliographer Michael Souliardos]," NE, vi (1909), 279–283.

6. See Johannes Irmscher, "Theodoros Gazes als griechischer Patriot [Theodore Gazes as a Greek Patriot]," *La Parola del passato*, xvi (1961), 161–173.

7. See Georgios Zoras, Γεώργιος ὁ Τραπεζούντιος καί αἱ πρός ἑλληνοτουρκικήν συνεννόησιν προσπάθειαι αὐτοῦ ('Η "Περί τῆς τῶν Χριστιανῶν πίστεως" ἀνέκδοτος πραγματεία [*George Trapezountios and His Efforts toward a Greco-Turkish Understanding (The Unpublished Treatise "On the Faith of the Christians")*] (Athens, 1954). Compare the Turkish view on the reconciliation of Christianity and Islam as expressed to Gregory Palamas: "Εἰς δέ τις ἐκείνων εἶπεν, ὡς ἔσται ποτε ὅτε συμφωνήσομεν ἀλλήλοις. Καί ἐγώ συνεθέμην καί ἐπευξάμην τάχιον ἥκειν τόν καιρόν ἐκεῖνον [And a certain one of them said that there will be a time when we shall get along with one another. And I agreed, and prayed that that opportunity come more quickly]" (Constantine I. Dyovouniotis, "Γρηγορίου Παλαμᾶ ἐπιστολή πρός Θεσσαλονικεῖς" (5:35), NE, xvi [1922], 19). On the important ideological movement later launched by Bedredin and his disciple, Berkludsh Mustafa, see Hieronymous Cotsonis, "Aus der Endzeit von Byzanz: Bürkludsche Mustafa [From the Final Period of Byzantium: Burkludsh Mustafa]," BZ, l (1957), 397–404.

8. See Angelo Mercati, "Le Due Lettere di Giorgio da Trebizonda a Maometto II," OCP, ix (1943), 65–99.

9. See Ludwig Mohler, *Kardinal Bessarion als Theologe, Humanist und Staatsmann*, i (Paderborn, 1923), 275–283; and Georg Voigt, *Enea Silvio de'Piccolomini, als Papst Pius der Zweite und sein Zeitalter* (15:21) (Berlin, 1863), iii, 56: "Wenn von den Leiden und Hoffnungen seiner griechischen Brüder die Rede war, zeigte Cardinal Bessarion stets einen drängenden Eifer. Er war eben kein weltkluger Mann, am wenigsten, wenn jene Grille ihn beherrschte [When the subject was the misfortunes and hopes of his Greek brothers, Cardinal Bessarion always showed a compulsive zeal. He was simply not a man wise to the world, least of all when that desire (to free his brothers) dominated him]."

10. See Mohler, *Kardinal Bessarion* (9), i, 285–303.

11. *Ibid.*, pp. 304–310.

12. *Ibid.*, pp. 310–324, 416–425.

13. See his speeches in PG, clxi, cols. 647–676. Note especially col. 667; and G. Fichet's exhortations to the leaders of the West to back Bessarion's plans (Émile Legrand, *Cent-dix Lettres grecques de François Filelfe* [Paris, 1892], pp. 251 ff.). Cf. Mohler, *Kardinal Bessarion* (9), i, 425–429; and

Othon Riemann, "Une Lettre d'un grec du quinzième siècle," AAEEG, xiii (1879), 124.

14. Émile Legrand, *Bibliographie hellénique ou description raisonnée des ouvrages publiés en grec par des Grecs au XVᵉ et XVIᵉ siècles* (Paris, 1885), i, clvi–clvii. See Elias Voutieridis, Ἱστορία τῆς νεοελληνικῆς λογοτεχνίας [*History of Modern Greek Literature*] (Athens, 1924), pp. 246–247. On Lascaris' travels in Greece, see Börje Knös, *Un Ambassadeur de l'hellénisme— Janus Lascaris—et la tradition gréco-byzantine dans l'humanisme français* (Uppsala-Stockholm-Paris, 1945), pp. 30–51, which contains the relevant bibliography. See also Lascaris' memorandum of 1508 to Pope Leo X, in Neculai Iorga, *Notes et extraits pour servir à l'histoire des Croisades au XVᵉ siècle* (Bucharest, 1916), 6th series (1501–1547), pp. 45–55.

15. See John Acciajuoli's poem to Charles V, "τοῦ πρωτοκόμητος Κορώνης [the chief leader of Korone]," in Georgios Zoras, Κάρολος ὁ Ε΄ τῆς Γερμανίας καὶ αἱ πρός ἀπελευθέρωσιν προσπάθειαι [*Charles V of Germany and the Efforts toward Liberation*] (Athens, 1953). This study, with the text of the poem, also appears in ΕΕΦΣΠΑ, ii, 5 (1954–1955), 420–472, and in a separate edition, Ἰωάννου Ἀζαγιώλου διήγησις συνοπτικὴ Καρόλου τοῦ Ε΄ [*A Brief Narrative on Charles V by John Acciajuoli*] (Athens, 1964). Note also the anonymous author of Θρῆνος τῆς Κωνσταντινουπόλεως [*Dirge for Constantinople*] (Adolf Ellissen, *Analekten der mittel- und neugriechischen Literatur* [9:8] [Leipzig, 1860], iii, 154). Antoine Gidel, *Études sur la litterature grecque moderne* (Paris, 1866), p. 66, believes that the author of the poem is Georgilas of Rhodes, though Émile Egger (*L'Hellénisme en France* [Paris, 1869], i, 439, fn. 1) has certain reservations as to its authorship. Note also that Francesco Filelfo in 1475 urged Demetrius Chalcocondyles to persuade Lorenzo de' Medici of Florence to launch a crusade against the Turks. See Legrand, *Cent-dix Lettres* (13), pp. 190–191.

16. Μονῳδία ἐπί τῇ δυστυχεῖ Κωνσταντινουπόλει, PG, clxi, col. 1139.

17. John Stavrakios, "κόντε Παλατῖνος καί καβελλάριος [Palatine count and chevalier]," was in fact one of Frederick's courtiers.

18. "Ἔκ τε τῆς ἀνάγκης αὐτῆς, ἥν Ἀδράστειαν ἐκάλεσαν οἱ φιλόσοφοι καί τῆς τῶν πραγμάτων περιφορᾶς τε καί παλιρροίας, ἀστάτων γε ὄντων καί ἐσαεί κινουμένων [And from that same need which the philosophers called 'Adrastian' and from the confusions and reversals of affairs, which were unstable and always in motion]." Basileios Laourdas, " Ἡ πρός τόν αὐτοκράτορα Φρειδερῖκον τόν τρίτον ἔκκλησις τοῦ Μιχαήλ Ἀποστόλη [The Appeal of Michael Apostolis to Emperor Frederick III]," Γέρας Ἀντωνίου Κεραμοπούλλου (Athens, 1953), p. 521.

19. *Ibid.*, pp. 516–527. See also the moving plea with which he closes his speech "Περί Ἑλλάδος καί Εὐρώπης [About Greece and Europe]" (Laourdas, "Μιχαήλ Ἀποστόλη λόγος περί Ἑλλάδος καί Εὐρώπης" (16:95), ΕΕΒΣ, xix [1949], 243–244).

20. Hippolyte Noiret, *Lettres inédites de Michel Apostolis* (Paris, 1889), pp. 110–111.

21. See Denis Zakythinos, "Μιχαήλ Μάρουλλος Ταρχανιώτης. Έλλην ποιητής τῶν χρόνων τῆς 'Αναγεννήσεως [Michael Maroullos Tarchaniotes. A Greek Poet of the Times of the Renaissance]," ΕΕΒΣ, v (1928), pp. 200–242.

22. See Alessandro Perosa, *Michaelis Marulli carmina* [*The Poems of Michael Maroullos*] (Verona, 1951), pp. 89–90, 98–99, and pp. xxxix–xliv, where a bibliography will be found. Note the epitaph to his father, Manilius:

Flens primum has auras hausi puer omine diro,
    Flebilis erepta vita fuit patria,
Nunc quoque flens morior nequid non flebile restet:
    Haec est humani conditio generis.

[Weeping and in evil times I as a child first breathed this air.
    Lamentable my life since my fatherland was seized.
Now also I die weeping, that nothing remains which is not to be wept for.
    Such is the state of human kind.]

23. *Ibid.*, pp. 41, 72.

24. *Ibid.*, pp. 72–73.

25. *Ibid.*, pp. 29, 77–78. Concerning Manilius (i.e., Manuel) Kavakes Ralles, see Legrand, *Cent-dix Lettres* (13), pp. viii–ix; Antonios Chatzis, Οἱ Ραούλ, Ράλ, Ράλαι (1080–1800) (Kirchhain, 1909), pp. 56–61; and Manoussos Manoussacas, "'Αρχιερεῖς Μεθώνης, Κορώνης καί Μονεμβασίας γύρω στά 1500 [The Bishops of Methone, Korone, and Monemvasia around 1500]," Πελοποννησιακά, ιιι (1959), 122–125.

26. Börje Knös considers this lack of faith a kind of snobbery. See his "Gemiste Pléthon et son souvenir," *Lettres d'humanité*, ix (1950), 152. For comments on the predilection of these scholars for magic, see Daniel Walker, *Spiritual and Demonic Magic from Ficino to Campanella* (London, 1958). Constantine Sathas' supposition, in Μεσαιωνική βιβλιοθήκη (2:23) (Venice-Paris, 1872–1894), viι, lvii, that the Byzantine scholars "ἐμύησαν εἰς τά μεγάλα τῆς ἀρχαιότητος μυστήρια τούς ἐν τῇ σκοτίᾳ τοῦ μεσαιωνικοῦ ρωμαϊσμοῦ καθεύδοντας λαούς [initiated into the great mysteries of antiquity those people who had been slumbering in the darkness of medieval Romanity]" is fanciful and unsupportable.

27. Zakythinos, "Μιχαήλ Μάρουλλος Ταρχανιώτης" (21), 225.

28. PG, clxi, col. 959.

29. *Ibid.*, col. 662.

INDEX

Academia Platonica, Florence, 241, 248

Academy of Florence ("Old Academy"), 247, 248

Academy Pontaniana, Naples, 254

Acarnania, 7, 15, 31, 78, 251, 312n18; Albanians in, 8, 10, 11, 116, 272n66

Acciajuoli family, 108, 109, 215

Acciajuoli, Antonio, duke of Athens, 134, 135

Acciajuoli, Donato, 245

Acciajuoli, Francesco, 211

Acciajuoli, John, 366n15

Acciajuoli, Nerio, ruler of Corinth, 105, 108, 110, 118, 313n35; Constantine XI and, 178; daughter of, 116

Achaia, 5, 10, 213, 215, 259, 266n9

Achelous, battle of (1359), 8, 112

Achelous River (Aspropotamos), 7, 14, 271n54, 272n72

Achilles, 44–45, 287n89

Achilles family, 201

Achris (Ochrida), 32, 50

Acrocorinth, 209, 210(fig.), 211

Acropolis, Athens, 24, 211, 312n33

Acta Conciliorum Oecumenicorum, 61

Actuarius, John, 47

Adrianople, 59, 243, 251; Ottoman Turks in, 76, 78–79, 190, 193, 200, 209, 211, 212, 215, 217, 218, 221, 227, 286n81, 329n1

Adriatic Sea, 161, 206

Aegean islands, 20, 22, 63, 190; Constantinopolitan refugees in, 76, 201, 202, 216; dialects of, 15, 81; Franks in, 43, 99, 106, 136, 137, 138; Mohammed II and, 213, 216–21, 222, 224, 231; piracy and, 69, 71, 298n8. See also specific islands

Aegina, island of, 4, 10, 109

Aeschines, 250

Aeschylus, 250

Aetolia, 29, 31, 78; Albanians in, 8, 10, 11, 12, 116, 272n66

Africa, 13

Against the Hellenes (Kata Hellenon . . . Scholarios), 171

Against Plato's Calumniator (In calumniatorem Platonis . . . Bessarion), 243

Agathias, monk, 82

Agathopolis (Aktopol), 79, 136

Agesilaos, Spartan general, 174

Agrafa, 153, 156, 165, 178; Armatoles in, 157, 158, 159

agriculture, 28, 34, 54–57, 130, 290n37; Constantine XI and, 172, 190; military service and, 129; Turkish invasions and, 62, 65, 71,

72, 76, 164, 165. *See also* land grants
Ahmed Pasha, quoted, 328n29
Aigion (Vostitsa), 209
Ainos (Enos), Asia Minor, 136, 184, 243; Ottoman Turks and, 213, 216, 219, 221
Akhis, 143
Ak Koyunlu Turcomans, 223, 226
Akritai, 22, 35, 64, 337n58
Akropolites, George, historian, 35
Aktopol (Agathopolis), on Black Sea, 79, 136
Ak-Tsaïrli Oğlu Mohammed Bey, 190
Alā ed-Din I Kaikobad, Sultan of Iconium, 64
Alaric, 19
Albania, 7, 8, 71, 269n40; Nicaea and, 38; Ottoman Turks and, 77, 78, 82, 149, 152, 179
Albanian people, 1, 6–12, 14, 16, 82, 269nn40–41, 270n45; Carlo I Tocco and, 11, 116, 272n66; Catalan armies and, 109, 110; languages of, 7, 269n40, 351n33; Peloponnesian revolts and, 207–209, 213, 215; Preliumbović and, 113. *See also* Arvanito-Vlachs
Aldja Kale (Kordyle), fortress, Asia Minor, 229
Aldus Academy, Venice, 252
Alexander (912–913), emperor, 3
Alexander the Great, 18, 35, 120, 175, 257; in folklore, 22–23, 47, 121
Alexander IV, pope, 95
Alexander Romance, 22–23, 24
Alexandria, Egypt, Sarapeum of, 19
Alexis, groom, 105
Alexius Angelos Philanthropenos, caesar of Greater Walachia and ruler of Thessaly, 114, 118
Alexius Comnenus, emperor of Trebizond, 221–22
Alexius I Comnenus, emperor, 2
Alexius Apocaucus, grand duke, 59, 194

Alfonso, copyist, 111
Alfonso I, king of Naples, 244, 253
Alfonso V, king of Aragon, 190
Ali Pasha of Ioannina, 180
Alighieri, Michael, 224
Almyros, 112, 165, 301n45
Amantos, Constantine, cited, 28, 202
Amasya, Asia Minor, 222, 225
Ambracia, 271n54
Amiroukes, George, philosopher, 226, 227, 228, 354n77
Amisus (Samsun), Asia Minor, 63, 223
Ammochostos (Famagusta), 95
Amphissa (Salona), 106, 109, 111
Anadolu Hisar, fortress, Asia Minor, 190
Anatolia, 65, 67, 68, 142, 223, 224
Anatolikon, 11
Anchialus (Pomoriye), on Black Sea, 136, 193
Ancona, Italy, 235, 362n63
Andrea of Cremona, 263
Andrew, saint, 215
Andritzopoulos, 306n30
Androni, brigand, 110
Andronicus, Akritic hero, 22
Andronicus I Comnenus, emperor, 221
Andronicus II Palaeologus, emperor, 41, 46, 57
Andronicus III Palaeologus, emperor, 8, 46, 147
Andronicus IV Palaeologus, emperor, 79
Andronicus Comnenus Ducas Palaeologus, 45
Andronicus Palaeologus, governor of Thessalonica, 146, 201
Andros, island of, 10, 20, 81
Angelokastron, 11
Angelokoma, 64
Angelina, Maria Radoslava, 315n57
Angelos family, 65
Angevin family, 8
Angiolello, Giovanni Maria degli, 121

Angistri, island of, 10

Anguillara, Count, of Rome, 220

Ankara, Turkey, 73, 201, 225

Ankara, battle of (1402), 85, 88, 125, 163; army reorganization after, 151; Byzantine and Ottoman empires after, 136–50

Anna of Savoy, empress, 59

Anselm, saint, 99

Anthimos, archbishop of Athens, 96

Antioch, Syria, 62

Antipsara, island of, 71

Antirretikos (*Rebuttal* . . . Gazes), 241

Anti-Taurus mountains, 21, 225

Antonios, archbishop of Heraclea, 139

Apano Castro, 81

Apocaucus, Alexius, grand duke, 59, 194

Apocaucus, John, metropolitan of Naupactus, 31–32, 297n1

Apollonius of Perga, 47

Apollonius of Rhodes, 251

Apostolis, Michael, 184–85, 241, 245, 336nn47, 49; quoted, 254, 260, 366nn18–19

Apsarades family of Ioannina, 313n43

Apulia, Italy, 167, 235, 244

Aquileia, Italy, 218

Arabs, 22, 60, 62, 69, 89

Aragon, 10, 109, 110

Aravantinos, Panaghiotis, cited, 180

Arcadia, 10

archaeology, 38, 49

Archimandreion monastery, Epirus, 113

architecture, 20, 38, 49, 50, 51(fig.); in Constantinople, 145, 194; in Crete, 97; mosques, 163, 200, 211, 231; in the Peloponnese, 82, 83(fig.), 84(fig.), 214(fig.), 284 n71; in Trebizond, 222, 231

Ardasa fortress, 228–29

Ardea, 6

Arethas, 24

Argolis, 10

Argonautica (Apollonius of Rhodes), 251

Argos, 4, 107, 209, 212, 256

Argyrokastron, Albania, 149

Argyropoulos, John, 208, 237, 245–47, 248, 254, 362nn67–68; quoted, 180, 183, 336n47

Argyros, Isaac, astronomer, 47

aristocracy, *see* nobility

Aristotle, 21, 39, 50, 100, 248, 249, 250; quoted, 147; Bessarion on, 243, 247; Gemistos on, 170, 171, 181, 184–85, 241; Hermonymos' codex to, 256; Hesychasm and, 57, 58; Petrarch and, 236

Armatoles, 157–60

Armenia, 63, 294n17; Turks in, 61, 68, 221–31

Armenopoulos, Constantine, jurist, 53, 148

armies: Catalan, 108, 109; of Constantine XI, 178–79, 190, 193, 194, 196, 197, 198; French, 252; Gemistos on organization of, 129, 132–33, 174; Macedonian, 123; mercenaries in, 8, 12, 30, 65–66, 71, 105, 341n41; military oligarchy and, 54–57, 74, 76, 123, 291n45; of Nicaea, 38, 40, 65; Ottoman, 12, 30, 60, 64, 65–66, 67, 73–74, 77, 78, 82, 125, 139–43, 145, 148, 149, 150, 151–60, 188, 190, 193, 194–99, 209, 212, 224–25, 226, 228, 258, 299nn23, 27–28, 318n 108, 323n25, 324nn31–33, 341n41, 349n15; prisoners of war and, 131, 174, 200–201, 221, 299n28, 320 n22; Roman, 273n80; Seljuk, 61; of Trebizond, 224, 225–26; of Venice, 202. *See also* janissaries

Armouris, Akritic hero, 22, 277n28, 278n33

Arnaea, plateau of, 4

art, 18, 19, 21–26; Cretan, 80, 97, 303n62; nationalism and, 21, 22, 26, 35, 38–39, 43–45, 82, 97,

112, 250, 260–62; Palaeologian renaissance, 46–49, 50, 58, 59, 82, 177, 222. *See also specific arts*

Arta, 11, 33, 111, 116, 251, 272*n*72

Artemision mountains, 209

Arvanito-Vlachs, 6, 10, 11, 14, 16, 111, 112, 116; Albania and, 7, 269*nn*40–42; Constantine XI and, 178–79, 180; Ottoman Turks and, 78, 82, 152, 154, 155, 156, 157, 164. *See also* Karagounides

Asanes, Alexander, 352*n*48

Asanes, Matthew, 209, 211, 221

Asanes, Michael, 352*n*48

Asarbey, 163

Ascension of Alexander the Great (bas-relief), 24, 25 (fig.)

Asia Minor, 61–68, 79, 136, 258–59, 324*n*35; Alexander the Great and, 18, 23; Athens and, 21–22; Byzantine Empire and, 16, 17, 20, 35, 40, 41, 50, 64–66, 88, 105; emigration (fourteenth century) from, 162–63; Greek peasant resettlement in, 56, 62–63; Mohammed II and, 224; its population exchange with Macedonia (1923), 164, 222; Romans in, 13; *sancaks* of, 206; Tamerlane and, 85. *See also specific cities*

Asiklar, 163

Aspropotamos (Achelous) River, 7, 14, 271*n*54, 272*n*72

"Assises of Romania," 107

Astakos (Dragomesto), Asia Minor, 11

astronomy, 47

Astypalaia, island of, 69–71

Atalante, 280*n*7

Athanasius, monk, 111

Athens, 18, 19, 20, 21, 243, 247, 267*n*16; Frankish rule and, 106, 108, 110, 134, 215, 280*n*7, 312*nn*18, 33; as Orthodox diocese, 21, 24, 32, 109, 110–11; Ottoman Turks in,

78, 104, 134–35, 169, 211, 232, 357*n*101

Atoumanos, Simon, archbishop of Thebes, 111, 236

Atramyttenos, Emmanuel, 260

Attica, 19, 98, 108, 178; Albanians in, 10, 11, 12, 110; language of, 26

Augustine, saint, 99

Auxentius, grand duke, 36

Avaro-Slavs, 2, 13

Avlaki, 145

Avlona (Valona), Albania, 7

Avret Hisar, 162

Axios River, 163

Aya Silonya, Thrace, fortress of, 162

Aydin, Asia Minor, 163

Badoer, Giacomo, 322*n*6

Balamout, 164

Balkan peninsula, 2, 16, 38, 59, 102; Ottoman Turks in, 67, 69–85, 149, 151, 152, 161, 162, 163–68. *See also specific place-names*

Balkan Wars (1912–1913), 5

ballads (*paralogai*), 21, 45

banditry, 78, 110, 236; seafaring, 69, 71, 298*n*8

Barbaro, Ermolao, 250

Barkan, Ömer Lûtfi, cited, 229; quoted, 355*nn*81, 88, 90

Barlaam, monk, 58, 59, 235

Basarab, Alexander, ruler of Walachia, 80

Basdar Haïreddin, 77

bas-reliefs, 24, 25 (fig.)

Bayezid I, sultan, 74, 78, 88, 144; occupation of Thessaly by, 152, 155–56, 162, 164; Thessalonica and, 123, 124, 125; Yuruks and, 163, 164, 165

Bayezid, son of Augustus, 155

Beck, Hans-Georg, 174; quoted, 288 *n*8

Bedreddin Bey, 77

Beldiceanu, Nicoara, cited, 328*n*21

Belesta, Jean de, quoted, 321*n*35

Belgrade, battle of (1456), 223
Belokoma (Bilecik), 64
Belon, Pierre, 121; quoted, 337n57
Benoît de Sainte-Maur, 44
Bessarion, Ioannis, archbishop of Nicaea, cardinal of Trebizond, 100, 201, 215, 237, 241–45, 249, 253, 362n61, 363n84; Argyropoulos and, 247; Constantine XI and, 169, 171, 172–78, 179, 204–205, 232, 334nn17, 19–21; crusade agitation of, 209, 218, 257–58, 259, 263, 365n9; on decline of faith, 87
Bessarion Academy, 243, 361n47
Bessoi tribe, 12
Bible, The, 87, 94; New Testament of, 91, 111, 250
Biblioteca Marciana, Codex CCVI, 256
Bibliothèque Nationale, Paris, 253
Biga, Asia Minor, 163
Bilecik (Belokoma), 64
bishops, 4, 32–33, 61–62; in the Athenian see, 21, 24, 32, 109, 110–11; Danubian, 81; judicial roles of, 147–48; Ottoman Turks and, 90, 94, 161; Roman Church and, 95, 96, 98, 138; in the see of Larissa, 314n47. See also individual names
Bithynia, Asia Minor, 34, 67, 68, 89, 101
Bitola (Monastir), 78
Bitrinitza (Tolophon), 110
Blachernae district, Constantinople, 194
Black Sea, 80, 136, 137, 193, 260; Theodore II Palaeologus on, 169, 170; Trebizond and, 222, 224; Venice and, 137, 190
Blastares, Matthew, monk, 53
Blemmydes, Nicephorus, 35, 39, 111–12; quoted, 38
Bobaljević, Vuk, 188, 338n6
Boccaccio, Giovanni, 235, 236
Boeotia, 10, 108, 178
Bogoslav's fief, Trikkala, 154

Bologna, Italy, 250
Bologna, Fra Lodovico da, 224
Bon, Antoine, on Corinth, 267n16
Boniface Castle, Crete, 36
Book of Titles (sancak), see sancaks
Bosnia, 227
Bosphorus, The, 17, 190; Golden Horn of, 194, 196
Boua tribe, 10
Boué, Ami, cited, 163
Bouïoi tribe, 7
Bourgos, Chandax, 298n8
Bracciolini, Poggio, 239
Bramante, Donato, 249
Branković, George, despot of Serbia, 188, 345n92
"Brief Chronicles," 2, 231
Brocquière, Bertrandon de la, cited, 101, 324n41, 329n1; quoted, 139, 141–42, 143, 152, 286n81, 324nn33, 35
Bruni, Leonardo, 239, 241, 319n11
Bryennios family, 65
Bryennios, Joseph, 20, 85, 88, 96, 121, 161, 185, 334n19; quoted, 87, 93, 100–101, 102, 125, 199
Bryennios, Manuel, 47
Budé, Guillaume, 249, 250, 252
Bulayir (Plagiarion), 72
Bulgaria, 38, 48, 53, 71; Ottoman Turks in, 76, 77, 152, 163, 164, 218–19
Bulgarian language, 3, 6, 268n32
Bulgarian people, 35; in battle of Klokotnitsa (1230), 33; invasion of Greece by, 4–5, 6, 30, 267n21, 274n84, 327n13
Bulla (Constitutio Cypria . . . Pope Alexander IV), 95
Buondelmonti, Christopher, cited, 71, 101, 138
Buondelmonti, Esau de, despot of Epirus, 113–14, 116, 118
Bürak Bey, 146, 163
Burgas (Pyrgos), 136, 193, 341n35
Burgundy, 179, 223–24

Bursa (Prusa), 62, 64, 144; Mohammed II in, 224, 228
Busleiden Collège des Trois Langues,
Louvain, 253
Byzantine Empire, 136, 337n56;
Alexander the Great and, 22–23,
24; class structure of, 54–57; eagle
emblem of, 40, 284n70; ethnic infusions in, 1–16; Hellenization of,
17–18, 20, 24–26, 28, 29–30, 37,
42–43, 101, 104–105, 106–107,
185–86, 232, 255, 256–63; Ottoman attack upon, 60, 64–66, 74,
76–77, 79, 85, 88, 137, 143–44,
145, 170, 187–205, 256–57; Palaeologian Renaissance in, 46–54, 59,
97, 137–38, 170, 222; Roman
foundation of, 17–20, 27–28, 29,
30, 37, 42–43, 49, 50, 100, 103,
175, 232. See also specific place-
names
Byzantios, Aristonymos, 260

Cádiz, Spain, 234
Caesarea, Cappadocia, 63
Caesarea, near Kozane, 3
Calabria, 57, 58, 235, 244, 254
Calecas, Manuel, 100, 236, 285n77;
quoted, 53, 124, 137–38
Calecas, Nicholas, quoted, 239
calligraphy, 50, 250, 252, 284n71
Callimachus, 251
Callimachus and Chrysorrhoe (An-
dronicus Comnenus Ducas Palae-
ologus), 45
Callipolis, 72
Callistus, Andronicus, 244, 247, 249,
250, 254, 358n20, 362n71, 364n91;
quoted, 245, 259–60
Callixtus III, pope, 208, 218, 219,
220, 253, 257
Cammelli, Giuseppe, quoted, 255,
358n20
Candia, 216, 251
Canea, 202
Cantacuzena, Irene, 345n92

Cantacuzenus, Demetrius, 80, 201
Cantacuzenus, Evdokia, 201, 345n92
Cantacuzenus, George, 170
Cantacuzenus, John, emperor, see
John VI Cantacuzenus
Cantacuzenus, John, in seige of Con-
stantinople, 201
Cantacuzenus, Manuel, despot of
Morea, see Manuel II Cantacuzenas
Cantacuzenus, Manuel, rebel leader
in Morea, 82, 208
Cantacuzenus, Matthew, 82, 106
Canterbury, England, 19–20
Capo di Matapan, 351n33
Cappadocia, 22, 50, 62, 63, 223;
Mordtmann in, 67–68. See also
specific place-names
Caratzas, Stamatis, cited, 235
Caraféria, 267n21
Carlo I Tocco, 11, 114, 116, 272n66,
315n65
Carlo II Tocco, 148, 179
Cassandrea (Potidaea), 146
Castel Nuovo (Kainourgion), 36
Castiglionchio, Lapo da, 241
Castiglione, Baldassar, 249
Castrenus, Demetrius, 358n20
Castriota, George ("Scanderbeg"),
208
Catalans, 69, 106, 107, 312n18;
Albanians and, 7, 10; laws of, 108–
109, 110; Orthodoxy and, 98, 110;
Ottoman Turks and, 77, 82; slave
trade of, 71
Catania, Sicily, 244, 364n90
Catherine, princess of Serbia, 345n92
Catherine (Theodora), princess of
Trebizond, 223, 227, 353n56
Caumont, Nompar II, Seigneur de,
cited, 71
Cayster River, 68
Cayir, 164
Cedrenus, George, cited, 20
Cephalonia, 11, 158, 202
Cephalonia and Leukas, duchess of,
113

Cephisus, battle of (1311), 108
Cephisus River, 98
Chadenos, provincial governor under Michael VIII Palaeologus, 64
Chalcedon, Asia Minor, 62
Chalcidice, 4, 81, 136
Chalcocondyles, Demetrius, 233, 237, 247–49, 362n63; Lorenzo de' Medici and, 248, 251, 366n15
Chalcocondyles, George, 134, 135, 169, 232
Chalcocondyles, Laonicos, 123, 134, 135, 232–33, 247, 357n101; cited, 5, 206, 207; quoted, 349n8
Chalcocondyles, Theophilus, 249
Chaldia (Ophis), 231
Chalil, Kara, 299n27
Chalkeon, Church of, Thessalonica, 50
Chandax (Herakleion), 96, 298n8
Charanis, Peter; quoted, 55; on Slav migrations, 266n8
Chariton, Metropolitan of Curtea-de-Argeş, 81
Charitonymos, Jerome, on Gemistos, 181, 183
Charles V, Holy Roman Emperor, 259, 366n15
Charles VII, king of France, 208
Charles VIII, king of France, 252, 259, 261
Charsianeites, monastery of, Constantinople, 187
Chatalja (Pharsala), see Pharsala
Cheroiana (Kanis), 231
Chios, island of, 107, 202, 216, 218, 219
Chlapen, Radoslav, 114, 315n57
Chlomos, Demetrius, copyist, 111
Chlomoutsi fortress, Peloponnesus, 213
Cholos, Peter (the Crippled), 207
Chomatianus, Demetrius, archbishop of Achris, 32
Choniates, Michael, archbishop of Athens, 21, 24, 26, 32

Choniates, Nicetas, historian, cited, 34–35; quoted, 28–29, 30, 54
Chora, monastery of, Constantinople, 47
Chortatzes, George, 41
Choumnos, Makarios, abbot of Nea Mone, 114
Choumnos, Nicephorus, 53
Christianity, 16, 17, 23; Albanians and, 12; anti-Semitism and, 257; Armatoles and, 157–60; compassion and, 86–87, 89–90, 127, 306n32; crusading zeal and, 209, 217–18; eschatalogical, 90–92; Gagauz, 274n89; Greek paganism and, 18–19, 26, 37, 39, 47, 48, 53, 57, 171, 184–85, 256, 262–63, 333n7; Holy War of Islam and, 60, 61–62, 64, 65, 66–68, 73, 76, 77, 78–79, 86, 88–89, 92, 143–44, 148, 149–50, 162, 203, 259, 292n59, 295n39, 296nn40–41, 44, 302nn53, 55, 365n7; janissary service and, 125, 151–52, 202; martyrdom and, 92, 93–95, 96, 200, 307n41; Slavs and, 3, 4; spahi service and, 149, 150, 152–57, 230–31, 355n90; Tamerlane and, 85. See also Orthodox Church; Roman Catholicism
Christodoulos, architect, 200, 344n86
Christoupolis, 78
Chronicle of Dryopis, 78
Chronicle of Galaxidi, 4, 104, 113
Chronicle (of Leontios Machairas), 105
Chronicle of Monemvasia, 2, 4
Chronicle of Morea, 43, 44
Chronicle of Proklos and Comnenus, 154
Chronicle (Sphrantzes), 216
Chrysoberges, Andrew, 100, 236
Chrysoberges, Maximus, 100, 101, 236
Chrysoberges, Nicholas, 111
Chrysoberges, Theodore, 100, 236

Chrysococces, George, astronomer, 47

Chrysoloras, Demetrius, quoted, 102

Chrysoloras, Manuel, 236, 237–41, 245, 248, 358n20, 364n91; teaching methods of, 240, 247, 249, 360n36; Union issue and, 100, 239

Chrysostom, John, saint, 230

Cilicia, 63, 294n17. *See also* Armenia

Çirmen, 77, 163

civil service, 40, 133, 175–76; in Cyprus, 133; Gemistos on, 128, 130; Turkish, 201, 206

Clavijo, Ruy Gonzales de, cited, 71, 222

Clement VII, pope, 259

Clement XVI, pope, 98

Cleopa Malatesta, princess, 132, 133

Colonia, Asia Minor, 14

Comnenus family, 54, 65. *See also* *individual rulers,* e.g., John IV Comnenus, emperor of Trebizond

Comnenus, Alexander, 227

Comnenus, Alexius (nephew of David), 227

Comnenus, Anna, 227

Comnenus, Constantine, 201

Comnenus, George, 227

Comnenus, Isaac, 201

Comparationes philosophorum Aristotelis et Platonis (Trapezountios), 243

Concerning the Book in Favor of Latin Dogma (*Pros to hyper tou latinikou dogmatos biblion . . .* Gemistos), 171

Congress of Mantua, 257

Constantin, Akritic hero, 22

Constantine I the Great, 17, 18, 19, 37, 232, 257, 260

Constantine VI, emperor, 3

Constantine VII Porphyrogenitus, emperor, 5, 24

Constantine XI Palaeologus, emperor, 145, 180–86, 232, 345n91; as despot of Morea, 134, 135, 169–

80, 190, 334n23; reign of, 180–86, 217; in siege of Constantinople, 187–205, 216, 343n74, 344n86

Constantine Lascaris, emperor of Nicaea, 34

Constantine Palaeologus, despot of Morea, *see* Constantine XI Palaeologus, emperor

Constantinople, 3, 62, 65, 87, 117, 126; Chrysoloras in, 237, 239, 240; Fourth Crusade and, 15, 29; Greek art in, 19, 24; Hesychast controversy in, 57, 58, 59; as Imperial seat, 17–18, 31, 32, 33, 34, 37, 42, 76–77, 136, 145, 180–81; Latin occupations of Greece and, 35, 40–41, 101, 104–105, 106–107, 148, 169; as Ottoman capital, 206, 207, 213, 221, 227, 228, 245, 251, 257–63; Palaeologian Renaissance in, 46, 53, 100, 137–38, 185, 222; Tamerlane and, 85; Turkish siege (1394), 79–80, 81–82, 302n58; Turkish siege (1422), 145; Turkish siege (1453) and capture, 93, 104, 139, 187–205, 216, 218, 234, 237, 250, 256, 280n13, 339n23, 340n28, 341n35, 342n51, 343n74, 344n86, 347nn114–15, 360n40; walls of, 125, 193–94, 195(*fig.*), 196, 197, 198, 199, 340n28, 342n51, 343n74

Constitutio Cypria (*Bulla*—Pope Alexander IV), 95

Constitution de Florence (Bruni), 319n11

copper mines, 225

Corfu, island of, 8, 32, 71, 107, 146, 202, 235; Janus Lascaris in, 251; Thomas Palaeologus and, 213, 215, 216

Corinth, 2, 3, 4, 18, 19, 105, 266n8, 267n16; Catalans and, 106, 110; fortification of Isthmus of, 128, 132, 172, 173, 174, 179, 317n90; Franks in, 10, 107; music and, 39; Ottoman invasions of, 207, 212, 349n15; silk industry of, 177

Corinthios, Manuel, 251

Coron (Korone), 41, 213

Council of Athens and Neopatras, 110

Council of Constance (1414–1418), 71, 239, 240

Council of Ferrara (1439), 241, 244, 245

Council of Florence (1439), 106; Church Union and, 138, 139, 187, 191; humanism and, 170, 171, 241, 244, 245

Council (synod) of 1450–1451, 187

Council (synod) of Santa Sophia (1412), 102

Council of Ten (1487), 311n11

Cousinéry, Esprit, 10; quoted, 267n21

Crete, 31, 41–42, 205, 251, 283n49, 285n75, 337n57; art in, 80, 97, 303n62; Byzantine refugees in, 202, 215–16, 228, 235, 260; orthodoxy in, 43, 87, 96–99, 106–107, 138, 323n16; rebellion of 1230 in, 35–36; serfdom abolitionists in, 134; Vlastos' revolt in, 311n3

Critobulus of Imbros, 216–17, 220–21; cited, 145–46, 211; quoted, 198, 199, 226, 352n44

Croesus, 262

Crusades, 60, 80, 172, 366n15; Aegean agitation for, 217, 219–21; Apostolis' agitation for, 260, 366nn18–19; Bessarion's agitation for, 178, 209, 218, 257–58, 259, 263, 365n9; Fourth, 15, 27, 28–31, 38, 54–55, 69

Crusius, Martinus, cited, 237

Crypto-Christianity, 66–68, 89–90, 150

Curtea-de-Argeş, 80

Cuyrataci, brigand, 110

Cyclades, The, 15, 71

Cyprus, 105, 231, 32n34; Orthodoxy in, 43, 95–96, 102, 133, 138, 139, 321n33

Cyriacus of Ancona, 170, 172

Cyrus, 175

Dacia, see Thrace

Dakybiza (Libyssa), Nicaea, 65

Dalmates, John, 199

Danişmend, Emir of Kastamonu, 21

Danişmendnāme, 22, 60

Danube River, 14, 80–81

Darius the Cretan, 185

David Comnenus, emperor of Trebizond, 221, 223–24, 225–27, 228, 229

Delir, 164

Delvino, 149

Demetrias (Volos), 112

Demetrius, son of Michael, Christian spahi, 153, 155

Demetrius, saint, 47, 89

Demetrius Palaeologus, ruler of the divided Morea, 180–81, 185, 190, 201, 336n53, 338n6; Aegean Islands and, 213, 216, 221; in Adrianople, 212–13, 215, 227, 350n24; revolt of (1455–58), 207, 208–209, 211

democracy, 49–50, 53–54

Demosthenes, 250

Demus, Otto, 49; quoted, 48

Dennis, G. T., cited, 118, 316n77

Derili, 164

Dervenochoria, villages, 212

dervishes, 66

Didymoteikhon, 76, 221

Dieterich, Karl, 63

Digenis, 22, 35, 44

Digenis Akritas, 22, 35, 44

Dionysios, metropolitan of Edessa and Pella, 307n41

Diplovatatzes family, 208

Diyarbakir, Mesopotamia, 223

Dobruja district, Rumania, 274n89

Docheiariou monastery, Mt. Athos, 24

Dodecanese islands, piracy in, 69, 71

Domanits, villages, 64

Domenico Gattilusi, ruler of Lesbos, 217, 218–19
Domeniko, 153
Dominican Order, 236, 240
Domokos, 10, 112, 114, 153
Doria, Zorzi, 201
Dorino I Gattilusi, ruler of Lesbos, 216, 217, 218
Dorino II Gattilusi, ruler of Ainos, 219
Dorotheos, archbishop of Trebizond, 139, 231
Dragomesto (Astakos), 11
Drama, Macedonia, 163
Dräseke, Johannes, quoted, 320n24
Dreux, Robert de, quoted, 148
Dryinoupolis, bishop of, 114
Dubrovnik (Ragusa), see Ragusa
Ducas family, see ruling individual members under their Christian names, e.g., Theodore Comnenus Ducas, despot of Epirus
Ducas, Stephen, 114
Ducas, Michael, 197, 198, 218; quoted, 106–107, 142–43
Dušan, Stephen, conquests of, 8, 77, 112, 114, 116, 154, 314n47, 327n13
Dvornik, Francis, quoted, 3

earthquake of 1354, in Callipolis, 72
ecclesiastical centers, 4, 16, 31–33, 306n27; art and, 49, 50, 59; Athenian, 109; Danubian, 80–81; Roman Church and, 95, 96; in Trebizond, 231; Turks and, 61–62, 63, 66, 78–79, 161. See also bishops; monasteries
Edessa, Virgin of, 307n41
education, 18, 46, 47, 58, 59, 170; in Athens, 19–20, 32; in Italy, 177, 235–36, 237, 239–40, 241, 243, 244, 245, 247–49, 250–51, 252–53, 254, 360n36, 363n84, 364n90; of janissaries, 125; of Theodore II Lascaris, 38, 39; in Thessalonica, 118, 120, 317n89; of Turkish civil

servants, 201; by tutors, 35, 245, 247, 363n84; Vlachs and, 15
Eer Baba, conqueror of Almyros, 301n45
Egypt, 80
Elbe River, 13
Eleavoulcos, castle of, 116
Eleusis, 19
Elis, 5, 10, 213
Elissaeus (teacher), 144, 171
England, 13, 19–20, 23, 248, 250, 254
Enos (Ainos), 136, 184, 243; Ottomans and, 213, 216, 219, 221
Eparchos, George, 251
Epidemia tou Mazari en Hadou (Sojourn of Mazaris in Hades . . . Gemistos), 126
Epirus, 7, 11, 29, 30; architecture and, 49; Church of, 31–32, 112–13, 281n20; Nicaean rivalry with, 31–36; Serbs in, 8, 111, 112–13, 114, 118, 148, 327n13; Slavs in, 2, 3, 5, 266n9, 274n84; Turks in, 10, 78, 104, 111, 114, 148–49, 328n19; Vlachs in, 13, 14, 111, 112, 116, 156, 180, 266n9. See also specific place-names
Epivatae, on Sea of Marmara, 193
Erasmus, Desiderius, 240, 250, 252, 253, 262
Ermeni Mountains, 64
Ermoniakus, K., poet, 33
Erotemata (Questions . . . Chrysoloras), 240
Erotocritus, 44–45
Ertoghrul Ghazi, 64
Erymanthos Mountains, 209
Erzurum, Asia Minor, 225
Esau de Buondelmonti, despot of Epirus, 113–14, 116, 118
Eski Mosque, Serrai, 77
Eskisehir, Asia Minor, 64
Estopañán, Sebastián Cirác, quoted, 327n13
ethnic groups, 1–16, 27, 114, 265n2, 272n72; in the Aegean Islands,

81–82; in Asia Minor, 63, 67–68; in Italy, 235, 358n9. *See also* *specific groups*

Euboea, 4, 10, 107, 216, 312n18; fall of, 258; Orthodoxy in, 43, 98

Euclid, 47

Eugenicus, Marc, 138, 139

Eugenius IV, pope, 178, 244; Church Union and, 138, 323n16

Euphrates River, 13, 206

Euripides, 250, 251

Europe, 29, 42–43, 49, 53, 174–75, 176; Aegean Islands and, 217–18; Asian refugees in, 71–72, 85; Constantine XI and, 178, 179, 190; Constantinople's fall and, 202–203, 205, 206, 245, 256, 257–63; feudalism of, 54–55, 143; Peloponnesian appeals to, 208–209, 212, 215; philosophy and, 39–40, 58, 99, 100, 170, 171, 185, 233, 234, 235, 236–37, 239, 241, 243–55, 263; Trebizond and, 226. *See also specific countries*

Eustathius, archbishop of Thessalonica, 20, 24, 33

Euthymios, abbot of Levkousias, 111, 313n41

Evagrius Scholasticus, 2, 286n83

Evdomon Palace, Constantinople, 194

Evrenos Bey, 77, 106, 146, 156, 163, 166

Ezeritai tribe, 5

Fallmerayer, Jakob Philipp, 1–2, 6, 167, 168, 265nn1–2

Famagusta (Ammochostos), 95

fatalism, 48

Fauriel, Claude, cited, 157

Feodosiya (Kaffa), 224

Ferrara, Italy, 241, 244, 245, 247

feudalism, 54–55, 107, 112, 127; cities and, 290n36; Ottoman, 64, 74, 78, 143, 145, 149–50, 152–57, 163, 165, 216–17, 219, 229, 230–31,

295n35, 355n81; *wakf* under, 123–24. *See also* land grants

Ficino, Marsiglio, 241, 248

Filelfo, Francesco, 245, 248, 366n15; quoted, 170, 253

Filelfo, Gian Mario, son of Francesco, 245

Flandanelas, Captain, at siege of Constantinople, 196

Florence, Italy, 105, 109, 113, 215, 234, 250, 366n15; Council of 1439 (*See* Council of Florence); French invasion of, 252; humanism in, 235–36, 237, 239, 241, 245, 247–49, 251, 319n11

Florence, University of, 235–36, 237, 245; chair of ancient Greek at, 247, 248–49, 251

Florimont (Aimé de Varennes), 22

Florius and Platziaflora, 45

folklore, 16, 44, 337n56; on the Albanians, 7; Alexander and, 22–23, 47, 121; on Catalan cruelty, 312n18; on crypto-Christians, 67, 68, 150; on fall of Constantinople, 203–205, 344n86, 347nn14–15; oracles in, 36, 91–92, 132–33, 172, 174, 197, 204, 205, 235, 260, 277n22, 306n30, 317n90, 347n114; paganism and, 19; on Peloponnesian revolts, 213, 215; on piracy, 69; songs and, 20, 21, 22, 27, 35, 157, 186, 226, 229, 230, 231, 277n22, 337n58; on Thessalonian resistance, 121; on Thrace, 72; on Trebizond, 227–28, 229–30; on Vlachs, 14; on Yuruks, 165

Fourth Crusade (1204), 15, 27, 28–31, 38, 69; feudalism and, 54–55; Orthodoxy and, 102

France, 22, 141, 208, 249, 250–53, 258, 259

Francès, E., quoted, 290n36

Francesca, wife of Carlo I Tocco, 116

Francesco Sforza, duke of Milan, 208

Francis I, king of France, 252, 253, 259

Franks, 15, 280n7, 284n71, 337n56; Catalans and, 10, 98, 108, 312n18; Church Union and, 138–39; Constantine XI and, 169, 177; hellenism and, 37, 39, 43, 45, 49, 99, 102, 104–11, 112, 133, 134, 231, 321nn33, 35; Ottoman Turks and, 77, 139–42, 143, 152, 205, 211, 218–19; Trebizond and, 222

Frederick III, emperor of Germany, 260, 262, 366n18

Frederick III, king of Sicily, 109

funeral pyres, 2

Gabriel, abbot of Archimandreion, 113

Gabriel, abbot of *Nea Mone*, 114

Gabriel, archbishop of Thessalonica, 125; quoted, 88–89

Gabrielopoulos family, 112

Gabrielopoulos, Michael, lord of Thessaly, 7, 33

Gagauz, 274n89

Galata, 202, 257, 302n58

Galen, 111

Galesiotes, Andronicus, 243, 250

Gallipoli peninsula, 162, 163, 234, 243; Turkish governors of, 217, 224

Gardiki, 213, 350n26

Gardner, Alice, 37

Gasmuli, 15, 43

Gaspo, Michael de, 98

Gato, I., bishop of Catania, 364n90

Gattilusi family, 136, 213, 216, 218–19, 352n44

Gattilusi, Domenico, ruler of Lesbos, 217, 218–19

Gattilusi, Dorino (I), ruler of Lesbos, 216, 217, 218

Gattilusi, Dorino (II), ruler of Ainos, 219

Gattilusi, Nicholas, ruler of Lemnos, 219

Gattilusi, Palamedes, ruler of Ainos, 216, 217, 219

Gazes, Theodore, 241, 244, 247, 253, 256, 358n20, 364n91; quoted, 187

Genitsa (Giannitsa), 162

Gemistos, George, 123, 126–35, 144, 169, 170, 232, 237, 263, 319n1, 362n67; Bessarion and, 172, 173, 174, 176, 177, 241, 243; Bruni and, 319n11; Gennadius and, 171–72, 184–85, 241, 256; Hexamilion, defeat at, and, 179–80; on Holy War of Islam, 333n7; his plan for reform of Morea, 128–32, 320nn24, 28, 335nn43–44; panegyrics on, 181, 183, 335nn43–44

Gennadius II, patriarch of Constantinople (George Kourtesis Scholarios), 138, 139; quoted, 92, 102, 184, 191, 192, 193, 241, 244, 336n53, 340nn24, 26–28, 360n40, 362n61; accession of Constantine XI and, 181, 187, 191; anti-Union riots and, 191, 339n21; Gemistos and, 171–72, 184–85, 241, 256; Hexamilion, defeat at, and, 179

Genoa, Italy, 59, 63, 69, 136, 137; Chios and, 107; Constantinople's siege and, 190, 196, 197, 202, 216; Mohammed II and, 217, 218, 219

George, the philosopher, 304n72

George the Swift, saint, 52(fig.)

George of Trebizond, 333n7, 358n20

Georgia, 222, 223, 224, 230

Georgilas of Rhodes, 366n15

Gercke, Alfred, 358n20

Germanus, patriarch of Nicaea, 32

Germany, 19, 40, 248, 250, 259, 260, 262; Bessarion in, 257–58; Chrysoloras in, 239, 240; Crete and, 36; Slavs and, 5

Geschichte der Halbinsel Morea wahrend des Mittelalters (*History of the Peninsula of Morea during the Middle Ages . . .* Fallmerayer), 1–2

ghazis, 64, 66, 73, 78, 163, 355n83

Giannitsa (Genitsa), 162

Giese, Friedrich, quoted, 296n41
Gislenos, saint, 19
Giustiniani family, 219
Giustiniani, John Longo, 190, 196, 198–99
Glabas, Isidore, metropolitan of Thessalonica, quoted, 92, 94–95, 120
Glarentza (Kyllene), 181
glass-making, 177
Gniaousta, 267n21
Golden Horn, 194, 196
Gordon, Thomas, cited, 6–7
Gostila, brigand, 110
Goths, 19
Gradenigo, Angelo, Venetian duke, 36
Gradenigo, Bartolomeo, Venetian duke, 36
Grammousta, 14
"Grand Comneni" of Trebizond, 31, 222, 227
Grant, John, German engineer, 191, 196
"Great Idea," 35. See also nationalism
Greco-Vlachs, 14–15
Greece, 136, 337nn56–57; Armatoles of, 157–60; Asia Minor wars and, 21–22, 35, 61–63; emigrations from, 3, 4, 8, 10–11, 81–82; Lascaris' journeys (1489–1492) in, 251, 258–59; Latin occupations of, 15–16, 28–31, 35–36, 37, 40, 41–42, 43–45, 49, 54–55, 82, 95–99, 104–11, 133–34; modern, 28, 49, 275n90; Moslem pirates in, 69; Ottoman conquest of, 78, 79, 104, 124–25, 154, 157–60, 161–68, 186, 256–63; revolution of 1821 in, 1, 6, 14, 127, 144, 158, 160, 213, 299n21; as Roman province, 17–20, 27–28, 29, 30; Vlachs in, 12–15, 16, 78, 273n80. See also specific place-names
Greek language: Aegean dialects of, 15, 81; Byzantium and, 16, 18, 20, 27; in Cappadocia, 63, 68, 94;

Catalans and, 110; Chalcocondyles on, 232, 233; in Cyprus, 133; ecclesiastical usage, 26, 38; in Epirus, 11, 13, 150; in France, 250; Gemistos and, 128, 170; in Italy, 235, 236, 237, 239–40, 243, 244, 245, 358n9; Kydones and, 53, 82; Slavs and, 6, 8, 10, 265n2, 268n32; vernacular literature and, 22, 26, 45
Greek people: Christianity and, 18–19, 67, 80–81; ethnic origins of, 1–16, 27, 265n2, 272n72; Turks and, 61–63, 67–68, 71, 77, 155, 257
Gregoras, Nicephorus, historian, 30, 47
Gregorios Stylites, monk, 111
Gregorovius, Ferdinand, cited, 134; quoted, 17–18, 19
Gregory, monk, on Gemistos, 127, 181
Gregory IX, pope, 37, 232
Gregory XI, pope, 77, 310n79
Gregory III Mammas, patriarch of Constantinople, 187, 192
Grevena, 32
Grocin, William, 248
Guarino da Verona, 237; quoted, 240, 360n36
Gulf of Corinth, 8, 209
Gulf of Messenia, 207
Gulf of Patras, 209
Gulf of Saros, 72
Gumuljina (Komotine), 77

Hackett, John, quoted, 138, 139
Hagia Sophia, 73, 192, 198, 199, 200, 344n86
hagiography, 47, 231
Hairoullah effendi, Grand Mufti, cited, 162–63
Halil, Tsantarli Kara, 77, 318n108
Halil Bey, 150
Hamza, Admiral of the Turkish fleet, 217
haraç, 167
Harmankaya, Asia Minor, 295n35

Hassan, janissary, 199

Hassan, Uzun, 223, 224, 225, 227, 228, 353n56

Hatun, Sara, mother of Uzun Hassan, 225, 228

Hebrus River, 77, 163

Hector, 262

Helen, empress of Trebizond, 227

Helen, princess of Serbia, 80

Helen, second wife of John II Lusignan, 105, 133, 138, 185, 321n33

hellenism, see hellenization; nationalism

hellenization: of the Albanians, 10, 14; Byzantine, 17–18, 20, 23, 24–26, 27, 28, 37, 42–43, 91, 101, 232, 255, 256; Danubian, 80–81; of Epirus, 33, 111–16; of the Latins, 15, 99, 106, 232, 253; in Macedonia, 116–25; in Nicaea, 35, 36–40; peasantry in, 30, 134, 290n37; of the Slavs, 3, 4–5, 6, 7, 14, 114, 267nn16, 18; of the Turks, 15–16, 61, 67, 211, 296n44

Hellespont, 68, 72, 73, 218

Hennegau, Germany, 19

Henry of Flanders, emperor of Constantinople, 104–105

Heptapyrgion Fortress, Constantinople, 227

Heraclius, emperor, 19, 194

Herakleia, on Sea of Marmara, 136, 180, 188, 193, 341n35

Herakleion (Chandax), 96, 298n8

Hermonymos, Charitonymos, bibliographer, quoted, 256

Hermonymos, George, copyist, 250, 252

Hermus River, 68

Herodotus, 170

Hesiod, 249, 250

Hesseling, Dirk, cited, 44

Hesychast controversy, 57–60, 102, 118, 235, 236

Heuzey, Léon, quoted, 269n40, 272n72

Hexabiblos (Armenopoulos), 53, 148

Hexamilion, Wall of, 128, 132, 172, 173, 174, 179

Hexapterygos, Theodoros, 35

Hierapetra, The, 260

Hierissos, 116

Hierosolymites, Nikon, priest, 80

Hill, Sir George Francis, 321nn33–34

Hisar-eri, 143

History of the Byzantine Empire (Amantos), 28

History of the Peninsula of Morea during the Middle Ages (Geschichte der Halbinsel Morea wahrend des Mittelalters . . . Fallmerayer), 1–2

Hitir, Pasha of Amasya, 222–23, 228

Hody, Umfredo, 358n20

Hofmann, Georg, quoted, 98

Hohenburg, Berthold von, 40

Holy Apostles, Church of the, Constantinople, 145, 200

Homer, 33, 236, 249

Hopf, Karl, 19; quoted, 294n17

horses, 141, 155

Hôtel de l'Ile, Constance, 240

How Aristotle Differs from Plato (Peri hon Aristoteles pros Platona diapheretai . . . Gemistos), 170, 241

humanism, 80, 99, 233, 254–55, 258, 260, 263; Athens and, 21; Barlaam and, 58; classical translation and, 46, 111, 240, 244; Florence and, 170, 171, 235–36; 237, 239, 241, 245, 247–49; French, 249, 250, 252, 253; pagan flavor of, 195; Rome and, 100, 234–35, 236, 237, 247; Theodore II Lascaris and, 38, 39–40

Hungary, 80, 178, 247; Turks in, 73, 188, 223

Hunyadi, John Corvinus, ruler of Transylvania, 178, 180, 188, 190

Hyakinthos, metropolitan of Curtea-de-Argeş, 81

Hydra, island of, 10, 215

Hypate, *see* Neopatras
Hypsomatheia, Constantinople, 200

Iberia, 188, 230
Ibrahim Bey, ruler of Karaman, 188, 190, 223, 338*n*9
icmâl, 150
iç oğlan, 201
Iconium (Konya), Asia Minor, 62, 64, 163, 164, 165
Idylls (Theocritus), 20
Iliad (Homer), 33, 44, 249
Illyria, 7, 12, 13
Imberius and Margarona, 45
Imbros, island of, 136, 352*nn*44, 48; Ottomans and, 213, 216–17, 218, 219, 220–21
Inalcik, Halil, cited, 149, 154
In calumniatorem Platonis (*Against Plato's Calumniator* . . . Bessarion), 243
India, 13
Ioannina, 8, 10, 11, 111, 116, 313*n*43, 314*n*48; fortification of, 29; Serbian occupation and, 112–13; Turkish capture of, 148–49; Yuruks in, 164
Ioasaph, abbot of Meteora, *see* John Ouroš Palaeologus, ruler of Thessaly and abbot of Meteora
Ionian islands, 231, 235
Ionian Sea, 158, 301*n*45; piracy on, 69, 71
Iphicrates, 120
Isaurian period (717–867), 63
Isidore, monk, 132, 133
Isidore, archbishop of Kiev, 191–92, 317*n*90
Isidore, archbishop of Thessalonica, 123, 124, 125
Islam, 274*n*89, 338*n*9; Albanians and, 12; Christian conversion to, 15–16, 66–68, 73, 79, 88, 89–90, 93, 148, 149–50, 153, 154, 155, 156, 162, 165, 259, 292*n*59, 295*n*39, 296*nn*40–41, 44, 302*n*53, 55, 328*n*19; Christian theological responses to, 74,

76, 86, 90–95, 139, 193, 203, 257, 302*n*53, 365*n*7; compassion and, 143–44, 292*n*59, 296*n*40, 324*n*35; Gemistos and, 171, 333*n*7; ghazi militarism and, 64–65, 73, 77–78, 163, 324*n*31; Ottoman conversion to, 60, 143; Tamerlane and, 85
Ismail, Turkish admiral, 221
Ismaïl Bey, Isfendiaroglou, prince of Kastamonu, 223, 225
Isocrates, 249
Istifa, *see* Thebes
Italy, 3, 13, 132, 141, 207, 358*n*9; Constantinople's fall and, 188, 190, 200–201, 218, 257, 258; crusaders and, 209, 217, 219–21, 258, 263; French invasion of (1494), 252; the Renaissance and Greek scholarship in, 58, 128, 172, 173, 175, 177, 234–55, 262, 360*n*36, 362*n*61, 364*n*90. *See also* specific placenames
Izlati, Bulgaria, 218–19

James I, Epistle of, quoted, 91
James the Persian, martyr, 90
janissaries, 74, 75(*fig.*), 125, 151–52, 156, 201, 258, 299*nn*23, 27–28, 318*n*108; Galata's exemption of, 202; salaries of, 207; in siege of Constantinople, 199; Trebizond and, 228
Jeremiah I, patriarch of Constantinople, 199
Jerusalem, 80
Jews, 144, 171; Turks and, 66, 148, 257
John, ruler of Thessaly, 56
John, metropolitan of Moscow, 187
John III Ducas Vatatzes, emperor of Byzantium and Nicaea, 34, 35, 43, 90, 175, 232, 283*n*49; quoted, 37–38; canonization of, 36, 306*n*27
John V Palaeologus, emperor, 53, 59, 71, 77, 99, 124, 234, 310*n*79; fiscal

policy of, 137; Ottoman Turks and, 76, 79, 117

John VI Cantacuzenus, emperor, 59, 71, 82, 99, 304n73

John VIII Palaeologus, emperor, 98, 140(fig.), 178, 192, 216, 341n41; Argyropoulos and, 245; Chrysoloras and, 239; Church Union and, 138, 139; Murad II and, 145, 146, 180

John de Brienne, Frankish emperor of Constantinople, 37

John IV ("the Good") Comnenus, emperor of Trebizond, 185, 188, 223, 353n56

John V Comnenus, emperor of Trebizond, 223

John II Lusignan, king of Cyprus, 105, 133, 321n33

John Ouroš Palaeologus, ruler of Thessaly and abbot of Meteora, 113, 114, 115(fig.), 164, 315n56

John II Ducas Orsini, despot of Epirus, 8, 33

John XIV Aprenos, patriarch of Constantinople, 89–90

John Apocaucus, metropolitan of Naupactus, 31–32, 297n1

John Chrysostom, saint, 230

John of Basingstoke, 21

John of Ephesus, 2

John of Ioannina, 93

Joseph of Ithaca, philosopher, 47

Julian ("the Apostate"), emperor, 185

Julius II, pope, 259

Justinian I, emperor, 3, 13, 19, 347n115

Justinian II, emperor, 3

Juvenal, monk, 183, 184

Kaffa (Feodosiya), 224

Kâfir-sipahiler, 65–66

Kainourgion (Castel Nuovo), 36

Kalamaria, 146, 162

Kalaphatis, Michael and Jacob, 201, 202

Kalarites, 7

Kalavryta, library of, 170

Kailar (Ptolemais), 163

Kale-eri, 143

Kallerges, Alexius, 41, 106

Kallerges, Andrew, 336n49

Kallerges, John, 106

Kallierges, Zachary, 252

Kalokyres, Constantine, quoted, 107

Kamariotes, Matthew, 251

Kamelos, Kosmas, monk, 111

Kananos, Lascaris, cited, 5

Kanis (Cheroiana), 231

Kapnion (Johann Reuchlin), 240, 248, 249, 250

Kara Chalil of Tsantarlı, 299n27

Karademilli, 164

Karagounides, 7. See also Arvanito-Vlachs

Karamania, Asia Minor, 74, 163, 188, 190, 324n35, 338n13; Trebizond and, 223

Karamtza, 163

Karasi, Asia Minor, 162, 163

Karatsoğlan, 164

Karatza Bey, Rumeli Valesi, general, 193

Karditsa, 7, 111, 155

Karpenision, 14

Karykes, Demetrios, archbishop of Ephesus, 35

Kasomoulis, Nikolaos, cited, 14

Kassim, governor of Gallipoli, 224, 228, 355n81

Kastamonu, 223

Kastoria, 50, 155

Kastrinos, Demetrius, 249, 251, 257; quoted, 253

Kastritsi fortress, Peloponnesus, 212, 213

Kata Hellenon (Against the Hellenes . . . Scholarios), 171

Katallactis, Jacob, John and George, 201

Kataphygion, 268n32

Kata tou Plethonos aporion ep' Aristotelei (Against the Doubts of

Plethon about Aristotle . . . Scholarios), 184–85
Kavakes family, 208
Kavakes, Demetrius Ralles, 185; quoted, 256
Kavasilas, Neilos, archbishop of Thessalonica, 53
Kavasilas, Nicholas, astronomer, 47, 53, 58; quoted, 50, 300n38
Kavazitis family, 222, 229
Kazaklar, 164
Kell Petros ("Scald-headed Peter"), 307n41
Keltzene province, 62
Keramopoullos, Antonios, on Vlach origins, 273n80
Kerassovo, 14
Kercoporta, of Constantinople, 197, 199
Kisalar, 163
Kissamos, 337n57
Kissling, Hans, quoted, 296n44
Kitros, 78
Kizilbashs, 355n84
Klette, Theodor, 358n20
Klisura, 268n32
Klokotnitsa, battle of, 33
"Knidia Athena" (Praxiteles), 19
Knights Hospitalers, of Rhodes, 217–18, 220
Knights of St. John of Jerusalem, 82, 106
Knös, Börje, quoted, 171
Koïnlu Hisar, 225
Kokkala, 213, 350n26
Kokkini Melia (Red Apple Tree), 204
Kolindros, 114
Kolokotrones, Theodore, 129
Komotine (Gumuljina), 77
Konitsa, 149
Konrad IV Hohenstaufen, emperor of Germany, 40
Konya (Iconium), Asia Minor, 62, 64, 163, 164, 165
Kopitar, Bartholomäus, quoted, 265n2

Köprülü, Fuad, cited, 67, 296n44
Koran, The, 143
Kordyle (Aldja Kale), fortress, Asia Minor, 229
Koritsa district, 78
Korone (Coron), 41, 213
Korthion, 81
Kosovo Polje, battle of (1389), 80, 163, 187
Kotyaeon (Kutahya), Asia Minor, 62
Koufala, 164
Kougeas, Socrates, quoted, 5
Koumas, Constantine, quoted, 13
Kozane, 3, 163
Kravari, 153
Kravaldi, spahi, 153
Kritoboulos of Imbros, *see* Critobulus of Imbros
Kritopoulos, Anthimos, metropolitan of Curtea-de-Argeş, 81
Kritopoulos, Mitrophanes, 358n20
Krokion, plain of, Thessaly, 165
Krystallis, Constantine, poet, 273n80
Kuru Dag, 72
Kutahya (Kotyaeon), Asia Minor, 62
Kydones, Demetrius, 48, 77, 79, 101, 102, 105, 120; quoted, 42, 50, 53, 58–59, 68, 72, 76, 82, 100, 118, 137, 234, 300n39, 301n45, 302nn53, 55–56, 304n73, 324n31, 358n18; in Italy, 234, 236, 237, 239, 358n18; Roman conversion of, 99–100, 309n73
Kydones, Prochoros, brother of Demetrius, 53
Kyllene (Glarentza), 181
Kynouria district, 81
Kyriakidis, Stilpon, cited, 147, 277 n28, 278nn30–31

Lacedemon district, 81
Lacedemonia (Laconia), 4, 135, 174, 175, 215, 256. *See* Sparta
Ladislaus, king of Hungary, 178
Lake Ioannina, 14
Lake Koroneia, 14, 163

Lala Sahin, Paşa, governor of Philippopolis, 166
La Marciana Library, Venice, 244
Lambros, Spyridon, 172, 313n41, 362n68; quoted, 26
Lamia (Zituni), 136, 145, 146, 155
Lampridio di Cremona, 253
Lampsacus, Asia Minor, 88
land grants, 98, 112–13, 291n45; hereditary, 34, 54–55, 143, 149, 154–55; monastic, 33, 56–57, 60, 85, 123, 127, 129–30, 165; Ottoman, 66–67, 74, 123–24, 143, 145, 153, 154, 155–57, 161, 163, 209, 213, 216–17, 227, 229, 230–31, 295n35; Turkish invasion threats and, 62, 64, 78, 149, 152–53, 165–66
languages, 13, 15, 81, 269n40; nationalism and, 16, 18, 20, 27, 30, 37, 38, 42, 43, 94, 183, 185–86, 232, 285nn77, 79, 286n80, 296n40, 316n77, 336nn47, 49, 337n58; place-names, 2, 4, 6, 12, 14, 19, 68, 79, 149, 153, 155, 163, 164, 213. See also specific languages
Laodicea, see of, Asia Minor, 62
Larissa, 112, 167, 314n47; Yuruks in, 162, 164–65, 331n25
Larissa, metropolitan of, quoted, 314 n47
Lascarids, 36–40, 202. See also individual ruling members under their Christian names, e.g., Theodore II Laścaris, emperor of Nicaea
Lascaris, Constantine, 243, 245, 249–50, 258; quoted, 253–54, 263, 364n90
Lascaris, Demetrius, 208
Lascaris, Emmanuel, 201
Lascaris, Janus, 237, 248, 249, 250–53, 258–59, 362n63
Lascaris, Manuel, 251
Lascaris, Matthew, 251
Lascaris, Theodore, 201

Lastiq, Jean de, commander of the Knights of Rhodes, 217–18
Latin language, 7, 111, 243, 245, 249; Quirinal College and, 252, 253; spread of, 13–14, 15
Latin occupations, 28–31, 40, 232; fall of Constantinople and, 202, 205, 218; feudalism and, 54–55; Roman Catholicism and, 15, 43, 95–99, 101–102, 133, 138, 321n33. See also specific conquering groups
law, 53; Catalan, 108–109, 110; Gemistos and, 126, 127, 128, 129, 130; judicial ethics and, 76, 87, 300nn38–39; in Thessalonica, 49–50, 117, 124, 146–47, 148, 149; in Thessaly, 33, 112–13, 156; Yuruk, 162
Laws (Nomoi . . . Gemistos), 171, 333n7
Lazare, saint, 80
Lefka, 105
Lefkousias, monastery of, Thessaly, 33, 111, 313n41
Legrand, Émile, 358n20
Lemnos, island of, 136; Ottomans and, 213, 216, 217, 218, 219, 220–21
Leo VI ("the Wise"), emperor, 3, 204, 205
Leo X, pope, 247, 252, 253, 259
Leon, mathematician, 20
Leonard of Chios, Bishop of Mytilene, 339n23
Leonardo da Vinci, 249
Leondari, 213
Lesbos, island of, 216, 217, 218, 219, 285n77
Leukas, archbishopric of, 116, 158
Levadia, 108–109, 154, 280n7
libraries, 20, 104, 111–12; French, 252, 253; Italian, 235, 243–44, 249, 251; of Kalavryta, 170; of Nicaea, 38; of Moschopoulos, 284n71; Turkish, 158
Libyssa (Dakybiza), Bithynia, 65
Lidorikion, 153, 179

Ligara, 164
Limassol, 95, 105
Linacre, Thomas, 248
"Linda Athena" (Praxiteles), 19
Liosa tribe, 10
literature, 20, 104, 111–12; classical revival in, 21, 30, 46–49, 53, 58, 82, 99, 170, 171, 233 (*See also* humanism); epic, 22, 26, 33, 35, 44, 144, 287n89, 337n58, 356n95; on fall of Constantinople, 203, 204, 259–63, 354n77, 366n15, 367n22; Frankish rule and, 43–45, 107–108, 232; hagiographic, 47, 231; Italian Renaissance and, 235–36, 241, 243, 249, 360n36; Janus Lascaris' collection of, 250–52, 253; Nicaea and, 38–39; painting and calligraphy and, 23–24, 50, 250, 252, 284n71; Serbian, 80; sermons as, 86, 89; translation skills and, 46, 111, 240, 243, 244. *See also* libraries; *and see specific titles*
Lluria, John de, 98
Lluria, Roger de, *fils*, 82, 98, 109
Loenertz, Raymond, cited, 113
London, England, 250
Lopadion (Olubad), Asia Minor, 199
Lorenzo de' Medici, 248, 251, 366n15
Loucaris, Cyril, 358n20
Louis XII, king of France, 252
Louvain, Flanders, 253
Lübeck, Germany, 5
Lucanis, Nicephorus, 209, 211
Luke the Younger, saint, 3–4
Lycurgus, 105, 121, 176
Lyvistros and Rhodamne, 45

Macedonia, 23, 38, 368n32; Fourth Crusade and, 30; Hesychast civil war and, 59; Latin in, 13; nobles expelled from, 127, 319n6; Ottoman Turks in, 72, 77, 107, 146–47, 159, 162, 163–64, 166, 190; Palaeologian Renaissance in, 49–54, 114, 116–25; Serbs in, 8, 77; Slavs in,

2, 3, 4, 5, 10, 274n84; Theodore Comnenus Ducas' conquest of, 33; toponyms of, 6, 155. *See also specific place-names*
Machairas, Leontios, 105
Maeander River, 62, 68
Magistros, Thomas, 46, 53
Magnesia, Asia Minor, 306n27
Magnesia, Asia Minor, "patriot monk" of, 90; quoted, 74, 76
Magnesia River, 90
Mahmud, Vizier, 213, 218, 226, 350n28
Mahmud II, sultan, 167
Maina, 5, 40, 98; Byzantine refugees in, 213, 215, 227, 351n33
Mainalon district, 209
Majorca, 71, 108
Makris, Makarios, 111, 317n89
Makrynitsa, 167
Malakasioi tribe, 7
Malazgirt, battle of (1071), 61
Malian Gulf, 136
Mamalakis, Ioannis, cited, 319n1
Mamelukes (Saracens), 49, 105
Mangaphas, nobleman, 113
Mängli, Muhammed ben, quoted, 292n59
Maniakes, Nicholakes, 109
Maniatai, 5
Manisa (Saruhan), Asia Minor, 163
Mantua, Italy, 257
Manuel II Palaeologus, emperor, and ruler of Thessalonica, 60, 99, 117(fig.), 192; quoted, 120–21; Aegean Islands and, 216; Chrysoloras and, 237; Gemistos and, 126, 127, 129, 131; Ottoman Turks and, 77, 85, 113, 114, 116, 117–18, 123, 124, 125, 145; Roman Church and, 102, 138, 139
Manuel II Cantacuzenus, despot of Morea, 10, 82, 105, 107, 109, 120
Manuel Angelos Philanthropenos, ruler of Thessaly, 114
Manutius, Aldus, 244, 250, 251, 252

Maria Melissene, duchess of Athens, 134–35

Marmara, Sea of, 65, 136, 180; piracy on, 69; siege of Constantinople and, 193, 194

Maroullos, Manuel, physician, 245, 367n22

Maroullos, Michael, poet, quoted, 367n22

Marsuppini, Carlo, 239

Masai, François, 319n1, 362n67; quoted, 319n11, 333n7

Mastrothodoros, Stephen, 98

mathematics, 47

Matthew, quoted, 91

Matthew, metropolitan of Ephesus, quoted, 86

Matthew, metropolitan of Ioannina, 113, 114

Matthew Corvinus, king of Hungary, 247

Maurice, emperor, 2, 3

Mavronicholas family, 108–109

Mavronicholas, Constantine, 109

Mavronicholas, Nicholas, 109

Maximilian I, of Germany, 259, 260

Mecca, Sherif of, 167

Medea, on Black Sea, 136

Medici family, 215, 247, 252

Medici, Lorenzo de', 248, 251, 366n15

medicine, 35, 47

Megale Porta, 33

Megara, 280n7

Megara, archbishop of, 110

Megara, battle of (1364), 82, 109

Meliarakis, Anthony, 37

Melingi tribe, 5

Melissene, Maria, duchess of Athens, 134

Melissinoi family, 35–36, 112, 134–35

Melitene province, 62

Meliteniotes, Theodore, 47

Memorabilia (Xenophon), 243

Menander, 2

Mentese, Emirate of, Asia Minor, 69

Mercati, Giovanni, 302n58; quoted, 285n79

mercenaries, 8, 12, 30, 65–66, 71, 105, 341n41

Merne, of Trebizond, 229, 355n88

Mesaritai tribe, 7

Mesembria (Nesebar), on Black Sea, 136, 193, 286n82

Mesochaldion, Trebizond, 222, 228

Mesopotamia, 62–63, 223

Mesopotamites, Isaac, monk, 31

Messenia, 10, 41, 107, 207, 213

Messina, Italy, 243, 249–50, 253

Metaphysics (Aristotle), 243

Metaphysics (Theophrastus), 243

Metaxas, Sergius, Antony, and Nicholas, 201, 202

Meteora, 69, 70(fig.), 111, 164, 251, 313nn41, 43

Methone (Modon), 41, 213; castle of, 214(fig.)

Metochites, Theodore, 47–48, 288n8; quoted, 49

Metsovon, 7

Meyendorff, Jean, quoted, 57–58

Meyer, Gustav, cited, 6

Michael, spahi, 153

Michael VIII Palaeologus, emperor, 46, 55, 62, 64; recapture of Constantinople by, 29, 40–41, 42

Michael, Czar of Bulgaria, 38

Michael I Comnenus Ducas, despot of Epirus, 29

Michael II Comnenus Ducas, despot of Epirus, 282n32

Michal, Köse, 295n35

Michal Oğlu Ali Bey, 150, 295n35

middle class, 55–56, 59; Gemistos on, 128, 129, 131

migrations: Albanian, 7, 10, 11, 12, 269nn40–42; Greek, 3, 4, 8, 10–11, 63, 67–68, 81–82; Slav, 2–3, 4–6, 7, 12, 13–14, 154, 266nn8–9, 274n84; Turkish, 162–63

Mikira-li district, 153

Milan, Italy, 234, 249, 250, 254

Miller, William, quoted, 275n90
Milutin, ruler of Serbia, 50
Mingrelia, 223, 224
Miracula Sancti Demitrii, 2
Misalar, 164
Mistra, 24, 40, 98, 106, 170; L. Chalcocondyles in, 232, 357n101; Gemistos in, 126, 127, 134, 319n1; iron mines of, 177; Mohammed II in, 212; palace of, 84(*fig.*), 181; Palaeologian Renaissance in, 46, 82, 178, 284n71
Modon (Methone), 41, 213; castle of, 214(*fig.*)
Moglena, 14
Mohammed, 91, 338n9
Mohammed I, sultan, 144, 155
Mohammed II, sultan, 66, 189(*fig.*), 207, 338n13; Aegean islands and, 213, 216–21, 222, 224, 231; Armatoles and, 157; capture of Constantinople by, 188, 190–202, 205, 257; land expropriations, 123, 153; Peloponnesian revolts and, 208–16, 221, 222, 223; Trebizond and, 221–31, 355nn81, 90
Mohammed Bey, son of Mandrominos, 201
monasteries, 4, 16, 19, 23, 32, 80, 83(*fig.*), 84(*fig.*), 271n59, 313n41; Danubian, 81; Hesychasm and, 57–60; Islamic, 66–67; in Italy, 235, 243, 244, 249; land rights of, 33, 56–57, 60, 85, 123, 127, 129–30, 165; libraries of, 20, 104, 111–12, 235; moral standards in, 87–88, 89; piracy and, 69; in Vagenetia, 8
Monasteriotes, archbishop of Ephesus, 35
Monastir (Bitola), 78
Monemvasia, 4, 40, 212, 213, 304n72; Pius II and, 350n24
Mongols, 62
Monodendrion (Only One Tree), 204
Montferrat family, 32
Montferrat, Boniface, 50

Mordtmann, A. D., quoted, 67–68
Morea, Despotate of, *see* Peloponnese, The
Morphou, 105
mosaics, 47
Moschopoulos, Manuel, 46
Moschopoulos, Nicephoros, metropolitan of Lacedemonia, 284n71
Moscopolis (Voskopojë), 14, 362n63
Moslems, *see* Islam
Mosque of the Conqueror, Athens, 211
Mosque of the Conqueror, Constantinople, 200
Mosque of Faith (the Conqueror), Trebizond, 231
Mouchlion, fortress of, Peloponnesus, 209, 211
Mount Athos, monastery of, 24, 50, 81, 251; Hesychasm and, 57, 59; Manuel II Palaeologus and, 123; Ottoman Turks and, 78, 146; pirates and, 69
Mount Hieron, 73
Mount Olympus, 165, 266n9
Mount Othrys, 165
Mount Parnassus, 108
Mount Parnon, 81
Mount Pelion, 167, 266n9
Mount Vermion, 166
Mousouros, Leo and Antony, 201, 202
Mousouros, Marcos, 251, 252–53
Mouziariko, 153
mufassal, the 150
Murad I, sultan, 71, 74, 76, 114, 152, 299n28, 318n18, Yuruks and, 162, 163
Murad II, sultan, 66, 136, 144–50, 188, 223, 338n13; army organization of, 151–52, 155, 157, 158, 159; Duchy of Athens and, 134, 135; Herakleia and, 180; tax policies of, 150, 157, 158, 159, 324n41; Yuruks and, 164
Murano, Italy, 177
Musa, son of Petko, 155
music, 39, 157

Mustafa, spahi, 153
Mustafa, son of Filatrino, spahi, 155
Mykonos, island of, 81, 107
Mylopotamos, 36
Myrepsos, Nicholas, physician, 47, 111
Mytilene, 218, 339n23; Crusaders in, 219–20

Naousa, 166
Naples, Italy, 190, 244, 249, 253, 254
Nardò, Italy, 235
Narrative of Achilles, 44–45
"Narrative concerning the Fall of Constantinople," Russian, 204
nationalism, 15, 16, 27–45, 111, 234–35, 285nn77, 79, 288n12; Albanian, 149, 179, 207; Armatoles and, 159–60; art and, 21, 22, 26, 35, 38–39, 43–45, 97, 112, 250, 260–62, 366n15, 367n22; Bessarion on, 172–78, 334n17; of Chalcocondyles, 232–33; Constantine XI and, 178–80, 183, 185–86, 203–205; Constantinople's fall and, 145–46, 200, 203–205, 222, 256–63, 280n13; Frankish rule and, 104–105, 133, 169, 311n8, 321nn33, 35, 337n56; Gemistos and, 123, 126–35, 169, 170–71, 172, 176, 181, 183, 184, 256, 263; Maina and, 215; Mistra and, 82; Nicaea and, 36–40, 46, 47–48, 49, 283n53; Ottoman Empire and, 77, 81, 88, 89, 104, 144, 337n56; peasant revolts and, 105; religion and, 18, 37, 41, 42, 43, 57, 58, 60, 88, 89, 90, 93, 94, 96, 97, 99, 102–103, 106–107, 118, 133, 183, 185–86, 187–88, 191–93, 231, 256, 257, 296n40, 311n11, 321n33; Roman tradition and, 100, 116, 120, 121, 123, 175, 183, 185, 232, 234–35, 255, 262, 337n56; Thessalonica's resistance and, 113, 114, 117–18, 120–21,

124–25, 146–47; Trebizond and, 222, 226, 229, 230, 231
Naupactus, 31, 32, 179; castle of, 8, 209, 267n18, 297n1
Nauplia, 107
Navarino (Pylos), 213
Navarre, 10, 105, 108, 109–10
Naxos, island of, 15, 71
Nea Mone of Thessalonica, 114
Nectarius, monk, 313n43
Neilos, patriarch of Constantinople, 111, 313n41
neoclassicism, *see* humanism
neo-Hellenism, *see* humanism; nationalism; neo-Platonism
Neopatras, 32, 108, 109, 110, 162, 167
Neophytos, monk, 109, 111
neo-Platonism, 19, 234; Gemistos and, 123, 127, 128, 170–71, 180, 181, 184–85, 241, 362n67; Hesychasm *versus*, 57, 58; Italian, 236, 243, 247, 248
Neroulos, Rizoz, cited, 158
Nesebar (Mesembria), on Black Sea, 136, 193, 286n82
Nesri, Mehemmed, cited, 163
Nevrokop, 155
Nicaea, Empire of, 31–43, 46, 62, 241; Epirus' rivalry with, 31–36, 281n20; Fourth Crusade and, 29, 30; Metochites in, 47–48, 49; Ottoman Turks in, 65, 89, 306n22. *See also specific place-names*
Nicephorus I, despot of Epirus, 3
Nicephorus II, despot of Epirus, 8, 112
Nicholas III, patriarch of Constantinople, 2
Nicholas V, pope, 138–39, 192, 253, 361n47; library of, 243–44; Turkish siege of Constantinople and, 188, 190, 191, 218
Nicholas Gattilusi, ruler of Lemnos, 219

Nicolitsa, 14

Nicomedia, Asia Minor, 46, 62, 65

Nicopolis, battle of 1396, 80

Nicosia, archbishop of, 98

Nidir, 163

nobility, the, 35, 53, 87; Catalan, 108–109; Cretan Venetian, 99, 106; in Epirus, 113, 116, 149; fall of Constantinople and, 28–29, 30, 137, 175, 197, 198, 200–202, 208, 302n55, 334n19; Frankish rule and, 105; Gemistos and, 126, 128, 129, 130, 173, 174; land grants of, 33, 34, 54–57, 65; in Macedonia, 59, 117, 124, 127, 146–47, 319n6; Peloponnesian intrigues of, 208, 212; spahi institution and, 149, 150, 152–57; Theodore II Lascaris and, 40; in Thessaly, 112, 153–56, 165, 207–208; of Trebizond, 227–28, 229, 230

nomadism, 15, 159; Albanian, 11, 154, 207; Turkish, 64, 162, 163, 164

Nomoi (Laws . . . Gemistos), 171, 333n7

Normans, 49

Notara, Anna, 200–201, 345n91

Notaras, Jacob, 200–201; quoted, 340 n33

Notaras, Lucas, grand duke, 181, 192–93, 200

Notaras, Matthew, 201

Notaras, Vlasios, 201

novels, 22–24, 44

Novo Brdo, Serbia, 80

Numa, 176

Nuremberg, Germany, 257

Ochrida (Achris), 32, 50

Ode on Constantinople's Misfortune (Callistus), 259–60

Odyssey (Homer), 249

Oenoe, 63

Oğlu, Balta, Turkish admiral, 196

Oises, Manuel Raul, 184

Old and New Romes: A Comparison (Chrysoloras), 239

Olovolos, Manuel, philosopher, 47

Olubad (Lopadion), Asia Minor, 199

Olympia, 2

Olympic Games, 172

Ömer, son of Turahan, 153, 208, 211

"On the Bravery of a Constantinopolitan Woman" (Tarhaniotes), 261

"On His Exile" (Tarhaniotes), 261

On Law (Peri nomon . . . Gemistos), 256

On the Sovereign Sun (Julian), 185

Ophis (Of), 63, 231

oral tradition, *see* folklore

Orchan, sultan, 64, 65, 66, 72, 162, 163; army reorganization by, 73, 299n28, 318n108

Orchan, prince, 190, 200, 338n13

"Order (*Orismos*) of Sinan Paşa," 149

Oreibasios, physician, 111

Oreine, 105

Orobe, island of, 4

Orthodox Church, 17, 26; autonomy in Russia, 187; Catalans and, 109, 110, 312n33; Epirotic, 31–32, 112–13; Gemistos and, 171–72, 184–85, 256, 333n7; Hesychasm and, 57–60, 102, 118, 236; lands of, 56–57, 60, 78–79; martyrs of, 93–95, 96, 203, 307n41; nationalism and, 16, 30, 41, 42, 43, 93, 94, 96, 97, 102–103, 106–107, 118, 133, 170, 184, 187–88, 311n11; Oecumenical Patriarchate of, 31, 61, 95, 96–97, 98, 102, 161, 314n47; Photian Schism of, 100, 102, 188, 203; Roman Catholic conversions from, 15, 95–99, 236, 239, 243, 253, 309n65, 310n79; Roman Union issue of, 95, 99–103, 118, 138–39, 180–81, 183, 185, 187–88, 191–93, 197, 235, 237, 239, 309n73, 310n79; Trebizond's fall and, 231; Turks and,

61–62, 66–68, 78–79, 80, 86–95, 99, 118, 149; Vatatzes' canonization by, 36, 306n27

Osman Bey, 295n35; ghazis under, 64

Ottoman Empire, 60, 64–68, 89, 252, 337n56; Aegean islands and, 36, 41–42, 69, 71, 213, 216–21, 222; army organization and, 12, 30, 73–74, 139–43, 151–60, 323n25, 324nn31–33 (*See also* armies, Ottoman); Athens and, 78, 104, 134–35, 169, 211, 232, 357n101; censuses of, 149, 150, 162, 163, 332n38; Christian theology and, 86, 91–95, 99, 139, 144, 203, 296n44; civil service of, 201; Constantine XI and, 178–80, 187–200, 203–205, 344n86; Constantinople's siege (1394) and, 79–80, 81–82, 302n58; crusade agitation against, 178, 190, 209, 217, 218, 219–21, 257–58, 259, 260, 263, 365n9, 366nn15, 18–19; Peloponnese's conquest by, 10–11, 29, 30, 41, 43, 78, 82, 104, 106, 114, 127, 132, 146–49, 169–86, 207–16, 222, 250, 258, 350n24, 351n33; Thessalonica's resistance to, 77, 78, 113, 114, 117–18, 120–21, 123, 124–25, 146–48, 300n42; Thessaly and, 14–15, 78, 104, 111, 114, 153–56, 158–59, 162, 164–68, 179, 180, 190, 207, 211; Thrace and, 72–73, 76, 77, 79, 161, 162–63, 218–19, 286n81, 299n21; Trebizond and, 221–31, 258, 353n56, 355nn81, 83; tribute exaction by, 64, 85, 137, 206–207, 217, 218, 221, 223, 224, 324n41

Pachymeres, George, 65; quoted, 285n75

Pacioti, brigand, 110

Padua, Italy, 245, 247, 250, 362n71

Padua, University of, 247–48, 249

Paean to the Handsome Demetrius (Kavasilas), 47

paganism, 18–19, 37, 39, 48, 53; Gemistos and, 171–72, 184–85, 256, 333n7; hagiography and, 47; Hesychasm *versus*, 57; Tarhaniotes and, 262–63

Pagomenos family, 208

painting, 48, 80, 303n62; fresco, 50, 97; miniature, 23–24, 50

Palaea Phocaea, Asia Minor, 219, 352n46

Palaeologian dynasty (1261–1453), 5, 46–60, 137, 222; neo-Hellenism of, 28, 35, 40, 42–43, 46–49, 57, 58, 60, 80, 81, 82, 99, 100, 102, 110, 116–25, 126–35, 169–86, 205, 235–37, 241. *See also individual rulers*

Palaeologina, Maria Angelina Ducaina, princess of Epirus, 113, 297n1

Palaeologus, Andrew, 215

Palaeologus, Constantine (Graetzas), 213

Palaeologus, Emmanuel, 201

Palaeologus, Emmanuel (son of Thomas), 215

Palaeologus, George, 219

Palaeologus, Murad, 201

Palaeologus, Symeon Uroš, ruler of Thessaly, 8, 114; quoted, 271n59

Palaeologus, Theophilus, 199

Palaeologus, Thomas, 363n84

Palaeologus, Zoë, 215

Palamas, Gregory, Archbishop of Thessalonica, 53; quoted, 72, 88, 365n7; Hesychasm of, 57, 58, 235

Palamedes Gattilusi, ruler of Ainos, 216, 217, 219

Palionaousta, 166

Panagia Chrysokephalos Cathedral, Trebizond, 231

Panegyric to Manuel and John VIII Palaeologus, 11, 121, 317n90

Paparrhegopoulos, Constantine, 27–28

Papoulia, Basilike, cited, 299n28, 318n108

Paramythia, 149

Pardo, Giovanni, Spanish philosopher and poet, 253
Parekvolai (Eustathius), 33
Paris, France, 250, 252, 253
Paris, University of, 250, 252
Parma, bishop of, quoted, 258
Parnon Mountains, 4
Parthenion Mountains, 209
Parthenon, The, 312n33
Paspatis, A., cited, 200
Patras, 3, 19, 209, 215
Patriarchs, 90, 96, 259; Oecumenical Patriarchate of, 31, 61, 95, 96–97, 98, 102, 161, 314n47. See also individual names
Patzinak tribe, 6
Paul, archbishop of Smyrna, 236
Paul, saint, quoted, 306n32
Paul II, pope, 257, 258
Paul VI, pope, 215
Pavia, battle of (1525), 259
peasantry, 53, 89, 121, 305n18, 327 n13; Bessarion on, 176; Catalans and, 108; Constantinople's siege and, 190; Gemistos and, 128, 134, 174; Hellenism and, 30, 134, 290n37; land grants and, 34, 54–57, 154; Ottoman Turks and, 65, 81–82, 137, 144, 154, 165–66; Saracens and, 105; of Trebizond, 226; urban refuges of, 59
"Peć and Serbia," archbishop of, 314 n47
Peloponnese (Morea), 31, 165; Albanians in, 7–12, 16, 109, 207–209, 213, 215, 269n41, 272n66; Constantine XI and, 169–80, 181, 190; Constantinople and, 17, 81–82, 170, 190, 202, 205, 213; division of 1449, 181, 208; Duchy of Athens and, 134, 135; Frankish rule in, 106, 312n18; Gemistos and, 126, 128–32, 133, 170, 173, 174, 320nn24, 28; piracy and, 69; Slavs in, 2–6, 7, 16, 266n8, 274n84; Thessalonian alliance with, 105–

106, 109, 114, 120; Turkish conquest of, 29, 30, 41, 43, 78, 82, 104, 106, 114, 127, 132, 146–49, 169–80, 207–16, 221, 222, 223, 250, 258, 350n24. See also specific place-names
Pergamon, 38
Peribleptos, monastery of, Mistra, 83 (fig.)
Peribleptos, monastery of, Constantinople, 200
Peri hon Aristoteles pros Platona diapheretai (How Aristotle Differs from Plato . . . Gemistos), 170, 241
Peri nomon (On Law . . . Gemistos), 256
Perinthos, 72
Peristeronas, 105
Pernot, Hubert, quoted, 278n35
Perotti, Niccolò, 243
Peroules, Demetrius, 111
Persians, 23, 60, 127, 263
Peter, saint, 94
Peter III, king of Aragon, 109, 110
Peter IV, king of Aragon, 10
Peter de Lusignan, king of Cyprus, 98
Petrarch, 235, 236
Petrobouas family, 208
Phacrases, dignitary of Thessalonica, 59
Phanarion, 33, 111, 112, 162; Albanians in, 7; Gemistos and, 131; spahis of, 153, 155
Pharsala, 10, 112, 114, 153, 162, 167
Phidias, 19, 260
Philadelphia, Asia Minor, 39
Philanthropenos family, 65, 114, 155, 315n57. See also individual ruling members
Philip, king of Macedonia, 22, 23, 120
Philip, duke of Burgundy, 223–24
Philippi, 121

Philippopolis (Plovdiv), 22, 23, 162, 166, 206; Mohammed II and, 218, 221, 225

philosophy, 19–20, 24, 244, 263; in Nicaea, 38, 39–40; Palaeologian Renaissance and, 46, 47, 50, 57–60, 100, 170, 184–85, 233, 234–37, 239, 241, 243–55. *See also* humanism; neo-Platonism

Philotheos, patriarch of Constantinople, 109, 314n47

Phlorina, 162

Phocas family, 65

Phocas, metropolitan of Sardes, 283n56

Phocas, Andronicus and Emmanuel, 201, 202

Phocis, 4

Phocylides, 250

Photian Schism, 100, 102, 188, 203

Photius, patriarch of Constantinople, 3

Phthiotis, 110

physics, 35

Piccolomini, Aeneas Sylvius, *see* Pius II, pope

Pieria district, 4, 267n21

Pilato, Leonzio, 235–36

Pincens, Jacob, Minorite monk, 334n20

Pindus Mountains, 7, 111, 149, 156, 165, 215; Vlachs in, 14, 154, 157, 159, 178–79, 180

Pinon, Carlier de, quoted, 351n33

Pisidia, 63

Pius II, pope, 201, 202, 215, 220, 253, 257, 258; Helen of Cyprus and, 133, 321n33; Monemvasia and, 350n24; Trebizond and, 224

Pizzicolli, Ciriaco de, 357n101

Plagiarion (Bulayir), 72

plague, 2, 164, 218, 223

Planoudes, Maximus, monk, 46

Platamon, 32, 153

Platana fortress, Asia Minor, 229

Plato, 24, 39, 50, 100, 170, 236; Bessarion on, 243, 247; Hesychasm and, 57, 58; Italian translations of, 241; on soldiers, 129

Plato's Academy, Athens, 19

Pléthon, *see* Gemistos, George

Plousiadenos, John, bibliographer, 138

Plovdiv, *see* Philippopolis

Plutarch, 47, 111, 250

poetry, 33; Akritic, 22, 26, 35, 44, 287n89, 337n58, 356n95; of Amiroukes, 354n77; nationalist, 260–62, 366n15, 367n22; romantic, 45. *See also* songs

Policastro, Calabria, 254

Poliziano, Angelo, 249

Polyphengon, fortress of, Peloponnesus, 209

Pomoriye (Anchialus), on Black Sea, 136, 193

Pontano, Giovanni, 254

Pontic Alps, 63, 223, 225, 226

Pontus, 63, 186, 230–31, 356n95

Poros, island of, 10

Porphyris, Akritic hero, 22

Porphyrogenitus, *see* Constantine VII Porphyrogenitus

Potamios, Theodore, quoted, 79

Potidaea (Cassandrea), 146

pottery, 24

Poulianos, Ares, cited, 6

Poulos, I. K., on Albanian colonies, 272n66

Pournar Daği, 162

Praxiteles, 19, 260

Preliumbović, Thomas, despot of Epirus, 10, 112–13, 114, 116, 118

Prëmeti district, 78

Priam, 262

Prilep, 162

Procheiron (Armenopoulos), 148

Promontorio de Campis, Iacopo, 341 n41

pronoia, see land grants

Prophet Elijah, Church of the, Corfu, 216

Propontis (Sea of Marmara), 136, 170, 193

Prosakon, 32, 116

Pros to hyper tou latinikou dogmatos biblion (Concerning the Book in Favor of the Latin Dogma . . . Gemistos), 171

Pros tas hyper tou Aristotelous Georgiou Scholariou antilepseis (The Views of George Scholarios in His Defense of Aristotle . . . Gemistos), 171

Protestantism, 258

Protobelissenos, George, copyist, 111

Prusa (Bursa), 62, 64, 144, 224, 228

Psara, island of, 71

Psellus, Michael, 24, 32, 276n15

Pseudo-Callisthenes, 22, 24

Pseudo-Nonnus, 24

Pseudo-Oppian, 24

Ptolemais (Kailar), 163

Ptolemy, 47

Pylos (Navarino), 213

Pyrgos (Burgas), 136, 193, 341n35

Pythia, Oracle of, 132–33

Questions (Erotemata . . . Chrysoloras), 240

Quirinal College, Rome, 252–53

Quirini, John, 71

Radenos, pupil of D. Kydones, 59

Radojčič, S., quoted, 48

Rafail, Antonije, 80

Ragusa (Dubrovnik), 50, 178, 188, 235, 362n63; Tarhaniotes in, 245, 260–61

raias (non-Moslem subjects), 16, 35, 40, 66, 166; Constantinople's fall and, 199, 200–202, 205; *haraç* and, 167, 206–207; janissary service of, 74 (*See also* janissaries); spahi service of, 149, 150, 152–57, 230–31

Ralles, Manuel, 262

Ranieri Zeno, doge of Venice, 41

Rantgoun, 164

Raul, Manuel, 208

Ravanica, monastery of, Serbia, 80

Ravenna, Italy, 258

Rebuttal (Antirretikos . . . Gazes), 241

Reformation, The, 258

Renaissance, The, 38, 58, 234–55, 262, 360n36; nationalism and, 256–63, 288n12; Palaeologian, 46–49. *See also* humanism

Rentes, Demetrius, Chancellor of Athens, 109

Republic (Plato), 129

Resava, monastery of, Serbia, 80

Rethymnon, 36

Reuchlin, Johann (Kapnion), 240, 248, 249, 250

Rhaedestos, 72

rhetoric, 35

Rhetoric (Aristotle), 21

Rhodes, island of, 43, 218, 219, 220

Rohlfs, Gerhard, cited, 235

Roman Catholicism, 236, 253, 346 n110; Bessarion's conversion to, 243, 363n84; Catalan, 98, 110, 312n33; Council of Ten (1487) and, 311n11; Helen of Cyprus and, 133, 321n33; Holy Roman Empire and, 259; Latin occupations and, 15, 43, 95–99, 101–102, 105, 107, 133, 138, 321n33; marriage laws and, 109; Orthodox Union issue and 95, 99–103, 118, 138–39, 180–81, 183, 185, 187–88, 191–93, 197, 235, 239, 309n73, 310n79; the Reformation and, 258; Venetian Senate (1425) and, 309n65

Roman Empire, 12, 92; Eastern Empire of, 17–20, 27–28, 29, 30, 37, 42–43, 49, 50, 100, 103, 175, 232, 273n80; Greek Byzantine nationalism and, 120, 121, 123, 175, 183, 185, 234–35, 255, 262; Latin spread and, 13, 14, 15. *See also* Byzantine Empire; Latin occupations

Romans, quoted, 94

Rome, city of, 17, 188, 239, 249;

Byzantine refugees in, 201, 202, 215, 234–35, 236, 237, 247, 250, 257, 358n18; publishing in, 252–53

Romulus, 262

Rouillard, Germaine, quoted, 290n37

Roustem, Kara, theologian, 74

Rozias, George C., 13; cited, 12, 273 n78

Rubió y Lluch, Antonio, 107; quoted, 108, 110

Rumanians, 12, 269n40

Rumeli Hisar, 190

Rumelia, 38, 43, 136, 142, 149, 163; castle guards of, 328n29; janissaries in, 151; Trebizond and, 228, 355 n81

Russia, 6, 53, 187; Constantinople's fall and, 204, 205; Hesychasm in, 59, 102

Russian Orthodox Church, 187

Rysion, on Sea of Marmara, 65

Saint Athanasius, Church of, Magnesia, 306n27

Saint Demetrios, Church of, Mistra, 284n71

Saint Dionysius, monastery of, Mt. Athos, 146

Saint Elias, Church of, Thessalonica, 51(fig.)

Saint George, Great Seal of, 108

Saint George of Zavlantia, monastery of, Thessaly, 56–57

Saint Mark, Cathedral of, Venice, 24

Saint Philip, Church of, Trebizond, 231

Saint Romanos, Church of, Constantinople, 199, 343n74

Saint Romanos Gate, Constantinople, 193, 196, 197, 199

Saint Stephanos (city), 136, 193

Saint Theodosia, Church of, Constantinople, 200

Saints Theodore, Church of the, Mistra, 284n71

Salamis, island of, 10

Salmenico Castle, Peloponnesus, 213

Salona (Amphissa), 106, 109, 111

Salonica, see Thessalonica

Salutati, Coluccio, 237

Samos, island of, 71

Samothrace, island of, 136; Ottoman Turks and, 213, 216, 219, 220, 221

Samsun (Amisus), 63, 223

sancaks, 149, 153, 154, 156, 159, 206; of Trebizond, 228, 229, 355n81

Sangarius district, 62

San Giovanni di Carbonara, Naples, 249

San Nicola di Casola, monastery of, southern Italy, 235

San Salvatore, monastery of, Messina, 243, 250

Sant'Agata di Goti, Church of, Rome, 253

Santameri fortress, Peloponnesus, 213

Santorini, island of, 15

Saracens, 49, 105

Sarakatsans, nomads, 15

Sarantaporos, 167

Sarapeum of Alexandria, 19

Sardes, 283n56

Sarigöl, 163

Saros, 299n21

Saruhan (Manisa), Asia Minor, 163

Sarutza Bey, 149, 163

Sathas, Constantine N., cited, 27, 340n27; quoted, 34, 367n26

Saxolo, 170

"Scald-headed Peter" (Kell Petros), 307n41

Scanderbeg (George Castriota), 208

Scarampi, Lodovico, patriarch of Aquileia, 218, 220

Scarlatos, Philippe, 201

Schiltberger, Johann, cited, 137; quoted, 347n115

Schirò, Giuseppe, quoted, 58

Scholarios, George, see Gennadius II, patriarch of Constantinople (George Kourtesis Scholarios)

science, 31, 35, 38, 47, 58, 177, 244
Scleros family, 65
sculpture, 19, 260; bas reliefs, 24, 25 (fig.)
Scyrus, 136, 202
Sea of Marmara (Propontis), 136, 170, 193
Sebastia (Sivas), Asia Minor, 225
Sebastianos, metropolitan of Ioannina, 112, 113, 314n48
Secundinus, Nicholas, 250
Seïdi Ahmet, vizier, 218
Selanik Yürükler Kanunname, 162
self-government, 280n7; Armatoles and, 158–60; Corfu, 107; Council of Athens and Neopatras and, 110; in Epirus, 149, 180; in Galata, 202; in Levadia, 108; in Maina, 215; in Thessalonica, 49–50, 53, 146–48; in Trebizond, 222; Vlachs and, 180
Selim I, sultan, 199
Seljuk Turks, 35, 61–62, 64, 67, 89
Selymbria, 136, 170, 202, 341n35
Seminara, Calabria, 235
Serbia, 10, 71; art of, 48, 50, 80; invasions of Greece by, 8, 30, 111, 112–13, 165, 313n41, 314n47, 327 n13; law in, 53; Ottoman Turks and, 77, 148, 152, 188
Serenus, 47
serfdom, 128, 129, 130, 134, 137, 165. *See also* peasantry
Serrai, 77, 116, 117, 155, 163, 227, 251
Servia, 162
Servopoulos, Frangoulios, 208, 254
Seyyid Battal, 22
Sforza, Francesco, duke of Milan, 208
Sforza, Lodovico, 249
Sgouropoulos, Demetrius, 251
Sgouros, Boua, Albanian chief, 11
shipbuilding, 177
Sicily, 3, 235, 244
Siderides, X. A., cited, 200
Siderokastron, 162
Silistra, 162

silk, 167–68, 177
Simavnaoglou, Turkish noble, 77
Simeonakis, John, 80
Sinai, monastery at, 80
Sinan Paşa, Valesi, governor of Rumelia, 149
Sinope, on Black Sea, 62, 224, 225
Siphnos, island of, 71
Sisojevac, church of, Serbia, 80
Sivas (Sebastia), Asia Minor, 225
Sixtus IV, pope, 247, 258
Skoplje (Üsküb), 206
Skordylai family, 35–36
Skylolimni, Trebizond, 226
slave trade, 71, 149, 187, 202, 329n1
Slavonia, 73
Slavs, 1, 2–6, 7, 16, 19, 265n2, 266n8, 274n84; in Corinth, 267n16; Fourth Crusade and, 29; piracy and, 69; in Thessaly, 2, 5, 8, 10, 114, 154, 155, 266n9, 267n18; Vlachs and, 12, 14
Smyrna, Asia Minor, 236
Socrates, 39
Sofia, Bulgaria, 218
Sogut district, 64, 67
Solon, 176
songs, 20, 21, 22, 27, 35, 186, 337n58; the Armatoles in, 157; as Christmas carols, 277n22; on Notaras family, 346n111; of Pontus resistance, 231, 356n95; of Trebizond, 226, 229–30; of the troubadours, 45. *See also* poetry
Sosandra, on Magnesia River, 90
Souliardos, Michael, coypist, quoted, 256
Soulis, George, on Albanians, 270n45
Sourmelis, Dionysius, cited, 12
Soviet Anthropological Institute, 6
Sozopolis, on Black Sea, 251
spahis, 149, 150, 152–57, 328n19; in Trebizond, 230–31, 355n90
Spain, 69, 108, 137, 254, 346n110. *See also* Catalans

Spandounis, Matthew, 345n92
Sparta, 5, 105, 174, 175, 250. *See*
Lacedemonia (Laconia)
Spata, Gin Boua, ruler of Aetolia, 12
Spata, Paul, brother of Gin Boua, 11–
12
Spetsai, island of, 10, 215
Sphrantzes, George, 216; cited, 134–
35, 139, 145; quoted, 151, 197–98,
211
Sporades islands, 136, 202
Stagai, monastery of, Meteora, 111
Stavrakios, John, 260, 366n17
Stein, Ernst, 358n20
Stephen Lazarević, despot of Serbia,
74, 80
Stephen II Uroš Milutin, despot of
Serbia, 245
Stephen of Surozh, saint, 20
Stiso, Sergio, 251
Stomeo, Paolo, cited, 287n89
Strabo, quoted, 274n84
Stradioti, 202
Strategopouloi family, 112
Strozzi, Palla, 241, 362n71
Strumica, 162
Strymon River, 136, 145, 146, 227
Stylis, 145
Suda (Suidas), 249
Şükrüllāh, cited, 74, 324n41; quoted,
66, 73, 295n39
Suleiman, sultan (1402–1410), 85,
296n41; Thrace and, 72–73, 162
Suleiman I the Magnificent, sultan
(1520–1566), 199, 332n38
sun worship, 185
Symeon, czar of Bulgaria, 4, 274n84
Symeon Uroš Palaeologus, ruler of
Thessaly, 8, 114; quoted, 271n59
Synada, 62
Synods, *see specific councils*
Syntagma kata Stoicheion (Blastares),
53
Syria, 105; migrations from, 63
Syros, island of, 15, 81

Tafur, Pero, 137; quoted, 143, 145,
320n22, 323n25, 324n32
Tamerlane, 85, 162, 175
tanning, 39
Tarchaniotes family, 65
Tarhaniotes, Michael Maroullos, 245;
quoted, 260–61
Tarsos, fortress of, Peloponnesus, 209
Tartars, 71
Tatar, 164
Taurus Mountains, 21, 228
taxation, 28, 33, 106, 137; Catalan,
110; Constantine XI and, 188,
338n6; Gemistos on, 129, 174; land
grant exemptions from, 55, 129,
152, 209; military, 60, 64, 129, 156–
57, 174; Ottoman, 64, 65, 85, 150,
156–57, 158, 159, 165, 166, 167,
206–207, 208, 212, 217, 324n41,
328n29, 332n38; Vatican, 247
Taygetus Mountains, 4, 126; paganism
in, 19; Slav settlements of, 5
Tenedos, island of, 69, 298n8
Tenos, island of, 15, 81, 107
Thalassinos, Leo and Andrea, 201
Thamar of Georgia, aunt of Alexius
Comnenus, 222
Thasos, island of, 136; Ottoman Turks
and, 213, 216, 217, 219, 220, 221
Thebes (Istifa), 18, 24, 82, 98, 109,
236; Constantine XI and, 178;
Council of 1373 in, 77; Frankish
occupation of, 280n7; Majorca and,
108; Turkish capture of, 134–35,
154
Themistocles, 121, 124
Theocritus, 20, 111
Theodora (Catherine), princess of
Trebizond, 223, 227, 353n56
Theodore, bishop of Alania, quoted,
280n13
Theodore I Lascaris, emperor of Ni-
caea, 34–35, 42
Theodore II Lascaris, emperor of Ni-
caea, 283n53, 286n82; quoted, 38,
39, 40, 42, 43, 283n56, 284n58

Theodore Comnenus Ducas, despot of Epirus, 31–32, 33, 34, 297n1

Theodore I Palaeologus, despot of Morea, 10, 105–106, 109, 114, 118

Theodore II Palaeologus, despot of Morea, 12, 98, 105, 169, 170, 201, 319n1; Gemistos and, 126, 127, 131, 132, 133

Theodore of Tarsus, archbishop of Canterbury, 19–20

Theodosius, 47

Theodosius I, emperor, 17, 18

Theodosius II, emperor, 194

Theoleptos I, patriarch of Constantinople, 199

Theon, 47

Theophanes, monk, 313n43

Theophanes, painter, 291n55

Theophrastus, 243

Thessalonians, quoted, 306n32

Thessalonica, 3, 87, 136, 243, 251; coronation of Theodore Comnenus Ducas in, 32; Councils of, 146–47, 148, 149; Fourth Crusade and, 28; Hesychasm and, 57, 58, 59, 235, 236; Klisura and, 268n32; Palaeologian Renaissance in, 46, 47, 49–54, 80, 116; pottery of, 24; Ottoman Turks and, 77, 78, 81, 85, 92, 94, 104, 105, 106, 107, 109, 113, 114, 117–18, 120–21, 123, 124–25, 146–48, 151, 162, 206, 300n42, 328n29; Vlachs in, 14; walls of the citadel of, 119(fig.); Yuruks in, 162, 163

Thessaly, 13, 31, 56, 111–16, 136, 251, 312n18; Albanians in, 7–8, 10, 33, 78, 111, 112, 153–56, 165, 207, 269n42; Hesychast civil war and, 59; Ottoman Turks in, 14–15, 78, 104, 111, 114, 153–56, 158–59, 162, 164–68, 179, 180, 190, 207, 211; Slavs in, 2, 5, 8, 10, 114, 154, 155, 266n9, 267n18; weaving in, 39, 166, 167–68. *See also specific place-names*

Thevet, André, cited, 215

Thomas Aquinas, saint, 99

Thomas Palaeologus, despot of divided Morea, 181, 190, 201, 258; Peloponnesian revolts and, 207, 208–209, 211, 212, 213

Thrace, 42–43, 136, 312n18; anti-Greek persecutions in (1906), 274 n89; Epirus and, 33; Gemistos and, 184; Hesychast civil war and, 59; Nicaea and, 38; Ottoman Turks in, 56, 72–73, 76, 77, 79, 161, 162–63, 218–19, 286n31, 299n21; piracy and, 69; Slavs in, 3, 5; Vlachs in, 12. *See also specific place-names*

Thucydides, 250

Tiferno, Gregorio da, 254

Timurtaş Bey, 150

Tocco family, 8, 158. *See also individual rulers*

Tocco, Leonardo, Count, 116

Tokat, Asia Minor, 225

Tophane, 196

Torsello, Marino Sanudo, 42, 43–44

Torzelo, J., cited, 152

Tozis, Giannis, quoted, 286nn82–83

trade, 4–5, 16, 108, 136–37; Italian, 59, 63, 188, 190, 202, 235; middle class and, 128, 131; monasteries and, 88; Trebizond and, 222, 225; Turkish invasions and, 76, 161

tragedy, 21

Transylvania, 73, 178

Trapezountios, George, 243, 244, 257

Traversari, Ambrogio, 239

Trebizond, 30, 31, 205, 243; Ottoman Turks and, 221–31, 258, 353n56, 355nn81, 83. *See also specific place-names*

Triclinios, Demetrius, 46, 287n2

Trikkala, 8, 111, 112, 159, 165; castle of, 9(fig.); spahis of, 153, 154, 155–56; Turahan's gifts to, 167

Trikkala, Order of 1520, 155

Tripolis, 209

Trissino, Gian Giorgio, 249

Trivolis, Demetrius, quoted, 256
Trojan War, The (chivalric novel), 44
Trojan War, The (Benoit de Sainte-Maur), 44
troubadours, 45
Truth of the Christian Faith, The (Trapezountios), 257
Tsakonia district, 4
Tschelebi, Evliya, 199; cited, 14, 163, 200
Turahan Bey, governor of Thessaly, 135, 153, 156, 163; Constantine XI and, 169, 190; land confiscations of, 165, 166; Peloponnesian invasions and, 207, 208; Tyrnavos and, 158, 164, 167–68
Turkey, 61, 88, 136, 258–59; exchange of Turkish population in Macedonia with Greek population in (1923), 164, 222; Romans in, 13. *See also* Asia Minor
Turkish Balıklı (Zoödochos Pege), Constantinople, 200
Turkish fleet, 196, 197; in the Aegean, 216, 217, 219, 220, 221; Trebizond and, 223, 224, 225, 227
Turkish language, 12, 66, 79, 254; Christian liturgy and, 94; personal names in, 338n9
Turks, 5, 22, 23, 57, 139–44, 323n25, 324nn31–33; Seljuk, 35, 61–62, 64, 67, 89; Yuruk, 64, 161–65, 179, 190, 331nn16, 25. *See also* Islam; Ottoman Empire
Tursun Bey, 150
Tyrnavos, 158, 164, 167
Tzapnides, 228, 355n84
Tzartzoulis, Nikolaos, on Vlachs, 273n80
Tzympe, 72, 162

Uğliesa, John, despot of Serbia, 314n47
Umur, son of Theodore, 155
Umur Bey, son of Sarutza Bey, 149, 163, 228, 355n81

Urban IV, pope, 41
Urban V, pope, 98
Urban VI, pope, 118
urbanization, 59, 290n36; Turkish invasions and, 62, 72, 161
Urquhart, David, cited, 158, 164
Uzunçarşılı, Ismail Hakki, cited, 151

Vagenetia, 8
Valona (Avlona), Albania, 7
Valtos, 158
Vardanis, George, metropolitan of Corfu, 32
Vardas family, 201, 202
Varennes, Aimé de, French poet, 22
Varlaam monastery, Meteora, 313n43
Varna (Stalin), 136, 145, 146, 274n89, 286n82
Varna, battle of (1444), 172, 178, 179, 187, 188; Galata and, 302n58
Vasmer, Max, cited, 3
Vatatzes family, 65. *See also individual ruling members*
Vatican Library, 244
Veles, 155
Vella, bishop of, 114
Velthandrus and Chrysantza, 45
Venice, 12, 24, 45, 82, 145, 158, 234; Bessarion library in, 243, 244; Byzantine refugees in, 201, 202, 228, 235, 250, 252, 259–60; Council of Ten (1487) and, 311n11; Cretan colony of, 35–36, 41–42, 80, 96–97, 98, 106–107, 134, 205, 215–16, 228, 235, 283n49, 285nn74–75, 311n8; Cyprus government and, 134; fleet of, 219–20; Greek trade and, 59, 63, 137, 188, 190, 235; Mohammed II and, 188, 196, 197, 213, 215, 219–20, 226; Morea and, 105, 178, 181; piracy and, 69, 298n8; publishing in, 240, 251, 252; Senate resolution (May 18, 1425), 309n65; Thessalonica's resistance to the Turks and, 118,

146–47, 148, 149; Turkish declaration of war on (1463), 258
Vergerio, Pier-Paolo, 239, 245
Vermion mountains, 4
Veroia, 50, 69; Ottoman Turks in, 77–78, 274n89
Vibius Quartus, G., cenotaph of, 121, 122(fig.)
Vienna, 257
Views of George Scholarios in His Defense of Aristotle, The (Pros tas hyper tou Aristotelous Georgiou Scholariou antilepseis . . . Gemistos), 171
Vinsauf, Walter, English chronicler, 23
Vizye, on Black Sea, 193
Vlach language, 7
Vlachia, *see* Thessaly
Vlachorynchini, 14
Vlachs, 6, 7, 10, 12–15, 16 266n9, 327n13, 328n21; ancient Greece and, 273n80; Constantine XI and, 334n23. *See also* Arvanito-Vlachs; Vlachorynchini
Vlastos, Rethemniot Sephes, 311n8
Voight, Georg, quoted, 365n9
Volos (Demetrias), 112
Vonitsa: castle of, 8; episcopal see of, 32
Voskopojë (Moscopolis), 14, 362n63
Vostitsa (Aigion), 209
Voyatzidis, Ioannis K., cited, 28, 40, 185, 288n12
Vryonis, Speros, on janissaries, 318 n108
Vryones, Palaeologus, 113

wakf institution, 123–24, 167
Walachia, 80–81, 114
wealth, 55, 59, 98, 206–207; Bessarion on, 175–76; Byzantine fiscal policy (1402–1421), 136–37, 145; Constantinople's siege and, 197, 198, 342n64; Gemistos on, 129–30, 131; monastic, 56, 60, 85, 88, 113, 123,

127, 129–30, 165; Turkish pillage and, 62, 64–65, 69, 71, 76, 78–79, 92, 99, 146, 161, 165, 200; Venetian crusaders and, 220. *See also* land grants; nobility; taxation; trade
weaving, 39, 166, 177; dyes and, 167, 332n39
Weigand, G., cited, 14
West, The, *see* Europe
World War II, 29
Worms, Germany, 257

Xanthopoulos, Nicephorus Kallistos, 53
Xanthopoulos, Theodore, 53
Xenophon, 243
Xeromero, 158, 337n56
Xylalas Palace, 191

Yakoub, Turkish admiral, 224
Yayakioï, 163
Yenice Vardar (Genitsa), 163
Yenisehir, *see* Larissa
Yenitzek, 165
Yiğit Bey, Pasha, 163
Ypsilantis, Athanasius, cited, 299n26, 341n35
Yugoslavia, 38. *See also* specific place-names
Yuruk Turks, 64, 161–65, 179, 190, 331nn16, 25

Zachary, pope, quoted, 19–20
Zacynthus, 11, 202
Zaganos, Turkish admiral, 221
Zakythinos, Denis, quoted, 262
Zambelios, Spyridon, on nationalism, 27
Zealots, 53, 124
"Zeus" (Phidias), 19
Zichna, Macedonia, 116, 274n89, 296n40
Zituni (Lamia), 136, 145, 146, 155
Zoödochos Pege (Turkish Balıklı), Constantinople, 200
Zorianos, Michael, 306n30
Zygos district, 5

MAPS

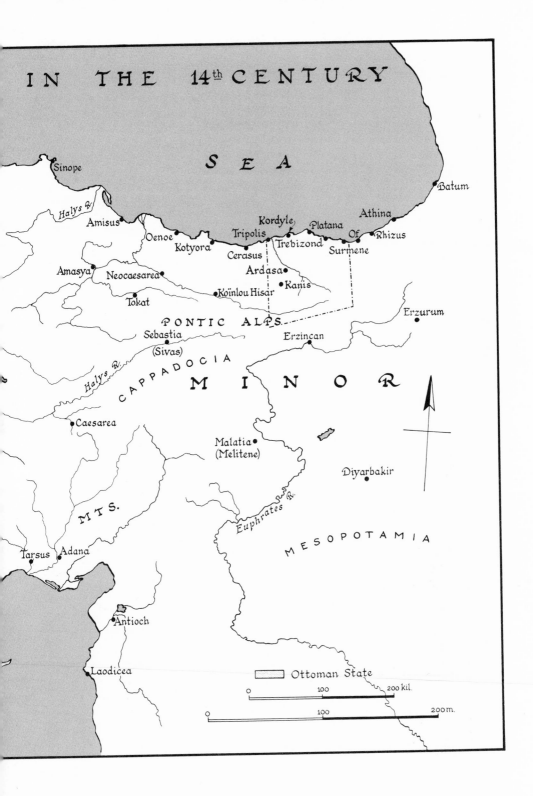

IN THE 14ᵗʰ CENTURY

SEA

Sinope

Batum

Halys R.

Amisus

Kordyle
Athina

Platana
Oenoe
Tripolis
Of
Rhizus

Kotyora
Trebizond
Surmene

Cerasus

Amasya
Neocaesarea
Ardasa

Koïnlou Hisar
Kanis

Erzurum

Tokat

PONTIC ALPS

Sebastia
Erzincan

(Sivas)

Halys R.

CAPPADOCIA
MINOR

Caesarea

Malatia
(Melitene)

Diyarbakir

MTS.

Euphrates R.

MESOPOTAMIA

Tarsus
Adana

Antioch

Laodicea

☐ Ottoman State

0   100   200 kil.

0   100   200 m.

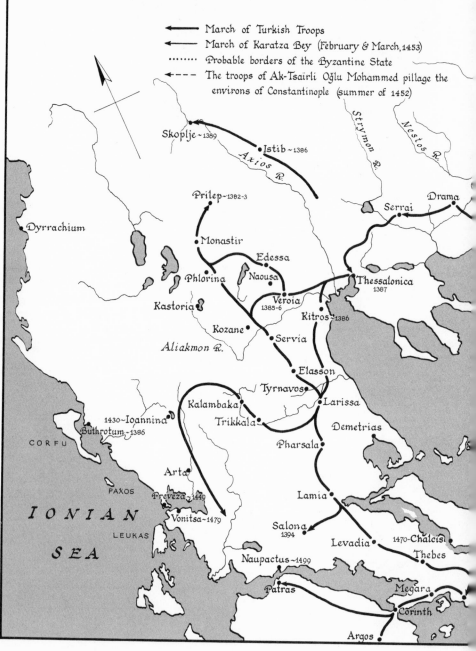

The Extension of the Ottoman Turks to the Greek Mainland (14ᵗʰ & 15ᵗʰ centuries)

← March of Turkish Troops
← March of Karatza Bey (February & March, 1453)
⋯⋯ Probable borders of the Byzantine State
←--- The troops of Ak-Tsaïrli Oğlu Mohammed pillage the environs of Constantinople (summer of 1452)

Strymon R.

Nestos R.

Skoplje ~1389
Istib ~1386
Axios R.

Prilep ~1382-3

Drama
Serrai

Dyrrachium

Monastir

Edessa
Naousa

Thessalonica
1387

Phlorina

Veroia
1385-6

Kastoria

Kitros ~1386

Kozane
Servia

Aliakmon R.

Elasson

Tyrnavos
Larissa

Kalambaka
Trikkala

Demetrias

1430~Ioannina
Buthrotum ~1386

Pharsala

CORFU

Arta

PAXOS
Preveza ~1449

Lamia

IONIAN

Vonitsa ~1479

LEUKAS

Salona
1394

Levadia

1470~Chalcis
Thebes

SEA

Naupactus ~1499

Megara

Patras

Corinth

Argos

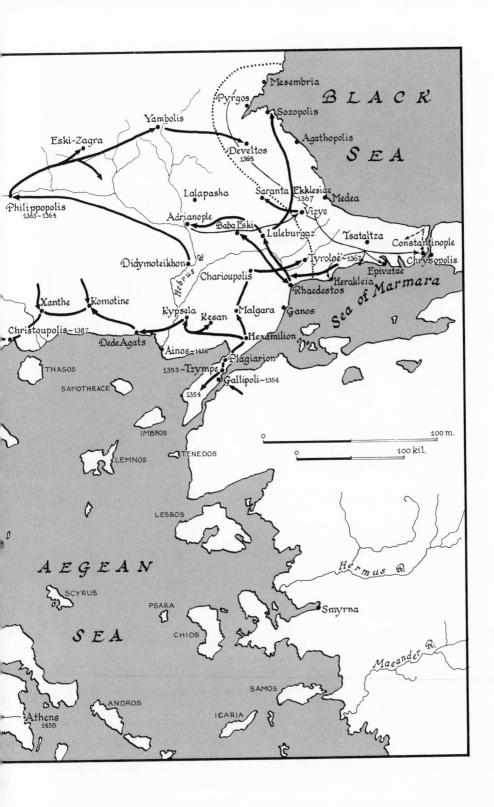

BLACK SEA

Mesembria

Pyrgos

Sozopolis

Agathopolis

Yambolis

Eski-Zagra

Develtos
1365

Philippopolis
1363~1364

Lalapasha

Saranta Ekklesiae
1367

Medea

Adrianople

Baba Eski

Vizye

Didymoteikhon

Charioupolis

Lüleburgaz

Tsataltza

Constantinople

Tyroloë~1367

Chrysopolis

Epivatae

Herakleia

Rhaedestos

Xanthe

Komotine

Kypsela

Kesan

Malgara

Ganos

Sea of Marmara

Christoupolis~1387

DedeAgats

Hexamilion

Ainos~1456

Plagiarion

Tzympe
1353~

Gallipoli~1354

1354

THASOS

SAMOTHRACE

IMBROS

LEMNOS

TENEDOS

LESBOS

AEGEAN

SEA

SCYRUS

PSARA

CHIOS

Hermus R.

Smyrna

100 m.

100 kil.

ANDROS

SAMOS

ICARIA

Maeander R.

Athens
1458

Main Points of Albanian Penetration

Dyrrachium (Durazzo)
Elbasan
Ochrida (Achris)
Monastir (Bitola)
Doiran
Serrai
Drama
Xanthe
Kavalla
Koritsa
Phlorina
Kastoria
Kailar
Thessalonica
THASOS
Kozane
LEMNOS
CORFU
Kalambaka
Ioannina
Larissa
AEGEAN
Trikkala
Demetrias
SEA
Pharsala (Chatalja)
SKIATHOS
SKOPELOS
Arta
Lamia (Zituni)
Preveza
LEUKAS
SCYRUS
Salona (Amphissa)
Naupactus (Lepanto)
Levadia
Chalcis
IONIAN
Thebes
CEPHALONIA
Patras
Athens
ANDROS
Corinth
SEA
Pyrgos
Argos
KEA
ZACYNTHUS
(ZANTE)
Nauplia
CYTHNOS
HYDRA
SERIPHOS
SPETSAI
Kalamata
Mistra
SIPHNOS
Methone (Modon)
Korone (Coron)
MELOS

0   100
Miles
0   100
Kilometers

CYTHERA

LEGEND

→ Penetration of Albanian and Arvanito~Vlach tribes

░░ Main points of Albanian establishment, approximated 14th~17th centuries

The areas marked in the map were not everywhere permanent establishments during the 14th through the 17th centuries, and they were not inhabited by Albanian immigrants only

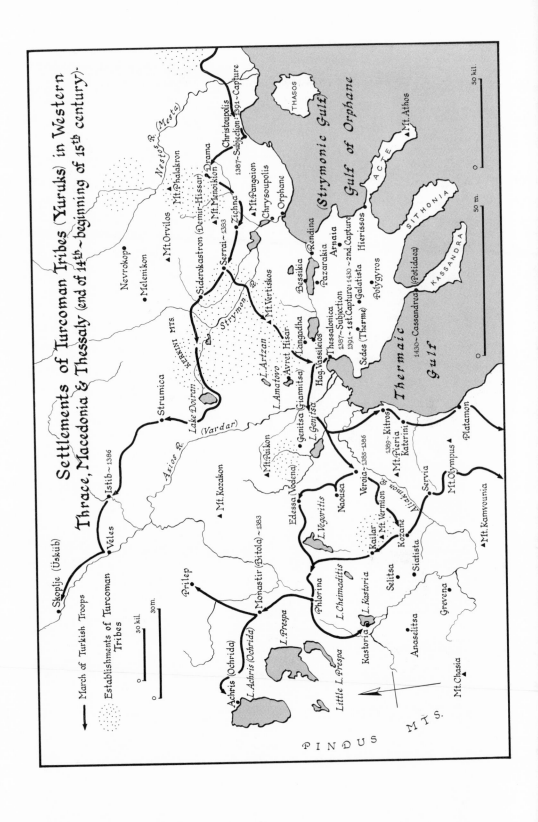

Settlements of Turcoman Tribes (Yuruks) in Western
Thrace, Macedonia & Thessaly (end of 14th ~ beginning of 15th century)·

→ — March of Turkish Troops

⋰⋱ — Establishments of Turcoman Tribes

Skopje (Üsküb)

Veles

Istib ~ 1386

Strumica

Prilep

Monastir (Bitola) ~ 1383

Achris (Ochrida)

L. Achris (Ochrida)

L. Prespa

Little L. Prespa

Phlorina

L. Cheimaditis

L. Kastoria

Kastoria

Selitsa

Siatista

Anaselitsa

Grevena

Mt.Chasia

Mt.Kamvounia

PINDUS   MTS.

Nevrokop

Melenikon

Mt.Orvilos

Siderokastron (Demir-Hissar)

Serrai ~ 1383

Zichna

Mt.Phalakron

Mt.Menoikion

Drama

Christoupolis 1387~Subjection 1391~Capture

Mt.Pangaion

Chrysoupolis

Orphane

THASOS

Mt.Athos

ACTE

SITHONIA

KASSANDRA

(Strymonic Gulf)

Gulf of Orphane

Rentina

Bessikia

Pazarakia

Arnaia

Galatista

Hierissos

Polygyros

1430~Cassandrea (Potidaea)

Thermaic

Gulf

Sedes (Therme)

Thessalonica 1387~Subjection 1391~1st.Capture 1430~2nd.Capture

Hag.Vassileios

Langadha

Avret Hisar

L.Amatovo

L.Artzan

Mt.Vertiskos

Genitsa (Giamitsa)

L.Genitsa

Edessa (Vodena)

Mt.Paikon

Naousa

L.Vgoritis

Mt.Kozakon

Kailar

Mt.Vermion & Milovon

Kozane

Veroia ~ 1385-1386

1389~Kitros

Mt.Pieria

Katerini

Servia

Mt.Olympus

Platamon

KERKINI MTS.

Nestos R. (Mesta)

Strymon R.

Axios R. (Vardar)

Lake Dcïran

30 kil.

30 m.

50 kil.

50 m.

The Greek Peninsula from 1402~1425

OTTOMAN EMPIRE

AEGEAN SEA

IONIAN SEA

Varna
Agathopolis
Medea
Constantinople
Herakleia
Dyrrachium (Durazzo)
Thessalonica
Thasos
Samothrace
Imbros
Lemnos
Larissa
Ioannina
Trikkala
Skopelos
Lesbos
Corfu
Paxos
Arta
Lamia (Zituni)
Vonitsa
Euboea
Chios
Leukas
Naupactus (Lepanto)
Thebes
Cephalonia
Patras
Athens
Samos
Corinth
Icaria
Argos
Tenos
Zacynthus (Zante)
Nauplia
Naxos
Kos
Melos
Rhodes
Crete

LEGEND

Arabaioi (Albanians)
Byzantine Empire
Despotate of Morea
Duchy of Thebes & Athens
Venetian Possessions
Principate of Achaia (Patras~Possession of Latin Archbishop)
Semi-independent populations of the Pindus Mountains
Areas belonging to various Albanian noble families, vassals of the sultan

Possessions of the Tocci
Possessions of the Giustiniani
Possessions of the Gattilusi
Knights of Rhodes
Possessions of various Frankish families

0   150
Miles

0   150
Kilometers

The Greek Peninsula and the Islands from 1453~1460

Kastoria •
Edessa •
Veroia •
Thessalonica •
Christoupolis (Kavalla)
THASOS
Buthrotum (v)
SAMOTHRACE
Athos 1456 (T)
CORFU
Ioannina •
Mt. Olympus ▲
IMBROS
Parga (v) •
Trikkala •
Kalambaka •
LEMNOS
Arta •
Larissa •
LESBOS
LEUKAS
Pharsala (Chatalja)
Demetrias (Volos) •
AEGEAN
SKIATHOS
Lamia (Zituni)
SKOPELOS
CEPHALONIA
Oreoi
SEA
Naupactus
Salona (Amphissa) •
Nea Phocaea
Patras •
Aigion •
Levadia •
Chalcis
Palaea Phocaea
Santameri •
Thebes •
CHIOS
ZANTE
Chlomoutsi •
Tarsos •
Athens 1458 (T)
Smyrna
Corinth
Karystos
Polyphengon
Nauplia •
ANDROS
SAMOS
IONIAN
AEGINA
TENOS
ICARIA
Leondari •
KEA
SEA
Gardiki •
HYDRA
KYTHNOS
SYROS
MYKONOS
Mistra •
SPETSAI
(Navarino) Pylos •
Kalamata •
SERIPHOS
PAROS
NAXOS
(Modon) Methone •
Korone (Coron)
Geraki •
SIPHNOS
AMORGOS
Monemvasia •
MELOS
IOS
Kilometers
CYTHERA
SANTORINI
ASTYPALAIA
Miles

LEGEND

- ▨ Possessions of the Gattilusi (until 1438) & of Demetrius Palaeologus (1458~1467)
- ▨ Possessions of the Giustiniani (1346~1566)
- ▨ Possessions of the Tocci (until 1479)
- ▨ Possessions of the Venetians (or under Venetian suzerainty)
- ▨ Arabaioi (Albanians)
- ▨ Armatoliki of Agrafa
- ▨ Possessions of various Frankish families
- .... District of Thebes conceded to the Duke of Athens (1458)
- – – – – Borders of the Duchy of Athens (1453~1458)
- •••••• Borders of the states of Thomas and Demetrius Palaeologus (after 1450)
- –••– Borders of the first Turkish occupation of the Peloponnese (1458~1460)

(T): Turkish ~ (v): Venetian

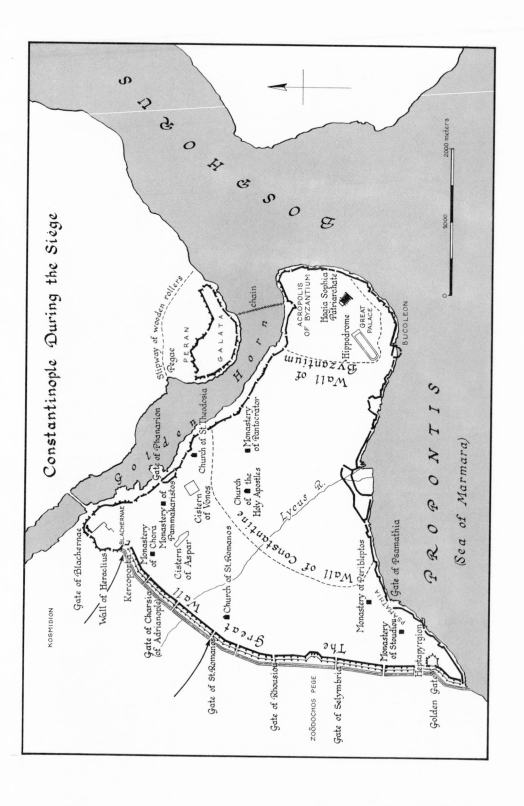

Constantinople During the Siège

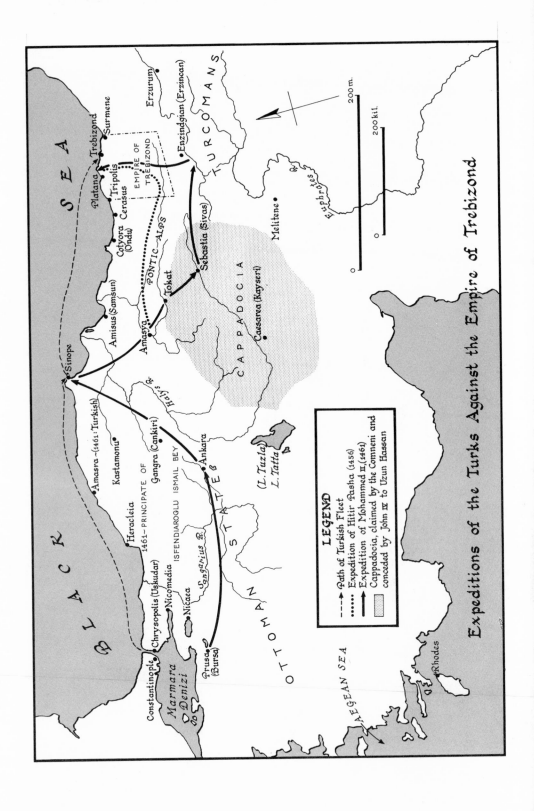

Expeditions of the Turks Against the Empire of Trebizond

The text of this book was set in Caledonia Linotype and printed by offset on P & S Old Forge manufactured by P. H. Glatfelter Co., Spring Grove, Pa. Composed, printed, and bound by Quinn & Boden Company, Inc., Rahway, New Jersey.